Family in Transition

Family in Transition

FOURTEENTH EDITION

Arlene S. Skolnick

New York University

Jerome H. Skolnick

New York University

Boston   New York   San Francisco
Mexico City   Montreal   Toronto   London   Madrid   Munich   Paris
Hong Kong   Singapore   Tokyo   Cape Town   Sydney

Senior Series Editor: *Jeff Lasser*
Series Editorial Assistant: *Erikka Adams*
Senior Marketing Manager: *Kelly May*
Editorial Production Service: *Omegatype Typography, Inc.*
Composition Buyer: *Linda Cox*
Manufacturing Buyer: *JoAnne Sweeney*
Electronic Composition: *Omegatype Typography, Inc.*
Cover Administrator: *Linda Knowles*

For related titles and support materials, visit our online catalog at www.ablongman.com.

Between the time website information is gathered and then published, it is not unusual
for some sites to have closed. Also, the transcription of URLs can result in typographical
errors. The publisher would appreciate notification where these errors occur so that they
may be corrected in subsequent editions.

Library of Congress Cataloging-in-Publication Data

Family in transition / [edited by] Arlene S. Skolnick, Jerome H. Skolnick — 14th ed.
    p.   cm.
    Includes bibliographic references.
    ISBN 0-205-48265-1 (paperbound)
    1. Family.   I. Skolnick, Arlene S.   II. Skolnick, Jerome H.

HQ518.F336   2007
306.85—dc22

                                                                2006043233

Printed in the United States of America

10   9   8   7   6   5   4   3   2   1   RRD VA   10   09   08   07   06

Contents

Preface   xi

Introduction   *1*

PART ONE • *The Changing Family*   **11**

1   *Families Past and Present*   **14**

■ READING 1
William J. Goode / The Theoretical Importance of the Family   14

■ READING 2
Anthony Giddens / The Global Revolution in Family and Personal Life   26

■ READING 3
Arlene Skolnick / The Life Course Revolution   32

■ READING 4
Donald J. Hernandez / Changes in the Demographics of Families over the Course of American History   40

2   *Public Debates and Private Lives*   **59**

■ READING 5
Sharon Hays / The Mommy Wars: Ambivalence, Ideological Work, and the Cultural Contradictions of Motherhood   59

■ READING 6
Janet Z. Giele / Decline of the Family: Conservative, Liberal, and Feminist Views   76

■ READING 7
George Chauncey / Why Do Gays Want to Marry?   95

PART TWO • *Sex and Gender*   *105*

3 *Changing Gender Roles*   *109*

■READING 8
Robert M. Jackson / Destined for Equality   109

■READING 9
Kathleen Gerson / Children of the Gender Revolution:
Some Theoretical Questions and Findings from the Field   117

4 *Sexuality and Society*   *129*

■READING 10
Amy T. Schalet / Raging Hormones, Regulated Love:
Adolescent Sexuality in the United States and the Netherlands   129

■READING 11
Beth Bailey / Sexual Revolution(s)   134

5 *Courtship and Marriage*   *151*

■READING 12
Paula England and Reuben J. Thomas / The Decline of the Date
and the Rise of the College Hook Up   151

■READING 13
Arlene Skolnick / Grounds for Marriage: How Relationships
Succeed or Fail   162

■READING 14
Lynne M. Casper and Suzanne M. Bianchi / Cohabitation   172

■READING 15
Frank F. Furstenberg, Jr. / Can Marriage Be Saved?   182

6 *Divorce and Remarriage*   *188*

■ READING 16

Karla B. Hackstaff / Divorce Culture: A Quest for Relational
Equality in Marriage   188

■ READING 17

Joan B. Kelly and Robert E. Emery / Children's Adjustment
Following Divorce: Risk and Resilience Perspectives   200

■ READING 18

Mary Ann Mason / The Modern American Stepfamily:
Problems and Possibilities   223

PART THREE • *Parents and Children*   *241*

7 *Parenthood*   *244*

■ READING 19

Philip Cowan and Carolyn Pape Cowan / New Families: Modern Couples
as New Pioneers   244

■ READING 20

Dan Clawson and Naomi Gerstel / Caring for Our Young:
Child Care in Europe and the United States   264

■ READING 21

Lawrence Friedman / Who Are Our Children?
Adoption, Past and Present   272

■ READING 22

Nicholas Townsend / The Four Facets of Fatherhood   282

8 *Childhood*   *291*

■ READING 23

Steven Mintz / Beyond Sentimentality: American Childhood
as a Social and Cultural Construct   291

■READING 24

Ellen Galinsky / What Children Think about Their
Working Parents   304

■READING 25

Vern L. Bengston, Timothy J. Biblarz, and Robert E. L. Roberts /
How Families Still Matter: A Longitudinal Study of Youth
in Two Generations   315

PART FOUR • *Families in Society*   325

9   *Work and Family Life*   329

■READING 26

Katherine S. Newman / Family Values against the Odds   329

■READING 27

Arlie Hochschild, with Anne Machung / The Second Shift: Working Parents
and the Revolution at Home   343

■READING 28

Kathleen Gerson and Jerry A. Jacobs / The Work-Home Crunch   350

10   *Family and the Economy*   360

■READING 29

Lillian B. Rubin / Families on the Fault Line   360

■READING 30

Harriet B. Presser / The Economy That Never Sleeps   377

■READING 31

Elizabeth Warren and Amelia Warren Tyagi / Why Middle-Class Mothers
and Fathers Are Going Broke   384

11 *Dimensions of Diversity*   *398*

■ **READING 32**

Ronald L. Taylor / Diversity within African American Families   398

■ **READING 33**

Maxine Baca Zinn and Barbara Wells / Diversity within Latino Families:
New Lessons for Family Social Science   422

■ **READING 34**

Judith Stacey / Gay and Lesbian Families: Queer Like Us   448

■ **READING 35**

Karen Pyke / "The Normal American Family" as an Interpretive
Structure of Family Life among Grown Children of Korean
and Vietnamese Immigrants   469

12 *Trouble in the Family*   *491*

■ **READING 36**

Jeremy Travis / Prisoners' Families and Children   491

■ **READING 37**

Kathryn Edin and Maria Kefalas / Unmarried with Children   505

■ **READING 38**

Denise A. Hines and Kathleen Malley-Morrison / Issues in the Definition
of Family Violence and Abuse   512

Preface

Once again, this new edition of *Family in Transition* has three aims. First, we looked for articles that help the reader make sense of current trends in family life. Second, we tried to balance excellent older articles with newer ones. Third, we have tried to select articles that are scholarly yet readable for an audience of undergraduates.

Among the new readings are the following:

- Donald J. Hernandez on the dramatic changes in the demography of families over the course of American history.
- George Chauncey explains how and why gays and lesbians came to want the right to marry.
- Paula England and Reuben J. Thomas examine the shift from "dating" to "hooking up" on college campuses (an original article written for this edition of *Family in Transition*).
- Frank F. Furstenberg, Jr. examines whether marriage really is an endangered institution, and whether children and society would be helped by restoring marriage to the status it enjoyed in the 1950s.
- Lawrence Friedman examines the dramatic shifts that have taken place over time in the meaning and practice of legal adoption.
- Harriet B. Presser explains why the demands of the 24/7 economy are hard on the families of those workers who have to keep it going.
- Elizabeth Warren and Amelia Warren Tyagi examine the economic pressures on middle class families today that make parental bankruptcy a more common experience for children than divorce.
- Judith Stacey examines the rise of gay and lesbian families and their implications for "straights."
- Jeremy Travis reveals how the huge increase in the prison population in recent years affects the children, families, and communities they leave behind—and return to.
- Kathryn Edin and Maria Kefalas explain why poor, unmarried young women have babies they can't afford.
- Denise A. Hines and Kathleen Malley-Morrison show why family violence and abuse are sometimes hard to define.

We would like to thank all those who have helped us with suggestions for this edition, as well as past ones. Thanks again to Rifat Salam, an NYU doctoral candidate, whose knowledge of the family research literature as well as the publishing process were enormously helpful.

Last but not least, thanks to the reviewers who offered many good suggestions for this edition: Jean Elson, University of New Hampshire; Denise McAdory, University of South Alabama; Mikki Meadows, Eastern Illinois University; Jeffrey P. Rosenfeld, Nassau Community College; Barbara Ryan, Widener University; and Suzanna Smith, University of Florida.

Family in Transition

Introduction
Family in Transition

The aim of this book is to help the reader make sense of American family life in the early years of the twenty-first century. Contrary to most students' expectations, "the family" is not an easy topic to study. One reason is that we know too much about it, because virtually everyone has grown up in a family. As a result there is a great temptation to generalize from our own experiences.

Another difficulty is that the family is a subject that arouses intense emotions. Not only are family relationships themselves deeply emotional, but family issues are entwined with strong moral and religious beliefs. And in the past several decades, "family values" has become a central battleground in American politics. Abortion, sex education, single parenthood, and gay rights are some of the issues that have have been debated since the 1980s.

Another problem is that the current state of the family is always being compared with the way families used to be. The trouble is, most people tend to have an idealized image of way families were in "the good old days." But no era ever looked like a golden age of family life to people actually living through it. That includes the 1950s, which many Americans now revere as the high point of American family life.

Finally, it's difficult to make sense about the state of the family from the statistics that constantly rain down from the media. For example, just before Father's Day in 2003, the Census Bureau issued a press release with the following headline: "Two Married Parents the Norm." It went on to state that, according to the Bureau's most recent survey, about 70 percent of children live with their two parents. Two months earlier, however, a report by a respected social science research organization contained the following headlines: "Americans Increasingly Opting Out of Marriage" and "Traditional Families Account for only 7 Percent of U.S. Households."

These are just a few examples of the confusing array of headlines and statistics about the family that the media are constantly serving up. Most often, the news tells of yet another fact or shocking incident that shows the alarming decline of the family. But every once in a while, the news is that the traditional family is making a comeback. No wonder one writer compared the family to a "great intellectual Rorschach blot" (Featherstone, 1979).

Everybody agrees that families have changed dramatically over the past several decades, but there is no consensus on what the changes mean. The majority of women, including mothers of young children, are now working outside the home. Divorce rates have risen sharply. (But they have leveled off since 1979.) Twenty-eight percent of children are living in single parent families. Cohabitation—once called "shacking up" or "living in sin"—is a widespread practice. The sexual double standard—the norm that demanded virginity for the bride, but not the groom—has largely disappeared from mainstream American culture. There are mother-only families, father-only families, grandparents raising grandchildren, and gay and lesbian families.

Indeed, the growing public acceptance of homosexuals is one of the most strikng trends of recent time, despite persisting stigma and the threat of violence. Local governments and some leading corporations have granted gays increasing recognition as domestic partners entitled to spousal benefits. In June of 2003, the Supreme Court struck down the last state laws that made gay sex a crime. The following November 18, the Massachusetts Supreme Judicial Court ruled that gays have the right to marry. These rulings have set off a national debate and a demand by conservatives to sponsor a Constitutional amendment forbidding same-sex marriage.

Does all of this mean the family is "in decline"? In crisis? Are we witnessing a moral meltdown? Why is there so much anxiety about the family? Why do so many families feel so much stress and strain? We can't answer these questions if we assume that family life takes place in a social vacuum. Social and economic circumstances have always had a profound impact on families, and when the world outside changes in important ways, families must also reshape themselves.

All these shifts in family life are part of an ongoing global revolution. All the industrialized nations, and many of the emerging ones, have experienced similar changes. In no other Western country, however, has family change been so traumatic and divisive as in the United States. For example, the two-earner family is the most common family pattern in the United States; 75 percent of mothers of children under 18 and over 60 percent of those with young children work outside the home. Yet the question of whether mothers "should" work is still a fiercely debated issue—except if the mother is on welfare.

Thus, the typical pattern for public discussion of family issues is a polarized, emotional argument. Lurching from one hot topic to another, every issue is presented as an either-or choice between two extreme positions: Which is better for children—two parents or one? Is divorce bad or good for children? Should mothers of young children work or not?

This kind of argument makes it difficult to discuss the issues and problems facing the family in a realistic way. It doesn't describe the range of views among family scholars, and it doesn't fit the research evidence. For example, the right question to ask about divorce is "Under what circumstances is divorce harmful or beneficial to children?" (Amato, 1994). In most public debates about divorce, however, that question is never asked, and the public never hears the useful information they should.

Still another problem with popular discourse about the family is that it exaggerates the amount of change that has actually occurred. For example, consider the statement above that only 7 percent of American households fit the model of the traditional family. This number, or something like it, is often cited by conservatives as proof that the institution is in danger of disappearing unless the government steps in to restore marriage and the two-parent family. At the opposite end of the political spectrum are those who celebrate the alleged decline of the traditional family and welcome the new family forms that have supposedly replaced it.

But is it true that only 7 percent of American households are traditional families? It all depends, as the saying goes, on how you define "traditional." The statement is true if you count only the families with children under 18 in which only the husband works outside the home. But if the wife works, too, as most married women now do, the family doesn't count as "traditional" by that definition. Neither does the recently married couple who do not have children yet. And the couple whose youngest child turns 18 is no longer counted as a "traditional" family either.

Despite the current high divorce rates (actually down from 1979), Americans have not abandoned the institution of marriage. The United States has the highest marriage rate in the industrial world. About 90 percent of Americans marry at some point in their lives, and virtually all who do either have, or want to have, children. Further, surveys repeatedly show that family is central to the lives of most Americans. Family ties are their deepest source of satisfaction and meaning, as well as the source of their greatest worries (Mellman, Lazarus, and Rivlin, 1990). In sum, family life in the United States is a complex mixture of both continuity and change.

While the transformations of the past three decades do not mean the end of family life, they have brought a number of new difficulties. For example, most families now depend on the earnings of wives and mothers, but the rest of society has not caught up to the new realities. For example, most schools are out of step with parents' working hours—they let out at 3:00, and still have the long summer vacations that once allowed children to work on the family farm. Most jobs, especially well-paying ones, are based on the male model; that is, a worker who can work full-time or longer without interruptions. In both blue-collar and white-collar jobs, there is still an earnings gap between men and women. Employed wives and mothers still bear most of the workload in the home.

UNDERSTANDING THE CHANGING FAMILY

During the same years in which the family was becoming the object of public anxiety and political debate, a torrent of new research on the family was pouring forth. The study of the family had come to excite the interest of scholars in a range of disciplines—history, demography, economics, law, psychology. As a result of this research, we now have much more information available about the families in past times, and our own, than we have ever had before.

The main outcome of this research has been to debunk myths about family life, both past and present. Nevertheless, the myths persist and help to fuel the cultural wars over family change.

The Myth of Universality

To say that the family is the same everywhere is in some sense true. Yet families also vary in many ways—in who is included as a family member, in emotional environments, living arrangements, ideologies, social and kinship networks, and economic and other functions. Although anthropologists have tried to come up with a single definition of family that would hold across time and place, they generally have concluded that doing so is not useful (Geertz, 1965; Stephens, 1963).

For example, although marriage is virtually universal across cultures, the definition of marriage is not the same. Although many cultures have weddings and notions of monogamy and permanence, some lack one or more of these attributes. In some cultures, the majority of people mate and have children without legal marriage and often without living together. In other societies, husbands, wives, and children do not live together under the same roof.

In our own society, the assumption of universality has usually defined what is normal and natural both for research and therapy and has subtly influenced our thinking to regard deviations from the nuclear family as sick or perverse or immoral. As Suzanne Keller (1971) once observed, "The fallacy of universality has done students of behavior a great disservice. By leading us to seek and hence to find a single pattern that has blinded us to historical precedents for multiple legitimate family arrangements."

The Myth of Family Harmony

"Happy families are all alike; each unhappy family is unhappy in its own way." This well-known quotation from Leo Tolstoy is a good example of the widespread tendency to divide families into two opposite types—happy or unhappy, good or bad, "normal" or "dysfunctional." The sitcom families of the 1950s—*Ozzie and Harriet, Leave It to Beaver,* and the rest—still serve today as models for how families ideally should be.

But few families, then or now, fit neatly into either category. For one thing, even the most loving relationships inevitably involve negative feelings as well as positive ones. It is this ambivalence that sets close relationships apart from less intimate ones. Indeed, from what we have learned about the Nelson family over the years, the real Ozzie and Harriet did not have an Ozzie and Harriet family.

Only in fairly recent times has the darker side of family life come to public attention. For example, child abuse was only "discovered" as a social problem in the 1960s. In recent years, family scholars have been studying family violence such as child abuse and wife beating to better understand the normal strains of family life. More police officers are killed and injured dealing with family fights than in dealing with any other kind of situation; of all the relationships between murderers and their victims, the family relationship is most common. Studies of family violence reveal that it is much more widespread than had been assumed, cannot easily be attributed to mental illness, and is not confined to the lower classes. Family violence seems to be a product of psychological tensions and external stresses that can affect all families at all social levels.

The study of family interaction has also undermined the traditional image of the happy, harmonious family. About three decades ago, researchers and therapists began to bring mental patients and their families together to watch how they behaved with one another. Oddly, researchers had not studied whole family groups before.

At first the family interactions were interpreted as pathogenic: a parent expressing affection in words but showing nonverbal hostility; alliances being made between different family members; families having secrets; or one family member being singled out as a scapegoat to be blamed for the family's troubles. As more and more families were studied, however, such patterns were found in many families, not just in those families with a schizophrenic child. Although this line of research did not uncover the cause of schizophrenia, it revealed that normal, ordinary families can often seem dysfunctional, or, in the words of one study, "difficult environments for interaction."

The Myth of Parental Determinism

The kind of family a child grows up in leaves a profound, lifelong impact. But a growing body of studies shows that early family experience is not the all-powerful, irreversible influence it has sometimes been thought to be. An unfortunate childhood does not doom a person to an unhappy adulthood. Nor does a happy childhood guarantee a similarly blessed future (Emde and Harmon, 1984; Macfarlane, 1964; Rubin, 1996).

Any parent knows that child rearing is not like molding clay or writing on a blank slate. Rather, it's a two-way process in which both parent and child influence each other. Children come into this world with their own temperament and other characteristics. Moreover, from a very early age children are active perceivers and thinkers. Finally, parents and children do not live in a social vacuum; children are also influenced in many ways, by the world around them and the people in it—relatives, family friends, the neighborhood, other children, the school, as well as the media.

The traditional view of parental determinism has been challenged by the extreme opposite view. Psychologist Judith Rich Harris asserts that parents have very little impact on their children's development. In her book, *The Nurture Assumption: Why Children Turn Out the Way They Do* (1998), Harris argues that genetics and peer groups, not parents, determine how a child will develop. As in so many debates about the family, both extremes oversimplify complex realities.

The Myth of a Stable Past

Laments about the current state of decay of the family imply some earlier era when the family was more stable and harmonious. Historians have not, in fact, located a golden age of the family. Nor have they found any time or place when families did not vary in many ways from whatever the standard model was. Indeed, they have found that premarital sexuality, illegitimacy, and generational conflict can best be studied as a part of family life itself rather than as separate categories of deviation.

The most shocking finding of recent years is the prevalence of child abandonment and infanticide throughout European history. It now appears that infanticide provided a major means of population control in all societies lacking reliable contraception, Europe included, and that it was practiced by families on legitimate children (Hrdy, 1999).

Rather than being a simple instinctive trait, having profound love for a newborn child seems to require two: the infant must have a decent chance of surviving, and the parents must feel that the infant is not competing with them and their older children in a struggle for survival. Throughout many centuries of European history, both of these conditions were lacking.

Another myth about the family is that it is a static, unchanging form, until recently, when it began to come apart. In reality, families have always been in flux; when the world around them changes, families have to change in response. At periods when a whole society undergoes some major transformation, family change may be especially rapid and dislocating.

In many ways, the era we are living through today resembles two earlier periods of family crisis and transformation in U.S. history (see Skolnick, 1991). The first occurred in the early nineteenth century, when the industrial era moved work out of the home (Ryan, 1981). In the older pattern, most people lived on farms. A father was not just the head of the household, but also boss of the family enterprise. Mother and children and hired hands worked under his supervision.

But when work moved out, so did the father and the older sons and daughters, leaving behind the mother and the younger children. These dislocations unleashed an era of personal stress and cultural confusion. Eventually, a new model of family emerged that not only reflected the new separation of work and family, but also glorified it.

The household now became idealized as "home sweet home," an emotional and spiritual shelter from the heartless world outside. Many of our culture's most basic ideas about the family and gender were formed at this time. And the mother-at-home, father-out-at-work model that most people think of as "traditional" was in fact the first version of the modern family.

Historians label this nineteenth century model of the family "Victorian" because it became influential in England and Western Europe as well as in the United States during the reign of Queen Victoria. It reflected, in idealized form, the nineteenth-century middle-class family. However, the Victorian model became the prevailing cultural definition of family. Few families could live up to the ideal in all its particulars; working-class, black, and ethnic families, for example, could not get by without the economic contributions of wives, mothers, and daughters. And even for middle-class families, the Victorian ideal prescribed a standard of perfection that was virtually impossible to fulfill (Demos, 1986).

Eventually, however, social change overtook the Victorian model. Beginning around the 1880s, another period of rapid economic, social, and cultural change unsettled Victorian family patterns, especially their gender arrangements. Several generations of so-called new women challenged Victorian notions of femininity.

They became educated, pursued careers, became involved in political causes—including their own—and created the first wave of feminism. This ferment culminated in the victory of the women's suffrage movement. It was followed by the 1920s' jazz-age era of flappers and flaming youth—the first, and probably the major, sexual revolution of the twentieth century.

Another cultural crisis ensued, until a new cultural blueprint emerged—the companionate model of marriage and the family. The new model was a modern, more relaxed version of the Victorian family; companionship and sexual intimacy were now defined as central to marriage.

This highly abbreviated history of family and cultural change forms the necessary backdrop for understanding the family upheavals of the late twentieth and early twenty-first centuries. As in earlier times, major changes in the economy and society have destabilized an existing model of family life and the everyday patterns and practices that have sustained it.

We have experienced a triple revolution: first, the move toward a postindustrial service and information economy; second, a life course revolution brought about by reductions in mortality and fertility; and third, a psychological transformation rooted mainly in rising educational levels. Although these shifts have profound implications for everyone, women have been the pacesetters of change. Most women's lives and expectations over the past three decades, inside and outside the family, have departed drastically from those of their own mothers. Men's lives today also are different from their fathers' generation, but to a much lesser extent.

THE TRIPLE REVOLUTION

The Postindustrial Family

A service and information economy produces large numbers of jobs that, unlike factory work, seem suitable for women. Yet as Jessie Bernard (1982) once observed, the transformation of a housewife into a paid worker outside the home sends tremors through every family relationship. It blurs the sharp contrast between men's and women's roles that mark the breadwinner/housewife pattern. It also reduces women's economic dependence on men, thereby making it easier for women to leave unhappy marriages.

Beyond drawing women out of the home, shifts in the nature of work and a rapidly changing globalized economy have unsettled the lives of individuals and families at all class levels. The well-paying industrial jobs that once enabled a blue-collar worker to own a home and support a family are no longer available. The once secure jobs that sustained the "organization men" and their families in the 1950s and 1960s have been made shaky by downsizing, an unstable economy, corporate takeovers, and a rapid pace of technological change.

The new economic uncertainty has also made the transition to adulthood increasingly problematic. In the postwar years, particularly in the United States, young people entered adulthood in one giant step. They found jobs, often out of high school, married young, left home, and had children quickly. Today, few young adults can afford to marry and have children in their late teens or early twenties. In an economy where a college degree is necessary to earn a living wage, early marriage impedes education for both men and women.

Those who do not go on to college have little access to jobs that can sustain a family. Particularly in the inner cities of the United States, growing numbers of young people have come to see no future for themselves at all in the ordinary world of work. In middle-class families, a narrowing opportunity structure has increased anxieties about downward mobility for offspring, and parents as well. The "incompletely launched young adult syndrome" has become common: Many young adults fail to launch careers and become successfully independent adults, and many even come home to crowd their parents' empty nest (Schnaiberg and Goldenberg, 1989).

The Life Course Revolution

We cannot hope to understand current predicaments of family life without understanding how drastically the basic realities of life and death have changed over the twentieth century. In 1900, average life expectancy was 47 years. Infants had the highest mortality rates, but young and middle-aged adults were often struck down by infectious diseases. Before the turn of the twentieth century, only 40 percent of women lived through all the stages of a normal life course: growing up, marrying, having children, and surviving with a spouse to the age of 50 (Uhlenberg, 1980).

Declining mortality rates have had a profound effect on women's lives. Women today are living longer and having fewer children. When infant and child mortality rates fall, women no longer have to have five, seven, or nine children to make sure that two or three will survive to adulthood. After rearing children, the average woman can look forward to three or four decades without maternal responsibilities.

One of the most important changes in contemporary marriage is the potential length of marriage and the number of years spent without children in the home. Our current high divorce rates may be a by-product of this shift. By the 1970s, the statistically average couple spent only 18 percent of their married lives raising young children, compared with 54 percent a century ago (Bane, 1976). As a result, marriage is becoming defined less as a union between parents raising a brood of children and more as a personal relationship between two individuals.

A Psychological Revolution

The third major transformation is a set of psychocultural changes that might be described as "psychological gentrification" (Skolnick, 1991). That is, cultural advantages once enjoyed only by the upper classes—in particular, education—have been extended to those lower down on the socioeconomic scale. Psychological gentrification also involves greater leisure time, travel, and exposure to information, as well as a general rise in the standard of living. Despite the persistence of poverty, unemployment, and economic insecurity in the industrialized world, far less of the population than in the historical past is living at the level of sheer subsistence.

Throughout Western society, rising levels of education and related changes have been linked to a complex set of shifts in personal and political attitudes. One of these is a more psychological approach to life—greater introspectiveness and a yearning for warmth and intimacy in family and other relationships (Veroff, Douvan, and Kulka, 1981). There is also evidence of an increasing preference on the part of both men and women for a more companionate ideal of marriage and a more democratic family. More broadly, these changes in attitude have been described as a shift to "postmaterialist values," emphasizing self-expression, tolerance, equality, and a concern for the quality of life (Inglehart, 1990).

The multiple social transformations of our era have brought both costs and benefits: Family relations have become both more fragile and more emotionally rich; mass longevity has brought us a host of problems as well as the gift of extended life. Although change has brought greater opportunities for women, persisting gender inequality means women have borne a large share of the costs of these gains. But we cannot turn the clock back to the family models of the past.

Despite the upheavals of recent decades, the emotional and cultural significance of the family persists. Family remains the center of most people's lives and, as numerous surveys show, a cherished value. Although marriage has become more fragile, the parent-child relationship—especially the mother-child relationship—remains a core attachment across the life course (Rossi and Rossi, 1990). The family, however, can be both "here to stay" and beset with difficulties.

Most European countries have recognized for some time that governments must play a role in supplying an array of supports to families' health care, children's allowances, housing subsidies, support for working parents and children (such as child care, parental leave, and shorter work days for parents), as well as an array of services for the elderly. Each country's response to these changes, as we've noted earlier, has been shaped by its own political and cultural traditions. The United States remains embroiled in a cultural war over the family; many social commentators and political leaders have promised to reverse the recent trends and restore the "traditional" family. In contrast, other Western nations, including Canada and the other English-speaking countries, have responded to family change by trying to remedy the problems brought about by economic and social transformations. As a result of these policies, these countries have been spared much of the poverty and other social ills that have plagued the United States in recent decades.

Looking Ahead

The world at the beginning of the twenty-first century is vastly different from what it was at the beginning, or even the middle, of the twentieth century. Families are struggling to adapt to new realities. The countries that have been at the leading edge of family change still find themselves caught between yesterday's norms, today's new realities, and an uncertain future. As we have seen, changes in women's lives have been a pivotal factor in recent family trends. In many countries there is a considerable difference between men's and women's attitudes and expectations of one another. Even where both partners accept a more equal division of labor in the home, there is often a gap between beliefs and behavior. In no country have employers, the government, or men fully caught up to the changes in women's lives.

Families have always struggled with outside circumstances and inner conflict. Our current troubles inside and outside the family are genuine, but we should never forget that many of the most vexing issues confronting us derive from benefits of modernization few of us would be willing to give up—for example, longer, healthier lives, and the ability to choose how many children to have and when to have them.

When most people died before they reached age 50, there was no problem of a large elderly population to care for. Nor was adolescence a difficult stage of life when children worked, education was a privilege of the rich, and a person's place in society was determined by heredity rather than choice.

In short, family life is bound up with the social, economic, and cultural circumstances of particular times and places. We are no longer peasants, Puritans, pioneers, or even suburbanites circa 1955. We face a world earlier generations could hardly imagine, and we must find new ways to cope with it.

A Note on the Family

Some family scholars have suggested that we drop the term *the family* and replace it with *families* or *family life*. The problem with *the family* is that it calls to mind the stereotyped image of the Ozzie and Harriet kind of family—two parents and their two or three minor children. But those other terms don't always work. In our own writing we use the term *the family* in much the same way we use *the economy*—a set of institutional arrangements through which particular tasks are carried out in a society. An economy deals with goods and service; the family deals with reproduction and child rearing, care and support for adults, and so on.

References

Amato, P. R. 1994. Life span adjustment of children to their parents' divorce. *The Future of Children* 4, no 1. (Spring).

Bane, M. J. 1976. *Here to Stay*. New York: Basic Books.

Bernard, J. 1982. *The Future of Marriage*. New York: Bantam.

Demos, J. 1986. *Past, Present, and Personal*. New York: Oxford University Press.

Emde, R. N., and R. J. Harmon, eds. 1984. *Continuities and Discontinuities in Development*. New York: Plenum Press.

Featherstone, J. 1979. Family matters. *Harvard Educational Review* 49, no. 1: 20–52.

Geertz, G. 1965. The impact of the concept of culture on the concept of man. In *New Views of the Nature of Man*, edited by J. R. Platt. Chicago: University of Chicago Press.

Harris, J. R. 1998. *The Nurture Assumption: Why Children Turn Out the Way They Do*. New York: Free Press.

Hrdy, S. B. 1999. *Mother Nature*. New York: Pantheon Books.

Inglehart, R. 1990. *Culture Shift*. N.J.: Princeton University Press.

Keller, S. 1971. Does the family have a future? *Journal of Comparative Studies*, Spring.

Macfarlane, J. W. 1964. Perspectives on personality consistency and change from the guidance study. *Vita Humana* 7: 115–126.

Mellman, A., E. Lazarus, and A. Rivlin. 1990. Family time, family values. In *Rebuilding the Nest*, edited by D. Blankenhorn, S. Bayme, and J. Elshtain. Milwaukee: Family Service America.

Rossi, A. S., and P. H. Rossi. 1990. *Of Human Bonding: Parent–Child Relations Across the Life Course*. Hawthorne, New York: Aldine de Gruyter.

Rubin, L. 1996. *The Transcendent Child*. New York: Basic Books.

Ryan, M. 1981. *The Cradle of the Middle Class*. New York: Cambridge University Press.

Schnaiberg, A., and S. Goldenberg. 1989. From empty nest to crowded nest: The dynamics of incompletely launched young adults. *Social Problems* 36, no. 3 (June): 251–269.

Skolnick, A. 1991. *Embattled Paradise: The American Family in an Age of Uncertainty*. New York: Basic Books.

Stephens, W. N. 1963. *The Family in Cross-Cultural Perspective*. New York: World.

Veroff, J., E. Douvan, and R. A. Kulka. 1981. *The Inner American: A Self-Portrait from 1957 to 1976*. New York: Basic Books.

I *The Changing Family*

The study of the family does not belong to any single scholarly field; genetics, physiology, archaeology, history, anthropology, sociology, psychology, and economics all touch on it. Religious and ethical authorities claim a stake in the family, and troubled individuals and families generate therapeutic demands on family scholarship. In short, the study of the family is interdisciplinary, controversial, and necessary for the formulation of social policy and practices.

Interdisciplinary subjects present characteristic problems. Each discipline has its own assumptions and views of the world, which may not directly transfer into another field. Some biologists and physically oriented anthropologists, for example, analyze human affairs in terms of individual motives and instincts; for them, society is a shadowy presence, serving mainly as the setting for biologically motivated individual action. Many sociologists and cultural anthropologists, in contrast, perceive the individual as an actor playing a role written by culture and society. One important school of psychology sees people neither as passive recipients of social pressures nor as creatures driven by powerful lusts, but as information processors trying to make sense of their environment. There is no easy way to reconcile such perspectives. Scientific paradigms—characteristic ways of looking at the world—determine not only what answers will be found, but also what questions will be asked. This fact has perhaps created special confusion in the study of the family.

There is the assumption that family life, so familiar a part of everyday experience, is easily understood. But familiarity may breed a sense of destiny—what we experience is transformed into the "natural." "We speak of families," R. D. Laing has observed, "as though we know what families are. We identify, as families, networks of people who live together over time, who have ties of marriage or kinship to one another" (Laing, 1971, p. 3).

Social scientists have been arguing for many years about how to define the family, even before the dramatic changes in the past three decades. Now the question of how to define the family has become a hot political issue. Is a mother and her child a family? A cohabiting couple? A cohabiting couple with children? A married couple without children? A grandmother who is raising her grandchildren? A gay couple? A gay couple with children?

In his article here, "The Theoretical Importance of the Family," William J. Goode defines *family* as a special kind of *relationship* between people rather than a particular kind of household or group, such as two married parents and their children. He argues that in all known societies, and under many social conditions, people develop family-like social patterns, a "familistic package," even when some of the traditional aspects of family are missing.

What is in this "familistic package?" Continuity is an essential element: the expectation that the relationship will continue. This makes it possible to share money and goods, and offer help to the other person, knowing that in the future that person will reciprocate. Familiarity is another benefit; family members know one another and their likes and dislikes. In other words, the family is something like a mutual aid society. It helps individuals meet their multiple needs, including the need for affection and companionship, and also serves as an insurance policy in times of sickness or other trouble.

Still another obstacle to understanding family life is that it is hard to see the links between the larger world outside the home and the individuals and families inside. Several of the selections in Part One aim to show us these links. For example, Anthony Giddens argues that there is a global revolution going on in sexuality, in marriage and the family, and in how people think of themselves and their relationships. He argues that we are living through another wave of technological and economic modernization that is having a profound impact on personal life. Further, he sees a strong parallel between the ideals of a democratic society and the emerging new ideals of family relationships. For example, a good marriage is coming to be seen as a relationship between equals. Giddens recognizes that many of the changes in family life are worrisome, but we can't go back to the family patterns of an earlier time.

Nor would most of us really want to. Nostalgic images of the family in earlier times typically omit the high mortality rates that prevailed before the twentieth century. Death could strike at any age, and was a constant threat to family stability. Arlene Skolnick's article reveals the profound impact of high mortality on family relationships.

The readings in Chapter 2 are concerned with the meaning of family in modern society. As women increasingly participate in the paid workforce, argues Sharon Hays, they find themselves caught up in a web of cultural contradictions that remain unresolved and indeed have deepened. There is no way, she further maintains, for contemporary women to get it "just right." Both stay-at-home and working mothers maintain an intensive commitment to motherhood, although they work it out in different ways. Women who stay at home no longer feel comfortable and fulfilled being defined by themselves and others as "mere housewives." Correspondingly, working women are frequently anxious about the time away from children and the complexities of balancing parental duties with the demands of serious employment.

The cultural contradictions that trouble motherhood can be seen as a part of the larger "cultural war" over the family. But there are more than two sides in the family wars. Janet Z. Giele carefully diagrams *three* positions on the family: the conservative, the liberal, and the feminist. The latter, for Giele, is the most promising for developing public policies that would combine conservative and liberal perspectives. The feminist vision, she argues, appreciates both the "premodern nature of the family" with the inevitable interdependence of family with a modern, fast-changing economy.

One of the major changes in American society over the past several decades has been the emergence of gays and lesbians from a history of ridicule, scorn, and persecution. Attitudes of heterosexual Americans towards gays have grown more tolerant. At the same time, however, there has been a dramatic increase in campaigns against gay rights, particulary the right to marry. Gay marriage became a battleground in the Presidential election of 2004.

Why do so many gay people want to marry at a time when marriage seems to be becoming less important to everyone else? It turns out that marriage is not "just a piece of paper." Rather, it brings with it a host of benefits, rights, and responsibilities that the average married couple scarcely thinks about. But as George Chauncy points out here, not being married brings a host of problems to gay partners in their dealings with employers, hospitals, schools, loan offices, and the like. For example, if one person had to be in the hospital for an illness or an operation, the other partner might not be allowed to visit. In addition to these practical benefits, marriage is important to gays because it symbolizes their personal commitment and gains them public recognition for their relationships.

In many ways, the marriage movement among gays may be the biggest boost the institution has received in years. So why does gay marriage provoke such fierce opposition? Chauncy argues that resistance to gay rights is rooted in the belief of some conservative religious denominations that homosexuality is a sinful choice. He also finds that opposition to gay rights is linked to opposition to gender equality.

References

Laing, R. D. 1971. *The Politics of the Family.* New York: Random House.

1 *Families Past and Present*

The Theoretical Importance of the Family

William J. Goode

Through the centuries, thoughtful people have observed that the family was disintegrating. In the past several decades, this idea has become more and more common. Many analysts have reported that the family no longer performs tasks once entrusted to it—production, education, protection, for example. From these and other data we might conclude that the family is on its way out.

But almost everyone who lives out an average life span enters the married state. Most eventually have children, who will later do the same. Of the increasing number who divorce, many will hopefully or skeptically marry again. In the Western nations, a higher percentage of people marry than a century ago. Indeed, the total number of years spent within marriage by the average person is higher now than at any previous time in the history of the world. In all known societies, almost everyone lives enmeshed in a network of family rights and obligations. People are taught to accept these rules through a long period of childhood socialization. That is, people come to feel that these family patterns are both right and desirable.

At the present time, human beings appear to get as much joy and sorrow from the family as they always have, and seem as bent as ever on taking part in family life. In most of the world, the traditional family may be shaken, but the institution will probably enjoy a longer life than any nation now in existence. The family does not seem to be a powerful institution, like the military, the church, or the state, but it seems to be the most resistant to conquest, or to the efforts people make to reshape it. Any specific family may appear to be fragile or unstable, but the family system as a whole is tough and resilient.

THE FAMILY: VARIOUS VIEWS

The intense emotional meaning of family relations for almost everyone has been observed throughout history. Philosophers and social analysts have noted that any

14

society is a structure made up of families linked together. Both travelers and anthropologists often describe the peculiarities of a given society by outlining its family relations.

The earliest moral and ethical writings of many cultures assert the significance of the family. Within those commentaries, the view is often expressed that a society loses its strength if people do not fulfill family obligations. Confucius thought that happiness and prosperity would prevail if everyone would behave "correctly" as a family member. This meant primarily that no one should fail in his filial obligations. That is, the proper relationship between ruler and subjects was like that between a father and his children. The cultural importance of the family is also emphasized in the Old Testament. The books of Exodus, Deuteronomy, Ecclesiastes, Psalms, and Proverbs, for example, proclaim the importance of obeying family rules. The earliest codified literature in India, the Rig-Veda, which dates from about the last half of the second millennium B.C., and the Law of Manu, which dates from about the beginning of the Christian era, devote much attention to the family. Poetry, plays, novels, and short stories typically seize upon family relationships as the primary focus of human passion, and their ideas and themes often grow from family conflict. Even the great epic poems of war have subthemes focusing on problems in family relations.[1]

From time to time, social analysts and philosophers have presented plans for societies that *might* be created (these are called utopias) in which new family roles (rights and obligations of individual members) are offered as solutions to traditional social problems. Plato's *Republic* is one such attempt. Plato was probably the first to urge the creation of a society in which all members, men and women alike, would have an equal opportunity to develop their talents to the utmost, and to achieve a position in society solely through merit. Since family patterns in all societies prevent selection based entirely on individual worth, to Plato's utopia the tie between parents and children would play no part, because knowledge of that link would be erased. Approved conception would take place at the same time each year at certain hymeneal festivals; children born out of season would be eliminated (along with those born defective). All children would be taken from their parents at birth and reared by specially designated people.

Experimental or utopian communities like Oneida, the Shakers, the Mormons, and modern communes have typically insisted that changes in family relations were necessary to achieve their goals. Every fundamental political upheaval since the French Revolution of 1789 has offered a program that included profound changes in family relations. Since World War II, most countries of the world have written new constitutions. In perhaps all of them, but especially in all the less developed nations, these new laws have been far more advanced than public opinion in those countries. They have aimed at creating new family patterns more in conformity with the leaders' views of equality and justice, and often antagonistic to traditional family systems. This wide range of commentary, analysis, and political action, over a period of twenty-five hundred years, suggests that throughout history we have been at least implicitly aware of the importance of family patterns as a central element in human societies.

---

1. See in this connection Nicholas Tavuchis and William J. Goode (eds.) *The Family through Literature* (Oxford University Press, 1973).

THE CENTRAL POSITION
OF THE FAMILY IN SOCIETY

In most tribal societies, kinship patterns form the major part of the whole social structure. By contrast, the family is only a small part of the social structure of modern industrial societies. It is nevertheless a key element in them, specifically linking individuals with other social institutions, such as the church, the state, or the economy. Indeed modern society, with its complex advanced technology and its highly trained bureaucracy, would collapse without the contributions of this seemingly primitive social agency. The class system, too, including its restrictions on education and opportunity, its high or low social mobility rates, and its initial social placement by birth, is founded on the family.

Most important, it is within the family that the child is first socialized to serve the needs of the society, and not only its own needs. A society will not survive unless its needs are met, such as the production and distribution of commodities, protection of the young and old or the sick and the pregnant, conformity to the law, and so on. Only if individuals are motivated to serve these needs will the society continue to operate, and the foundation for that motivation is laid by the family. Family members also participate in informal social control processes. Socialization at early ages makes most of us wish to conform, but throughout each day, both as children and as adults, we are often tempted to deviate. The formal agencies of social control (such as the police) are not enough to do more than force the extreme deviant to conform. What is needed is a set of social pressures that provide feedback to the individual whenever he or she does well or poorly and thus support internal controls as well as the controls of the formal agencies. Effectively or not, the family usually takes on this task.

The family, then, is made up of individuals, but it is also a social unit, and part of a larger social network. Families are not isolated, self-enclosed social systems; and the other institutions of society, such as the military, the church, or the school system, continually rediscover that they are not dealing with individuals, but with members of families. Even in the most industrialized and urban of societies, where it is sometimes supposed that people lead rootless and anonymous lives, most people are in continual interaction with other family members. Men and women who achieve high social position usually find that even as adults they still respond to their parents' criticisms, are still angered or hurt by a sibling's scorn. Corporations that offer substantial opportunities to rising executives often find that their proposals are turned down because of objections from family members.

So it is through the family that the society is able to elicit from the individual his or her contributions. The family, in turn, can continue to exist only if it is supported by the larger society. If these two, the smaller and the larger social system, furnish each other the conditions necessary for their survival, they must be interrelated in many important ways. Thus, the two main themes in this [reading] will be the relations among family members, and the relations between the family and the society.

PRECONCEPTIONS ABOUT THE FAMILY

The task of understanding the family presents many difficulties, and one of the greatest barriers is found in ourselves. We are likely to have strong emotions about the family. Because of our own deep involvement in family relationships, objective analysis is not easy. When we read about other types of family behavior, in other classes or societies, we are likely to feel that they are odd or improper. We are tempted to argue that this or that type of family behavior is wrong or right, rather than to analyze it. Second, although we have observed many people in some of their family behavior, usually we have had very limited experience with what goes on behind the walls of other homes. This means that our sample of observations is very narrow. It also means that for almost any generalization we create or read about, we can often find some specific experience that refutes it, or fits it. Since we feel we "already know," we may not feel motivated to look for further data against which to test generalizations.

However, many supposedly well-known beliefs about the family are not well grounded in fact. Others are only partly true and must be studied more precisely if they are to be understood. One such belief is that "children hold the family together." Despite repeated attempts to affirm it, this generalization does not seem to be very strong. A more correct view seems to be that there is a modest association between divorce and not having children, but it is mostly caused by the fact that people who do not become well adjusted, and who may for some reasons be prone to divorce, are also less likely to have children.

Another way of checking whether the findings of family sociology are obvious is to present some research findings, and ask whether it was worth the bother of discovering them since "everybody knew them all along." Consider the following set of facts. Suppose a researcher had demonstrated those facts. Was it worthwhile to carry out the study, or were the facts already known?

1. Because modern industrial society breaks down traditional family systems, one result is that the age of marriage in Western nations (which was low among farmers) has risen greatly over many generations.
2. Because of the importance of the extended family in China and India, the average size of the household has always been large, with many generations living under one roof.
3. In polygynous societies, most men have several wives, and the fertility rate is higher than in monogamous societies.

Although these statements sound plausible to many people, and impressive arguments have been presented to support them, in fact they are all false. For hundreds of years, the age at marriage among farmers in Western nations has been relatively high (25–27 years), and though it rises and falls somewhat over time, there seems to be no important trend in any particular direction. With reference to multifamily households, every survey of Chinese and Indian households has shown that even generations ago they were relatively modest in size (from four to six persons, varying by region and time period). Only under special historical circumstances will large, extended households be common. As to polygyny, the fact is that except under special circumstances, almost all men in all societies must be content with only one wife, and the fertility rate of polygynous marriages (one man married to several wives) is lower than that for monogamous marriages. Thus we see that with reference to the incorrect findings just cited, common beliefs did require testing, and they were wrong.

On the other hand, of course, many popular beliefs about how families work *are* correct. We cannot assume their correctness, however. Instead, we have to examine our observations, and make studies on our own to see how well these data fit in order to improve our understanding of the dynamics of family processes in our own or in other societies. If we emphasize the problems of obtaining facts, we should not lose sight of the central truth of any science: vast quantities of figures may be entirely meaningless, unless the search is guided by fruitful hypotheses or broad conceptions of social behavior. What we seek is organized facts, a structure of propositions, in which theory and fact illuminate one another. If we do not seek actual observation, we are engaged in blind speculation. If we seek facts without theoretical guidance, our search is random and often yields findings that have no bearing on anything. Understanding the family, then, requires the same sort of careful investigation as any other scientific endeavor.

WHY THE FAMILY IS THEORETICALLY SIGNIFICANT

Because the family is so much taken for granted, we do not often stop to consider the many traits that make it theoretically interesting. A brief consideration of certain peculiarities of the family will suggest why it is worthwhile exploring this social unit.

The family is the only social institution other than religion that is formally developed in all societies: a specific social agency is in charge of a great variety of social behaviors and activities. Some have argued that legal systems did not exist in preliterate or technologically less developed tribes or societies because there was no formally organized legislative body or judiciary. Of course, it is possible to abstract from concrete behavior the legal *aspects* of action, or the economic aspects, or the political dynamics, even when there are no explicitly labeled agencies formally in control of these areas in the society. However, kinship statuses and their responsibilities are the object of both formal and informal attention in societies at a high or a low technological level.

Family duties are the direct role responsibility of everyone in the society, with rare exceptions. Almost everyone is both born into a family and founds one of his or her own. Each individual is kin to many others. Many people, by contrast, may escape the religious duties others take for granted, or military or political burdens. Moreover, many family role responsibilities cannot usually be delegated to others, while in a work situation specialized obligations can be delegated.

Taking part in family activities has the further interesting quality that though it is not backed by the formal punishments supporting many other obligations, almost everyone takes part nonetheless. We must, for example, engage in economic or productive acts, or face starvation. We must enter the army, pay taxes, and appear before courts, or face money penalties and force. Such punishments do not usually confront the individual who does not wish to marry, or refuses to talk with his father or brother. Nevertheless, so pervasive are the social pressures, and so intertwined with indirect or direct rewards and punishments, that almost everyone conforms, or claims to conform, to family demands.

Although the family is usually thought of as an *expressive* or emotional social unit, it serves as an *instrumental* agency for the larger social structures, and all other institutions and agencies depend upon its contributions. For example, the role behavior learned within the family becomes the model or prototype for behavior required in other segments of the society. Inside the family, the content of the *socialization* process is the cultural tradition of the larger society. Families are also themselves *economic* units with respect to production and allocation. With reference to *social control,* each person's total range of behavior, and how his or her time and energies are budgeted, is more easily visible to family members than to outsiders. They can evaluate how the individual is allocating his or her time and money, and how well he or she is carrying out various duties. Consequently, the family acts as a source of pressure on the individual to adjust—to work harder and play less, or go to church less and study more. In all these ways, the family is partly an instrument or agent of the larger society. If it fails to perform adequately, the goals of the larger society may not be effectively achieved.

Perhaps more interesting theoretically is the fact that the various *tasks of the family are all separable* from one another, but in fact are not separated in almost all known family systems. We shall discuss these functions or tasks in various contexts in this book, so no great elaboration is needed at this point. Here are some of the contributions of the family to the larger society: reproduction of young, physical maintenance of family members, social placement of the child, socialization, and social control.

Let us consider how these activities could be separated. For example, the mother could send her child to be fed in a neighborhood mess hall, and of course some harassed mothers do send their children to buy lunch in a local snack bar. Those who give birth to a child need not socialize the child. They might send the child to specialists, and in deed specialists do take more responsibility for this task as the child grows older. Parents might, as some eugenicists have suggested, be selected for their breeding qualities, but these might not include any great talent for training the young. Status placement might be accomplished by random drawing of lots, by IQ tests or periodic examinations in physical and intellectual skills, or by popularity polls. This assignment of children to various social positions could be done without regard to an individual's parents, those who socialized or fed the child, or others who might supervise the child's daily behavior.

Separations of this kind have been suggested from time to time, and a few hesitant attempts have been made here and there in the world to put them into operation. However, three conclusions relevant to this kind of division can be drawn: (1) In all known societies, the *ideal* (with certain qualifications to be noted) is that the family be entrusted with all these functions. (2) When one or more family tasks are entrusted to another agency by a revolutionary or utopian society, the change can be made only with the support of much ideological fervor, and usually political pressure as well. (3) These experiments are also characterized by a gradual return to the more traditional type of family. In both the Israeli *kibbutzim* and the Russian experiments in relieving parents of child care, the ideal of completely communal living was once urged. Husband and wife were to have only a personal and emotional tie with one another: divorce would be easy. The children were to see their parents at regular intervals but look to their nursery attendants and mother surrogates for affection and direction during work hours. Each individual was to contribute his or her best skills to the cooperative unit without regard to family ties or sex status (there would be few or no "female" or "male" tasks). That ideal was attempted in a modest way, but behavior gradually dropped away from the ideal. The only other country in which the pattern has been attempted on a large scale is China. Already

Chinese communes have retreated from their high ambitions, following the path of the *kibbutz* and the Russian *kolkhoz*.

Various factors contribute to these deviations from attempts to create a new type of family, and the two most important sets of pressures cannot easily be separated from each other. First is the problem, also noted by Plato, that individuals who develop their own attitudes and behaviors in the usual Western (European and European-based) family system do not easily adjust to the communal "family" even when they believe it is the right way. The second is the likelihood that when the family is radically changed, the various relations between it and the larger society are changed. New strains are created, demanding new kinds of adjustments on the part of the individuals in the society. Perhaps the planners must develop somewhat different agencies, or a different blueprint, to transform the family.

These comments have nothing to do with "capitalism" in its current political and economic argument with "communism." They merely describe the historical fact that though various experiments in separating the major functions of the family from one another have been conducted, none of these evolved from a previously existing family system. In addition, the several modern important attempts at such a separation, including the smaller communes that were created in the United States during the 1960s and 1970s, mostly exhibit a common pattern, a movement *away* from the utopian blueprint of separating the various family activities and giving each of them to a different social unit.

It is possible that some of these activities (meals) can be more easily separated than others; or that some family systems (for example, matrilineal systems) might lend themselves to such a separation more easily than others. On the other hand, we have to begin with the data that are now available. Even cautiously interpreted, they suggest that the family is a rather stable institution. On the other hand, we have not yet analyzed what this particular institution is. In the next section we discuss this question.

DEFINING THE FAMILY: A MATTER OF MORE OR LESS

Since thousands of publications have presented research findings on the family, one might suppose that there must be agreement on what this social unit is. In fact, sociologists and anthropologists have argued for decades about how to define it. Indeed, creating a clear, formal definition of any object of study is sometimes more difficult than making a study of that object. If we use a *concrete* definition, and assert that "a family is a social unit made up of father, mother, and children," then only about 35 percent of all U.S. households can be classed as a family. Much of the research on the family would have to exclude a majority of residential units. In addition, in some societies, one wife may be married to several husbands, or one husband to several wives. The definition would exclude such units. In a few societies there have been "families" in which the "husband" was a woman; and in some, certain "husbands" were not expected to live with their "wives." In the United States, millions of households contain at least one child, but only one parent. In a few communes, every adult male is married to all other adult females. That is, there are many kinds of social units that seem to be like a family, but do not fit almost any concrete definition that we might formulate.

We can escape such criticisms in part by claiming that most adults eventually go through such a *phase* of family life; that is, almost all men and women in the United States marry at some time during their lives, and most of them eventually have children. Nevertheless, analysis of the family would be much thinner if we focused only on that one kind of household. In ordinary language usage, people are most likely to agree that a social unit made up of father, mother, and child or children is a genuine family. They will begin to disagree more and more, as one or more of those persons or social roles is missing. Few people would agree that, at the other extremes, a household with only a single person in it is a family. Far more would think of a household as a family if it comprised a widow and her several children. Most people would agree that a husband-wife household is a family if they have children, even if their children are now living somewhere else. However, many would not be willing to class a childless couple as a family, especially if that couple planned never to have children. Very few people would be willing to accept a homosexual couple as a family.

What can we learn from such ordinary language usage? First, that *family* is not a single thing, to be captured by a neat verbal formula. Second, many social units can be thought of as "more or less" families, as they are more or less similar to the traditional type of family. Third, much of this graded similarity can be traced to the different kinds of role relations to be found in that traditional unit. Doubtless the following list is not comprehensive, but it includes most of those relationships: (1) At least two adult persons of opposite sex reside together. (2) They engage in some kind of division of labor; that is, they do not both perform exactly the same tasks. (3) They engage in many types of economic and social exchanges; that is, they do things for one another. (4) They share many things in common, such as food, sex, residence, and both goods and social activities. (5) The adults have parental relations with their children, as their children have filial relations with them; the parents have some authority over their children, and both share with one another, while also assuming some obligation for protection, cooperation, and nurturance. (6) There are sibling relations among the children themselves, with, once more, a range of obligations to share, protect, and help one another. When all these conditions exist, few people would deny that the unit is a family. As we consider households in which more are missing, a larger number of people would express some doubt as to whether it really is a family. Thus, if two adults live together, but do nothing for each other, few people would agree that it is a family. If they do not even live together, fewer still would call the couple a family.

Individuals create all sorts of relations with each other, but others are more or less likely to view them as a family to the extent that their continuing social relations exhibit some or all of the role patterns noted above. Most important for our understanding of the family is that in all known societies, and under a wide range of social conditions, some kinds of familistic living arrangements seem to emerge, with some or all of these traits. These arrangements can emerge in prisons (with homosexual couples as units), under the disorganized conditions of revolution, conquest, or epidemic; or even when political attempts are made to reduce the importance of the family, and instead to press people to live in a more communal fashion. That is, people create and re-create some forms of familistic social patterns even when some of those traditional elements are missing.

This raises the inevitable question: Why does this happen? Why do people continue to form familistic relations, even when they are not convinced that it is the ideal social arrangement? Why is *this* and not some *other* social pattern so widespread? Of course, this is not an argument for the *universality* of the conjugal family. Many other kinds of relations between individuals are created. Nevertheless, some approximation of these familistic relationships do continue to occur in the face of many alternative temptations and opportunities as well as counterpressures. Unless we are willing to assert that people are irrational, we must conclude that these relationships must offer some *advantages*. What are they?

ADVANTAGES OF THE "FAMILISTIC PACKAGE"

We suppose that the most fundamental set of advantages is found in the division of labor and the resulting possibility of social exchanges between husband and wife (or members of a homosexual couple), as well as between children and parents. This includes not only economic goods, but help, nurturance, protection, and affection. It is often forgotten that the modern domestic household is very much an *economic* unit even if it is no longer a farming unit. People are actually producing goods and services for one another. They are buying objects in one place, and transporting them to the household. They are transforming food into meals. They are engaged in cleaning, mowing lawns, repairing, transporting, counseling,—a wide array of services that would have to be paid for in money if some member of the family did not do them.

Families of all types also enjoy some small economies of scale. When there are two or more members of the household, various kinds of activities can be done almost as easily for everyone as for a single person; it is almost as easy to prepare one meal for three or four people as it is to prepare a similar meal for one person. Thus, the cost of a meal is less per person within a family. Families can cooperate to achieve what an individual cannot, from building a mountain cabin to creating a certain style of life. Help from all members will make it much easier to achieve that goal than it would be for one person.

All the historic forms of the family that we know, including communal group marriages, are also attractive because they offer *continuity*. Thus, whatever the members produce together, they expect to be able to enjoy together later. Continuity has several implications. One is that members do not have to bear the costs of continually searching for new partners, or for new members who might be "better" at various family tasks. In addition, husband and wife, as well as children, enjoy a much longer line of social credit than they would have if they were making exchanges with people outside the family. This means that an individual can give more at one time to someone in the family, knowing that in the longer run this will not be a loss: the other person will remain long enough to reciprocate at some point, or perhaps still another member will offer help at a later time.

Next, the familistic mode of living offers several of the advantages of any informal group.[2] It exhibits, for example, a very short line of communication; everyone is close by,

2. For further comparisons of bureaucracy and informal groups, see Eugene Litwak, "Technical Innovation and Theoretical Functions of Primary Groups and Bureaucratic Structures," *American Journal of Sociology*, 73 (1968), 468–481.

and members need not communicate through intermediaries. Thus they can respond quickly in case of need. A short line of communication makes cooperation much easier. Second, everyone has many idiosyncratic needs and wishes. In day to day interaction with outsiders, we need not adjust to these very much, and they may be a nuisance; others, in turn, are likely not to adjust to our own idiosyncracies. However, within the familistic mode of social interaction, people learn what each other's idiosyncratic needs are. Learning such needs can and does make life together somewhat more attractive because adjusting to them may not be a great burden, but does give pleasure to the other. These include such trivia as how strong the tea or coffee should be, how much talk there will be at meals, sleep and work schedules, levels of noise, and so on. Of course with that knowledge we can more easily make others miserable, too, if we wish to do so.

Domestic tasks typically do not require high expertise, and as a consequence most members of the family can learn to do them eventually. Because they do learn, members derive many benefits from one another, without having to go outside the family unit. Again, this makes a familistic mode of living more attractive than it would be otherwise. In addition, with reference to many such tasks, there are no outside experts anyway (throughout most of world history, there have been no experts in childrearing, taking care of small cuts or bruises, murmuring consoling words in response to some distress, and so on). That is, the tasks within a family setting are likely to be tasks at which insiders are at least as good as outsiders, and typically better.

No other social institutions offer this range of complementarities, sharing, and closely linked, interwoven advantages. The closest possible exception might be some ascribed, ritual friendships in a few societies, but even these do not offer the range of exchanges that are to be found in the familistic processes.

We have focused on advantages that the *members* of families obtain from living under this type of arrangement. However, when we survey the wide range of family patterns in hundreds of societies, we are struck by the fact that this social unit is strongly supported by *outsiders*—that is, members of the larger society.

It is supported by a structure of norms, values, laws, and a wide range of social pressures. More concretely, other members of the society believe such units are necessary, and they are concerned about how people discharge their obligations within the family. They punish members of the family who do not conform to ideal behavior, and praise those who do conform. These intrusions are not simply whimsical, or a matter of oppression. Other members of the society do in fact have a stake in how families discharge their various tasks. More broadly, it is widely believed that the collective needs of the whole society are served by some of the activities individual families carry out. In short, it is characteristic of the varieties of the family that participants on an average enjoy more, and gain more comfort, pleasure, or advantage from being in a familistic arrangement than from living alone; and *other* members of the society view that arrangement as contributing in some measure to the survival of the society itself. Members of societies have usually supposed it important for most *other* individuals to form families, to rear children, to create the next generation, to support and help each other—whether or not individual members of specific families do in fact feel they gain real advantages from living in a familistic arrangement. For example, over many centuries, people opposed legal divorces, whether or not they themselves were happily married, and with little regard for the marital happiness of others.

This view of what makes up the "familistic social package" explains several kinds of widely observable social behavior. One is that people experiment with different kinds of arrangements, often guided by a new philosophy of how people ought to live. They do so because their own needs have not been adequately fulfilled in the traditional modes of family arrangements available to them in their own society. Since other people have a stake in the kinds of familistic arrangements people make, we can also expect that when some individuals or groups attempt to change or experiment with the established system, various members of the society will object, and may even persecute them for it. We can also see why it is that even in a high-divorce society such as our own, where millions of people have been dissatisfied or hurt by their marriages and their divorces, they nevertheless move back into a marital arrangement. That is, after examining various alternatives, the familistic social package still seems to offer a broader set of personal advantages, and the outside society supports that move. And, as noted earlier, even when there are strong political pressures to create new social units that give far less support for the individual family, as in China, Russia, and the Israeli *kibbutzim*, we can expect that people will continue to drift back toward some kind of familistic arrangement.

A SOCIOLOGICAL APPROACH TO FAMILY RESEARCH

The unusual traits the family exhibits as a type of social subsystem require that some attention be paid to the analytic approach to be used in studying it. First, neither ideal nor reality can be excluded from our attention. It would, for example, be naive to suppose that because some 40 percent of all U.S. couples now marrying will eventually divorce, they do not cherish the ideal of remaining married to one person. Contemporary estimates suggest that about half of all married men engage in extramarital intercourse at some time, but public opinion surveys report that a large majority of both men and women in the United States, even in these permissive times, approve of the ideal of faithfulness. On a more personal level, every reader of these lines has lied at some time, but nevertheless most believe in the ideal of telling the truth.

A sociologist ascertains the ideals of family systems partly because they are a rough guide to behavior. Knowing that people prefer to have their sons and daughters marry at least at the same class level, we can expect them to try to control their children's mate choices if they can do so. We can also specify some of the conditions under which they will have a greater or lesser success in reaching that goal. We also know that when a person violates the ideal, he or she is likely to conceal the violation if possible. If that is not possible, people will try to find some excuse for the violation, and are likely to be embarrassed if others find out about it.

The sociology of the family cannot confine itself only to contemporary urban (or suburban) American life. Conclusions of any substantial validity or scope must include data from other societies, whether these are past or present, industrial or nonindustrial, Asian or European. Data from the historical past, such as Periclean Athens or imperial Rome, are not often used because no sociologically adequate account of their family systems has as yet been written.[3] On the other hand, the last two decades have seen the appearance of many studies about family systems in various European cities of the last five centuries.

The study of customs and beliefs from the past yields a better understanding of the possible range of social behavior. Thereby, we are led to deny or at least to qualify a finding that might be correct if limited only to modern American life (such as the rise in divorce rates over several decades). The use of data from tribal societies of the past or present helps us in testing conclusions about family systems that are not found at all in Western society, such as matrilineal systems or polygyny. Or, an apparently simple relationship may take a different form in other societies. For example, in the United States most first marriages are based on a love relationship (whatever else they may be based on), and people are reluctant to admit that they have married someone with whom they were not in love. By contrast, though people fall in love in other societies, love may play a small or a large part in the marriage system. . . .

It is possible to study almost any phenomenon from a wide range of viewpoints. We may study the economic aspects of family behavior, or we may confine ourselves to the biological factors in family patterns. A full analysis of any concrete object is impossible. Everything can be analyzed from many vantage points, each of them yielding a somewhat different but still limited picture. Everything is infinitely complex. Each science limits its perspective to the range of processes that it considers important. Each such approach has its own justification. Here we examine the family mainly from a sociological perspective.

The sociological approach focuses on the family as a social institution, the peculiar and unique quality of family interaction as *social*. For example, family systems exhibit the characteristics of legitimacy and authority, which are not biological categories at all. The values and the prescribed behavior to be found in a family, or the rights and duties of family statuses such as father or daughter, are not psychological categories. They are peculiar to the theoretical approach of sociology. Personality theory is not very useful in explaining the particular position of the family in Chinese and Japanese social structures, although it may help us understand how individuals respond emotionally to those rights and obligations. If we use a consistently sociological approach, we will miss some important information about concrete family interaction. The possible gain when we stay on one theoretical level may be the achievement of some increased systematization, and some greater rigor.

At a minimum, however, when an analyst moves from the sociological to the psychological level of theory, he or she ought at least to be conscious of it. If the investigation turns to the impact of biological or psychological factors on the family, they should be examined with reference to their *social* meaning. For example, interracial marriage appears to be of little biological significance, but it has much social impact on those who take part in such a marriage. A sociologist who studies the family is not likely to be an expert in the *psychodynamics* of mental disease, but is interested in the effect of mental disease on the social relations in a particular family or type of family, or in the adjustment different family types make to it.

---

3. However, Keith Hopkins has published several specialized studies on various aspects of Roman families. See his *Conquerors and Slaves* (Cambridge, Eng.: Cambridge University Press, 1978).

■READING 2

The Global Revolution in Family and Personal Life

Anthony Giddens

Among all the changes going on today, none are more important than those happening in our personal lives—in sexuality, emotional life, marriage and the family. There is a global revolution going on in how we think of ourselves and how we form ties and connections with others. It is a revolution advancing unevenly in different regions and cultures, with many resistances.

As with other aspects of the runaway world, we don't know what the ratio of advantages and anxieties will turn out to be. In some ways, these are the most difficult and disturbing transformations of all. Most of us can tune out from larger problems for much of the time. We can't opt out, however, from the swirl of change reaching right into the heart of our emotional lives.

There are few countries in the world where there isn't intense discussion about sexual equality, the regulation of sexuality and the future of the family. And where there isn't open debate, this is mostly because it is actively repressed by authoritarian governments or fundamentalist groups. In many cases, these controversies are national or local—as are the social and political reactions to them. Politicians and pressure groups will suggest that if only family policy were modified, if only divorce were made harder or easier to get in their particular country, solutions to our problems could readily be found.

But the changes affecting the personal and emotional spheres go far beyond the borders of any particular country, even one as large as the United States. We find the same issues almost everywhere, differing only in degree and according to the cultural context in which they take place.

In China, for example, the state is considering making divorce more difficult. In the aftermath of the Cultural Revolution, very liberal marriage laws were passed. Marriage is a working contract, that can be dissolved, I quote: "when husband and wife both desire it."

Even if one partner objects, divorce can be granted when "mutual affection" has gone from the marriage. Only a two week wait is required, after which the two pay $4 and are henceforth independent. The Chinese divorce rate is still low as compared with Western countries, but it is rising rapidly—as is true in the other developing Asian societies. In Chinese cities, not only divorce, but cohabitation is becoming more frequent.

In the vast Chinese countryside, by contrast, everything is different. Marriage and the family are much more traditional—in spite of the official policy of limiting childbirth through a mixture of incentives and punishment. Marriage is an arrangement between two families, fixed by the parents rather than the individuals concerned.

A recent study in the province of Gansu, which has only a low level of economic development, found that 60% of marriages are still arranged by parents. As a Chinese saying has it: "meet once, nod your head and marry." There is a twist in the tail in modernising China. Many of those currently divorcing in the urban centres were married in the traditional manner in the country.

In China there is much talk of protecting the family. In many Western countries the debate is even more shrill. The family is a site for the struggles between tradition and modernity, but also a metaphor for them. There is perhaps more nostalgia surrounding the lost haven of the family than for any other institution with its roots in the past. Politicians and activists routinely diagnose the breakdown of family life and call for a return to the traditional family.

Now the "traditional family" is very much a catch-all category. There have been many different types of family and kinship systems in different societies and cultures. The Chinese family, for instance, was always distinct from family forms in the West. Arranged marriage was never as common in most European countries, as in China, or India. Yet the family in non-modern cultures did, and does, have some features found more or less everywhere.

The traditional family was above all an economic unit. Agricultural production normally involved the whole family group, while among the gentry and aristocracy, transmission of property was the main basis of marriage. In mediaeval Europe, marriage was not contracted on the basis of sexual love, nor was it regarded as a place where such love should flourish. As the French historian, Georges Duby, puts it, marriage in the middle ages was not to involve "frivolity, passion, or fantasy."

The inequality of men and women was intrinsic to the traditional family. I don't think one could overstate the importance of this. In Europe, women were the property of their husbands or fathers—chattels as defined in law.

In the traditional family, it wasn't only women who lacked rights—children did too. The idea of enshrining children's rights in law is in historical terms relatively recent. In premodern periods, as in traditional cultures today, children weren't reared for their own sake, or for the satisfaction of the parents. One could almost say that children weren't recognised as individuals.

It wasn't that parents didn't love their children, but they cared about them more for the contribution they made to the common economic task than for themselves. Moreover, the death rate of children was frightening. In Colonial America nearly one in four infants died in their first year. Almost 50% didn't live to age 10.

Except for certain courtly or elite groups, in the traditional family sexuality was always dominated by reproduction. This was a matter of tradition and nature combined. The absence of effective contraception meant that for most women sexuality was inevitably closely connected with childbirth. In many traditional cultures, including in Western Europe up to the threshold of the 20th Century, a woman might have 10 or more pregnancies during the course of her life.

Sexuality was regulated by the idea of female virtue. The sexual double standard is often thought of as a creation of the Victorian period. In fact, in one version or another it was central to almost all non-modern societies. It involved a dualistic view of female sexuality—a clear cut division between the virtuous woman on the one hand and the libertine on the other.

Sexual promiscuity in many cultures has been taken as a positive defining feature of masculinity. James Bond is, or was, admired for his sexual as well as his physical heroism. Sexually adventurous women, by contrast, have nearly always been beyond the pale, no matter how much influence the mistresses of some prominent figures might have achieved.

Attitudes towards homosexuality were also governed by a mix of tradition and nature. Anthropological surveys show that homosexuality—or male homosexuality at any rate—has been tolerated, or openly approved of, in more cultures than it has been outlawed.

Those societies that have been hostile to homosexuality have usually condemned it as specifically unnatural. Western attitudes have been more extreme than most; less than half a century ago homosexuality was still widely regarded as a perversion and written up as such in manuals of psychiatry.

Antagonism towards homosexuality is still widespread and the dualistic view of women continues to be held by many—of both sexes. But over the past few decades the main elements of people's sexual lives in the West have changed in an absolutely basic way. The separation of sexuality from reproduction is in principle complete. Sexuality is for the first time something to be discovered, moulded, altered. Sexuality, which used to be defined so strictly in relation to marriage and legitimacy, now has little connection to them at all. We should see the increasing acceptance of homosexuality not just as a tribute to liberal tolerance. It is a logical outcome of the severance of sexuality from reproduction. Sexuality which has no content is by definition no longer dominated by heterosexuality.

What most of its defenders in Western countries call the traditional family was in fact a late, transitional phase in family development in the 1950's. This was a time at which the proportion of women out at work was still relatively low and when it was still difficult, especially for women, to obtain divorce without stigma. On the other hand, men and women by this time were more equal than they had been previously, both in fact and in law. The family had ceased to be an economic entity and the idea of romantic love as basis for marriage had replaced marriage as an economic contract.

Since then, the family has changed much further. The details vary from society to society, but the same trends are visible almost everywhere in the industrialised world. Only a minority of people now live in what might be called the standard 1950's family—both parents living together with their children of the marriage, where the mother is a full time housewife, and the father the breadwinner. In some countries, more than a third of all births happen outside wedlock, while the proportion of people living alone has gone up steeply and looks likely to rise even more.

In most societies, like the U.S., marriage remains popular—the U.S. has aptly been called a high divorce, high marriage society. In Scandinavia, on the other hand, a large proportion of people living together, including where children are involved, remain unmarried. Moreover, up to a quarter of women aged between 18 and 35 in the U.S. and Europe say they do not intend to have children—and they appear to mean it.

Of course in all countries older family forms continue to exist. In the U.S., many people, recent immigrants particularly, still live according to traditional values. Most family life, however, has been transformed by the rise of the couple and coupledom. Marriage and the family have become what I termed in an earlier lecture shell institutions. They are still called the same, but inside their basic character has changed.

In the traditional family, the married couple was only one part, and often not the main part, of the family system. Ties with children and other relatives tended to be equally or even more important in the day to day conduct of social life. Today the couple, married or unmarried, is at the core of what the family is. The couple came to be at the centre of family life as the economic role of the family dwindled and love, or love plus sexual attraction, became the basis of forming marriage ties.

A couple once constituted has its own exclusive history, its own biography. It is a unit based upon emotional communication or intimacy. The idea of intimacy, like so many other familiar notions I've discussed in these lectures, sounds old but in fact is very new. Marriage was never in the past based upon intimacy—emotional communication. No doubt this was important to a good marriage but it was not the foundation of it. For the couple, it is. Communication is the means of establishing the tie in the first place and it is the chief rationale for its continuation.

We should recognise what a major transition this is. "Coupling" and "uncoupling" provide a more accurate description of the arena of personal life now than do "marriage and the family." A more important question for us than "are you married?" is "how good is your relationship?"

The idea of a relationship is also surprisingly recent. Only 30 or so years ago, no one spoke of "relationships." They didn't need to, nor did they need to speak in terms of intimacy and commitment. Marriage at that time was the commitment, as the existence of shotgun marriages bore witness. While statistically marriage is still the normal condition, for most people its meaning has more or less completely changed. Marriage signifies that a couple is in a stable relationship, and may indeed promote that stability, since it makes a public declaration of commitment. However, marriage is no longer the chief defining basis of coupledom.

The position of children in all this is interesting and somewhat paradoxical. Our attitudes towards children and their protection have altered radically over the past several generations. We prize children so much partly because they have become so much rarer, and partly because the decision to have a child is very different from what it was for previous generations. In the traditional family, children were an economic benefit. Today in Western countries a child, on the contrary, puts a large financial burden on the parents. Having a child is more of a distinct and specific decision than it used to be, and it is a decision guided by psychological and emotional needs. The worries we have about the effects of divorce upon children, and the existence of many fatherless families, have to be understood against the background of our much higher expectations about how children should be cared for and protected.

There are three areas in which emotional communication, and therefore intimacy, are replacing the old ties that used to bind together people's personal lives—in sexual and love relations, parent-child relations and in friendship.

To analyse these, I want to use the idea of what I call the "pure relationship." I mean by this a relationship based upon emotional communication, where the rewards derived from such communication are the main basis for the relationship to continue.

I don't mean a sexually pure relationship. Also I don't mean anything that exists in reality. I'm talking of an abstract idea that helps us understand changes going on in the world. Each of the three areas just mentioned—sexual relationships, parent-child relations and friendship—is tending to approximate to this model. Emotional communication or intimacy, in other words, are becoming the key to what they are all about.

The pure relationship has quite different dynamics from more traditional social ties. It depends upon processes of active trust—opening oneself up to the other. Self-disclosure is the basic condition of intimacy.

The pure relationship is also implicitly democratic. When I was originally working on the study of intimate relationships, I read a great deal of therapeutic and self-help literature on the subject. I was struck by something I don't believe has been widely noticed or remarked upon. If one looks at how a therapist sees a good relationship—in any of the three spheres just mentioned—it is striking how direct a parallel there is with public democracy.

A good relationship, of course, is an ideal—most ordinary relationships don't come even close. I'm not suggesting that our relations with spouses, lovers, children or friends aren't often messy, conflictful and unsatisfying. But the principles of public democracy are ideals too, that also often stand at some large distance from reality.

A good relationship is a relationship of equals, where each party has equal rights and obligations. In such a relationship, each person has respect, and wants the best, for the other. The pure relationship is based upon communication, so that understanding the other person's point of view is essential.

Talk, or dialogue, are the basis of making the relationship work. Relationships function best if people don't hide too much from each other—there has to be mutual trust. And trust has to be worked at, it can't just be taken for granted.

Finally, a good relationship is one free from arbitrary power, coercion or violence.

Every one of these qualities conforms to the values of democratic politics. In a democracy, all are in principle equal, and with equality of rights and responsibilities comes mutual respect. Open dialogue is a core property of democracy. Democratic systems substitute open discussion of issues—a public space of dialogue—for authoritarian power, or for the sedimented power of tradition. No democracy can work without trust. And democracy is undermined if it gives way to authoritarianism or violence.

When we apply these principles—as ideals, I would stress again—to relationships, we are talking of something very important—the possible emergence of what I shall call, a democracy of the emotions in everyday life. A democracy of the emotions, it seems to me, is as important as public democracy in improving the quality of our lives.

This holds as much in parent-child relations as in other areas. These can't, and shouldn't, be materially equal. Parents must have authority over children, in everyone's interests. Yet they should presume an in-principle equality. In a democratic family, the authority of parents should be based upon an implicit contract. The parent in effect says to the child: "If you were an adult, and knew what I know, you would agree that what I ask you to do is legitimate."

Children in traditional families were—and are—supposed to be seen and not heard. Many parents, perhaps despairing of their children's rebelliousness, would dearly like to resurrect that rule. But there isn't any going back to it, nor should there be. In a democracy of the emotions, children can and should be able to answer back.

An emotional democracy doesn't imply lack of discipline, or absence of authority. It simply seeks to put them on a different footing.

Something very similar happened in the public sphere, when democracy began to replace arbitrary government and the rule of force. And like public democracy the democratic family must be anchored in a stable, yet open, civil society. If I may coin a phrase—"It takes a village."

A democracy of the emotions would draw no distinctions of principle between heterosexual and same-sex relationships. Gays, rather than heterosexuals, have actually been pioneers in discovering the new world of relationships and exploring its possibilities. They have had to be, because when homosexuality came out of the closet, gays weren't able to depend upon the normal supports of traditional marriage. They have had to be innovators, often in a hostile environment.

To speak of fostering an emotional democracy doesn't mean being weak about family duties, or about public policy towards the family. Democracy, after all, means the acceptance of obligations, as well as rights sanctioned in law. The protection of children has to be the primary feature of legislation and public policy. Parents should be legally obliged to provide for their children until adulthood, no matter what living arrangements they enter into. Marriage is no longer an economic institution, yet as a ritual commitment it can help stabilise otherwise fragile relationships. If this applies to heterosexual relationships, I don't see why it shouldn't apply to homosexual ones too.

There are many questions to be asked of all this—too many to answer in a short lecture. I have concentrated mainly upon trends affecting the family in Western countries. What about areas where the traditional family remains largely intact, as in the example of China with which I began? Will the changes observed in the West become more and more global?

I think they will—indeed that they are. It isn't a question of whether existing forms of the traditional family will become modified, but when and how. I would venture even further. What I have described as an emerging democracy of the emotions is on the front line in the struggle between cosmopolitanism and fundamentalism that I described in the last lecture. Equality of the sexes, and the sexual freedom of women, which are incompatible with the traditional family, are anathema to fundamentalist groups. Opposition to them, indeed, is one of the defining features of religious fundamentalism across the world.

There is plenty to be worried about in the state of the family, in Western countries and elsewhere. It is just as mistaken to say that every family form is as good as any other, as to argue that the decline of the traditional family is a disaster.

I would turn the argument of the political and fundamentalist right on its head. The persistence of the traditional family—or aspects of it—in many parts of the world is more worrisome than its decline. For what are the most important forces promoting democracy and economic development in poorer countries? Well, they are the equality and education of women. And what must be changed to make these possible? Most importantly, what must be changed is the traditional family.

In conclusion, I should emphasise that sexual equality is not just a core principle of democracy. It is also relevant to happiness and fulfilment.

Many of the changes happening to the family are problematic and difficult. But surveys in the U.S. and Europe show that few want to go back to traditional male and female roles, much less to legally defined inequality.

If ever I were tempted to think that the traditional family might be best after all, I remember what my great aunt said. She must have had one of the longest marriages of anyone. She married young, and was with her husband for over 60 years. She once confided to me that she had been deeply unhappy with him the whole of that time. In her day there was no escape.

READING 3

The Life Course Revolution

Arlene Skolnick

Many of us, in moments of nostalgia, imagine the past as a kind of Disneyland—a quaint setting we might step back into with our sense of ourselves intact, yet free of the stresses of modern life. But in yearning for the golden past we imagine we have lost, we are unaware of what we have escaped.

In our time, for example, dying before reaching old age has become a rare event; about three-quarters of all people die after their sixty-fifth birthday. It is hard for us to appreciate what a novelty this is in human experience. In 1850, only 2 percent of the population lived past sixty-five. "We place dying in what we take to be its logical position," observes the social historian Ronald Blythe, "which is at the close of a long life, whereas our ancestors accepted the futility of placing it in any position at all. In the midst of life we are in death, they said, and they meant it. To them it was a fact; to us it is a metaphor."

This longevity revolution is largely a twentieth-century phenomenon. Astonishingly, two-thirds of the total increase in human longevity since prehistoric times has taken place since 1900—and a good deal of that increase has occurred in recent decades. Mortality rates in previous centuries were several times higher than today, and death commonly struck at any age. Infancy was particularly hazardous; "it took two babies to make one adult," as one demographer put it. A white baby girl today has a greater chance of living to be sixty than her counterpart born in 1870 would have had of reaching her first birthday. And after infancy, death still hovered as an ever-present possibility. It was not unusual for young and middle-aged adults to die of tuberculosis, pneumonia, or other infectious diseases. (Keats died at twenty-five, Schubert at thirty-one, Mozart at thirty-five.)

These simple changes in mortality have had profound, yet little-appreciated effects on family life; they have encouraged stronger emotional bonds between parents and children, lengthened the duration of marriage and parent-child relationships, made grandparenthood an expectable stage of the life course, and increased the number of grandparents whom children actually know. More and more families have four or even five generations alive at the same time. And for the first time in history, the average couple has more parents living than it has children. It is also the first era when most of the parent-child relationship takes place after the child becomes an adult.

In a paper entitled "Death and the Family," the demographer Peter Uhlenberg has examined some of these repercussions by contrasting conditions in 1900 with those in 1976. In 1900, for example, half of all parents would have experienced the death of a child; by 1976 only 6 percent would. And more than half of all children who lived to the age of fifteen in 1900 would have experienced the death of a parent or sibling, compared with less than 9 percent in 1976. Another outcome of the lower death rates was a decline in the number of orphans and orphanages. Current discussions of divorce rarely take into account the almost constant family disruption children experienced in "the good old days." In 1900, 1 out of 4 children under the age of fifteen lost a parent; 1 out of 62 lost both. The corresponding figures for 1976 are, respectively, 1 out of 20 and 1 out of 1,800.

Because being orphaned used to be so common, the chances of a child's not living with either parent was much greater at the turn of the century than it is now. Indeed, some of the current growth in single-parent families is offset by a decline in the number of children raised in institutions, in foster homes, or by relatives. This fact does not diminish the stresses of divorce and other serious family problems of today, but it does help correct the tendency to contrast the terrible Present with an idealized Past.

Today's children rarely experience the death of a close relative, except for elderly grandparents. And it is possible to grow into adulthood without experiencing even that loss. "We never had any deaths in my family," a friend recently told me, explaining that none of her relatives had died until she was in her twenties. In earlier times, children were made aware of the constant possibility of death, attended deathbed scenes, and were even encouraged to examine the decaying corpses of family members.

One psychological result of our escape from the daily presence of death is that we are ill prepared for it when it comes. For most of us, the first time we feel a heightened concern with our own mortality is in our thirties and forties when we realize that the years we have already lived outnumber those we have left.

Another result is that the death of a child is no longer a sad but normal hazard of parenthood. Rather, it has become a devastating, life-shattering loss from which a parent may never fully recover. The intense emotional bonding between parents and infants that we see as a sociobiological given did not become the norm until the eighteenth and nineteenth centuries. The privileged classes created the concept of the "emotionally priceless" child, a powerful ideal that gradually filtered down through the rest of society.

The high infant mortality rates of premodern times were partly due to neglect, and often to lethal child-rearing practices such as sending infants off to a wet nurse* or, worse, infanticide. It now appears that in all societies lacking reliable contraception, the careless treatment and neglect of unwanted children acted as a major form of birth control. This does not necessarily imply that parents were uncaring toward all their children; rather, they seem to have practiced "selective neglect" of sickly infants in favor of sturdy ones, or of later children in favor of earlier ones.† In 1801 a writer observed of Bavarian peasants:

> The peasant has joy when his wife brings forth the first fruit of their love, he has joy with the second and third as well, but not with the fourth. . . . He sees all children coming

---

*Wet-nursing—the breastfeeding of an infant by a woman other than the mother—was widely practiced in premodern Europe and colonial America. Writing of a two-thousand-year-old "war of the breast," the developmental psychologist William Kessen notes that the most persistent theme in the history of childhood is the reluctance of mothers to suckle their babies, and the urgings of philosophers and physicians that they do so. Infants were typically sent away from home for a year and a half or two years to be raised by poor country women, in squalid conditions. When they took in more babies than they had milk enough to suckle, the babies would die of malnutrition.

The reluctance to breast-feed may not have reflected maternal indifference so much as other demands in premodern, precontraceptive times—the need to take part in the family economy, the unwillingness of husbands to abstain from sex for a year and a half or two. (Her milk would dry up if a mother became pregnant.) Although in France and elsewhere the custom persisted into the twentieth century, large-scale wet-nursing symbolizes the gulf between modern and premodern sensibilities about infants and their care.

†The anthropologist Nancy Scheper-Hughes describes how impoverished mothers in northeastern Brazil select which infants to nurture.

thereafter as hostile creatures, which take the bread from his mouth and the mouths of his family. Even the heart of the most gentle mother becomes cold with the birth of the fifth child, and the sixth, she unashamedly wishes death, that the child should pass to heaven.

Declining fertility rates are another major result of falling death rates. Until the baby boom of the 1940s and 1950s, fertility rates had been dropping continuously since the eighteenth century. By taking away parents' fear that some of their children would not survive to adulthood, lowered early-childhood mortality rates encouraged careful planning of births and smaller families. The combination of longer lives and fewer, more closely spaced children created a still-lengthening empty-nest stage in the family. This in turn has encouraged the companionate style of marriage, since husband and wife can expect to live together for many years after their children have moved out.

Many demographers have suggested that falling mortality rates are directly linked to rising divorce rates. In 1891 W. F. Willcox of Cornell University made one of the most accurate social science predictions ever. Looking at the high and steadily rising divorce rates of the time, along with falling mortality rates, he predicted that around 1980, the two curves would cross and the number of marriages ended by divorce would equal those ended by death. In the late 1970s, it all happened as Willcox had predicted. Then divorce rates continued to increase before leveling off in the 1980s, while mortality rates continued to decline. As a result, a couple marrying today is more likely to celebrate a fortieth wedding anniversary than were couples around the turn of the century.

In statistical terms, then, it looks as if divorce has restored a level of instability to marriage that had existed earlier due to the high mortality rate. But as Lawrence Stone observes, "it would be rash to claim that the psychological effects of the termination of marriage by divorce, that is by an act of will, bear a close resemblance to its termination by the inexorable accident of death."

THE NEW STAGES OF LIFE

In recent years it has become clear that the stages of life we usually think of as built into human development are, to a large degree, social and cultural inventions. Although people everywhere may pass through infancy, childhood, adulthood, and old age, the facts of nature are "doctored," as Ruth Benedict once put it, in different ways by different cultures.

The Favorite Age

In 1962 Phillipe Ariès made the startling claim that "in medieval society, the idea of childhood did not exist." Ariès argued not that parents then neglected their children, but that they did not think of children as having a special nature that required special treatment; after the age of around five to seven, children simply joined the adult world of work and play. This "small adult" conception of childhood has been observed by many anthropologists in preindustrial societies. In Europe, according to Ariès and others, childhood was discovered, or invented, in the seventeenth and nineteenth centuries, with the emergence of the private, domestic, companionate family and formal schooling. These institutions created distinct roles for children, enabling childhood to emerge as a distinct stage of life.

Despite challenges to Ariès's work, the bulk of historical and cross-cultural evidence supports the contention that childhood as we know it today is a relatively recent cultural invention; our ideas about children, child-rearing practices, and the conditions of children's lives are dramatically different from those of earlier centuries. The same is true of adolescence. Teenagers, such a conspicuous and noisy presence in modern life, and their stage of life, known for its turmoil and soul searching, are not universal features of life in other times and places.

Of course, the physical changes of puberty—sexual maturation and spurt in growth—happen to everyone everywhere. Yet, even here, there is cultural and historical variation. In the past hundred years, the age of first menstruation has declined from the mid-teens to twelve, and the age young men reach their full height has declined from twenty-five to under twenty. Both changes are believed to be due to improvements in nutrition and health care, and these average ages are not expected to continue dropping.

Some societies have puberty rites, but they bring about a transition from childhood not to adolescence but to adulthood. Other societies take no note at all of the changes, and the transition from childhood to adulthood takes place simply and without social recognition. Adolescence as we know it today appears to have evolved late in the nineteenth century; there is virtual consensus among social scientists that it is "a creature of the industrial revolution and it continues to be shaped by the forces which defined that revolution: industrialization, specialization, urbanization . . . and bureaucratization of human organizations and institutions, and continuing technological development."

In America before the second half of the nineteenth century, youth was an ill-defined category. Puberty did not mark any new status or life experience. For the majority of young people who lived on farms, work life began early, at seven or eight years old or even younger. As they grew older, their responsibility would increase, and they would gradually move toward maturity. Adults were not ignorant of the differences between children and adults, but distinctions of age meant relatively little. As had been the practice in Europe, young people could be sent away to become apprentices or servants in other households. As late as the early years of this century, working-class children went to work at the age of ten or twelve.

A second condition leading to a distinct stage of adolescence was the founding of mass education systems, particularly the large public high school. Compulsory education helped define adolescence by setting a precise age for it; high schools brought large numbers of teenagers together to create their own society for a good part of their daily lives. So the complete set of conditions for adolescence on a mass scale did not exist until the end of the nineteenth century.

The changed family situations of late-nineteenth- and early-twentieth-century youth also helped make this life stage more psychologically problematic. Along with the increasing array of options to choose from, rapid social change was making one generation's experience increasingly different from that of the next. Among the immigrants who were flooding into the country at around the time adolescence was emerging, the generation gap was particularly acute. But no parents were immune to the rapid shifts in society and culture that were transforming America in the decades around the turn of the century.

Further, the structure and emotional atmosphere of middle-class family life was changing also, creating a more intimate and emotionally intense family life. Contrary to the view that industrialization had weakened parent-child relations, the evidence is that family ties between parents and adolescents intensified at this time: adolescents lived at home until they married, and depended more completely, and for a longer time, on their parents than in the past. Demographic change had cut family size in half over the course of the century. Mothers were encouraged to devote themselves to the careful nurturing of fewer children.

This more intensive family life seems likely to have increased the emotional strain of adolescence. Smaller households and a more nurturing style of child rearing, combined with the increased contact between parents, especially mothers, and adolescent children, may have created a kind of " 'Oedipal family' in middle class America."

The young person's awakening sexuality, particularly the young male's, is likely to have been more disturbing to both himself and his parents than during the era when young men commonly lived away from home. . . . There is evidence that during the Victorian era, fears of adolescent male sexuality, and of masturbation in particular, were remarkably intense and widespread.

Family conflict in general may have been intensified by the peculiar combination of teenagers' increased dependence on parents and increased autonomy in making their own life choices. Despite its tensions, the new emotionally intense middle-class home made it more difficult than ever for adolescents to leave home for the heartless, indifferent world outside.

By the end of the nineteenth century, conceptions of adolescence took on modern form, and by the first decades of the twentieth century, *adolescence* had become a household word. As articulated forcefully by the psychologist G. Stanley Hall in his 1904 treatise, adolescence was a biological process—not simply the onset of sexual maturity but a turbulent, transitional stage in the evolution of the human species: "some ancient period of storm and stress when old moorings were broken and a higher level attained."

Hall seemed to provide the answers to questions people were asking about the troublesome young. His public influence eventually faded, but his conception of adolescence as a time of storm and stress lived on. Adolescence continued to be seen as a period of both great promise and great peril: "every step of the upward way is strewn with the wreckage of body, mind and morals." The youth problem—whether the lower-class problem of delinquency, or the identity crises and other psychological problems of middle-class youth—has continued to haunt America, and other modern societies, ever since.

Ironically, then, the institutions that had developed to organize and control a problematic age ended by heightening adolescent self-awareness, isolating youth from the rest of society, and creating a youth culture, making the transition to adulthood still more problematic and risky. Institutional recognition in turn made adolescents a more distinct part of the population, and being adolescent a more distinct and self-conscious experience. As it became part of the social structure of modern society, adolescence also became an important stage of the individual's biography—an indeterminate period of being neither child nor adult that created its own problems. Any society that excludes youth from adult work, and offers them what Erikson calls a "moratorium"—time and space to try out identities and lifestyles—and at the same time demands extended schooling as the route to success is likely to turn adolescence into a "struggle for self." It is also likely to run the risk of increasing numbers of mixed-up, rebellious youth.

But, in fact, the classic picture of adolescent storm and stress is not universal. Studies of adolescents in America and other industrialized societies suggest that extreme rebellion and rejection of parents, flamboyant behavior, and psychological turmoil do not describe most adolescents, even today. Media images of the youth of the 1980s and 1990s as a deeply troubled, lost generation beset by crime, drug abuse, and teenage pregnancy are also largely mistaken.

Although sexual activity and experimenting with drugs and alcohol have become common among middle-class young people, drug use has actually declined in recent years. Disturbing as these practices are for parents and other adults, they apparently do not interfere with normal development for most adolescents. Nevertheless, for a significant minority, sex and drugs add complications to a period of development during which a young person's life can easily go awry—temporarily or for good.

More typically, for most young people, the teen years are marked by mild rebelliousness and moodiness—enough to make it a difficult period for parents but not one of a profound parent-child generation gap or of deep alienation from conventional values. These ordinary tensions of family living through adolescence are exacerbated in times of rapid social change, when the world adolescents confront is vastly different from the one in which their parents came of age. Always at the forefront of social change, adolescents in industrial societies inevitably bring discomfort to their elders, who "wish to see their children's adolescence as an enactment of the retrospectively distorted memory of their own. . . . But such intergenerational continuity can occur only in the rapidly disappearing isolation of the desert or the rain forest."

If adolescence is a creation of modern culture, that culture has also been shaped by adolescence. Adolescents, with their music, fads, fashions, and conflicts, not only are conspicuous, but reflect a state of mind that often extends beyond the years designated for them. The adolescent mode of experience—accessible to people of any age—is marked by "exploration, becoming, growth, and pain."

Since the nineteenth century, for example, the coming-of-age novel has become a familiar literary genre. Patricia Spacks observes that while Victorian authors looked back at adolescence from the perspective of adulthood, twentieth-century novelists since James Joyce and D. H. Lawrence have become more intensely identified with their young heroes, writing not from a distance but from "deep inside the adolescence experience." The novelist's use of the adolescent to symbolize the artist as romantic outsider mirrors a more general cultural tendency. As Phillipe Ariès observes, "Our society has passed from a period which was ignorant of adolescence to a period in which adolescence is the favorite age. We now want to come to it early and linger in it as long as possible."

The Discovery of Adulthood

Middle age is the latest life stage to be discovered, and the notion of mid-life crisis recapitulates the storm-and-stress conception of adolescence. Over the course of the twentieth century, especially during the years after World War II, a developmental conception of childhood became institutionalized in public thought. Parents took it for granted that children passed through ages, stages, and phases: the terrible twos, the teenage rebel. In recent years the idea of development has been increasingly applied to adults, as new stages of adult life are discovered. Indeed much of the psychological revolution of recent years—the tendency to look at life through psychological lenses—can be understood in part as the extension of the developmental approach to adulthood.

In 1976 Gail Sheehy's best-selling *Passages* popularized the concept of mid-life crisis. Sheehy argued that every individual must pass through such a watershed, a time when we reevaluate our sense of self, undergo a crisis, and emerge with a new identity. Failure to do so, she warned, can have dire consequences. The book was the most influential pop-ular attempt to apply to adults the ages-and-stages approach to development that had long been applied to children. Ironically, this came about just as historians were raising questions about the universality of those stages.

Despite its popularity, Sheehy's book, and the research she reported in it, have come under increasing criticism. "Is the mid-life crisis, if it exists, more than a warmed-over identity crisis?" asked one review of the research literature on mid-life. In fact, there is lit-tle or no evidence for the notion that adults pass through a series of sharply defined stages, or a series of crises that must be resolved before passing from one stage to the next.

Nevertheless, the notion of a mid-life crisis caught on because it reflected shifts in adult experience across the life course. Most people's decisions about marriage and work are no longer irrevocably made at one fateful turning point on the brink of adulthood. The choices made at twenty-one may no longer fit at forty or fifty—the world has changed; par-ents, children, and spouses have changed; working life has changed. The kind of issue that makes adolescence problematic—the array of choices and the need to fashion a coherent, continuous sense of self in the midst of all this change—recurs throughout adulthood. As a Jules Feiffer cartoon concludes, "Maturity is a phase, but adolescence is forever."

Like the identity crisis of adolescence, the concept of mid-life crisis appears to re-flect the experience of the more educated and advantaged. Those with more options in life are more likely to engage in the kind of introspection and reappraisal of previous choices that make up the core of the mid-life crisis. Such people realize that they will never fulfill their earlier dreams, or that they have gotten what they wanted and find they are still not happy. But as the Berkeley longitudinal data show, even in that segment of the population, mid-life crisis is far from the norm. People who have experienced fewer choices in the past, and have fewer options for charting new directions in the future, are less likely to encounter a mid-life crisis. Among middle Americans, life is dominated by making ends meet, coping with everyday events, and managing unexpected crises.

While there may be no fixed series of stages or crises adults must pass through, mid-dle age or mid-life in our time does have some unique features that make it an unsettled time, different from other periods in the life course as well as from mid-life in earlier eras. First, as we saw earlier, middle age is the first period in which most people today confront death, illness, and physical decline. It is also an uneasy age because of the in-creased importance of sexuality in modern life. Sexuality has come to be seen as the core of our sense of self, and sexual fulfillment as the center of the couple relationship. In mid-life, people confront the decline of their physical attractiveness, if not of their sexuality.

There is more than a passing resemblance between the identity problems of ado-lescence and the issues that fall under the rubric of "mid-life crisis." In a list of themes recurring in the literature on the experience of identity crisis, particularly in adolescence, the psychologist Roy Baumeister includes: feelings of emptiness, feelings of vagueness, generalized malaise, anxiety, self-consciousness. These symptoms describe not only ado-lescent and mid-life crises but what Erikson has labeled identity problems—or what has, of late, been considered narcissism.

Consider, for example, Heinz Kohut's description of patients suffering from what he calls narcissistic personality disorders. They come to the analyst with vague symptoms, but eventually focus on feelings about the self—emptiness, vague depression, being drained of energy, having no "zest" for work or anything else, shifts in self-esteem, heightened sensitivity to the opinions and reactions of others, feeling unfulfilled, a sense of uncertainty and purposelessness. "It seems on the face of it," observes the literary critic Steven Marcus, "as if these people are actually suffering from what was once called unhappiness."

The New Aging

Because of the extraordinary revolution in longevity, the proportion of elderly people in modern industrial societies is higher than it has ever been. This little-noticed but profound transformation affects not just the old but families, an individual's life course, and society as a whole. We have no cultural precedents for the mass of the population reaching old age. Further, the meaning of *old age* has changed—indeed, it is a life stage still in process, its boundaries unclear. When he came into office at the age of sixty-four, George [H. W.] Bush did not seem like an old man. Yet when Franklin Roosevelt died at the same age, he did seem to be "old."

President Bush illustrates why gerontologists in recent years have had to revise the meaning of "old." He is a good example of what they have termed the "young old" or the "new elders"; the social historian Peter Laslett uses the term "the third age." Whatever it is called, it represents a new stage of life created by the extension of the life course in industrialized countries. Recent decades have witnessed the first generations of people who live past sixty-five and remain healthy, vigorous, alert, and, mostly due to retirement plans, financially independent. These people are "pioneers on the frontier of age," observed the journalist Frances Fitzgerald, in her study of Sun City, a retirement community near Tampa, Florida, "people for whom society had as yet no set of expectations and no vision."

The meaning of the later stages of life remains unsettled. Just after gerontologists had marked off the "young old"—people who seemed more middle-aged than old—they had to devise a third category, the "oldest old," to describe the fastest-growing group in the population, people over eighty-five. Many if not most of these people are like Tithonus, the mythical figure who asked the gods for eternal life but forgot to ask for eternal youth as well. For them, the gift of long life has come at the cost of chronic disease and disability.

The psychological impact of this unheralded longevity revolution has largely been ignored, except when misconstrued. The fear of age, according to Christopher Lasch, is one of the chief symptoms of this culture's alleged narcissism. But when people expected to die in their forties or fifties, they didn't have to face the problem of aging. Alzheimer's disease, for example, now approaching epidemic proportions, is an ironic by-product of the extension of the average life span. When living to seventy or eighty is a realistic prospect, it makes sense to diet and exercise, to eat healthy foods, and to make other "narcissistic" investments in the self.

Further, "the gift of mass longevity," the anthropologist David Plath argues, has been so recent, dramatic, and rapid that it has become profoundly unsettling in all postindustrial societies: "If the essential cultural nightmare of the nineteenth century was to be in poverty, perhaps ours is to be old and alone or afflicted with terminal disease."

Many people thus find themselves in life stages for which cultural scripts have not yet been written; family members face one another in relationships for which tradition provides little guidance. "We are stuck with awkward-sounding terms like 'adult children' and . . . 'grandson-in-law.' " And when cultural rules are ambiguous, emotional relationships can become tense or at least ambivalent.

A study of five-generation families in Germany reveals the confusion and strain that result when children and parents are both in advanced old age—for example, a great-great-grandmother and her daughter, who is herself a great-grandmother. Who has the right to be old? Who should take care of whom? Similarly, Plath, who has studied the problems of mass longevity in Japan, finds that even in that familistic society the traditional meaning of family roles has been put into question by the stretching out of the life span. In the United States, some observers note that people moving into retirement communities sometimes bring their parents to live with them. Said one disappointed retiree: "I want to enjoy my grandchildren; I never expected that when I was a grandparent I'd have to look after my parents."

■READING 4

Changes in the Demographics of Families over the Course of American History

Donald J. Hernandez

America's families have undergone three major transformations: the first between the beginning of the Industrial Revolution and the Great Depression, the second after World War II, and the third beginning now. In this [reading], I examine the profound transformations in each of these time periods, and I use children as the lens through which to view, analyze, and evaluate them.

The first reason for using children as my focal point is that much of the growing interest and concern about changes in the work-family nexus arise from apparent incompatibilities between work and parenting in America. These tensions often have potentially detrimental consequences not only for the work roles of parents but also for the current well-being and future prospects of children. Second, children, as compared to adults, have relatively little control over the forces and decisions that impair or improve their circumstances.

Third, the family is the institution most directly responsible for children's well-being because parents make the day-to-day decisions that determine the quality of care—plus the quality of the nutrition, clothing, housing, health care, schools, and neighborhoods—available to children. But the choices parents make are shaped by opportunities and constraints flowing from social and economic forces as well as from federal, state, and local public policies. Most notably for present purposes, the resources that parents can make available to their children are determined largely by parents' access to paid employment, as well as by the timing and financial rewards associated with their paid work.

Finally, I focus on children because they are at the leading edge of the current demographic transformation of the American family and society, which is creating a new

American majority. Historically, racial and ethnic minorities, including Hispanics, blacks, Asians, American Indians, and other nonwhite groups, have constituted only a small portion of the American population. But taken as a whole, these racial and ethnic minorities are growing much more rapidly than the non-Hispanic white population, and these groups are destined to become the numerical majority within the lifetime of today's children. The emergence of racial and ethnic minorities as the majority population is occurring most rapidly, and will become a reality first, among children.

REVOLUTIONARY TRANSFORMATIONS FROM THE CIVIL WAR TO WORLD WAR II

The lives of children were completely altered between the mid-1800s and the mid-1900s by three revolutionary changes in the family: a radical change in fathers' work, the approaching extinction of the large nuclear family, and the flowering of mass education. In the mid-1800s, 70 percent of children lived in two-parent farm families, a majority lived in families with seven or more siblings, and only about one-half attended school (Figures 1 and 2). By 1930, only 30 percent of children lived on farms, 55 percent lived in two-parent families with a breadwinner father and a homemaker mother, and most children had only one or two brothers or sisters in the home. By 1940, the length of the school

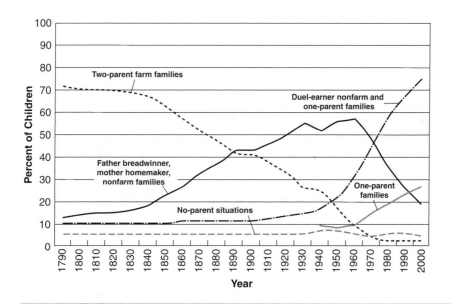

FIGURE 1 *Children Ages 0–17 in Farm Families, Father-as-Breadwinner Families, and Dual-Earner Families, 1790–2000*

Two parent farm families were estimated at 2 percent for year 2000. Estimates are for ten-year intervals from 1970 to 2000.

Source: D. J. Hernandez, *America's Children: Resources from Family, Government and the Economy* (New York: Russell Sage Foundation, 1993).

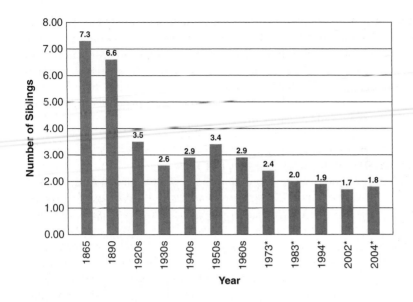

FIGURE 2   *Median Number of Siblings, 1865–2004*

*Expected

Source: D. J. Hernandez, *America's Children: Resources from Family, Government, and the Economy* (New York: Russell Sage Foundation, 1993) and unpublished census tabulations kindly provided by Martin O'Connell.

year had doubled, and about 90 percent of children ages seven to seventeen were enrolled in school.

During the mid-1800s, then, most children spent little time in school, and they lived in two-parent farm families, working side by side with their fathers and mothers and a large number of siblings to sustain themselves in small farming communities. By the 1930s and 1940s, most children lived in nonfarm families where the fathers left home for most of the day to earn the income required to support their families, while mothers remained in the home to care for their children and to perform unpaid household labor. After age six, children spent most of the day and the year in school. Although a hundred years may seem like a long time, it is important to note that the life expectancy of middle-aged adults today is more than seventy-five years. Consequently, the hundred-year transformation in the family economy, family size, and schooling occurred in little more than a single human lifetime, by today's standards.

Explaining the Transformation of Fathers' Work, Family Size, and Schooling

What explains these three revolutionary changes in the family lives of children? During the first century of the Industrial Revolution, these changes reflected the three major pathways available to parents who wanted either to improve their family's relative social and economic status or to keep from losing too much ground compared to others who were taking advantage of emerging economic opportunities.[1] First, as the mechanization of agriculture created an increasingly precarious economic situation for many rural families, the attraction of comparatively well-paid jobs for fathers in the expanding urban-industrial economy motivated mass migration from farms to urban areas. Thus the rise of capitalism in the late nineteenth and twentieth centuries increasingly drew workers, especially fathers, into expanding urban areas, serving as an engine not only for the transformation of fathers' work but also for the transformations in fertility and schooling that followed.

But the move to urban areas meant that food, clothing, and other necessities had to be purchased, making the costs of supporting each child more demanding. Meanwhile, laws restricting child labor and mandating universal education, along with comparatively low wages for children in urban areas, greatly reduced the potential economic contributions of children to their urban families. Also, as the quality and quantity of consumer products and services increased with economic growth, expected consumption standards rose; people had to spend more money simply to maintain the new "normal" standard of living, and the newly available goods and services competed with children for parental time and money. For all these reasons, more and more parents limited their family size to a comparatively small number of children, allowing available income to be spread less thinly.

Schooling increased dramatically for three broad reasons. First, as the economic value of children's work declined relative to adults', parents became less motivated to keep their children in the labor force. Second, the child protection movement and labor unions successfully sought legislation restricting child labor and mandating universal schooling.[2] Third, as time passed and higher educational attainments became increasingly necessary to obtain jobs that offered higher incomes and greater prestige, parents encouraged and fostered higher educational attainments for their children as a path to success in adulthood.

REVOLUTIONARY TRANSFORMATIONS SINCE WORLD WAR II

The post-World War II era was marked by three additional revolutionary changes: the expansion of mothers' participation in the paid labor force, the rise of one-parent-family living arrangements, and the drop and subsequent rise in child poverty.

The Rise of Mothers' Labor Force Participation

During the last half of the twentieth century, children witnessed an enormous increase in the proportion of mothers working for pay (Figure 3), just as the children in an earlier era had experienced a massive movement by fathers out of the home to work in the urban-industrial economy. The revolution in mothers' work occurred twice as fast, however. The decline for children in the two-parent farm family from 60 percent to 10 percent occurred from 1860 to 1960. But the corresponding rise in working mothers from 10 percent to 60 percent required only half that time—from 1940 to 1990. By 2000, seven in ten children lived with mothers who worked for pay.

What caused this revolutionary increase in mothers' labor force participation? Much of the answer lies in the earlier historic changes in the family and the economy.

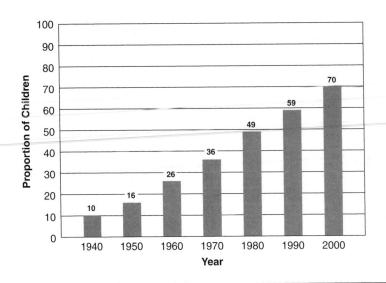

FIGURE 3   *Proportion of Children with Mothers in the Labor Force, 1940–2000*

Data for 2000 are from U.S. Bureau of the Census, Current Population Survey, 2000.

Source: D. J. Hernandez, *America's Children: Resources from Family, Governments, and the Economy* (New York: Russell Sage Foundation, 1993).

Before 1940, many parents had three major avenues for maintaining, improving, or regaining their economic status. They could move off the farm for fathers to obtain comparatively well-paid jobs, they could have fewer children to allow available income to be spread less thinly, or they could increase their education. But by 1940, only 23 percent of Americans lived on farms, and 70 percent of parents had only one or two dependent children in the home. In addition, many adults found it difficult or impractical to pursue additional schooling after age twenty-five. Thus, the historical avenues to improving the relative economic status of their families had already effectively closed for a large majority of parents age twenty-five or older.

However, a fourth major possibility for improving the relative economic status of their families emerged between 1940 and 1960. In the post–World War II economy, white-collar jobs for women were increasingly open, and comparatively few unmarried women were available to take these jobs.[3] Meanwhile, mothers were becoming increasingly available and increasingly well qualified for paid employment, for at least three reasons. First, the historic increases in school enrollment and in the school year's length had effectively released mothers from personal child care responsibilities for the equivalent of about two-thirds of an eight-hour workday, for about two-thirds of a full-time adult workyear. Second, many mothers were highly educated, because their educational attainments, along with men's, had increased historically (Figure 4).

Third, immediate economic insecurity and need, associated with fathers' lack of access to full-time employment, made mothers' work attractive. Full-time year-round work increased for fathers after the Great Depression. But through the subsequent decades up

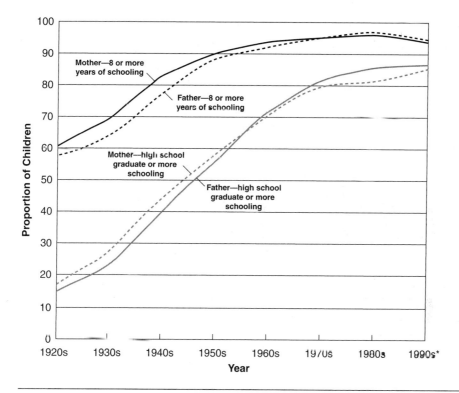

FIGURE 4 *Proportion of Children Born between 1920s and 1990s Whose Parents Have Specified Educational Attainment*

*Nine or more years of schooling

Source: D. J. Hernandez, *America's Children: Resources from Family, Government, and the Economy* (New York: Russell Sage Foundation, 1993).

to 1990, and despite the enormous increase in mother-only families, at least one-fifth of children lived with fathers who, during any given year, experienced part-time work or joblessness (Figure 5). This has been a powerful incentive for mothers to enter the paid labor market. It also is plausible that paid work offered an attractive hedge for some women against the increasingly likely economic disaster of losing most or all of their husbands' incomes through divorce. In addition, the Equal Pay Act in 1963 and the prohibition of sex discrimination under Title VII of the 1964 Civil Rights Act facilitated the rise in mothers' paid employment by easing legal barriers to women's employment that initially had been erected in the late 1800s; the women's movement of the 1970s, meanwhile, served to legitimate and encourage mothers' labor force participation.[4]

The Rise of Mother-Only Families

Twenty years after mothers' labor force participation began to expand, another revolution in family life began—an unprecedented increase in mother-only families. A

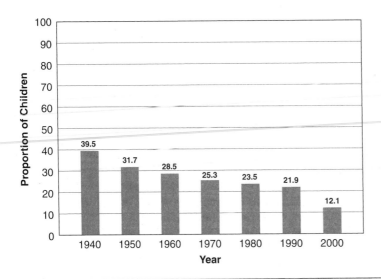

FIGURE 5 *Proportion of Children Living with a Father Who Works Less Than Full Time Year-Round, 1940–2000*

Data for 2000 are from U.S. Bureau of the Census, Current Population Survey, 2000.

Source: D. J. Hernandez, *America's Children: Resources from Family, Government, and the Economy* (New York: Russell Sage Foundation, 1993).

remarkably steady increase in divorce occurred between the 1860s and 1960s, with only three short-lived jumps around the world wars and the Great Depression (Figure 6). Expanding urban employment for fathers fueled the increase in divorce.[5] Preindustrial farming had literally required fathers and mothers to work together to support the family. But as fathers obtained nonfarm jobs, they could, if they wanted, leave the family home and take their incomes with them. At the same time, in moving to urban areas, husbands and wives left behind the small-town social controls that had once censured divorce. The economic interdependence of husbands and wives was weakened further by the revolutionary rise in mothers' labor force participation after 1940. With a non-farm job, a mother could, if she and her husband separated or divorced, support herself with her own income. This fact contributed to the rapidly rising divorce rates during the late 1960s and 1970s.[6]

Economic insecurity and need also have contributed greatly to the rise in separation and divorce. Glen Elder, Rand Conger, and their colleagues have shown that instability in fathers' work and resulting drops in family incomes lead to increased hostility between husbands and wives, reduced quality of the marital relationship, and increased risk of divorce.[7] In fact, each of the three economic recessions between 1970 and 1982, as compared to each preceding nonrecessionary period, led to sharp increases in mother-only families.[8]

Between 1940 and 1960, however, black children experienced much larger increases than white children in mother-only families with separated or divorced mothers, and especially after 1970, they experienced extremely large increases in mother-only

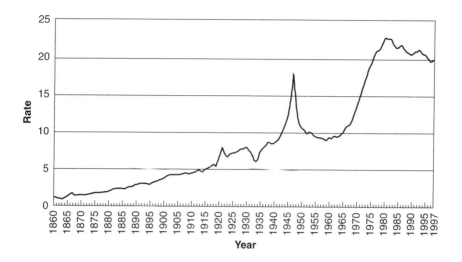

FIGURE 6   *Divorce Rates 1860–1997 (rate per 1,000 married women age 15 and older)*

Source: Reprinted from National Center for Health Statistics, "Advance Report of Final Divorce Statistics, 1988," *Monthly Vital Statistics Report* 39, no. 12, supp. 2, May 21, 1991.

families with never-married mothers.[9] The much higher proportion of black children who lived in mother-only families between 1940 and 1960 may be accounted for by disruptions associated with the startling drop in the proportion of blacks living on farms following the Great Depression, from 44 percent in 1940 to only 11 percent by 1960, and by the extraordinary economic pressures black families confronted as they moved to urban areas.

Turning to the rise in out-of-wedlock childbearing, the second component of the rise in mother-only families—and a major contributing factor—has been, as suggested by William Julius Wilson, the lack of employment among young men, especially black men.[10] In 1955, black men and white men ages sixteen to twenty-four were nearly equal in their chances of having a job (Figure 7). But by the late 1970s and 1980s, young black men were 15 percent to 25 percent more likely than young white men to be without a job, representing a large and rapid reduction in the availability of young-adult black men (that is, those of the main family-building ages) who might provide significant support to families.[11] The size of this racial gap in employment is at least two-thirds as large as the 23 percentage point increase between 1960 and 1988 in the comparative proportion of black and white children living in mother-only families with never-married mothers.

The proportion of children with a mother but no father in the home jumped from the narrow range of 6 percent or 8 percent during the 1940s and 1950s to 23 percent in 2000. Little change occurred before 1960, because, during the prior century, the effect of increasing divorce had been counterbalanced by declines in parental death rates. From a child life-course perspective, however, very high proportions of children, historically, spent at least part of their childhood living with fewer than two parents, at about 30

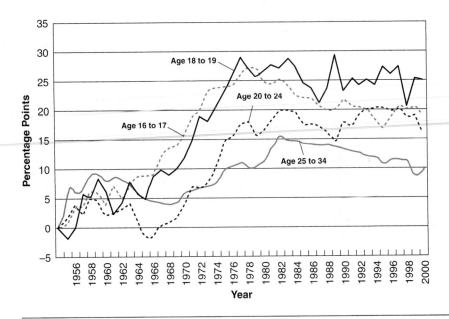

FIGURE 7 *Percentage Points by Which White Male Employment Exceeds Black Male Employment, 1955–2000*

U.S. Bureau of Statistics (2001).

Source: D. J. Hernandez, *America's Children: Resources from Family, Government, and the Economy* (New York: Russell Sage Foundation, 1993).

percent for whites and between 55 percent and 60 percent for blacks, mainly because of parental death or divorce (Figure 8).

The Myth of the Traditional Ozzie and Harriet Family

Drawing together the changes in fathers' and mothers' employment and family structure, we can then calculate estimates—for any given time period—of the proportion of children living in families where the father worked full time year-round, the mother was a full-time homemaker without paid employment, and all the children were born after the parents' only marriage. These are the so-called traditional Ozzie and Harriet families.[12] Taking into account the effects not only of divorce, out-of-wedlock childbearing, and mothers' employment but also of instability in fathers' employment, we see that never since the Great Depression have a majority of children lived in the idealized Ozzie and Harriet families that have remained a myth throughout the postwar era [Figure 9]. While 31 percent of seventeen-year-olds lived in these mythologized families in 1920, the prevalence of such families fell over time to only 15 percent in 1960, and less than one-half of U.S. children have been born into such families since at least 1940. In fact, the fraction of children born into these families fell from 44.5 percent in the 1950s to only 27.4 percent in 1980.

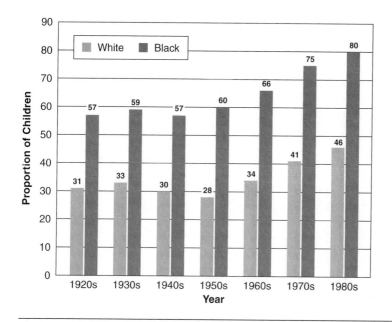

FIGURE 8 *White and Black Children Ever Living with Fewer than Two Parents by Age 17, 1920s to 1980s Cohorts*

More recent estimates cannot be calculated from the decennial census because of changes in data collection. Since 1980, however, the proportions of white and black children ever living with fewer than two parents may have increased and almost surely have not declined. Parental divorce and births to unmarried women are the primary determinants of these trends. Although the divorce rate has changed little since 1980, the proportion of all births accounted for by unmarried women increased substantially between 1980 and 2000 from 10 to 29 percent for whites and from 49 to 68 percent for blacks.

Source: D. J. Hernandez, *America's Children: Resources from Family, Government, and the Economy* (New York: Russell Sage Foundation, 1993).

Furthermore, the limited evidence available for earlier times regarding marital dissolution and women's work suggests that it was never the case that a majority of children lived in such idealized families. About one-fifth of newborns in 1940 and 1950 were not living in intact, two-parent families, and from 1920 to 1950 about one-third of seventeen-year-olds were not living in such families.[13] In addition, the overall rate of marital dissolution was steady between 1860 and 1960 because declining mortality rates were counterbalanced by rising divorce rates.[14] Therefore, it is likely that as far back as 1860 roughly one-fifth of children were not born into intact, two-parent families, and that by age seventeen this proportion increased to about one-third. Insofar as mortality rates were still higher before 1860, the proportion of children not living in intact, two-parent families may also have been greater prior to the middle of the nineteenth century.

Mothers' employment was also substantial prior to 1940, if work that was not counted as employment in historical census data collection is included. For example, the

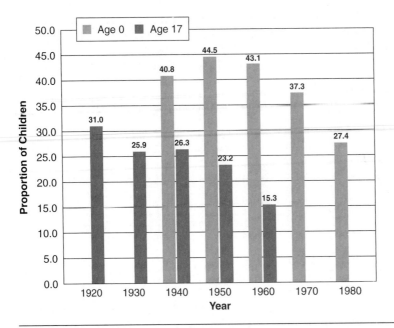

FIGURE 9   *Children in Ozzie and Harriet Families at Ages 0 and 17,*
1920s to 1980s Cohorts

More recent estimates cannot be calculated from the decennial census because of changes in data collection. The proportion of children ages 0 and 17 living in Ozzie and Harriet families has, however, no doubt declined further since 1980, when the most recent estimates in this figure were calculated. A primary determinant of decline in Ozzie and Harriet families has been the fall in the proportion with two parents in the home where the father works full time year-round and the mother did not work last year, which by 2000 had dropped for children ages 0 and 17, respectively, to 18 percent and 11 percent. These proportions are less than the corresponding estimates of the proportions in Ozzie and Harriet families of 27 percent and 15 percent, respectively, calculated as of 1980. If it were possible to take into account parental divorce and births to unmarried women, the proportions as of 2000 would be smaller still.

Source: D. J. Hernandez, *America's Children: Resources from Family, Government, and the Economy* (New York: Russell Sage Foundation, 1993).

1900 census counted only 22.5 percent of women as employed in the formal economy, but the rate of women's employment rises to 46.4 percent if work is defined as including the taking in of boarders and lodgers, along with the uncounted work of women in factories, family shops, and family farms.[15] Women on family farms at the turn of the century, and earlier, contributed substantial labor to their families' enterprises,[16] and most of the increase in female employment in 1900 that is associated with counting informal work (16.9 percent of 23.9 percent) results from considering as employed those women on family farms whose husbands were counted as labor force participants because they were family farmers.[17]

While historical evidence strongly suggests that never in U.S. history have a majority of children been born into or lived in families where all of the children were born after the parents' only marriage and where the mother acted only as a homemaker and it was exclusively the father who provided economic support to the family by working full time year-round, the reasons for this fact have shifted over time. Prior to and during the early years of the Industrial Revolution, most children lived on farms where fathers and mothers both worked in the family enterprise to support themselves and their children, and high parental mortality rates exposed many children to one-parent families. As farming diminished and mortality declined, levels of often-insecure urban employment for fathers increased and were followed by mothers' increased employment in the formal labor market, as well as rising levels of divorce and, then, out-of-wedlock child-bearing. Though the series of revolutionary changes in children's family lives during the past two centuries was not without its moments of continuity, what is important nevertheless is that from the perspective of children's actual living situations, the idealized vision of traditional family life has been a myth.

The Fall and Rise of Child Poverty

The third postwar revolution in children's lives has involved income and poverty trends. Median family income more than doubled between 1947 and 1973, but it increased by only 7 percent in the next twenty years, despite the enormous jump in mothers' paid work in the formal economy. Not until the seven years spanning 1993 to 2000 did a sustained increase of 18 percent occur in median family income.

With regard to poverty, social perceptions about what income levels were "normal" and "adequate" changed substantially because of the enormous increase in real income and the real standard of living between 1940 and 1973. The relative nature of judgments about what income level is sufficient has been noted for more than two hundred years. In *Wealth of Nations*, for example, Adam Smith emphasized that poverty must be defined in comparison to contemporary standards of living. He defined economic hardship as the experience of being unable to consume commodities that "the custom of the country renders it indecent for creditable people, even of the lowest order, to be without."[18] In 1958, the economist John Kenneth Galbraith also argued, "A people are poverty-stricken when their income, even if adequate for survival, falls markedly behind that of the community. Then they cannot have what the larger community regards as the minimum necessary for decency; and they cannot wholly escape, therefore, the judgment of the larger community that they are indecent. They are degraded for, in a literal sense, they live outside the grades or categories which the community regards as respectable."[19]

Historical changes in public perceptions about the amount of income needed by families have generally mirrored actual changes in family income.[20] In a review of evidence spanning 1937 through the 1960s, Rainwater found that throughout the era, Americans had viewed a "low" or "poverty-level" income in any given year as an amount equal to less than 50 percent of median family (disposable) income in that year; "enough to get along" as an amount equal to at least 50 percent of the median but less than 75 percent of it; "comfortable or prosperous" as an amount equal to at least 75 percent of the median but less than 150 percent of it; and "rich or super-rich" as an amount at least 150 percent of the median.[21] Therefore, the relative poverty measure adopted here sets the value of the poverty threshold at one-half of median family income in specific years, with adjustment for family size.[22]

According to this measure, child poverty declined sharply during the 1940s and then more slowly during the 1950s and 1960s. But after 1979, child poverty increased sharply, and it has since remained at high levels (Figure 10). The 1999 relative poverty rate for children of 27 percent was identical to the rate experienced by children in 1949. Meanwhile, the proportion of children living in official poverty also increased from a low of about 14 percent in 1969 to a high of 21 to 23 percent between 1990 and 1996, although official child poverty subsequently declined to 16 percent as of 2000.[23]

Why did childhood poverty increase between the early 1970s and early 1980s and then remain at high levels through the early 1990s? One important and sometimes overlooked relevant change has been the large declines in the incomes of working men, especially those in the prime ages for fathering and rearing children. Large increases have occurred since the early 1970s—but especially since 1979—in the extent to which men working full time year-round have earnings that are less than the official poverty level for a four-person family. From 1992 to 1994, the proportions of men working full time year-round with such low incomes were 40 percent for ages eighteen to twenty-four, 13 percent for ages twenty-five to thirty-four, and 8 percent for ages thirty-five to fifty-four. Despite small declines sub-

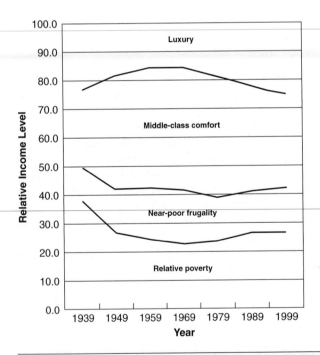

FIGURE 10   *Children Ages 0 to 17 Years by Relative Income Level, 1939–1999*

Data for 1999 are from U.S. Bureau of the Census, Current Population Survey, 2000.

Source: D. J. Hernandez, *America's Children: Resources from Family, Government, and the Economy* (New York: Russell Sage Foundation, 1993).

sequently, the proportions remained high in 1997, at 35 percent, 12 percent, and 8 percent, respectively.[24]

Of course, the amount of income available to children from their fathers is substantially less for children living in mother-only families than for children living with two parents. The best available evidence indicates, however, that only about one-third of the increase in child poverty during the 1980s could be accounted for by the rise in mother-only families, while about two-thirds of the increase was directly accounted for by declining income.[25] Thus, trends in childhood poverty have not mainly followed patterns in mother-only families that are independent of economic factors. Instead, trends in poverty have changed mainly because of the economic and employment experiences of fathers and mothers.

THE NEW AMERICAN MAJORITY OF THE TWENTY-FIRST CENTURY

Looking to the future, the U.S. fertility rate is near or below the level required to replace the population, and the baby boom generation is moving beyond childbearing age. Consequently, driven by population growth in other countries and U.S. economic opportunities, future growth in the U.S. population will occur primarily through immigration and births to current and future immigrants and their descendants. As of 2000, 20 percent of children in the United States were children of immigrants, with one or both parents foreign-born; more than three-fifths of these children were Hispanic, and more than one-fifth were Asian (Figure 11).

Because most children in immigrant families are Hispanic or non-white, Census Bureau projections indicate that children younger than eighteen who are Hispanic, black, Asian, or of some other racial minority will grow to account for more than one-half of the child population before 2040. But the timing of growth among racial and ethnic minorities varies greatly by age. The most recent projections by the U.S. Census Bureau indicate that in the year 2030, when the baby boom generation born between 1946 and 1964 will be in the retirement-age range of sixty-six to eighty-four years, 74 percent of the elderly will be non-Hispanic whites, compared to only 59 percent of working-age adults and 52 percent of children (Figure 12).[26] Consequently, as the growing elderly population of the predominantly white baby boom generation reaches retirement age, its members will increasingly depend on the productive activities and civic participation (that is, voting) of working-age adults who are members of racial and ethnic minorities (many of whom lived in immigrant families as children) for their economic support during retirement.

The Outlook for Immigrant Children's Families

A critical question for the future, then, is: What are the circumstances of children in immigrant families today? A recent study by the National Academy of Sciences' Institute of Medicine and the National Research Council found the following.[27] Children in immigrant families were, as of the 1990 census, less likely than children in U.S.-born families to have only one parent in the home. The overwhelming majority of children in

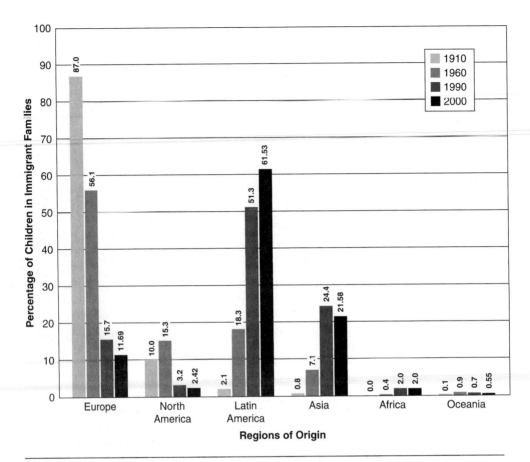

FIGURE 11   *Children in Immigrant Families from Various Regions of Origin: 1910, 1960, 1990, and 2000*

Data for 2000 are from U.S. Bureau of the Census, Current Population Survey, 2000.

Source: D. J. Hernandez and K. Darke, "The Well-Being of Immigrant Children, Native-Born Children with Immigrant Parents, and Native-Born Children with Native-Born Parents," in *Trends in the Well-Being of America's Children and Youth* (Washington, DC: Office of the Assistant Secretary for Planning and Evaluation, U.S. Department of Health and Human Services, 1998.)

immigrant families, like those in U.S.-born families, had fathers who were in the labor force—at 88 percent to 95 percent across the generations—and they were nearly as likely to have mothers in the labor force. This suggests that children in immigrant families are more likely to benefit from stable two-parent family situations than are children in U.S.-born families, and that the families of children of immigrants and those native-born have equally strong work ethics. The proportions with college-educated parents also were quite similar for children in immigrant and in U.S.-born families. But children in immigrant families were, on average, more likely to be exposed to socioeconomic risks. For example, children in immigrant families experienced higher poverty

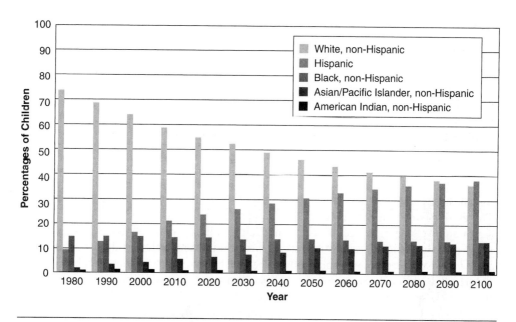

FIGURE 12 *Past and Projected Percentages of Children in Specified Race/Ethnic Groups*
Source: Population Projections Program, Population Division, U.S. Census Bureau, January 13, 2000.

rates, and much higher proportions of their parents had completed eight years of schooling or less.

The higher levels of poverty among children in immigrant families are, however, highly concentrated among children from only twelve countries of origin. Five of these countries are the source of many officially recognized refugees: the former Soviet Union, Cambodia, Laos, Thailand, and Vietnam. Immigrants from four of the twelve nations have fled countries experiencing war or political instability: El Salvador, Guatemala, Nicaragua, and Haiti. Two others are small countries sending many migrants who seek unskilled work: Honduras and the Dominican Republic. The twelfth country is Mexico, which currently sends the largest number of both legal and illegal immigrants, and which has been an important source of unskilled labor for the U.S. economy throughout the twentieth century. The overall official poverty rate for children in immigrant families from these twelve countries was 35 percent in the 1990 census.

With regard to work issues in these families, 90 percent of children in immigrant families from these twelve countries had fathers who were in the labor force. But, in sharp contrast, 40 percent had fathers who did not work full time year-round, 46 percent had fathers with eight years of schooling or less, and 40 percent lived in linguistically isolated households where no one in the home age fourteen or older spoke English exclusively or very well. Thus, the much higher poverty rate for children from these twelve countries is not strongly related to a lack of labor force participation by fathers but instead is strongly associated with a lack of full-time year-round work among fathers, with extremely low educational attainments among parents, and with linguistic isolation from English-speaking society.

Available evidence suggests, then, that compared to third- and later-generation children, those in immigrant families were, on average, exposed to greater socioeconomic risks, particularly if their origins were in Southeast Asia, the former Soviet Union, Central America, or Mexico. In addition, children in immigrant families had less access to health insurance and health care, and those living at greatest socioeconomic risk were less likely to live in families receiving a range of welfare benefits and services.

Surprisingly, then, children in immigrant families were doing at least as well as or better than third- and later-generation children for a wide variety of indicators measuring physical health, mental health, and school adjustment.[28] This conclusion must be tempered, however, for three reasons.[29] First, although available evidence regarding the health and well-being of children in immigrant families is consistent across a wide variety of domains, it is limited both in its quality and in the number of domains for which research exists. Second, available evidence suggests there is enormous variability across children with different countries of origin for many indicators.[30] Third, health and well-being of children in immigrant families appear to deteriorate through time and across generations.[31] Since children in immigrant families are the fastest-growing component of the new American majority, the prospects for them are enormously important to the nation's future.

PUBLIC POLICIES FOR CHILDREN AND FAMILIES IN THE TWENTY-FIRST CENTURY

. . . [T]he number of children living in families in which all adults work has important implications for the creation of a private and public system that universally provides the resources children and families require for their current well-being, their future success, and their basic human dignity. What kind of system might this be? Four components appear essential: paid parental leave, pre-kindergarten early education and care, guaranteed income supports, and access to health insurance and health care.

Universal paid leave for parents with infants is essential if parents are to have the time necessary for the care and nurturing of their newborns while working.[32] Currently, the United States has a two-class system in which a small group of parents can afford to take time off to be with their babies, whereas a very large second tier is effectively shut off from the opportunity of spending significant time with their newborns. All newborns would benefit from universal paid parental leave.

Universal pre-kindergarten early education and care programs would also benefit all children and families.[33] The United States has experienced two child care revolutions: the first for children age five or six and older as fathers entered the urban-industrial labor market, and the second for preschool-age children as mothers entered the paid labor force. The first child care revolution was legally mandated and funded by the government through universal public education systems that provided the intellectual foundation for the enormously successful American economy. Are the development, education, and success of America's youngest children any less important today as the nation competes for well-paid jobs in the global economy?

Public support for child care is currently a two-class system. For middle-income and high-income families, federal tax credits are available. But the working poor and working near-poor have access only to stigmatized and inadequate child care services and vouchers, or to no public child care resources at all. Reliance on the corporate world is not likely to reduce inequality of access to child care, because only the most successful companies with highly paid employees have the resources to provide such child care benefits. A caring society will provide early care and education, universally, for its children.

Guaranteed income supports are also essential. While nearly all families in America are working families, many live in poverty because their wages are low or their jobs are part-time or part-year. The single most successful policy to reduce poverty among working Americans during the past decade has been the earned income tax credit. Refundable earned income tax credits have proven to be a politically viable vehicle for creating an income floor for working Americans.

Closely related is the need for a refundable child care credit for parents of many working-poor families who must work nonstandard hours to support themselves. Among all employed women ages eighteen to thirty-four in 1991 with children younger than fourteen, for example, only 60 percent worked a fixed daytime weekdays-only schedule. These workers are especially likely to provide many services in the American economy, working as cashiers, waitresses, or cooks; nursing aides, orderlies, or attendants; supervisors or proprietors in sales occupations; hairdressers or cosmetologists; or maids, janitors, or cleaners.[34] In order to survive, these workers must work nights, weekends, or irregular hours, which pose special difficulties for making child care arrangements. For these families, universal, refundable child care credits are an essential adjunct to universal pre-kindergarten early education.

Lastly, access to health insurance and health care is needed. For the past half century, Americans have relied primarily on employers to provide health care coverage for their families, with a limited public system only for the most destitute. Yet 29 percent of children in 2000 were not covered by employee-based private insurance, and including government-supported coverage, 12 percent remain uninsured. Among poor children, 76 percent were not covered by employee-based private insurance, and 33 percent had no coverage from either private or government sources.[35] Low-income working families often do not have access to health insurance. Children and adults require health care to survive and thrive. As one of the wealthiest nations in the world, the United States can surely afford health care for all.

CONCLUSION

In sum, if Americans care about all their children and families, then universal approaches to meeting their needs may be not only appropriate but also essential because the piecemeal approaches of the past have left many children and families without adequate child care, without adequate income, and without adequate health care. As the new American majority emerges, the work and family experiences of non-Hispanic whites and of racial, ethnic, and cultural minorities are becoming bound together ever more tightly, and the future of each is increasingly becoming the future of all.

Editors' Note: *Notes and references for this reading can be found in the original source.*

2

Public Debates and Private Lives

■READING 5

The Mommy Wars: Ambivalence, Ideological Work, and the Cultural Contradictions of Motherhood

Sharon Hays

I have argued that all mothers ultimately share a recognition of the ideology of intensive mothering. At the same time, all mothers live in a society where child rearing is generally devalued and the primary emphasis is placed on profit, efficiency, and "getting ahead." If you are a mother, both logics operate in your daily life.

But the story is even more complicated. Over half of American mothers participate directly in the labor market on a regular basis; the rest remain at least somewhat distant from that world as they spend most of their days in the home. One might therefore expect paid working mothers to be more committed to the ideology of competitively maximizing personal profit and stay-at-home mothers to be more committed to the ideology of intensive mothering. As it turns out, however, this is not precisely the way it works.

Modern-day mothers are facing two socially constructed cultural images of what a good mother looks like. Neither, however, includes the vision of a cold, calculating businesswoman—that title is reserved for childless career women. If you are a good mother, you *must* be an intensive one. The only "choice" involved is whether you *add* the role of paid working woman. The options, then, are as follows. On the one side there is the portrait of the "traditional mother" who stays at home with the kids and dedicates her energy to the happiness of her family. This mother cheerfully studies the latest issue of *Family Circle*, places flowers in every room, and has dinner waiting when her husband comes home. This mother, when she's not cleaning, cooking, sewing, shopping, doing the laundry, or comforting her mate, is focused on attending to the children and ensuring their proper development. On the other side is the image of the successful "supermom." Effortlessly juggling home and work, this mother can push a stroller with one hand and carry a briefcase in the other. She is always properly coiffed, her nylons have no runs, her suits are freshly pressed, and her home has seen the white tornado. Her children are immaculate and well mannered but not passive, with a strong spirit and high self-esteem.

Although both the traditional mom and the supermom are generally considered socially acceptable, their coexistence represents a serious cultural ambivalence about how mothers should behave. This ambivalence comes out in the widely available indictments of the failings of both groups of women. Note, for instance, the way Mecca, a welfare mother, describes these two choices and their culturally provided critiques:

> The way my family was brought up was, like, you marry a man, he's the head of the house, he's the provider, and you're the wife, you're the provider in the house. Now these days it's not that way. Now the people that stay home are classified, quote, "lazy people," we don't "like" to work.
>
> I've seen a lot of things on TV about working mothers and nonworking mothers. People who stay home attack the other mothers 'cause they're, like, bad mothers because they left the kids behind and go to work. And, the other ones aren't working because we're lazy. But it's not lazy. It's the lifestyle in the 1990s it's, like, too much. It's a demanding world for mothers with kids.

The picture Mecca has seen on television, a picture of these two images attacking each other with ideological swords, is not an uncommon one.

It is this cultural ambivalence and the so-called choice between these paths that is the basis for what Darnton (1990) has dubbed the "mommy wars." Both stay-at-home and paid working mothers, it is argued, are angry and defensive; neither group respects the other. Both make use of available cultural indictments to condemn the opposing group. Supermoms, according to this portrait, regularly describe stay-at-home mothers as lazy and boring, while traditional moms regularly accuse employed mothers of selfishly neglecting their children.

My interviews suggest, however, that this portrait of the mommy wars is both exaggerated and superficial. In fact, the majority of mothers I spoke with expressed respect for one another's need or right to choose whether to go out to work or stay at home with the kids. And, as I have argued, they also share a whole set of similar concerns regarding appropriate child rearing. These mothers have not formally enlisted in this war. Yet the rhetoric of the mommy wars draws them in as it persists in mainstream American culture, a culture that is unwilling, for various significant reasons, to unequivocally embrace either vision of motherhood, just as it remains unwilling to embrace wholeheartedly the childless career woman. Thus, the charges of being lazy and bored, on the one hand, or selfish and money-grubbing, on the other, are made available for use by individual mothers and others should the need arise.

What this creates is a no-win situation for women of child-bearing years. If a woman voluntarily remains childless, some will say that she is cold, heartless, and unfulfilled as a woman. If she is a mother who works too hard at her job or career, some will accuse her of neglecting the kids. If she does not work hard enough, some will surely place her on the "mommy track" and her career advancement will be permanently slowed by the claim that her commitment to her children interferes with her workplace efficiency (Schwartz 1989). And if she stays at home with her children, some will call her unproductive and useless. A woman, in other words, can never fully do it right.

At the same time that these cultural images portray all women as somehow less than adequate, they also lead many mothers to feel somehow less than adequate in their daily lives. The stay-at-home mother is supposed to be happy and fulfilled, but how can she be when she hears so often that she is mindless and bored? The supermom is supposed to be able to juggle her two roles without missing a beat, but how can she do either job as well as she is expected if she is told she must dedicate her all in both directions? In these circumstances, it is not surprising that many supermoms feel guilty about their inability to carry out both roles to their fullest, while many traditional moms feel isolated and invisible to the larger world.

Given this scenario, both stay-at-home and employed mothers end up spending a good deal of time attempting to make sense of their current positions. Paid working mothers, for instance, are likely to argue that there are lots of good reasons for mothers to work in the paid labor force; stay-at-home mothers are likely to argue that there are lots of good reasons for mothers to stay at home with their children. These arguments are best understood not as (mere) rationalizations or (absolute) truths but rather as socially necessary "ideological work." Berger (1981a) uses this notion to describe the way that all people make use of available ideologies in their "attempt to cope with the relationship between the ideas they bring to a social context and the practical pressures of day-to-day living in it" (15). People, in other words, select among the cultural logics at their disposal in order to develop some correspondence between what they believe and what they actually do. For mothers, just like others, ideological work is simply a means of maintaining their sanity.

The ideological work of mothers, as I will show, follows neither a simple nor a straightforward course. First, as I have pointed out, both groups face two contradictory cultural images of appropriate mothering. Their ideological work, then, includes a recognition and response to both portraits. This duality is evident in the fact that the logic the traditional mother uses to affirm her position matches the logic that the supermom uses to express ambivalence about her situation, and the logic that the employed mother uses to affirm her position is the same logic that the stay-at-home mother uses to express ambivalence about hers. Their strategies, in other words, are mirror images, but they are also incomplete—both groups are left with some ambivalence. Thus, although the two culturally provided images of mothering help mothers to make sense of their own positions, they simultaneously sap the strength of mothers by making them feel inadequate in one way or the other. It is in coping with these feelings of inadequacy that their respective ideological strategies take an interesting turn. Rather than taking divergent paths, as one might expect, both groups attempt to resolve their feelings of inadequacy by returning to the logic of the ideology of intensive mothering.

THE FRUMPY HOUSEWIFE AND THE PUSH TOWARD THE OUTSIDE WORLD

Some employed mothers say that they go out to work for pay because they need the income. But the overwhelming majority also say that they *want* to work outside the home. First, there's the problem of staying inside all day: "I decided once I started working that I need that. I need to work. Because I'll become like this big huge hermit frumpy person if I stay home." Turning into a "big huge hermit frumpy person" is connected to the feeling of being confined to the home. Many women have had that experience at one time or another and do not want to repeat it:

> When I did stay home with him, up until the time when he was ten months old, I wouldn't go out of the house for three days at a time. Ya know, I get to where I don't want to get dressed, I don't care if I take a shower. It's like, what for? I'm not going anywhere.

Not getting dressed and not going anywhere are also tied to the problem of not having a chance to interact with other adults:

> I remember thinking, "I don't even get out of my robe. And I've gotta stay home and breast-feed and the only adult I hear is on *Good Morning America*—and he's not even live!" And that was just for a couple of months. I don't even know what it would be like for a couple of years. I think it would be really difficult.

Interacting with adults, for many paid working mothers, means getting a break from the world of children and having an opportunity to use their minds:

> When I first started looking for a job, I thought we needed a second income. But then when I started working it was like, this is great! I do have a mind that's not *Sesame Street!* And I just love talking with people. It's just fun, and it's a break. It's tough, but I enjoyed it; it was a break from being with the kids.

If you don't get a break from the kids, if you don't get out of the house, if you don't interact with adults, and if you don't have a chance to use your mind beyond the *Sesame Street* level, you might end up lacking the motivation to do much at all. This argument is implied by many mothers:

> If I was stuck at home all day, and I did do that 'cause I was waiting for day care, I stayed home for four months, and I went crazy, I couldn't stand it. I mean not because I didn't want to spend any time with her, but because we'd just sit here and she'd just cry all day and I couldn't get anything done. I was at the end of the day exhausted, and feeling like shit.

Of course, it is exhausting to spend the day meeting the demands of children. But there's also a not too deeply buried sense in all these arguments that getting outside the home and using one's mind fulfill a longing to be part of the larger world and to be recognized by it. One mother made this point explicitly:

> [When you're working outside the home] you're doing something. You're using your mind a little bit differently than just trying to figure out how to make your day work with your kid. It's just challenging in a different way. So there's part of me that wants to be, like, *recognized.* I think maybe that's what work does, it gives you a little bit of a sense of recognition, that you don't feel like you get [when you stay home].

Most employed mothers, then, say that if they stay at home they'll go stir-crazy, they'll get bored, the demands of the kids will drive them nuts, they won't have an opportunity to use their brains or interact with other adults, they'll feel like they're going nowhere, and they'll lose their sense of identity in the larger world. And, for many of these mothers, all these points are connected:

> Well, I think [working outside is] positive, because I feel good about being able to do the things that I went to school for, and keep up with that, and use my brain. As they grow older, [the children are] going to get into things that they want to get into, they're going to be out with their friends and stuff, and I don't want to be in a situation where my whole life has been wrapped around the kids. That's it. Just some outside interests so that I'm not so wrapped up in how shiny my floor is. [She laughs.] Just to kind of be out and be stimulated. Gosh, I don't want this to get taken wrong, but I think I'd be a little bit bored. And the other thing I think of is, I kind of need a break, and when you're staying at home it's constant. It's a lot harder when you don't have family close by, [because] you don't get a break.

In short, paid working mothers feel a strong pull toward the outside world. They hear the world accusing stay-at-home moms of being mindless and unproductive and of lacking an identity apart from their kids, and they experience this as at least partially true.

Stay-at-home mothers also worry that the world will perceive them as lazy and bored and watching television all day as children scream in their ears and tug at their sleeves. And sometimes this is the way they feel about themselves. In other words, the same image that provides working mothers with the reasons they should go out to work accounts for the ambivalence that stay-at-home mothers feel about staying at home.

A few stay-at-home mothers seem to feel absolutely secure in their position, but most do not. Many believe that they will seek paid work at some point, and almost all are made uncomfortable by the sense that the outside world does not value what they do. In all cases, their expressions of ambivalence about staying at home mimic the concerns of employed mothers. For instance, some women who stay at home also worry about becoming frumpy: "I'm not this heavy. I'm, like, twenty-seven pounds overweight. It sounds very vain of me, in my situation. It's like, I'm not used to being home all the time, I'm home twenty-four hours. I don't have that balance in my life anymore." And some stay-at-home mothers feel as if they are physically confined inside the home. This mother, for example, seems tired of meeting the children's demands and feels that she is losing her sense of self:

> There's a hard thing of being at home all the time. You have a lot of stress, because you're constantly in the house. I think having a job can relieve some of that stress and to make it a lot more enjoyable, to want to come home all the time. . . . My outings are [limited]. I'm excited when I have to go grocery shopping. Everything I pick is what they eat, everything they like, or what they should eat. Me, I'm just *there*. I'm there for them. I feel that I'm here for them.

Both of these stay-at-home mothers, like over one-third of the stay-at-home mothers in my sample, plan to go out to work as soon as they can find paid employment that offers sufficient rewards to compensate (both financially and ideologically) for sending the kids to day care. Most of the remaining mothers are committed to staying at home with the children through what they understand as formative years. The following mother shares that commitment, while also echoing many paid working mothers in her hopes that one day she will have a chance to be around adults and further her own growth:

> Well, we could do more, we'd have more money, but that's really not the biggest reason I'd go back to work. I want to do things for myself, too. I want to go back and get my master's [degree] or something. I need to grow, and be around adults, too. I don't know when, but I think in the next two years I'll go back to work. The formative years—their personality is going to develop until they're about five. It's pretty much set by then. So I think it's pretty critical that you're around them during those times.

One mother stated explicitly that she can hardly wait until the kids are through their formative years:

> At least talking to grown-ups is a little more fulfilling than ordering the kids around all day. My life right now is just all theirs. Sometimes it's a depressing thought because I think, "Where am I? I want my life back." . . . I mean, they are totally selfish. It's like an ice cream. They just gobble that down and say, "Let me have the cinnamon roll now."
> . . . [But] I had them, and I want them to be good people. So I've dedicated myself to them right now. Later on I get my life back. They won't always be these little sponges. I don't want any deficiency—well, nobody can cover all the loopholes—but I want to be comfortable in myself to know that I did everything that I could. It's the least I can do to do the best I can by them.

Mothers, she seems to be saying, are like confections that the kids just gobble down—and then they ask for more.

Thus, many stay-at-home moms experience the exhaustion of meeting the demands of children all day long, just as employed mothers fear they might. And many stay-at-home mothers also experience a loss of self. Part of the reason they feel like they are losing their identity is that they know the outside world does not recognize a mother's work as valuable. This woman, committed to staying at home until her youngest is at least three years old, explains:

> You go through a period where you feel like you've lost all your marbles. Boy, you're not as smart as you used to be, and as sharp as you used to be, and not as respected as you used to be. And those things are really hard to swallow. But that's something I've discussed with other mothers who are willing to stay home with their kids, and we've formed a support group where we've said, "Boy, those people just don't know what they're talking about." We're like a support group for each other, which you have to have if you've decided to stay at home, because you have so many people almost pushing you to work, or asking "Why don't you work?" You're not somehow as good as anybody else 'cause you're staying at home; what you're doing isn't important. We have a lot of that in this society.

Another mother, this one determined to stay at home with her kids over the long haul, provides a concrete example of the subtle and not-so-subtle ways in which society pushes mothers to participate in the paid labor force, and of the discomfort such mothers experience as a result:

> As a matter of fact, somebody said to me (I guess it was a principal from one of the schools) . . . "Well, what do you *do*? Do you have a *job*?" And it was just very funny to me that he was so uncomfortable trying to ask me what it was in our society that I did. I guess that they just assume that if you're a mom at home that it means nothing. I don't know, I

just don't consider it that way. But it's kind of funny, worrying about what you're gonna say at a dinner party about what you do.

And it's not just that these mothers worry about being able to impress school principals and people at cocktail parties, of course. The following mother worries about being "interesting" to other women who do not have children:

> I find myself, now that I'm not working, not to have as much in common [with other women who don't have children]. We don't talk that much because I don't have that much to talk about. Like I feel I'm not an interesting person anymore.

In short, the world presents, and mothers experience, the image of the lazy, mindless, dull housewife—and no mother wants to be included in that image.

THE TIME-CRUNCHED CAREER WOMAN AND THE PULL TOWARD HOME

Stay-at-home mothers use a number of strategies to support their position and combat the image of the frumpy housewife. Many moms who are committed to staying at home with their kids often become part of formal or informal support groups, providing them an opportunity to interact with other mothers who have made the same commitment. Others, if they can afford the cost of transportation and child care, engage in a variety of outside activities—as volunteers for churches, temples, and community groups, for instance, or in regular leisure activities and exercise programs. They then have a chance to communicate with other adults and to experience themselves as part of a larger social world (though one in which children generally occupy a central role).

But the primary way that stay-at-home mothers cope with their ambivalence is through ideological work. Like paid working mothers, they make a list of all the good reasons they do what they do. In this case, that list includes confirming their commitment to good mothering, emphasizing the importance of putting their children's needs ahead of their own, and telling stories about the problems that families, and especially children, experience when mothers go out to work for pay.

Many stay-at-home mothers argue that kids require guidance and should have those cookies cooling on the kitchen counter when they come home from school:

> The kids are the ones that suffer. The kids need guidance and stuff. And with two parents working, sometimes there isn't even a parent home when they come home from school. And that's one thing that got me too. I want to be home and I want to have cookies on the stove when they come home from school. Now we eat meals together all the time. It's more of a homey atmosphere. It's more of a *home* atmosphere.

Providing this homey atmosphere is difficult to do if one works elsewhere all day. And providing some period of so-called quality time in the evening, these mothers tell me, is not an adequate substitute. One mother elaborates on this point in response to a question about how she would feel if she was working outside the home:

Oh, guilty as anything. I know what I'm like after dinner, and I'm not at my best. And neither are my kids. And if that's all the time I had with them, it wouldn't be, quote, "quality time." I think it's a bunch of b.s. about quality time.

And quality time, even if it *is* of high quality, cannot make up for children's lack of a quantity of time with their mothers. This argument is often voiced in connection with the problem of paid caregiver arrangements. Most mothers, whether they work for pay or not, are concerned about the quality of day care, but stay-at-home mothers often use this concern to explain their commitment to staying at home. This mother, for example, argues that children who are shuffled off to a series of day-care providers simply will not get the love they need:

> I mean, if I'm going to have children I want to *raise* them. I feel really strongly about that. Really strongly. I wish more people did that. Myself, I think it's very underestimated the role the mother plays with the child. I really do. From zero to three [years], it's like their whole self-image. [Yet, working mothers will say,] "Well, okay, I've got a caretaker now," "Well, that nanny didn't work out." So by the time the children are three years old they've had four or five people who have supposedly said "I'll love you forever," and they're gone. I think that's really tough on the kids.

Since paid caregivers lack that deep and long-lasting love, I'm told, they won't ever be as committed to ministering to the child's needs as a mom will:

> I don't think anybody can give to children what a mother can give to her own children. I think there's a level of willingness to put up with hard days, crying days, cranky days, whining days, that most mothers are going to be able to tolerate just a little bit more than a caretaker would. I think there's more of a commitment of what a mother wants to give her children in terms of love, support, values, etcetera. A caretaker isn't going to feel quite the same way.

Stay-at-home mothers imply that all these problems of kids who lack guidance, love, and support are connected to the problem of mothers who put their own interests ahead of the interests of their children. A few stay-at-home mothers will explicitly argue, as this one does, that employed mothers are allowing material and power interests to take priority over the well-being of their kids:

> People are too interested in power, they just aren't interested in what happens to their kids. You know, "Fine, put them in day care." And I just feel sad. If you're so interested in money or a career or whatever, then why have kids? Why bring them into it?

Putting such interests ahead of one's children is not only somehow immoral; it also produces children with real problems. The following mother, echoing many stories about "bad mothers" that we have heard before, had this to say about her sister:

> My sister works full-time—she's a lawyer. And her kids are the most obnoxious, whiny kids. I can't stand it. They just hang on her. She thinks she's doing okay by them because they're in an expensive private school and they have expensive music lessons and they have expensive clothes and expensive toys and expensive cars and an expensive house. I don't

know. Time will tell, I guess. But I can't believe they're not going to have some insecurities. The thing that gets me is, they don't need it. I mean, he's a lawyer too. Basically, it's
like, "Well, I like you guys, but I don't really want to be there all day with you, and I don't
want to have to do the dirty work."

These are serious indictments indeed.

It is just these sorts of concerns that leave paid working mothers feeling inadequate
and ambivalent about *their* position. Many of them wonder at times if their lives or the
lives of their children might actually be better if they stayed at home with the kids. Above
all, many of them feel guilty and wonder, "Am I doing it right?" or "Have I done all I can
do?" These are the mothers who, we're told, have it all. It is impossible to have it all,
however, when "all" includes two contradictory sets of requirements. To begin to get a
deeper sense of how these supermoms do not always feel so super, two examples might
be helpful.

Angela is a working-class mother who had expected to stay home with her son
through his formative years. But after nine months she found herself bored, lonely, and
eager to interact with other adults. She therefore went out and got a full-time job as a
cashier. She begins by expressing her concern that she is not living up to the homemaking
suggestions she reads in *Parenting* magazine, worrying that she may not be doing it right:

> I get *Parenting* magazine and I read it. I do what is comfortable for me and what I can do.
> I'm not very creative. Where they have all these cooking ideas, and who has time to do
> that, except for a mother who stays home all day? Most of this is for a mother who has
> five, six hours to spend with her child doing this kind of thing. I don't have time for that.
> So then that's when I go back to day care. And I know that she's doing this kind of
> stuff with him, teaching him things. You know, a lot of the stuff that they have is on school-
> ing kinds of things, flash cards, that kind of thing. Just things that I don't do. That makes
> me feel bad. Then I think, "I should be doing this" and "Am I doing the right thing?" I
> know I have a lot of love for him.

Although she loves her son and believes that this is probably "the most important thing,"
she also feels guilty that she may not be spending a sufficient amount of time with him,
simply because she gets so tired:

> I think sometimes that I feel like I don't spend enough time with him and that's my biggest
> [concern]. And when I am with him, sometimes I'm not really up to being with him. Even
> though I am with him, sometimes I want him to go away because I've been working all
> day and I'm exhausted. And I feel sometimes I'll stick him in bed early because I just don't
> want to deal with him that day. And I feel really guilty because I don't spend enough time
> with him as it is. When I do have the chance to spend time with him, I don't want to spend
> time with him, because I'm so tired and I just want to be with myself and by myself.

Even though Angela likes her paid work and does not want to give it up, the problems of
providing both a quantity of time and the idealized image of quality time with her child,
just like the challenge of applying the creative cooking and child-rearing ideas she finds
in *Parenting* magazine, haunt her and leave her feeling both inadequate and guilty.

Linda is a professional-class mother with a well-paying and challenging job that
gives her a lot of satisfaction. She spent months searching for the right preschool for her

son and is relieved that he is now in a place where the caregivers share her values. Still, she worries and wonders if life might be better if she had made different choices:

> I have a friend. She's a very good mom. She seems very patient, and I never heard her raise her voice. And she's also not working. She gets to stay home with her children, which is another thing I admire. I guess I sort of envy that too. There never seems to be a time where we can just spend, like, playing a lot. I think that's what really bothers me, that I don't feel like I have the time to just sit down and, in a relaxing way, play with him. I can do it, but then I'm thinking "Okay, well I can do this for five minutes." So that's always in the back of my mind. Time, time, time. So I guess that's the biggest thing.
>
> And just like your question, "How many hours a day is he at preschool and how many hours do you spend per day as the primary caregiver?" just made me think, "Oh my gosh!" I mean they're watching him grow up more than I am. They're with him more than I am. And that makes me feel guilty in a way, and it makes me feel sad in a way. I mean I can just see him, slipping, just growing up before me. Maybe it's that quality-time stuff. I don't spend a lot of time, and I don't know if the time I do spend with him is quality.
>
> [But] if I just stay at home, I'll kind of lose, I don't know if I want to say my sense of identity, but I guess I'll lose my career identity. I'm afraid of that I guess. . . . My friend who stays at home, she had a career before she had her children, but I forget what it was. So that whole part of her, I can't even identify it now.

On the one hand, Linda envies and admires stay-at-home moms and worries about not spending enough quality time with her son, or enough play time. She is also upset that her day-care provider spends more hours with her son each day than she can. On the other hand, Linda worries that if she did stay at home she'd lose her identity as a professional and a member of the larger society. "Time, time, time," she says, there's never enough time to do it all—or at least to do it all "right."

The issue of time is a primary source of paid working mothers' ambivalence about their double shift. Attempting to juggle two commitments at once is, of course, very difficult and stressful. This mother's sense of how time pressures make her feel that she is always moving too fast would be recognizable to the majority of paid working mothers:

> I can see when I get together with my sister [who doesn't have a paid job] . . . that she's so easygoing with the kids, and she takes her time, and when I'm with her, I realize how stressed out I am sometimes trying to get things done.
>
> And I notice how much faster I move when I shop. . . . She's so relaxed, and I think I kind of envy that.

The problem of moving too fast when shopping is connected to the problem of moving too fast when raising children. Many paid working mothers envy those who can do such things at a more relaxed pace.

For a few employed mothers (two out of twenty in my sample) the problems of quality and quantity time outweigh the rewards of paid work, and they intend to leave their jobs as soon as they can afford to do so. This woman is one example:

> I believe there's a more cohesive family unit with maybe the mother staying at home. Because a woman tends to be a buffer, mediator, you name it. She pulls the family together.

But if she's working outside the home, sometimes there's not that opportunity anymore for her to pull everyone together. She's just as tired as the husband would be and, I don't know, maybe the children are feeling like they've been not necessarily abandoned but, well, I'm sure they accept it, especially if that's the only life they've seen. But my daughter has seen a change, even when I was only on maternity leave. I've seen a change in her and she seemed to just enjoy it and appreciate us as a family more than when I was working. So now she keeps telling me, "Mom, I miss you."

When this mother hears her daughter say "I miss you," she feels a tremendous pull toward staying at home. And when she talks about the way a family needs a mother to bring its members together, she is pointing to an idealized image of the family that, like quality and quantity time, weighs heavily in the minds of many mothers.

The following paid working mother also wishes she could stay at home with the kids and wishes she could be just like the television mom of the 1950s who bakes cookies every afternoon. But she knows she has to continue working for financial reasons:

Yes. I want to be Donna Reed, definitely. Or maybe Beaver Cleaver's mother, Jane Wyatt. Anybody in an apron and a pretty hairdo and a beautiful house. Yes. Getting out of the television set and making the most of reality is really what I have to do. Because I'll always have to work.

But the majority of paid working mothers, as I have stated, not only feel they need to work for financial reasons but also *want* to work, as Angela and Linda do. Nonetheless, their concerns about the effects of the double shift on their children match the concerns of those employed moms who wish they could stay at home as well as mimicking those of mothers who actually do stay at home. This mother, for instance, loves her paid work and does not want to give it up, but she does feel guilty, wondering if she's depriving her kids of the love and stimulation they need, particularly since she does not earn enough to justify the time she spends away:

Honestly, I don't make that much money. So that in itself brings a little bit of guilt, 'cause I know I work even though we don't have to. So there's some guilt associated. If kids are coming home to an empty house every day, they're not getting the intellectual stimulation [and] they're not getting the love and nurturing that other mothers are able to give their kids. So I think in the long run they're missing out on a lot of the love and the nurturing and the caring.

And this mother does not want it to seem that she is putting her child second, but she feels pressure to live up to the image of a supermom:

I felt really torn between what I wanted to do. Like a gut-wrenching decision. Like, what's more important? Of course your kids are important, but you know, there's so many outside pressures for women to work. Every ad you see in magazines or on television shows this working woman who's coming home with a briefcase and the kids are all dressed and clean. It's such a lie. I don't know of anybody who lives like that.

There's just a lot of pressure that you're not a fulfilled woman if you're not working outside of the home. But yet, it's just a real hard choice.

This feeling of being torn by a gut-wrenching decision comes up frequently:

> I'm constantly torn between what I feel I should be doing in my work and spending more time with them. . . . I think I would spend more time with them if I could. Sometimes I think it would be great not to work and be a mom and do that, and then I think, "well?"
>
> I think it's hard. Because I think you do need to have contact with your kid. You can't just see him in the morning and put him to bed at night because you work all day long. I think that's a real problem. You need to give your child guidance. You can't leave it to the schools. You can't leave it to churches. You need to be there. So, in some ways I'm really torn.

The overriding issue for this mother is guidance; seeing the children in the morning and putting them to bed at night is just not enough.

This problem, of course, is related to the problem of leaving kids with a paid caregiver all day. Paid working mothers do not like the idea of hearing their children cry when they leave them at day care any more than any other mother does. They are, as we have seen, just as concerned that their children will not get enough love, enough nurturing, enough of the right values, enough of the proper education, and enough of the right kind of discipline if they spend most of their time with a paid caregiver. To this list of concerns, paid working mothers add their feeling that when the kids are with a paid caregiver all day, it feels as if someone else is being the mother. One woman (who stayed at home until her son was two years old) elaborates:

> Well, I think it's really sad that kids have to be at day care forty hours a week. Because basically the person who's taking care of them is your day-care person. They're pretty much being the mother. It's really sad that this other person is raising your child, and it's basically like having this other person *adopting* your child. It's *awful* that we have to do that. I just think it's a crime basically. I wish we didn't have to do it. I wish everybody could stay home with their kids and have some kind of outlet. . . .
>
> And I think having a career is really important, but I think when it comes time to have children, you can take that time off and spend it with your kid. Because you can't go backwards, and time does fly with them. It's so sad . . . I hear people say, "Oh, my day-care lady said that so-and-so walked today or used a spoon or something." I mean it's just so devastating to hear that you didn't get to see that.

Leaving one's child with a paid caregiver for hours on end is therefore a potential problem not only because that "other mother" may not be a good mother but also because the real mother misses out on the joys that come from just being with the child and having a chance to watch him or her grow. This is a heart rending issue for many mothers who work outside the home.

Once again, the arguments used by stay-at-home mothers to affirm their commitment to staying home are mimicked by the arguments paid working mothers use to express their ambivalence about the time they spend away from their children. And again, though the reasoning of these women is grounded in their experiences, it is also drawn from a widely available cultural rhetoric regarding the proper behavior of mothers.

THE CURIOUS COINCIDENCE OF PAID WORK AND THE IDEOLOGY OF INTENSIVE MOTHERING

Both paid working moms and stay-at-home moms, then, do the ideological work of making their respective lists of the reasons they should work for pay and the reasons they should stay at home. Yet both groups also continue to experience and express some ambivalence about their current positions, feeling pushed and pulled in two directions. One would assume that they would cope with their ambivalence by simply returning to their list of good reasons for doing what they do. And stay-at-home mothers do just that: they respond to the push toward work in the paid labor force by arguing that their kids need them to be at home. But, as I will demonstrate, working mothers do not use the mirror strategy. The vast majority of these women do not respond to the pull toward staying at home by arguing that kids are a pain in the neck and that paid work is more enjoyable. Instead, they respond by creating a new list of all the reasons that they are good mothers even though they work outside the home. In other words, the ideological work meant to resolve mothers' ambivalence generally points in the direction of intensive mothering.

Most paid working mothers cope with the ambivalence by arguing that their participation in the labor force is ultimately good for their kids. They make this point in a number of ways. For instance, one mother thinks that the example she provides may help to teach her kids the work ethic. Another says that with the "outside constraints" imposed by her work schedule, she's "more organized and effective" as a mom. Yet another mother suggests that her second child takes just as much time and energy away from her first child as her career does:

> I think the only negative effect [of my employment] is just [that] generally when I'm over-stressed I don't do as well as a mother. But work is only one of the things that gets me overstressed. In fact it probably stresses me less than some other things. I think I do feel guilty about working 'cause it takes time away from [my oldest daughter]. But it struck me that it's acceptable to have a second child that takes just as much time away from the other child. *That* I'm not supposed to feel guilty about. But in some ways this [pointing to the infant she is holding] takes my time away from her more than my work does. Because this is constant.

More often, however, paid working mothers share a set of more standard explanations for why their labor-force participation is actually what's best for their kids. First, just as Rachel feels that her income provides for her daughter's toys, clothing, outings, and education, and just as Jacqueline argues, "I have weeks when I don't spend enough time with them and they suffer, but those are also the weeks I bring home the biggest paychecks," many mothers point out that their paid work provides the financial resources necessary for the well-being of their children:

> How am I supposed to send her to college without saving up? And also the money that I make from working helps pay for her toys, things that she needs, clothes. I never have to say, "Oh, I'm on a budget, I can't go buy this pair of shoes." I want the best for her.

Some mothers express a related concern—namely, what would happen to the family if they did not have paying jobs and their husbands should die or divorce them? One woman expressed it this way:

> Well, my dad was a fireman, so I guess there was a little bit of fear, well, if anything happened to him, how are we gonna go on? And I always kind of wished that [my mother] had something to fall back on. I think that has a lot to do with why I continue to work after the kids. I've always just felt the need to have something to hold on to.

The second standard argument given by employed mothers is that paid caregiver arrangements can help to further children's development. With respect to other people's kids, I'm told, these arrangements can keep them from being smothered by their mothers or can temporarily remove them from bad family situations. With reference to their own children, mothers emphasize that good day care provides kids with the opportunity to interact with adults, gives them access to "new experiences" and "different activities," "encourages their independence," and allows them to play with other kids—which is very important, especially now that neighborhoods no longer provide the sort of community life they once did:

> They do say that kids in preschool these days are growing up a little more neurotic, but I don't think that my daughter would have had a better life. In fact I think her life would have been a thousand times worse if I was a low-income mother who stayed home and she only got to play with the kids at the park. Because I think that preschool is really good for them. Maybe not a holding tank, but a nice preschool where they play nice games with them and they have the opportunity to play with the same kids over and over again. I think that's really good for them. Back in the 1950s, everybody stayed home and there were kids all over the block to play with. It's not that way now. The neighborhoods are deserted during the week.

Third, several mothers tell me that the quality of the time they spend with their kids actually seems to increase when they have a chance to be away from them for a part of the day. Listen to these mothers:

> When I'm with them too long I tend to lose my patience and start yelling at them. This way we both get out. And we're glad to see each other when we come home.

> If women were only allowed to work maybe ten to fifteen hours a week, they would appreciate their kids more and they'd have more quality time with them, rather than having to always just scold them.

> I think I have even less patience [when I stay home with the children], because it's like, "Oh, is this all there is?" . . . Whereas when I go to work and come home, I'm glad to see him. You know, you hear people say that they're better parents when they work because they spend more quality time, all those clichés, or whatever. For me that happens to be true.

> And now when I come home from work (although I wish I could get off earlier from work), I think I'm a better mom. There you go! Because when I come home from work, I don't

have *all* day, just being with the kids. It's just that when I'm working I feel like I'm competent, I'm a person!

Getting this break from the kids, a break that reinforces your feeling of competence and therefore results in more rewarding time with your children is closely connected to the final way paid working mothers commonly attempt to resolve their ambivalence. Their children's happiness, they explain, is dependent upon their *own* happiness as mothers. One hears this again and again: "Happy moms make happy children"; "If I'm happy in my work then I think I can be a better mom"; and "I have to be happy with myself in order to make the children happy." One mother explains it this way:

> In some ways working is good. It's definitely got its positive side, because I get a break. I mean, now what I'm doing [working part-time] is perfect. I go to work. I have time to myself. I get to go to the bathroom when I need to go to the bathroom. I come home and I'm very happy to see my kids again. What's good for the mother and makes the mother happy is definitely good for the kids.

In all these explanations for why their participation in the paid labor force is actually good for their kids, these mothers want to make it clear that they still consider children their primary interest. They are definitely not placing a higher value on material success or power, they say. Nor are they putting their own interests above the interests of their children. They want the children to get all they need. But part of what children need, they argue, is financial security, the material goods required for proper development, some time away from their mothers, more quality time when they are with their mothers, and mothers who are happy in what they do. In all of these statements, paid working mothers clearly recognize the ideology of intensive mothering and testify that they are committed to fulfilling its requirements.

To underline the significance of this point, let me remind the reader that these paid working mothers use methods of child rearing that are just as child-centered, expert-guided, emotionally absorbing, labor-intensive, and financially expensive as their stay-at-home counterparts; they hold the child just as sacred, and they are just as likely to consider themselves as primarily responsible for the present and future well-being of their children. These are also the very same mothers who put a tremendous amount of time and energy into finding appropriate paid caregiver arrangements. Yet for all that they do to meet the needs of their children, they still express some ambivalence about working outside the home. And they still resolve this ambivalence by returning to the logic of intensive mothering and reminding the observer that ultimately they are most interested in what is best for their kids. This is striking.

CONTINUING CONTRADICTIONS

All this ideological work is a measure of the power of the pushes and pulls experienced by American mothers today. A woman can be a stay-at-home mother and claim to follow tradition, but not without paying the price of being treated as an outsider in the larger public world of the market. Or a woman can be a paid worker who participates in that larger world, but she must then pay the price of an impossible double shift. In both cases, women are enjoined to maintain the logic of intensive mothering. These contradictory pressures mimic the contradictory logics operating in this society, and almost all mothers experience them. The complex strategies mothers use to cope with these contradictory logics highlight the emotional, cognitive, and physical toll they take on contemporary mothers.

As I have argued, these strategies also highlight something more. The ways mothers explain their decisions to stay at home or work in the paid labor force, like the pushes and pulls they feel, run in opposite directions. Yet the ways they attempt to resolve the ambivalence they experience as a result of those decisions run in the *same* direction. Stay-at-home mothers, as I have shown, reaffirm their commitment to good mothering, and employed mothers maintain that they are good mothers even though they work. Paid working mothers do not, for instance, claim that child rearing is a relatively meaningless task, that personal profit is their primary goal, and that children are more efficiently raised in child-care centers. If you are a mother, in other words, although both the logic of the workplace and the logic of mothering operate in your life, the logic of intensive mothering has a *stronger* claim.

This phenomenon is particularly curious. The fact that there is no way for either type of mother to get it right would seem all the more reason to give up the logic of intensive mothering, especially since both groups of mothers recognize that paid employment confers more status than motherhood in the larger world. Yet images of freshly baked cookies and *Leave It to Beaver* seem to haunt mothers more often than the housewives' "problem that has no name" (Friedan 1963), and far more often than the image of a corporate manager with a big office, a large staff, and lots of perks. Although these mothers do not want to be defined as "mere" housewives and do want to achieve recognition in the outside world, most would also like to be there when the kids come home from school. Mothers surely try to balance their own desires against the requirements of appropriate child rearing, but in the world of mothering, it is socially unacceptable for them (in word if not in deed) to place their own needs above the needs of their children. A good mother certainly would never simply put her child aside for her own convenience. And placing material wealth or power on a higher plane than the well-being of children is strictly forbidden. It is clear that the two groups come together in holding these values as primary, despite the social devaluation of mothering and despite the glorification of wealth and power.

The portrait of the mommy wars, then, is overdrawn. Although the ideological strategies these groups use to explain their choice of home or paid work include an implicit critique of those "on the other side," this is almost always qualified, and both groups, at least at times, discuss their envy or admiration for the others. More important, as should now be abundantly clear, both groups ultimately share the same set of beliefs and the same set of concerns. Over half the women in my sample explicitly state that the choice between home and paid work depends on the individual woman, her interests, desires, and circumstances. Nearly all the rest argue that home is more important than paid work because children are simply more important than careers or the pursuit of financial gain. The paid working women in my sample were actually twice as likely as their stay-at-home counterparts to respond that home and children are more important and rewarding than paid work. Ideologically speaking, at least, home and children actually seem to become more important to a mother the more time she spends away from them.

There *are* significant differences among mothers—ranging from individual differences to more systematic differences of class, race, and employment. But in the present context, what is most significant is the commitment to the ideology of intensive mothering that women share in spite of their differences. In this, the cultural contradictions of motherhood persist.

The case of paid working mothers is particularly important in this regard, since these are the very mothers who, arguably, have the most to gain from redefining motherhood in such a way as to lighten their load on the second shift. As we have seen, however, this is not exactly what they do. It is true, as Gerson (1985) argues, that there are ways in which paid working mothers do redefine motherhood and lighten their load—for instance, by sending their kids to day care, spending less time with them than their stay-at-home counterparts, legitimating their paid labor-force participation, and engaging in any number of practical strategies to make child-rearing tasks less energy- and time-consuming. But, as I have argued, this does not mean that these mothers have given up the ideology of intensive mothering. Rather, it means that, whether or not they actually do, they feel they should spend a good deal of time looking for appropriate paid caregivers, trying to make up for the lack of quantity time by focusing their energy on providing quality time, and remaining attentive to the central tenets of the ideology of intensive child rearing. It also means that many are left feeling pressed for time, a little guilty, a bit inadequate, and somewhat ambivalent about their position. These stresses and the strain toward compensatory strategies should actually be taken as a measure of the persistent strength of the ideology of intensive mothering.

To deepen the sense of paradox further, one final point should be repeated. There are reasons to expect middle-class mothers to be in the vanguard of transforming ideas about child rearing away from an intensive model. First, middle-class women were historically in the vanguard of transforming child-rearing ideologies. Second, while many poor and working-class women have had to carry a double shift of wage labor and domestic chores for generations, middle-class mothers have had little practice, historically speaking, in juggling paid work and home and therefore might be eager to avoid it. Finally, one could argue that employed mothers in the middle class have more to gain from reconstructing ideas about appropriate child rearing than any other group—not only because their higher salaries mean that more money is at stake, but also because intensive mothering potentially interferes with their career trajectories in a more damaging way than is true of less high-status occupations. But, as I have suggested, middle-class women are, in some respects, those who go about the task of child rearing with the greatest intensity.

When women's increasing participation in the labor force, the cultural ambivalence regarding paid working and stay-at-home mothers, the particular intensity of middle-class mothering, and the demanding character of the cultural model of appropriate child rearing are taken together, it becomes clear that the cultural contradictions of motherhood have been deepened rather than resolved. The history of child-rearing ideas demonstrates that the more powerful the logic of the rationalized market became, so too did its ideological opposition in the logic of intensive mothering. The words of contemporary mothers demonstrate that this trend persists in the day-to-day lives of women.

Editors' Note: *References for this reading can be found in the original source.*

■ READING 6

Decline of the Family: Conservative, Liberal, and Feminist Views

Janet Z. Giele

In the 1990s the state of American families and children became a new and urgent topic. Everyone recognized that families had changed. Divorce rates had risen dramatically. More women were in the labor force. Evidence on rising teenage suicides, high rates of teen births, and disturbing levels of addiction and violence had put children at risk.

Conservatives have held that these problems can be traced to a culture of toleration and an expanding welfare state that undercut self-reliance and community standards. They focus on the family as a caregiving institution and try to restore its strengths by changing the culture of marriage and parenthood. Liberals center on the disappearance of manual jobs that throws less educated men out of work and undercuts their status in the family as well as rising hours of work among the middle class that makes stable two-parent families more difficult to maintain. Liberals argue that structural changes are needed outside the family in the public world of employment and schools.

The feminist vision combines both the reality of human interdependence in the family and individualism of the workplace. Feminists want to protect diverse family forms that allow realization of freedom and equality while at the same time nurturing the children of the next generation.

THE CONSERVATIVE EXPLANATION: SELFISHNESS AND MORAL DECLINE

The new family advocates turn their spotlight on the breakdown in the two-parent family, saying that rising divorce, illegitimacy, and father absence have put children at greater risk of school failure, unemployment, and antisocial behavior. The remedy is to restore religious faith and family commitment as well as to cut welfare payments to unwed mothers and mother-headed families.

Conservative Model

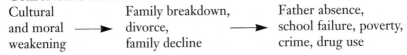

Cultural and moral weakening ⟶ Family breakdown, divorce, family decline ⟶ Father absence, school failure, poverty, crime, drug use

Cultural and Moral Weakening

To many conservatives, the modern secularization of religious practice and the decline of religious affiliation have undermined the norms of sexual abstinence before marriage and the prohibitions of adultery or divorce thereafter. Sanctions against illegitimacy or divorce have been made to seem narrow-minded and prejudiced. In addition, daytime television and the infamous example of Murphy Brown, a single mother having a child out of wedlock, helped to obscure simple notions of right and wrong. Barbara Dafoe Whitehead's controversial article in the *Atlantic* entitled "Dan Quayle Was Right" is an example of this argument.[1]

Gradual changes in marriage law have also diminished the hold of tradition. Restrictions against waiting periods, race dissimilarity, and varying degrees of consanguinity were gradually disappearing all over the United States and Europe.[2] While Mary Ann Glendon viewed the change cautiously but relativistically—as a process that waxed and waned across the centuries—others have interpreted these changes as a movement from status to contract (i.e., from attention to the particular individual's characteristics to reliance on the impersonal considerations of the market place).[3] The resulting transformation lessened the family's distinctive capacity to serve as a bastion of private freedom against the leveling effect and impersonality of public bureaucracy.

Erosion of the Two-Parent Family

To conservatives, one of the most visible causes of family erosion was government welfare payments, which made fatherless families a viable option. In *Losing Ground,* Charles Murray used the rise in teenage illegitimate births as proof that government-sponsored welfare programs had actually contributed to the breakdown of marriage.[4] Statistics on rising divorce and mother-headed families appeared to provide ample proof that the two-parent family was under siege. The proportion of all households headed by married couples fell from 77 percent in 1950 to 61 percent in 1980 and 55 percent in 1993.[5] Rising cohabitation, divorce rates, and births out of wedlock all contributed to the trend. The rise in single-person households was also significant, from only 12 percent of all households in 1950 to 27 percent in 1980, a trend fed by rising affluence and the undoubling of living arrangements that occurred with the expansion of the housing supply after World War II.[6]

The growth of single-parent households, however, was the most worrisome to policymakers because of their strong links to child poverty. In 1988, 50 percent of all children were found in mother-only families compared with 20 percent in 1950. The parental situation of children in poverty changed accordingly. Of all poor children in 1959, 73 percent had two parents present and 20 percent had a mother only. By 1988, only 35 percent of children in poverty lived with two parents and 57 percent lived with a mother only. These developments were fed by rising rates of divorce and out-of-wedlock births. Between 1940 and 1990, the divorce rate rose from 8.8 to 21 per thousand married women. Out-of-wedlock births exploded from 5 percent in 1960 to 26 percent in 1990.[7]

To explain these changes, conservatives emphasize the breakdown of individual and cultural commitment to marriage and the loss of stigma for divorce and illegitimacy. They understand both trends to be the result of greater emphasis on short-term gratification and on adults' personal desires rather than on what is good for children. A young woman brings a child into the world without thinking about who will support it. A husband divorces his wife and forms another household, possibly with other children, and leaves children of the earlier family behind without necessarily feeling obliged to be present in their upbringing or to provide them with financial support.

Negative Consequences for Children

To cultural conservatives there appears to be a strong connection between erosion of the two-parent family and the rise of health and social problems in children. Parental investment in children has declined—especially in the time available for supervision and companionship. Parents had roughly 10 fewer hours per week for their children in 1986 than in 1960, largely because more married women were employed (up from 24 percent in 1940 to 52 percent in 1983) and more mothers of young children (under age six) were working (up from 12 percent in 1940 to 50 percent in 1983). By the late 1980s just over half of mothers of children under a year old were in the labor force for at least part of the year.[8] At the same time fathers were increasingly absent from the family because of desertion, divorce, or failure to marry. In 1980, 15 percent of white children, 50 percent of black children, and 27 percent of children of Hispanic origin had no father present. Today 36 percent of children are living apart from their biological fathers compared with only 17 percent in 1960.[9]

Without a parent to supervise children after school, keep them from watching television all day, or prevent them from playing in dangerous neighborhoods, many more children appear to be falling by the wayside, victims of drugs, obesity, violence, suicide, or failure in school. During the 1960s and 1970s the suicide rate for persons aged fifteen to nineteen more than doubled. The proportion of obese children between the ages of six and eleven rose from 18 to 27 percent. Average SAT scores fell, and 25 percent of all high school students failed to graduate.[10] In 1995 the Council on Families in America reported, "Recent surveys have found that children from broken homes, when they become teenagers, have 2 to 3 times more behavioral and psychological problems than do children from intact homes."[11] Father absence is blamed by the fatherhood movement for the rise in violence among young males. David Blankenhorn and others reason that the lack of a positive and productive male role model has contributed to an uncertain masculine identity which then uses violence and aggression to prove itself. Every child deserves a father and "in a good society, men prove their masculinity not by killing other people, impregnating lots of women, or amassing large fortunes, but rather by being committed fathers and loving husbands."[12]

Psychologist David Elkind, in *The Hurried Child*, suggests that parents' work and time constraints have pushed down the developmental timetable to younger ages so that small children are being expected to take care of themselves and perform at levels which are robbing them of their childhood. The consequences are depression, discouragement, and a loss of joy at learning and growing into maturity.[13]

Reinvention of Marriage

According to the conservative analysis, the solution to a breakdown in family values is to revitalize and reinstitutionalize marriage. The culture should change to give higher priority to marriage and parenting. The legal code should favor marriage and encourage parental responsibility on the part of fathers as well as mothers. Government should cut back welfare programs which have supported alternate family forms.

The cultural approach to revitalizing marriage is to raise the overall priority given to family activities relative to work, material consumption, or leisure. Marriage is seen as the basic building block of civil society, which helps to hold together the fabric of volunteer activity and mutual support that underpins any democratic society.[14] Some advocates are unapologetically judgmental toward families who fall outside the two-parent mold. According to a 1995 *Newsweek* article on "The Return of Shame," David Blankenhorn believes "a stronger sense of shame about illegitimacy and divorce would do more than any tax cut or any new governmental program to maximize the life circumstances of children." But he also adds that the ultimate goal is "to move beyond stigmatizing only teenage mothers toward an understanding of the terrible message sent by all of us when we minimize the importance of fathers or contribute to the breakup of families."[15]

Another means to marriage and family revitalization is some form of taking a "pledge." Prevention programs for teenage pregnancy affirm the ideal of chastity before marriage. Athletes for Abstinence, an organization founded by a professional basketball player, preaches that young people should "save sex for marriage." A Baptist-led national program called True Love Waits has gathered an abstinence pledge from hundreds of thousands of teenagers since it was begun in the spring of 1993. More than 2,000 school districts now offer an abstinence-based sex education curriculum entitled "Sex Respect." Parents who are desperate about their children's sexual behavior are at last seeing ways that society can resist the continued sexualization of childhood.[16]

The new fatherhood movement encourages fathers to promise that they will spend more time with their children. The National Fatherhood Initiative argues that men's roles as fathers should not simply duplicate women's roles as mothers but should teach those essential qualities which are perhaps uniquely conveyed by fathers—the ability to take risks, contain emotions, and be decisive. In addition, fathers fulfill a time-honored role of providing for children as well as teaching them.[17]

Full-time mothers have likewise formed support groups to reassure themselves that not having a job and being at home full-time for their children is an honorable choice, although it is typically undervalued and perhaps even scorned by dual-earner couples and women with careers. A 1994 *Barron's* article claimed that young people in their twenties ("generation X") were turning away from the two-paycheck family and scaling down their consumption so that young mothers could stay at home. Although Labor Department statistics show no such trend but only a flattening of the upward rise of women's employment, a variety of poll data does suggest that Americans would rather spend less time at work and more time with their families.[18] Such groups as Mothers at Home (with 15,000 members) and Mothers' Home Business Network (with 6,000 members) are trying to create a sea change that reverses the priority given to paid work outside the home relative to unpaid caregiving work inside the family.[19]

Conservatives see government cutbacks as one of the major strategies for strengthening marriage and restoring family values. In the words of Lawrence Mead, we have "taxed Peter to pay Paula."[20] According to a *Wall Street Journal* editorial, the "relinquishment of personal responsibility" among people who bring children into the world without any visible means of support is at the root of educational, health, and emotional problems of children from one-parent families, their higher accident and mortality rates, and rising crime.[21]

The new congressional solution is to cut back on the benefits to young men and women who "violate social convention by having children they cannot support."[22] Sociologist Brigitte Berger notes that the increase in children and women on welfare coincided with the explosion of federal child welfare programs—family planning, prenatal and postnatal care, child nutrition, child abuse prevention and treatment, child health and guidance, day care, Head Start, and Aid to Families with Dependent Children (AFDC), Medicaid, and Food Stamps. The solution is to turn back the debilitating culture of welfare dependency by decentralizing the power of the federal government and restoring the role of intermediary community institutions such as the neighborhood and the church. The mechanism for change would be block grants to the states which would change the welfare culture from the ground up.[23] Robert Rector of the American Heritage Foundation explains that the states would use these funds for a wide variety of alternative programs to discourage illegitimate births and to care for children born out of wedlock, such as promoting adoption, closely supervised group homes for unmarried mothers and their children, and pregnancy prevention programs (except abortion).[24]

Government programs, however, are only one way to bring about cultural change. The Council on Families in America puts its hope in grassroots social movements to change the hearts and minds of religious and civil leaders, employers, human service professionals, courts, and the media and entertainment industry. The Council enunciates four ideals: marital permanence, childbearing confined to marriage, every child's right to have a father, and limitation of parents' total work time (60 hours per week) to permit adequate time with their families.[25] To restore the cultural ideal of the two-parent family, they would make all other types of family life less attractive and more difficult.

ECONOMIC RESTRUCTURING: LIBERAL ANALYSIS OF FAMILY CHANGE

Liberals agree that there are serious problems in America's social health and the condition of its children. But they pinpoint economic and structural changes that have placed new demands on the family without providing countervailing social supports. The economy has become ever more specialized with rapid technological change undercutting established occupations. More women have entered the labor force as their child-free years have increased due to a shorter childbearing period and longer lifespan. The family has lost economic functions to the urban workplace and socialization functions to the school. What is left is the intimate relationship between the marital couple, which, unbuffered by the traditional economic division of labor between men and women, is subject to even higher demands for emotional fulfillment and is thus more vulnerable to breakdown when it falls short of those demands.

Liberal Model

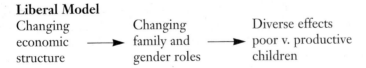

Changing economic structure ⟶ Changing family and gender roles ⟶ Diverse effects poor v. productive children

The current family crisis thus stems from structural more than cultural change—changes in the economy, a pared-down nuclear family, and less parental time at home. Market forces have led to a new ethic of individual flexibility and autonomy. More dual-earner couples and single-parent families have broadened the variety of family forms. More single-parent families and more working mothers have decreased the time available for parenting. Loss of the father's income through separation and divorce has forced many women and children into poverty with inadequate health care, poor education, and inability to save for future economic needs. The solution that most liberals espouse is a government-sponsored safety net which will facilitate women's employment, mute the effects of poverty, and help women and children to become economically secure.

Recent Changes in the Labor Market

Liberals attribute the dramatic changes in the family to the intrusion of the money economy rather than cultural and moral decline. In a capitalist society individual behavior follows the market. Adam Smith's "invisible hand" brings together buyers and sellers who maximize their satisfaction through an exchange of resources in the marketplace. Jobs are now with an employer, not with the family business or family farm as in preindustrial times. The cash economy has, in the words of Robert Bellah, "invaded" the diffuse personal relationships of trust between family and community members and transformed them into specific impersonal transactions. In an agricultural economy husbands and wives and parents and children were bound together in relationships of exchange that served each others' mutual interests. But modern society erodes this social capital of organization, trust among individuals, and mutual obligation that enhances both productivity and parenting.[26]

The market has also eroded community by encouraging maximum mobility of goods and services. Cheaper labor in the South, lower fuel prices, and deeper tax breaks attracted first textile factories, then the shoe industry, and later automobile assembly plants which had begun in the North. Eventually, many of these jobs left the country. Loss of manufacturing jobs has had dramatic consequences for employment of young men without a college education and their capacity to support a family. In the 1970s, 68 percent of male high school graduates had a full-time, year-round job compared with only 51 percent in the 1980s. Many new jobs are located in clerical work, sales, or other service occupations traditionally associated with women. The upshot is a deteriorating employment picture for less well educated male workers at the same time that there are rising opportunities for women. Not surprisingly, even more middle income men and women combine forces to construct a two-paycheck family wage.[27]

Changing Family Forms

Whereas the farm economy dictated a two-parent family and several children as the most efficient work group, the market economy gives rise to a much wider variety of family forms. A woman on the frontier in the 1800s had few other options even if she were married to a drunken, violent, or improvident husband. In today's economy this woman may have enough education to get a clerical job that will support her and her children in a small apartment where the family will be able to use public schools and other public amenities.[28]

Despite its corrosive effect on family relations, the modern economy has also been a liberating force. Women could escape patriarchal domination; the young could seek their fortune without waiting for an inheritance from their elders—all a process that a century ago was aligned with a cultural shift that Fred Weinstein and Gerald Platt termed "the wish to be free."[29] Dramatic improvements took place in the status of women as they gained the right to higher education, entry into the professions, and the elective franchise.[30] Similarly, children were released from sometimes cruel and exploitive labor and became the object of deliberate parental investment and consumption.[31] Elders gained pensions for maintenance and care that made them economically independent of their adult children. All these developments could be understood as part of what William J. Goode has referred to as the "world revolution in family patterns" which resulted in liberation and equality of formerly oppressed groups.[32]

The current assessment of change in family forms is, however, mostly negative because of the consequences for children. More parental investment in work outside the family has meant less time for children. According to liberals, parents separate or divorce or have children outside of marriage because of the economic structure, not because they have become less moral or more selfish. Young women have children out of wedlock when the young men whom they might marry have few economic prospects and when the women themselves have little hope for their own education or employment.[33] Change in the family thus begins with jobs. Advocates of current government programs therefore challenge the conservatives' assertion that welfare caused the breakup of two-parent families by supporting mothers with dependent children. According to William Julius Wilson, it is partly the lack of manual labor jobs for the would-be male breadwinner in inner-city Chicago—the scarcity of "marriageable males"—which drives up the illegitimacy rate.[34]

Among educated women, it is well known that the opportunity costs of foregone income from staying home became so high during the 1950s and 1960s that ever increasing numbers of women deserted full-time homemaking to take paid employment.[35] In the 1990s several social scientists have further noted that Richard Easterlin's prediction that women will return to the home during the 1980s never happened. Instead, women continued in the labor force because of irreversible normative changes surrounding women's equality and the need for women's income to finance children's expensive college education.[36] Moreover, in light of globalization of the economy and increasing job insecurity in the face of corporate downsizing, economists and sociologists are questioning Gary Becker's thesis that the lower waged worker in a household (typically the woman) will tend to become a full-time homemaker while the higher waged partner becomes the primary breadwinner. Data from Germany and the United States on the trend toward women's multiple roles suggests that uncertainty about the future has made women invest more strongly than ever in their own careers. They know that if they drop out for very long they will have difficulty reentering if they have to tide over the family when the main breadwinner loses his job.[37]

Consequences for Children

The ideal family in the liberal economic model, according to political philosopher Iris Young, is one which has sufficient income to support the parents and the children and "to foster in those children the emotional and intellectual capacities to acquire such well-paid, secure jobs themselves, and also sufficient to finance a retirement."[38] Dependent families do not have self-sufficient income but must rely on friends, relatives, charity, or the state to carry out their contribution to bringing up children and being good citizens.

Among liberals there is an emerging consensus that the current economic structure leads to two kinds of underinvestment in children that are implicated in their later dependency—material poverty, characteristic of the poor, and "time" poverty, characteristic of the middle class.

Thirty years ago Daniel Patrick Moynihan perceived that material poverty and job loss for a man put strain on the marriage, sometimes to the point that he would leave. His children also did less well in school.[39] Rand Conger, in his studies of Iowa families who lost their farms during the 1980s, found that economic hardship not only puts strain on the marriage but leads to harsh parenting practices and poorer outcomes for children.[40] Thus it appears possible that poverty may not just be the result of family separation, divorce, and ineffective childrearing practices; it may also be the *cause* of the irritability, quarrels, and violence which lead to marital breakdown. Material underinvestment in children is visible not just with the poor but in the changing ratio of per capita income of children and adults in U.S. society as a whole. As the proportion of households without children has doubled over the last century (from 30 to 65 percent), per capita income of children has fallen from 71 percent of adult income in 1870 to 63 percent in 1930 and 51 percent in 1983.[41]

The problem of "time" poverty used to be almost exclusively associated with mothers' employment. Numerous studies explored whether younger children did better if their mother was a full-time homemaker rather than employed outside the home but found no clear results.[47] Lately the lack of parental time for children has become much more acute because parents are working a total of twenty-one hours more per week than in 1970 and because there are more single-parent families. In 1965 the average child spent about thirty hours a week interacting with a parent, compared with seventeen hours in the 1980s.[43] Moreover, parents are less dependent on their children to provide support for them during old age, and children feel less obligated to do so. As skilled craftsmanship, the trades, and the family farms have disappeared, children's upbringing can no longer be easily or cheaply combined with what parents are already doing. So adults are no longer so invested in children's futures. The result is that where the social capital of group affiliations and mutual obligations is the lowest (in the form of continuity of neighborhoods, a two-parent family, or a parent's interest in higher education for her children), children are 20 percent more likely to drop out of high school.[44]

It is not that parents prefer their current feelings of being rushed, working too many hours, and having too little time with their families. Economist Juliet Schor reports that at least two-thirds of persons she surveyed about their desires for more family time versus more salary would take a cut in salary if it could mean more time with their families. Since this option is not realistically open to many, what parents appear to do is spend more money on their children as a substitute for spending more time with them.[45]

Fixing the Safety Net

Since liberals believe in a market economy with sufficient government regulation to assure justice and equality of opportunity, they support those measures which will eradicate the worst poverty and assure the healthy reproduction of the next generation.[46] What particularly worries them, however, is Charles Murray's observation that since

1970 the growth of government welfare programs has been associated with a *rise* in poverty among children. Payments to poor families with children, while not generous, have nevertheless enabled adults to be supported by attachment to their children.[47] Society is faced with a dilemma between addressing material poverty through further government subsidy and time poverty through policies on parental leave and working hours. It turns out that the United States is trying to do both.

Measures for addressing material poverty would stimulate various kinds of training and job opportunities. The Family Support Act of 1988 would move AFDC mothers off the welfare rolls by giving them job training and requiring them to join the labor force. Such action would bring their economic responsibility for supporting their children into line with their parental authority. A whole program of integrated supports for health insurance, job training, earned income tax credits for the working poor, child support by the noncustodial parent, and supported work is put forward by economist David Ellwood in *Poor Support*.[48] An opposite strategy is to consolidate authority over children with the state's economic responsibility for their care by encouraging group homes and adoption for children whose parents cannot support them economically.[49]

Means for addressing time poverty are evident in such legislative initiatives as the Family and Medical Leave Act of 1993. By encouraging employers to grant parental leave or other forms of flexible work time, government policy is recognizing the value of parents having more time with their children, but the beneficiaries of such change are largely middle-class families who can afford an unpaid parental leave.[50] Another tactic is to reform the tax law to discourage marital splitting. In a couple with two children in which the father earns $16,000 annually and the mother $9,000, joint tax filing gives them no special consideration. But if they file separately, each taking one child as a dependent, the woman will receive about $5,000 in Earned Income Tax Credit and an extra $2,000 in food stamps.[51] Changing the tax law to remove the incentives for splitting, establishing paternity of children born out of wedlock, and intensifying child support enforcement to recover economic support from fathers are all examples of state efforts to strengthen the kinship unit.

INTERDEPENDENCE: THE FEMINIST VISION OF WORK AND CAREGIVING

A feminist perspective has elements in common with both conservatives and liberals: a respect for the family as an institution (shared with the conservatives) and an appreciation of modernity (valued by the liberals). In addition, a feminist perspective grapples with the problem of women's traditionally subordinate status and how to improve it through both a "relational" and an "individualist" strategy while also sustaining family life and the healthy rearing of children.[52] At the same time feminists are skeptical of both conservative and liberal solutions. Traditionalists have so often relied on women as the exploited and underpaid caregivers in the family to enable men's activities in the public realm. Liberals are sometimes guilty of a "male" bias in focusing on the independent individual actor in the marketplace who does not realize that his so-called "independence," is possible only because he is actually *dependent* on all kinds of relationships that made possible his education and life in a stable social order.[53]

By articulating the value of caregiving along with the ideal of women's autonomy, feminists are in a position to examine modern capitalism critically for its effects on families and to offer alternative policies that place greater value on the quality of life and human relationships. They judge family strength not by their *form* (whether they have two-parents) but by their functioning (whether they promote human satisfaction and development) and whether both women and men are able to be family caregivers as well as productive workers. They attribute difficulties of children less to the absence of the two-parent family than to low-wage work of single mothers, inadequate child care, and inhospitable housing and neighborhoods.

Feminist Model

Lack of cooperation among community, family, and work → Families where adults are stressed and overburdened → Children lack sufficient care and attention from parents

Accordingly, feminists would work for reforms that build and maintain the social capital of volunteer groups, neighborhoods, and communities because a healthy civil society promotes the well-being of families and individuals as well as economic prosperity and a democratic state. They would also recognize greater role flexibility across the life cycle so that both men and women could engage in caregiving, and they would encourage education and employment among women as well as among men.

Disappearance of Community

From a feminist perspective, family values have become an issue because individualism has driven out the sense of collective responsibility in our national culture. American institutions and social policies have not properly implemented a concern for all citizens. Comparative research on family structure, teenage pregnancy, poverty, and child outcomes in other countries demonstrates that where support is generous to help *all* families and children, there are higher levels of health and general education and lower levels of violence and child deviance than in the United States.[54]

Liberal thinking and the focus on the free market have made it seem that citizens make their greatest contribution when they are self-sufficient, thereby keeping themselves off the public dole. But feminist theorist Iris Young argues that many of the activities that are basic to a healthy democratic society (such as cultural production, caretaking, political organizing, and charitable activities) will never be profitable in a private market. Yet many of the recipients of welfare and Social Security such as homemakers, single mothers, and retirees are doing important volunteer work caring for children and helping others in their communities. Thus the social worth of a person's contribution is not just in earning a paycheck that allows economic independence but also in making a social contribution. Such caretaking of other dependent citizens and of the body politic should be regarded as honorable, not inferior, and worthy of society's support and subsidy.[55]

In fact it appears that married women's rising labor force participation from 41 percent in 1970 to 58 percent in 1990 may have been associated with their withdrawal from unpaid work in the home and community.[56] Volunteer membership in everything from the PTA to bowling leagues declined by over 25 percent between 1969 and 1993. There is now considerable concern that the very basis that Alexis de Tocqueville thought necessary to democracy is under siege.[57] To reverse this trend, social observers suggest that it will be necessary to guard time for families and leisure that is currently being sucked into the maw of paid employment. What is needed is a reorientation of priorities to give greater value to unpaid family and community work by both men and women.

National policies should also be reoriented to give universal support to children at every economic level of society, but especially to poor children. In a comparison of countries in the Organization for Economic Cooperation and Development, the United States ranks at the top in average male wages but near the bottom in its provision for disposable income for children. In comparison with the $700 per month available to children in Norway, France, or the Netherlands in 1992, U.S. children of a single nonemployed mother received only slightly under $200.[58] The discrepancy is explained by very unequal distribution of U.S. income, with the top quintile, the "fortunate fifth," gaining 47 percent of the national income while the bottom fifth receives only 3.6 percent.[59] This sharp inequality is, in turn, explained by an ideology of individualism that justifies the disproportionate gains of the few for their innovation and productivity and the meager income of the poor for their low initiative or competence. Lack of access to jobs and the low pay accruing to many contingent service occupations simply worsen the picture.

Feminists are skeptical of explanations that ascribe higher productivity to the higher paid and more successful leading actors while ignoring the efforts and contribution of the supporting cast. They know that being an invisible helper is the situation of many women. This insight is congruent with new ideas about the importance "social capital" to the health of a society that have been put forward recently by a number of social scientists.[60] Corporations cannot be solely responsible for maintaining the web of community, although they are already being asked to serve as extended family, neighborhood support group, and national health service.

Diversity of Family Forms

Those who are concerned for strengthening the civil society immediately turn to the changing nature of the family as being a key building block. Feminists worry that seemingly sensible efforts to reverse the trend of rising divorce and single parenthood will privilege the two-parent family to the detriment of women; they propose instead that family values be understood in a broader sense as valuing the family's unique capacity for giving emotional and material support rather than implying simply a two–parent form.

The debate between conservatives, liberals, and feminists on the issue of the two-parent family has been most starkly stated by sociologist Judith Stacey and political philosopher Iris Young.[61] They regard the requirement that all women stay in a marriage as an invitation to coercion and subordination and an assault on the principles of freedom and self-determination that are at the foundation of democracy. Moreover, as Christopher Jencks and Kathryn Edin conclude from their study of several hundred welfare families, the current welfare reform rhetoric that no couple should have a child unless they can support it, does not take into account the uncertainty of life in which people who start out married or with adequate income not always remain so. In the face of the worldwide dethronement of the two-parent family (approximately one-quarter to one-third of all families around the globe are headed by women), marriage should not be seen as the cure for child poverty. Mothers should not be seen as less than full citizens if they are not married or not employed (in 1989 there were only 16 million males between the ages of 25 and 34 who made over $12,000 compared with 20 million females of the same age who either had a child or wanted one).[62] National family policy should instead begin with a value on women's autonomy and self-determination that includes the right to bear children. Mother-citizens are helping to reproduce the next generation for the whole society, and in that responsibility they deserve at least partial support.

From a feminist perspective the goal of the family is not only to bring up a healthy and productive new generation; families also provide the intimate and supportive group of kin or fictive kin that foster the health and well-being of every person—young or old, male or female, heterosexual, homosexual, or celibate. Recognition as "family" should therefore not be confined to the traditional two-parent unit connected by blood, marriage, or adoption, but should be extended to include kin of a divorced spouse (as Stacey documented in her study of Silicon Valley families), same-sex partnerships, congregate households of retired persons, group living arrangements, and so on.[63] Twenty years ago economist Nancy Barrett noted that such diversity in family and household form was already present. Among all U.S. households in 1976, no one of the six major types constituted more than 15–20 percent: couples with and without children under eighteen with the wife in the labor force (15.4 and 13.3 percent respectively); couples with or without children under 18 with the wife not in the labor force (19.1 and 17.1 percent); female- or male-headed households (14.4 percent); and single persons living alone (20.6 percent).[64]

Such diversity both describes and informs contemporary "family values" in the United States. Each family type is numerous enough to have a legitimacy of its own, yet no single form is the dominant one. As a result the larger value system has evolved to encompass beliefs and rules that legitimate each type on the spectrum. The regressive alternative is "fundamentalism" that treats the two-parent family with children as the only legitimate form, single-parent families as unworthy of support, and the nontraditional forms as illegitimate. In 1995 the general population appears to have accepted diversity of family forms as normal. A Harris poll of 1,502 women and 460 men found that only 2 percent of women and 1 percent of men defined family as "being about the traditional nuclear family." One out of ten women defined family values as loving, taking care of, and supporting each other, knowing right from wrong or having good values, and nine out of ten said society should value all types of families.[65] It appears most Americans believe that an Aunt Polly single-parent type of family for a Huck Finn that provides economic support, shelter, meals, a place to sleep and to withdraw, is better than no family at all.

Amidst gradual acceptance of greater diversity in family form, the gender-role revolution is also loosening the sex-role expectations traditionally associated with breadwinning and homemaking. Feminists believe that men and women can each do both.[66] In addition, women in advanced industrial nations have by and large converged upon a new life pattern of multiple roles by which they combine work and family life. The negative outcome is an almost universal "double burden" for working women in which they spend eighty-four hours per week on paid and family work, married men spend seventy-two hours, and single persons without children spend fifty hours.[67] The positive consequence, however, appears to be improved physical and mental health for those women who, though stressed, combine work and family roles.[68] In addition, where a woman's husband helps her more with the housework, she is less likely to think of getting a divorce.[69]

The Precarious Situation of Children

The principal remedy that conservatives and liberals would apply to the problems of children is to restore the two-parent family by reducing out-of-wedlock births, increasing the presence of fathers, and encouraging couples who are having marital difficulties to avoid divorce for the sake of their children. Feminists, on the other hand, are skeptical that illegitimacy, father absence, or divorce are the principal culprits they are made out to be. Leon Eisenberg reports that over half of all births in Sweden and one-quarter of births in France are to unmarried women, but without the disastrous correlated effects observed in the United States. Arlene Skolnick and Stacey Rosencrantz cite longitudinal studies showing that most children recover from the immediate negative effects of divorce.[70]

How then, while supporting the principle that some fraction of women should be able to head families as single parents, do feminists analyze the problem of ill health, antisocial behavior, and poverty among children? Their answer focuses on the *lack of institutional supports* for the new type of dual-earner and single-parent families that are more prevalent today. Rather than attempt to force families back into the traditional mold, feminists note that divorce, lone-mother families, and women's employment are on the rise in every industrialized nation. But other countries have not seen the same devastating decline in child well-being, teen pregnancy, suicides and violent death, school failure, and a rising population of children in poverty. These other countries have four key elements of social and family policy which protect all children and their mothers: (1) work guarantees and other economic supports; (2) child care; (3) health care; and (4) housing subsidies. In the United States these benefits are scattered and uneven; those who can pay their way do so; only those who are poor or disabled receive AFDC for economic support, some help with child care, Medicaid for health care, and government-subsidized housing.

A first line of defense is to raise women's wages through raising the minimum wage, then provide them greater access to male-dominated occupations with higher wages. One-half of working women do not earn a wage adequate to support a family of four above the poverty line. Moreover, women in low-wage occupations are subject to frequent lay-offs and lack of benefits. Training to improve their human capital, provision of child care, and broadening of benefits would help raise women's capacity to support a family. Eisenberg reports that the Human Development Index of the United Nations (HDI), which ranks countries by such indicators as life expectancy, educational levels, and per capita income, places the United States fifth and Sweden sixth in the world. But when the HDI is recalculated to take into account equity of treatment of women, Sweden rises to first place and the United States falls to ninth. Therefore, one of the obvious places to begin raising children's status is to "raise the economic status and earning power of their mothers."[71]

A second major benefit which is not assured to working mothers is child care. Among school-age children up to thirteen years of age, one-eighth lack any kind of after-school child care. Children come to the factories where their mothers work and wait on the lawn or in the lobby until their mothers are finished working. If a child is sick, some mothers risk losing a job if they stay home. Others are latchkey kids or in unknown circumstances such as sleeping in their parents' cars or loitering on the streets. Although 60 percent of mothers of the 22 million preschool children are working, there are only 10 million child care places available, a shortfall of one to three million slots.[72] Lack of good quality care for her children not only distracts a mother, adds to her absences from work, and makes her less productive, it also exposes the child to a lack of attention and care that leads to violent and antisocial behavior and poor performance in school.

Lack of medical benefits is a third gaping hole for poor children and lone-parent families. Jencks and Edin analyze what happens to a Chicago-area working woman's income if she goes off welfare. Her total income in 1993 dollars on AFDC (with food stamps, unreported earnings, help from family and friends) adds up to $12,355, in addition to which she receives Medicaid and child care. At a $6 per hour full-time job, however, without AFDC, with less than half as much from food stamps, with an Earned Income Tax Credit, and help from relatives, her total income would add to $20,853. But she would have to pay for her own medical care, bringing her effective income down to $14,745 if she found free child care, and $9,801 if she had to pay for child care herself.[73]

Some housing subsidies or low-income housing are available to low-income families. But the neighborhoods and schools are frequently of poor quality and plagued by violence. To bring up children in a setting where they cannot safely play with others introduces important risk factors that cannot simply be attributed to divorce and single parenthood. Rather than being protected and being allowed to be innocent, children must learn to be competent at a very early age. The family, rather than being child-centered, must be adult-centered, not because parents are selfish or self-centered but because the institutions of the society have changed the context of family life.[74] These demands may be too much for children, and depression, violence, teen suicide, teen pregnancy, and school failure may result. But it would be myopic to think that simply restoring the two-parent family would be enough to solve all these problems.

Constructing Institutions for the Good Society

What is to be done? Rather than try to restore the two-parent family as the conservatives suggest or change the economy to provide more jobs as recommended by the liberals, the feminists focus on the need to revise and construct institutions to accommodate the new realities of work and family life. Such an undertaking requires, however, a broader interpretation of family values, a recognition that families benefit not only their members but the public interest, and fresh thinking about how to schedule work and family demands of everyday life as well as the entire life cycle of men and women.

The understanding of family values has to be extended in two ways. First, American values should be stretched to embrace all citizens, their children and families, whether they are poor, white, or people of color, or living in a one-parent family. In 1977, Kenneth Keniston titled the report of the Carnegie Commission on Children *All Our Children.* Today many Americans still speak and act politically in ways suggesting that they *disown* other people's children as the next generation who will inherit the land and support the economy. Yet in the view of most feminists and other progressive reformers, all these children should be embraced for the long-term good of the nation.[75] By a commitment to "family values" feminists secondly intend to valorize the family as a distinctive intimate group of many forms that is needed by persons of all ages but especially children. To serve the needs of children and other dependent persons, the family must be given support and encouragement by the state to carry out its unique functions. Iris Young contends that marriage should not be used to reduce the ultimate need for the state to serve as a means to distribute needed supports to the families of those less fortunate.[76] Compare the example of the GI Bill of Rights after World War II, which provided educational benefits to those who had served their country in the military. Why should there not be a similar approach to the contribution that a parent makes in raising a healthy and productive youngster?[77]

At the community level families should be embraced by all the institutions of the civil society—schools, hospitals, churches, and employers—as the hidden but necessary complement to the bureaucratic and impersonal workings of these formal organizations. Schools rely on parents for the child's "school readiness." Hospitals send home patients who need considerable home care before becoming completely well. The work of the church is carried out and reinforced in the family; and when families fail, it is the unconditional love and intimacy of family that the church tries to replicate. Employers depend on families to give the rest, shelter, emotional support, and other maintenance of human capital that will motivate workers and make them productive. Increasingly, the professionals and managers in these formal organizations are realizing that they need to work more closely with parents and family members if they are to succeed.

Feminists would especially like to see the reintegration of work and family life that was torn apart at the time of the industrial revolution when productive work moved out of the home and into the factory. Several proposals appear repeatedly: parental leave (which now is possible through the Family and Medical Leave Act of 1993); flexible hours and part-time work shared by working parents but without loss of benefits and promotion opportunities; home-based work; child care for sick children and after-school supervision. Although some progress has been made, acceptance of these reforms has been very slow. Parental leave is still *unpaid*. The culture of the workplace discourages many persons from taking advantage of the more flexible options which do exist because they fear they will be seen as less serious and dedicated workers. In addition, most programs are aimed at mothers and at managers, although there is growing feeling that fathers and hourly workers should be included as well.[78]

Ultimately these trends may alter the shape of women's and men's life cycles. Increasingly, a new ideal for the life course is being held up as the model that society should work toward. Lotte Bailyn proposes reorganization of careers in which young couples trade off periods of intense work commitment with each other while they establish their families so that either or both can spend more time at home.[79] Right now both women and men feel they must work so intensely to establish their careers that they have too little time for their children.[80] For the poor and untrained, the problem is the opposite: childbearing and childrearing are far more satisfying and validating than a low-paying, dead-end job. The question is how to reorient educators or employers to factor in time with family as an important obligation to society (much as one would factor in military service, for example). Such institutional reorganization is necessary to give families and childrearing their proper place in the modern postindustrial society.

CONCLUSION

A review of the conservative, liberal, and feminist perspectives on the changing nature of the American family suggests that future policy should combine the distinctive contributions of all three. From the conservatives comes a critique of modernity that recognizes the important role of the family in maintaining child health and preventing child failure. Although their understanding of "family values" is too narrow, they deserve credit for raising the issue of family function and form to public debate. Liberals see clearly the overwhelming power of the economy to deny employment, make demands on parents as workers, and drive a wedge between employers' needs for competitiveness and families' needs for connection and community.

Surprising although it may seem, since feminists are often imagined to be "way out," the most comprehensive plan for restoring family to its rightful place is put forward by the feminists who appreciate both the inherently premodern nature of the family and at the same time its inevitable interdependence with a fast-changing world economy. Feminists will not turn back to the past because they know that the traditional family was often a straightjacket for women. But they also know that family cannot be turned into a formal organization or have its functions performed by government or other public institutions that are incapable of giving needed succor to children, adults, and old people which only the family can give.

The feminist synthesis accepts both the inherent particularism and emotional nature of the family and the inevitable specialization and impersonality of the modern economy. Feminists are different from conservatives in accepting diversity of the family to respond to the needs of the modern economy. They are different from the liberals in recognizing that intimate nurturing relationships such as parenting cannot all be turned into a safety net of formal care. The most promising social policies for families and children take their direction from inclusive values that confirm the good life and the well-being of every individual as the ultimate goal of the nation. The policy challenge is to adjust the partnership between the family and its surrounding institutions so that together they combine the best of private initiative with public concern.

Notes

1. Barbara Dafoe Whitehead, "Dan Qayle Was Right," *Atlantic Monthly* (April 1993): 47. Her chapter in [*Promises to Keep: Decline and Renewal of Marriage in America*, edited by D. Popenoe, J. B. Elshtain, and D. Blankenhorn] on the "Story of Marriage" continues the theme of an erosion of values for cultural diversity.

2. Mary Ann Glendon, "Marriage and the State: The Withering Away of Marriage," *Virginia Law Review* 62 (May 1976): 663–729.

3. See chapters by Milton Regan and Carl Schneider in [*Promises to Keep: Decline and Renewal of Marriage in America*, edited by D. Popenoe, J. B. Elshtain, and D. Blankenhorn].

4. Charles A. Murray, *Losing Ground: American Social Policy: 1950–1980* (New York: Basic Books, 1984). Critics point out that the rise in out-of-wedlock births continues, even though welfare payments have declined in size over the last several decades, thereby casting doubt on the perverse incentive theory of rising illegitimacy.

5. U.S. Bureau of the Census. *Statistical Abstract of the United States: 1994*, 114th ed. (Washington, DC: 1994), 59.

6. Suzanne M. Bianchi and Daphne Spain, *American Women in Transition* (New York: Russell Sage Foundation, 1986), 88.

7. Donald J. Hernandez, *America's Children: Resources from Family, Government, and the Economy* (New York: Russell Sage Foundation, 1993), 284, 70. Janet Zollinger Giele, "Woman's Role Change and Adaptation: 1920–1990," in *Women's Lives through Time: Educated American Women of the Twentieth Century*, ed. K. Hulbert and D. Schuster (San Francisco: Jossey-Bass. 1993), 40.

8. Victor Fuchs, "Are Americans Underinvesting in Children?" in *Rebuilding the Nest*, ed. David Blankenhorn, Stephen Bayme, and Jean Bethke Elshtain (Milwaukee. Family Service America, 1990), 66. Bianchi and Spain, *American Women in Transition*, 141, 201, 226. Janet Zollinger Giele, "Gender and Sex Roles," in *Handbook of Sociology*, ed. N. J. Smelser (Beverly Hills, CA: Sage Publications, 1988), 300.

9. Hernandez, *America's Children*, 130. Council on Families in America, *Marriage in America* (New York: Institute for American Values. 1995), 7.

10. Fuchs, "Are Americans Underinvesting in Children?" 61. Some would say, however, that the decline was due in part to a larger and more heterogeneous group taking the tests.

11. Council on Families in America, *Marriage in America*, 6. The report cites research by Nicholas Zill and Charlotte A. Schoenborn, "Developmental, Learning and Emotional Problems: Health of Our Nation's Children, United States, 1988." *Advance Data*, National Center for Health Statistics, Publication #120, November 1990. See also, Sara McLanahan and Gary Sandefur, *Growing Up with a Single Parent* (Cambridge, MA: Harvard University Press, 1994).

12. Edward Gilbreath, "Manhood's Great Awakening," *Christianity Today* (February 6, 1995): 27.

13. David Elkind, *The Hurried Child: Growing Up Too Fast Too Soon* (Reading, MA: Addison-Wesley, 1981).

14. Jean Bethke Elshtain, *Democracy on Trial* (New York: Basic Books, 1995).

15. Jonathan Alter and Pat Wingert, "The Return of Shame," *Newsweek* (February 6, 1995): 25.

16. Tom McNichol, "The New Sex Vow: 'I won't' until 'I do'," USA Weekend, March 25–27, 1994, 4 ff. Lee Smith. "The New Wave of Illegitimacy," *Fortune* (April 18, 1994): 81 ff.

17. Susan Chira, "War over Role of American Fathers," *New York Times*, June 19, 1994, 22.

18. Juliet Schor, "Consumerism and the Decline of Family and Community: Preliminary Statistics from a Survey on Time, Money, and Values." Harvard Divinity School, Seminar on Families and Family Policy, April 4, 1995.

19. Karen S. Peterson, "In Balancing Act, Scale Tips toward Family," *USA Today*, January 25, 1995.

20. Lawrence Mead, "Taxing Peter to Pay Paula," *Wall Street Journal*, November 2, 1994.

21. Tom G. Palmer, "English Lessons: Britain Rethinks the Welfare State," *Wall Street Journal*, November 2, 1994.

22. Robert Pear, "G.O.P. Affirms Plan to Stop Money for Unwed Mothers," *New York Times*, January 21, 1995, 9.

23. Brigitte Berger. "Block Grants: Changing the Welfare Culture from the Ground Up," *Dialogue* (Boston: Pioneer Institute for Public Policy Research), no. 3, March 1995.

24. Robert Rector, "Welfare," *Issues '94: The Candidate's Briefing Book* (Washington, DC: American Heritage Foundation, 1994), chap. 13.

25. Council on Families in America, *Marriage in America*, 13–16.

26. Robert Bellah, "Invasion of the Money World," in *Rebuilding the Nest*, ed. David Blankenhorn, Steven Bayme, and Jean Bethke Elshtain (Milwaukee: Family Service America, 1990), 227–36. James Coleman, *Foundations of Social Theory* (Cambridge, MA: Harvard University Press, 1990).

27. Sylvia Nasar, "More Men in Prime of Life Spend Less Time Working," *New York Times*, December 1, 1994, A1.

28. John Scanzoni, *Power Politics in the American Marriage* (Englewood Cliffs, NJ: Prentice-Hall, 1972). Ruth A. Wallace and Alison Wolf, *Contemporary Sociological Theory* (Englewood Cliffs, NJ: Prentice-Hall, 1991), 176.

29. Fred Weinstein and Gerald M. Platt, *The Wish to Be Free: Society, Psyche, and Value Change* (Berkeley, CA: University of California Press, 1969).

30. Kingsley Davis, "Wives and Work: A Theory of the Sex-Role Revolution and Its Consequences," in *Feminism, Children, and the New Families*, ed. S. M. Dornbusch and M. H. Strober (New York: Guilford Press. 1988), 67–86. Janet Zollinger Giele, *Two Paths to Women's Equality: Temperance, Suffrage, and the Origins of American Feminism* (New York: Twayne Publishers, Macmillan, 1995).

31. Vivianna A. Zelizer, *Pricing the Priceless Child: The Changing Social Value of Children* (New York: Basic Books, 1985).

32. William J. Goode, *World Revolution in Family Patterns* (New York: The Free Press, 1963).

33. Constance Willard Williams, *Black Teenage Mothers: Pregnancy and Child Rearing from Their Perspective* (Lexington, MA: Lexington Books, 1990).

34. William Julius Wilson, *The Truly Disadvantaged: The Inner City, the Underclass, and Public Policy* (Chicago: University of Chicago Press, 1987).

35. Jacob Mincer, "Labor-Force Participation of Married Women: A Study of Labor Supply," in *Aspects of Labor Economics*, Report of the National Bureau of Economic Research (Princeton, NJ: Universities-National Bureau Committee of Economic Research, 1962). Glen G. Cain. *Married Women in the Labor Force: An Economic Analysis* (Chicago: University of Chicago Press, 1966).

36. Richard A. Easterlin, *Birth and Fortune: The Impact of Numbers on Personal Welfare* (New York: Basic Books, 1980). Valerie K. Oppenheimer, "Structural Sources of Economic Pressure for Wives to Work—Analytic Framework," *Journal of Family History* 4, no. 2 (1979): 177–99. Valerie K. Oppenheimer, *Work and the Family: A Study in Social Demography* (New York: Academic Press, 1982).

37. Janet Z. Giele and Rainer Pischner, "The Emergence of Multiple Role Patterns Among Women: A Comparison of Germany and the United States," *Vierteljahrshefte zur Wirtschaftsforschung* (Applied Economics Quarterly) (Heft 1–2, 1994). Alice S. Rossi, "The Future in the Making," *American Journal of Orthopsychiatry* 63, no. 2 (1993): 166–76. Notburga Ott, *Intrafamily Bargaining and Household Decisions* (Berlin: Springer-Verlag, 1992).

38. Iris Young, "Mothers, Citizenship and Independence: A Critique of Pure Family Values," *Ethics* 105, no. 3 (1995): 535–56. Young critiques the liberal stance of William Galston, *Liberal Purposes* (New York: Cambridge University Press, 1991).

39. Lee Rainwater and William L. Yancey, *The Moynihan Report and the Politics of Controversy* (Cambridge, MA: MIT Press, 1967).

40. Glen H. Elder, Jr., *Children of the Great Depression* (Chicago: University of Chicago Press, 1974). Rand D. Conger, Xiao-Jia Ge, and Frederick O. Lorenz, "Economic Stress and Marital Relations," in *Families in Troubled Times: Adapting to Change in Rural America*, ed. R. D. Conger and G. H. Elder, Jr. (New York: Aldine de Gruyter, 1994), 187–203.

41. Coleman, *Foundations of Social Theory*, 590.

42. Elizabeth G. Menaghan and Toby L. Parcel, "Employed Mothers and Children's Home Environments," *Journal of Marriage and the Family* 53, no. 2 (1991): 417–31. Lois Hoffman, "The Effects on Children of Maternal and Paternal Employment," in *Families and Work*, ed. Naomi Gerstel and Harriet Engel Gross (Philadelphia: Temple University Press, 1987), 362–95.

43. Juliet Schor, *The Overworked American: The Unexpected Decline of Leisure* (New York: Basic Books, 1991). Robert Haveman and Barbara Wolfe, *Succeeding Generations: On the Effects of Investments in Children* (New York: Russell Sage Foundation, 1994), 239.

44. Coleman, *Foundations of Social Theory*, 596–97.

45. Schor, "Consumerism and Decline of Family."

46. Iris Young, "Mothers, Citizenship and Independence," puts Elshtain, Etzioni, Galston, and Whitehead in this category.

47. Coleman, *Foundations of Social Theory*, 597–609.

48. Sherry Wexler, "To Work and To Mother: A Comparison of the Family Support Act and the Family and Medical Leave Act" (Ph.D. diss. draft, Brandeis University, 1995). David T. Ellwood, *Poor Support: Poverty in the American Family* (New York: Basic Books, 1988).

49. Coleman, *Foundations of Social Theory*, 300–21. Coleman, known for rational choice theory in sociology, put forward these theoretical possibilities in 1990, fully four years ahead of what in 1994 was voiced in the Republican Contract with America.

50. Wexler, "To Work and To Mother."

51. Robert Lerman, "Marketplace," National Public Radio, April 18, 1995.

52. Karen Offen, "Defining Feminism: A Comparative Historical Approach," *Signs* 14, no. 1 (1988): 119–51.

53. Young, "Mothers, Citizenship and Independence."

54. Robert N. Bellah et al., *Habits of the Heart* (Berkeley, CA: University of California Press, 1985), 250–71. Gosta Esping-Andersen, *The Three Worlds of Welfare Capitalism* (Princeton, NJ: Princeton University Press, 1990). Susan Pedersen, *Family, Dependence, and the Origins of the Welfare State: Britain and France, 1914–1945* (New York: Cambridge University Press, 1993).

55. Young, "Mothers, Citizenship and Independence."

56. Giele, "Woman's Role Change and Adaptation" presents these historical statistics.

57. Elshtain, *Democracy on Trial.* Robert N. Bellah et al., *The Good Society* (New York: Knopf, 1991), 210. Robert D. Putnam, "Bowling Alone: America's Declining Social Capital," *Journal of Democracy* 4, no. 1 (1995): 65–78.

58. Heather McCallum, "Mind the Gap" (paper presented to the Family and Children's Policy Center colloquium, Waltham, MA, Brandeis University, March 23, 1995). The sum was markedly better for children of employed single mothers, around $700 per mother in the United States. But this figure corresponded with over $1,000 in eleven other countries, with only Greece and Portugal lower than the U.S. Concerning the high U.S. rates of teen pregnancy, see Planned Parenthood advertisement, "Let's Get Serious About Ending Teen Childbearing," *New York Times,* April 4, 1995, A25.

59. Ruth Walker, "Secretary Reich and the Disintegrating Middle Class," *Christian Science Monitor,* November 2, 1994, 19.

60. For reference to "social capital," see Coleman, *Foundations of Social Theory*; Elshtain, *Democracy on Trial*; and Putnam, "Bowling Alone." For "emotional capital," see Arlie Russell Hochschild, *The Managed Heart: The Commercialization of Human Feeling* (Berkeley, CA: University of California Press, 1983). For "cultural capital," see work by Pierre Bourdieu and Jurgen Habermas.

61. Judith Stacey, "Dan Quayle's Revenge: The New Family Values Crusaders," *The Nation,* July 25/August 1, 1994, 119–22. Iris Marion Young, "Making Single Motherhood Normal," *Dissent* (Winter 1994): 88–93.

62. Christopher Jencks and Kathryn Edin, "Do Poor Women Have a Right to Bear Children," *The American Prospect* (Winter 1995): 43–52.

63. Stacey, "Dan Quayle's Revenge." Arlene Skolnick and Stacey Rosencrantz, "The New Crusade for the Old Family," *The American Prospect* (Summer 1994): 59–65.

64. Nancy Smith Barrett, "Data Needs for Evaluating the Labor Market Status of Women," in *Census Bureau Conference on Federal Statistical Needs Relating to Women,* ed. Barbara B. Reagan (U.S. Bureau of the Census, 1979), Current Population Reports, Special Studies, Series P-23, no. 83, pp. 10–19. These figures belie the familiar but misleading statement that "only 7 percent" of all American families are of the traditional nuclear type because "traditional" is defined so narrowly—as husband and wife with two children under 18 where the wife is not employed outside the home. For more recent figures and a similar argument for more universal family ethic, see Christine Winquist Nord and Nicholas Zill, "American Households in Demographic Perspective," working paper no. 5, Institute for American Values, New York, 1991.

65. Tamar Levin, "Women Are Becoming Equal Providers," *New York Times,* May 11, 1995, A27.

66. Marianne A. Ferber and Julie A. Nelson, *Beyond Economic Man: Feminist Theory and Economics* (Chicago: University of Chicago Press, 1993).

67. Fran Sussner Rodgers and Charles Rodgers, "Business and the Facts of Family Life," *Harvard Business Review,* no. 6 (1989): 199–213, especially 206.

68. Ravenna Helson and S. Picano, "Is the Traditional Role Bad for Women?" *Journal of Personality and Social Psychology* 59 (1990): 311–20. Rosalind C. Barnett, "Home-to-Work Spillover Revisited: A Study of Full-Time Employed Women in Dual-Earner Couples," *Journal of Marriage and the Family* 56 (August 1994): 647–56.

69. Arlie Hochschild, "The Fractured Family," *The American Prospect* (Summer 1991): 106–15.

70. Leon Eisenberg, "Is the Family Obsolete?" *The Key Reporter* 60, no. 3 (1995): 1–5. Arlene Skolnick and Stacey Rosencrantz, "The New Crusade for the Old Family," *The American Prospect* (Summer 1994): 59–65.

71. Roberta M. Spalter-Roth, Heidi I. Hartmann, and Linda M. Andrews, "Mothers, Children, and Low-Wage Work: The Ability to Earn a Family Wage," in *Sociology and the Public Agenda,* ed. W. J. Wilson (Newbury Park, CA: Sage Publications, 1993), 316–38.

72. Louis Uchitelle, "Lacking Child Care, Parents Take Their Children to Work," *New York Times,* December 23, 1994, 1.

73. Jencks and Edin, "Do Poor Women Have a Right," 50.

74. David Elkind, *Ties That Stress: The New Family in Balance* (Boston: Harvard University Press, 1994).

75. It is frequently noted that the U.S. is a much more racially diverse nation than, say, Sweden, which has a concerted family and children's policy. Symptomatic of the potential for race and class division that impedes recognition of all children as the nation's children is the book by Richard J. Herrnstein and Charles A. Murray, *The Bell Curve: Intelligence and Class Structure in American Life* (New York: The Free Press, 1994).

76. Young, "Making Single Motherhood Normal," 93.

77. If the objection is that the wrong people will have children, as Herrnstein and Murray suggest in *The Bell Curve*, then the challenge is to find ways for poor women to make money or have some other more exciting career that will offset the rewards of having children, "such as becoming the bride of Christ or the head of a Fortune 500 corporation," to quote Jencks and Edin, "Do Poor Women Have a Right," 48.

78. Beth M. Miller, "Private Welfare: The Distributive Equity of Family Benefits in America" (Ph.D. thesis, Brandeis University, 1992). Sue Shellenbarger, "Family-Friendly Firms Often Leave Fathers Out of the Picture," *Wall Street Journal*, November 2, 1994. Richard T. Gill and T. Grandon Gill, *Of Families, Children, and a Parental Bill of Rights* (New York: Institute for American Values, 1993). For gathering information on these new work-family policies, I wish to acknowledge help of students in my 1994–95 Family Policy Seminar at Brandeis University, particularly Cathleen O'Brien, Deborah Gurewich, Alissa Starr, and Pamela Swain, as well as the insights of two Ph.D students, Mindy Fried and Sherry Wexler.

79. Lotte Bailyn, *Breaking the Mold: Women, Men and Time in the New Corporate World* (New York: The Free Press, 1994).

80. Penelope Leach, *Children First: What Our Society Must Do and Is Doing* (New York: Random House, 1994).

■ READING 7

Why Do Gays Want to Marry?

by George Chauncey

WHAT MARRIAGE MEANT

Why did getting married matter so much to so many people in a culture that seemed no longer to place much stock in the institution?

Many people waiting in line that night in Cambridge and the next morning in Boston pointed to the problems they and their partners had faced in their dealings with hospitals, loan offices, schools, and employers. After eighteen years together, Peter and John were annoyed that they still couldn't get family insurance. They worried about what would happen to the house they'd bought together when one of them died. And they remembered how when Peter's grandmother passed away, John couldn't attend the entire funeral with him. "John's been part of my family," Peter recalled. "Both our families are very close, and he was the only one that couldn't take bereavement leave off of work to be there. All my sisters, their husbands, they got to be there. He had to miss the morning part of the funeral, couldn't come for the wake, couldn't come until later." Everyone wondered why he couldn't be there. So did they. "You know," he said, "these injustices come up."

Kate had also been with her partner for eighteen years. There had been times when one of them was working and the other was in school and they'd sit down at tax time and calculate "what taxes we would have paid, had we been married. Then we figured out what taxes we paid separately, and we called it the lesbian tax. Every year it was like, hmm, was it worth $3,000 to be lesbians this year?" They always agreed "it was worth it, but we've both been very aware of the financial impact" of the fact that they couldn't get married.

Two women who'd been together for nineteen years told of the time one of them went into the hospital for breast surgery and her partner "wasn't allowed in there." They "had to fight, and fight," and "I ended up signing myself out." Another woman had tried to renegotiate her partner's student loans with an agency. "I get on the phone and talk to these people, and they say, well, who are you? And I say, I'm her partner. And they go, so what." So she "had to send in a form that says its okay for me to talk for her," a different form for each loan. "This is insane," she thought.

In San Francisco, Portland, and Boston alike, significantly more women than men got marriage licenses. In Massachusetts, two-thirds of the 752 couples to get marriage licenses on the first day were lesbian, and 40 percent of those couples had children living with them.[3] This shouldn't be surprising, since having children raised the stakes for everyone. When their kids were born they had taken care of all the paperwork—the wills and health proxies and trusts—many of them had never bothered with before. But "while that's there, you never really know that those legal documents would uphold in a court of law," one mother commented. And she wondered about all the gay parents who didn't have the money or time to get those documents prepared. What would happen to them "when there's some sort of tragedy?" Another woman remembered that when she got a job with health insurance she couldn't put her partners' children on it, even though they had raised the children together for years.

But the people waiting in line didn't just want the rights, protections, and benefits that married couples had. They wanted to be recognized as fully equal. The fierce resistance to same-sex marriage had impressed on people the power of marriage to symbolize that equality. Especially in San Francisco, waiting in line to get a license came to feel like an act of civil disobedience as numerous government officials and right-wing legal groups raced to shut the line down. But even in Massachusetts, no one could forget how hard Governor Romney, the Catholic Church, and many legislators had fought to keep them from getting there.

"This isn't just benefits, and it isn't just the legal issue," Robert insisted as he waited outside Boston City Hall. He regarded the freedom to marry as a sign of his full equality and humanity. "I woke up a couple of days ago," he remembered, "and said to myself, oh my God, we're going to be equal to other human beings." Deb said she "was sitting on the subway this morning coming in here, and I'm looking around, thinking, okay, I'll be just like them. . . .We're no longer second-class citizens. That's what it really means."

The sudden possibility of getting married made many people wonder if they had been complicit before with their second-class citizenship. They had accepted and taken for granted that they would never have the rights and protections of marriage, and now wondered why. Domestic partnership and civil unions, which had once seemed like a huge advance, even preferable to some as an alternative to marriage, now seemed unacceptably "separate and unequal," as people took to saying. Why had they put up with it? "There's so many ways in which we know we have had second-class citizenship because of our lack of access to this civil institution," one woman mused.

Some people in line said they had always wanted to get married, even though they never expected it would actually be possible. Others had never thought of doing it at all—until they suddenly could. "When you knew that you couldn't do it, you didn't think about it, because it was sort of painful," Anne commented. "So I don't think I realized how much I wanted to do it, until I could do it. My parents have been married for forty years, my sister's been married for fourteen years, it's something we do in our family. So once it was real, I realized it was something I really wanted to do."

The rush to marry bore testimony to the continuing power of marriage as a symbol of personal commitment and as a means of gaining recognition for that commitment from others. "First and foremost, I love this woman and she loves me," one woman said to explain why she was in line, and marriage was "the best sign of a commitment that you can make." Another woman commented on how many of the "younger people" at her job had gotten married. "It's a long process of their planning it, and sharing that with people, and being excited, and doing it with their families." She'd been with her partner for more than twenty-five years, and now that she was planning her own wedding she was struck by how much it meant to her to "be able to talk about that with people, and have people involved in that." She noticed even more than before the "power of marriage as a social institution that gives people credibility within the community."

Still, not everyone raced to get married. For many couples, the fact that it suddenly was an option—that they suddenly *could* and *had* to make a choice about getting married—led to soul-searching about the meaning of marriage for their relationship as well as thoughtful debate about what securing this right might mean for the larger movement for social justice.

Some people who decided to get married, especially feminists, continued to be critical of how marriage allocated benefits and served to elevate some relationships over others. "We're progressive people who have really thought a lot about what the pros and cons are of this, which is something that I don't think a lot of heterosexuals think about," Karen commented. Getting married was "not going to have a big impact in our lives personally, quite honestly, because we're deeply committed to each other, we're deeply loyal to our friends and our family and each other." But she, too, thought it was important to be there, because so long as marriage rights were denied, "the inequalities can only ferment and seep through our system of justice," and "equality can't happen." Another woman agreed that she had "mixed feelings" about marriage. "But then, like everybody, when it happened, it just felt like a door opened, and it's momentous and historic and important. I've had my commitment ceremony, so I'm not doing this for the sanction of the state, but because it has made it clearer that this is about second-class citizenship."

Shortly after she got married, Evelynn Hammond wrote some friends about her complex reactions to the experience:

> As I walked to my office I thought—nothing will ever be the same and yet picking up the license was the same experience anyone straight would have had. I wish I had adequate words to describe all the events of last week—but I don't yet. My feelings aren't really

about the personal aspects of same-sex marriage. I don't feel any differently about Alexandra or my commitment to her than I did before last week. It is the historic aspect of this that feels strange, pleasant, and disquieting. I keep ruminating on what it means to be "normal" versus "not normal"; "different" and "not-different." I feel like I was a part of the dismantling of the Berlin Wall—the dismantling of something that was literally both concrete and ideological.

WHAT IS DEFENDED BY THE "DEFENSE OF MARRIAGE ACT"?

The images of joyous lesbian and gay couples and their kids that filled America's television sets in the winter of 2004 produced widely varying responses. Their ordinary humanity and devotion to one another touched many Americans. But their audacity in claiming the right to marry horrified many others, especially religious conservatives. On February 24, just two weeks after Mayor Newsom had thrown open the doors of City Hall, President Bush himself called for a constitutional amendment that would shut those doors forever.

Why did marriage galvanize such strident opposition, as well as such excitement? For all the ferocity of the debate unleashed by the developments in San Francisco and Boston, the debate over marriage was only the latest stage in a long-running debate over gay equality. The fiercest opponents of same-sex marriage had pushed the Defense of Marriage Act through Congress eight years earlier and had been fighting gay rights for more than a generation. Long before proposing a constitutional amendment to ban same-sex marriage, they had opposed gay rights ordinances, the right of gay couples to adopt children, and the appearance of gay characters in the media. For more than twenty years they had led referendum campaigns against gay rights ordinances. In 1996, the Southern Baptist Convention had called for a boycott of Disney because Disneyland hosted gay theme nights and the company had established a domestic partnership program that "accepts and embraces homosexual relationships for the purpose of insurance benefits." In 2001, Focus on the Family had opposed the decision of New York Governor George Pataki to make benefits available to the gay partners as well as the spouses of victims of the September 11 terrorist attacks.[4] Many of the arguments they made against same-sex marriage—that it would harm children and undermine the sanctity of marriage, the nation's morality, and very idea of gender difference—echoed the arguments they had once made against gay rights measures that now enjoyed wide popular support.

Still, "defending marriage" as the union of one man and one woman had special symbolic significance for the opponents of gay rights. Many of its opponents saw "gay marriage" as both the ultimate sign of gay equality and the final blow to their traditional ideal of marriage, which had been buffeted by thirty years of change. Their arguments reflected this, and even as they recapitulated old themes, they registered the profound change that had taken place in American attitudes toward gay people.

The link between the "defense of marriage" and opposition to gender equality was especially noteworthy. The association of homosexuality with gender inversion and role reversal has shaped public attitudes toward both gay people and gender conventions throughout the twentieth century. At times that association has produced a compelling mixture of fascination and awe, which was palpable among the thousands of heterosexuals who flocked to see the female and male impersonators at Harlem's drag balls in the 1920s and 1930s, and among the millions who danced to the disco beat of Sylvester and RuPaul half a century later. But at times of dramatic change in gender roles, opponents of change have often used that association to attack those changes and to stigmatize gay people. This could be seen in the early twentieth century, when many doctors condemned women's quest for equality as a sign of degeneration. And it could be seen in the simultaneous enactment of laws restricting women's employment and gay people's visibility in response to the crisis in the male-dominated family caused by the Great Depression of the 1930s. Over the course of the twentieth century, advances and reversals in the rights of lesbians and gay men have almost always been linked to similar changes in the status of women.

After the rise of the women's movement and gay movement in the 1960s and 1970s, the opponents of both linked them as much as many of their participants did. The specter of "homosexual marriage" was part of what doomed the battle to ratify the Equal Rights Amendment. The Amendment easily passed both houses of Congress in 1972 and was ratified by thirty of the necessary thirty-eight states within a year. But in the next two years, conservatives brought that momentum to a halt. Some of their most effective arguments warned that the ERA would not just end sex discrimination but would also challenge the very notion of difference between men and women by rendering unconstitutional the legal recognition of such differences. Three claims about how the ERA would subvert everyday common sense about gender differences were especially evocative: it would require unisex toilets, the drafting of women into the military, and the recognition of "homosexual marriage."[5] ERA supporters rejected those arguments but could not overcome them. Indeed, the effectiveness of these arguments against the ERA is probably one reason few gay activists imagined that marriage rights were possible to pursue in the 1970s.

Beginning in the 1970s, the growing Christian Right linked changes in women's roles to the growing freedom of gay people in more powerful and enduring ways. A fundamentalist revival characterized the 1960s and 1970s as much as the sexual revolution did. In 1979, leaders of several "superchurches" at the forefront of that revival organized the Moral Majority to counteract what they saw as the nation's slide into immorality. Drawing on a strong base in independent fundamentalist churches and the power of evangelical television shows and networks to communicate their message, the movement rapidly grew. The Traditional Values Coalition, Focus on the Family, Christian Coalition, and other groups formed in its wake shared its central belief that restoring the Christian family was the key to restoring the nation's moral order.[6]

In his 1980 book *Listen, America!*, Jerry Falwell, the founder of the Moral Majority, warned that changes in gender roles and the growth of the gay movement were two sides of the same coin: "We would not be having the present moral crisis regarding the homosexual movement if men and women accepted their proper roles as designated by God," he contended. "In the Christian home the father is responsible to exercise spiritual control and to be the head over his wife and children; 'for the husband is the head of the wife, even as Christ is the head of the church' (Ephesians 5:23). . . . In the Christian home the woman is to be submissive; 'wives, submit yourselves unto your own husbands, as unto the Lord' (Ephesians 5:22). Homosexuality is Satan's diabolical attack upon the family, God's order in Creation."[7] The link was so obvious to Falwell that he didn't need to explain it.

Stated in these stark terms, such arguments were unlikely to persuade a majority of Americans by the beginning of the twenty-first century, but they found a powerful constituency in the movement for "traditional family values." That movement's concern that, as Rev. Falwell put it, "feminists desire to eliminate God-given differences that exist between the sexes"[8] helped inspire its fervent opposition to granting marriage rights to gay couples. Glenn Stanton of Focus on the Family warned in 2003 that "homosexual marriage" would mean "the terms 'husband' and 'wife' would become merely words with no meaning. . . . Gender would become nothing."[9] The movement's "defense of marriage" as something available only to a man and woman was premised on the belief that God had ordained certain roles in marriage exclusively to men as "husbands" and women as "wives." The movement's opposition to "homosexual marriage" was inspired in good part by its fear that allowing two people of the same sex to marry would ratify the transformation of marriage over the last thirty years into an institution of legal equality and gender neutrality, in which most people expect and are expected to negotiate the terms of their own relationships free of legally mandated gender roles.

Such concerns stood behind many of the arguments made against gay marriage. Since most Americans were unprepared to accept fundamentalist prescriptions for wifely behavior, anti-marriage activists typically sought to frame their arguments in ways that would appeal to what seemed common-sense ideas about marriage's purpose. In the debate over DOMA (Defense of Marriage Act) and the federal constitutional amendment, religious leaders and quite a few congressmen cited scripture to argue that the purpose of marriage was procreation. This had a certain "commonsense" ring to it, even though neither the capacity nor the intention to procreate had ever been a requirement of marriage. GLAD conclusively demonstrated this in the Massachusetts case, and adoption as well as the new reproductive technologies had given every couple, gay or straight, fertile or infertile, the capacity to bring children into their lives. But when religious conservatives referred to "procreation," they often used it as shorthand for a larger set of assumptions about the roles of husbands and wives, including women's need to accept that their primary duty in life is to be mothers.

The right wing's most resonant arguments opposed gay couples' marriage rights under the guise of defending the interests of children. "Unisex marriages," as some foes took to calling them, simply did not create a good environment for raising children, they claimed, despite all of the evidence to the contrary.

Such arguments built on a long tradition of antigay rhetoric, but also diverged from it in ways that revealed just how far the country had moved on gay issues. A decade before arguments about the fitness of gay couples as parents moved to the center of the marriage debate, they got an extensive airing as growing numbers of couples sought joint adoption of children. Along with the growing acceptance of gay people, the research studies showing no ill effects on children seem to have influenced public opinion as well as the courts. In 1977, only 14 percent of Americans thought gay people should be allowed to adopt children. That number doubled to 29 percent by 1992, and it jumped to almost 50 percent just eight years later, in one more sign of the dramatic change in attitudes in the 1990s.[10]

Fears about whether or not the children of gay couples would turn out alright often indirectly expressed fears about whether or not those children would become homosexual themselves, notwithstanding a generation of research showing that was not the case. But these fears also expressed the lingering anxiety of some heterosexuals that the legitimization or normalization of homosexuality would have an effect on their own children as well, causing their children to become gay. For decades, many of the most strident opponents of gay rights had been inspired by such fears and made them central to their depiction of the "homosexual threat."

Public authorities and hate groups alike have often stigmatized social outsiders—be they Jews or gypsies or homosexuals—as child stealers or child molesters, because concern about children links people's broadest fears about the reproduction of the familiar social order to their deepest and most intimate fears about the safety of their own children—and about whether their children will reproduce their way of life, be it their religion, race, or sexuality. In her 1977 campaign against Miami's gay rights ordinance, Anita Bryant brilliantly mobilized that demonic image of homosexuals through newspaper ads and the very name of her organization, "Save Our Children." In the antigay hate literature that flooded states and municipalities during the referendum campaigns of the late 1980s and 1990s, homosexuals were often depicted in this way. Christian Right organizations distributed thousands of copies of "The Gay Agenda," a video that effectively juxtaposed discussions of pedophilia with images of gay teachers and gay parents marching with their children in Gay Pride parades, which made it easy for viewers to imagine they were molesters showing off their prey.

Those demonic stereotypes became less effective as people became more familiar with gay people, as their friends and relatives came out to them and as they saw gay people treated in more humane and respectful ways in the media. In 1977, two-thirds of Americans objected to lesbians or gay men being hired as elementary school teachers, the last place a child molester should be (two-thirds expressed no concern about gay salespersons). Fifteen years later, in 1992, half still rejected the idea of their child having a gay elementary school teacher. A decade later, about 60 percent were willing to see gay elementary school teachers, and two-thirds found gay high school teachers acceptable. The experience of knowing someone gay had an enormous impact on people's opinions. A 1993 survey found that two-thirds of the respondents who had a close gay friend or family member would not worry if their child's teacher were gay or lesbian; only a third of those without a close gay friend or relative said the same thing.[11]

But such concerns continue to animate the fiercest opposition to gay rights. Indeed, much of the debate over same-sex marriage and gay rights more generally hinges on the cultural divide in American society between modernist and fundamentalist views of human nature. Many scholars now argue that the ancient belief that homosexuality was a form of sinful behavior in which anyone might engage was superceded in the late nineteenth century by the modernist understanding that the homosexual was a distinct category of person. As Michel Foucault famously described this evolution, "the sodomite had been a temporary aberration; the homosexual was now a species."[12] But many Americans never accepted this new understanding of sexuality.

By and large, Americans who support gay rights tend to believe sexual identity is a stable, intrinsic, and enduring condition over which people have no control, whereas those who disapprove of homosexuality are much more likely to believe it is a choice, and a sinful one at that. A major Pew Foundation study conducted in early 2004 found that a person's belief or disbelief in the mutability of homosexual identity was a more powerful predictor of their attitudes toward gay people than education, knowing someone gay, or "general ideological beliefs." Two-thirds of those who believed someone could change their homosexuality had an unfavorable view of gay people, whereas 60 percent of those who believed that being gay was an immutable condition over which people had no choice were favorably disposed.[13]

By the winter of 2003–2004, when the marriage issue briefly dominated American political debate, the country was evenly divided on this question. Two out of five Americans thought homosexuality was something people were born with or was fixed so early in life they had no control over it. But an equal number, another two out of five, believed it was simply a choice or preference, which people could change. Half of Americans with an opinion on the matter, in other words, simply do not believe homosexuals are a discrete minority of people. One of President Bush's first public statements on the marriage debate in July 2003 suggests the prevalence of such views. In a tortured comment in which he sought to appear tolerant while also appealing to his backers on the Christian Right, he cautioned Americans that homosexuals shouldn't be singled out, since, as he put it, "we're all sinners."[14]

The belief that homosexuality is a sinful choice instead of a minority status is especially pronounced among people with a fundamentalist or evangelical worldview. Fundamentalist Protestants are more than twice as likely to believe that someone can change their sexual orientation than either mainline Protestants or Catholics (65 percent compared to 26 and 30 percent, respectively). Indeed, almost three-quarters of evangelicals who are deeply involved in their churches and religious life believe that homosexuals can change, and 93 percent of them believe homosexuality is an immoral choice.

As a result, evangelicals are more likely to fear that any government, religious, or media legitimization of homosexuality threatens the stability of heterosexuality itself by making homosexuality seem a more acceptable, even appealing choice. They worry especially about youth being exposed to such temptation, so take great care to prevent their children from having any exposure to gay people. More than two-thirds of Catholics would permit their children to play in the home of a friend who has a gay parent; but only a fifth of evangelicals would. Almost 60 percent of Catholics would hire a gay babysitter, but only 10 percent of Protestant fundamentalists would. Fundamentalists are twice as likely as most Americans to keep books with gay characters away from their children.

During the 1996 debate over the Employment Non-Discrimination Act, which would have banned antigay discrimination in hiring, some of its opponents evoked its potential consequences for young people to explain their opposition. Senator John Ashcroft, for one, opposed the bill because engaging "in a homosexual lifestyle . . . is a choice which can be made and unmade," and ending discrimination in employment might result in boys coming into contact with gay men who would influence them to make a bad choice. "I am worried about youngsters in our society," he argued. "I think there are times when young men are unsure about themselves when they are in transition, when they have identified perhaps more with their mothers than with their fathers, and they move from boyhood to manhood. Those are critical times when role models are very important. I think Senator Nickles was on target when he said that we have to be careful of who we have in the Boy Scouts."[15]

Most gay people found it difficult to believe that anyone could think their sexual orientation was a choice or that granting equal rights to gay people would influence children to become gay. Many could tell stories about how they had discovered and then resisted their own sexual orientation, given the social pressures against being gay. Being raised by heterosexuals hadn't turned them into heterosexuals, so why should the reverse be true? Then many came to resent the implication of the question itself, since gay life did no harm and for them was a positive good, and even if some people could change their sexual orientation (like their religion), it would not justify discrimination against gay people.

But the question of choice became an increasingly important element of the national debate over gay equality in the 1990s. A steady barrage of stories in the media about research studies showing that homosexuality was genetically or biologically determined was countered by an equally steady campaign by antigay activists to insist that homosexuals could change—that, in effect, homosexuals could be converted to heterosexuality just as Jews or Muslims could be converted to Christianity. Most famously, in the late 1990s Christian Right leaders began publicizing "reparative therapy" programs that they claimed could "convert" homosexuals into heterosexuals. The focus of these programs on "saving" individual souls from homosexuality allowed the Right to moderate its image when its outright demonization of homosexuals became less plausible and acceptable to most Americans.[16] The programs drew on psychological theories that had long been discredited by the American Psychological Association and were condemned by most mainline Protestant and Catholic leaders, and the "ex-gay" movement was regularly embarrassed by "ex-ex-gays" who deserted and denounced it as a sham. But the Christian Right's new focus on the claim that homosexuality was a choice reinforced old stereotypes about homosexual seduction and provided the right with a subtle but powerful argument to use against any arrangement—from domestic partnership to marriage—that might seem to give social support to a sinfully chosen "lifestyle."

Editors' Note: *Notes and references for this reading can be found in the original source.*

II *Sex and Gender*

U.S. society has experienced both a sexual revolution and a gender revolution. The first has liberalized attitudes toward erotic behavior and expression; the second has changed the roles and status of women and men in the direction of greater equality. Both revolutions have been brought about by the rapid social changes in recent years, and both revolutions have challenged traditional conceptions of marriage.

The traditional idea of sexuality defines sex as a powerful biological drive continually struggling for gratification against restraints imposed by civilization. The notion of sexual instincts also implies a kind of innate knowledge: A person intuitively knows his or her own identity as male or female, he or she knows how to act accordingly, and he or she is attracted to the "proper" sex object—a person of the opposite gender. In other words, the view of sex as biological drive pure and simple implies "that sexuality has a magical ability, possessed by no other capacity, that allows biological drives to be expressed directly in psychological and social behaviors" (Gagnon and Simon, 1970, p. 24).

The whole issue of the relative importance of biological versus psychological and social factors in sexuality and sex differences has been obscured by polemics. On the one hand, there are the strict biological determinists who declare that anatomy is destiny. On the other hand, there are those who argue that all aspects of sexuality and sex-role differences are matters of learning and social construction.

There are two essential points to be made about the nature-versus-nurture argument. First, modern genetic theory views biology and environment as interacting, not opposing forces. Second, both biological determinists and their opponents assume that if a biological force exists, it must be overwhelmingly strong. But the most sophisticated evidence concerning both gender development *and* erotic arousal suggests that physiological forces are gentle rather than powerful. Despite all the media stories about a "gay gene" or "a gene for lung cancer," the scientific reality is more complicated. As one researcher wrote recently, "the scientists have identified a number of genes that may, under certain circumstances, make an individual more or less susceptible to the action of a variety of environmental agents" (cited in Berwick, 1998, p. 4).

In terms of scholarship, the main effect of the gender and sexual revolutions has been on awareness and consciousness. Many sociologists and psychologists used to take it for granted that women's roles and functions in society reflect universal physiological and temperamental traits. Since in practically every society women were subordinate to men, inequality was interpreted as an inescapable necessity of organized social life. Such analysis suffered from the same intellectual flaw as the idea that discrimination against nonwhites implies their innate inferiority. All such explanations failed to analyze the so-cial institutions and forces producing and supporting the observed differences.

But as Robert M. Jackson points out, modern economic and political institutions have been moving toward gender equality. For example, both the modern workplace and the state have increasingly come to treat people as workers or voters without regard for their gender or their family status. Educational institutions from nursery school to grad-uate school are open to both sexes. Whether or not men who have traditionally run these institutions were in favor of gender inequality, their actions eventually improved women's status in society. Women have not yet attained full quality, but in Jackson's view, the trend in that direction is irreversible.

One reason the trend toward greater gender equality will persist is that young peo-ple born since the 1970s have grown up in a more equal society than their parents' gen-eration. Kathleen Gerson reports on a number of findings from her study of 18- to 30-year-old "children of the gender revolution." First, she finds that a mother's em-ployment status and the number of parents in the home are not the major determinants of children's experience in the home. What seems to matter is, first, family process—how family members interact with one another. Second, life changes such as a major ill-ness, alcoholism, job loss, or family move can have a major impact on a child, but can occur in any family structure. She finds that young adults of both sexes have similar high aspirations for themselves in work and family, valuing both commitment and autonomy. They understand that these are difficult goals, and that there is a lack of social and com-munity resources, such as child care, in support of working families. But Gerson finds a loss of political vision in this generation; they see only private solutions to work and family issues.

For many Americans, the most worrisome aspect of the sexual revolution is the in-crease in teenage sexual activity. But in her study comparing Dutch and U.S. parents, Amy T. Schalet finds strikingly different attitudes toward teenage sexuality. "Would you permit your 16-year-old child to have a boy- or girlfriend sleep over at home?" she asks, among other questions. For U.S. parents, the answer is clearly "no." Teenage sex is so obviously wrong and dangerous that they feel their opposition to it needs no explanation. In contrast, Dutch parents tend to "normalize" teen sexuality; they don't view it as dan-gerous in itself, as long as the adolescents have a close relationship and behave responsi-bly. Schalet argues that Dutch parents are not simply more "permissive" than their U.S. counterparts; rather, these attitudes are part of a larger set of cultural differences.

In her article, Beth Bailey presents a historian's overview of the most recent sexual revolution. She finds that it was composed of at least three separate strands. First, there has been a gradual increase, over the course of the twentieth century, in sexual imagery and openness about sexual matters in the media and in public life generally. Second, in the 1960s and 1970s, premarital sex, which had always been part of dating, came to in-clude intercourse, and even living together before or without marriage. The flamboyant sex radicals of the sixties' counterculture were the loudest but the least numerous part of the sexual revolution.

Both the sexual revolution and gender revolution have reshaped the ways young men and women get together. In their study of the current college social scene, Paula England and Reuben Thomas find that the traditional "date" seems to be on the way out on college campuses. A "date" used to mean that a man called a woman in advance to invite her out to dinner or a movie or some other event. The "tradition" is not very old, however: Dating was "invented" in the 1920s. Earlier, the young man would come to "court" the young woman at her home, while her parents looked on. When dating replaced the home visit, the older generational was shocked.

Today, college students apply the term "dating" only to couples who are already in a romantic relationship. "Hanging out," often in groups, and "hooking up" have replaced the "old fashioned" date. A "hook-up" means the couple go off somewhere to be by themselves. It implies that something sexual happened, but not necessarily intercourse. England and Thomas conclude that the college sexual scene is marred by gender inequality.

Despite all the changes, marriage remains a cherished U.S. institution; the Census Bureau estimates that 90 percent of Americans will marry at some point in their lives. And very few do so expecting that the marriage will end in divorce. So what does make a marriage break down? In her article here, Arlene Skolnick shows that in recent years, researchers have found out a great deal about couple relationships, and some of the findings are contrary to widespread assumptions. For example, happy families are not all alike. And every marriage contains within it two marriages—a happy marriage and an unhappy one.

One of the reasons many people think marriage is a dying institution is the growth of cohabitation in recent years. Is living together going to replace marriage eventually? In their article here, Lynne M. Casper and Suzanne Bianchi look at the demographic evidence on cohabitation—how widespread is it, who does it, and what it means for "traditional marriage." They conclude, as have other researchers, that cohabitation will not replace marriage in the United States. In some European countries, living together has become a standard living arrangement for raising children. But in America, people cohabit for diverse reasons. For many couples, living togther is a step on the way to a planned marriage. Some cohabit because they are uncommitted or unsure about a future together. Young couples with low incomes may live together and put off marriage because they feel they can't afford a wedding or a house to live in.

Frank Furstenberg observes that Americans are far more alarmed about recent trends in premarital sex, cohabitation, and single parenthood than Europeans. Worry about the state of marriage has struck a "raw political nerve" in America. The Bush administration is trying to reverse these trends and promote marriage in a variety of ways. These policies assume that the only family form that can lead to children's healthy development is two married biological parents. Furstenberg analyzes the social science evidence behind these claims and finds it unconvincing. Moreover, he finds that economic inequality has much to do with today's marital patterns. He concludes that the best way to promote both stable marriage and child well-being is to support children and their families with the array of supports and services they need.

What does it mean for married couples to be living in a time when divorce has become a commonplace, no longer shameful, event? Do high divorce rates signify a decline in such family values as commitment and responsibility? Karla Hackstaff explores these questions through in-depth interviews contrasting couples who married in the 1950s and those who married in the 1970s. She finds that the issue of divorce is inseparably intertwined with the issue of gender equality. Historically, marriage has been a male-dominated institution. The '50s wives accepted this, yet they tended to think about divorce far more than their husbands did. The '70s couples try to work out more egalitarian arrangements, and have developed a "marital work ethic" to counter the threat of divorce. Hackstaff concludes that today's "divorce culture" may be a temporary phenomenon, part of the transition toward greater equality in all aspects of marriage.

In recent years, there has been a backlash against divorce, especially for couples with children. The media have featured dramatic stories about the devastating, life-long scars that parental divorce supposedly inflicts on children. Legislators in some states have been considering making divorce harder to get. Joan Kelly and Robert Emery, reviewing the growing social science literature on the effects of divorce, offer a far more complex picture. Divorce does increase the risk for psychological and social problems, but most children are resilient—they do as well as those from intact families. Kelly and Emery discuss the factors that can protect children from the risks.

Because most divorced people remarry, more children will live with stepparents than in the recent past. As Mary Ann Mason points out in her article here, although stepfamilies are a large and growing part of American family life, their roles in the family are not clearly defined. Moreover, stepfamilies are largely ignored by public policymakers, and they exist in a legal limbo. She suggests a number of ways to remedy the situation.

Despite all its difficulties, marriage is not likely to go out of style in the near future. Ultimately we agree with Jessie Bernard (1982), who, after a devastating critique of traditional marriage from the point of view of a sociologist who is also a feminist, said this:

> The future of marriage is as assured as any social form can be. . . . For men and women will continue to want intimacy, they will continue to want to celebrate their mutuality, to experience the mystic unity which once led the church to consider marriage a sacrament. . . . There is hardly any probability such commitments will disappear or that all relationships between them will become merely casual or transient. (p. 301)

References

Bernard, Jessie. 1982. *The Future of Marriage*. New York: World.
Berwick, Robert C. 1998. The doors of perception. *The Los Angeles Times Book Review*. March 15.
Gagnon, J. H., and W. Simon. 1970. *The Sexual Scene*. Chicago: Aldine/Transaction.

3 *Changing Gender Roles*

Destined for Equality

Robert M. Jackson

Over the past two centuries, women's long, conspicuous struggle for better treatment has masked a surprising condition. Men's social dominance was doomed from the beginning. Gender inequality could not adapt successfully to modern economic and political institutions. No one planned this. Indeed, for a long time, the impending extinction of gender inequality was hidden from all.

In the middle of the nineteenth century, few said that equality between women and men was possible or desirable. The new forms of business, government, schools, and the family seemed to fit nicely with the existing division between women's roles and men's roles. Men controlled them all, and they showed no signs of losing belief in their natural superiority. If anything, women's subordination seemed likely to grow worse as they remained attached to the household while business and politics became a separate, distinctively masculine, realm.

Nonetheless, 150 years later, seemingly against all odds, women are well on the way to becoming men's equals. Now, few say that gender equality is impossible or undesirable. Somehow our expectations have been turned upside down.

Women's rising status is an enigmatic paradox. For millennia women were subordinate to men under the most diverse economic, political, and cultural conditions. Although the specific content of gender-based roles and the degree of inequality between the sexes varied considerably across time and place, men everywhere held power and status over women. Moreover, people believed that men's dominance was a natural and unchangeable part of life. Yet over the past two centuries, gender inequality has declined across the world.

The driving force behind this transformation has been the migration of economic and political power outside households and its reorganization around business and political interests detached from gender. Women (and their male supporters) have fought against prejudice and discrimination throughout American history, but social conditions governed the intensity and effectiveness of their efforts. Behind the very visible conflicts between women and male-dominated institutions, fundamental processes concerning economic and political organization have been paving the way for women's success. Throughout these years, while many women struggled to improve their status and many men resisted those efforts, institutional changes haltingly, often imperceptibly, but persistently undermined gender inequality. Responding to the emergent imperatives of large-scale, bureaucratic organizations, men with economic or political power intermittently adopted policies that favored greater equality, often without anticipating the implications of their actions. Gradually responding to the changing demands and possibilities of households without economic activity, men acting as individuals reduced their resistance to wives and daughters extending their roles, although men rarely recognized they were doing something different from their fathers' generation.

Social theorists have long taught us that institutions have unanticipated consequences, particularly when the combined effect of many people's actions diverges from their individual aims. Adam Smith, the renowned theorist of early capitalism, proposed that capitalist markets shared a remarkable characteristic. Many people pursuing only selfish, private interests could further the good of all. Subsequently, Karl Marx, considering the capitalist economy, proposed an equally remarkable but contradictory assessment. Systems of inequality fueled by rational self-interest, he argued, inevitably produce irrational crises that threaten to destroy the social order. Both ideas have suffered many critical blows, but they still capture our imaginations by their extraordinary insight. They teach us how unanticipated effects often ensue when disparate people and organizations each follow their own short-sighted interests.

Through a similar unanticipated and uncontrolled process, the changing actions of men, women, and powerful institutions have gradually but irresistibly reduced gender inequality. Women had always resisted their constraints and inferior status. Over the past 150 years, however, their individual strivings and organized resistance became increasingly effective. Men long continued to oppose the loss of their privileged status. Nonetheless, although men and male-controlled institutions did not adopt egalitarian values, their actions changed because their interests changed. Men's resistance to women's aspirations diminished, and they found new advantages in strategies that also benefited women.

Modern economic and political organization propelled this transformation by slowly dissociating social power from its allegiance to gender inequality. The power over economic resources, legal rights, the allocation of positions, legitimating values, and setting priorities once present in families shifted into businesses and government organizations. In these organizations, profit, efficiency, political legitimacy, organizational stability, competitiveness, and similar considerations mattered more than male privileges vis-à-vis females. Men who had power because of their positions in these organizations gradually adopted policies ruled more by institutional interests than by personal prejudices. Over the long run, institutional needs and opportunities produced policies that worked against gender inequality. Simultaneously, ordinary men (those without economic or political power) resisted women's advancements less. They had fewer resources to use against the women in their lives, and less to gain from keeping women subordinate. Male politicians seeking more power, businessmen pursuing wealth and success, and ordinary men pursuing their self-interest all contributed to the gradual decline of gender inequality.

Structural developments produced ever more inconsistencies with the requirements for continued gender inequality. Both the economy and the state increasingly treated people as potential workers or voters without reference to their family status. To the disinterested, and often rationalized, authority within these institutions, sex inequality was just one more consideration with calculating strategies for profit and political advantage. For these institutions, men and women embodied similar problems of control, exploitation, and legitimation.

Seeking to further their own interests, powerful men launched institutional changes that eventually reduced the discrimination against women. Politicians passed laws giving married women property rights. Employers hired women in ever-increasing numbers. Educators opened their doors to women. These examples and many others show powerful men pursuing their interests in preserving and expanding their economic and political power, yet also improving women's social standing.

The economy and state did not systematically oppose inequality. On the contrary, each institution needed and aggressively supported some forms of inequality, such as income differentials and the legal authority of state officials, that gave them strength. Other forms of inequality received neither automatic support nor automatic opposition. Over time, the responses to other kinds of inequality depended on how well they met institutional interests and how contested they became.

When men adopted organizational policies that eventually improved women's status, they consciously sought to increase profits, end labor shortages, get more votes, and increase social order. They imposed concrete solutions to short-term economic and political problems and to conflicts associated with them. These men usually did not envision, and probably did not care, that the cumulative effect of these policies would be to curtail male dominance.

Only when they were responding to explicitly egalitarian demands from women such as suffrage did men with power consistently examine the implications of their actions for gender inequality. Even then, as when responding to women's explicit demands for legal changes, most legislators were concerned more about their political interests than the fate of gender inequality. When legislatures did pass laws responding to public pressure about women's rights, few male legislators expected the laws could dramatically alter gender inequality.

Powerful men adopted various policies that ultimately would undermine gender inequality because such policies seemed to further their private interests and to address inescapable economic, political, and organizational problems. The structure and integral logic of development within modern political and economic institutions shaped the problems, interests, and apparent solutions. Without regard to what either women or men wanted, industrial capitalism and rational legal government eroded gender inequality.

MAPPING GENDER INEQUALITY'S DECLINE

When a band of men committed to revolutionary change self-consciously designed the American institutional framework, they did not imagine or desire that it would lead toward gender equality. In 1776 a small group of men claimed equality for themselves and similar men by signing the Declaration of Independence. In throwing off British sovereignty, they inaugurated the American ideal of equality. Yet after the success of their revolution, its leaders and like-minded property-owning white men created a nation that subjugated women, enslaved blacks, and withheld suffrage from men without property.

These men understood the egalitarian ideals they espoused through the culture and experiences dictated by their own historical circumstances. Everyone then accepted that women and men were absolutely and inalterably different. Although Abigail Adams admonished her husband that they should "remember the ladies," when these "fathers" of the American nation established its most basic rights and laws, the prospect of fuller citizenship for women was not even credible enough to warrant the effort of rejection. These nation builders could not foresee that their political and economic institutions would eventually erode some forms of inequality much more emphatically than had their revolutionary vision. They could not know that the social structure would eventually extend egalitarian social relations much further than they might ever have thought desirable or possible.

By the 1830s, a half-century after the American Revolution, little had changed. In the era of Jacksonian democracy, women still could not vote or hold political office. They had to cede legal control of their inherited property and their income to their husbands. With few exceptions, they could not make legal contracts or escape a marriage through divorce. They could not enter college. Dependence on men was perpetual and inescapable. Household toil and family welfare monopolized women's time and energies. Civil society recognized women not as individuals but as adjuncts to men. Like the democracy of ancient Athens, the American democracy limited political equality to men.

Today women enjoy independent citizenship; they have the same liberty as men to control their person and property. If they choose or need to do so, women can live without a husband. They can discard an unwanted husband to seek a better alternative. Women vote and occupy political offices. They hold jobs almost as often as men do. Ever more women have managerial and professional positions. Our culture has adopted more affirmative images for women, particularly as models of such values as independence, public advocacy, economic success, and thoughtfulness. Although these changes have not removed all inequities, women now have greater resources, more choices in life, and a higher social status than in the past.

In terms of the varied events and processes that have so dramatically changed women's place in society, the past 150 years of American history can be divided into three half-century periods. The *era of separate spheres* covers roughly 1840–1890, from the era of Jacksonian democracy to the Gilded Age. The *era of egalitarian illusions*, roughly 1890–1940, extends from the Progressive Era to the beginning of World War II. The third period, the *era of assimilation*, covers the time from World War II to the present (see Table 1).

Over the three periods, notable changes altered women's legal, political, and economic status, women's access to higher education and to divorce, women's sexuality, and the cultural images of women and men. Most analysts agree that people's legal, political, and economic status largely define their social status, and we will focus on the changes in these. Of course, like gender, other personal characteristics such as race and age also define an individual's status, because they similarly influence legal, political, and economic rights and resources. Under most circumstances, however, women and men are

TABLE 1   *The Decline of Gender Inequality in American Society*

	1840–1890 The Era of Separate Spheres	1890–1940 The Era of Egalitarian Illusions	1940–1990 The Era of Assimilation	1990–? Residual Inequities
Legal and political status	Formal legal equality instituted	Formal political equality instituted	Formal economic equality instituted	Women rare in high political offices
Economic opportunity	Working-class jobs for single women only	Some jobs for married women and educated women	All kinds of jobs available to all kinds of women	"Glass ceiling" and domestic duties hold women back
Higher education	A few women admitted to public universities and new women's colleges	Increasing college; little graduate or professional education	Full access at all levels	Some prestigious fields remain largely male domains
Divorce	Almost none, but available for dire circumstances	Increasingly available, but difficult	Freely available and accepted	Women typically suffer greater costs
Sexuality and reproductive control	Repressive sexuality; little reproductive control	Positive sexuality but double standard; increasing reproductive control	High sexual freedom; full reproductive control	Sexual harassment and fear of rape still widespread
Cultural image	Virtuous domesticity and subordination	Educated motherhood, capable for employment & public service	Careers, marital equality	Sexes still perceived as inherently different

not systematically differentiated by other kinds of inequality based on personal characteristics, because these other differences, such as race and age, cut across gender lines. Educational institutions have played an ever-larger role in regulating people's access to opportunities over the last century. Changes in access to divorce, women's sexuality, and cultural images of gender will not play a central role in this study. They are important indicators of women's status, but they are derivative rather than formative. They reveal inequality's burden.

The creation of separate spheres for women and men dominated the history of gender inequality during the first period, 1840–1890. The cultural doctrine of separate spheres emerged in the mid-nineteenth century. It declared emphatically that women and men belonged to different worlds. Women were identified with the household and maintenance of family life. Men were associated with income-generating employment and public life. Popular ideas attributed greater religious virtue to women but greater civic virtue to men. Women were hailed as guardians of private morality while men were regarded as the protectors of the public good. These cultural and ideological inventions were responses to a fundamental institutional transition, the movement of economic activity out of households into independent enterprises. The concept of separate spheres legitimated women's exclusion from the public realm, although it gave them some autonomy and authority within their homes.

Women's status was not stagnant in this period. The cultural wedge driven between women's and men's worlds obscured diverse and significant changes that did erode inequality. The state gave married women the right to control their property and income. Jobs became available for some, mainly single, women, giving them some economic independence and an identity apart from the household. Secondary education similar to that offered to men became available to women, and colleges began to admit some women for higher learning. Divorce became a possible, though still difficult, strategy for the first time and led social commentators to bemoan the increasing rate of marital dissolution. In short, women's opportunities moved slowly forward in diverse ways.

From 1890 to 1940 women's opportunities continued to improve, and many claimed that women had won equality. Still, the opportunities were never enough to enable women to transcend their subordinate position. The passage of the Woman Suffrage Amendment stands out as the high point of changes during this period, yet women could make little headway in government while husbands and male politicians belittled and rejected their political aspirations. Women entered the labor market in ever-increasing numbers, educated women could get white-collar positions for the first time, and employers extended hiring to married women. Still, employers rarely considered women for high-status jobs, and explicit discrimination was an accepted practice. Although women's college opportunities became more like men's, professional and advanced degree programs still excluded women. Married women gained widespread access to effective contraception. Although popular opinion expected women to pursue and enjoy sex within marriage, social mores still denied them sex outside it. While divorce became more socially acceptable and practically available, laws still restricted divorce by demanding that one spouse prove that the other was morally repugnant. Movies portrayed glamorous women as smart, sexually provocative, professionally talented, and ambitious, but even they, if they were good women, were driven by an overwhelming desire to marry, bear children, and dedicate themselves to their homes.

Writing at the end of this period, the sociologist Mirra Komarovsky captured its implications splendidly. After studying affluent college students during World War II, Komarovsky concluded that young women were beset by "serious contradictions between two roles." The first was the feminine role, with its expectations of deference to men and a future focused on familial activities. The second was the "modern" role that "partly obliterates the differentiation in sex," presumably because the emphasis on education made the universal qualities of ability and accomplishment seem the only reasonable limitations on future activities. Women who absorbed the egalitarian implications of modern education felt confused, burdened, and irritated by the contrary expectations that they display a subordinate femininity. The intrinsic contradictions between these two role expectations could only end, Komarovsky declared, when women's real adult role was redefined to make it "consistent with the socioeconomic and ideological modern society."[1]

Since 1940, many of these contradictions have been resolved. At an accelerating pace, women have continually gained greater access to the activities, positions, and statuses formerly reserved to men.

Despite the tremendous gains women have experienced, they have not achieved complete equality, nor is it imminent. The improvement of women's status has been uneven, seesawing between setbacks and advances. Women still bear the major responsibility for raising children. They suffer from lingering harassment, intimidation, and disguised discrimination. Women in the United States still get poorer jobs and lower income. They have less access to economic or political power. The higher echelons of previously male social hierarchies have assimilated women slowest and least completely. For example, in blue-collar hierarchies they find it hard to get skilled jobs or join craft unions; in white-collar hierarchies they rarely reach top management; and in politics the barriers to women's entry seem to rise with the power of the office they seek. Yet when we compare the status of American women today with their status in the past, the movement toward greater equality is striking.

While women have not gained full equality, the formal structural barriers holding them back have largely collapsed and those left are crumbling. New government policies have discouraged sex discrimination by most organizations and in most areas of life outside the family. The political and economic systems have accepted ever more women and have promoted them to positions with more influence and higher status. Education at all levels has become equally available to women. Women have gained great control over their reproductive processes, and their sexual freedom has come to resemble that of men. It has become easy and socially acceptable to end unsatisfactory marriages with divorce. Popular culture has come close to portraying women as men's legitimate equal. Television, our most dynamic communication media, regularly portrays discrimination as wrong and male abuse or male dominance as nasty. The prevailing theme of this recent period has been women's assimilation into all the activities and positions once denied them.

This book [this reading was taken from] focuses on the dominant patterns and the groups that had the most decisive and most public roles in the processes that changed women's status: middle-class whites and, secondarily, the white working class. The histories of gender inequality among racial and ethnic minorities are too diverse to address adequately here.[2] Similarly, this analysis neglects other distinctive groups, especially lesbians and heterosexual women who avoided marriage, whose changing circumstances also deserve extended study.

While these minorities all have distinctive histories, the major trends considered here have influenced all groups. Every group had to respond to the same changing political and economic structures that defined the opportunities and constraints for all people in the society. Also, whatever their particular history, the members of each group understood their gender relations against the backdrop of the white, middle-class family's cultural preeminence. Even when people in higher or lower-class positions or people in ethnic communities expressed contempt for these values, they were familiar with the middle-class ideals and thought of them as leading ideas in the society. The focus on the white middle classes is simply an analytical and practical strategy. The history of dominant groups has no greater inherent or moral worth. Still, except in cases of open, successful rebellion, the ideas and actions of dominant groups usually affect history much more than the ideas and actions of subordinate groups. This fact is an inevitable effect of inequality.

THE MEANING OF INEQUALITY AND ITS DECLINE

We will think differently about women's status under two theoretical agendas. Either we can try to evaluate how short from equality women now fall, or we can try to understand how far they have come from past deprivations.

Looking at women's place in society today from these two vantage points yields remarkably different perspectives. They accentuate different aspects of women's status by altering the background against which we compare it. Temporal and analytical differences separate these two vantage points, not distinctive moral positions, although people sometimes confuse these differences with competing moral positions.

If we want to assess and criticize women's disadvantages today, we usually compare their existing status with an imagined future when complete equality reigns. Using this ideal standard of complete equality, we would find varied shortcomings in women's status today. These shortcomings include women's absence from positions of political or economic power, men's preponderance in the better-paid and higher-status occupations, women's lower average income, women's greater family responsibilities, the higher status commonly attached to male activities, and the dearth of institutions or policies supporting dual-earner couples.

Alternatively, if we want to evaluate how women's social status has improved, we must turn in the other direction and face the past. We look back to a time when women were legal and political outcasts, working only in a few low-status jobs, and always deferring to male authority. From this perspective, women's status today seems much brighter. Compared with the nineteenth century, women now have a nearly equal legal and political status, far more women hold jobs, women can succeed at almost any occupation, women usually get paid as much as men in the same position (in the same firm), women have as much educational opportunity as men, and both sexes normally expect women to pursue jobs and careers.

As we seek to understand the decline of gender inequality, we will necessarily stress the improvements in women's status. We will always want to remember, however, that gender inequality today stands somewhere between extreme inequality and complete equality. To analyze the modern history of gender inequality fully, we must be able to look at this middle ground from both sides. It is seriously deficient when measured against full equality. It is a remarkable improvement when measured against past inequality.

Editors' Note: *Notes for this reading can be found in the original source.*

■ R E A D I N G   9

Children of the Gender Revolution: Some Theoretical Questions and Findings from the Field

Kathleen Gerson

As a new century commences, it is clear that fundamental changes in family, work, and gender arrangements have transformed the experience of growing up in American society. Only several decades ago, an American child was likely to grow to adulthood in a two-parent home with a mother who worked outside the home either intermittently or not at all. No such common situation unites children today. With less than fourteen percent of American households containing a married couple with a breadwinning husband and homemaking wife, children living in a "traditional family" now form a distinct minority (Ahlburg and De Vita, 1992; Gerson, 1993). Regardless of race, ethnicity, or class, most younger Americans have lived, or will live, in a family situation that departs significantly from a pattern once thought to be enduring. Many have grown up in a two-parent home in which both parents have pursued strong and sustained ties to work outside the home. Others have lived through marital disruptions and perhaps the remarriage of one or both parents. Still others have been raised by a single mother who never married the father of her children. Most of these children have experienced shifting circumstances, in which some substantial change occurred in their family situation before they left their parents' home.

This revolution in the experience of childhood has provided an unprecedented opportunity to unravel the processes of human development and better understand the consequences of growing up in diverse family situations. We are living through a natural social experiment that makes it possible to assess the effects of family arrangements as well as other social and cultural institutions on the lives of children. As the recipients of widespread gender and family change, this generation is ideally positioned to shed light on a number of important theoretical questions.

First, what is the relationship between family composition and children's welfare? Is family structure, as measured by the household's composition and gender division of labor, the most consequential aspect of a child's developmental environment, as has been generally assumed, or is family form mediated by other factors, such as interactional processes within the home and contextual factors outside it? Second, what are the links between parental choices and children's reactions? How do children make sense of their family situations and their parents' circumstances, and what strategies do they develop to cope with their situations? Are children inclined to adopt their parents' choices and beliefs, and when and under what circumstances are they more likely to reject or modify them?

Third, what part do institutions outside the family, and especially community, educational, and labor market structures, play in shaping a child's outlook and developmental trajectory? And, finally, as new generations of women and men respond to widespread cultural changes outside the home and shifting dynamics within it, what personal, social, and political strategies are they developing to cope with the new contingencies wrought by the family and gender revolutions? What do the experiences of this pivotal generation portend for the future of gender—as a cultural belief and a lived experience?

The "children of the gender revolution" have grown to adulthood in a wide range of circumstances, and their experiences offer a window through which to glimpse both general processes of human development and historically embedded social shifts. By taking a careful look at the developmental paths and personal conflicts of this generation, we can untangle the role that family structure plays in children's lives and discover the other processes and factors that either mitigate or explain its effects. And since members of this generation are now negotiating the transition to adulthood and thus poised to craft their own work and family strategies, they offer important clues to the future course of the transformation in family, work, and gender patterns begun by their parents.

CHANGES IN CHILDREN'S LIVES: CONTENDING WITH THEORETICAL APPROACHES AND THE "FAMILY VALUES" DEBATE

The diversification of family forms has produced disputes among American social scientists (as well as among politicians and ordinary citizens) about the effects of family and gender transformations on the welfare of children. These debates have been framed in "either/or" terms, in which those who decry the decline of the homemaker–breadwinner family have clashed with those who defend and, to some extent, celebrate the rise of alternative family forms.

Analysts concerned that family and gender transformations threaten children's welfare and undermine the larger social fabric have developed a perspective that emphasizes "family decline." (See, for example, Blankenhorn, 1994; Popenoe, 1989 and 1996; Whitehead, 1997.) This approach tends to view the "traditional family," characterized by permanent heterosexual commitment and a clear sexual division of labor between stay-at-home mothers and breadwinning fathers, as the ideal family form. The rise in divorce, out-of-wedlock parenthood, and employment among mothers thus represent a serious family breakdown that is putting new generations of younger Americans at risk. From this perspective, "nontraditional families," such as dual-earner and single-parent households, are part of a wider moral breakdown, in which the spread of an individualistic ethos has encouraged adults to pursue their own self-interest at the expense of children.

While compelling, the "family decline" contains both logical and empirical deficiencies. First, it treats family change as if it were a cause rather than an effect. Yet new family forms are inescapable reactions to basic economic and social shifts that have propelled women into the workplace and expanded the options for personal development in adulthood. By idealizing the mid-twentieth century homemaker–breadwinner household, this perspective also tends to downplay the positive aspects of change and especially the expansion of options for women. We now know, however, that family life in the past rarely conformed to our nostalgic images and that many homemaker–breadwinner families were rife with unhappiness and abuse (Coontz, 1992).

In response to the critique of family change, less pessimistic analysts have responded that family life is not declining but rather adapting, as it has always done in response to new social and economic exigencies. These analysts point out that a return to family forms marked by significant gender inequality is neither possible nor desirable and would not solve the predicaments parents and children now face. (See, for example, Skolnick, 1991; Stacey, 1990 and 1996; Coontz, 1997.) The roots of the family and gender revolution extend deep into the foundations of the economy, the society, and the culture. Single parents and employed mothers have thus become scapegoats for social ills with deeper economic and political roots.

Despite the polarized nature of the American "family values" debate, both perspectives have tended to focus on family structure as the crucial arena of contention. Yet research suggests that family structure, taken alone, cannot explain or predict outcomes for children. While children living with both biological parents appear on average to fare better than children in one-parent homes, most of the difference can be traced to the lower economic and social resources available to single parents as well as to factors such as high family conflict that promote parental break-up in the first place (Cherlin et al., 1991; McLanahan and Gary Sandefur, 1994).

In the case of employed mothers, circumstantial factors also appear to trump family structure. Despite the persisting concern that children are harmed when their mothers work outside the home, decades of research have yielded virtually no support for this claim. Instead, the critical ingredients in providing for children's welfare are such factors as a mother's satisfaction with her situation, the quality of care a child receives, and the involvement of fathers and other supportive caretakers (Barnett and Rivers, 1996; Hoffman, 1987). Even comparisons between oft-labeled "traditional" and "nontraditional" families show that diversity within family types is generally as large as differences between them (Acock and Demo, 1994).

The focus on family structure has thus obscured a number of more basic questions about the short- and long-run consequences of these complicated and deeply rooted social changes. While it is clear that a return to a world marked by a clear sexual division of labor, an unquestioned acceptance of gender inequality, and the predominance of patriarchal families, is neither desirable nor possible, it is less clear what new social forms will or should emerge. To understand this process, we need to delve beneath the polarized controversy over family values to clarify the consequences of diversifying family forms, increasing female autonomy, and shifting adult commitments to those who are the most direct recipients of change. How has the generation born during this period of rapid and tumultuous change experienced, interpreted, and responded to the gender revolution forged by their parents?

UNDERSTANDING THE CHILDREN OF THE GENDER REVOLUTION

To answer these questions, I have interviewed a group that can be considered the "children of the gender revolution." These late adolescents and young adults, between the ages of 18 and 30, are members of the generation that is young enough to have experienced the dynamics of family change at close hand, yet old enough to have a perspective on their childhood circumstances and to be formulating their own plans for the future. Since family change may have been experienced differently in different economic and social contexts, the group has been drawn from a range of racial and ethnic backgrounds and a variety of poor, working-class, and middle-class communities. Of the 120 people interviewed, approximately 56% are non-Hispanic white, 20% are African-American, 18% are Hispanic, and 6% are Asian. They were randomly selected from a range of urban and suburban neighborhoods in the New York metropolitan area. (Most respondents were selected by a random sampling procedure as part of a larger study of the children of immigrants and native-born Americans.) To ensure that the parents of my respondents had been born and grown up amid the changing family circumstances of American society, my sample was drawn entirely from the native-born group. (See Mollenkopf et al. for a description of the study and sampling techniques.)

To illuminate how these "children of the gender revolution" have made sense of their childhoods and are formulating strategies for adulthood, in-depth, life-history interviews elicited information on their experiences growing up, their strategies for coping with past and present difficulties, and their outlooks on the future. Most lived in some form of "nontraditional" family arrangement before reaching eighteen. About a third lived in a single-parent home at some point in their childhood, and an additional 40% grew up in homes in which both parents held full-time jobs for a sustained period of time. Even the remaining group, who described their families as generally "traditional," were likely to grow up in homes that underwent some form of notable change as mothers went to work or marriages faced crises. As a whole, this diverse group experienced the full range of changes now emerging in U.S. family and gender arrangements.

The experiences of these strategically placed young women and men call into question a number of long-held assumptions about the primacy of family structure in human development. Their life paths and outlooks point, instead, to the importance of processes of family change, the shape of opportunities outside the family, and children's active strategies to cope with their circumstances amid inescapable but uncertain social shifts.

FAMILY STRUCTURE OR FAMILY TRAJECTORIES?

Despite the theoretical focus on "family structure," which generally refers to the composition and division of labor in the household, these young women and men offer a different view of how they formed their sense of self and their outlook on the future. From their perspective, what matters instead are more subtle family processes and pathways. Indeed, simple family typologies, based on differences among homemaker–breadwinner, dual-earner, and single-parent homes, mask important variations within such family forms. Indeed, regardless of the apparent "structure" of the household, most children experience some form of change in their family life over time. While a minority can point to stable, supportive family environments marked by few noticeable changes, the more common experience involves transitions, sometimes abrupt and always consequential, from one "family environment" to another. Surprisingly, this experience of change applies to many whose parents remained married and not just to those whose households underwent a break-up. More important than household structure at one point in time are the "trajectories" that families follow as they develop throughout the life of a child.

From the time a child is born to the time she or he leaves home, the family environment can develop in different ways. From the point of view of the child, these family experiences assume the form of family trajectories, or pathways, that can either remain stable or move in different directions over time. A "stable" trajectory may remain relatively harmonious, supportive, and secure, or it may remain chronically conflictual and unsupportive. A "changing" trajectory may become more stable and supportive as family conditions improve over the span of childhood and adolescence, or it may become more conflictual and insecure as family conditions deteriorate.

These trajectories are important, but they are not closely linked to prevailing notions of "traditional" and "nontraditional" family structures. While classical theories might predict that traditional households would be more stable and harmonious than nontraditional ones, the experiences of these young women and men reveal no such clear relationship. For example, a number of apparently stable "traditional" households are actually marked by chronic conflict or some kind of less readily noticeable change. In one case, a family's outward stability masked chronic parental addictions and abuse that never improved, despite their status as a two-parent home. In another case, a drug-addicted, distant father moved out of the family home in response to his wife's demand that he break his addiction or leave. Several years later, after a successful recovery, he returned to become a supportive, involved parent. This outwardly stable but internally riven "traditional" family thus became more harmonious and secure over time.

A comparable diversity of processes and practices can be found in nontraditional households. While all children undergo some kind of change if their parents separate or divorce, the transition can bring improvement or deterioration. One young woman, for example, felt relieved when her father divorced her neglectful, emotionally abusive mother, and she found stability and support when he remarried a nurturing, economically successful woman.

Static categories of "family type" thus offer limited clues about the dynamics between parents and children or the unfolding nature of family life. Children rarely perceive their families as fixed arrangements, but rather as a range of situations in flux, which either offer or deny them support over time. These processes are important in providing for a child's welfare, but they are not simple reflections of family structure. A breadwinner–homemaker arrangement does not guarantee a stable or supportive home, and those with dual-earning, single, or stepparents are clearly able to provide support and care.

EMPLOYED MOTHERS AND OTHER PARENTS

If family process is more important than family structure, then a mother's well-being is also more important than whether or not she works outside the home. While most of these young women and men grew up in homes in which their mothers were strongly involved in earning a living, the fact of working or not working mattered less than whether or not mothers (and fathers) appeared satisfied with their lives as workers and parents.

Young women and men reared by work-committed mothers generally agreed that the ensuing benefits outweighed any hypothetical losses. In many cases, a mother's job kept the family from falling into poverty, and in some, it helped propel the household up the class ladder. A mother's employment also gave both parents increased autonomy and appeared to enhance parental equality. While some worried that their mothers and fathers had to toil at difficult, demanding, and low-paying jobs, no one felt neglected. To the contrary, they were appreciative of their mothers' efforts to provide for their own and their family's welfare. Working outside the home thus provided a way for mothers as well as fathers to become "good" parents.

Those whose mothers did not pursue independent avenues outside the domestic sphere expressed more ambivalence. While some were pleased to have their mothers' attention focused exclusively on home and family, others were concerned that the choice had been an unnecessary sacrifice. In these cases, when a homemaking mother seemed frustrated or unhappy, the child's reaction was more likely to center on guilt and minor resentment than on gratitude.

More important than the choice to work or stay home, however, is the child's perception about why the choice was made. When a parent, whether mother or father, appeared to work for the family's welfare as well as his or her own needs, the child accepted these choices as unproblematic. If, in contrast, a mother's choice appeared to contradict her family's needs or her own desires, the child responded with concern and doubt. Children felt supported when parents made choices that provided for everyone's needs and did not pit the wishes of mothers against the needs of children. They fared better, however, when contextual supports helped working parents resolve the conflicts between family and work. Most important were reliable, neighborhood-based child care resources, involvement from committed fathers, and satisfying and flexible jobs for both parents.

BEYOND FAMILY STRUCTURE: FAMILY PROCESSES AND OPPORTUNITY CONTEXTS

How did children from these diverse family situations fare as they negotiated the challenges and dangers of childhood and adolescence? Their diverse fates ranged from successful young adults who were able to launch promising college and work careers to those who became entangled in less felicitous patterns, such as school failure, involvement in crime, and early parenthood. Why were some able to negotiate the risks of adolescence while others were propelled down perilous paths? While it may be tempting to attribute these disparate outcomes to family structure, that does not appear to be the explanation. Not only were people from all types of families, including traditional ones, socially and emotionally sidetracked, but many from "nontraditional" households were able to avoid or overcome the dangers they faced.

Several important, interacting factors influence individual trajectories. First, processes within the family either provided or denied emotional and social support to the child. Second, social and economic resources outside the family, including neighborhood-based resources such as peer groups and schools and class-based resources such as economic support, provided or denied financial and "social capital" to either avoid or escape dangerous situations. Structural and cultural contexts outside the family thus influenced children's outlooks and trajectories, regardless of the kinds of families in which they lived.

School experiences, for example, ranged from academic involvement and success to minor alienation to school failure. Those who fared poorly were likely to have parents who lacked either the will, the skills, or the money to make a special effort to hold the child to reasonable standards, to fight for a child in the face of an indifferent bureaucracy, or to make financial sacrifices (such as choosing a parochial or private school). Those who succeeded, on the other hand, were fortunate in a variety of ways. Most possessed either class-related resources that provided access to good schools and the social pressures and expectations of school success. In the absence of class resources, the support of only one person who believed in and would fight for the child could made a crucial difference.

Yet single mothers, many of whom were poor, and dual-income parents with time-consuming jobs were just as likely as traditional families to provide these pressures and supports. For example, one young man attributed his college and graduate degrees to his struggling but feisty single mother, who fought against a school bureaucracy determined to consign him to the category of "learning disabled."

Experiences outside of school also ranged from engagement in constructive activities, such as organized sports and social service, to involvement in dangerous pursuits, such as crime, drugs, and sexual risk-taking. While opportunities to experiment in risky ways were more prevalent in poor and minority communities, there were inducements in all types of neighborhoods. Those who fell prey to more dangerous lifestyles were not more likely to live in nontraditional homes, but they were more likely to become integrated into peer groups that countered a family's influence. Indeed, avoiding risky behavior often required resisting local temptations, such as a street culture centered around illicit activities. Neighborhoods matter and can thwart the efforts of parents to protect their children from the influences of a burgeoning youth culture outside the home.

Class resources, however, offer a consequential buffer. Middle-class children were more likely to be shielded by their parents and their communities while they passed through a stage of adolescent experimentation, whether it involved drugs, sex, or petty crimes. Poor and minority children were more likely to "get caught," to become ensnared in a punitive system, and to pay a higher long-term price for youthful indiscretions. In all of these ways, class resources and family processes (especially in the form of parental support) provide the context for family life and tend to supercede family structure as crucial shapers of children's life chances and developmental trajectories.

CHILDREN'S INTERPRETIVE FRAMEWORKS AND COPING STRATEGIES

Family processes and class resources form the context for children's experiences, but these contexts are always sifted through a child's interpretive framework and personal coping strategies. These strategies and frameworks represent active efforts on the part of children to give meaning to the actions of others and to craft their own choices amid the uncertainties of changing circumstances.

As this strategic generation has confronted the ideas, opportunities, and models of work and family institutions in flux, most people have had to cope with a world in which high hopes and aspirations are colliding with subtle fears and constricted realities. Regardless of race or class position, most women and men strongly support those aspects of change that have opened up opportunities for women and created new possibilities for redefining gender. Yet these hopes co-exist with concerns about the difficulty of combining work and family, the dangers of economic insecurity, and the lack of institutionalized supports for nontraditional choices. Whether the issue is work, family, or how to combine the two, the men and women emerging from the gender revolution perceive both new opportunities and a new set of dilemmas with few clear resolutions. While most hold egalitarian and pluralist ideals, at least in the abstract, they are less sanguine about whether or how these ideals can be achieved. (In a study of children living in gender-equal families, Risman, 1998, also finds a gap between children's egalitarian ideals and their identities.)

Work

Among women and men of all classes, almost everyone aspires to better jobs than their parents secured or they have yet been able to find. However, if the desire for a good, well-paying, white-collar job or career is nearly universal, the expectation of achieving it is not. Rather, these young women and men are divided in their optimism about the future. These divisions reveal blurring gender boundaries even as class boundaries persist. Women and men alike thus hold high aspirations for work careers, although those with constricted opportunities are less confident about reaching them. Optimism seems well-founded for some (e.g., college-educated whites) and ill-founded for others (e.g., young, single mothers and high school drop-outs). Most are hoping to find "satisfying jobs," willing to settle for "economic security," and not confident that they will be able to achieve either.

The skepticism about long-term economic prospects is reflected in men's and women's expectations of each other. Both groups view their economic prospects in "individualist" terms. Since men generally do not expect to earn enough to support wives and families alone, and women do not expect to be able to rely on male breadwinners, both groups believe their economic fate depends on their own job market achievements rather than on forging a lasting commitment with one partner. Women are thus as likely as men to express high job aspirations, and men are as likely as women to long for respite from the demands of earning a living. Despite these shared aspirations, women remain aware that their opportunities are more constricted than men's. A common refrain is thus that, "Women have it better today than in the past, but men still have it better and probably always will."

Marriage

If economic security and job options remain a concern, most nevertheless believe it is easier to shape their own labor market fate than to control the fate of their personal relationships. The vast majority of women *and* men view egalitarian marriage as the ideal, not only because dual-earner marriages appear to provide the best economic alternative but also because they offer the best hope for balancing personal autonomy with mutual commitment. These are high standards for defining a "good marriage," and many are skeptical that they will be able to achieve it.

Gender provides a lens through which similar expectations are experienced differently. While women and men are equally skeptical of creating lasting commitments, women are more aware of the consequences for work and family. They are more likely to see the possibility of raising children alone and more likely to link this possibility to the need for economic autonomy. Yet women agree with men that it is better to go it alone than to become enmeshed in an unhappy or narrowly confining commitment. Even those few—mostly men—who view traditional marriage as the ideal are more wishful than certain. In the face of these ideals, however, women remain skeptical that men can be counted on to shoulder their fair share, and men doubt they will have the job flexibility to do so.

Parenthood

Changing views of marriage provide the context for shifting orientations toward parenthood. For most women and men, the best parenting appears to be equal parenting. The rise of employed mothers and dual-earning couples thus appears to be good for children—bringing in more family income, fostering happier marriages, and providing better examples of women's autonomy and gender justice. Most (though not all) have concluded that "ideal mothers" and "ideal fathers" are fundamentally indistinguishable, and, across races and classes, the majority are skeptical of family arrangements based on rigid or insurmountable gender differences.

Regardless of their own family experience, moreover, everyone agrees that a committed partnership and happy marriage provide the best context for raising a child. The problem, however, is that a happy marriage is difficult to achieve. Most also agree, therefore, in the context of a deteriorating or chronically conflictual marriage, a child cannot thrive. The key for this generation is that both parents remain involved and supportive even if they find they cannot sustain a commitment to each other.

Views of Gender

Larger cultural shifts, and especially the rising acceptance of and need for women's economic independence, have permeated everywhere, leaving children from all classes and family situations exposed to changing definitions of gender and new work and family options. Most support these changes, arguing that while women have gained considerable opportunities, they have not done so at men's expense.

Women as well as men place a high value on autonomy, and men are equally likely to espouse egalitarian ideals at home and at work. These ideals clash, however, with institutional options that put many of them out of reach. If egalitarian ideologies, support for diversity, and a desire for personal choice predominate, behavioral strategies may stray far from these ideals.

Despite the desire to span the perceived gap between goals and opportunities, few can envision effective social, institutional, or political resolutions to these intractable dilemmas. When asked whether employers or the government can or should help families, most reply that individuals in American society are on their own. The protracted political battle over "family values" has left this generation with little faith that political action can make a difference or that "personal" problems can have social causes and institutional solutions.

Self and Society amid the Gender Revolution

A diverse and shifting set of experiences are sending these children of the gender revolution in a variety of new and unclear directions. Most hold high aspirations for the future but are also skeptical about the possibilities for achieving their fondest dreams. And because they do not generally see the link between their own seemingly intractable dilemmas and the larger social–structural forces that are shaping the contours of change, they lack a vision of the possibilities for social solutions to what are experienced as very personal problems.

Prepared to face a gap between ideals and options, they are determined to exercise some choice over which trade-offs to make—between work and family, parenthood and career, marriage and going it alone. If their work and family ideals prove to be false promises, they reserve the right to change their circumstances. Despite the uncertainty ahead, however, most agree that the future will not and should not bring a return to the idealized past of separate spheres for men and women. From their perspective, the era when most marriages were permanent, women stayed home with children, and men wielded unquestioned power is irretrievable and undesirable.

BEYOND THE "FAMILY VALUES" DEBATE

The emergence of diverse family arrangements in the United States offers a unique opportunity to develop a better theoretical grasp of the link between the institutions of child rearing, the experiences of growing up, and the long-term trajectories of children. While debate has focused on the importance of family structure, the developmental trajectories of those who have grown up amid these changes reveals a more complicated picture. The lessons gleaned from these lives suggest expansions to and reformulations of prevailing theoretical frameworks.

First, family processes and trajectories matter more than family structure. Not only can conflict and neglect be found in all types of families, including those that may appear outwardly stable and secure, but processes of nurturance and support also emerge in a range of family contexts. More important than a family's structure at one point in time are processes of family change over time. Does a child's family context involve increasing support and declining conflict or, in contrast, declining support and continuing or rising conflict? From the child's perspective, what matters in the long run are emotional and economic sustenance, mutually respectful dynamics within the home, and caring bonds with their parents and other caretakers. Traditional families cannot guarantee these conditions, and nontraditional ones are often able to provide them.

Similarly, the employment status of mothers matters less than the overall context in which mothers—and fathers—create their lives. Across classes and gender groups, children are less concerned about whether their mothers work outside the home than about why their mothers work (or do not work), how their mothers feel about working (or not working), and what kind of caretaking arrangements their mothers and fathers can rely on. On balance, children see their mothers' employment as a benefit on many levels. Mothers' jobs offer families greater economic security and increased resources, enhance mothers' satisfaction and autonomy, and provide an example worthy of emulation. Children do worry, however, about their mothers' and fathers' abilities to obtain jobs with good economic prospects, supportive working conditions, and enough flexibility for combining work with family life.

Given the varied and ambiguous influence of family structure, it is time to focus theoretical attention on the institutional arrangements and social processes that matter for children, regardless of the family form in which they happen to live. Community and economic resources are crucial, providing the context for family life and either opening opportunities or posing risks and dangers. Resources such as educational and work opportunities, child care services, and personal networks of adults and peers help shape parents' strategies for rearing their children and children's abilities to cope with difficult circumstances.

Finally, children are not passive recipients of parental and social influences. They actively interpret and respond to their social worlds, often in unexpected ways. As social actors facing unforeseen contingencies, they must make new sense out of received messages and develop a variety of innovative coping strategies. They are crafting these strategies in a changing cultural context, where new views of gender and shifting work and family opportunities are as likely to influence their outlooks as are immediate family experiences.

The trajectories and experiences of these "children of the gender revolution" suggest that a search for one "best" family form provides neither a fruitful theoretical avenue nor a useful practical agenda. Instead, the challenge is to understand how children experience and respond to family conditions that are usually in flux and always embedded in wider institutions. Regardless of a child's family circumstance, contextual supports are essential for enabling parents and children to cope with change in a satisfying way.

For those who have grown to adulthood during this era of fluid personal paths and family arrangements, the fundamental aspects of change appear irreversible and, on balance, desirable. The dismantling of the homemaker–breadwinner ideal has widened options that few are prepared to surrender. These changes in family life and women's options have not, however, been met with comparable changes in the workplace and community life. And although most have adopted nontraditional, egalitarian ideals, few can envision support from employers or the government for achieving their goals. Lacking faith in work or political institutions, they are resolved to seek individual solutions to unprecedented social dilemmas and to develop new ways of negotiating adulthood. The experiences and responses of this new generation are especially important in this era of irrevocable but incomplete transformation. They may be the inheritors of change, but their strategies for responding to their parents' choices and their own dilemmas will shape their future course.

References

Acock, Alan C., and David H. Demo. 1994. *Family Diversity and Well-Being.* Thousand Oaks, CA: Sage Publications.

Ahlburg, Dennis A., and Carol J. De Vita. 1992. "New Realities of the American Family." *Population Bulletin* 47 (2) (August): 1–44.

Barnett, Rosalind, and Caryl Rivers. 1996. *She Works/He Works: How Two-Income Families Are Happier, Healthier, and Better Off.* San Francisco, CA: HarperSanFrancisco.

Blankenhorn, David. 1994. *Fatherless America: Confronting Our Most Urgent Social Problem.* New York: Basic Books.

Cherlin, Andrew, et al. 1991. "Longitudinal Studies of Effects of Divorce on Children in Great Britain and the United States." *Science* 252 (June): 1386–1389.

Coontz, Stephanie. 1992. *The Way We Never Were: American Families and the Nostalgia Trap.* New York: Basic Books.

———. 1997. *The Way We Really Are: Coming to Terms with America's Changing Families.* New York: Basic Books.

Crosby, Faye J., ed. 1987. *Spouse, Parent, Worker: On Gender and Multiple Roles.* New Haven: Yale University Press.

Gerson, Kathleen. 1993. *No Man's Land: Men's Changing Commitments to Family and Work.* New York: Basic Books.

Hoffman, Lois. 1987. "The Effects on Children of Maternal and Paternal Employment." Pp. 362–395 in *Families and Work*, edited by Naomi Gerstel and Harriet Engel Gross. Philadelphia: Temple University Press.

McLanahan, Sara, and Gary Sandefur. 1994. *Growing Up with a Single Parent: What Hurts, What Helps.* Cambridge, MA: Harvard University Press.

Mollenkopf, John, Philip Kasinitz, and Mary Waters. 1997. "The School to Work Transition of Second Generation Immigrants in Metropolitan New York: Some Preliminary Findings." Paper presented at Levy Institute Conference on the Second Generation (October). New York: Bard College.

Popenoe, David. 1989. *Disturbing the Nest: Family Change and Decline in Modern Societies.* New York: Aldine de Gruyter.

———. 1996. *Life without Father: Compelling New Evidence that Fatherhood and Marriage Are Indispensable for the Good of Children and Society.* New York: Free Press.

Risman, Barbara J. 1998. *Gender Vertigo: American Families in Transition.* New Haven and London: Yale University Press.

Skolnick, Arlene. 1991. *Embattled Paradise: The American Family in an Age of Uncertainty.* New York: Basic Books.

Stacey, Judith. 1990. *Brave New Families: Stories of Domestic Upheaval in Late 20th Century America.* New York: Basic Books.

———. 1996. *In the Name of the Family: Rethinking Family Values in a Postmodern Age.* Boston: Beacon Press.

Whitehead, Barbara D. 1997. *The Divorce Culture.* New York: Alfred A. Knopf.

4 Sexuality and Society

Raging Hormones, Regulated Love: Adolescent Sexuality in the United States and the Netherlands

Amy T. Schalet

Researchers have noted large differences among advanced industrial societies in public attitudes towards adolescent sexuality (Ester et al., 1993; Halman, 1991; Jones et al., 1986; Rademakers, 1997). Public attitudes towards adolescent sexuality in the US have been characterized as "restrictive" and "non-accepting," and those in the Netherlands as occupying a midway position between the permissiveness of Scandinavian countries and the restrictiveness of southern Europe and the US (Rademakers, 1997). The clearest indicator of a sharp difference between the US and Netherlands comes from the European Value Systems Study Group. In 1981 this survey group found that 65 percent of the American public believed sex between people under the age of 18 was never justified while only 25 percent of the Dutch public agreed with this statement (Halman, 1991). The sexual practices, particularly the contraceptive behavior, of Dutch and American adolescents display an equally striking contrast. Although they become sexually active at roughly the same age, American teenage girls are nine times more likely to become pregnant than their Dutch counterparts. While teenage pregnancy is a rare occurrence in the Netherlands, 20 percent of American girls who are sexually active become pregnant each year (Brugman et al., 1995; Delft and Ketting, 1992; *Facts in Brief*, 1998).

THE STUDY

Between September 1991 and February 1992, I interviewed 14 American and 17 Dutch parents of teenagers. In each country I contacted half of the interviewees via a high-school parent organization and the other half through referrals from personal networks. The parents I interviewed all lived near or in a middle-sized university city in a metropolitan area.

In both countries the parents differed from the national average since almost all were married, more than half were Catholic (although many Dutch interviewees describe themselves as non-religious), all were white, and most were well educated. Nine Dutch and ten American parents, had at least an MA degree. Two parents in each country had degrees from junior colleges. Six Dutch and two American parents had high-school degrees or less. Most of my interviews were with mothers but in each country some fathers participated. Their children were all around 16 years old and were as often boys as they were girls.

The interviews I conducted were semi-structured and centered around topics that concern parents of adolescents: school, work, friends, alcohol, sexuality, family and transitions into adulthood. My initial goal was to explore general differences and similarities in the way these Dutch and American parents constructed adolescence as a phase of life. Only in the course of these interviews did sexuality emerge as the most significant and clear point of divergence between the two sets of parents. Taking this divergence as a point of departure, I systematically compared the interview transcripts of the Dutch and American parents by topic. By counting the quantifiable answers and tracing the words, expressions and forms of reasoning parents used, I was able to reconstruct their different cultural logics. The presentation that follows combines description with interpretation to illuminate these logics. First, I discuss how the American and Dutch parents conceptualize adolescent sexuality. Then I turn to their strategies for managing it within the parental home.

THE DRAMATIZATION
OF ADOLESCENT SEXUALITY

Even before the interview turns to the subject of sexuality, 11 out of 14 American parents mention sex as something that characterizes and complicates the period of adolescence. They often refer to the sexual desire of an adolescent as "drives" or "urges" which they attribute to the physical processes of puberty. Puberty confuses the child, burdening him with a load of hormonally produced sexual feelings. One mother thinks the physical transition adolescents experience is

> . . . difficult for them, very difficult. Their bodies are changing, and they are experiencing feelings that they have never had before, and they are getting interested in the opposite sex per se and having feelings to deal with that they never had.

Expressions such as "raging hormones" and "hormones that are acting up" suggest that adolescent sexuality emerges from a biological source within the individual and possesses a disruptive power.

While many parents say it is normal for a teenager to experience sexual feelings, all of them also say that at 16 their child is not ready for a relationship involving sex. When parents talk about teenage sex, they usually refer to *other* teenagers, not to their own children. Parents describe teenage sexual involvement as an individual condition or activity; teenagers are "sexually active" or engaged in "sexual activity." American parents do not usually refer to a relational or emotional context when talking about the sexual activity of teenagers. One reason they do not associate teenage sexuality with love or an emotionally meaningful relationship is the widespread belief that 16-year-olds are unable to form deep or steady romantic attachments. One American mother says point-blank, "They're not mature enough to handle a serious relationship." Another doesn't think "a 16-year-old is going to be committed to that extent. I mean maybe this month, but next month it could be someone else." Even when long-term romantic attachments do exist between adolescents, parents do not believe sex is warranted. A mother whose daughter had dated the same boy throughout high school does not think "someone who is 16 is mature enough to really have a relationship that would be a meaningful relationship, one that would involve sex."

This dissociation of teenage sexuality from contexts of love and commitment explains why American parents often refer to teenage sexual activity as experimental, promiscuous, immoral or exclusively pleasure-driven. It is not uncommon, in fact, for parents to mention teenage sex in the same breath as drugs, excessive drinking or vandalism. However, parents do not attribute such negative qualities to sexuality in general. Adult sexuality is different from the sexual activity of "kids." "I very strongly feel that sex is not a child—shouldn't be an activity for children," says one mother. "I just think sex is another thing that's for adults and not for kids." The developmental maturity, economic independence or marital status of "adults" distinguishes them from "kids" and sanctions their "adult" sexual activity. Because teenagers lack these attributes, their motivations for engaging in sex and their sexual desires, motivations and experiences are thought to have a different, lesser value. "It's not that we don't approve of sex," says one mother. "It's that we don't approve of sex at a certain time in life."

Some religious parents believe that sexual intercourse, regardless of its consequences, poses a threat to the individual because pre-marital sex is wrong. Most parents, however, do not refer to sin but rather emphasize the negative consequences that sex can entail. One mother says that "sex is not good for a kid" and that with the spread of AIDS "it's terribly, terribly dangerous." Another father would disapprove of his son's becoming sexually involved because "tied in with that is this whole horror show of AIDS and related diseases." One mother feels her daughter is "at risk": "And [you worry] that their lives can get messed up more. If a girl gets pregnant, she has to deal with an abortion or a baby." Another mother says that her son could risk his future by getting sexually involved. Her advice to him: "You're really blessed. Don't blow it. You know. Don't throw it out the window on some cheap thrill because what's it going to get you?" Another father believes one should tell teenagers, "Don't do it. You're crazy. You're playing with a loaded gun. There's no other way that I can put it. You're going to ruin your life."

American parents assume that teenagers cannot guard against unwanted consequences of sexual involvement—for instance, by using contraceptives. They suggest that teenagers are unable to regulate their sexual impulses, making any sexual involvement tantamount to irresponsibility. The parents express similar notions about the inability of teenagers to exercise self-restraint when they discuss alcohol consumption. Eleven parents believe 16-year-olds should not be allowed to drink alcohol without parental supervision because they "would not know their limitations," "do not have any idea of their capacity" or "are not mature enough to be able to control something like that." Parents suggest that if teenagers are given free access to alcohol they will consume excessively rather than in moderation because they "don't know how to make those distinctions."

The notion that a teenager cannot restrain herself is related to the belief that she lacks a fully solidified internal reference point or a reliable moral compass. Like the biological process of puberty, the period of adolescence is thought to disrupt and confuse a person and to make one extremely susceptible to influences outside oneself. This "inner unreliability" renders teenagers unaccountable for their actions. Thus, many American parents explain the drinking and sexual behavior of teenagers not as a consequence of free will but as a result of "being pushed" or "forced" by others. "Too often a kid ends up having sex because it's a peer thing rather than something he's honestly ready for," one mother says. A father believes, "These kids get wrapped up in it. It's a trap. It's peer pressure." The *dramatization* of teenage sexuality thus involves the interplay of internal urges, external pressures and a self unable yet to direct or protect itself.

THE NORMALIZATION OF ADOLESCENT SEXUALITY

While the American parents emphasize how teenage sexuality is disruptive, the Dutch parents describe teenage sexuality as something that does not and should not present many problems. They often speak jokingly about the relationships and sexuality of teenage children. One mother tells of her amusement when her son said to her one day, "Now I want a girlfriend, the time is ripe for that." Another father describes how, as a joke for Christmas, he and his wife gave their children gold-colored condoms, which they had bought in Berkeley, California. Such jokes indicate the *normality* with which the Dutch parents approach the issue of adolescent sexuality. Dutch parents believe that sexuality should be talked about and dealt with in a "normal" way, meaning that it should not be made taboo or the cause of unnecessary difficulty. "We have always talked openly, normally about [reproduction and contraception]," says one mother. Another mother favors sex education at school because that way "it becomes very normal to talk about it."

The onset of sexual desire in teenagers is usually discussed in relation to a boyfriend or girlfriend, or in terms of being *verliefd* (in love or infatuated) with another person. In other words, Dutch parents think about the sexuality of teenagers in the context of a relationship and their emotional involvement with another person. Adolescents are not said to be "sexually active"; rather they "go to bed with each other" or have "sexual contact." "Yes, I do think that is a result of having a boyfriend or a girlfriend for a long time, that you surely have a sexual, thus an intimate, relationship," one mother says. Another mother explains why a young person would want to be sexual with a partner: "If you love each other, then you want to be together, don't you, to have that warmth."

This relationship-based conception of adolescent sexuality is not only descriptive, it is prescriptive. Dutch parents say that teenagers *should* view sexuality in the context of their emotions for and relationships with other people. One mother approves of sex education in school "as long as it is indeed about relationships, and not just sex, pure sex." When sex education is about "dealing with each other, having understanding for each other," then she finds it "extremely good." Another mother reiterates that sex education should include talking about "feelings, clearly taking the other person into account, for boys as well as for girls." It is the presence of a "relationship" which determines whether

Dutch parents approve of teenagers having sex. A number of them indicate that the depth and stability of the relationship, rather than age or any other condition, are the criteria that make sex acceptable. One mother approves of sex at 16 "as long as they have a steady relationship, not every week with another person." Another mother says that young people should not have sex based on a momentary attraction but

> . . . if you are sixteen, and there comes a period of four or five months of going out really steadily, and you don't do any crazy things, then I would think it all right. . . . Yes. . . . As long as they have a steady girlfriend, or a steady boyfriend, then I think it is all right.

Parents stress that a person should be *er aan toe*. *Er aan toe zijn* means "to be ready for" or "at the right moment." Such readiness is the result of a gradual mental and physical process of development. What distinguishes the Dutch parents from the American parents is their belief that teenagers are capable of being *er aan toe*, or ready for a sexual relationship. Although most Dutch parents do not think their own 16-year-old is ready, eight think it is possible for a person to be *er aan toe* at 16. Another six think this can be the case at 17 or 18. Relative to their American counterparts, Dutch parents have little anxiety about their child becoming sexually involved prematurely. It is generally thought that if a person is not *er aan toe*, he or she will not want to have sex. The assumption behind the concept *er aan toe zijn* is that when a person feels ready and wants to have sex, he is indeed ready.

Unlike their American counterparts, Dutch parents do not envision a battle between bodily drives and rational control. Sexual desire and the personal development which makes it possible to experience sex in a good way are thought to go together. For that reason, parents trust that "the right moment" will best be recognized by a teenager herself. "You should ask him that," one mother responds when asked whether she thinks her son is ready for a relationship involving sex. "That is something he should decide for himself, whether he is ready or not." One father says his daughter was ready for sex at 16 "because she herself indicated she was ready." He had always told his daughters:

> I will never have any objection [to a sexual relationship] when they—really out of their own free will, and never because they have to do it or because of coercion or because they feel that they have to belong, or because otherwise the boyfriend won't like them anymore—but only when they themselves feel the need for that, and when they are themselves ready for it. And when that is, I don't know.

Dutch parents do not view adolescent sexuality as being dangerous in and of itself. They stress that teenagers should use contraceptives, and frequently mention their own role in urging their children to do so. "Without a condom, I will not allow them to make love," says one mother. One father would object if his daughter wanted to become sexually involved at 16. He says nonetheless, "When she has a boyfriend for a while, [her mother] says, 'Shall we go to the doctor to get the pill?' " One mother continually points out the necessity of contraceptives to her son because "it must become an automatism." If her daughter had continued to go steady with her boyfriend, one other mother says, she would have told her, "You must go on the pill." The Dutch parents do not regard sex as inherently risky because they expect their children will use contraceptives to protect themselves against unwanted consequences of sex. Asked whether he is worried about his daughter's sexual behavior, one father responds, "I do have that trust that if she were to do it, she would use contraceptives, she has a good enough head on her shoulders."

When they discuss drinking Dutch parents express a similar trust that their child will use common sense. Asked if their 16-year-old is old enough to drink, parents usually respond "yes, in moderation," implying that a 16-year-old is capable of self-imposed moderation. One mother says her son had "become acquainted with alcohol" on a school trip to Rome, where he had gotten "good and drunk." As a consequence he decided "out of himself" not to drink to excess in the future. In a similar way, the mechanism that moderates sexual desire and prevents pregnancy and disease is thought to be internal, within an adolescent. The notion that teenagers possess the ability to restrain themselves and to commit to others enables Dutch parents to normalize adolescent sexuality, to treat it, in other words, as something that neither is nor should be a problem.

Editors' Note: References and Notes for this reading can be found in the original source.

■READING 11

Sexual Revolution(s)

Beth Bailey

In 1957 America's favorite TV couple, the safely married Ricky and Lucy Ricardo, slept in twin beds. Having beds at all was probably progressive—as late as 1962 June and Ward Cleaver did not even have a bedroom. Elvis's pelvis was censored in each of his three appearances on the *Ed Sullivan Show* in 1956, leaving his oddly disembodied upper torso and head thrashing about on the TV screen. But the sensuality in his eyes, his lips, his lyrics was unmistakable, and his genitals were all the more important in their absence. There was, likewise no mistaking, Mick Jagger's meaning when he grimaced ostentatiously and sang "Let's spend some *time* together" on *Ed Sullivan* in 1967. Much of the audience knew that the line was really "Let's spend the night together," and the rest quickly got the idea. The viewing public could see absence and hear silence—and therein lay the seeds of the sexual revolution.

What we call the sexual revolution grew from these tensions between public and private—not only from tensions manifest in public culture, but also from tensions between private behaviors and the public rules and ideologies that were meant to govern behavior. By the 1950s the gulf between private acts and public norms was often quite wide—and the distance was crucial. People had sex outside marriage, but very, very few acknowledged that publicly. A woman who married the only man with whom she had had premarital sex still worried years later: "I was afraid someone might have learned that we had intercourse before marriage and I'd be disgraced." The consequences, however, were not just psychological. Young women (and sometimes men) discovered to be having premarital sex were routinely expelled from school or college; gay men risked all for engaging in consensual sex. There were real penalties for sexual misconduct and while many deviated from the sexual orthodoxy of the day, all but a few did so furtively, careful not to get "caught."

Few episodes demonstrate the tensions between the public and private dimensions of sexuality in midcentury America better than the furor that surrounded the publication of the studies of sexual behavior collectively referred to as the "Kinsey Reports." Though a dry, social scientific report, *Sexual Behavior in the Human Male* (1948) had sold over a quarter of a million copies by 1953, when the companion volume on the human female came out. The male volume was controversial, but the female volume was, in *Look* magazine's characterization, "stronger stuff." Kinsey made it clear that he understood the social implications of his study, introducing a section on "the pre-marital coital behavior of the female sample which has been available for this study" with the following qualification: "Because of this public condemnation of pre-marital coitus, one might believe that such contacts would be rare among American females and males. But this is only the overt culture, the things that people openly confess to believe and do. Our previous report (1948) on the male has indicated how far publicly expressed attitudes may depart from the realities of behavior—the covert culture, what males actually do."

Kinsey, a biologist who had begun his career with much less controversial studies of the gall wasp, drew fire from many quarters, but throughout the criticism is evident concern about his uncomfortable juxtaposition of public and private. "What price biological science . . . to reveal intimacies of one's private sex life and to draw conclusions from inscriptions on the walls of public toilets?" said one American in a letter to the editor of *Look* magazine.

Much of the reaction to Kinsey did hinge on the distance between the "overt" and the "covert." People were shocked to learn how many men and women were doing what they were not supposed to be doing. Kinsey found that 50 percent of the women in his sample had had premarital sex (even though between 80 percent and 89 percent of his sample disapproved of premarital sex on "moral grounds"), that 61 percent of college-educated men and 84 percent of men who had completed only high school had had premarital sex, that over one-third of the married women in the sample had "engaged in petting" with more than ten different men, that approximately half of the married couples had engaged in "oral stimulation" of both male and female genitalia, and that at least 17 percent of American men had had "some homosexual experience" during their lifetimes.

By pulling the sheets back, so to speak, Kinsey had publicized the private. Many people must have been reassured by the knowledge that they were not alone, that their sexual behaviors were not individual deviant acts but part of widespread social trends. But others saw danger in what Kinsey had done. By demonstrating the distance between the overt and the covert cultures, Kinsey had further undermined what was manifestly a beleaguered set of rules. *Time* magazine warned its readers against the attitude that "there is morality in numbers," the *Chicago Tribune* called Kinsey a "menace to society," and the *Ladies' Home Journal* ran an article with the disclaimer: "The facts of behavior reported . . . are not to be interpreted as moral or social justification for individual acts."

Looking back to the century's midpoint, it is clear that the coherence of (to use Kinsey's terms) covert and overt sexual cultures was strained beyond repair. The sexual revolution of the 1960s emerged from these tensions, and to that extent it was not revolutionary, but evolutionary. As much as anything else, we see the overt coming to terms with the covert. But the revision of revolution to evolution would miss a crucial point. It is not historians who have labeled these changes "sexual revolution"—it was people at the time, those who participated and those who watched. And they called it that before much of what we would see as revolutionary really emerged—before gay liberation and the women's movement and Alex Comfort's *The Joy of Sex* (1972) and "promiscuity" and singles' bars. The term was in general use by 1963—earlier than one might expect.

To make any sense of the sexual revolution, we have to pay attention to the label people gave it. Revolutions, for good or ill, are moments of danger. It matters that a metaphor of revolution gave structure to the myriad changes taking place in American society. The changes in sexual mores and behaviors could as easily have been cast as evolutionary—but they were not.

Looking back, the question of whether or not the sexual revolution was revolutionary is not easy to answer; it depends partly on one's political (defined broadly) position. Part of the trouble, though, is that the sexual revolution was not one movement. It was instead a set of movements, movements that were closely linked, even intertwined, but which often made uneasy bedfellows. Here I hope to do some untangling, laying out three of the most important strands of the sexual revolution and showing their historical origins, continuities, and disruptions.

The first strand, which transcended youth, might be cast as both evolutionary and revolutionary. Throughout the twentieth century, picking up speed in the 1920s, the 1940s and the 1960s, we have seen a sexualization of America's culture. Sexual images have become more and more a part of public life, and sex—or more accurately, the representation of sex—is used to great effect in a marketplace that offers Americans fulfillment through consumption. Although the blatancy of today's sexual images would be shocking to someone transported from an earlier era, such representations developed gradually and generally did not challenge more "traditional" understandings of sex and of men's and women's respective roles in sex or in society.

The second strand was the most modest in aspect but perhaps the most revolutionary in implication. In the 1960s and early 1970s an increasing number of young people began to live together "without benefit of matrimony," as the phrase went at the time. While sex was usually a part of the relationship (and probably a more important part than most people acknowledged), few called on concepts of "free love" or "pleasure" but instead used words like "honesty," "commitment," and "family." Many of the young people who lived together could have passed for young marrieds and in that sense were pursuing fairly traditional arrangements. At the same time, self-consciously or not, they challenged the tattered remnants of a Victorian epistemological and ideological system that still, in the early 1960s, fundamentally structured the public sexual mores of the American middle class.

The third strand was more self-consciously revolutionary, as sex was *actively claimed* by young people and used not only for pleasure, but also for power in a new form of cultural politics that shook the nation. As those who threw themselves into the "youth revolution" (a label that did not stick) knew so well, the struggle for America's future would take place not in the structure of electoral politics, but on the battlefield of cultural meaning. Sex was an incendiary tool of a revolution that was more than political. But not even the cultural revolutionaries agreed on goals, or on the role and meaning of sex in the revolution.

These last two strands had to do primarily with young people, and that is signifi-cant. The changes that took place in America's sexual mores and behaviors in the sixties were *experienced* and *defined* as revolutionary in large part because they were so closely tied to youth. The nation's young, according to common wisdom and the mass media, were in revolt. Of course, the sexual revolution was not limited to youth, and sex was only one part of the revolutionary claims of youth. Still it was the intersection of sex and youth that signaled danger. And the fact that these were often middle-class youths, the ones reared in a culture of respectability (told that a single sexual misstep could jeopardize their bright futures), made their frontal challenges to sexual mores all the more inex-plicable and alarming.

Each of these strands is complex, and I make no pretense to be exhaustive. Thus, rather than attempting to provide a complete picture of changes in behaviors or ideolo-gies, I will examine several manifestations of seemingly larger trends. The sexualization of culture (the first strand) is illustrated by the emergence of *Playboy* and *Cosmo* maga-zines. For the "modest revolutionaries" (the second strand), I look to the national scan-dal over a Barnard College junior's "arrangement" in 1968 and the efforts of University of Kansas students to establish a coed dormitory. Finally, the cultural radicals (the third strand) are represented by the writings of a few counterculture figures.

By focusing on the 1960s, we lose much of the "sexual revolution." In many ways, the most important decade of that revolution was the 1970s, when the "strands" of the 1960s joined with gay liberation, the women's movement, and powerful assertions of the importance of cultural differences in America. Yet, by concentrating on the early years of the sexual revolution, we see its tangled roots—the sexual ideologies and behaviors that gave it birth. We can also understand how little had been resolved—even begun—by the end of the 1960s.

BEFORE THE REVOLUTION: YOUTH AND SEX

Like many of the protest movements that challenged American tranquility in the sixties, the sexual revolution developed within the protected space and intensified atmosphere of the college campus. An American historian recalls returning to Harvard University in 1966 after a year of postgraduate study in England. Off balance from culture shock and travel fatigue, he entered Harvard Yard and knew with absolute certainty that he had "missed the sexual revolution." One can imagine a single symbolic act of copulation sig-naling the beginning of the revolution (it has a nicely ironic echo of "the shot heard round the world"). The single act and the revolution complete in 1966 are fanciful constructions; not everything began or ended at Harvard even in those glory years. But events there and at other elite colleges and universities, if only because of the national attention they re-ceived, provide a way into the public intersections of sex, youth and cultural politics.

Harvard had set a precedent in student freedom in 1952, when girls (the contem-porary term) were allowed to visit in Harvard men's rooms. The freedom offered was not supposed to be sexual—or at least not flagrantly so. But by 1963 Dean Jon Monro complained that he was "badly shaken up by some severe violations," for a once "pleas-ant privilege" had come to be "considered a license to use the college rooms for wild parties or sexual intercourse." The controversy went public with the aid of *Time* magazine, which fanned the flames by quoting a senior's statement that "morality is a relative concept projecting certain mythologies associated with magico-religious beliefs." The Parietals Committee of the Harvard Council for Undergraduate Affairs, according to the *Boston Herald*, concluded that "if these deep emotional commitments and ties occasionally lead to sexual intercourse, surely even that is more healthy than the situation a generation ago when 'nice girls' were dated under largely artificial circumstances and sexual needs were gratified at a brothel." Both justifications seemed fundamentally troubling in different ways, but at least the controversy focused on men. The sexual double standard was strong. When the spotlight turned on women, the stakes seemed even higher.

The media had a field day when the president of Vassar College, Sarah Blanding, said unequivocally that if a student wished to engage in premarital sex she must withdraw from the college. The oft-quoted student reply to her dictum chilled the hearts of middle-class parents throughout the country: "If Vassar is to become the Poughkeepsie Victorian Seminary for young Virgins, then the change of policy had better be made explicit in admissions catalogs."

Such challenges to authority and to conventional morality were reported to eager audiences around the nation. None of this, of course, was new. National audiences had been scandalized by the panty raid epidemic of the early 1950s, the antics and petting parties of college youth had provided sensational fodder for hungry journalists in the 1920s. The parents—and grandparents—of these young people had chipped away at the system of sexual controls themselves. But they had not directly and publicly denied the very foundations of sexual morality. With few exceptions, they had evaded the controls and circumvented the rules, climbing into dorm rooms through open windows, signing out to the library and going to motels, carefully maintaining virginity in the technical sense while engaging in every caress known to married couples. The evasions often succeeded, but that does not mean that the controls had no effect. On the contrary, they had a great impact on the ways people experienced sex.

There were, in fact, two major systems of sexual control, one structural and one ideological. These systems worked to reinforce one another, but they affected the lives of those they touched differently.

The structural system was the more practical of the two but probably the less successful. It worked by limiting opportunities for the unmarried to have intercourse. Parents of teenagers set curfews and promoted double dating, hoping that by preventing privacy they would limit sexual exploration. Colleges, acting in loco parentis, used several tactics: visitation hours, parietals, security patrols, and restrictions on students' use of cars. When Oberlin students mounted a protest against the college's policy on cars in 1963, one male student observed that the issue was not transportation but privacy: "We wouldn't care if the cars had no wheels, just so long as they had doors."

The rules governing hours applied only to women and, to some extent, were meant to guarantee women's safety by keeping track of their comings and goings. But the larger rationale clearly had to do with sexual conduct. Men were not allowed in women's rooms but were received in lounges or "date rooms," where privacy was never assured. By setting curfew hours and requiring women to sign out from their dormitories, indicating who they were with and where they were going, college authorities meant to limit possibilities for privacy. Rules for men were not deemed necessary—because of a sexual double standard, because men's safety and well-being seemed less threatened in general, and because the colleges and universities were primarily concerned with controlling their own populations. If women were supervised or chaperoned and in by 11:00 P.M., the men would not have partners—at least, not partners drawn from the population that mattered.

Throughout the 1950s, the structural controls became increasingly complex; by the early 1960s they were so elaborate as to be ludicrous. At the University of Michigan in 1962, the student handbook devoted nine of its fifteen pages to rules for women. Curfews varied by the night of the week, by the student's year in college, and even, in some places, by her grade point average. Students could claim Automatic Late Permissions (ALPs) but only under certain conditions. Penalties at Michigan (an institutional version of "grounding") began when a student had eleven "late minutes"—but the late minutes could be acquired one at a time throughout the semester. At the University of Kansas in the late 1950s, one sorority asked the new dean of women to discipline two women who had flagrantly disregarded curfew. The dean, investigating, discovered that the women in question had been between one and three minutes late signing in on three occasions.

The myriad of rules, as anyone who lived through this period well knows, did not prevent sexual relations between students so much as they structured the times and places and ways that students could have sexual contact. Students said good-nights on the porches of houses, they petted in dormitory lounges while struggling to keep three feet on the floor and clothing in some semblance of order, and they had intercourse in cars, keeping an eye out for police patrols. What could be done after eleven could be done before eleven, and sex need not occur behind a closed door and in a bed—but this set of rules had a profound impact on the *ways* college students and many young people, living in their parents' homes *experienced sex*.

The overelaboration of rules, in itself, offers evidence that the controls were beleaguered. Nonetheless, the rules were rarely challenged frontally and thus they offered some illusion of control. This system of rules, in all its inconsistency, arbitrariness, and blindness, helped to preserve the distinction between public and private, the coexistence of overt and covert, that defines midcentury American sexuality.

The ideological system of controls was more pervasive than the structured system and probably more effective. This system centered on ideas of difference: men and women were fundamentally different creatures, with different roles and interests in sex. Whether one adopted a psychoanalytic or an essentialist approach, whether one looked to scholarly or popular analysis, the final conclusion pointed to *difference*. In sex (as in life), women were the limit setters and men the aggressors.

The proper limits naturally depended on one's marital status, but even within marriage sex was to be structured along lines of difference rather than of commonality. Marital advice books since the 1920s had the importance of female orgasm, insisting that men must satisfy their wives, but even these calls for orgasm equality posited male and female pleasure as competing interests. The language of difference in postwar America, which was often quite extreme, can be seen as a defensive reaction to changing gender roles in American society.

One influential psychoanalytic study, provocatively titled *Modern Woman: The Lost Sex*, condemned women who tried to be men and argued the natural difference between men and women by comparing their roles in sexual intercourse. The woman's role is "passive," the authors asserted. "[Sex] is not as easy as rolling off a log for her. It is easier. It is as easy as being the log itself. She cannot fail to deliver a masterly performance, by doing nothing whatever except being duly appreciative and allowing nature to take its course." For the man, in contrast, sexuality is "overt, apparent and urgent, outward and ever-present," fostered by psychological and physiological pressures toward orgasm. Men might experiment sexually with few or no consequences and no diminution of pleasure. Women, on the other hand, could not: "The strong desire for children or lack of it in a woman has a crucial bearing on how much enjoyment she derives from the sexual act. . . . Women can-not make . . . pleasure an end in itself without inducing a decline in the pleasure."

These experts argued from a psychoanalytic framework, but much less theoretical work also insisted on the fundamental difference between men and women, and on their fundamentally different interests in sex. Texts used in marriage courses in American high schools and college typically included chapters on the difference between men and women—and these difference were not limited to their reproductive systems.

Women did in fact have a different and more imperative interest in controlling sex than men, for women could become pregnant. Few doctors would fit an unmarried woman with a diaphragm, though one might get by in the anonymity of a city with a cheap "gold" ring from a drugstore or by pretending to be preparing for an impending honeymoon. Relying on the ubiquitous condom in the wallet was risky and douching (Coca-Cola had a short-lived popularity) even more so. Abortion was illegal, and though many abortions took place, they were dangerous, expensive, and usually frightening and degrading experiences. Dependable and *available* birth control might have made a dif-ference (many could later attribute "the sexual revolution" to the "pill"), but sexual be-haviors and sexual mores were not based simply on the threat of illegitimate pregnancy. Kinsey found that only 44 percent of the women in his sample said that they restricted their pre-marital coitus "because of fear of pregnancy," whereas 80 percent cited "moral reasons." Interestingly, 44 percent of the sample also noted their "fear of public opinion."

Women who were too "free" with sexual favors could lose value and even threaten their marriageability. In this society, a woman's future socioeconomic status depended primarily on her husband's occupation and earning power. While a girl was expected to "pet to be popular," girls and women who went "too far" risked their futures. Advice books and columns from the 1940s and 1950s linked girls' and women's "value" to their "virtue," arguing in explicitly economic terms that "free" kisses destroyed a woman's value in the dating system: "The boys find her easy to afford. She doesn't put a high value on herself." The exchange was even clearer in the marriage market. In chilling language, a teen adviser asked: "Who wants second hand goods?"

It was not only the advisers and experts who equated virtue and value. Fifty percent of the male respondents in Kinsey's study wanted to marry a virgin. Even though a rela-tively high percentage of women had intercourse before marriage, and a greater number engaged in "petting," most of these women at least *expected* to marry the man, and many did. Still, there might be consequences. Elaine Tyler May, who analyzed responses to a large, ongoing psychological study of married couples in the postwar era, found that many couples struggled with the psychological burdens of premarital intimacy for much of their married lives. In the context of a social/cultural system that insisted that "nice girls don't," many reported a legacy of guilt or mistrust. One woman wrote of her hus-band: "I think he felt that because we had been intimate before marriage that I could be as easily interested in any man that came along."

Of course, sexual mores and behaviors were highly conditioned by the sexual double standard. Lip service was paid to the ideal of male premarital chastity, but that ideal was usually obviated by the notion, strong in peer culture and implicity acknowledged in the larger culture, that sexual intercourse was a male rite of passage. Middle-class boys pushed at the limits set by middle-class girls but they generally looked elsewhere for "experience." A man who went to high school in the early 1960s (and did not lose his virginity until his first year of college) recalls the system with a kind of horror: "You slept with one kind of woman, and dated another kind, and the women you slept with, you didn't have much respect for, generally."

The distinction was often based on class—middle-class boys and men had sex with girls and women of the lower classes, or even with prostitutes. They did not really expect to have intercourse with a woman of their own class unless they were to be married. Samuel Hynes, in his memoir of coming of age as a navy flier during World War II, describes that certain knowledge: "There were nice girls in our lives, too. Being middle-class is more than a social station, it's kind of destiny. A middle-class boy from Minneapolis will seek out nice middle-class girls, in Memphis or anywhere else, will take them out on middle-class dates and try to put their hand inside their middle-class underpants. And he will fail. It was all a story that had already been written."

Dating, for middle-class youth, was a process of sexual negotiation. "Good girls" had to keep their virginity yet still contend with their own sexual desires or with boys who expected at least some petting as a "return" on the cost of the date. Petting was virtually universal in the world of heterosexual dating. A 1959 *Atlantic* article, "Sex and the College Girl," described the ideal as having "done every possible kind of petting without actually having intercourse."

For most middle-class youth in the postwar era, sex involved a series of skirmishes that centered around lines and boundaries: kissing, necking, petting above the waist, petting below the waist, petting through clothes, petting under clothes, mild petting, heavy petting. The progression of sexual intimacy had emerged as a highly ordered system. Each act constituted a stage, ordered in a strict hierarchy (first base, second base, and so forth), with vaginal penetration as the ultimate step. But in their attempts to preserve technical virginity, many young people engaged in sexual behaviors that, in the sexual hierarchy of the larger culture, should have been more forbidden than vaginal intercourse. One woman remembers: "We went pretty far, very far; everything but intercourse. But it was very frustrating. . . . Sex was out of the question. I had it in mind that I was going to be a virgin. So I came up with oral sex. . . . I thought I invented it."

Many young men and women acted in defiance of the rules, but that does not make the rules irrelevant. The same physical act can have very different meanings depending on its emotional and social/cultural contexts. For America's large middle class and for all those who aspired to "respectability" in the prerevolutionary twentieth century, sex was overwhelmingly secret or furtive. Sex was a set of acts with high stakes and possibly serious consequences, acts that empasized and reinforced the different roles of men and women in American society. We do not know how each person felt about his or her private acts, but we do know that few were willing or able to publicly reject the system of sexual controls.

The members of the generation that would be labeled "the sixties" were revolutionary in that they called fundamental principles of sexual morality and control into question. The system of controls they had been inherited and lived within was based on a set of presumptions rooted in the previous century. In an evolving set of arguments and actions (which never became thoroughly coherent or unified), they rejected a system of sexual controls organized around concepts of difference and hierarchy.

Both systems of control—the structural and the ideological—were firmly rooted in a Victorian epistemology that had, in most areas of life, broken down by the early twentieth century. This system was based on a belief in absolute truth and a passion for order and control. Victorian thought, as Joseph Singal has argued persuasively, insisted on "preserving absolute standards based on a radical dichotomy between that which was deemed 'human' and that regarded as 'animal.' " On the "human" side were all forces of civilization; on the "animal," all instincts, passions, and desires that threatened order and self-control. Sex clearly fell into the latter category. But the Victorian romance was not restricted to human versus animal, civilized versus savage. The moral dichotomy "fostered a tendency to see the world in polar terms." Thus we find rigid dichotomous pairs not only of good and evil, but of men and women, body and soul, home and world, public and private.

Victorian epistemology, with its remarkably comfortable and comforting certainties and its stifling absolutes, was shaken by the rise of a new science that looked to "dynamic process" and "relativism" instead of the rigid dichotomies of Victorian thought. It was challenged from within by those children of Victorianism who "yearned to smash the glass and breathe freely," as Jackson Lears argued in his study of antimodernism. And most fundamentally, it was undermined by the realities of an urban industrial society. American Victorian culture was, as much as anything, a strategy of the emerging middle classes. Overwhelmed by the chaos of the social order that had produced them and that they sought to manage, the middling classes had attempted to separate themselves from disorder and corruption. This separation, finally, was untenable.

The Victorian order was overthrown and replaced by a self-consciously "modern culture." One place we point to demonstrate the decline of Victorianism is the change in sexual "manners and mores" in the early twentieth century. Nonetheless, sex may be the place that Victorian thought least relinquished its hold. This is not to say that prudishness reigned—the continuity is more subtle and more fundamental. Skirts rose above the knee, couples dated and petted, sexologists and psychologists acknowledged that women were not naturally "passionless," and the good judge Ben Lindsey called for the "companionate marriage." But the systems of control that regulated and structured sex were Victorian at their core, with science replacing religion to authorize absolute truth, and with inflexible bipolar constructions somewhat reformulated but intact. The system of public controls over premarital sex was based on rigid dichotomous pairings: men and women, public and private. This distinction would be rejected—or at least recast—in the cultural and sexual struggles of the sixties.

REVOLUTIONARIES

All those who rejected the sexual mores of the postwar era did not reject the fundamental premises that gave them shape. *Playboy* magazine played an enormously important (if symbolic) role in the sexual revolution, or at least in preparing the ground for the sexual revolution. *Playboy* was a men's magazine in the tradition of *Esquire* (for which its founder had worked briefly) but laid claim to a revolutionary stance partly by replacing *Esquire's* airbrushed drawings with airbrushed flesh.

Begun by Hugh Hefner in 1953 with an initial print run of 70,000, *Playboy* passed the one million circulation mark in three years. By the mid-1960s Hefner had amassed a fortune of $100 million, including a lasciviously appointed forty-eight-room mansion staffed by thirty Playboy "bunnies" ("fuck like bunnies" is a phrase we have largely left behind, but most people at the time caught the allusion). Playboy clubs, also staffed by large-breasted and long-legged women in bunny ears and cottontails, flourished throughout the country. Though *Playboy* offered quality writing and advice for those aspiring to sophistication, the greatest selling point of the magazine was undoubtedly its illustrations.

Playboy, however, offered more than masturbatory opportunities. Between the pages of coyly arranged female bodies—more, inscribed in the coyly arranged female bodies—flourished a strong and relatively coherent ideology. Hefner called it a philosophy and wrote quite a few articles expounding it (a philosophy professor in North Carolina took it seriously enough to describe his course as "philosophy from Socrates to Hefner").

Hefner saw his naked women as "a symbol of disobedience, a triumph of sexuality, an end of Puritanism." He saw his magazines as an attack on "our ferocious anti-sexuality, our dark antieroticism." But his thrust toward pleasure and light was not to be undertaken in partnership. The Playboy philosophy according to Hefner, had less to do with sex and more to do with sex roles. American society increasingly "blurred distinctions between the sexes . . . not only in business, but in such diverse realms as household chores, leisure activities, smoking and drinking habits, clothing styles, upswinging homosexuality and the sex-obliterating aspects of togetherness," concluded the "Playboy Panel" in June 1962. In Part 19 of his extended essay on the Playboy philosophy, Hefner wrote: "PLAYBOY stresses a strongly heterosexual concept of society—in which the separate roles of men and women are clearly defined and compatible."

Read without context, Hefner's call does not necessarily preclude sex as a common interest between men and women. He is certainly advocating heterosexual sex. But the models of sex offered are not partnerships. Ever innovative in marketing and design, *Playboy* offered in one issue a special "coloring book" section. A page featuring three excessively voluptuous women was captioned "Make one of the girls a blonde. Make one of the girls a brunette. Make one of the girls a redhead. It does not matter which is which. The girls' haircolors are interchangeable. So are the girls."

Sex, in the Playboy mode, was a contest—not of wills, in the model of the male seducer and the virtuous female, but of exploitative intent, as in the playboy and the would-be wife. In *Playboy's* world, women were out to ensnare men, to entangle them in a web of responsibility and obligation (not the least of which was financial). Barbara Ehrenreich has convincingly argued that *Playboy* was an integral part of a male-initiated revolution in sex roles, for it advocated that men reject burdensome responsibility (mainly in the shape of wives) for lives of pleasure through consumption. Sex, of course, was part of this pleasurable universe. In *Playboy*, sex was located in the realm of consumption, and women were interchangeable objects, mute, making no demands, each airbrushed beauty supplanted by the next month's model.

It was not only to men that sexual freedom was sold through exploitative visions. When Helen Gurley Brown revitalized the traditional women's magazine that was *Cosmopolitan* in 1965, she compared her magazine to *Playboy*—and *Cosmo* did celebrate the pleasures of single womanhood and "sexual and material consumerism." But before Brown ran *Cosmo*, she had made her contribution to the sexual revolution with *Sex and the Single Girl*, published in May 1962. By April 1963, 150,000 hard-cover copies had been sold, garnering Brown much media attention and a syndicated newspaper column, "Woman Alone."

The claim of *Sex and the Single Girl* was, quite simply, "nice, single girls *do*." Brown's radical message to a society in which twenty-three-year-olds were called old maids was that singleness is good. Marriage, she insisted, should not be an immediate goal. The Single Girl sounds like the Playboy's dream, but she was more likely a nightmare revisited. Marriage, Brown advised, is "insurance for the worst years of your life. During the best years you don't need a husband." But she quickly amended that statement: "You do need a man every step of the way, and they are often cheaper emotionally and more fun by the dozen." That fun explicitly included sex, and on the woman's terms. But Brown's celebration of the joys of single life still posed men and women as adversaries. "She need never be bored with one man per lifetime," she enthused. "Her choice of partners is endless and they seek *her* . . . Her married friends refer to her pursuers as wolves, but actually many of them turn out to be lambs—to be shorn and worn by her."

Brown's celebration of the single "girl" actually began with a success story—her own. "I married for the first time at thirty-seven. I got the man I wanted," begins *Sex and the Single Girl*. Brown's description of that union is instructive: "David is a motion picture producer, forty-four, brainy, charming and sexy. He was sought after by many a Hollywood starlet as well as some less flamboyant but more deadly types. And I got him! We have two Mercedes-Benzes, one hundred acres of virgin forest near San Francisco, a Mediterranean house overlooking the Pacific, a full-time maid and a good life."

While Brown believes "her body wants to" is a sufficient reason for a man to have an "affair," she is not positing identical interests of men and women in sex. Instead, she asserts the validity of women's interests—interests that include Mercedes-Benzes, full-time maids, lunch ("Anyone can take you to lunch. How bored can you be for an hour?"), vacations, and vicuna coats. But by offering a female version of the Playboy ethic, she greatly strengthened its message.

Unlike the youths who called for honesty, who sought to blur the boundaries between male and female, *Playboy* and *Cosmo* offered a vision of sexual freedom based on difference and deceit, but within a shared universe of an intensely competitive market economy. They were revolutionary in their claiming of sex as a legitimate pleasure and in the directness they brought to portraying sex as an arena for struggle and exploitation that could be enjoined by men and women alike (though in different ways and to different ends). Without this strand, the sexual revolution would have looked very different. In many ways *Playboy* was a necessary condition for "revolution," for it linked sex to the emerging culture of consumption and the rites of the marketplace. As it fed into the sexual reconfigurations of the sixties, *Playboy* helped make sex more—or less—than a rite of youth.

In the revolutionary spring of 1968, *Life* magazine looked from the student protests at Columbia across the street to Barnard College: "A sexual anthropologist of some future century, analyzing the pill, the drive-in, the works of Harold Robbins, the Tween-Bra and all the other artifacts of the American Sexual Revolution, may consider the case of Linda LeClair and her boyfriend, Peter Behr, as a moment in which the morality of an era changed."

The LeClair affair, as it was heralded in newspaper headlines and syndicated columns around the country, was indeed such a moment. Linda LeClair and Peter Behr were accidental revolutionaries, but as *Life* not so kindly noted "history will often have its little joke. And so it was this spring when it found as its symbol of the revolution a champion as staunch, as bold and as unalluring as Linda LeClair." The significance of the moment is not to be found in the actions of LeClair and Behr, who certainly lacked revolutionary glamour despite all the headlines about "Free Love," but in the contest over the meaning of those actions.

The facts of the case were simple. On 4 March 1968 the *New York Times* ran an article called "An Arrangement: Living Together for Convenience, Security, Sex." (The piece ran full-page width; below it appeared articles on "How to Duck the Hemline Issue" and "A Cook's Guide to the Shallot.") An "arrangement," the author informs us, was one of the current euphemisms for what was otherwise known as "shacking up" or, more innocuously, "living together." The article, which offers a fairly sympathetic portrait of several unmarried student couples who lived together in New York City, features an interview with Barnard sophomore, "Susan," who lived with her boyfriend "Peter" in an off campus apartment. Though Barnard had strict housing regulations and parietals (the curfew was midnight on weekends and ten o'clock on weeknights, and students were meant to live either at home or in Barnard housing), Susan had received permission to live off campus by accepting a job listed through Barnard's employment office as a "live-in maid." The job had, in fact, been listed by a young married woman who was a good friend of "Susan's."

Not surprisingly, the feature article caught the attention of Barnard administrators, who had little trouble identifying "Susan" as Linda LeClair. LeClair was brought before the Judiciary Council—not for her sexual conduct, but for lying to Barnard about her housing arrangements. Her choice of roommate was certainly an issue; if she had been found to be living alone or, as one Barnard student confessed to the *Times*, with a female cat, she would not have been headline-worthy.

Linda, however, was versed in campus politics, and she and Peter owned a mimeograph machine. She played it both ways, appearing for her hearings in a demure, knee-length pastel dress and churning out pamphlets on what she and Peter called "A Victorian Drama." She and Peter distributed a survey on campus, garnering three hundred replies, most of which admitted to some violation of Barnard's parietals or housing regulations. Sixty women were willing to go public and signed forms that read: "I am a student of Barnard College and I have violated the Barnard Housing Regulations. . . . In the interest of fairness I request that an investigation be made of my disobedience."

Linda LeClair had not done anything especially unusual, as several letters from alumnae to Barnard's president, Martha Peterson, testified. But her case was a symbol of change, and it tells us much about how people understood the incident. The president's office received over two hundred telephone calls (most demanding LeClair's expulsion) and over one hundred letters; editorials ran in newspapers, large and small, throughout the country. Some of the letters were vehement in their condemnation of LeClair and of the college. Francis Beamen of Needham, Massachusetts, suggested that Barnard should be renamed "BARNYARD"; Charles Orsinger wrote (on good quality letterhead), "If you let Linda stay in college, I can finally prove to my wife with a front page news story about that bunch of glorified whores going to eastern colleges." An unsigned letter began: "SUBJECT: Barnard College—and the kow-tow to female students' who practice prostitution, PUBLICLY!"

Though the term "alley cat" cropped up more than once, a majority of the letters were thoughtful attempts to come to terms with the changing morality of America's youth. Many were from parents who understood the symbolic import of the case. Overwhelmingly, those who did not simply rant about "whoredom" structured their comments around concepts of public and private. The word *flaunt* appeared over and over in the letters to President Peterson. Linda was flaunting her sneering attitude"; Linda and Peter were "openly flaunting their disregard of moral codes"; they were "openly flaunting rules of civilized society." Mrs. Bruce Bromley, Jr., wrote her first such letter on a public issue to recommend, "Do not let Miss LeClair attend Barnard as long as she flaunts immorality in your face." David Abrahamson, M.D., identifying himself as a former Columbia faculty member, offered "any help in this difficult case." He advised President Peterson, "Undoubtedly the girl's behavior must be regarded as exhibitionism, as her tendency is to be in the limelight which clearly indicates some emotional disturbance or upset."

The public-private question *was* the issue in this case—the letter writers were correct. Most were willing to acknowledge that "mistakes" can happen; many were willing to allow for some "discreet" sex among the unmarried young. But Linda LeClair *claimed* the right to determine her own "private" life; she rejected the private—public dichotomy *as it was framed around sex*, casting her case as an issue of individual right versus institutional authority.

But public response to the case is interesting in another way. When a woman wrote President Peterson that "it is time for these young people to put sex back in its proper place, instead of something to be flaunted" and William F. Buckley condemned the "delinquency of this pathetic little girl, so gluttonous for sex and publicity," they were not listening. Sex was not what Linda and Peter talked about. Sex was not mentioned. Security was, and "family." "Peter is my family," said Linda. "It's a very united married type of relationship—it's the most important one in each of our lives. And our lives are very much intertwined."

Of course they had sex. They were young and in love, and their peer culture accepted sex within such relationships. But what they claimed was partnership—a partnership that obviated the larger culture's insistence on the difference between men and women. The letters suggesting that young women would "welcome a strong rule against living with men to protect them against doing that" made no sense in LeClair's universe. When she claimed that Barnard's rules were discriminatory because Columbia men had no such rules, that "Barnard College was founded on the principle of equality between women and men," and asked, "If women are able, intelligent people, why must we be supervised and curfewed?" she was denying that men and women had different interests and needs. Just as the private-public dichotomy was a cornerstone of sexual control in the postwar era, the much-touted differences between men and women were a crucial part of the system.

Many people in the 1960s and 1970s struggled with questions of equality and difference in sophisticated and hard-thought ways. Neither Peter Behr nor Linda LeClair was especially gifted in that respect. What they argued was commonplace to them—a natural language and set of assumptions that nonetheless had revolutionary implications. It is when a set of assumptions becomes natural and unself-conscious, when a language appears in the private comments of a wide variety or people that it is worth taking seriously. The unity of interests that Behr and LeClair called upon as they obviated the male-female dichotomy was not restricted to students in the progressive institutions on either coast.

In 1969 the administration at the University of Kansas (KU), a state institution dependent on a conservative, though populist, legislature for its funding, attempted to establish a coed dormitory for some of its scholarship students. KU had tried coed living as an experiment in the 1964 summer session and found students well satisfied, though some complained that it was awkward to go downstairs to the candy machines with one's hair in curlers. Curlers were out of fashion by 1969, and the administration moved forward with caution.

A survey on attitudes toward coed housing was given to those who lived in the scholarship halls, and the answers of the men survive. The results of the survey go against conventional wisdom about the provinces. Only one man (of the 124 responses recorded) said his parents objected to the arrangement ("Pending further discussion," he noted). But what is most striking is the language in which the men supported and opposed the plan. "As a stereotypical answer," one man wrote, "I already am able to do all the role-playing socially I need, and see communication now as an ultimate goal." A sophomore who listed his classification as both "soph." and "4-F I hope" responded: "I believe that the segregation of the sexes is unnatural. I would like to associate with women on a basis other than dating roles. This tradition of segregation is discriminatory and promotes inequality of mankind." One man thought coed living would make the hall "more homey." Another said it would be "more humane." Many used the word "natural." The most eloquent of the sophomores wrote: "[It would] allow them to meet and interact with one another in a situation relatively free of sexual overtones; that is, the participating individuals would be free to encounter one another as human beings, rather than having to play the traditional stereotyped male and female roles. I feel that coed living is the only feasible way to allow people to escape this stereotypical role behavior."

The student-generated proposal that went forward in December 1970 stressed these (as they defined them) "philosophical" justifications. The system would NOT be an arrangement for increased boy-meets-girl contact or for convenience in finding dates," the committee insisted. Instead, coed living would "contribute to the development of each resident as a full human being." Through "interpersonal relationships based on friendship and cooperative efforts rather than on the male/female roles we usually play in dating situations" students would try to develop "a human concern that transcends membership in one or the other sex."

While the students disavowed " 'boy-meets-girl' contact" as motivation, no one seriously believed that sex was going to disappear. The most cogently stated argument against the plan came from a young man who insisted: "[You] can't ignore the sexual overtones involved in coed living, after all, sex is the basic motivation for your plan. (I didn't say lust, I said sex)." Yet the language in which they framed their proposal was significant: they called for relationships (including sexual) based on a common humanity.

Like Peter Behr and Linda LeClair, these students at the University of Kansas were attempting to redefine both sex and sex roles. Sex should not be negotiated through the dichotomous pairings of male and female, public and private. Instead, they attempted to formulate and articulate a new standard that looked to a model of "togetherness" undreamed of and likely undesired by their parents. The *Life* magazine issue with which this essay began characterized the "sexual revolution" as "dull." "Love still makes the world go square," the author concluded, for the revolutionaries he interviewed subscribed to a philosophy "less indebted to *Playboy* than Peanuts, in which sex is not so much a pleasure as a warm puppy." To his amusement, one "California girl" told him: "Besides being my lover, Bob is my best friend in all the world," and a young man insisted, "We are not sleeping together, we are living together."

For those to whom *Playboy* promised revolution, this attitude was undoubtedly tame. And in the context of the cultural revolution taking place among America's youth, and documented in titillating detail by magazines such as *Life*, these were modest revolutionaries indeed, seeming almost already out of step with their generation. But the issue, to these "dull" revolutionaries, as to their more flamboyant brothers and sisters, was larger than sex. They understood that the line between public and private had utility; that the personal was political.

In 1967, The Summer of Love

It was a "holy pilgrimage," according to the Council for a Summer of Love. In the streets of Haight-Ashbury, thousands and thousands of "pilgrims" acted out a street theater of costumed fantasy, drugs and music and sex that was unimaginable in the neat suburban streets of their earlier youth. Visionaries and revolutionaries had preceded the deluge; few of them drowned. Others did. But the tide flowed in the vague countercultural yearnings, drawn by the pop hit "San Francisco (Be Sure to Wear Flowers in Your Hair)" and its promise of a "love-in," by the pictures in *Life* magazine or in *Look* magazine or in *Time* magazine, by the proclamations of the underground press that San Francisco would be "the love-guerilla training school for drop-outs from mainstream America . . . where the new world, a human world of the 21st century is being constructed." Here sexual freedom would be explored; not cohabitation, not "arrangements," not "living together" in ways that looked a lot like marriage except for the lack of a piece of paper that symbolized the sanction of the state. Sex in the Haight was revolutionary.

In neat suburban houses on neat suburban streets, people came to imagine this new world, helped by television and by the color pictures in glossy-paper magazines (a joke in the Haight told of "bead-wearing *Look* reporters interviewing bead-wearing *Life* reporters"). Everyone knew that these pilgrims represented a tiny fraction of America's young, but the images reverberated. America felt itself in revolution.

Todd Gitlin, in his soul-searching memoir of the sixties, argues the cultural significance of the few:

> Youth culture seemed a counterculture. There were many more weekend dope-smokers than hard-core "heads"; many more readers of the *Oracle* than writers for it; many more co-habitors than orgiasts; many more turners-on than droppers-out. Thanks to the sheer number and concentration of youth, the torrent of drugs, the sexual revolution, the trau-

matic war, the general stampede away from authority, and the trend-spotting media, it was easy to assume that all the styles of revolt and disaffection were spilling together tributaries into a common torrent of youth and euphoria, life against death, joy over sacrifice, now over later, remaking the whole bleeding world.

Youth culture and counterculture, as Gitlin argues so well, were not synonymous, and for many the culture itself was more a matter of lifestyle than revolutionary intent. But the strands flowed together in the chaos of the age, and the few and the marginal provided archetypes that were read into the youth culture by an American public that did not see the lines of division. "Hippies, yippies, flippies," said Mayor Richard Daley of Chicago. "Free Love," screamed the headlines about Barnard's Linda LeClair.

But even the truly revolutionary youths were not unified, no more on the subject of sex than on anything else. Members of the New Left, revolutionary but rarely countercultural, had sex but did not talk about it all the time. They consigned sex to a relatively "private" sphere. Denizens of Haight-Ashbury lived a Dionysian sexuality, most looking nowhere but to immediate pleasure. Some political-cultural revolutionaries, however, claimed sex and used it for the revolution. They capitalized on the sexual chaos and fears of the nation, attempting to use sex to politicize youth and to challenge "Amerika."

In March 1968 the *Sun,* a Detroit people's paper put out by a "community of artists and lovers" (most notably John Sinclair of the rock group MC5), declared a "Total Assault on the Culture." Sinclair, in his "editorial statement," disavowed any prescriptive intent but informed his readers: "We *have* found that there are three essential human activities of the greatest importance to all persons, and that people are well and healthy in proportion to their involvement in these activities: rock and roll, dope, and fucking in the streets. . . . We suggest the three in combination, all the time."

He meant it. He meant it partly because it was outrageous, but there was more to it. "Fucking" helps you "escape the hangups that are drilled into us in this weirdo country"—it negates "private lives," "feels good," and so destroys an economy of pain and scarcity. Lapsing into inappropriately programmatic language, Sinclair argued:

> Our position is that all people must be free to fuck freely, whenever and wherever they want to, or not to fuck if they don't wanna—in bed, on the floor, in the chair, on the streets, in the parks and fields, "back seat boogie for the high school kids" sing the Fugs who brought it all out in the open on stage and on records, fuck whoever wants to fuck you and everybody else do the same. America's silly sexual "mores" are the end-product of thousands of years of deprivation and sickness, of marriage and companionship based on the ridiculous misconception that one person can "belong" to another person, that "love" is something that has to do with being "hurt," sacrificing, holding out, "teardrops on your pillow," and all that shit.

Sinclair was not alone in his paean to copulation. Other countercultural seekers believed that they had to remake love and reclaim sex to create community. These few struggled, with varying degrees of honesty and sincerity, over the significance of sex in the beloved community.

For others, sex was less a philosophy than a weapon. In the spring of 1968, the revolutionary potential of sex also suffused the claims of the Yippies as they struggled to stage a "Festival of Life" to counter the "Death Convention" in Chicago. "How can you separate politics and sex?" Jerry Rubin asked with indignation after the fact. Yippies lived by that creed. Sex was a double-edged sword, to be played two ways. Sex was a lure to youth; it was part of their attempt to tap the youth market, to "sell a revolutionary consciousness." It was also a challenge, "flaunted in the face" (as it were) of America.

The first Yippie manifesto, released in January 1968, summoned the tribes of Chicago. It played well in the underground press, with its promise of "50,000 of us dancing in the streets, throbbing with amplifiers and harmony . . . making love in the parks." Sex was a politics of pleasure, a politics of abundance that made sense to young middle-class whites who had been raised in the world without limits that was postwar America.

Sex was also incendiary, and the Yippies knew that well. It guaranteed attention. Thus the "top secret" plans for the convention that Abbie Hoffman mimeographed and distributed to the press promised a barbecue and lovemaking by the lake, followed by "Pin the Tail on the Donkey," "Pin the Rubber on the Pope," and "other normal and healthy games." Grandstanding before a crowd of Chicago reporters, the Yippies presented a city official with an official document wrapped in a *Playboy* centerfold inscribed, "To Dick with love, the Yippies." The *Playboy* centerfold in the Yippies' hands was an awkward nexus between the old and the new sexuality. As a symbolic act, it did not proffer freedom so much as challenge authority. It was a sign of disrespect—to Mayor Richard Daley and to straight America.

While America was full of young people sporting long hair and beads, the committed revolutionaries (of cultural stripe) were few in number and marginal at best. It is telling that the LeClair affair could still be a scandal in a nation that had weathered the Summer of Love. But the lines were blurred in sixties America. One might ask with Todd Gitlin, "What was marginal anymore, where was the mainstream anyway?" when the Beatles were singing, "Why Don't We Do It in the Road?"

CONCLUSION

The battles of the sexual revolution were hard fought, its victories ambiguous, its outcome still unclear. What we call the sexual revolution was an amalgam of movements that flowed together in an unsettled era. They were often at odds with one another, rarely well thought out, and usually without a clear agenda.

The sexual revolution was built on equal measures of hypocrisy and honesty, equality and exploitation. Indeed, the individual strands contain mixed motivations and ideological charges. Even the most heartfelt or best intentions did not always work out for the good when put into practice by mere humans with physical and psychological frailties. As we struggle over the meaning of the "revolution" and ask ourselves who, in fact, *won*, it helps to untangle the threads and reject the conflation of radically different impulses into a singular revolution.

5 Courtship and Marriage

■ READING 12

The Decline of the Date and the Rise of the College Hook Up

Paula England and Reuben J. Thomas

In 2002, an undergraduate student came to the first author's (England's) office and said that he wanted to do a research paper on why students on campus didn't date much anymore. She said, amazed, "They don't?" A query in a large class that afternoon confirmed that dates aren't very common. Students said that people mostly hang out with friends or hook up. Being over 50, England had never heard of a "hook up"! The students said they believed that dating was still common on *other* campuses, but thought something unique made it rare on their campus. A graduate student, recently graduated from a small liberal arts college, supplied the information that students at her alma mater also thought that their school was unique in how dead the old-fashioned date was. A colleague at a large state university said the same thing was going on there. It seemed a national trend, but we could find few studies on the phenomenon.[1]

Intrigued by this social change, in 2005, the two of us, England (a professor of sociology) and Thomas (a doctoral student working as her research assistant), set out to study the college hook up scene. We used the medium-sized private university where we work as a case study.

We had over 615 students answer an on-line survey with closed-ended questions amenable to statistical analysis. We had a team of students do in-depth qualitative interviews with 270 fellow undergraduate students. In this article, we present the first report of findings from this study.[2] Here we only describe the undergraduate, heterosexual scene; we hope in future studies to also explore what is happening with gay, lesbian, and

---

1. Glenn and Marquant, 2001; Paul et al., 2000; Armstrong, 2005.

2. While we will provide statistics, the reader should remember that this was not a probability sample, so we cannot say that it is representative of the University's population. And, while we know similar trends are apparent on other campuses, they may be somewhat different in the patterns described here. We especially suspect that patterns are different when college students live with their parents.

151

bisexual students and with graduate students. Based on talking to students and faculty on many campuses—large state universities, private universities, and small colleges—we believe that the demise of the date and the rise of the hook up is a national trend, probably starting in the 1980s, and that something similar to what we describe in this article is happening on many campuses.

IS THE TRADITIONAL DATE DYING?

The traditional date started with a man asking a woman at least several days in advance if she wanted to go to a movie, dinner, a concert, a dance, a party, or some other event. Dating isn't ancient, however; it was an "invention" of the 1920s and was helped along by the invention of the automobile and commercial spots, like movie theatres, where youth could go.[3] Before that, young men often had to "court" women in their homes under the supervision of parents. At first the practice of dating outraged the older generation, who had grown up in the Victorian era with the previous courtship pattern. After the advent of dating as a social form, dates were the pathway into romantic relationships, but not every date involved serious romantic interest on either side. Sometimes he just wanted someone to take to the dance, or she thought it would be fun to go to the party. Dates were a way to get to know each other, although the gender norms of the 1950s and 1960s worked against male and female college students having as much in common as they do today. If you wanted sex, except for the unusual "pick up" or "one night stand" situation, dates were pretty much the only way to move in that direction. In the 1950s and before, the social norm was that sexual intercourse was to be reserved for marriage. Of course, the norm was sometimes violated, but usually not until the couple planned to get married. If the woman got unexpectedly pregnant (birth control was harder to obtain then, especially for single people), a "shot gun marriage" might ensue. Thus, dates were sometimes casual, sometimes led to serious relationships and even marriage. Sometimes they involved something physical—making out or more, but not always.

Today, on college campuses, the students in our study told us, the traditional date is nearly dead. Either male or female students sometimes invite a date to a fraternity, sorority, athletic team, or dorm event. Those are dates, but somehow they aren't seen as "real dates" in the traditional sense. In fact, students tend to use the term "dating" to refer to the activities of couples who have already decided that they are in an exclusive romantic relationship.

In our survey, we asked students how many dates they had been on since they came to college with someone they weren't already in a relationship with, excluding dorm or Greek events. Although the average student in the survey had been in college two years already, over half of both the men and women had been on fewer than five dates. Twenty-one percent of the men and 32% of the women hadn't been on any dates. Only 7% had been on more than 10. But when we asked how many dates they had been on since coming to college with someone they were in an exclusive relationship with, the numbers were much higher. About 30% of each sex had been on none, but 45% had been on more than 10, showing that dating is much more common after than before exclusive rela-

3. Bailey, 1998.

tionships are formed. As one male student told us, "So there's no such thing as causally going out to . . . gauge the other person. . . . I mean you can hang out. . . . But we're only dating once we've decided we like each other . . . and want to be in a relationship."

THE HOOK UP

What is a "hook up"? Two people are hanging out in the dorm or see each other at a party, start talking or dancing, and, sometime during the evening, go somewhere private (often a dorm room or apartment), and something sexual happens. Often they have been drinking. Hooking up with someone doesn't necessarily imply an interest in a relationship, although sometimes it leads to relationships; in this way the hook up is similar to the old-fashioned date.

We asked students in the survey how many hook ups they had been on. A little more than 20% had never been on one. A quarter had hooked up at least once but no more than 4 times. About 20% had had 5–10 hookups, and over a third had hooked up more than 10 times.

We asked questions to get an in-depth portrait of each respondent's most recent hook up. About half (47%) started at a party. Fraternities often host such parties, but dorm or house parties are also common. About a quarter (23%) started when two people were hanging out in the dorm. Others started at bars or miscellaneous settings.

Students make jokes about "random hook ups," where the two had never met before that night, but these are unusual on our campus. Only 14% said they didn't know the person they hooked up with before that night, at least a little. Over half said they knew the person moderately or very well. In fact, slightly over half of those reporting on a recent hook up said they had hooked up with this same person before.[4] Interviews revealed that sometimes a sequence of multiple hook ups ultimately leads to an exclusive relationship. Other times, people become what some call "friends with benefits"—two people who regularly have sex together but do not define themselves as boyfriend and girlfriend.

Hook ups often follow lots of drinking. We asked respondents how many drinks (beers, glasses of wine, shots, mixed drinks, or malt liquors) they had had the night of the hook up. Men averaged 5 and women 3 drinks. Because we had asked them their weight, we were able to apply a formula used by the U.S. Department of Transportation to estimate blood alcohol content. Almost half (46%) reported drinking little enough that they were not significantly impaired. Thirteen percent were impaired but under the legal limit. Another 13% were over the legal limit with a blood alcohol content between .08 and .12. Finally, 28% were extremely drunk, with a blood alcohol content estimated at .12 or over. In the qualitative interviews, students talked about the role of alcohol two ways. Sometimes they said being drunk caused them to do things they wish they hadn't afterwards—going farther sexually than is consistent with their values, or just getting so drunk that they got sick and were miserable. Other times they admitted that they liked being under the influence because it took away inhibitions and helped them do things they wanted to but were too self-conscious to do sober.

---

4. This was coded from the qualitative interviews where we asked the story about how the hook up with this person came about. The question wasn't asked in the survey.

As students use the term, a hook up implies that something sexual happened, but not necessarily that you "had sex," by which students mean sexual intercourse. Oral sex is not seen as "having sex," something that surprises many over-50 adults. We gave students a checklist and asked them to check any of the specific sexual behaviors they had engaged in on their most recent hook up since they came to college, whether with a person from their school or not. We categorized all hook ups according to how far things went sexually. About a third (34%) of hook ups involved no more than kissing and some touching that didn't involve genitals. Nineteen percent involved hand stimulation of one or both person's genitals, but nothing more (we considered oral sex or vaginal or anal intercourse to be "more"). Twenty-two percent involved oral sex, but not intercourse. About the same number, 23%, involved sexual intercourse.[5] (See Figure 1.) In the cases

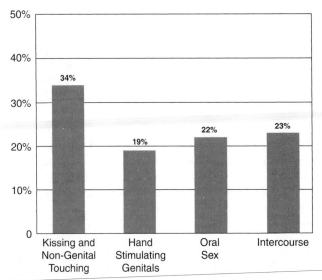

Levels of Sexual Behavior

FIGURE 1   *Percent of Hook Ups Involving Levels of Sexual Behavior*
Higher categories may have also included behaviors lower on the list but not vice versa.

5. Hook ups are classified by assuming a hierarchy where kissing and nongenital touching is first, hand stimulation of genitals next, oral sex next, and intercourse going "farthest." (Vaginal and anal intercourse are classified together, although there were only two cases of anal sex reported among heterosexual hook ups.) A hook up is classified according to the highest point on this hierarchy that occurred. For example, if a couple kissed, one stimulated the other's genitals by hand, and they had oral sex, it would be classified in the "oral sex" category. Considering oral sex as "going farther" than hand stimulation of genitals is somewhat arbitrary. We made this decision because often mouth–genital contact is considered more intimate than hand–genital contact, and because our data show that oral sex more often leads to orgasm and hand stimulation is rarely conducted to the point of orgasm (see Figure 3). Hook ups were classified into oral and hand stimulation categories irrespective of which partner was performing or receiving the stimulation.

where things stopped with oral sex, 49% of the time it was mutual, but where it was not, it was much more often the young men than women receiving oral sex (37% versus 14% of the oral sex cases).

WHERE DO RELATIONSHIPS COME FROM?

If hook ups don't imply interest in a relationship, where do relationships come from on campus today? In the era of the date, while most dates didn't lead to exclusive relationships, nonetheless, most exclusive relationships came through dates. Now that the date is on the wane, are there no relationships? To the contrary, we found that many students form exclusive relationships. We asked on the survey if students had ever been in a relationship that lasted at least six months that started since they came to college. Over a third (36% of men and 40% of women) said yes. If we included relationships with a fellow high school student that lasted into their college years, the percent was even higher.

How do relationships get started? In the qualitative interviews, we asked students the story of how their relationships started and then coded the data for whether a date or a hook up (if either) came first. About a third started with a traditional date. But 44% had one or more hook ups first; sometimes this was followed by some dating before things were really defined as "exclusive" or "official." As one woman said,

> "In . . . the college hook up culture, it tends to start with . . . a crush already there. . . . Then . . . alcohol or the party setting . . . helps bring it together and people tend to . . . hook up, and if they're really into each other . . . that first hook up tends to lead straight into . . . more intense dating which can qualify as relationships. . . ."

One male respondent reflected on this sequence: "A lot of my guy friends aren't looking for relationships . . . but when they meet those girls, it's often been within the group of friends. . . . And then . . . you try to hook up with them. And then you can start dating. . . ." Another guy said, "For a time it was more like a regular hook up and then we . . . started getting attracted to each other and our relationship actually ended up happening."

The remainder of the pathways into relationships were varied—including cases where students went almost seamlessly from meeting or being friends to falling for each other and being an exclusive couple without anything in between that they defined as a hook up. As one woman said, "We met my sophomore year through a friend, and then he'd just come up and talk to me . . . And we were . . . friends for, like, almost a year before we started dating." A man said: "We had to hang out because we were in the show, and so we became really good friends, and then there was just a point where we realized we were dating. . . ."

Relationships were often made "official" or exclusive via "the talk"—where one of the two people sought to define the relationship more clearly. Some students call this a "DTR" or "define the relationship" talk. Others just call it "the talk." Students told us these talks are often initiated after several hook ups by the woman who wants to know where she stands with the guy. Guys then can agree that they are in a relationship or say that they really don't want to go beyond hooking up—we heard quite a few reports of the latter happening. One woman talked about wanting to find out where she stood, but hesitating: "I feel like it's . . . the stereotypical girl thing to do, like . . . the guy feels like the girl is boxing him into a relationship, and I don't want to be . . . that girl. . . . If we continue to see each other . . . I probably will bring it up eventually . . . "

But sometimes the beginning of a "relationship" is more ambiguous. One woman said, "We had been hooking up for a year and a half before finally he said that he loved me. And so then I was like 'Well I guess that means that we're going out, right?' And he said 'Yeah.' We never . . . had . . . the relationship defining talk."

Relationships include doing things together, "dating," and usually having sex. Just over three-quarters of our respondents said that they had had intercourse when describing a current or most recent relationship that lasted at least 6 months. Nonetheless, it is notable that a quarter had been in a relationship for 6 months and had not had intercourse. Obviously, some groups of students, for reasons either of religious belief or just wanting to take it slow, do not consider relationships to imply sex.

GENDER AND THE HOOK UP

When norms about what is permissive sexually liberalize, is this a form of women's liberation or not? Feminists still debate this question. On first glance it seems obvious—if it is accepted (at least in some groups) for women to do more sexually, but they retain the choice to say no, it must be an expansion of their freedom and a victory from a feminist point of view. In one sense this is true. Consider a young woman who hooked up and had oral sex with two or more guys in a year, ended up in a relationship with one of them, had sex with him, broke up with him, and had sex with another partner before marrying him. In 1960 she would have been strongly stigmatized in most social circles. Today, while some groups (often those taking a conservative interpretation of Christian, Jewish, Islamic, or other religions) are very much against sex before marriage, in many social circles, this young woman's behavior would be unremarkable. Cultural changes have given women the option of more sexual behavior than in the past. Options have thereby increased for men too; when "good girls" wouldn't even think of performing oral sex on the first date (and the hook up didn't exist), men were much less likely to have easily accessible sexual satisfaction.

Equal Opportunity Orgasms?

We asked respondents whether they had an orgasm on their most recent hook up, and whether they thought their partner did. Whether we use women's or men's report, about 40% say the man had an orgasm. But a much lower percent of women had an orgasm, even by men's report, but it also appears that men often think the woman has an orgasm when she doesn't! Men reported that their female partners had an orgasm in 30% of the most recent hook ups, but only 14% of the women reported an orgasm.

If we believe each gender's report of their own orgasm, hook ups involve orgasm for men twice as often as for women. The orgasm disparity is much worse than sex gap in pay in the labor market; women have less than half the orgasms of men on hook ups, but women earn more than three-quarters as much as men![6] Why does this gap exist?

One reason is probably that women are receiving less genital stimulation conducive to orgasm than men in hook ups. For example, in hook ups involving oral sex but no intercourse, men had over two and a half times the probability of receiving unreciprocated oral sex than women did. (As mentioned above, where couples stopped with oral sex, 49% of the time it was mutual, 37% only the man received it, and only 14% of the time only the women received it.)

Sometimes the disparity is because women are uncomfortable receiving oral sex outside a relationship. One male respondent described it this way: "I think that girls don't go into a situation expecting that the first time, [that] the guy is gonna go down . . . they feel that's a bigger deal. . . . The female feels a little more protective of herself. . . . Whereas, the guy . . .—there's no shame in . . . having the girl have her hand down your pants. . . ."

Other times, the problem is that men are unwilling or unskilled at performing cunnilingus. One female respondent complained: "He did that thing where . . . they put their hand on the top of your head . . . and I hate that! . . . Especially 'cause there was not an effort made to, like, return that favor." One woman complained about the inequity in emphasis on female pleasure, saying, "Most usually guys don't give me head. Usually I give them head. . . . And that sucks." Another said:

> He wanted me to go down on him . . . which you know I had no problem, I actually rather enjoyed. . . . And then we finish . . . I don't want to say 'my turn,' but. . . . Next morning . . . he turns over and . . . wants to start making out again. . . . So I'm gonna assert my wants this time. . . . I'm taking his hand and trying to move it down there and he goes for maybe for thirty seconds and then stops . . .and he expects me to repeat the night before. . . . I was, like, 'I'm sorry.'

We see the orgasm gap as well when we look at reports of orgasm within specific types of hook ups. For example, in the fifth of hook ups involving intercourse, women and men agree that men have an orgasm more than 80% of the time, but, by women's report these hook ups lead to her orgasm only a third of the time. (Men, however, report that their female intercourse partner orgasmed 70% of the time.) In hook ups where he received oral sex, men and women agree that he has an orgasm about 80% of the time, but in hook ups where he performs oral sex on her, only 30% of the women who had such hook ups said they had orgasm (men estimate women had orgasms in 61% of these). Thus, by anyone's report, women have substantially fewer orgasms than men. (See Figure 2 which uses respondents' reports of their own orgasms.)

If we believe women's reports of their own orgasms, men are vastly overestimating the frequency of their partners' orgasms (see Figure 3.) Why might this be? A number of women talked about faking orgasms to shore up the guy's ego. So, in some cases, men may be receiving misleading information. One man, in the dark about whether a woman he's had sex with several times has an orgasm says, "I'm just not really sure. But she makes a lot of noises . . . so I think I'm doing the right thing. . . ."

---

6. Institute for Women's Policy Research, 2005. In 2004, among U.S. full-time, year-round workers, women's median annual earnings was $31,223, 76.5% of men's median, which was $40,798. These figures include only full-time, year-round workers, but are not adjusted for differences in years of experience or occupation.

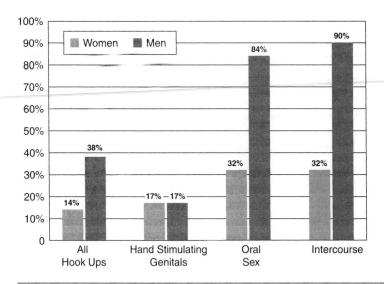

FIGURE 2   *Percent of Men and Women Reporting Having an Orgasm in Hook Ups Involving Various Sexual Behaviors*

Statistics include only men's report of men's orgasm and women's report of women's orgasm. Women's orgasm for hook ups involving oral sex include only those where she received oral sex, whether he did or not, and exclude those involving intercourse. Men's orgasm for hook ups involving oral sex include only those where he received oral sex, whether she did or not, and exclude those involving intercourse. Analogously, hook ups involving hand stimulation of her genitals may or may not involve her hand stimulation of his genitals, and vice versa, but both exclude any involving intercourse or oral sex.

Reputations and the Double Standard

In qualitative interviews, students often talked about how women get a bad reputation—among men and women—if they hook up too much, or with too many men who know each other, or have sex too easily. Men who do the same thing sometimes get a bad reputation among women, but it doesn't last as long, they said. Meanwhile, men gain status from talking to other men about their exploits. It would seem more consistent with "equal opportunity feminism" if *both* men and women both got an equally bad (or elevated) reputation for the same behavior, or if *neither* got a bad reputation at all. The double standard is an area where cultural changes have not liberated women much at all.

One male respondent reflected on the double standard, saying, "I definitely see some girls out there just wanting to hook up." The interviewer asked "And ... those girls, ... are they treated differently?" He reflected, "Sometimes they're called 'slutty.' ... I guess it's ... less stigmatic for a guy to go out and be, like, 'I'm gonna go get some ass' than for a girl. ... I mean not myself. ... Women are sexual creatures too; they can do what they want. But ... there's still that ... 'preserve the women' attitude, or denounce them. ..." He continues: "There's a lot of times where they ... see this girl and go ... there's no way I can date her, but ... she's hot for a hook up." One woman talked about the stigma of being seen coming home from a hook up, saying, "Then I take the

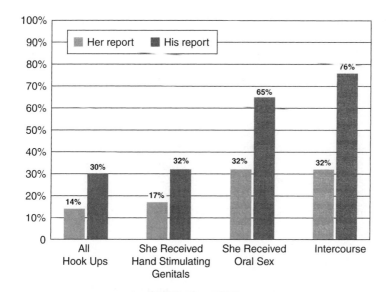

FIGURE 3 *Men's and Women's Perceptions of the* **Woman's** *Orgasm in Hook Ups Involving Various Sexual Behaviors*

Statistics for hook ups involving oral sex for her may or may not include oral sex for him, and vice versa, but both exclude those including intercourse. Analogously, hook ups involving hand stimulation of her genitals may or may not involve her hand stimulation of his genitals, and vice versa, but both exclude any involving intercourse or oral sex. Numbers are percent of hook ups in which women reported to have orgasms.

ultimate walk of shame home at 10:00 in the morning. . . . As people are going to class, I'm walking in heels and a dress, completely hung-over, makeup smeared."

The double standard came out in survey responses as well. Asked whether they had ever hooked up with someone and then respected the person less because of hooking up with the respondent, 37% of the men said yes (compared to only 27% of the women). Asked if they ever thought someone they hooked up with had respected them less after the hook up, 51% of the women said yes (but only 25% of men).

Relational versus Recreational Sex

A national study of adults a decade ago found that most respondents of both sexes think sex should be limited to relationships, but more men than women thought casual sex is okay.[7] In our study, women showed more interest in turning hook ups into relationships than men, and more women wanted to limit sexual intercourse to relationships. For example, asked to agree or disagree with the statement that they would not have sex with someone unless they were in love with the person, 62% of the women agreed or strongly agreed, but only 36% of the men. This may reflect that women have internalized different values than men. Or it may be because women are subjected to more judgment—the

7. Michael et al., 1995.

double standard discussed above—if they are sexual too easily. One woman reflected: "That's not something that I'd ever thought that a decent person should do. . . . I wanted to think that we had a relationship . . . but, it really wasn't . . . because we didn't actually see each other except when we were hooking up."

Gender differences in relational orientation may also reflect differences how much women have been socialized to have skills at intimate relationships. Whatever the source, if women want relationships more than men, it puts men in a stronger bargaining position about starting relationships.[8] One female respondent described hanging out in a fraternity and hearing guys tease brothers who were too into their relationships, saying "There are two girls in that relationship." The implication seemed to be that "real men" are not supposed to care about relationships. Of course there were cases of women just wanting casual hook ups too. But the sentiments of the woman below were expressed by many more women than men. Asked how she felt after a hook up, she said:

> Fricken sweet! I was so happy . . . with the new prospect. . . . I don't . . . know where this relationship will go . . . , how serious it would be. But . . . I heard from his friend that he usually doesn't pursue people . . . so . . . the fact that he's called me up a bunch . . . bodes well.

Another woman said, "He calls me like everyday. . . . Hopefully it's something more than a hook up." One man described a mismatch in relational interest: "I'm still interested in pursuing her in the purely physical manner but definitely nothing emotional or romantic, where she might be interested in something emotional or romantic."

WHAT HAS CHANGED?[9]

The 1960s and 1970s are known for both the sexual revolution and changes in gender inequality. Both of these affected the path of change in romantic and sexual behavior. The advent and legalization of the birth control pill in the 1960s, and the legalization of abortion with a Supreme Court decision in 1973 made it possible to have sex without fear of having an unwanted birth. Ideas that women should be free to choose careers—even in traditionally male fields—may have spilled over into the idea that women as well as men had a right to sexual freedom. Whereas the norm had been that sex was reserved for marriage, and some groups still uphold this view, the dominant view came to be that sex was okay in an exclusive romantic relationship, whether or not it led to marriage. That view

8. One might think that an analogous thing would be true about sex. If men want sex before there is really a relationship, and women don't, women are in a sense empowered in the area of sex because they can get what they want. There is some truth to this, but the cost of having sex early—or of just hooking up too much absent intercourse—is greater for women than for men. This is not only because of the risk of pregnancy, but, also because of the double standard that means women get a bad reputation more than men for the same behavior.

9. The data from our study deal only with the present, not how we got here over the past several decades. In this section, we use our knowledge of the history of recent decades to speculate on how the changes leading to the present situation happened.

was popular among the cohorts in college in the 1970s. Indeed, there was some movement toward acceptance of sex in even casual relationships. But, then the pendulum swung back, and the government began promoting abstinence-only sex education programs in public schools. (By contrast, in Europe students are taught about and offered contraceptives.) The AIDS epidemic increased fear about casual sex.

Whether because of conservative backlash, fear of AIDS, or because the culture was simply not going to accept casual "sex" as mainstream, a curious thing happened. Oral sex, which used to be less common, and practiced largely by couples who were already having intercourse, came to be seen as much less serious or intimate. Oral sex then became accepted in the younger generation in relatively casual relationships, such as hook ups, while intercourse was retained as something many save for relationships. As one male respondent put it, "There are all these little lines . . . gradations, then there's a BIG . . . line between oral sex and intercourse."

People are marrying later, and this, too, probably contributed to the rise of the hook up. Average age at first marriage in the U.S. at the turn of the 21st century was just over 25 for women and 27 for men, up about 4 years from 1960.[10] In our sample, most said they wanted to marry and said they thought it would be at ages even older than these current national averages. With fewer marrying right after college, there is less rush to settle into a relationship. Of course, the increased acceptance of cohabitation and easier availability of sex outside marriage may have contributed to putting marriage off longer. In the 1950s and 1960s, one thing pushing young people into marriage earlier was that it was controversial to have sex or live together before marriage.

In sum, among college students traditional dating is on the wane. The hook up is more common. With hand–genital stimulation and oral sex fairly easily available through hook ups, and friendship easily available in coed dorms, many men see little reason to ask women on formal dates, to the lament of some women. One might have thought that the gender revolution would lead to women asking men out on dates. Instead, the date has almost died. The term "dating" has come to refer more to couples already in an exclusive relationship.

Hook up culture disadvantages women who want relationships before any sexual contact, because the hook up, defined by some sexual activity, is the main pathway into relationships today. Hook up culture hasn't gotten rid of relationships, which remain quite common. Some relationships start with an old-fashioned traditional date. But more common is relationships that start with a series of hook ups, sometimes preceded by friendship and "hanging out."

One might have thought the gender revolution would lead to equality in concern for male and female sexual pleasure, or to equal treatment of men's and women's sexual experiences in forming reputations. But it did not. The sexual double standard and practices that prioritize men's over women's sexual pleasure have not changed much. In the past, men could have sex outside marriage with less loss to reputation than women experienced. Today, in most social circles, neither men nor women are expected to be virgins at marriage. But women get a bad reputation more readily than men from having sex with or hooking up with too many people. Hook up sex does not seem to be "equal

---

10. Caplow et al., 2000, Chapter 4.

opportunity" when it comes to orgasm; women have orgasms less frequently than men. It appears that equal opportunity for women has gone farther in the educational and ca reer world than in the college sexual scene.

References

Armstrong, Elizabeth A., Laura Hamilton, and Brian Sweeney. 2005. "Sexual Assault on Campus: A Gender Structure Explanation of Party Rape." Unpublished paper, Indiana University.

Bailey, Beth. 1988. *From Front Porch to Back Seat: Courtship in Twentieth-Century America*. Baltimore: Johns Hopkins University Press, 1988.

Caplow, Theodore, Louis Hicks, and Ben J. Wattenberg. 2000. *The First Measured Century: An Illustrated Guide to Trends in America, 1900–2000*. Washington D.C.: American Enterprise Institute.

Glenn, Norval and Elizabeth Marquardt. 2001. *Hooking Up, Hanging Out, and Hoping for Mr. Right: College Women on Dating and Mating Today*. New York: Institute for American Values, 2001.

Institute for Women's Policy Research. 2005. *The Gender Wage Ratio*. Washington D.C.: IWPR. Accessed 9-10-05 at www.iwpr.org.

Robert T. Michael, John H. Gagnon, Edward O. Laumann, and Gina Kolata. 1995. *Sex in America: A Definitive Survey*. New York: Little Brown.

Paul, Elizabeth L., Brian McManus, and Allison Hayes. 2000. "Hook Ups: Characteristics and Correlates of College Students' Spontaneous and Anonymous Sexual Experiences." *Journal of Sex Research* 37, 1: 76–88.

■ READING 13

Grounds for Marriage: How Relationships Succeed or Fail

Arlene Skolnick

> The home made by one man and one woman bound together "until death do ye part" has in large measure given way to trial marriage.
> Chauncy J. Hawkins (1907)

> Marriage has universally fallen into awful disrepute.
> Martin Luther (1522)

On June 2, 1986, *Newsweek* magazine featured a cover story that proclaimed that a woman over 40 had a greater chance of being "killed by a terrorist" than of getting married. The story, based on one study, set off a media blitz, along with a wave of alarm and anxiety among single women. Eventually, however, after the furor died down, other researchers pointed to serious flaws in the study *Newsweek* had relied on for the story. The study had relied on trends in earlier generations of women to make predictions about the future of unmarried women today.

In the summer of 1999, another report about the alarming state of marriage was released (National Marriage Project Report, 1999). Exhibit A was a finding that, between 1960 and 1990, the marriage rate among young adults had gone down 23 percent. Again a widely publicized "finding" had to be corrected. The problem this time was including teenagers as young as 15 as "young adults" in 1960 and 1996. Teenagers were far more likely to get married in the 1950s than the 1990s or at any previous time in American history.

The death of marriage has been proclaimed many times in American history, but in the first years of the twenty-first century, the institution is still alive. Despite today's high divorce rates, the rise in one-parent families, and other trends, the United States today has the highest marriage rate among the advanced industrial countries. The Census Bureau estimates that about 90 percent of Americans will eventually marry.

The combination of both high marriage and high divorce rates seems paradoxical, but actually represents two sides of the same coin: the importance of the emotional relationship between the partners. Marriage for love was not unknown in earlier eras, but other, more practical considerations usually came first—economic security, status, and the interests of parents and kin.

Even in the 1950s, the heyday of the marital "togetherness" ideal, researchers found that so-called "empty shell" or "disengaged" marriages were widespread. Such couples lived under one roof, but seemed to have little or no emotional connection to one another. Some of these spouses considered themselves happily married, but others, particularly women, lived in quiet desperation.

Couples today have much higher expectations. Between the 1950s and the 1970s, American attitudes toward marriage changed dramatically as part of what has been called a "psychological revolution"—a transformation in the way people look at marriage, parenthood, and their lives in general (Veroff, Donvan, and Kulka, 1981). In 1957, people judged themselves and their partners in terms of how well the partners fulfilled their social roles in marriage. Is he a good provider? Is she a good homemaker?

By the 1970s, people had become more psychologically oriented, seeking emotional warmth and intimacy in marriage. Why the change? The shift is linked to higher educational levels. In the 1950s, the psychological approach to relationships was found among the relatively few Americans who had been to college. By the 1970s the psychological approach to marriage and family life had become, as the authors put it, "common coin."

In an era when divorce has lost its stigma and remaining married has become as much a choice as getting married in first place, it's not surprising that a loving and rewarding relationship has become the gold standard for marital success. Although they know the statistics, few if any couples go to the altar expecting that their own relationship will break down. How do relationships become unhappy? What is the process that transforms happy newlyweds into emotional strangers? In the rest of this paper, I discuss my own research on marriage in the context of what others have been learning in answer to these questions.

THE STUDY OF MARRIAGE
PAST AND PRESENT

In recent years, there have been great advances in the study of couple relationships. Until the 1970s there were many studies of what was called marital "adjustment," "happiness," "success," or "satisfaction." This research was usually based on large surveys in which people's ratings of their own marital happiness were correlated with other characteristics. The best-established correlates were demographic factors, such as occupation, education, income, age at marriage, religious participation, and the like. There was little theorizing about why these links might exist.

The use of self-reported ratings to study marriage came under a lot of criticism. Some researchers argued that the concept of marital happiness was hopelessly vague; others questioned the validity of simply asking people to rate their own marriages. But there were deeper problems with these earlier studies. Even the best self-report measure can hardly capture what goes on in the private psychosocial theater of married life.

In the 1970s, a new wave of marital research began to breach the wall of marital privacy. Psychologists, clinicians, and social scientists began to observe families interacting with one another in laboratories and clinics, usually through one-way mirrors. The new technology of videotaping made it possible to preserve these interactions for later analysis. Behavioral therapists and researchers began to produce a literature describing the behavior of happy and unhappy couples. At the same time, social psychologists began to study close relationships of various kinds.

During this period I began my own research into marriage, using couples who had taken part in the longitudinal studies carried out at the Institute of Human Development (IHD) at the University of California at Berkeley. One member of the couple had been part of the study since childhood, and had been born either in 1921 or 1928. Each spouse had been interviewed in depth in 1958, when the study members were 30 or 37 years old. They were interviewed again in 1970 and 1982.

Despite the richness of the longitudinal data, it did not include observations of the spouses interacting with one another, a method of research that did not come on the scene until the study was decades old. On the other hand, few of the new observational studies of marriage have included the kind of in-depth material on the couples' lives as did the longitudinal study. It seemed to me that the ideal study of marriage, assuming cost was not an issue, would include both observational and interview data as well as a sort of ethnography of the couples' lives at home. A few years ago, I was offered the opportunity to be involved in a small version of such a project in a study of the marriages of police officers. I will discuss this study later on.

The new wave of research has revealed a great deal about the complex emotional dynamics of marriage, and perhaps most usefully, revealed that some widespread beliefs about couple relations are incorrect. But there is still a great deal more to learn. There is as yet no grand theory of marriage, no one royal road to understanding marriage, no one size fits all prescriptions for marital success. But we have gained some important insights to marital (and marriage-like) relationships. And there seems to be a striking convergence of findings emerging from different approaches to studying couples. Here are some of these insights.

For Better and For Worse

The sociologist Jesse Bernard argued that every marriage contains two marriages, the husband's and the wife's (1972), and that his is better than hers. Bernard's claims have been controversial, but in general, her idea that husbands and wives have different perspectives on their marriage has held up over time.

But apart from gender differences, marital relationships also seem to divide in two another way: every marriage contains within it both a good marriage and bad marriage. Early studies of marital quality assumed that all marriages could be lined up along a single dimension of satisfaction, adjustment or happiness—happy couples would be at one end of the scale, unhappy ones at the other, and most couples would fall somewhere in between.

More recently, marriage researchers have found that that you need two separate dimensions to capture the quality of a relationship, a positive dimension and a negative one. The key to marital happiness is the balance between the good marriage and the bad one. The finding emerges in different ways in studies using different methods.

In my own research, I came across this same "good marriage–bad marriage" phenomenon among the Berkeley longitudinal couples (Skolnick, 1981). First, we identified couples ranging from high and low in marital satisfaction based on ratings of the marriage each spouse had made, combined with ratings made by clinical interviewers who had seen each separately. Later we examined transcripts of the clinical interviews to see how people who had scored high or low on measures of marital quality described their marriages. In the course of the interview, each person was asked about his or her satisfactions and dissatisfactions in the relationship.

Surprisingly, looking only at statements about dissatisfaction, it was hard to tell the happily married from their unhappy counterparts. None of the happy spouses were without some complaints or irritations. One husband went on at length at what a terrible homemaker his wife was. The wife in one of the most highly rated marriages reported having "silent arguments"—periods of not speaking to one another—which lasted about a week. "People always say you should talk over your differences," the wife said, "but it doesn't work in our family."

Only in descriptions of the satisfactions of the marriage did the contrast emerge. The happy couples described close, affectionate, and often romantic relationships. One man remarked after almost 30 years of marriage, "I still have stars in my eyes." A woman said, "I just can't wait for him to get home every night; just having him around is terrific."

The most systematic evidence for this good marriage/bad marriage model emerges from the extensive program of studies of marital interaction carried out by Gottman, Levenson, and associates (1992, 1998). Their research is based on videotaped observations of couple discussions in a laboratory setting. These intensive studies not only record facial expressions, gestures, and tone of voice, but also monitor heart rates and other physiological indicators of stress.

Surprisingly, these studies do not confirm the widespread notion that anger is the great destroyer of marital relationships. Among the indicators that do predict marital distress and eventual divorce are high levels of physiological arousal, that is stress, as couples interact with one another, a tendency for quarrels to escalate in intensity, and a tendency to keep the argument going even after the other person has tried to "make up" and end it.

As noted earlier, the key factor in the success of a marriage is not the amount of anger or other negative emotion in the relationship—no marriage always runs smoothly and cheerfully—but the balance between positive and negative feelings and actions. Indeed, Gottman gives a precise estimate of this ratio in successful marriages—five to one. In other words, the "good" marriage has to be five times better than the "bad" marriage is bad.

It seems as if the "good" marriage acts like a reservoir of positive feelings that can keep arguments from escalating out of control. In virtually every marriage and family, "emotional brushfires" are constantly breaking out. Whether these flare-ups develop into major bonfires depends on the balance between the good marriage and the bad one.

Gottman identifies a set of four behavioral patterns, that he calls "the four horsemen of the apocalypse;" they constitute a series of escalating signs of marital breakdown. These include: criticism (not just complaining about a specific act, but denouncing the spouse's whole character); contempt (insults, name calling, mockery); then defensiveness (each spouse feeling hurt, mistreated and misunderstood by the other); and finally, stonewalling (one or both partners withdraws into silence and avoidance).

Tolstoy Was Wrong: Happy Marriages Are Not All Alike

The most common approach to understanding marriage, as we have seen, is to correlate ratings of marital happiness with other variables. But focusing on *variables* masks an enormous amount of *individual* variation. Some studies over the years, however, have looked at differences among marriages at a given level of satisfaction. Among the first was a widely cited study published in 1965. John Cuber and Peggy Harroff interviewed 437 successful upper-middle-class men and women about their lives and marriages. These people had been married for at least 15 years to their original spouses, and reported themselves as being satisfied with their marriages. Yet the authors found enormous variation in marital style among these stable, contented upscale couples.

Only one out of six marriages in the sample conformed to the image of what marriage is supposed to be—that is, a relationship based on strong emotional bonds of love and friendship. The majority of others, however, did not fit the ideal model. Some couples were "conflict habituated," the bickering, battling spouses often portrayed in plays, movies, and television. Yet they were content with their marriages and did not define their fighting as a problem.

A second group of couples were in "devitalized" marriages; starting out in close, loving relationships, they had drifted apart over the years. In the third "passive congenial" type of relationship, the partners were never in love or emotionally close in the first place. Marriage for these couples was a comfortable and convenient lifestyle, leaving them free to devote their energy to their careers or other interests.

The most recent studies of marital types come from the research of John Gottman and his colleagues, described earlier. Along with identifying early warning signs of later marital trouble and divorce, Gottman also observed that happy, successful marriages were not all alike. Moreover, he also found that much of the conventional wisdom about marriage is misguided.

For example, marital counselors and popular writings on marriage often advocate what Gottman calls a "validation" or "active-listening" model. They recommend that when couples have a disagreement, they should speak to one another as a therapist speaks to a client. For example, a wife is supposed to state her complaints directly to the husband, in the form of "I" statements, for example, "I feel you're not doing your share of the housework." Then he is supposed to calmly respond by paraphrasing what she has said, and empathize with her feelings, "Sounds like you're upset about this."

To their surprise, Gottman and his colleagues found that very few couples actually fit this therapeutically approved, "validating" model of marriage. Like Cuber and Harroff, they found that people can be happily married even if they fight a lot; Gottman calls these "volatile" marriages. At the opposite extreme, were "avoidant" couples, who did not argue or even talk about their conflicts. These happily married couples also defied conventional wisdom about the importance of "communication" in marriage.

In my own study, I too found a great deal of variation among the longitudinal couples. Apart from the deep friendship that typified all the happy couples they differed in many other ways. Some spent virtually 24 hours a day together, others went their own ways, going off to parties or weekends alone. Some were very traditional in their gender patterns, others egalitarian. Some were emotionally close to their relatives, some were distant. Some had a wide circle of friends, some were virtual hermits.

They could come from happy or unhappy families. The wife in one of the happiest marriages had a very difficult relationship with her father; she grew up "hating men" and planned never to marry. Her husband also grew up in an unhappy home where the parents eventually divorced. In short, if the emotional core of marriage is good, it seems to matter very little what kind of lifestyle the couple chooses to follow.

Marriage Is a Movie, Not a Snapshot

The ancient Greek philosopher Heroclitis once said that you can never step into the same river twice, because it is always moving. The same is true of marriage. A variety of studies show that over a relatively short period of time, marriages and families can change in the ways they interact and in their emotional atmosphere. In studies of police officer couples, to be described in more detail below, the same marriage could look very different from one laboratory session to the next, depending on how much stress the officer had experienced on each day.

The IHD longitudinal studies made it possible to follow the same couples over several decades. Consider the following examples, based on the first two adult follow-ups around 1960 and the early 1970s (Skolnick, 1981):

Seen in 1960, when they were in their early 30s, the marriage of Jack and Ellen did not look promising. Jack was an aloof husband and uninvolved father. Ellen was overwhelmed by caring for three small children. She had a variety of physical ailments, and needed a steady dose of tranquilizers to calm her anxieties. Ten years later, however, she was in good health and enjoying life. She and Jack had become a warm, loving couple.

Martin and Julia were a happily married couple in 1960. They had two children they adored, an active social life, and were fixing up a new home they had bought.

Martin was looking forward to a new business venture. A decade later, Martin had developed a severe drinking problem that had disrupted every aspect of their relationship. Thinking seriously about divorce, Julia said it all had started when the business had started to fail and ultimately went bankrupt.

Perhaps the most striking impression from following these marriages through long periods of time is the great potential for change in intimate relationships. Those early interviews, suggest that many couples had what would today be called "dysfunctional" marriages. At the time, it seemed to the spouses, as well as to the interviewers, that the source of the trouble was psychological problems in the husband or wife or both, or else that they were incompatible.

For some couples, such explanations were valid: at later interviews the same emotional or personality difficulties were clear. Some people, however, had divorced and married again to people with whom they were a better fit. One man who had seemed emotionally immature all his life finally found happiness in his third marriage. He married a younger woman who was both nurturing to him and yet a "psychological age mate," as he put it.

Although close to a third of the IHD marriages eventually did end in divorce, all the IHD couples were married years before the divorce revolution of the 1970s made divorce legally easier to obtain, as well as more common and socially acceptable. Many unhappy couples remained married long enough to outgrow their earlier difficulties, or advance past the circumstances that were causing the difficulties in the first place. Viewed from a later time, marital distress at one period or stage in life seemed to be rooted in situational factors: problems at work, trouble with in-laws or money, bad housing, or too many babies too close together. In the midst of these strains, however, it was easy to blame problems on a husband's or a wife's basic character. Only later, when the situation had changed, did it seem that there was nothing inherently wrong with the couple's relationship.

The Critical Events of a Marriage May Not Be inside the Marriage

The longitudinal data, as noted above, revealed a striking amount of change for better or worse depending on a large variety of life circumstances. While the impact of such external factors remains a relatively understudied source of marital distress, there has been growing interest in the impact of work and working conditions—especially job stress—on family life. One of the most stressful occupations, police work, also suffers from very high rates of divorce, domestic violence, and alcoholism. In 1997, Robert Levenson and I took part in collaboration between the University of California and a West Coast urban police department (Levenson, Roberts, and Bellows, 1998; Skolnick, 1998). We focused on job stress and marriage. This was a small, exploratory study, using too few couples—eleven—for statistical analysis, but it yielded some striking preliminary findings.

Briefly, Levenson's part of the study looked at the impact of stress on couple interaction in the laboratory. His procedures called for each spouse keep a stress diary every day for 30 days. Once a week for four weeks, the couples came to the laboratory at the end of the work day, after eight hours of being apart. Their interaction was videotaped, and physiological responses of each spouse were monitored continuously.

In my part of the project, we used an adaptation of the IHD clinical interview with officers and their wives in their homes. (The sample did not include female officers or police couples.) The aim was to examine their perceptions of police work and its impact on their marriages, their general life circumstances, and the sources of stress and support in their lives. I discovered that these officers and their wives were making heroic efforts to do well in their work and family lives against enormous odds. The obvious dangers and disasters police must deal with are only part of the story; sleep deprivation, frustration with the department bureaucracy, and inadequate equipment were some of the other factors adding up to an enormous stress.

In spite of their difficult lives, these couples seemed to have good, well-functioning marriages, at home and in the laboratory, except on high stress days. Levenson's study was able to examine the direct effects of different levels of stress on the face-to-face interaction of these couples—something that had not been done before. The findings were striking. Variations in the husband's work stress had a marked impact on both couple interaction and the physiological indicators of emotional arousal.

More surprising, it was not just the police officer who showed evidence of stress, but the partner as well. Even before either partner had said a word, while they were just sitting quietly, both the officer and the spouse showed signs of physiological arousal. In particular, there was a kind of "paralysis of the positive emotion system" in both partners (Levenson, Roberts, and Bellows, 1998). Looking at the videotapes, you didn't need the physiological measures to see what was going on. The husband's restless agitation was clear, as was the wife's tense and wary response to it. The wives seemed frozen in their seats, barely able to move. In fact, just watching the couples on videotape is enough to make a viewer also feel tense and uneasy.

Recall that these couples did not look or act this way on the days they were not under high job stress. However, on high stress days, the couples were showing the same warning signs that Gottman and Levenson had found in their earlier studies to be predictors of divorce. The "paralysis of the positive emotion system" means that the "good" aspects of the marriage were unavailable just when they were most needed. Repeated often enough, such moments can strain even a good marriage; they create an emotional climate where tempers can easily flare, hurtful things may be said, and problems go unsolved. Police work may be an extreme example of a high-pressure occupation, but it is far from the only one. "What's the difference between a stressed-out business executive and a stressed-out police officer?" asked a New York columnist not long ago, after a terrible case of domestic violence in a police family. "The officer," he went on, "brings home a loaded gun."

CAN MARRIAGE BE SAVED?

The notion that marriage is a dying institution is remarkably persistent among the American public. Politicians and social critics, particularly conservative ones, insist that divorce, cohabitation, single parenthood, and other recent trends signal moral decline and the unraveling of the social fabric. Some family scholars agree with these pessimistic conclusions. Others argue that marriage and the family are not collapsing but simply becoming more diverse.

A third possibility is that American families are passing through a cultural lag, a difficult in-between period, as they adapt to new social and economic conditions. While a rapidly changing world outside the home has moved towards greater gender equality, the roles of men and women inside the home have changed relatively little. Across the twentieth century, schools, businesses, the professions, and other institutions have become increasingly neutral about gender. Moreover, legal and political trends in modern democracies have undermined the legitimacy of gender and other forms of caste-like inequality, at least in principle.

To be sure, we have not yet achieved full equality. But we have become used to seeing women in the workplace, even in such formerly all-male institutions as the police, the military, the Congress, and the Supreme Court. The family remains the one institution still based on separate and distinct roles for men and women. Despite the vast social and economic changes that have transformed our daily lives, the old gender roles remain deeply rooted in our cultural assumptions and definitions of masculinity and femininity. At the same time, a more equal or "symmetrical" model of marriage is struggling to be born. Surveys show that most Americans, especially young people, favor equal rather than traditional marriage.

But the transition to such a model has been difficult, even for those committed to the idea of equal partnerships. The difficulties of raising children, and men's continuing advantages in the workplace, make it hard for all but the most dedicated couples to live up to their own ideals.

Adding to the difficulties are the economic shifts of recent years—growing economic inequality, the demise of the well-paying blue-collar job, and the end of the stable career of the 1950s "organization man." The long hours and working weeks that have replaced the nine-to-five corporate workplace take their toll on relationships.

Traditionally, marriage has always been linked to economic opportunity—a young man had to be able to support a wife to be considered eligible to marry. The high rates of marriage in the 1950s were sustained in part by rising wages and a relatively low cost of living; the average 30-year-old man could afford to buy an average-priced house for less than 20 percent of his salary. Today, marriage is becoming something of a "luxury item," a form of "having" available mainly to those already enjoying economic advantages (Furstenberg, 1996). The vast majority of low income men and women would like the "luxury" model, but feel they can't afford it.

Inside marriage, conflicts stemming from gender issues have become the leading cause of divorce (Nock, 1999). Studies of couples married since the 1970s reveal the dynamics of these conflicts. Arlie Hochchild, for example, has found that the happiest marriages are those where the husband does his share of the "second shift," the care of home and children. Another recent study shows that today's women also expect their husbands to do their share of the emotional work of marriage—monitoring and talking about the relationship itself; this "marital work ethic" has emerged in middle class couples married since the 1970s, in response to easy and widespread divorce (Hackstaff, 2000).

Dominance is another sore point in many of today's marriages. Gottman and his colleagues (1998) have found that a key factor in predicting marital happiness and divorce is a husband's willingness to accept influence from his wife; but to many men, the loss of dominance in marriage doesn't feel like equality, it feels more like a shift in power that leaves their wives dominant over them. Studies of battered women show that domestic violence may be the extreme form of this common problem—the man's attempt to assert what he sees as his prerogative to dominate and control his partner.

Still, change is happening, even while men lag behind in the gender revolution. Today's men no longer expect to be waited on in the home the way their grandfathers were by their grandmothers. Middle class norms demand a more involved kind of father than those of a generation ago. The sight of a man with a baby in his arms or on his back is no longer unusual.

In sum, marriage today is passing through a difficult transition to a new economy and a new ordering of gender relations. Those who sermonize about "family values" need to recall that the family is also about "bread and butter" issues and back up their words with resources. And while some people believe that equality and stable marriage are incompatible, the evidence seems so far to show the opposite. As one therapist and writer puts it:

> The feminist revolution of this century has provided the most powerful challenge to traditional patterns of marriage. Yet paradoxically, it may have strengthened the institution by giving greater freedom to both partners, and by allowing men to accept some of traditionally female values. (Rubenstein, 1990)

References

Bernard, J. 1972. *The Future of Marriage*. New York: Bantam Books.

Furstenberg, F. 1996. The future of marriage. *American Demographics* (June): 34–40.

Gottman, J. M. and R. W. Levenson. 1992. Marital processes predictive of later dissolution: behavior, physiology and health. *Journal of Personality and Social Psychology* 63:221–33.

Gottman, J. M., J. Coan, S. Carrere, and C. Swanson. 1998. Predicting marital happiness and stability from newlywed interactions. *Journal of Marriage and the Family* 60:5–22.

Hackstaff, K. 2000. *Marriage in a Culture of Divorce*. Boston: Beacon Press.

Levenson, R. W., N. Roberts, and S. Bellows. 1998. Report on police marriage and work stress study. Unpublished paper, University of California, Berkeley.

National Marriage Project. 1999. *Report on Marriage*. Rutgers University.

Nock, S. L. 1999. The problem with marriage. *Society* 36, No. 5 (July/August).

Rubinstein, H. 1990. *The Oxford Book of Marriage*. New York: Oxford University Press.

Skolnick, A. 1981. Married lives: longitudinal perspectives on marriage. In *Present and Past in Middle Life*, edited by D. H. Eichorn, J. A. Clausen, N. Haan, M. P. Honzik, and P. H. Mussen, 269–298. New York: Academic Press.

———. 1993. His and her marriage in longitudinal perspective. In *Feminine/Masculine: Gender and Social Change*. Compendium of Research Summaries. New York: The Rockefeller Foundation.

———. 1998. Sources and processes of police marital stress. Paper presented at National Conference on Community Policing. November. Arlington, Va.

Veroff, J. G., E. Douvan, and R. A. Kulka. 1981. *The Inner American: A Self-Portrait from 1957–1976*. New York: Basic Books.

■READING 14

Cohabitation

Lynne M. Casper and Suzanne M. Bianchi

Shacking up. Living in sin. Living together. Persons of the opposite sex sharing living quarters. Doubling up. Sleeping together. All of these expressions have been used to describe the living arrangement that demographers refer to as cohabitation. Some of these terms are more value laden than others, and the one an individual chooses to describe this living arrangement can say a great deal about how he or she views unmarried sexual partners. Although *cohabitation* can refer to same-sex couples, most of the demographic research conducted to date has been concerned with opposite-sex partners.

The increase in heterosexual cohabitation that has accompanied the delay in marriage and increase in divorce is one of the most significant changes in family life to take place in the latter half of the 20th century (Seltzer 2000; Smock 2000). Some observers believe that the increase in cohabitation has eroded commitment to marriage and "traditional" family life (e.g., Waite and Gallagher 2000). One of the best examples of this view is presented in a report titled *Should We Live Together? What Young Adults Need to Know About Cohabitation Before Marriage*, published by the National Marriage Project (Popenoe and Whitehead 1999). This controversial report paints an overwhelmingly negative picture of cohabitation, asserting that "cohabiting unions tend to weaken the institution of marriage and pose clear and present dangers to women and children."

Most adults in the United States eventually marry: 91 percent of women ages 45 to 54 in 1998 had been married at least once (Bianchi and Casper 2000:15), and an estimated 88 percent of women in younger cohorts are likely to marry eventually (Raley 2000). But the meaning and permanence of marriage may be changing as cohabitation increases.

Marriage used to be the demographic event that almost exclusively marked the formation of a new household, the beginning of sexual relations, and the birth of a child. Marriage also typically implied that each partner had one sexual partner and identified the two individuals who would parent any child born of the union. The increasing social acceptance of cohabitation outside marriage has meant that these linkages can no longer be assumed. Also, what it means to be "married" or "single" is changing as the personal lives of unmarried couples come to resemble those of their married counterparts in some ways but not in others (Seltzer 2000; Smock 2000).

Cohabiting and marital relationships have much in common: coresidence; emotional, psychological, and sexual intimacy; and some degree of economic interdependence. But the two relationships differ in other important ways. Marriage is a relationship between two people of opposite sexes that adheres to legal, moral, and social rules, a social institution that rests upon common values and shared expectations for appropriate behavior within the partnership (Nock 1998b). Society upholds and enforces appropriate marital behavior both formally and informally. In contrast, there is no widely recognized social blueprint or script for the appropriate behavior of cohabitors, or for the behavior of the friends, families, and other individuals and institutions with whom they interact. There is no common term in use for referring to one's nonmarital live-in lover, whereas the terms *spouse, husband,* and *wife* are institutionalized. Most important, there is far greater societal acceptance of marriage—and far more ambivalence about cohabitation—as a desirable adult relationship for the rearing of children.

We begin this chapter with the intriguing story of the growth in cohabitation in the latter decades of the 20th century. Tracking trends in cohabitation has been difficult because until recently there was no direct measurement of the numbers of unmarried partners living together. Until the late 1980s, when national surveys began the routine collection of information on cohabitation, researchers relied on indirect estimates to document the increase in cohabitation. The 1987–88 National Survey of Families and Households (NSFH) collected the first cohabitation histories. The 1990 Census was the first census enumeration that included "unmarried partner" among a list of categories from which a respondent could choose in identifying his or her household relationship. Beginning in 1995, the Current Population Survey (CPS) also included the category "unmarried partner" as a possible response to the household relationship question, and the National Survey of Family Growth began to obtain detailed data on cohabitation.

In the discussion that follows, we use CPS data and indirect estimates to examine the growth in cohabitation since the late 1970s. In an effort to understand more about the meaning of cohabitation, we review relevant research on this topic, compare cohabitors with married and single people, and examine how cohabitors view themselves. We also investigate whether cohabitors are becoming more like married people over time as cohabitation becomes a more common experience and gains wider social acceptance. We describe the linkages between cohabitation and other demographic events and the potential positive and negative consequences they engender. We conclude the chapter with a discussion of what demographers know about cohabitation and what this implies for the future of marriage and family life in the United States.

WHO COHABITS AND HOW HAS THIS CHANGED OVER TIME?

Unmarried heterosexual cohabitation began to capture national attention during and after the period of well-publicized student unrest on college campuses in the late 1960s and early 1970s. The image of the time was of sexually promiscuous college students experimenting with new family forms by living with their boyfriends or girlfriends rather than marrying, often trying to keep their arrangements secret from their disapproving parents. In the 1970s, Paul Glick and Arthur Norton (1977) of the U.S. Census Bureau were the first to use information on household composition from the decennial census and CPS to define cohabitors as "persons of the opposite sex sharing living quarters," or POSSLQs for short.

Figure 1 shows changes in cohabitation using a modified version of the indirect POSSLQ measure (Casper and Cohen 2000). The proportion of unmarried women who were cohabiting tripled, from 3 percent to 9 percent, between 1978 and 1998. Increases

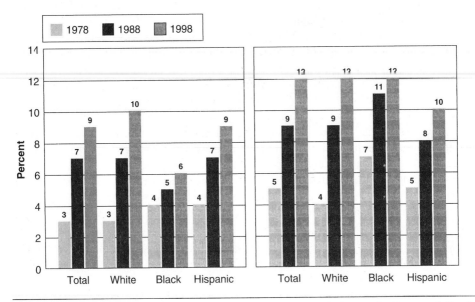

FIGURE 1 *Percentages of Unmarried Men and Women Cohabiting, by Race and Gender: 1978–1998*

Race/ethnicity categories are white, non-Hispanic; black, non-Hispanic; and Hispanic.

Source: Current Population Survey, March supplements, 1978, 1988, 1998.

were similar among unmarried men—from 5 percent to nearly 12 percent—with men more likely than women to cohabit, both in 1978 and in 1998.

These estimates of cohabitation may seem low, especially considering the heightened concern of some observers that cohabitation is eroding commitment to marriage and family life. The rates are low, in part, because they represent only those who are cohabiting at a given point in time. A much larger proportion of people have ever cohabited, and the likelihood of cohabiting appears to be increasing over time. Only 8 percent of first marriages in the late 1960s were preceded by cohabitation, compared with 49 percent in 1985–86 (Bumpass 1990) and 56 percent by the early to mid-1990s (Bumpass and Lu 2000). Thus, young couples today are more likely to begin their coresidential relationships in cohabitation than in marriage.

Why has cohabitation increased so much? A number of factors, including increased uncertainty about the stability of marriage, the erosion of norms against cohabitation and sexual relations outside of marriage, the availability of reliable birth control, and the weakening of religious and other normative constraints on individuals' family decisions, seem to be ending the taboo against living together without marrying. For example, by the mid-1990s, a majority of high school seniors thought that living together prior to marriage was a good idea (Axinn and Thornton 2000).

Some argue that cohabitation reduces the costs of partnering, especially if one is uncertain about a potential mate, and allows a couple to experience the benefits of an intimate relationship without committing to marriage (Willis and Michael 1994). If a cohabiting relationship is not successful, one can simply move out; if a marriage is not successful, one suffers through a sometimes lengthy and messy divorce.

Meanwhile, the development of effective contraceptives has given childbearing-age couples greater freedom to engage in sexual intercourse without the risk of unwanted pregnancy. The availability of reliable birth control has increased the prevalence of premarital sex. As premarital sex has become more common, it has become more widely accepted, and so has living with a partner before marriage (Bumpass and Sweet 1989a). Widespread availability of contraception also makes it easier to avoid unwanted pregnancy if one chooses to live with a partner after separation or divorce from a previous marriage.

Shifting norms mean that adults today are more likely to believe that cohabitation and divorce are acceptable and less likely to believe that marriage is a lifelong commitment than was true in the past (Thornton 1989; Thornton and Freedman 1983). Thus the normative barrier that once discouraged cohabitation has begun to wither away. Increasingly, American values have shifted from those favoring family commitment and self-sacrifice to those favoring self-fulfillment, individual growth, and personal freedom (Lasch 1979; Lesthaeghe 1995; McLanahan and Casper 1995).

Early estimates suggested that college students were in the vanguard of attitudinal and behavior changes that fostered the growth in cohabitation. Glick and Norton (1977:34), for example, highlighted the fact that a greater proportion of unmarried than married couples (8 percent versus 5 percent) included two partners who were college students and that, in 1970, one-fourth of unmarried couples had at least one partner who was enrolled in college. Subsequent research, however, has documented that cohabitation is a behavior that is prevalent among less educated individuals. Larry Bumpass and James Sweet (1989b), in discussing the first direct estimates of cohabitation, note: "Contrary to a common view of cohabitation as college student behavior, education is strongly and negatively related to rates of cohabitation before first marriage. The highest rates are found among the least educated" (p. 622).

CPS trends, based on indirect estimates, indicate that about 16 percent of men who cohabit are college graduates; this figure has remained quite stable over time (see Table 1). Among women, the estimate in 1998 was 17 percent, up from 13 percent in 1978 and 1988. Other estimates of the likelihood that an individual will ever cohabit suggest that increases in the rates of cohabitation continue to be greater for those with only a high school education than for those with a college education (Bumpass and Lu 2000).

Who cohabits defies stereotypes in other ways as well. For example, increasingly, cohabitation is not a phenomenon confined to early adulthood. Although more than 60 percent of cohabiting men and almost two-thirds of women in unmarried partnerships were under age 35 in 1978, these proportions have declined. In 1998, a relatively high percentage of cohabitors were in their mid-30s or older (almost 50 percent of men and more than 40 percent of women in 1998). As age at first marriage increases, the average age of cohabitors also appears to be increasing. In addition, living together without marrying is common after first marriages end as well as before they begin. In 1998, 45 percent of the men and 51 percent of the women in heterosexual unmarried couples had been previously married, with the vast majority either separated or divorced.

One of the biggest compositional shifts that is occurring among unmarried couples is the increase in the presence of children in these households, either children born to the couple or those that one of the partners has from a prior relationship. In 1978, about 28 percent of cohabitor households included children under age 18 (see Table 1). By 1998, the proportion had increased to 37 percent. About two-fifths of all children spend at least some years during their childhoods living with a parent and the parent's unmarried partner, according to recent estimates by Bumpass and Lu (2000:35). This percentage is high both because of the popularity of cohabitation after separation and divorce, where children from a prior marriage may be present, and because more births outside marriage are to mothers who are living with their partners.

TABLE 1 *Presence of Children, Age, and Marital Status among Unmarried Couples: 1978–1998 (in percentages)*

	All Couples		
	1978	1988	1998
Age			
Men			
Total	100.0	100.0	100.0
15–24	21.2	18.2	15.1
25–34	40.3	40.5	37.2
35+	38.5	41.3	47.7
Women			
Total	100.0	100.0	100.0
15–24	35.5	25.8	21.8
25–34	29.9	39.4	34.4
35+	34.6	34.8	43.8
Marital status			
Men			
Total	100.0	100.0	100.0
Separated/divorced	46.9	45.3	42.2
Widowed	6.5	3.3	3.2
Never married	46.7	51.4	54.6
Women			
Total	100.0	100.0	100.0
Separated/divorced	39.3	44.2	44.9
Widowed	15.1	8.0	5.7
Never married	45.7	47.9	49.4
Children in the household	27.6	33.8	37.1
College graduates			
Men	15.8	16.0	16.3
Women	13.4	13.3	17.1

Unmarried partners estimated with adjusted POSSLQ measure (see Casper and Cohen 2000).

Source: Current Population Survey, March supplements, 1978, 1988, 1998.

The proportion of births to unmarried mothers who are actually living with their partners (often their children's fathers) increased from 29 percent in the mid-1980s to near 40 percent in the mid-1990s (Bumpass and Lu 2000:35). In some European countries, most notably Scandinavian countries, cohabitation increasingly seems to function as a substitute for marriage, with couples unlikely to marry before the birth of their children. In the United States, the likelihood of marriage with the birth of a child is declining but seems to be a far smaller component of the increase in children in cohabiting unions than in Europe.

As more women spend time in cohabiting relationships, the time "at risk" of a pregnancy while a women is living with an unmarried partner goes up. Most of the increase in births to cohabitors (as much as 70 percent) is due to this factor (Raley 2001). Cohabiting women who become pregnant have become a little less likely to marry before the birth, and single women who become pregnant have become more likely to move in with the father of the child rather than remain single or marry. Yet these two changes in behavior—staying in a cohabiting arrangement rather than marrying if one becomes pregnant or moving in with a partner rather than marrying if one becomes pregnant while single—account for only about 10 percent of the increase in births to cohabiting women (Raley 2001:66).

The increased recognition that many unmarried couples are raising children is leading to greater attention to the ways in which children's lives may be affected by the marital status of their parents. For example, children born to unmarried couples have a higher risk of experiencing their parents' separation than do children born to married couples (Bumpass, Raley, and Sweet 1995). The ties that bind fathers to their children may also be weaker in cohabiting than in marital relationships: After parents separate, children whose parents never married see their fathers less often and are less likely to be financially supported by their fathers than are children born to married parents (Cooksey and Craig 1998; Seltzer 2000)....

COHABITATION AND MARRIAGE

Much of the demographic research on cohabitation has been oriented around one question: How similar is (heterosexual) cohabitation to marriage? Economic theorists often view marriage as an institution in which individual goals are replaced by altruism and the subordination of self-interest in favor of goals that benefit the family (e.g., Becker 1991). Married couples supposedly maximize benefits for their families by specializing in different activities—wives tend to specialize in homemaking and husbands tend to specialize in breadwinning. This gender role difference has meant that women tend to seek spouses with higher education and earnings than themselves—men who would be good breadwinners. Men, by contrast, tend to look for women who will be good mothers and homemakers.

Evidence suggests that cohabitation may attract individuals who value more egalitarian, less specialized, gender roles. Gender-differentiated roles are not absent from cohabiting unions; for example, cohabiting couples with higher-earning male (but not female) partners are the ones that proceed more quickly to marriage (Sanchez, Manning, and Smock 1998). Yet research has found that cohabiting relationships endure longer when partners' employment patterns and earnings are more similar than different (Brines and Joyner 1999). Cohabiting couples also tend to divide housework in a more egalitarian fashion than do married couples (South and Spitze 1994), and cohabitors are less likely to espouse traditional gender roles (Clarkberg, Stolzenberg, and Waite 1995; Lesthaeghe and Surkyn 1988).

Cohabitation may also be especially attractive to those with more individualistic, more materialistic, and less family-oriented outlooks on life. Cohabitors are more likely than others to believe that individual freedom is important in a marriage (Thomson and Colella 1992). Men and women are more likely to choose cohabitation as their first union if it is important to them to have "lots of money" in life (Clarkberg et al. 1995). Women who value their careers are more likely than other women to cohabit for their first union, whereas those who think that finding the right person to marry and having a happy family life is important are more likely than others to begin their first union with marriage (Clarkberg et al. 1995).

Cohabitors are also more accepting of divorce. They are less likely than married persons to disapprove of divorce (Lesthaeghe and Surkyn 1988), with those who disapprove of divorce more likely to begin their first union with marriage (Axinn and Thornton 1992). Children of divorced parents are more likely to cohabit than are children of married parents (Cherlin, Kiernan, and Chase-Lansdale 1995), in part because people whose mothers divorced tend to hold attitudes that are more approving of cohabitation (Axinn and Thornton 1996).

To the extent that cohabitation is an "incomplete institution" lacking clear normative standards (Nock 1995), it may provide a more comfortable setting than marriage for less conventional couples. Perhaps the strongest indicator of this is the higher percentage of cohabiting than married couples who cross the racial divide in their partnerships (see Table 2). Cohabiting couples are more than twice as likely to be of different races than married couples—13 percent compared with 5 percent. About half of interracial cohabiting couples are made up of a white woman and a man of another race (data not shown).

Schoen and Weinick (1993) argue that because cohabiting relationships tend to be short-term relationships, cohabiting partners are less concerned with the ascribed characteristics of their partners than are the partners in married couples. Half of all cohabitations last a year or less; only about one-sixth of cohabitations last at least 3 years, and only one-tenth last 5 years or more (Bumpass and Lu 2000). Thus an individual's choosing a partner of the same age, race, and religion as him- or herself is not as important in cohabitation as it is in marriage, because cohabitation does not necessarily entail a long-term commitment or the accompanying normative standards such a relationship implies.

It is much more common in cohabiting than in marital relationships for the female partner to be older and better educated than her male partner (see Table 2). Women are more than 2 years older than their partners in 24 percent of unmarried couples but in only 12 percent of married couples, and women have a higher educational level in 21 percent of cohabiting couples compared with only 16 percent of married couples.

The data displayed in Table 2 support the notion that cohabiting couples are more egalitarian in terms of their labor force participation and earnings. Almost four out of

TABLE 2   *Characteristics of Cohabiting and Married Couples: 1998*

	Cohabiting	Married
Total number of couples (thousands)	3,142	54,317
% of couples in which		
Woman is of different race/ethnicity than man	13	5
Woman is at least 2 years older than man	24	12
Woman has more education than man	21	16
Both man and woman worked for pay	77	60
Woman worked more hours[a]	24	16
Woman's contribution to couple's 1997 income (% of total income)[b]	41	37

A cohabiting couple is defined as an unmarried couple who maintains a household together. Race/ethnicity categories are white, non-Hispanic; black, non-Hispanic; and Hispanic.

a. Woman worked more hours than her partner in the preceding year.

b. Calculated for couples in which both partners were employed.

Source: Current Population Survey, March supplement, 1998.

five cohabiting couples have both partners employed, compared with only three in five married couples. Men tend to work more hours than their partners in cohabiting and marital relationships, but women's hours of employment exceed their partners' hours in a greater percentage of cohabiting (24 percent) than married (16 percent) couples. When employed, women and men have earnings that are closer to equality in cohabiting than in married couples; women in cohabiting couples contribute 41 percent of the couple's annual earnings, compared with 37 percent, on average, for married women.

Some of the differences shown in Table 2 reflect the fact that unmarried couples tend to be younger, on average, than married couples, and younger generations have more egalitarian attitudes toward the labor force roles of men and women and are more likely to choose partners with different racial backgrounds. However, the evidence in Table 2, combined with the attitudinal and family background differences between unmarried and married couples noted in other research, suggests that cohabitation provides a living arrangement that suits couples who may be somewhat uncertain about whether their partnerships can be sustained over the long term. These may be couples who must work out issues that surround partnering across racial lines, couples who defy patterns that are considered "normal" in the larger society (such as when an "older" woman partners with a "younger" man or a more educated woman partners with a less educated mate), or couples for whom an equal economic partnership is a priority and who may be concerned that marriage will propel them into a gendered division of labor that will make it difficult to sustain their egalitarianism. . . .

CONCLUSION

Cohabitation has increased dramatically over a relatively short period of time, raising concerns about the effects of this new family form on the institutions of marriage and the family in the United States. Currently, the majority of individuals live with partners before they marry. Hence the lines that differentiate marriage from being single have faded over time. The effects of cohabitation on the institution of marriage are likely to vary according to how cohabitors view their relationships. Some cohabitors have definite plans to marry their partners and end up doing so, whereas others live together in relationships of convenience with low levels of commitment—these couples often separate.

Not only is cohabitation increasing among people who have not entered a first marriage, it is also slowing the rate of remarriage after divorce or separation. Almost one-half of those cohabiting at any given point in time are doing so after rather than before a first marriage. In part due to the role cohabitation is playing after marriages end, the characteristics of cohabitors are changing. Compared with 20 years ago, more of them are older than age 35 and more cohabiting households include children. And, although cohabitation was initially linked to experimentation among college students, its increase has been widespread and its popularity today is as great or greater among those with less education.

As cohabitation continues to increase and to become more normative, will it replace marriage as the preferred living arrangement for raising children in the United States, as it seems to have done in some countries, most notably Sweden? The answer still seems to be no. Although unmarried partners do not necessarily rush to marry if the woman becomes pregnant, and single women who become pregnant may move in with their partners rather than marry them, these behaviors are still not widespread in the United States, at least not among the majority white population. And only 1 in 10 cohabitors believes that the cohabiting relationship is a substitute for marriage. The largest factor explaining why more births occur in cohabiting relationships today than two decades ago is merely that so many more people cohabit before and after marriage. What this means, however, is that a significant percentage of the babies born to unmarried mothers—perhaps as large a proportion as 40 percent—actually begin life residing with both parents, who live together but are not married.

Demographers are only beginning to study the heterogeneity of cohabiting relationships. New estimates suggest that about 4 percent of cohabiting couples are in same-sex relationships. One-fifth of lesbian-couple and about 5 percent of gay-couple households include children, often from one partner's previous heterosexual union. Heterosexual cohabitation is on the rise among all racial groups, although estimates of the prevalence among different groups vary by whether the percentages are calculated for all adults, unmarried adults, or all unions. Blacks have a high portion of all unions that are unmarried partnerships, but black unmarried women have relatively low rates of living with partners. The gender gap in rates of cohabitation is greatest for blacks because black unmarried men have rates of partnering as great as or greater than other racial groups. Also, more unmarried than married heterosexual couples are mixed-race couples.

Cohabiting couples defy gender stereotypes more often than do married couples: Women's and men's labor force roles are more similar and the woman's age, education, and hours of market work more often exceed the man's in cohabiting than in marital unions. Partly this is because cohabitors are younger than married couples and younger cohorts have more gender-egalitarian attitudes. Yet cohabitation also seems to be chosen as a first relationship more often by women who value career goals than by other women and by couples who either value an equal economic partnership or defy gender stereotypes in other ways (such as having a female partner who is older than the male partner).

Although researchers have been preoccupied with comparisons of cohabitation to marriage (or, in some cases, to singlehood), the reality is that cohabitation is serving a diverse set of couples with an array of reasons for living together rather than marrying. About one-half of cohabitors indicate strong intentions to marry their partners, and 1 in 10 claims that the unmarried partnership is a substitute for marrying. The remainder seem uncertain about their compatibility with their current partners, their future plans, and/or marriage as an institution. Not surprisingly, whether cohabitors marry, break up, or continue living together as unmarried couples varies by how they see their relationships. And partners often disagree on the quality of the relationship, with the partnership more likely to dissolve if the woman is unhappy and more likely to continue as a cohabitation but not proceed to marriage if the man is unhappy.

Finally, although one might think that couples' living together before or instead of marrying should make marriages more stable, because partners can discover irreconcilable differences before they tie the knot, one of the strongest findings is that those who cohabit prior to marriage divorce more often than those who do not. The debate is over whether living together makes such couples more "irreverent" toward the institution of marriage or whether they have characteristics and attitudes that are more accepting of divorce in the first place. The evidence to date suggests it is more the latter than the former, and the question is whether cohabitation will become less selective of certain types of individuals. If living together is increasingly "what one does" before marrying or remarrying, and as marital partnerships change as well, those who cohabit may become less distinct from those who marry. On economic dimensions such as labor force participation and earnings, married and unmarried partners seem less differentiated today than they were 20 years ago. Still, among whites, educational attainment may be diverging between the two groups. How cohabitation alters the future of marriage will ultimately rest on whether unmarried cohabiting couples are increasingly a distinct group of persons who doubt the possibility of long-term commitment or are merely couples captured at different points in their relationships than those who have married, but who nonetheless continue to aspire to the goal of committed family life.

Editors' Note: *References for this reading can be found in the original source.*

■ **READING 15**

Can Marriage Be Saved?

Frank F. Furstenberg, Jr.

A growing number of social scientists fear that marriage may be on the rocks and few doubt that the matrimony, as we have known it, has undergone a wrenching period of change in the past several decades. Andrew Cherlin, a leading sociologist of the family, speaks of "the de-institutionalization of marriage," conceding a point to conservative commentators who have argued that marriage and the family have been in a state of freefall since the 1960s.

Western Europe has experienced many of the same trends—declining rates of marriage, widespread cohabitation, and rising levels of nonmarital childbearing—but has largely shrugged them off. By contrast, concern about the state of marriage in the United States has touched a raw, political nerve. What ails marriage and what, if anything, can be done to restore this time-honored social arrangement to its former status as a cultural invention for assigning the rights and responsibilities of reproduction including sponsorship and inheritance.

On the left side of the political spectrum, observers believe that the institutional breakdown of marriage has its roots in economic and social changes brought about by shifts in home-based production, structural changes in the economy, and the breakdown of the gender-based division of labor—trends unlikely to be reversed. The other position, championed by most conservatives, is that people have lost faith in marriage because of changes in cultural values that could be reversed or restored through shifts in the law, changes in administrative policies and practices, and public rhetoric to alter beliefs and expectations.

The Bush administration is trying to put into place a set of policies aimed at reversing the symptoms of retreat from marriage: high rates of premarital sex, nonmarital childbearing, cohabitation, and divorce. Do their policies make sense and do they have a reasonable prospect of success? To answer this question, I want to begin with the trends that Americans, including many social scientists, have found so alarming and then turn to the question of how much public policy and what kinds of policies could help to strengthen marriage.

DEMOGRAPHIC CHANGES AND POLITICAL INTERPRETATION

When compared to the 1950s, the institution of marriage seems to be profoundly changed, but is the middle of the twentieth century an appropriate point of comparison? It has been widely known since the baby boom era that the period after the Second World War was unusual demographically: the very early onset of adult transitions; unprecedented rates of marriage; high fertility; an economy that permitted a single wage earner to support a family reasonably well; and the flow of federal funding for education, housing, and jobs distinguished the 1950s and early 1960s as a particular historical moment different from any previous period and certainly different from the decades after the Vietnam War era. For a brief time, the nuclear family in the United States and throughout much of Europe reigned supreme.

If we use the middle of the twentieth century as a comparison point, it might appear that we have been witnessing a deconstruction of the two-parent biological family en masse. But such a view is historically shortsighted and simplistic. The nuclear family, though long the bourgeois ideal, had never been universally practiced, at least as it was in the middle of the last century. Only in the 1950s—and then for a very brief time—did it become the gold standard for what constitutes a healthy family. Indeed, sociologists at that time fiercely debated whether this family model represented a decline from the "traditional" extended family. Even those who argued against this proposition could not agree whether this family form was desirable ("functional" in the language of the day) or contained fatal flaws that would be its undoing.

During the 1960s and 1970s, anthropological evidence indicated that family diversity is universal, and findings from the new field of historical demography revealed that families in both the East and the West had always been changing in response to economic, political, demographic and social conditions. In short, the nuclear family was cross-culturally and historically not "the natural unit," that many wrongly presume today.

Although it was widely known that the family had undergone considerable changes from ancient times and during the industrial revolution, that family systems varied across culture, and that social-class differences created varied forms of the family within the same society, it was not until the 1960s, when historians began to use computers to analyze census data, that the extent of this variation came into clearer focus. For the first time, family scholars from several disciplines could see the broad outlines of a new picture of how family forms and functions are intimately related to the social, cultural, and perhaps especially the economic contexts in which household and kinship systems are embedded.

From this evidence, students of the family can assert three points. First, no universal form of the family constitutes the appropriate or normative arrangement for reproduction, nurturance, socialization, and economic support. Both across and within societies, family forms, patterns, and practices vary enormously. Second, change is endemic to all family systems, and at least in the West, where we have the best evidence to date, family systems have always been in flux. Typically, these changes create tensions and often ignite public concern. Since colonial times, the family has been changing and provoking public reaction from moralists, scientists, and, of course, public authorities. Finally, family systems do not evolve in a linear fashion but become more or less complex and more elemental in different eras or among different strata of society depending on the economic and social conditions to which families must adapt.

Does this mean that we are seeing a continuation of what has always been or something different than has ever occurred in human history—the withering of kinship as an organizing feature of human society? The decline of marriage suggests to some that this round of change is unique in human history or that its consequences for children will be uniquely unsettling to society.

Many scholars weighed in on these questions. It is fair to say that there are two main camps: (1) those who have decided that the family is imperiled as a result of changes in the marriage system, a position held by such respectable social scientists as Linda Waite, Norvel Glenn, and Judith Wallerstein; and (2) those who remain skeptical and critical of those sounding the alarm, a position held by the majority of social scientists. Many in this second camp take seriously the concerns of the "alarmists" that children's welfare may be at risk if the current family regime continues. Still, they doubt that the family can be coaxed back into its 1950s form and favor adaptations in government policy to assist new forms of the family—an approach followed by most European nations.

Some portion of those skeptics are not so alarmed by changes in the family, believing that children's circumstances have not been seriously compromised by family change. They contend that children's well-being has less to do with the family form in which they reside than the resources possessed to form viable family arrangements. Lacking these resources (material and cultural), it matters little whether the children are born into a marriage, cohabitation, or a single-parent household, because they are likely not to fare as well as those whose parents possess the capacity to realize their goals.

I place myself in this latter group. Of course, children will fare better when they have two well-functioning, collaborative parents than one on average, but one well-functioning parent with resources is better than two married parents who lack the resources or skills to manage parenthood. Moreover, parents with limited cultural and material resources are unlikely to remain together in a stable marriage. Because the possession of such psychological, human, and material capital is highly related to marital stability, it is easy to confuse the effects of stable marriage with the effects of competent parenting. Finally, I believe that the best way to foster marriage stability is to support children with an array of services that assist parents and children, regardless of the family form in which they reside.

MARRIAGE AND GOOD OUTCOMES FOR CHILDREN

A huge number of studies have shown that children fare better in two-biological-parent families than they do in single-biological-parent families, leading most family researchers to conclude that the nuclear family is a more effective unit for reproduction and socialization. Yet this literature reveals some troubling features that have not been adequately examined by social scientists. The most obvious of these is that such findings rule out social selection.

If parents with limited resources and low skills are less likely to enter marriage with a biological parent and remain wed when they do (which we know to be true), then it follows that children will do worse in such single-parent households than in stable marriages. We have known about this problem for decades, but researchers have not been equipped adequately to rule out selection. The standard method for doing so is by statistically controlling for prior differences, but this method is inadequate for ruling out differences because it leaves so many sources of selection unmeasured, such as sexual compatibility, substance abuse, and so on. Newer statistical methods have been employed to correct for unmeasured differences, but strong evidence exists that none of these techniques is up to the challenge. Nevertheless, it is *theoretically* possible to examine social experiments such as those being mounted in the marriage-promotion campaign and assess their long-term effects on children.

Another useful approach is to examine macro-level differences at the state or national level that would be less correlated with social selection and hence more revealing of the impact of marriage arrangements on children's well-being. To date, there is little evidence supporting a correlation between family form and children's welfare at the national level. Consider first the historical data showing that children who grew up in the 1950s (baby boomers) were not notably free of problem behavior. After all, they were the cohort who raised such hell in the 1960s and 1970s from 1955 to 1975, indicators of social problems among children (test scores, suicide, homicide, controlled-substance use, crime) that can be tracked by vital statistics all rose. These indicators accompanied, and in some cases preceded rather than followed, change in the rates of divorce, the decline of marriage, and the rise of nonmarital childbearing during this period. Conversely, there is no evidence that the cohort of children who came of age in the 1990s and early part of this century are doing worse than previous cohorts because they are more likely to have grown up in single-parent families. Of course, compensatory public policies or other demographic changes such as small family size, higher parental education, or lower rates of poverty may have offset the deleterious effects of family form, but such an explanation concedes that family form is not the most potent source of children's well-being as so many observers seem to believe.

We might also gain some purchase on this issue by comparing the success of children under different family regimes. Do the countries with high rates of cohabitation, low marriage, high divorce, and high nonmarital fertility have the worst outcomes for children? We don't know the answer to this question, but we do know that various indicators of child well-being—health, mental health, educational attainment—do show higher scores in northern than in Southern Europe. They appear to be linked to the level of investment in children, not the family form (which is certainly more intact in Southern Europe). Still, this question deserves more attention than it has received.

Significantly, many of the countries that continue to adhere to the nuclear model have some of the world's lowest rates of fertility—a problem that seems worse in countries with very low rates of nonmarital childbearing. I am not claiming that nonmarital childbearing is necessarily desirable as a social arrangement for propping up fertility, but it is a plausible hypothesis that nonmarital childbearing helps to keep the birth rate up in countries that would otherwise be experiencing a dangerously low level of reproduction.

Finally, it is important to recognize that family change in the United States (and in most Western countries, it appears) has not occurred evenly among all educational groups. In this country, marriage, divorce, and nonmarital childbearing have jumped since the 1960s among the bottom two-thirds of the educational distribution but have not changed much at all among the top third consisting, today, of college graduates and postgraduates. Though marriage comes later to this group, they are barely more likely to have children out of wedlock, have high levels of marriage, and, if anything, lower levels of divorce than were experienced several decades ago. In other words, almost all the change has occurred among the segment of the population that has either not gained economically or has lost ground over the past several decades. Among the most socially disadvantaged and most marginalized segments of American society, marriage has become imperiled and family conditions have generally deteriorated, resulting in extremely high rates of union instability. The growing inequality in the United States may provide some clues for why the family, and marriage in particular, is not faring well and what to do about it.

MARRIAGE AND PUBLIC POLICY

The logic of the Bush administration's approach to welfare is that by promoting and strengthening marriage, children's well-being, particularly in lower-income families will be enhanced. At first blush, this approach seems to make good sense. Economies of scale are produced when two adults live together. Two parents create healthy redundancies and perhaps help build social capital both within the household and by creating more connections to the community. The prevalence of marriage and marital stability is substantially higher among well-educated and more stably employed individuals than among those with less than a college education and lower incomes. Wouldn't it be reasonable to help the less educated enjoy the benefits of the nuclear family?

There are several reasons to be skeptical of this policy direction. First, we have the experience of the 1950s, when marriages did occur in abundance among low-income families. Divorce rates were extremely high during this era, and many of these families dissolved their unions when they had an opportunity to divorce because of chronic problems of conflict, disenchantment, and scarcity. In my own study of marriages of teen parents in the 1960s, I discovered that four out of every five women who married the father of their children got divorced before the child reached age eighteen; the rate of marital stability among those who married a stepfather was even higher. Certainly, encouraging marriage among young couples facing a choice of nonmarital childbearing or wedlock is not an easy choice when we knew the outcome of the union is so precarious. If divorce is a likely outcome, it is not clear whether children are better off if their parents marry and divorce than remain unmarried, knowing as we do that family conflict and flux have adverse effects on children's welfare.

What about offering help to such couples before or after they enter marriage? This is a good idea, but don't expect any miracles from the current policies. Strong opposition exists to funding sustained and intensive premarital and postmarital counseling among many proponents of marriage-promotion programs. Conservative constituencies largely believe that education, especially under the aegis of religious or quasi-religious sponsorship is the best proscription for shoring up marriage. Yet, the evidence overwhelmingly shows that short-term programs that are largely didactic will not be effective in preserving marriages. Instead, many couples need repeated bouts of help both before and during marriage when they run into difficult straits. Most of these couples have little or no access to professional counseling.

The federal government has funded several large-scale experiments combining into a single program marital education or counseling *and* social services including job training or placement. These experiments, being conducted by the Manpower Research Demonstration Corporation, will use random assignment and have the best hope of producing some demonstrable outcomes. Yet, it is not clear at this point that even comprehensive programs with sustained services will be effective in increasing partner collabo-ration and reducing union instability.

There is another approach that I believe has a better prospect of improving both children's chances and probably at least an equal chance of increasing the viability of mar-riages or marriage-like arrangements. By directing more resources to low-income chil-dren regardless of the family form they live in through such mechanisms as access to quality child care, health care, schooling, and income in the form of tax credits, it may be plausible to increase the level of human, social, and psychological capital that children receive. And, by increasing services, work support, and especially tuition aid for adoles-cents and young adults to attend higher education, Americans may be able to protect chil-dren from the limitations imposed by low parental resources. Lending this type of assistance means that young adults are more likely to move into higher paying jobs and acquire through education the kinds of communication and problem-solving skills that are so useful to making marriage-like relationships last.

When we invest in children, we are not only likely to reap the direct benefits of in-creasing human capital but also the indirect benefits that will help preserve union stabil-ity in the next generation. This approach is more likely to increase the odds of success for children when they grow up. If I am correct, it probably follows that direct investment in children and youth has a better prospect of strengthening marriage and marriage-like relationships in the next generation by improving the skills and providing the resources to make parental relationships more rewarding and enduring.

So it comes down to a choice in strategy: invest in strengthening marriage and hope that children will benefit or invest in children and hope that marriages will benefit. I place my bet on the second approach.

6 Divorce and Remarriage

Divorce Culture: A Quest for Relational Equality in Marriage

Karla B. Hackstaff

When people marry they do not simply tie a knot, but weave a complex of relationships according to pre-existing patterns. In U.S. history, the institution of marriage has been like a loom through which several threads of social relations have been woven. Marriage has been a monogamous, lifelong commitment that has regulated gender, sexuality, and the physical and social reproduction of the generations. This Western marital pattern is being redesigned. We are still responding to the tapestry of old, but the various threads are being disaggregated and rewoven. Our society is deeply divided regarding the value and meaning of these new and partially woven designs.

Over the past decade, family scholars have debated whether we should be optimistic or pessimistic about marital and family life (Glenn 1987, 349).[1] Optimistic theorists have argued that families are not falling apart, but simply changing and adapting to new socio-economic conditions (Riley 1991; Scanzoni 1987; Skolnick 1991). They stress the value of embracing family diversity and removing structural obstacles for the well-being of all families. Optimists emphasize the oppression that has attended women's sacrifices in marriage and point to the potential for greater self-determination and happier relationships today (Cancian 1987; Coontz 1992, 1997; Riessman 1990; Skolnick 1991; Stacey 1990, 1996). These theorists are concerned about threads that have regulated gender and sexuality and have subordinated women in marriage.

Pessimistic theorists have argued that the institution of marriage is a cause for concern—that divorce rates signify an unraveling of social bonds (Bellah et al. 1985; Glenn 1987; Lasch 1979; Popenoe 1988; Popenoe, Elshtain, and Blankenhorn 1996; Spanier 1989; Whitehead 1997a). Above all, pessimists argue that divorce suggests an increasingly tenuous thread of commitment and a growing "individualism" among today's adults, particularly since marital dissolution by divorce, rather than death, entails individual choice. In this view, marriage represents the singular commitment that sustains intergenerational family relationships, especially parenthood. Indeed, several recent books urge a return to lifelong marriage for the sake of children (Blankenhorn 1995a, 1995b; Popenoe, Elshtain, and Blankenhorn 1996; Whitehead 1997a).

Pessimists fear that with the advent of divorce culture we have forsaken nurturance, commitment, and responsibility. Because these are the very virtues that have traditionally been valorized in women, these divorce debates are always implicitly, if not explicitly, about gender. As one optimistic scholar has argued, "when commentators lament the collapse of traditional family commitments and values, they almost invariably mean the uniquely female duties associated with the doctrine of separate spheres for men and women" (Coontz 1992, 40). Critics of divorce do not always or necessarily reject gender equality in marriage, but they do tend to set it apart. Many scholars assume that the thread of gender ideology can be easily disentangled from the thread of commitment.

The middle-class '50s and '70s couples in this study, in combination with those in other studies, enhance our knowledge of the newly constructed meanings of marriage. Among the '70s spouses, I found a reproduction of divorce culture among the married, a growth in a marital work ethic, and fluid, even contradictory, beliefs regarding marital and gender ideologies. These findings validate the concerns of both optimists and pessimists.

Pessimists may be dismayed by the sense of contingency in the talk of married couples and may be confirmed in their belief that commitments are unraveling. On the other hand, optimists may feel validated in their views that spouses do not take divorce lightly; rather, "working" on marriages is the prevailing belief among spouses—though wives are still trying to equalize this work. A full-blown marital work ethic has arisen because of divorce anxiety and marital instability, yet it has also arisen because of instabilities in beliefs about gender. Spouses must be reflexive about the nature of marriage since the authority of marriage culture and male dominance have lost their hegemonic hold. The fluid beliefs among '70s spouses suggest that spouses do not wholly embrace either marriage or divorce culture. This may disturb pessimists more—at least those who would like to see marriage culture regain the hegemony of generations past.

At this point in time, marriage does not seem to be forever for almost half of all marriages. Is this a result of culture and the decline of values such as commitment, or are there other factors contributing to marital contingency today? Could divorce culture be transitional—a means to the goals of equality and new tapestries of commitment, rather than an end in itself? While the individualism of divorce culture has brought new problems, we should neither overlook the structural sources of these troubles nor forget the costs of marriage culture, particularly to women.

THE COSTS OF MARRIAGE CULTURE

Women's greater participation in the labor force, increased activity in the political sphere, and greater initiation of divorces suggest that women like Mia Turner and Roxanne Kason-Morris are claiming their rights and appropriating a model of individualism. However, my research suggests that women's increasing "individualism" needs to be understood in context. Because we proceed from a history of male-dominated marriages, individualism does not *mean* the same thing for women as for men.

Historically, we know that as heads of the household, even when not primary bread-winners, most husbands have had greater authority, and therefore greater freedom to be independent, than wives. Economic and legal structures have not only firmly anchored a white man's family authority in the public sphere, but have recognized and applauded his individualism. His autonomy, integrity, rights, and self-expression were never con-strained to the same degree as those of wives, though he carried heavy financial respon-sibilities. Not all men have been able to accomplish or benefit from the provider role—working-class men and men of color have often been thwarted by economic and racial injustice. However, for those able to realize the ideal of the male provider role, these responsibilities have optimized men's freedoms and prerogatives.

Wives who are more individualistic are often trying to counter the legacy of male dominance in marriage. At face value, "contingent marriage" dilutes commitment by making it conditional. Marital commitment and contingency stand in an uneasy relation to one another. The unconditional commitment requires flexibility and a long-range view of reciprocity and rewards over time; it permits conflict, serendipity, and unforeseen developments without threatening the commitment; it builds trust that only a sustained history can provide. Yet, "marriage as forever" can also obscure the latent terms of com-mitment that have prevailed under conditions of male dominance. Paradoxically, a sense of contingency can enable wives to elicit values such as commitment, responsibility, care-taking, and equality. In short, it provides a powerful lever to set the terms of marriage.[2]

Of course, both men and women can use the lever of contingency in heterosexual marriage. Indeed, a male-dominated divorce culture may be a greater threat to the val-ues of responsibility, caretaking, and equality than a male-dominated marriage culture. Yet, as I have suggested, securing power through individualism is not a new means for men within divorce culture. Thus, this lever is more important for women, who have had less economic and political power in the marital relationship. In fact, contingent mar-riage may be crucial for redefining marriage in an egalitarian direction. Most women are hungry not for power but for "the absence of domination" (M. Johnson 1988, 261). Yet, how can wives challenge domination without engaging the power of individualism?

A belief in equality is more widespread today—the '70s spouses did not generally embrace male dominance as their '50s counterparts did, but rather voiced support for gender equality.[3] Yet, ongoing conflicts over gender equality are apparent in husbands' and wives' "hidden agendas." When there is evidence of rights equality—such as a wives' participation in the labor force—husbands tend to assume that equality has been achieved; they are unaware of ongoing inequalities, such as marital work, and their en-during privileges to set the terms of marriage. Rights equality has more often been a mas-culinist discourse in U.S. law and culture (Arendell 1995; Coltrane and Hickman 1992; Weitzman 1985).

Many wives also embrace rights equality, yet women's conventional responsibilities for caretaking, child rearing, kin work, and marital work continue to incline women to-ward a vision of equality that focuses upon relational responsibilities, expressiveness, eq-uity, and interdependence. Relational equality has been more often feminized in U.S. society (Cancian 1987; Riessman 1990). It is not that women are "essentially" relational, but rather that they have been expected and positioned to accomplish relationality. While some women are undoubtedly more individualistic today, as critics of divorce culture argue (Hewlett and West 1998, 200; Whitehead 1997a, 172, 181), more women increasingly want to share the marital and family labors that optimists have documented. Women are frustrated by men's lack of participation in marital work—and the emotion work, kin work, and housework that such reflexive assessment encompasses (Blaisure and Allen 1995; Cancian 1987; DeVault 1987; di Leonardo 1987; Goldscheider and Waite 1991; Hochschild 1983; Hochschild with Maching 1989; Oliker 1989; Thompson and Walker 1989; Thompson 1991).

These gendered marital visions are also apparent in the retrospective accounts of the divorced. Among divorced women and men, Riessman (1990, 164–65, 184) found that "freedom" encapsulated the positive meaning of divorce, but this gateway to freedom did not necessarily hold the same meaning. Women reported a freedom from subordination and the freedom for self-development—reflecting limits to equality in marriage; men reported freedom from obligations demanded by wives and a freedom from wives' scrutiny—reflecting some dissatisfaction with marital labors. Also, while former wives described their "transformations in identity" as learning to balance relatedness with self-reliance, former husbands discovered the value of "talk" and becoming more relational (199). This latter change by some husbands is ironic for former wives if, as I have argued, relational inequality contributes to marital instability and contingency.

In their suburban divorced sample, Kitson and Holmes (1992) found that ex-husbands and ex-wives similarly ranked a "lack of communication or understanding" as the top marital complaint (though wives ranked this higher) and similarly ranked "joint conflict over roles" as a key complaint.[4] Most interesting, however, was a notable gender difference on the marital complaint "not sure what happened"; for ex-husbands it ranked third, for ex-wives it ranked 28th (123). This suggests that men were less attuned to what the marriage lacked—a prerequisite for doing marital work.

Some '70s husbands—such as Robert Leonetti, Gordon Walker, and Paul Nakato—do marital work. Yet, more often than not, wives initiate and try to redistribute the actual "marital work" of communicating, caring, fulfilling needs, adjusting, and planning for marital well-being. To advocate shared marital work is to de-gender the rights and responsibilities conventionally attached to marital practices, to challenge male authority, and to disrupt power relations. Recent research that aims to predict marital happiness and divorce, as well as to improve the efficacy of marital therapy, reveals that a husband's refusal to accept influence from his wife is a key factor for predicting divorce (Gottman et al. 1998, 14, 19).

The above research suggests that marital work and the relational equality that it entails may be as important as rights equality for wives in a culture of divorce. The cultural irony is that even though wives may want a relational marriage, they may need to draw upon individualism to secure it. If secured, that is, if husbands keep up with wives' changes, wives may change the power dynamics of their marriage. Yet, ultimately what many wives want is not freedom from commitment, but freedom within an egalitarian and relational marriage. However, if relationality is unsecured, these wives may choose the gateway of divorce.

It is worth recalling that it was primarily the wives and not the husbands who thought about divorce among '50s couples ensconced in marriage culture. What does this reveal about the gendered costs of marriage culture? Writing about marriage and the nuclear family, Stacey (1996, 69) noted: "It seems a poignant commentary on the benefits to women of that family system that, even in a period when women retain primary responsibility for maintaining children and other kin, when most women continue to earn significantly less than men with equivalent cultural capital, and when women and their children suffer substantial economic decline after divorce, that in spite of all this, so many regard divorce as the lesser of evils." In light of women's postdivorce commitments to children, to charge such mothers with an egoistic or self-centered individualism reveals a refusal to recognize the costs of marriage culture to women.

Are there no costs for men in marriage culture? While research continues to find that marriage is better for men than women in terms of overall health and mortality rates (Hu and Goldman 1990), men are adjusting to new gender ideologies and practices too. Historically, the ability to provide and the ability to head a household have rooted men's identities. Working women and growing beliefs in equality are increasingly uprooting these means to manhood, as distinct from womanhood. As Furstenberg (1988, 239) has observed: "Men looking at marriage today may sense that it offers them a less good deal than it once did. This is the inevitable result of reducing male privileges, female deference to men, and a range of services that were customarily provided as part of the conjugal bargain. The loss of these privileges has persuaded some men to opt out of family life altogether." Paul Nakato's observation that some '70s men would rather be "right" than "married"—echoes Goode (1992, 124) on the sociology of superordinates: "Men view even small losses of deference, advantages, or opportunities as large threats and losses." Craig Kason-Morris felt increasingly underappreciated for all his work; yet his solution was to devote more energy to breadwinning, risking the relational needs of his marriage.

If we ignore the emotional costs of marriage culture and its connection to gender inequality, we will fail to see that divorce culture is a transitional phenomenon. We will also advance the costs of divorce culture—the impoverished single mothers, estranged fathers, and affected children—of concern to pessimists and optimists alike.

THE COSTS OF DIVORCE CULTURE

The gendered patterns of divorce follow from those of marriage. Just as women usually do the primary parenting during a marriage, they generally obtain custody of children after divorce. Fathers are overwhelmingly noncustodial parents—only 14 percent of custodial parents are fathers (Sugarman 1998, 15). Just as fathers help support children during marriage, they are expected to contribute to child support upon divorce. Yet, many noncustodial fathers have become estranged from their children and delinquent on child support. Single, custodial mothers must often raise children on one slim paycheck. More widespread divorce seems to have increased women's and children's impoverishment, undermined fathers' economic and emotional commitment to children, and deprived children of the emotional and economic goods that two parents can provide.

Pessimists acknowledge structural impediments to marital commitments—the decline of the male wage and the need for two wage earners in a postindustrial economy. Yet, they see the decline in cultural and family values, such as commitment, as the more pivotal factor fostering these new social problems. On the other hand, optimists regularly argue that our failure to respond to the new global and postindustrial economy—the low priority given to families by corporate and government entities—is more basic to these problems, and that these new conditions demand solutions that do not discriminate on the basis of marital status. Although structural solutions are central, optimists are also concerned with cultural and family values—though the values of equality or justice are of greater concern than commitment.

Optimists and pessimists alike are concerned about the economic costs of divorce for mothers and their children. About a third of female-headed households are in poverty—six times the rate of married-couple households (U.S. Bureau of the Census 1995, P60-187). A re-evaluation of one study's claims about the economic consequences of divorce a year after divorce, finds that women's standard of living declines by 27 percent and men's increases by 10 percent (Peterson 1996, 534).[5]

A key solution to poverty for many pessimistic family scholars is reinforcing marriage and the nuclear family structure (Blankenhorn 1995b; Hewlett and West 1998; Popenoe et al. 1996; Whitehead 1997a). Marriage has functioned to redistribute economic resources in the past.[6] Also, today more than ever, two earners are necessary to secure a middle-class standard of living. However, to imply that unmarried motherhood or divorce are the *cause* of poverty among women and children, and marriage the only solution, is to use family structure to solve problems generated by the social structure. Such an approach overlooks the enduring gender inequality in economic structures. Also, marriage does not necessarily reverse poverty, particularly for working-class women and women of color. For instance, Brewer (1988, 344) noted that "an emphasis on female-headed households misses an essential truth about black women's poverty: black women are also poor in households with male heads." Higher wages in female-dominated jobs may be a more effective solution than marriage. This would not only help married, nuclear family households, but all families and households.

Similarly, marriage culture will not solve the larger economic problem of declining wages for working- and middle-class men brought by a postindustrial, service, and global economy.[7] Indeed, we could transform divorce culture by repairing wage declines for those most disadvantaged by this postindustrial economy—including many working-class men, especially men of color. This could remove sources of conflict and resentment within and across family groups. Yet, to address structural sources of inequality would only mitigate, and not reverse, divorce culture unless we attend to cultural beliefs about gender as well.

Pessimists advocate marriage culture in part because it would seem to solve so many problems of divorce culture at once, most especially divorced men's failure to provide and care for their children. Of all policies, child support has received the most attention by legislators and media over the last two decades. Only about half of custodial mothers with child support orders receive the full amount (Arendell 1995, 39). In 1991 the "average monthly child support paid by divorced fathers contributing economic support" was only $302 (for an estimated 1.5 children), and "child support payments amounted to only about 16% of the incomes of divorced mothers and their children" (Arendell 1997, 162). As a result of the Family Support Act of 1988, the mechanisms for securing child support from fathers have become more rigorous (Furstenberg and Cherlin 1991, 109); there are established formulas for calculating child support payments and, since 1994, all new child support payments are withheld from the paychecks of absent parents (mostly fathers). Yet, as Hewlett and West (1998, 180) observe, in spite of all the policies and prison terms, "the number of deadbeat dads has declined only slightly since 1978."[8]

We need new ways to address fathers' "failure to provide"—clearly, some fathers partly withdraw from marriage and children because they cannot be "good providers."[9] Yet, to focus on the provider role is to limit fatherhood to a model that evolved during the industrial era and is at odds with a postindustrial economy. One could say that this approach merely exchanges a "fragmented" fatherhood for its predecessor: a "shrinking" fatherhood (Blankenhorn 1995a).[10] Indeed, to focus on providing alone will only sustain men's detachment from parenting. "Studies do show that fathers who visit more regularly pay more in child support" (Furstenberg and Cherlin 1991, 274). Whether these payments are due to visiting or greater commitment, attention to the relational aspects of fathering would seem crucial.

Both optimistic and pessimistic scholars are concerned about the lack of paternal participation in children's lives. Most research shows a substantial and unacceptable decline over time in father-child contact after a divorce (Furstenberg and Cherlin 1991). Data from the recent National Survey of Families and Households reveals that about 30 percent of children of divorce have not seen their fathers at all in the preceding year and many more see their fathers irregularly and infrequently (Arendell 1995, 38). Speaking of unmarried as well as divorced fathers, Hewlett and West (1988, 168) report that "close to half of all fathers lose contact with their children." —> ages? definition?

Thus, all family scholars see a need to revitalize and redefine fatherhood. For example, a supporter of divorce culture, Arendell (1995, 251) protests: "Why should it be so difficult to be a nurturing, engaged father? Where are the institutional and ideological supports for parenting?" Arendell adds: "That caring fathers are subject to criticism and stigmatization points to a seriously flawed ideological system" (251). Also, advocates of marriage culture Hewlett and West (1998, 173) assert that "a withering of the father-child bond devastates children, stunts men, and seriously erodes our social capital." In spite of shared concerns, the means to a revitalized fatherhood are contested.

Just as critics of divorce culture suggest that marriage will alleviate the impoverishment of single mothers, they argue that fathers cannot be effective parents outside of the marriage structure (Blankenhorn 1995a; Hewlett and West 1998; Popenoe 1996; Wallerstein and Blakeslee 1989; Whitehead 1997a). For example, Hewlett and West (1998, 171–72) note that single males are more likely to die prematurely due to self-neglect, more likely to abuse drugs and alcohol, and are responsible for a disproportionate share of violence—including murder, robbery, and rape. They reason, like Durkheim, that marriage and children have a "civilizing" effect upon men.[11] In Blankenhorn's (1995a) view, both co-residence and a parental alliance with the mother are preconditions for effective fatherhood.

Undoubtedly, co-residence assists in the building of relationships—including, and especially, parent-child relationships. Yet, there is evidence to suggest it is not a precondition for effective fatherhood. In her study of divorced fathers, Arendell (1995) describes "innovative" divorced fathers (not all of whom had single custody) who were able to detach being a father from being a partner, separate anger at an ex-wife from their love for their children, focus on the children's needs rather than adult rights, and combine breadwinning with caretaking in ways that developed their nurturing and relational skills. While such fathers are too rare, fathers who parent effectively after divorce suggest that marriage or co-residence are not prerequisites—though alliances between parents do seem to be important whether outside or inside the marriage structure. Further, studies on nonresidential mothers show they are more active participants in their children's lives (Maccoby and Mnookin 1992, 212; Arendell 1997, 170). Finally, even if custody determinations were divided equally between women and men, co-residence would not always be an option for father and child. Suggesting marriage as the solution for divorce—and effective fathering—is empty advice for those compelled to divorce.[12]

Divorced fathers' flagging commitment seems to have exposed a tenuous responsibility for children in the first place. This may represent a "male flight from commitment" that started in the 1950s (Ehrenreich 1984); even so, this too should be understood as a legacy of separate spheres that identified masculinity with the provider role and devalued men's caretaking capacities (Bernard 1981; Coontz 1992). Since women still do the bulk of child rearing during a marriage, many divorced fathers have to learn how to be a primary parent after divorce (Arendell 1997, 163). As optimists and pessimists alike have observed, men appear to depend upon wives to mediate their relationship to their children (Arendell 1995, 33; Furstenberg and Cherlin 1991, 275; Wallerstein and Blakeslee 1989; Whitehead 1997b).[13] This may explain why marriage seems like the only solution for effective fathering for the pessimists.

Another route for expanding paternal participation—and overcoming the historical equivalence between breadwinning and masculinity[14]—would be to construct men as nurturers, caretakers, and responsible fathers. Arendell (1995, 251) calls for "a more vocal and widespread critique of the conventions of masculinity." A construction of masculinity that goes beyond putting all of men's eggs into one "breadwinner" basket (Bernard 1981) is long overdue. Perhaps marriage has an important "civilizing function" for men because of a flawed construction of masculinity in the first place; men have been deprived of the expectation or opportunity to advance their relationality—from boyhood to manhood.

Reinforcing marriage by compelling "divorce as a last resort" would obscure, not solve, this paternal disability. Rather than advocating marriage or reinforcing the provider role as pessimists do, many optimists argue that men need to combine providing with caretaking just as women have combined caretaking with providing. In the aggregate, women are changing faster than men. To keep up with wives' changes means that husbands must be willing to recognize the legitimacy of a wife's relational concerns, embrace what has been largely a devalued sphere, and to share power with their wives.

If a redistribution of relational responsibilities were to take place in marriage, this might extend fathers' involvement with their children in the event of divorce. More important, this could prevent divorces based on relational inequalities in the first place.[15] Indeed, in my research, paternal participation is part of the "marital labor" that egalitarian wives wanted to share. Reconstructing masculinity (and therefore gender in marriage) might provide the stronger deterrent to divorce for which pessimists have been searching.

IS DIVORCE EVER A GATEWAY FOR CHILDREN?

Given children's attenuated relations with their fathers and the downward mobility most children share with their mothers, is divorce ever a gateway for children? Not only do two-thirds of divorces involve children (U.S. Bureau of the Census 1995, P60-187), but few people object to divorce by childless couples today. Because it is children that electrify the divorce debates, I only sampled married parents. Are children paying the price for adults' individualism and lapsed family values, as the critics of divorce culture would argue? Or, could they be paying the costs of marriage culture and the quest for equality—interpersonal and institutional—that I have described?

Divorce is rarely experienced as a "gateway" for children—even perhaps, when it should be. It is, however, a turning point that is distinct from the adult experience. There is a tendency in the debates about the effects of divorce upon children to project adult experiences and capacities onto children. One recent study found that parents' and children's experiences were generally "out of synch" (Stewart et al. 1997, cited in Arendell 1998, 227). Parents may overestimate their child's well-being. Kitson with Holmes (1992, 227) found that most parents attribute very low levels of distress to their children, even though we know that the early period is hard for children. Whether divorce is due to a spouse's adultery, violence, or self-centeredness, the decision is not the child's to make. Of course, children survive and thrive after the temporary crisis of parental divorce, just as they survive other crises. Yet, the assumption that children are resilient should be tempered with the view that the endurance of parental relationships (even if they divorce) matters to children. Neither "divorce as a last resort" nor "divorce as a gateway" capture the divorce turning point for children, because they both presume some choice in the matter.[16]

Many studies agree upon some costs borne by children after a parental divorce, yet the source, extent, and meaning of these costs are fiercely debated (Wallerstein and Kelly 1980; Wallerstein and Blakeslee 1989; Amato and Booth 1997; Maccoby and Mnookin 1992; Hetherington, Law, and O'Connor 1993; Furstenberg and Cherlin 1991; Whitehead 1997a). The conditions preceding, surrounding, and following divorce matter a great deal, including the quality of parent-child relationships, custodial arrangements, the quality of the ex-spousal and coparenting relationships, the economic and social supports available, and the child's own psychological strengths (Furstenberg and Cherlin 1991; Kelly 1988, 134). The age and gender of the child may matter—though gender effects have been questioned (Arendell 1997, 175; Wallerstein and Kelly 1980; Kelly 1988; Wallerstein and Blakeslee 1989). Remarriage and new stepfamily relations affect a child's adjustment over time; indeed, some research suggests remarriage may be more of an adjustment than divorce (Ahrons and Rodgers 1987, 257).

Drawing upon an analysis of 92 studies involving 13,000 children, Amato (1994, 145) reports consistent findings that children of divorce experience "lower academic achievement, more behavioral problems, poorer psychological adjustment, more negative self-concepts, more social difficulties, and more problematic relationships with both mothers and fathers." Also, children of divorce are reported to become pregnant outside of marriage, marry young, and divorce upon becoming adults (McLanahan and Bumpass 1988; Glenn and Kramer 1987).

Taken together, these findings would seem to be alarming. The pessimists are alarmed. Yet, we should not assume that divorce is the "cause" when divorce is correlated with undesirable effects among children. Research on the adverse effects of divorce for children consistently finds that other factors that accompany divorce may be more important than the divorce itself. For example, "income differences account for almost 50 percent of the disadvantage faced by children in single-parent households" (McLanahan and Sandefur 1994; Coontz 1997, 101). Changes of residence and schools help to explain the other 50 percent of disadvantage. Above all, prospective and longitudinal studies of families suggest that marital conflict is more crucial than divorce in explaining behavioral and emotional problems for those children who are troubled (Amato and Booth 1996, 1997; Block, Block, and Gjerde, 1986; Coontz 1997, 102). Longitudinal studies have discovered that children's problems are apparent over a decade before the parents' divorce. Thus, in some cases, divorce and a single-parent household is better for children than continued marital conflict (Amato, Loomis, and Booth 1995).

Furthermore, Amato's (1994) analysis of multiple studies also reveals that the effects of divorce are very weak and that differences between children of divorce and children in continuously intact families are quite small (Amato and Keith 1991; Amato 1994; Amato and Booth 1996, 1997). As the optimist Coontz (1997, 99) clarifies, this research does not suggest that children of divorced parents have *more problems*, rather that *more children* of divorced parents have problems than do children of married parents. Yet, children of divorce show greater variability in their adjustment (Amato 1994). This means that some children of divorce do better than children of married parents. Children from all kinds of families fare well and poorly. When we focus on the difference between family structures, we overlook the extensive overlap in children's well-being across family structures. Further, research increasingly suggests that the quality and consistency of family life, and not family structure, influence children's well-being (Arendell 1997, 187).

Most of the '70s couples I interviewed did not believe in staying together "for the sake of the children" if there was marital conflict. Parents sense that if their marriage is continuously in conflict, then this harms children too. Divorce is not a singular solution to conflict or violence since both can be exacerbated upon separation and divorce (Arendell and Kurz, 1999). Yet the gateway is crucial for such troubled marriages. Recall that the '50s Dominicks stayed together miserably for thirty years in spite of extramarital affairs, separation, and indications of violence—all for the sake of the children. These were justifiable conditions under the terms of marriage culture. One wonders to what degree the "sake of the children," among other deterrents, inhibited divorces that should have been when marriage culture reigned uncontested.[17]

Kurz's (1995, 52) random sample of divorced mothers revealed that 19 percent pursued divorce specifically because of violence; however, an astonishing 70 percent reported at least one incident of violence during the marriage or separation. Most research shows that violence remains a graver problem for wives than husbands—particularly in terms of injuries (Gelles and Straus 1988; Kurz 1989; Straton 1994). Also, research increasingly finds that witnessing spouse abuse *is* child abuse—even when a child is not physically violated (Holden, Geffner, and Jouriles 1998). Thus, removing children from the perpetrator, however much he (or she) is loved, is arguably for the sake of the children.

Believers in "divorce as a gateway" may want to make parental happiness equivalent to children's happiness when it is not. Pessimists correctly stress that the child's experience of divorce is distinct from the parents' experience. Thus, scholars are increasingly advocating parenting education classes for divorcing parents (Arendell 1995; Wallerstein 1998). Yet, believers in "divorce as a last resort" also mistakenly presume that the maintenance of marriage and a nuclear family is equivalent to children's happiness. We should not ignore the injuries that have attended marriage culture—particularly a male-dominated marriage culture. When egalitarian spouses become parents there is often a shift toward "increased traditionality of family and work roles in families of the 1980s and 1990s," and this "tends to be associated with *more* individual and marital distress for parents" (Cowan and Cowan 1998, 184). This represents the pinch between egalitarian beliefs and the structural impediments to equality in practice. Further, to the degree that we idealize a male-dominated, nuclear family model we cannot fail to reproduce such constructions of inequality among children. While some children are paying a price for the quest for equality, children also pay a price when the thread of commitment is tangled with the thread of male dominance. Moreover, children do find happiness and another vision of equality in alternative family forms.

THE FUTURE OF DIVORCE CULTURE

From Durkheim (1961) to Giddens (1979, 1991), sociologists have regularly addressed transitional periods such as our own. Norms, ideals, and authorities that guided our marital practices in the past are inadequate to families' needs in today's socioeconomic context. Could divorce culture represent a new tapestry of ideals and norms for guiding today's family lives? Even as the practices of '70s spouses are shaped by novel conditions, spouses attempt to shape them in turn—drawing alternatively, selectively, and even haphazardly on available ideologies and practices. Although divorce culture seems to be replacing marriage culture, it should be seen as a transitional means for "people to make sense of the circumstances in which they find themselves" (Mullings 1986), providing alternative strategies for action when marriage culture falls short. Still, like the '70s spouses, many people are ambivalent about divorce culture. Moreover, marriage culture endures.

Because divorce culture is new and unsettling there is a tendency to inflate its power and prevalence. Marriage culture is widely embraced. "Marriage as forever" is a belief that is not only sustained by married couples, but also the divorced (Riessman 1990). The reintroduction of grounds in "covenant marriages" represents a political effort to value the old tapestry that sustained "divorce as a last resort." Finally, "marrying as a given" lives on. While rates of marriage and remarriage have decreased since the mid-1960s (U.S. Bureau of the Census, 1992, P23-180, 8)—suggesting that fewer people experience marriage as an imperative—the majority of people eventually marry. Also, the two-parent family continues to be the predominant family form—so concern with its decline can be overstated (Cowan and Cowan 1998, 189).

Marriage culture also lives on in the next generation's aspirations. The majority of young people say they value marriage and plan to marry (Landis-Kleine et al. 1995). A 1992 survey showed that of all extremely important goals in life, the most valued by 78 percent of the high school respondents was "having a good marriage and family life" (Glenn 1996, 21). "Being able to find steady work" was ranked a close second by 77 percent of these students, and "being successful in my line of work" and "being able to give my children better opportunities than I've had" tied for third, at 66 percent.

Will the '90s spouses continue, reverse, or transcend the advance of divorce culture? How will they cope with the rise of divorce culture and its problems? Because a culture of divorce creates "divorce anxiety," premarital counseling would seem to be increasingly important. One valuable component of "covenant marriage" advanced by pessimists (in spite of critiques of therapeutic culture) has been to encourage religious or secular premarital counseling. Instituting therapy before marriage might prepare '90s spouses for the reflexive process and the marital work that characterizes marriage in an era of change, choice, and uncertainty.[18] Such counseling should not only attune spouses to one another's hopes, dreams, and desires, but should also provide information on the social conditions faced by married couples today. For example, the arrival of children is a vulnerable period of transition in marriage even when children are deeply desired (Cowan and Cowan 1998). Also, '90s spouses should know that aspirations for lifetime marriage, for thriving children, and a good job are not new; most people getting married share these hopes for themselves even as they harbor doubts about others. What thwarts their resolve and aspirations? Do they simply become individualistic?

This analysis of divorce culture has tried to situate the charges that a high divorce rate represents increased individualism in recent generations. On the one hand, like the pessimists, I agree that divorce culture is marked by individualism. Individualism clearly links and underlies the tenets of divorce culture: the choice to marry, to set conditions, and the chance to unmarry all speak to the primacy of the individual to redesign his or her life. However, my research complicates these claims. Individualism is not in a zero-sum relationship with commitment. It can be morally responsible rather than egoistic, it has not been absent for men in marriage culture, and it is not necessarily an end in itself. Divorce culture exposes how the terms of marital commitment reflect a legacy of male dominance. For married women, individualism can be a tool to resist old and enforce new terms of marital commitment—including nurturance, commitment, and relational responsibility shared by both spouses. When mothers use the power of individualism for relational ends—by working to provide, by removing children from violent households, or by refusing to be subordinated—individualism is neither an end in itself nor easily severed from committed responsibility. The meaning of pulling the individualistic lever of divorce culture cannot be stripped from interactional or institutional contexts. Thus '90s spouses would also do well to take the insights of optimists into account. Our quest for equality is ongoing.

Finally, an overemphasis on the individualism of women or men diverts our attention from the ways our social structures obstruct this quest for equality. The variety of families today may not represent a failure of commitment as much as individuals' valiant struggles to sustain commitments in a society that withholds structural supports from workers and families. Indeed, until the 1993 Family and Medical Leave Act, the United States had no family policy at all.[19] Other scholars have suggested an array of family policies—from easing work and family conflicts to providing economic and social supports—for today's burdened families, which I will not repeat here (see Arendell 1995; Burggraf 1997; Hewlett and West 1998; Hochschild 1997; Mason, Skolnick, and Sugarman 1998). Yet, two things are clear—when we allow corporate and government policies to neglect the needs of working parents, we are undermining marriage culture, and when we ignore enduring gender inequalities we advance divorce culture.

While divorce culture is flawed, I see it as a means to propel marital and family relationships in an egalitarian direction. Both "optional marriage" and "divorce as a gateway" recognize commitments apart from marriage, expose the costs of marriage culture, and legitimate diverse family arrangements. Critics of divorce culture advocate a return to the singular design of the nuclear family structure; however, in many ways this sustains a white, middle-class ethnocentrism,[20] and a heterosexism[21] that has marked our family ideals. By challenging "marriage as a given" and "divorce as a last resort," divorce culture helps to destigmatize unmarried families.

As we reconstruct the terms of marriage culture with the tool of divorce culture, we risk sacrificing relationality for rights equality. Rights language is essential for justice, dignity, and self-determination. Yet, it is not an unmitigated good, and only the young, childless, wealthy, or powerful can indulge in a sense of independence and obscure interdependence by relying upon others to sustain the illusion. Only when the relational responsibilities, still constructed as "feminine," are practiced and valued by men, and by the society at large, will we be able to move beyond the individualism of divorce culture and beyond a notion of equality limited to individual rights and obscuring relational responsibilities. Whether divorce culture eventually supplants rather than contests marriage culture, or generates "family cultures" that transcend this contestation, will depend upon social structural change and the quest for relational equality in the next generation.

Editors' Note: References and Notes for this reading can be found in the original source.

■ READING 17

Children's Adjustment Following Divorce: Risk and Resilience Perspectives

Joan B. Kelly and Robert E. Emery

Parental divorce has been viewed for 40 years as the cause of a range of serious and enduring behavioral and emotional problems in children and adolescents. Divorced families have been widely portrayed by the media, mental health professionals, and conservative political voices as seriously flawed structures and environments, whereas, historically, married families were assumed to be wholesome and nurturing environments for children (Popenoe, Elshtain, & Blankenhorn, 1996; Whitehead, 1998). Although, on average, children fare better in a happy two-parent family than in a divorced family, two essential caveats that distinguish our position from the stereotypical view are underscored. First, unfortunately, many two-parent families do not offer a happy environment for parents or for children (e.g., Cummings & Davies, 1994; Amato, Loomis, & Booth, 1995). Second, although there are differences in the average psychological well-being of children from happy married families and divorced families, it also is true that the majority of children from divorced families are emotionally well-adjusted (Amato, 1994, 2001; Hetherington, 1999).

A continuing stream of sophisticated social science and developmental research has contributed a more complex understanding of factors associated with children's positive outcomes and psychological problems in the context of both marriage and divorce. As a result, most social scientists relinquished a simplistic view of the impact of divorce more than a decade ago. Research demonstrating that children's behavioral symptoms and academic problems could be identified, in some instances, for a number of years before their parents' divorces was particularly important in facilitating this conceptual shift (Block, Block, & Gjerde, 1986; Cherlin et al., 1991). However, compelling stories of negative outcomes for children of divorce continued to be reported by the media in the past decade, stimulated in part by a 10-year longitudinal study of divorced families that emphasized the enduring psychological damage for children of divorce (Wallerstein & Blakeslee, 1989). More recently, two longitudinal studies that report quite different long-term outcomes for children and young adults (Hetherington & Kelly, 2002; Wallerstein, Lewis, & Blakeslee, 2000) have interested the media in taking a more discriminating look at divorce research, although the preference in the media for drama and simple dichotomous answers remain evident (e.g., *Time* Magazine, September 25, 2000).

We believe that social science researchers need to look more closely at the varied evidence on children and divorce within and across disciplines and across methodological approaches. Among the basic empirical issues of concern are (a) the confounding of correlation with cause such that any psychological problems found among children from divorced families often are portrayed as "consequences" of divorce, whereas both logic and empirical evidence demonstrate otherwise; (b) the overgeneralization of results from relatively small, unrepresentative, often highly select samples, most notably clinical or troubled samples as in the widely discussed work of Wallerstein; (c) the too ready acceptance of the null hypothesis of no differences in the face of limited and sometimes superficial assessment, particularly in large, often representative samples; and (d) the failure to distinguish between normative outcomes and individual differences in drawing implications for practice and policy, for example, by noting that the majority of children from divorced families are not "at risk" and that family processes *after* divorce are strong predictors of risk versus resilience. These methodological considerations are of vital importance for the conduct of research, and they point to an interpretation of empirical findings that offers a more nuanced and, we think, more complete understanding of the psychological meaning of divorce for children.

Here we review the empirical research literature on the adjustment of children of divorce from the perspective of the stressors that divorce generally presents for children, the type and extent of risk observed in divorced children when compared with those in still married families, and factors that have been demonstrated to ameliorate risk for children during and after divorce. A third dimension of children's postdivorce outcomes, that of painful memories and experiences, is distinguished from the presence of pathology, and some of the differences and controversies between quantitative and clinical research reports regarding longer-term adjustment are highlighted.

STRESSORS OF THE DIVORCE PROCESS

More than two decades ago, divorce was reconceptualized as a process extending over time that involved multiple changes and potential challenges for children, rather than as a single event (Hetherington, 1979; Wallerstein & Kelly, 1980). The number, severity, and duration of separation and divorce-engendered stressors were observed to vary from child to child, from family to family, and over time. The nature of the initial separation, parental adjustment and resources, parental conflict and cooperation, repartnering of one or both parents, stability of economic resources, and children's own individual resources are central to how these stressors affect children's short- and longer-term reactions and outcomes. It is anticipated that unalleviated and multiple stressors encumber children's attempts to cope with divorce and are more likely to result in increased risk and psychological difficulties over time.

Stress of the Initial Separation

Independently of the longer-term consequences of divorce, the initial period following separation of parents is quite stressful for the vast majority of children and adolescents (Hetherington, 1979; Wallerstein & Kelly, 1980). For some children, their stress predates separation because of chronic high conflict and or violence in the marriage. However, the majority of children seem to have little emotional preparation for their parents' separation, and they react to the separation with distress, anxiety, anger, shock, and disbelief (Hetherington, Cox, & Cox, 1982; Wallerstein & Kelly). In general, these crisis-engendered responses diminish or disappear over a period of 1 or 2 years (Hetherington & Clingempeel, 1992; Wallerstein & Kelly).

Complicating children's attempts to cope with the major changes initiated by separation, most children are inadequately informed by their parents about the separation and divorce. They are left to struggle alone with the meaning of this event for their lives, which can cause a sense of isolation and cognitive and emotional confusion (Dunn, Davies, O'Connor, & Sturgess, 2001; Smart & Neale, 2000; Wallerstein & Kelly, 1980). The majority of parents fail to communicate their thoughts with each other regarding effective custody and access arrangements for their children (Kelly, 1993), and they seem even less able or willing to provide important information to their children about immediate and far-reaching changes in family structure, living arrangements, and parent-child relationships. In one study of parent-child communications about divorce, 23% of children said no one talked to them about the divorce, and 45% said they had been given abrupt one- or two-line explanations ("Your dad is leaving"). Only 5% said they had been fully informed and encouraged to ask questions (Dunn et al.).

Intensifying children's stress is the abrupt departure of one parent, usually the father, from the household. In the absence of temporary court orders, some children do not see their nonresident parents for weeks or months. For those children with strong attachments to caring parents, the abrupt and total absence of contact is quite distressing and painful (Wallerstein & Kelly, 1980). Those children who have legal or informal permission to see nonresident parents must begin to deal with the logistics and emotions of transitioning between two households. They must integrate and adapt to unfamiliar schedules and physical spaces imposed on them often without consultation (Kelly, 2002; McIntosh, 2000; Smart, 2002; Smart & Neale, 2000), as well as decide what clothes, toys, and resource materials should be with them in each household. They also must shift from one psychological space to another, in which parents may have different rules and levels of anger toward the other parent (Smart). Children must adapt to unaccustomed absences from both parents without the ability to communicate on an at-will basis. Visiting arrangements that are not developmentally attuned to children's developmental, social, and psychological needs also may be a stressor, particularly for very young children who lack the cognitive, language, and emotional maturity to ask questions about, understand, and cope with the large changes in their lives (Kelly & Lamb, 2000).

Parental Conflict

A major stressor for children is persistent conflict between parents following separation and divorce (Emery, 1982; Johnston, 1994; Johnston & Roseby, 1997). Children in divorcing families have widely varying histories of exposure to marital conflict and violence. Although it often is assumed that parents in high-conflict marriages continue their conflict after separation and divorce, predivorce conflict is far from perfect as a predictor of the amount of postdivorce conflict (Booth & Amato, 2001). Between 20–25% of children experience high conflict during their parents' marriage (Booth & Amato; Hetherington, 1999), and some of these couples reduce their conflict once separated or divorced, whereas others continue to remain entrenched in conflict patterns. Approximately one quarter of divorced parents report low marital conflict (Booth & Amato; Hetherington, 1999; Wallerstein & Kelly, 1980). In some of these families, intense anger and conflict is ignited by the separation itself and the impact of highly adversarial legal processes (Johnston & Campbell, 1988; Kelly, 2002; Kelly & Johnston, 2001; Wallerstein & Kelly). Thus, some children will be burdened by continuing or intensified conflict, whereas others will experience significantly less conflict on a daily basis.

Although the association between intense marital conflict and children's poor adjustment has been repeatedly demonstrated, findings from studies of the impact of postdivorce conflict and children's adjustment have been mixed. Booth and Amato (2001) reported no association between postdivorce conflict and later adjustment in young adults. Others have found that marital conflict is a more potent predictor of postdivorce adjustment than is postdivorce conflict (Booth & Amato; Buehler et al., 1998; Kline, Johnston, & Tschann, 1990), whereas Hetherington (1999) found that postdivorce conflict had more adverse effects than did conflict in the married families. The varied findings may reflect the use of different measures of conflict and adjustment, a failure to differentiate between types of conflict after divorce, parental styles of conflict resolution, and the extent of direct exposure of the child to anger and conflict.

High conflict is more likely to be destructive postdivorce when parents use their children to express their anger and are verbally and physically aggressive on the phone or in person (Buchanan, Maccoby, & Dornbusch, 1991; Johnston, 1994). Parents who express their rage toward their former spouse by asking children to carry hostile messages, by denigrating the other parent in front of the child, or by prohibiting mention of the other parent in their presence are creating intolerable stress and loyalty conflicts in their children. Not surprisingly, such youngsters were more depressed and anxious when compared with high-conflict parents who left their children out of their angry exchanges (Buchanan et al.). When parents continued to have conflict but encapsulated their conflict and did not put their children in the middle, their children did not differ from children whose parents had low or no conflict (Buchanan et al.; Hetherington, 1999). Although high conflict postdivorce is generally assumed to be a shared interaction between two angry, culpable parents, our clinical, mediation, and arbitration experience in high conflict post-divorce cases indicates that it is not uncommon to find one enraged or defiant parent and a second parent who no longer harbors anger, has emotionally disengaged, and attempts to avoid or mute conflict that involves the child.

Diminished Parenting after Divorce

A related stressor for children is the impact of inept parenting both prior to and following divorce. Whereas intense marital conflict by itself has modest negative effects on children's adjustment, the negative impact of high conflict on children's adjustment is substantially mediated through significant problems in the parenting of both mothers and fathers. In particular, mothers in high-conflict marriages are reported to be less warm, more rejecting, and use harsher discipline, and fathers withdraw more from and engage in more intrusive interactions with their children compared with parents in low-conflict marriages (Belsky, Youngblade, Rovine, & Volling, 1991; Cummings & Davies, 1994; Hetherington, 1999; Krishnakumar & Buehler, 2000). Further, living with a depressed, disturbed, or character-disordered parent after divorce clearly places children at risk and is associated with impaired emotional, social, and academic adjustment (Emery, Waldron, Kitzmann, & Aaron, 1999; Hetherington, 1999; Kalter, Kloner, Schreiser, & Okla, 1989; Kline et al., 1990). After divorce, there are few opportunities for competent nonresident parents to buffer the more pernicious effects of behaviors of emotionally troubled custodial parents, and the influence of the nonresident parent on children's adjustment diminishes over time (Hetherington, 1999).

Coupled with this is the frequent deterioration in the parenting of both custodial and nonresident parents in the first several years after separation (Hetherington et al., 1982; Wallerstein & Kelly, 1980). Parents are preoccupied with their own emotional responses to divorce, as well as the demands of integrating single parenting with work and social needs. Not only are divorced parents more prone to emotional liability, but depression, alcoholism, drug abuse, and psychosomatic complaints are more frequent compared with married parents. Some children and adolescents become the sole emotional support for their distraught and needy parents (Wallerstein & Kelly, 1980; Hetherington, 1999). Boys appear to experience more angry exchanges and contentious relationships with their custodial mothers compared with girls (Hetherington, 1999). Boys also experience a greater decline in the quality of the home environment following separation than girls, not only because of more coercive mother-son relationships, but also because fathers typically spend more time with their sons than with their daughters during marriage. These emotional and physical interactions are curtailed or cease following separation (Mott, Kowaleski-Jones, & Menaghan, 1997). Most characteristic of diminished parenting is that children experience less positive involvement with their custodial parent, including less affection and time spent and more erratic and harsh discipline (Hetherington). The children's own increased anger and upset makes it even more difficult for distressed single parents to maintain effective parenting practices.

Loss of Important Relationships

Children from divorced families also face the risk of longer-term erosion or loss of important relationships with close friends, extended and new family members, and, particularly, nonresident parents, who typically are their fathers. Children accustomed to seeing their nonresident parents every day prior to separation often see them 4 days per month following separation and divorce. For many children this may lead to a diminished view of their father's importance in their lives and an erosion of closeness and meaning in these parent-child relationships (Amato, 1987; Amato & Booth, 1996; Kelly & Lamb, 2000; Thompson & Laible, 1999; Wallerstein & Kelly, 1980). Between 18% and 25% of children have no contact with their fathers 2–3 years after divorce (Braver & O'Connell, 1998; Hetherington & Kelly, 2002; Maccoby & Mnookin, 1992; Seltzer, 1998).

The significant reduction in the time children spend with their nonresident parents is due to a number of psychological, interparental, and institutional barriers. Many fathers reduce their involvement or cease contact with their children following divorce because of their own personality limitations (Arendell, 1995; Dudley, 1996; Emery, 1994; Hetherington, 1999; Kruk, 1992; Wallerstein & Kelly, 1980). Some of these fathers were minimally involved during marriage, whereas others become distracted by new partners after separation. Another group of fathers describe a painful depression about the loss of contact with their children that leads to diminished contact (Arendell; Braver et al., 1993; Kruk; Wallerstein & Kelly). Ambiguities in the visiting parent role, including a lack of clear definitions as to how part-time parents are to behave, and paternal role identity issues contribute to reduced paternal involvement (Hetherington & Stanley-Hagan, 1997; Madden-Derdich & Leonard, 2000; Minton & Pasley, 1996; Thompson & Laible, 1999). Maternal remarriage also typically diminishes contacts between children and their fathers (Bray & Berger, 1993; Hetherington & Clingempeel, 1992).

Adversarial processes that restrict timely and regular contacts with fathers also limit more extensive involvement and paternal responsibility (Emery, Laumann-Billings, Waldron, Sbarra, & Dillon, 2001; Kelly, 1991, 1993), as do written or informal guidelines recommending restricted visiting plans that were based on unsubstantiated theory (e.g., Hodges, 1991), rather than empirical research (Kelly, 2002; Kelly & Lamb, 2000; Lamb & Kelly, 2001; Warshak, 2000a). Considerable research has indicated that many children, particularly boys, want more time with their fathers than is traditionally negotiated or ordered; that children and young adults describe the loss of contact with a parent as the primary negative aspect of divorce; and that children report missing their fathers over time (Fabricius & Hall, 2000; Healy, Malley, & Stewart, 1990; Hetherington, 1999; Hetherington et al., 1982; Laumann-Billings & Emery, 2000; Wallerstein & Kelly, 1980). Despite such findings, court policy and practice has been slow to change. Compared with nonresident fathers, nonresident mothers are more likely to visit frequently, assume more parenting functions, and less often cease contact with their children (Depner, 1993; Hetherington, 1999; Maccoby & Mnookin, 1992), particularly when mothers endorse the custodial arrangement. In part, this may be related to the different role expectations of mothers in our society.

Moving after divorce is common and may interfere substantially with the contacts and relationships between children and their nonmoving parents (Braver, Ellman, & Fabricius, 2003; Kelly & Lamb, 2003; Warshak, 2000b). In Arizona, 30% of custodial parents moved out of the area within 2 years after separation (Braver et al.). In Virginia, the average distance between fathers and their children 10 years after divorce was 400 miles (Hetherington & Kelly, 2002). Relocations of more than 75–100 miles may create considerable barriers to continuity in father-child relationships, because distance requires more time and expense to visit and results in the erosion of closeness in the relationships, particularly with very young children (Hetherington & Kelly; Kelly & Lamb). Paternal remarriage and the demands of new children also diminish paternal commitment to the children of the prior marriage (Hetherington & Clingempeel, 1992; Hetherington, 1999).

Aside from the psychological and institutional barriers experienced by fathers, maternal attitudes regarding fathers maintaining postdivorce relationships with their children are influential. Evidence shows that mothers may function as gatekeepers to father involvement after divorce, as they have been found to do during marriage (Pleck, 1997). Maternal hostility at the beginning of divorce predicts less visitation and fewer overnights 3 years later (Maccoby & Mnookin, 1992), and, according to one study, 25–35% of custodial mothers interfere with or sabotage visiting (Braver & O'Connell, 1998). Maternal anger and dissatisfaction with higher levels of father contact, regardless of conflict level, is associated with poorer adjustment in children compared with children whose mothers were satisfied with high father involvement (King & Heard, 1999). In this latter study, it is difficult to know whether mothers' dissatisfaction was caused by poor fathering or by their own upset and anger with their former spouse, although a longitudinal study found that maternal anger/hurt about the divorce and concerns about parenting each predicted maternal perceptions of visiting problems (Wolchik, Fenaughty, & Braver, 1996).

Children themselves also influence the extent of paternal involvement following divorce. Some children limit contact with nonresident parents for both developmentally appropriate and psychologically inappropriate reasons (Johnston, 1993). In response to observing or hearing violence in marriages, frightened and angry children may refuse to visit abusive parents after separation. This choice to reduce or avoid contact may be a healthy response for children who have become realistically estranged, a choice not possible in the married family (Kelly & Johnston, 2001). Some youngsters avoid or reluctantly visit mentally ill parents or those whose disinterest, extreme narcissism, or selfishness interferes with meaningful parent-child relationships. Still other children refuse to visit after separation because they are alienated from a parent with whom they previously had an adequate or better relationship (Gardner, 1998). Although Gardner described this pathological adaptation primarily as the result of an alienating parent's efforts to sabotage the child's other parent-child relationship, a more recent formulation portrays the behaviors of the rejected parent as contributing also to the child's alienation (Johnston, in press; Kelly & Johnston). Mostly, these children (preadolescents and adolescents) are responding to a complex set of factors following separation, including the parents' personality problems and parenting deficits; the hostile, polarizing, and denigrating behaviors of the parents, which encourages alienation; the child's own psychological vulnerabilities and anger; and the extreme hostility generated by the divorce and the adversarial process (Johnston; Kelly & Johnston).

Economic Opportunities

Whereas contradictory findings exist (e.g., Braver & O'Connell, 1998), most scholars report that divorce substantially reduces the standard of living for custodial parents and children, and to a lesser extent, the nonresident parent (Duncan & Hoffman, 1985). Census bureau surveys show that one third of custodial parents entitled to support by court order are not receiving it (*San Francisco Chronicle*, 2002). Although divorce has generally been blamed for this decline in income, it also is apparent that marriages that end in divorce are more likely to have lower incomes prior to separation compared with parents who did not divorce in the same period (Clarke-Stewart, Vandell, McCartney, Owen, & Booth, 2000; Pong & Ju, 2000, Sun, 2001). Divorce further accelerates the downward standard of living. The consequences of reduced economic circumstances may be a significant stressor for many children through disruptive changes in residence, school, friends, and child care arrangements. Booth and Amato (2001) found that 46% of young adults recalled moving in the year following separation, and 25% reported changing schools. On average, the women in the Virginia longitudinal study moved four times in the first 6 years, but poorer women moved seven times (Hetherington & Kelly, 2002). Additionally, because child support generally is structured to pay for the basic necessities, children may not be able to participate in sports, lessons, and organizations that brought significant meaning to their lives prior to separation. This is particularly true if there are limited resources, high parent conflict, and poor cooperation.

Remarriage and Repartnering

Divorce creates the potential for children to experience a continuing series of changes and disruptions in family and emotional relationships when one or both parents introduce new social and sexual partners, cohabitate, remarry, and/or redivorce. The effect of serial attachments and losses may hinder more mature and intimate attachments as young adults. Estimates suggest that three quarters of divorced men and two thirds of divorced women eventually remarry (Bumpass, Sweet, & Castro-Martin, 1990), and 50% of divorced adults cohabit before remarriage, whereas others cohabit instead of remarriage. It is estimated that approximately one third of children will live in a remarried or cohabitating family before the age of 18 (Bumpass, Raley, & Sweet, 1995). For some, these new relationships are accompanied by family conflict, anger in the stepparent-child relationship, and role ambiguities (Bray, 1999; Hetherington & Clingempeel, 1992). Repartnering may be most stressful and problematic for children when entered into soon after divorce (Hetherington & Kelly, 2002).

DIVORCE AS RISK FOR CHILDREN

A large body of empirical research confirms that divorce increases the risk for adjustment problems in children and adolescents (for reviews, see Amato, 2000; Emery, 1999; Hetherington, 1999; Kelly, 2000, McLanahan, 1999; Simons et al., 1996). Children of divorce were significantly more likely to have behavioral, internalizing, social, and academic problems when compared with children from continuously married families. The extent of risk is at least twice that of children in continuously married families (Hetherington, 1999; McLanahan; Zill, Morrison, & Coiro, 1993). Although 10% of children in continuously married families also have serious psychological and social problems, as measured on objective tests, estimates are that 20–25% of children from divorced families had similar problems (Hetherington & Kelly, 2002; Zill & Schoenborn, 1990). The largest effects are seen in externalizing symptoms, including conduct disorders, antisocial behaviors, and problems with authority figures and parents. Less robust differences are found with respect to depression, anxiety, and self-esteem. Whereas preadolescent boys were at greater risk for these negative outcomes than girls in several studies (see Amato, 2001; Hetherington, 1999), no gender differences specifically linked to divorce were found in other studies (Sun, 2001; Vandewater & Lansford, 1998). The complex interaction between gender, age at separation, preseparation adjustment, sex of custodial parent, quality of relationships with both parents, and extent of conflict confounds efforts to clarify findings regarding gender.

Children in divorced families have lower academic performance and achievement test scores compared with children in continuously married families. The differences are modest and decrease, but do not disappear, when income and socioeconomic status are controlled (for review, see McLanahan, 1999). Children from divorced families are two to three times more likely to drop out of school than are children of intact families, and the risk of teenage childbearing is doubled. However, it appears that youngsters are already at risk for poorer educational performance and lowered expectations well before separation. For example, the risk for school dropout is associated with poverty or low income prior to separation, and this may be exacerbated by the further decline in economic resources following separation (Pong & Ju, 2000). Further, in looking at parental resources available to children prior to separation, parents provided less financial, social, human, and cultural capital to their children compared with parents who remained married (Sun & Li, 2001), and parent-child relationships were less positive (Sun, 2001). Adolescents from divorced families scored lower on tests of math and reading both prior to and after parental separation compared with adolescents in married families, and their parents were less involved in their adolescents' education (Sun & Li, 2002).

The increased risk of divorced children for behavioral problems is not diminished by remarriage. As with divorce, children in stepfamily homes are twice as likely to have psychological, behavioral, social, and academic problems than are children in nondivorced families (Bray, 1999; Hetherington & Kelly, 2002; Zill, 1998; Zill & Schoenborn, 1990).

Children from divorced families have more difficulties in their intimate relationships as young adults. Compared with young adults in continuously married families, young adults from divorced families marry earlier, report more dissatisfaction with their marriages, and are more likely to divorce (Amato, 1999, 2000; Chase-Lansdale, Cherlin, & Kierman, 1995). Relationships between divorced parents and their adult children also are less affectionate and supportive than those in continuously married families (Amato & Booth, 1996; Zill et al., 1993). When divorced parents denigrated the other parent in front of the children, young adults were more likely to report angry and less close relationships with the denigrating parents (Fabricius & Hall, 2000). Somewhat surprising is the finding that young adults whose parents had low-conflict marriages and then divorced had more problems with intimate relationships, less social support of friends and relatives, and lower psychological well-being compared with children whose high-conflict parents divorced (Booth & Amato, 2001). Parents in low-conflict marriages who divorced differed in certain dimensions, including less integration in the community and more risky behaviors, and this may place their children at greater risk. Further research is needed to understand the aspects of parenting and parent-child relationships in these low-conflict marriages that negatively affect the later relationships of their offspring.

Higher divorce rates for children of divorced families compared with those in still-married families are substantiated in a number of studies (Amato, 1996; McLanahan &

Sandefur, 1994; Wolfinger, 2000). The risk of divorce for these young adults is related to socioeconomic factors, as well as life course decisions such as cohabitation, early marriage, and premarital childbearing; attitudes toward marriage and divorce; and interpersonal behaviors, all of which are associated with marital instability (Amato, 1996, 2000). The number and cumulative effect of family structure transitions is linked to the higher probability of divorce; three or more transitions (divorce, remarriage, redivorce greatly increase the risk of offspring divorce (Wolfinger).

PROTECTIVE FACTORS REDUCING RISK FOR CHILDREN OF DIVORCE

In the last decade, researchers have identified a number of protective factors that may moderate the risks associated with divorce for individual children and that contribute to the variability in outcomes observed in children of divorce. These include specific aspects of the psychological adjustment and parenting of custodial parents, the type of relationships that children have with their nonresident parents, and the extent and type of conflict between parents.

Competent Custodial Parents and Parenting

Living in the custody of a competent, adequately functioning parent is a protective factor associated with positive outcomes in children. Overall, one of the best predictors of children's psychological functioning in the marriage (Cummings & Davies, 1994; Keitner & Miller, 1990) and after divorce (Emery et al., 1999; Hetherington, 1999; Johnston, 1995; Kalter et al., 1989; Kline et al., 1990) is the psychological adjustment of custodial parents (usually mothers) and the quality of parenting provided by them. A particular cluster of parenting behaviors following divorce is an important protective factor as well. When custodial parents provide warmth, emotional support, adequate monitoring, discipline authoritatively, and maintain age-appropriate expectations, children and adolescents experience positive adjustment compared with children whose divorced custodial parents are inattentive, less supportive, and use coercive discipline (Amato, 2000; Buchanan et al., 1996; Hetherington, 1999; Krishnakumar & Buehler, 2000; Maccoby & Mnookin, 1992).

Nonresident Parents

There is a potential protective benefit from the timely and appropriate parenting of nonresident parents. Frequency of visits between fathers and children generally is not a reliable predictor of children's outcomes, because frequency alone does not reflect the quality of the father-child relationship. In one study, boys and younger children, but not girls or older children, were better adjusted with frequent and regular contact with their fathers (Stewart, Copeland, Chester, Malley, & Barenbaum, 1997). In the context of low conflict, frequent visits between fathers and children is associated with better child adjustment, but where interparental conflict is intense, more frequent visits were linked to poorer adjustment, presumably because of the opportunities for more direct exposure of the children to parental aggression and pressures (Amato & Rezac, 1994; Hetherington & Kelly, 2002; Johnston, 1995).

Frequency of contact also has beneficial effects when certain features of parenting are present in nonresident parents. A meta-analysis of 57 studies found that children who had close relationships with their fathers benefited from frequent contacts when their fathers remained actively involved as parents (Amato & Gilbreth, 1999). When fathers helped with homework and projects, provided authoritative parenting, and had appropriate expectations for their children, the children had more positive adjustment and academic performance than did those with less involved fathers. More paternal involvement in children's schooling was also associated with better grades and fewer repeated grades and suspensions (Nord, Brimhall, & West, 1997). The combination of fathers engaging in activities with their children and providing financial support was associated with increased probability of completing high school and entering college compared with activities alone or activities combined with very low financial support (Menning, 2002). Indeed, when both parents engage in active, authoritative, competent parenting, adolescent boys from divorced families had no greater involvement in delinquent behavior than did those in continuously married families (Simon et al., 1996).

New reports about joint custody, compared with sole custody, also suggest a protective effect for some children. A meta-analysis of 33 studies of sole- and joint-physical custody studies reported that children in joint-custody arrangements were better adjusted on multiple objective measures, including general adjustment, emotional and behavioral adjustment, and academic achievement compared with children in sole-custody arrangements (Bausermann, 2002). In fact, children in joint custody were better adjusted regardless of the level of conflict between parents, and they did not differ in adjustment from the children in still-married families. Although the joint-custody parents had less conflict prior to separation and after divorce than did sole-custody parents, these differences did not affect the advantage of joint custody. Lee (2002) also reported positive effects of dual residence on children's behavioral adjustment, although the effects were suppressed by high interparental conflict and children's sadness.

In sharp contrast to the 1980s, some findings suggest that between 35% and 40% of children may now have at least weekly contacts with their fathers, particularly in the first several years after divorce (Braver & O'Connell, 1998; Hetherington, 1999; Seltzer, 1991, 1998). This may reflect changes in legal statutes and social contexts that now encourage shared legal decision-making, less restrictive views of paternal time with children, and greater opportunities for interested fathers to engage more fully in active parenting. Mothers also are more satisfied with higher levels of paternal involvement than they were 20 years ago (King & Heard, 1999), possibly reflecting changing cultural and work-related trends and the increased role of the father in raising children (Doherty, 1998; Pleck, 1997).

Diminished Conflict between Parents Following Divorce

Low parental conflict is a protective factor for children following divorce. Although we know little about the thresholds at which conflict becomes a risk factor following divorce in different families, some conflict appears to be normative and acceptable to the parties (King & Heard, 1999). Young adults whose parents had low conflict during their earlier years were less depressed and had fewer psychological symptoms compared with those whose parents had continued high conflict (Amato & Keith, 1991; Zill et al., 1993). When parents have continued higher levels of conflict, protective factors include a good relationship with at least one parent or caregiver; parental warmth (Emery & Forehand, 1994; Neighbors, Forehand, & McVicar, 1993; Vandewater & Lansford, 1998); and the ability of parents to encapsulate their conflict (Hetherington, 1999). Several studies found no differences in the amount of conflict between parents in sole- or joint-custody arrangements (Braver & O'Connell, 1998; Emery et al., 1999; Maccoby & Mnookin, 1992), although results from a meta-analysis found more conflict in sole-custody families prior to and after divorce (Bausermann, 2002).

Most parents diminish their conflict in the first 2–3 years after divorce as they become disengaged and establish their separate (or remarried) lives. Studies indicate that between 8% and 12% of parents continue high conflict 2–3 years after divorce (Hetherington, 1999; King & Heard, 1999; Maccoby & Mnookin, 1992). The relatively small group of chronically contentious and litigating parents are more likely to be emotionally disturbed, character-disordered men and women who are intent on vengeance and or on controlling their former spouses and their parenting (Johnston & Campbell, 1988; Johnston & Roseby, 1997). Such parents use disproportionate resources and time in family courts, and their children are more likely to be exposed to parental aggression. When one or both parents continue to lash out during transitions between households, mediation experience indicates that children can be protected from this exposure through access arrangements that incorporate transfers at neutral points (e.g., school, day care).

Related to the level of conflict between parents postdivorce is the effect of the coparental relationship. Research shows that between 25% and 30% of parents have a cooperative coparental relationship characterized by joint planning, flexibility, sufficient communication, and coordination of schedules and activities. However, more than half of parents engage in parallel parenting, in which low conflict, low communication, and emotional disengagement are typical features. Although there are distinct advantages of cooperative coparenting for children, children thrive as well in parallel parenting relationships when parents are providing nurturing care and appropriate discipline in each household (Hetherington, 1999; Hetherington & Kelly, 2002; Maccoby & Mnookin, 1992; Whiteside & Becker, 2000).

RESILIENCE OF CHILDREN OF DIVORCE

Despite the increased risk reported for children from divorced families, the current consensus in the social science literature is that the majority of children whose parents divorced are not distinguishable from their peers whose parents remained married in the longer term (Amato, 1994, 2001; Chase-Lansdale et al., 1995; Emery, 1999; Emery & Forehand, 1994; Furstenberg & Kiernan, 2001; Hetherington, 1999; Simons et al., 1996; Zill et al., 1993). There is considerable overlap between groups of children and adolescents in married and postdivorce families, with some divorced (and remarried) children functioning quite well in all dimensions, and some children in married families experiencing severe psychological, social, and academic difficulties (Amato, 1994, 2001; Hetherington, 1999). Whereas a slight widening of the differences between children from married and divorced families is found in studies in the 1990s, the magnitude of the differences remains small (Amato, 2001). Both large-scale studies with nationally representative samples and multimethod longitudinal studies using widely accepted psychological and social measures and statistics indicate that the majority of children of divorce continue to fall within the average range of adjustment (Amato, 2001; Hetherington & Kelly, 2002; Zill et al., 1993).

Not to minimize the stresses and risk to children that separation and divorce create, it is important to emphasize that approximately 75–80% of children and young adults do not suffer from major psychological problems, including depression; have achieved their education and career goals; and retain close ties to their families. They enjoy intimate relationships, have not divorced, and do not appear to be scarred with immutable negative effects from divorce (Amato, 1999, 2000; Laumann-Billings & Emery, 2000; McLanahan, 1999; Chase-Lansdale et al., 1995). In fact, Amato (1999) estimated that approximately 42% of young adults from divorced families in his study had well-being scores above the average of young adults from nondivorced families.

As we indicated here, the differences in children's lives that determine their longer-term outcomes are dependent on many circumstances, among them their adjustment prior to separation, the quality of parenting they received before and after divorce, and the amount of conflict and violence between parents that they experienced during marriage and after divorce. Children from high-conflict and violent marriages may derive the most benefit from their parents' divorces (Amato et al., 1995; Booth & Amato, 2001) as a result of no longer enduring the conditions that are associated with significant adjustment problems in children in marriages. Once freed from intense marital conflict, these findings suggest that parenting by custodial parents improves, although research is needed to explain more specifically what aspects of parent-child relationships and family functioning facilitate recovery in these youngsters. Clearly, the links between level of marital conflict and outcomes for children are complex. For children whose parents reported marital conflict in the mid-range, divorce is associated with only slightly lower psychological well-being (Booth & Amato, 2001). If this midrange marital conflict represents approximately 50% of the families that divorce, as others have found, then the large number of resilient children seen in the years following divorce is not surprising.

UNDERSTANDING CONTRADICTORY FINDINGS ON ADULT CHILDREN OF DIVORCE

These broadly based findings of long-term resiliency are at odds with the 25-year longitudinal study that has received wide-spread attention. In *The Unexpected Legacy of Divorce* (Wallerstein et al., 2000), the authors report that children of divorce, interviewed in young adulthood, do not survive the experience of divorce and that the negative effects are immutable. These young adults are described as anxious, depressed, burdened, failing to reach their potential, and fearful of commitment and failure.

What accounts for these enormously disparate findings? Many of these differences can be traced to methodological issues and may relate as well to the clinical interpretations of participant interviews about their experiences as divorced young adults. An essential methodological concern is that this study (Wallerstein & Kelly, 1980; Wallerstein & Blakeslee, 1989; Wallerstein et al., 2000) was a qualitative study, used a clinical sample, and no comparison group of married families existed from the start. The data were collected in clinical interviews by experienced therapists, and no standardized or objective measures of psychological adjustment, depression, anxiety, self-esteem, or social relationships were used. The goal of the study, initiated in 1969 when information about children of divorce was extremely limited, was to describe in detail the responses of children and parents to the initial separation and divorce, and then to see how they fared over the first 5 years in comparison with their initial reports and behaviors (Wallerstein & Kelly).

The parents in the original sample of 60 families had severe psychological and relationship problems, suggesting that this sample of families was not "normal," as has been widely asserted by Wallerstein in the media (Waters, 2001). Only one third of the parents were clinically rated as functioning psychologically at an adequate or better level during the marriage; approximately one half of the mothers and fathers were "moderately disturbed" or "frequently incapacitated by disabling neuroses and addictions," including chronic depression, suicide attempts, alcoholism, severe relationship problems, or problems in controlling rage. Additionally, 15–20% of the parents were "severely disturbed," including those diagnosed with severe manic depression, paranoid ideation, and bizarre thinking and behaviors (see Wallerstein & Kelly, 1980, Appendix A, pp. 328–329). In part, the pervasive parent pathology found in the original sample may be the basis for the descriptions presented in the 25-year follow-up of inattentive, selfish, narcissistic, abandoning parents intent on self-gratification. In contrast, in Hetherington's multimethod, longitudinal studies using married families as a comparison group, most divorced parents eventually became as competent as the still-married parents and were caring toward their children in the years following divorce (Hetherington, 1999; Hetherington & Kelly, 2002).

It has been stated in the most recent report (Wallerstein et al., 2000) and in personal interviews that the children in the original sample were carefully prescreened, "asymptomatic," and developmentally on track (Waters, 2001, p. 50). In fact, 17% of the children were clinically rated as having severe psychological, social, and/or developmental problems (Wallerstein & Kelly, 1980, p. 330) and were retained in the sample. The nonrepresentative sample of convenience was referred from a variety of sources, including lawyers, therapists, and the court, or were self-referred. The parents participated in a free, 6-week divorce counseling intervention from which the data were gathered (see Kelly & Wallerstein, 1977; Wallerstein & Kelly, 1977), and the children were seen for three to four sessions by child-trained therapists.

Objective data are limited in the 25-year report (Wallerstein et al., 2000), and few statistical analyses were available. The qualitative findings were presented primarily as six composites; however, without sufficient data, it is impossible for the reader to determine whether the composites were representative of the whole sample. With rare exception, these composites present stark, failed outcomes. The emotional pain and failures of these young adults has been presented in a consistently negative manner, so the overall impression is one of pervasive pathology. Based on the limited data found in the earlier follow-up, one would expect that among the 93 young adults interviewed at the 25-year follow-up there were some subjects without pain, anger, and depression who were enjoying successful marriages and parent-child relationships. We believe that in the absence of objective questionnaires, standardized measures, and statistical analyses, clinical research is particularly vulnerable to a focus on psychopathology to the exclusion of more adaptive coping sand resilience. Certainly, the sweeping generalizations in the 25-year report that none of these youngsters escaped the permanently damaging effects of parental divorce are not consistent with the limited data in an endnote in *The Unexpected Legacy of Divorce* (2000, p. 333), which indicates that 70% of the sample of adult children of divorce scored either in the "average" or "very well to outstanding" range on an overall measure of psychological well-being. Without standardized adjustment measures, it is difficult to compare these numbers with the findings of other divorce research.

Aside from sampling and methodological concerns, another explanation for the marked divergence in longer-term outcomes of divorce offspring may be a confusion of pain and pathology. Like young adults participating in more objective assessments of pain, participants in the Wallerstein study may have reported considerable distress in reflecting upon their parents' divorce. However, painful reflections on a difficult past are not the same as an inability to feel and function competently in the present.

PAINFUL MEMORIES AS LONGER-TERM RESIDUES OF DIVORCE

A third perception of the short- and longer-term effects of divorce may be a useful complement and balance to risk and resilience perspectives. Painful memories and experiences may be a lasting residue of the divorce (and remarriage) process for many youngsters and young adults. However, it is important to distinguish pain or distress about parental divorce from longer-term psychological symptoms or pathology. Clearly, divorce can create lingering feelings of sadness, longing, worry, and regret that coexist with competent psychological and social functioning. Substantial change and relationship loss, when compounded for some by continuing conflict between parents, represents an ongoing unpleasant situation over which the child or adolescent may have no control. Research that includes standardized and objective measures of both psychological adjustment and painful feelings is useful in disentangling differences in long-term outcomes reported in young adults from divorced families. Such research may help to explain some of the apparent conflict between studies using clinical and quantitative methods.

A decade after divorce, well-functioning college students reported continued pain and distress about their parents' divorces (Laumann-Billings & Emery, 2000). Compared with students in still-married families, they reported more painful childhood feelings and experiences, including worry about such things as their parents attending major events and wanting to spend more time with their fathers. They did not blame themselves for parental divorce, and 80% thought that the divorce was right for their parents. Feelings of loss were the most prevalent of the painful feelings, and the majority reported they missed not having their father around. Many questioned whether their fathers loved them. Despite these painful feelings and beliefs, these young adults did not differ on standardized measures of depression or anxiety from a comparison sample of students in still-married families. These findings were replicated in a second sample of low-income young adults who were not college students. Among factors associated with more pain among children from divorced families were living in sole mother or father custody, rather than a shared custody arrangement, and higher levels of postdivorce parental conflict. When children's parents continued their high conflict, these young adults reported greater feelings of loss and paternal blame and were more likely to view their lives through the filter of divorce (Laumann-Billings & Emery). Young adults in both samples also reported lower levels of loss when they had lived in joint physical custody and were less likely to see life through the filter of divorce. As would be expected, there is no question that divorce impacted the lives of many of these young adults and that parental attitudes and behavior affected the degree of painful feelings lingering after divorce. Although tempting, this impact should not be confused with or portrayed as poor psychological adjustment.

Feelings of loss also were reported by half of 820 college students a decade after divorce in another study (Fabricius & Hall, 2000). Subjects indicated that they had wanted to spend more time with their fathers in the years after divorce. They reported that their mothers were opposed to increasing their time with fathers. When asked which of nine living arrangements would have been best for them, 70% chose "equal time" with each parent, and an additional 30% said a "substantial" number of overnights with their fathers, preferences that were similar in a sample of young adults in nondivorced families. The typical amount of contact reported in this and other studies between children and their fathers was every other weekend. One can infer from these findings that for many years, many of these students experienced some degree of painful longing for the absent parent that might have been alleviated with more generous visiting arrangements. An analysis of the amount of contact and closeness to fathers indicated that with each increment of increased contact between these children and their fathers, there was an equal increase in young adults reporting closeness to their fathers and a corresponding decrease in anger toward their fathers. Further, the increased feelings of closeness toward fathers did not diminish their reported closeness to mothers (see Fabricius, 2003). Further, increasing increments of father contact were linked to incremental amounts of support paid by fathers for their children's college (Fabricius, Braver, & Deneau, 2003). In fact, students who perceived their parents as opposed to or interfering with contact with the nonresident parent were more angry and less close to those parents than were students who reported their parents as more supportive of contact with the nonresident parents.

Another source of pain may be the extent to which adult children feel that they had no control over their lives following divorce. As indicated earlier, the majority of children and adolescents are not adequately informed about the divorce and its implications for their lives (Dunn et al., 2001). They also are not consulted for their ideas regarding access arrangements and how they are working for them, both emotionally and practically (Kelly, 2002; McIntosh, 2000; Smart & Neale, 2000). The young adults cited earlier who longed to spend increased time with their fathers either perceived that they had no control over this arrangement or in reality did not have control. In lacking a voice in these divorce arrangements, not only did they miss their fathers over an extended period, but they were left with lingering doubts as to whether their fathers loved them. The substantial presence of involved nonresident parents in children's lives after divorce may be an important indicator to many children that they are valued and loved.

Transitions between two households constitute another arena where many children do not have sufficient input and control, particularly as they move into adolescence, and this may cause lingering angry or painful feelings. Whereas 25% of youngsters had *some to many* negative feelings about transitions between households, 73% had *some to many* positive feelings about the transitions. There was a significant association between positive feelings about transitions and being given a voice or role in some decision-making about the arrangements (Dunn et al., 2001). Although some research calls attention to the importance of children having a voice in formulating or shaping postdivorce parenting plans, there is the danger of burdening children with decisions that the adults cannot make. Giving children the right to be heard, if not done with sensitivity and care, may give children the responsibility for making an impossible choice between their two parents. There is a distinction between providing children with the possibility of input regarding their access arrangements and the inherent stresses of decision-making—a distinction with which children themselves seem quite familiar and comfortable (Kelly, 2002; McIntosh, 2000; Smart & Neale, 2000).

IMPLICATIONS FOR PRACTICE AND INTERVENTIONS

There are a number of important implications for practice and intervention that derive from this analysis of children's adjustment following divorce. Rather than communicating a global or undifferentiated view of the impact of divorce, research has begun to identify particular factors that increase children's risk following divorce and, equally important, those that are protective and promote resiliency in children and adolescents. Understanding this literature is central to promoting policies and developing and assessing services that have the potential to help mitigate family problems so that adjustment problems among children from divorced families are diminished. There are few better examples than the importance of adopting a systems approach (including family systems and broader social and legal systems) to helping these children. Whatever its specific nature or focus, interventions are more likely to benefit children from divorced families if they seek to contain parental conflict, promote authoritative and close relationships between children and *both* of their parents, enhance economic stability in the postdivorce family, and, when appropriate, involve children in effective interventions that help them have a voice in shaping more individualized and helpful access arrangements (Kelly, 2002).

Among the hierarchy of interventions available that strive toward some of these ends are parent education programs for parents and children, divorce mediation, collaborative lawyering, judicial settlement conferences, parenting coordinator or arbitration programs for chronically litigating parents, and family and group therapy for children and parents (Kelly, 2002). Clearly, there is a need for more research on these sorts of interventions; at present, only mediation enjoys a solid base of research support regarding the benefits to divorcing and divorced families (Emery, 1994; Emery, Kitzmann, & Waldron, 1999; Kelly, 1996, 2002). The potential benefits of mediation are substantial in both the short term (e.g., reduced parental conflict and improved parent support and communications; Kelly, 1996) and longer term. For example, a randomized trial of an average of 5 hours of custody mediation led to significant and positive effects on parent-child and parent-parent relationships 12 years later (Emery et al., 2001), including more sustained contact between fathers and children, compared with those in the litigation sample.

Divorce education programs for parents and children have proliferated in the United States in the past decade, particularly those associated with family courts (Geasler & Blaisure, 1999). They are generally limited to one to two sessions in the court sector and four to six sessions in the community or schools. Research on this newer preventive intervention is more limited and has focused primarily on parent satisfaction and parental self-reports of the impact of the interventions on their behavior (Kelly, 2002). Programs that are research-based and focused on skill development showed more promise in educating parents and promoting change than did those that are didactic or affect-based (Kelly, 2002). However, few studies of these programs are designed to demonstrate their efficacy in preventing or reducing psychological or social adjustment problems for children of divorce, or in actually modifying parental behaviors associated with poor child outcomes. Several experimental or quasi-experimental studies of lengthier, research-based programs designed to facilitate children's postdivorce adjustment have been conducted that show promising behavioral and psychological changes in both parents and children (for review, see Haine, Sandler, Wolchik, Tein, & Dawson-McClure, 2003). The child-focused programs, incorporating aspects of risk and resiliency factors described in their article, have demonstrated significant reductions at follow-up in child externalizing and internalizing behaviors and child self-esteem compared with nontreatment controls. Several investigations of mother-focused programs also found reductions in child psychological and behavioral problems, improvements in mother-child relationship quality and discipline, and changed attitudes toward father-child relationships and visiting (Haine et al., 2003). Few programs and research have focused on fathers to test the efficacy of providing newer empirical information regarding the benefits of active, competent parenting among nonresident parents, rather than the more permissive, weekend entertainment model that so frequently emerges after divorce; however, new research is promising (Braver, Griffin, Cookson, Sandler, & Williams, in press).

Another important implication of these findings for practice is as a reminder to practitioners of several seemingly obvious but easily overlooked points. Children and young people from divorced families seen in counseling or psychotherapy are a select group who surely differ from the general population of children of divorce. We must be careful in generalizing to all children from those in small, unrepresentative, or clinical samples, particularly when contributing to public education or policy. We believe that the public education message needs to acknowledge that when divorce occurs, parents and legal systems designed to assist families can utilize particular research knowledge and skills to reduce the risks associated with divorce for children. Although we also wish to promote more happy marriages, we conclude that although some children are harmed by parental divorce, the majority of findings show that most children do well. To suggest otherwise is to provide an inaccurate interpretation of the research findings. Further, such misrepresentation[s] of research are potentially harmful in creating stigma, helplessness, and negative expectations for children and parents from divorced families. Practitioners and educators need to be reminded and remind others that the painful memories expressed by young people from divorced families are not evidence of pathology. At the same time, we should encourage researchers to develop objective, reliable, and valid measures of the important struggles associated with divorce that might be apparent first in schools or clinical practice.

References

Amato, P. (1987). Family processes in one-parent, step-parent and intact families. The child's point of view. *Journal of Marriage and the Family, 49,* 327–337.

Amato, P. R. (1994). Life-span adjustment of children to their parents' divorce. *Future of Children: Children and Divorce, 4,* 143–164.

Amato, P. (1996). Explaining the intergenerational transmission of divorce. *Journal of Marriage and the Family, 58,* 628–640.

Amato, P. (1999). Children of divorced parents as young adults. In E. M. Hetherington (Ed.), *Coping with divorce, single parenting, and remarriage* (pp. 147–164). Mahway, NJ: Erlbaum.

Amato, P. (2000). The consequences of divorce for adults and children. *Journal of Marriage and Family, 62,* 1269–1287.

Amato, P. R. (2001). Children of divorce in the 1990s: An update of the Amato and Keith (1991) meta-analysis. *Journal of Family Psychology, 15,* 355–370.

Amato, P., & Booth, A. (1996). A prospective study of divorce and parent-child relationships. *Journal of Marriage and the Family, 58,* 356–365.

Amato, P., & Gilbreth, J. (1999). Nonresident fathers and children's well-being: A meta-analysis. *Journal of Marriage and the Family, 61,* 557–573.

Amato, P. & Keith, B. (1991). Parental divorce and adult well-being: A meta-analysis. *Journal of Marriage and the Family, 53,* 43–58.

Amato, P. R., Loomis, L., & Booth, A. (1995). Parental divorce, parental marital conflict, and offspring well-being during early adulthood. *Social Forces, 73,* 895–916.

Amato, P. R., & Rezac, S. (1994). Contact with residential parents, interparental conflict, and children's behavior. *Journal of Family Issues, 12,* 578–599.

Arendell, T. (1995). *Fathers and divorce.* Thousand Oaks, CA: Sage.

Bausermann, R. (2002). Child adjustment in joint-custody versus sole-custody arrangements: A meta-analytic review. *Journal of Family Psychology, 16,* 91–102.

Belsky, J., Youngblade, L., Rovine, M., & Volling, B. (1991). Patterns of marital change and parent-child interaction. *Journal of Marriage and the Family, 53,* 487–498.

Block. J., Block, J., & Gjerde, P. (1986). The personality of children prior to divorce: A prospective study. *Child Development, 57,* 827–840.

Booth, A., & Amato, P. R. (2001). Parental predivorce relations and offspring postdivorce well-being. *Journal of Marriage and Family, 63,* 197–212.

Braver, S. L., Ellman, I. M., & Fabricius, W. V. (2003). Relocation of children after divorce and children's best interests: New evidence and legal considerations. *Journal of Family Psychology, 17,* 206–219.

Braver, S. L., Griffin, W. A., Cookston, J. T., Sandier, I. N., & Williams, J. (in press). Promoting better fathering among divorced nonresident fathers. In W. M. Pinsof & J. Lebow, (Eds.), *Family psychology: The art of the science.* New York: Oxford University Press.

Braver, S. L., & O'Connell, E. (1998). *Divorced dads: Shattering the myths.* New York: Tarcher, Putnam.

Braver, S. L., Wolchik, S. A., Sandler, I. N., Sheets, V., Fogas, B., & Bay, R. C. (1993). A longitudinal study of noncustodial parents: Parents without children. *Journal of Family Psychology, 7,* 9–23.

Bray, J. H. (1999). From marriage to remarriage and beyond: Findings from the Developmental Issues in Stepfamilies research project. In E. M. Hetherington (Ed), *Coping with divorce, single parenting, and remarriage: A risk and resiliency perspective* (pp. 253–272). Mahwah, NJ: Lawrence Erlbaum.

Bray, J. H., & Berger, S. H. (1993). Nonresident family-child relationships following divorce and remarriage. In C. E. Depner & J. H. Bray (Eds). *Non-residential parenting: New vistas in family living* (pp. 156–181). Newbury Park, CA: Sage.

Buchanan, C., Maccoby, E., & Dornbusch, S. (1991). Caught between parents: Adolescents' experience in divorced homes. *Child Development, 62,* 1008–1029.

Buehler, C., Krishnakumar, A., Stone, G., Anthony, C., Pemberton, S., Gerard, J., & Barber, B. K. (1998). Interparental conflict styles and youth problem behaviors: A two-sample replication study. *Journal of Marriage and the Family, 60,* 119–132.

Bumpass, L. L., Raley, R. K., & Sweet, J. A. (1995). The changing character of stepfamilies: Implications of cohabitation and nonmarital childbearing. *Demography, 32,* 425–436.

Bumpass, L. L., Sweet, J. A., & Castro-Martin, T. (1990). Changing patterns of remarriage. *Journal of Marriage and the Family, 52,* 747–756.

Chase-Lansdale, P. L., Cherlin, A. J., & Kierman, K. E. (1995). The long-term effects of parental divorce on the mental health of young adults: A developmental perspective. *Child Development, 66,* 1614–1634.

Cherlin, A., Furstenberg, F., Jr., Lindsay, P., Chase-Lansdale, P., Kiernan, K., Robins, P., Morrison, D., & Teitler, J. (1991). Longitudinal studies of the effects of divorce on children in Great Britain and the United States. *Science, 252,* 1386–1389.

Clark-Stewart, K. A., Vandell, D. L., McCartney, K., Owen, M. T., & Booth, C. (2000). Effects of parental separation and divorce on very young children. *Journal of Family Psychology, 14,* 304–326.

Cummings, E., & Davies, P. (1994). *Children and marital conflict.* New York: Guilford Press.

Depner, C. E. (1993). Parental role reversal: Mothers and non-residential parents. In C. E. Depner & J. H. Bray (Eds.), *Nonresidential parenting: New vistas in family living* (pp. 37–57). Newbury Park, CA: Sage.

Doherty, W. J. (1998). Responsible fathering: An overview and conceptual framework. *Journal of Marriage and the Family, 60,* 277–292.

Dudley, J. R. (1996). Noncustodial fathers speak about their parental role. *Family and Conciliation Courts Review, 34,* 410–426.

Duncan, G. J., & Hoffman, S. D. (1985). Economic consequences of marital instability. In M. David & T. Smeeding (Eds.), *Horizontal equity, uncertainty and well-being* (pp. 427–469). Chicago: University of Chicago Press.

Dunn, J., Davies, L., O'Connor, T., & Sturgess, W. (2001). Family lives and friendships: The perspectives of children in step-, single-parent, and nonstop families. *Journal of Family Psychology, 15,* 272–287.

Emery, R. E. (1982). Interparental conflict and the children of discord and divorce. *Psychological Bulletin, 92,* 310–330.

Emery, R. E. (1994). *Renegotiating family relationships: Divorce, child custody, and mediation.* New York: Guilford.

Emery, R. E. (1999). *Marriage, divorce, and children's adjustment* (2nd ed.). Thousand Oaks, CA: Sage.

Emery, R. E., & Forehand, R. (1994). Parental divorce and children's well-being: A focus on resilience. In R. J. Haggerty, L. Sherrod, N. Garmezy, & M. Rutter (Eds.), *Risk and resilience in children* (pp. 64–99). London: Cambridge University Press.

Emery, R. E., Kitzmann, K. M., & Waldron, M. (1999). Psychological interventions for separated and divorced families. In E. M. Hetherington (Ed.), *Coping with divorce, single parenting, and remarriage* (pp. 323–344). Mahwah, NJ: Erlbaum.

Emery, R. E., Laumann-Billings, L., Waldron, M., Sbarra, D. A., & Dillon, P. (2001). Child custody mediation and litigation: Custody, contact, and co-parenting 12 years after initial dispute resolution. *Journal of Consulting and Clinical Psychology, 69,* 323–332.

Emery, R. E., Waldron, M., Kitzmann, K. M., & Aaron, J. (1999). Delinquent behavior, future divorce or nonmarital childbearing, and externalizing behavior among offspring: A 14-year prospective study. *Journal of Family Psychology, 13,* 568–579.

Fabricius, W. V. (2003). Listening to divorce: New findings that diverge from Wallerstein, Lewis, and Blakeslee. *Family Relations, 52,* 385–396.

Fabricius, W. V., Braver, S. L., & Deneau, K. (2003). Divorced parents' financial support of their children's college expenses. *Family Court Review, 41,* 224–241.

Fabricius, W. V., & Hall, J. (2000). Young adults' perspectives on divorce: Living arrangements. *Family and Conciliation Courts Review, 38,* 446–461.

Furstenberg, F. F., & Kiernan, K. E. (2001). Delayed parental divorce: How much do children benefit? *Journal of Marriage and Family, 63,* 446–457.

Gardner, R. A. (1998). *The parental alienation syndrome* (2nd ed.). Creskill. NJ: Creative Therapeutics.

Geasler, M. J., & Blaisure, K. R. (1999). 1998 Nationwide survey of court-connected divorce education programs. *Family and Conciliation Courts Review, 37,* 36–63.

Haine, R. A., Sandler, I. N., Tein, J. Y., & Dawson-McClure, S. R. (2003). Changing the legacy of divorce: Evidence from prevention programs and future directions. *Family Relations, 52*, 397–405.

Healy, J., Malley, J., & Stewart, A. (1990). Children and their fathers after parental separation. *American Journal of Orthopsychiatry, 60*, 531–543.

Hetherington, E. M. (1979). Divorce: A child's perspective. *American Psychologist. 34*, 851–858.

Hetherington, E. M. (1999). Should we stay together for the sake of the children? In E. M. Hetherington (Ed.). *Coping with divorce, single parenting, and remarriage* (pp. 93–116). Mahwah, NJ: Erlbaum.

Hetherington, E. M., & Clingempeel, W. G. (1992). Coping with marital transitions: A family systems perspective. *Monographs of the Society for Research in Child Development, 57*.

Hetherington, E. M., Cox, M., & Cox, R. (1982). Effects of divorce on parents and children. In M. Lamb (Ed.), *Nontraditional families* (pp. 233–288). Hillsdale, NJ: Erlbaum.

Hetherington, E. M., & Kelly, J. (2002). *For better or for worse*. New York: Norton.

Hetherington, E. M., & Stanley-Hagan, M. M. (1997). The effects of divorce on fathers and their children. In M. Lamb (Ed.), *The role of the father in child development* (pp. 191–211). New York: Wiley.

Hodges, W. (1991). *Interventions for children of divorce: Custody, access, and psychotherapy*. New York: Wiley.

Johnston, J. R. (1993). Children of divorce who refuse visitation. In C. Depner & J. Bray (Eds.). *Nonresident parenting: New vistas in family living* (pp. 109–135). Newbury Park: CA Sage.

Johnston, J. R. (1994). High-conflict divorce. *Future of Children, 4*, 165–182.

Johnston, J. R. (1995). Research update: Children's adjustment in sole custody compared to joint custody families and principles for custody decision making. *Family and Conciliation Courts Review, 33*, 415–425.

Johnston, J. R. (in press). Parental alignments and rejection: An empirical study of alienation in children of divorce. *Journal of the American Academy of Psychiatry and the Law.*

Johnston, J. R., & Campbell, L. (1988). *Impasses of divorce: The dynamics and resolution of family conflict*. New York: Free Press.

Johnston, J. R., & Roseby, V. (1997). *In the name of the child. A developmental approach to understanding and helping children of conflict and violent divorce*. New York: Free Press.

Kalter, N., Kloner, A., Schreiser, S., & Okla, K. (1989). Predictors of children's post-divorce adjustment. *American Journal of Orthopsychiatry, 59*, 605–618.

Keitner, G. L., & Miller, I. W. (1990). Family functioning and major depression: An overview. *American Journal of Psychiatry, 147*, 1128–1137.

Kelly, J. B. (1991). Parent interaction after divorce: Comparison of mediated and adversarial divorce processes. *Behavioral Sciences and the Law, 9*, 387–398.

Kelly, J. B. (1993). Developing and implementing post-divorce parenting plans: Does the forum make a difference? In J. Bray & C. Depner (Eds.), *Non-residential parenting: New vistas in family living* (pp. 136–155). Newbury Park, CA: Sage.

Kelly, J. B. (1994). The determination of child custody. *Future of Children: Children and Divorce, 4*, 121–242.

Kelly, J. B. (1996). A decade of divorce mediation research: Some answers and questions. *Family and Conciliation Courts Review, 34*, 373–385.

Kelly, J. B. (2000). Children's adjustment in conflicted marriage and divorce: A decade review of research. *Journal of Child and Adolescent Psychiatry, 39*, 963–973.

Kelly, J. B. (2002). Psychological and legal interventions for parents and children in custody and access disputes: Current research and practice. *Virginia Journal of Social Policy and Law, 10*, 129–163.

Kelly, J. B., & Johnston. J. R. (2001). The alienated child: A reformulation of parental alienation syndrome. *Family Court Review, 39*, 249–266.

Kelly, J. B., & Lamb, M. E. (2000). Using child development research to make appropriate custody and access decisions. *Family and Conciliation Courts Review, 38*, 297–311.

Kelly, J. B., & Lamb, M. E. (2003). Developmental issues in the resolution of relocation cases involving young children: When, whether. and how? *Journal of Family Psychology, 17*, 193–205.

Kelly, J. B., & Wallerstein, J. S. (1977). Brief interventions with children in divorcing families. *American Journal of Orthopsychiatry, 47*, 23–29.

King, V., & Heard, H. E. (1999). Nonresident father visitation, parental conflict, and mother's satisfaction: What's best for child well-being? *Journal of Marriage and the Family, 61,* 385–396.

Kirn, W. (2000. September 25). Should you stay together for the kids? *Time, 156,* 74–82.

Kline, M., Johnston, J., & Tschann, J. (1990). The long shadow of marital conflict: A model of children's postdivorce adjustment. *Journal of Marriage and the Family, 53,* 297–309.

Krishnakamur, A., & Buehler, C. (2000). Interparental conflict and parenting behaviors: A meta-analytic review. *Family Relations, 49,* 25–44.

Kruk, E. (1992). Psychological and structural factors contributing to the disengagement of noncustodial fathers after divorce. *Family and Conciliation Courts Review, 30,* 81–101.

Lamb, M. E., & Kelly, J. B. (2001). Using the empirical literature to guide the development of parenting plans for young children: A rejoinder to Solomon and Biringen. *Family Court Review, 39,* 365–371.

Laumann-Billings, L., & Emery, R. E. (2000). Distress among young adults in divorced families. *Journal of Family Psychology, 14,* 671–687.

Lee, M. Y. (2002). A model of children's postdivorce behavioral adjustment in maternal and dual-residence arrangements. *Journal of Family Issues, 23,* 672–697.

Maccoby, E., & Mnookin, R. (1992). *Dividing the child.* Cambridge, MA: Harvard University Press.

Madden-Derdich, D. A., & Leonard, S. A. (2000). Parental role identity and fathers' involvement in coparental interaction after divorce: Fathers' perspectives. *Family Relations, 49,* 311–318.

Madden-Derdich, D. A., & Leonard, S. A. (2001). Shared experiences, unique realities: Formerly married mothers' and fathers' perceptions of parenting and custody after divorce. *Family Relations. 51,* 37–45.

McIntosh, J. (2000). Child-inclusive divorce mediation: Report on a qualitative research study. *Mediation Quarterly, 18,* 55–70.

McLanahan, S. S. (1999). Father absence and children's welfare. In E. M. Hetherington (Ed). *Coping with divorce, single parenting, and remarriage: A risk and resiliency perspective* (pp. 117–146). Mahwah. NJ: Lawrence Erlbaum.

McLanahan, S. S., & Sandefur, G. (1994). *Growing up with a single parent.* Cambridge. MA: Harvard University Press.

Menning, C. L. (2002). Absent parents are more than money: The joint effects of activities and financial support on youths' educational attainment. *Journal of Family Issues, 23,* 648–671.

Minton, C., & Pasley, K. (1996). Fathers' parenting role identity and father involvement: A comparison of nondivorced and divorced resident fathers. *Journal of Family Issues, 17,* 26–45.

Mott, F., Kowaleski-Jones, L., & Meneghan, E. (1997). Parental absence and child behavior: Does a child's gender make a difference? *Journal of Marriage and the Family, 59,* 103–118.

Neighbors, B., Forehand, R., & McVicar, D. (1993). Resilient adolescents and interparental conflict. *American Journal of Orthopsychiatry, 63,* 462–471.

Nord, C. W., Brimhall, D., & West, J. (1997). *Fathers involvement in their children's schools.* Washington, DC: National Center for Education Statistics.

Pleck, J. H. (1997). Paternal involvement: level, sources, and consequences. In M. E. Lamb (Ed.), *The role of the father in child development* (3rd ed.; pp. 66–103). New York: Wiley.

Pong, S. L., & Ju, D. B. (2000). The effects of change in family structure and income on dropping out of middle and high school. *Journal of Family Issues, 21,* 147–169.

Popenoe, D., Elshtain, J. B., & Blankenhorn, D. (1996). *Promises to keep: Decline and renewal of marriage in America.* Langham, MD: Rowman & Littlefield.

Seltzer, J. (1991). Relationships between fathers and children who live apart: The father's role after separation. *Journal of Marriage and the Family, 53,* 79–101.

Seltzer, J. (1998). Father by law: Effects of joint legal custody on nonresident fathers' involvement with children. *Demography, 35,* 135–146.

Simons, R. L., & Associates (1996). *Understanding differences between divorced and intact families: Stress, interaction, and child outcome.* Thousand Oaks, CA: Sage.

Smart, C. (2002). From children's shoes to children's voices. *Family Court Review, 40,* 307–319.

Smart, C., & Neale, B. (2000). 'It's my life too'—Children's perspectives on post-divorce parenting. *Family Law, 30,* 163–169.

Stewart, A., Copeland, A., Chester, N., Malley, J., & Barenbaum, N. (1997). *Separating together: How divorce transforms families.* New York: Guilford.

Sun, Y. (2001). Family environment and adolescents' well-being before and after parents' marital disruption: A longitudinal analysis. *Journal of Marriage and Family, 63,* 697–713.

Sun, Y., & Li, Y. (2001). Marital disruption, parental investment, and children's academic achievement. *Journal of Family Issues, 22,* 27–62.

Sun, Y., & Li, Y. (2002). Children's well-being during parents' marital disruption process: A pooled time-series analysis. *Journal of Marriage and Family, 64,* 472–488.

Thompson, R., & Laible, D. (1999). Noncustodial parents. In M. E. Lamb (Ed.), *Parenting and child development in nontraditional families* (pp. 103–124). Mahwah, NJ: Lawrence Erlbaum.

Vandewater, E., & Lansford, J. (1998). Influences of family structure and parental conflict on children's well-being. *Family Relations, 47,* 323–330.

Wallerstein, J. S., & Blakeslee, S. (1989). *Second chances: Men, women and children a decade after divorce.* New York: Tiekner & Fields.

Wallerstein, J. S., & Kelly, J. B. (1977). Divorce counseling: A community service for families in the midst of divorce. *American Journal of Orthopsychiatry, 47,* 4–22.

Wallerstein, J. S., & Kelly, J. B. (1980). *Surviving the breakup: How children and parents cope with divorce.* New York: Basic Books.

Wallerstein, J. S., Lewis, J. M., & Blakeslee, S. (2000). *The unexpected legacy of divorce: A 25 year landmark study.* New York: Hyperion.

Warshak, R. A. (2000a). Blanket restrictions: Overnight contacts between parents and young children. *Family and Conciliation Courts Review, 38,* 422–445.

Warshak, R. A. (2000b). Social science and children's best interests in relocation cases: Burgess revisited. *Family Law Quarterly, 34,* 83–113.

Waters, R. (2001). The 30 years war. *Psychotherapy Networker, March/April,* 40–52.

Whitehead, B. D. (1998). *The divorce culture: Rethinking our commitments to marriage and family.* New York: Knopf.

Whiteside, M. F., & Becker, B. J. (2000). Parental factors and young child's post-divorce adjustment: A meta-analysis with implications for parenting arrangements. *Journal of Family Psychology, 14,* 5–26.

Wolchik, S. A., Fenaughty, A. M., & Braver, S. L. (1996). Residential and non-residential parents' perspectives on visitation problems. *Family Relations, 45,* 230–237.

Wolfinger, N. H. (2000). Beyond the intergenerational transmission of divorce: Do people replicate the patterns of marital instability they grew up with? *Journal of Family Issues, 21,* 1061–1086.

Zill, N. D. (1988). Behavior, achievement, and health problems among children in stepfamilies: Findings from a national survey of child health. In E. M. Hetherington & J. D. Arasteh (Eds.), *Impact of divorce, single parenting, and stepparenting on children* (pp. 325–368). Hillsdale, NJ: Lawrence Erlbaum.

Zill, N., Morrison, D., & Coiro, M. (1993). Long term effects of parental divorce on parent-child relationships, adjustment, and achievement in young adulthood. *Journal of Family Psychology, 7,* 91–103.

Zill, N., & Schoenborn, C. A. (1990). *Developmental, learning, and emotional problems: Health of our nation's children, United States, 1988.* Advance data from Vital and Health Statistics, No. 190. Washington, DC: National Center for Health Statistics.

■**READING 18**

The Modern American Stepfamily: Problems and Possibilities

Mary Ann Mason

Cinderella had one, so did Snow White and Hansel and Gretel. Our traditional cultural myths are filled with the presence of evil stepmothers. We learn from the stories read to us as children that stepparents, particularly stepmothers, are not to be trusted. They may pretend to love us in front of our biological parent, but the moment our real parent is out of sight they will treat us cruelly and shower their own children with kindnesses. Few modern children's tales paint stepparents so harshly, still the negative image of stepparents lingers in public policy. While the rights and obligations of biological parents, wed or unwed, have been greatly strengthened in recent times, stepparents have been virtually ignored. At best it is fair to say that as a society we have a poorly formed concept of the role of stepparents and a reluctance to clarify that role.

Indeed, the contrast between the legal status of stepparents and the presumptive rights and obligations of natural parents is remarkable. Child support obligations, custody rights, and inheritance rights exist between children and their natural parents by virtue of a biological tie alone, regardless of the quality of social or emotional bonds between parent and child, and regardless of whether the parents are married. In recent years policy changes have extended the rights and obligations of natural parents, particularly in regard to unwed and divorced parents, but have not advanced with regard to stepparents. Stepparents in most states have no obligation during the marriage to support their stepchildren, nor do they enjoy any right of custody or control. Consistent with this pattern, if the marriage terminates through divorce or death, they usually have no rights to custody or even visitation, however longstanding their relationship with their stepchildren. Conversely, stepparents have no obligation to pay child support following divorce, even if their stepchildren have depended on their income for many years. In turn, stepchildren have no right of inheritance in the event of the stepparent's death (they are, however, eligible for Social Security benefits in most cases).[1]

Policymakers who spend a great deal of time worrying about the economic and psychological effects of divorce on children rarely consider the fact that about 70 percent of mothers are remarried within six years. More over, about 28 percent of children are born to unwed mothers, many of whom eventually marry someone who is not the father of their child. In a study including all children, not just children of divorce, it was estimated that one-fourth of the children born in the United States in the early 1980s will live with a stepparent before they reach adulthood.[2] These numbers are likely to increase in the future, at least as long as the number of single-parent families continues to grow. In light of these demographic trends, federal and state policies affecting families and children, as well as policies governing private-sector employee benefits, insurance, and other critical areas of everyday life, may need to be adapted to address the concerns of modern stepfamilies.

In recent years stepfamilies have received fresh attention from the psychological and social sciences but little from legal and policy scholars. We now know a good deal about who modern stepfamilies are and how they function, but there have been few attempts to apply this knowledge to policy. This [reading] first of all reviews the recent findings on the everyday social and economic functioning of today's stepfamilies, and then examines current state and federal policies, or lack of them in this arena. Finally, the sparse set of current policy recommendations, including my own, are presented. These proposals range from active discouragement of stepfamilies[3] to a consideration of stepparents as de facto parents, with all the rights and responsibilities of biological parents during marriage, and a limited extension of these rights and responsibilities following the breakup of marriage or the death of the stepparent.[4]

THE MODERN STEPFAMILY

The modern stepfamily is different and more complex than Cinderella's or Snow White's in several important ways. First, the stepparent who lives with the children is far more likely to be a stepfather than a stepmother, and in most cases the children's biological father is still alive and a presence, in varying degrees, in their lives. Today it is divorce, rather than death, which usually serves as the background event for the formation of the stepfamily, and it is the custodial mother who remarries (86 percent of stepchildren live primarily with a custodial mother and stepfather),[5] initiating a new legal arrangement with a stepfather.[6]

Let us take the case of the Jones-Hutchins family. Sara was eight and Josh five when their mother and father, Martha and Ray Jones divorced. Three years later Martha married Sam Hutchins, who had no children. They bought a house together and the children received health and other benefits from Sam's job, since Martha was working part time at a job with no benefits.

Theoretically, this new parental arrangement was a triangle, since Ray was still on the scene and initially saw the children every other weekend. In most stepfamilies the noncustodial parent, usually the father, is still alive (only in 25 percent of cases is the non-custodial parent dead, or his whereabouts unknown). This creates the phenomenon of more than two parents, a situation that conventional policymakers are not well equipped to address. However, according to the National Survey of Families and Households (NSFH), a nationally representative sample of families, contact between stepchildren and their absent natural fathers is not that frequent. Contact falls into four broad patterns: roughly one-quarter of all stepchildren have no association at all with their fathers and receive no child support; one-quarter see their fathers only once a year or less often and receive no child support; one-quarter have intermittent contact or receive some child support; and one-quarter may or may not receive child support but have fairly regular contact, seeing their fathers once a month or more. Using these data as guides to the quality and intensity of the father-child relationship, it appears that relatively few stepchildren are close to their natural fathers or have enough contact with them to permit the fathers to play a prominent role in the children's upbringing. Still, at least half of natural fathers do figure in their children's lives to some degree.[7] The presence of the noncustodial parent usually precludes the option of stepparent adoption, a solution that would solve the legal ambiguities, at least, of the stepparent's role.

In size, according to the National Survey of Families and Households, modern residential stepfamilies resemble modern nondivorced families and single-parent families, with an average of two children per family. Only families with two stepparents (the rarest type of stepfamily, in which both parents had children from previous relationships, and both are the custodial parents) are larger, with an average of 3.4 children per household. In part because divorce and remarriage take time, children are older. In the NSFH households, the youngest stepchildren in families are, on average, aged eleven, while the youngest children in nondivorced families are six and a half.[8]

There are also, of course, nonresidential stepparents (the spouses of noncustodial parents), usually stepmothers. In our case, Ray married again, the year after Martha married Sam. Ray's new wife, Leslie, was the custodial parent of Audrey, age twelve. This marriage complicated the weekend visits. The Jones children were resentful of their new stepmother, Leslie, and her daughter, Audrey. Ray found it easier to see them alone, and his visits became less frequent.

Some children may spend a good deal of time with nonresidential stepparents, and they may become significant figures in the children's lives, unlike Leslie in our example. But for our purpose of reassessing the parental rights and obligations of stepparents, we will focus only on residental stepparents, since they are more likely to be involved in the everyday support and care of their stepchildren. Moreover, the wide variety of benefits available to dependent children, like Social Security and health insurance, are usually attached only to a residential stepparent.

The modern stepfamily, like those of Cinderella and Snow White, also has stresses and strains. This was certainly true for the Jones-Hutchins family. Sara was eleven and Josh seven when their mother married Sam. At first Sara refused to talk to Sam and turned her face away when he addressed her. Josh was easier. He did not say much, but was willing to play catch or go an on errand with Sam if encouraged by Sam to do so. Sara grew only slightly more polite as she developed into adolescence. She spoke to Sam only if she needed something. But, as her mother pointed out to Sam, she hardly spoke to her either. Josh continued to be pleasant, if a little distant, as he grew older. He clearly preferred his mother's attention.

The classic longitudinal studies by Heatherington and colleagues,[9] spanning the past two decades, provide a rich source of information on how stepfamilies function. Heatherington emphasizes that stepchildren are children who have experienced several marital transitions. They have usually already experienced the divorce of their parents (although the number whose mothers have never before wed is increasing) and a period of life in a single-parent family before the formation of the stepfamily. In the early stages of all marital transitions, including divorce and remarriage, child-parent relations are often disrupted and parenting is less authoritative than in nondivorced families. These early periods, however, usually give way to a parenting situation more similar to nuclear families.[10]

The Heatherington studies found that stepfathers vary in how enthusiastically and effectively they parent their stepchildren, and stepchildren also vary in how willingly they permit a parental relationship to develop. Indeed, many stepfather-stepchild relationships are not emotionally close. Overall, stepfathers in these studies are most often disengaged and less authoritative as compared with nondivorced fathers. The small class of residential stepmothers exhibits a similar style.[11] Conversely, adolescent children tend to perceive their stepfathers negatively in the early stages of remarriage, but over time, they too become disengaged. In an interesting twist on fairy tale lore, adolescent children in stepfamilies experience less conflict with their residential stepmothers than do children in nondivorced families with their own mothers.[12]

The age and gender of the child at the time of stepfamily formation are critical in his or her adjustment. Early adolescence is a difficult time in which to have remarriage occur, with more sustained difficulties in stepfather-stepchild relations than in remarriages where the children are younger. Young (preadolescent) stepsons, but not necessarily stepdaughters, develop a closer relationship to their stepfathers after a period of time; this is not as likely with older children.[13]

Other researchers have found that in their lives outside the family, stepchildren do not perform as well as children from nondivorced families, and look more like the children from single-parent families. It seems that divorce and remarriage (or some factors associated with divorce and remarriage) increase the risk of poor academic, behavioral, and psychological outcomes.[14]

The difficulties of the stepfamily relationship are evident in the high divorce rate of such families. About one-quarter of all remarrying women separate from their new spouses within five years of the second marriage, and the figure is higher for women with children from prior relationships. A conservative estimate is that between 20 percent and 30 percent of stepchildren will, before they turn eighteen, see their custodial parent and stepparent divorce.[15] This is yet another disruptive marital transition for children, most of whom have already undergone at least one divorce.

Other researchers look at the stepfamily more positively. Amato and Keith analyzed data comparing intact, two-parent families with stepfamilies and found that while children from two-parent families performed significantly better on a multifactored measure of well-being and development, there was a significant overlap. A substantial number of children in stepfamilies actually perform as well or better than children in intact two-parent families. As Amato comments, "Some children grow up in well-functioning intact families in which they encounter abuse, neglect, poverty, parental mental illness, and parental substance abuse. Other children grow up in well-functioning stepfamilies and have caring stepparents who provide affection, effective control and economic support."[16] Still other researchers suggest that it may be the painful transitions of divorce and economically deprived single-parenthood which usually precede the formation of the stepfamily that explain the poor performance of stepchildren.[17]

Perhaps a fairer comparison of stepchildren's well-being is against single-parent families. Indeed, if there were no remarriage, (or first marriage, in the case of unmarried birth mothers), these children would remain a part of a single-parent household. On most psychological measures of behavior and achievement, stepchildren look more like children from single-parent families than children from never-divorced families, but on economic measures it is a different story. The National Survey of Families and Households (NSFH) data show that stepparents have slightly lower incomes and slightly less education than parents in nuclear families, but that incomes of all types of married families with children are three to four times greater than the incomes of single mothers. Custodial mothers in stepfamilies have similar incomes to single mothers (about $12,000 in 1987). If, as seems plausible, their personal incomes are about the same before they married as after, then marriage has increased their household incomes more than threefold. Step-fathers' incomes are, on average, more than twice as great as their wives', and account for nearly three-fourths of the family's income.[18]

In contrast to residential stepparents, absent biological parents only rarely provide much financial or other help to their children. Some do not because they are dead or cannot be found; about 26 percent of custodial, remarried mothers and 28 percent of single mothers report that their child's father is deceased or of unknown whereabouts. Yet even in the three-quarters of families where the noncustodial parent's whereabouts are known, only about one-third of all custodial mothers (single and remarried) receive child support or alimony from former spouses, and the amounts involved are small compared to the cost of raising children. According to NSFH data, remarried women with awards receive on average $1780 per year, while single mothers receive $1383. Clearly, former spouses cannot be relied on to lift custodial mothers and their children out of poverty.[19]

The picture is still more complex, as is true with all issues relating to stepfamilies. Some noncustodial fathers, like Ray Jones in our scenario, have remarried and have stepchildren themselves. These relationships, too, are evident in the NSFH data. Nearly one-quarter (23 percent) of residential stepfathers have minor children from former relationships living elsewhere. Two-thirds of those report paying child support for their children.[20] In our case, Ray Jones did continue his child support payments, but he felt squeezed by the economic obligation of contributing to two households. This is a growing class of fathers who frequently feel resentful about the heavy burden of supporting two households, particularly when their first wife has remarried.

In sum, although we have no data that precisely examine the distribution of resources within a stepfamily, it is fair to assume that stepfathers' substantial contributions to family income improve their stepchildren's material well-being by helping to cover basic living costs. For many formerly single-parent families, stepfathers' incomes provided by remarriage are essential in preventing or ending poverty among custodial mothers and their children. (The data are less clear for the much smaller class of residential stepmothers.)

While legal dependency usually ends at eighteen, the economic resources available to a stepchild through remarriage could continue to be an important factor past childhood. College education and young adulthood are especially demanding economic events. The life-course studies undertaken by some researchers substantiate the interpersonal trends seen in stepfamilies before the stepchildren leave home. White reports that viewed from either the parent's or the child's perspective, relationships over the life-course between stepchildren and stepparents are substantially weaker than those between biological parents and children. These relationships are not monolithic, however; the best occur when the stepparent is a male, there are no stepsiblings, the stepparent has no children of his own, and the marriage between the biological parent and the stepparent is intact.[21] On the other end, support relationships are nearly always cut off if the stepparent relationship is terminated because of divorce or the death of the natural parent.

The Jones children were fortunate. Martha and Sam enjoyed a good marriage, in spite of the stress of stepparenting, and Sam was glad to help them with college expenses. Their biological father, Ray, felt he had his own family to support; his stepdaughter,

Audrey, also needed money for college. As Sara grew older she grew more accepting of Sam. And after her first child was born, she seemed happy to accept Sam as a grandfather for her child. Josh continued on good terms with Sam.

Again, one might ask to compare these findings to single-parent households where there are no stepparents to provide additional support. The data here are less available. While we do know that stepchildren leave home earlier and are less likely to attend college than children from intact families, the comparison with single-parent families is not clear.[22] One study of perceived normative obligation to stepparents and stepchildren suggests that people in stepfamilies have weaker, but still important, family ties than do biological kin.[23] In terms of economic and other forms of adult support, even weak ties cannot be discounted. They might, instead, become the focus of public policy initiatives.

STEPFAMILIES IN LAW AND PUBLIC POLICY

Both state and federal law set policies that affect stepfamilies. Overall, these policies do not reflect a coherent policy toward stepparents and stepchildren. Two competing models are roughly evident. One, a "stranger" model, followed by most states, treats the residential stepparent as if he or she were a legal stranger to the children, with no rights and no responsibilities. The other, a "dependency" model, most often followed by federal policymakers, assumes the residential stepfather is, in fact, supporting the stepchildren and provides benefits accordingly. But there is inconsistency in both state and federal policy. Some states lean at times toward a dependency model and require support in some instances, and the federal government sometimes treats the stepparent as if he or she were a stranger to the stepchildren, and ignores them in calculating benefits.

State law governs the traditional family matters of marriage, divorce, adoption, and inheritance, while federal law covers a wide range of programs and policies that touch on the lives of most Americans, including stepfamilies. As the provider of benefits through such programs as Temporary Aid for Needy Families (TANF) and Social Security, the federal government sets eligibility standards that affect the economic well-being of many stepfamilies. In addition, as the employer of the armed forces and civil servants, the federal government establishes employee benefits guidelines for vast numbers of American families. And in its regulatory role, the federal government defines the status of stepfamilies for many purposes ranging from immigration eligibility to tax liability.

Not covered in this [reading] or, to my knowledge, yet systematically investigated are the wide range of private employee benefit programs, from medical and life insurance through educational benefits. These programs mostly take their lead from state or federal law. Therefore, it is fair to guess that they suffer from similar inconsistencies.

State Policies

State laws generally give little recognition to the dependency needs of children who reside with their stepparent; they are most likely to treat the stepparent as a stranger to the children, with no rights or obligations. In contrast to the numerous state laws obligating parents to support natural children born out of wedlock or within a previous marriage, only a few states have enacted statutes which specifically impose an affirmative duty on stepparents. The Utah stepparent support statute, for example, provides simply that, "A stepparent shall support a stepchild to the same extent that a natural or adoptive parent is required to support a child."[24] This duty of support ends upon the termination of the marriage. Most states are silent on the obligation to support stepchildren.[25]

A few states rely on common law, the legal tradition stemming from our English roots. The common law tradition leans more toward a dependency model. It dictates that a stepparent can acquire the rights and duties of a parent if he or she acts *in loco parentis* (in the place of a parent). Acquisition of this status is not automatic; it is determined by the stepparent's intent. A stepparent need not explicitly state the intention to act as a parent; he or she can "manifest the requisite intent to assume responsibility by actually providing financial support or by taking over the custodial duties."[26] Courts, however, have been reluctant to grant *in loco* parental rights or to attach obligations to unwilling stepparents. In the words of one Wisconsin court, "A good Samaritan should not be saddled with the legal obligations of another and we think the law should not with alacrity conclude that a stepparent assumes parental relationships to a child."[27]

At the extreme, once the status of *in loco parentis* is achieved, the stepparent "stands in the place of the natural parent, and the reciprocal rights, duties, and obligations of parent and child subsist." These rights, duties, and obligations include the duty to provide financial support, the right to custody and control of the child, immunity from suit by the stepchild, and, in some cases, visitation rights after the dissolution of the marriage by death or divorce.

Yet stepparents who qualify as *in loco parentis* are not always required to provide support in all circumstances. A subset of states imposes obligation only if the stepchild is in danger of becoming dependent on public assistance. For example, Hawaii provides that:

> A stepparent who acts in loco parentis is bound to provide, maintain, and support the stepparent's stepchild during the residence of the child with the stepparent if the legal parents desert the child or are unable to support the child, thereby reducing the child to destitute and necessitous circumstances.[28]

Just as states do not regularly require stepparents to support their stepchildren, they do not offer stepparents the parental authority of custody and control within the marriage. A residential stepparent generally has fewer rights than a legal guardian or a foster parent. According to one commentator, a stepparent "has no authority to make decisions about the child—no authority to approve emergency medical treatment or even to sign a permission slip for a field trip to the fire station."[29]

Both common law and state statutes almost uniformly terminate the stepparent relationship upon divorce or the death of the custodial parent. This means that the support obligations, if there were any, cease, and that the stepparent has no rights to visitation or custody. State courts have sometimes found individual exceptions to this role, but they have not created any clear precedents. Currently only a few states authorize stepparents to seek visitation rights, and custody is almost always granted to a biological parent upon divorce. In the event of the death of the stepparent's spouse, the noncustodial, biological parent is usually granted custody even when the stepparent has, in fact, raised the child. In one such recent Michigan case, *Henrickson v. Gable*,[30] the children, aged nine and ten when their mother died, had lived with their stepfather since infancy and had rarely seen their biological father. In the ensuing custody dispute, the trial court left the children with their stepfather, but an appellate court, relying upon a state law that created a strong preference for biological parents, reversed this decision and turned the children over to their biological father.

Following the stranger model, state inheritance laws, with a few complex exceptions, do not recognize the existence of stepchildren. Under existing state laws, even a dependent stepchild whose stepparent has supported and raised the child for many years is not eligible to inherit from the stepparent if there is no will. California provides the most liberal rule for stepchild recovery when there is no will, but only if the stepchild meets relatively onerous qualifications. Stepchildren may inherit as the children of a deceased stepparent only if "it is established by clear and convincing evidence that the stepparent would have adopted the person but for a legal barrier."[31] Very few stepchildren have been able to pass this test. Similarly a stepchild cannot bring a negligence suit for the accidental death of a stepparent. In most instances, then, only a biological child will inherit or receive legal compensation when a stepparent dies.

Federal Policies

The federal policies that concern us here are of two types: federal benefit programs given to families in need, including TANF and Supplemental Security Income (SSI), and general programs not based on need, including Social Security was well as civil service and military personnel employee benefits. Most of these programs follow the dependency model. They go further than do most states in recognizing or promoting the actual family relationship of residential stepfamilies. Many of them (although not all) assume that residential stepparents support their stepchildren and accordingly make these children eligible for benefits equivalent to those afforded to other children of the family.

Despite the fact that federal law generally recognizes the dependency of residential stepchildren, it remains wanting in many respects. There is a great deal of inconsistency in how the numerous federal programs and policies treat the stepparent-stepchild relationship, and the very definitions of what constitutes a stepchild are often quite different across programs. Most of the programs strive for a dependency-based definition, such as living with or receiving 50 percent of support from a stepparent. However, some invoke the vague definition, "actual family relationship," and some do not attempt any definition at all, thus potentially including nonresidential stepchildren among the beneficiaries. In some programs the category of stepchild is entirely absent or specifically excluded from the list of beneficiaries for some programs.

Even where program rules permit benefits for dependent stepchildren as for natural children, the benefits to stepchildren are typically severed by death or divorce.[32] While Social Security does cover dependent stepchildren in the event of death, several programs specifically exclude stepchildren from eligibility for certain death benefits. Under the Federal Employees' Retirement System, stepchildren are explicitly excluded from the definition of children in determining the default beneficiary, without concern for the stepchild's possible dependency. All stepchildren are similarly excluded from eligibility for lump-sum payments under the Foreign Service Retirement and Disability System and the CIA Retirement and Disability program.[33]

Stepchildren are even more vulnerable in the event of divorce. Here the stranger model is turned to. As with state law, any legally recognized relationship is immediately severed upon divorce in nearly all federal programs. The children and their stepparents become as strangers. Social Security does not provide any cushion for stepchildren if the deceased stepparent is divorced from the custodial parent. Under Social Security law, the stepparent-stepchild relationship is terminated immediately upon divorce and the stepchild is no longer eligible for benefits even if the child has in fact been dependent on the insured stepparent for the duration of a very long marriage.[34] If the divorce were finalized the day before the stepparent's death the child would receive no benefits.

In sum, current federal policy goes part way toward defining the role of the stepparent by assuming a dependency model in most programs, even when state law does not, and providing benefits to stepchildren based on this assumption of stepparent support. However, as described, existing federal stepparent policy falls short in several critical areas. And state laws and policies fall far short of federal policies in their consideration of stepfamilies, for the most part treating stepparents as strangers with regard to their stepchildren.

NEW POLICY PROPOSALS

Proposals for policy reform regarding stepfamilies are scant in number and, so far, largely unheard by policymakers. Most of the proposals come from legal scholars, a few from social scientists. Stepparents have not been organized to demand reform, nor have child advocates. All the reforms have some disagreements with the existing stranger and dependency models, but few offer a completely new model.

All of the proposals I review base their arguments to a greater or lesser degree on social science data, although not always the same data. The proposers may roughly be divided into three camps. The first, and perhaps smallest camp, I call *negativists*. These are scholars who view stepfamilies from a sociobiological perspective, and find them a troublesome aberration to be actively discouraged. The second, and by far largest group of scholars, I term *voluntarists*. This group acknowledges both the complexity and the often distant nature of stepparent relationships, and largely believes that law and policy should leave stepfamilies alone, as it does now. If stepparents wish to take a greater role in their stepchildren's lives, they should be encouraged to do so, by adoption or some other means. The third camp recognizes the growing presence of stepfamilies as an alternate family form and believes they should be recognized and strengthened in some important ways. This group, I call them *reformists*, believes the law should take the lead in providing more rights or obligations to stepparents. The few policy initiatives from this group range from small specific reforms regarding such issues as inheritance and visitation to my own proposal for a full-scale redefinition of stepparents' rights and obligations.

The negativist viewpoint on stepparenting, most prominently represented by sociologist David Popenoe, relies on a sociobiological theory of reproduction. According to this theory, human beings will give unstintingly to their own biological children, in order to promote their own genes, but will be far less generous to others. The recent rise in divorce and out-of-wedlock births, according to Popenoe, has created a pattern of essentially fatherless households that cannot compete with the two-biological-parent families.

Popenoe believes the pattern of stepparent disengagement revealed by many researchers is largely based on this biological stinginess.

> If the argument . . . is correct, and the family is fundamentally rooted in biology and at least partly activated by the "genetically selfish" activities of human beings, childbearing by non relatives is inherently problematic. It is not that unrelated individuals are unable to do the job of parenting, it is just that they are not as likely to do the job well. Stepfamily problems, in short, may be so intractable that the best strategy for dealing with them is to do everything possible to minimize their occurrence.

Moreover, Popenoe cites researchers on the greatly increased incidence of child abuse by stepfathers over natural fathers, who suggest that "stepchildren are not merely 'disadvantaged' but imperiled."[35] This argument is not so farfetched, he claims, in fact it is the stuff of our folk wisdom. Snow White and Hansel and Gretel had it right; stepparents are not merely uncaring, they may be dangerous.

Popenoe goes beyond the stranger model, which is neutral as to state activity, and suggests an active discouragement of stepparent families. He believes the best way to obstruct stepfamilies is to encourage married biological two-parent families. Premarital and marital counseling, a longer waiting period for divorce, and a redesign of the current welfare system so that marriage and family are empowered rather than denigrated are among his policy recommendations. He is heartened by what he calls the "new familism," a growing recognition of the need for strong social bonds, which he believes can best be found in the biological two-parent family.[36]

The second group of scholars, whom I call voluntarists, generally believe that the stepparent relationship is essentially voluntary and private and the stranger model most clearly reflects this. The legal bond formed by remarriage is between man and wife—stepchildren are incidental; they are legal strangers. Stepparents may choose, or not choose, to become more involved with everyday economic and emotional support of their stepchildren; but the law should not mandate this relationship, it should simply reflect it. These scholars recognize the growth of stepfamilies as a factor of modern life and neither condone nor condemn this configuration. Family law scholar David Chambers probably speaks for most scholars in this large camp when he says,

> In most regards, this state of the law nicely complements the state of stepparent relationships in the United States. Recall the inescapable diversity of such relationships—residential and non-residential, beginning when the children are infants and when they are teenagers, leading to comfortable relationships in some cases and awkward relationships in others, lasting a few years and lasting many. In this context it seems sensible to permit those relationships to rest largely on the voluntary arrangements among stepparents and biologic parents. The current state of the law also amply recognizes our nation's continuing absorption with the biologic relationship, especially as it informs our sensibilities about enduring financial obligations.[37]

Chambers is not enthusiastic about imposing support obligations on stepparents, either during or following the termination of a marriage, but is interested in promoting voluntary adoption. He would, however, approve some middle ground where biological parents are not completely cut off in the adoption process.

Other voluntarists are attracted by the new English model of parenting, as enacted in the Children Act of 1989. Of great attraction to American voluntarists is the fact that under this model a stepparent who has been married at least two years to the biological parent may voluntarily petition for a residence order for his or her spouse's child. With a residence order the stepparent has parental responsibility toward the child until the age of sixteen. But this order does not extinguish the parental responsibility of the non-custodial parent.[38] In accordance with the Children Act of 1989, parents, biological or otherwise, no longer have parental rights, they have only parental responsibilities, and these cannot be extinguished upon the divorce of the biological parents. In England, therefore, it is possible for three adults to claim parental responsibility. Unlike biological parental responsibility, however, stepparent responsibility does not usually extend following divorce. The stepparent is not normally financially responsible following divorce, but he or she may apply for a visitation order.

The third group, whom I call reformists, believe that voluntary acts on the part of stepparents are not always adequate, and that it is necessary to reform the law in some way to more clearly define the rights and responsibilities of stepparents. The American Bar Association Family Law Section has been working for some years on a proposed Model Act to suggest legislative reforms regarding stepparents' obligations to provide child support and rights to discipline, visitation, and custody. A Model Act is not binding anywhere; it is simply a model for all states to consider. Traditionally, however, Model Acts have been very influential in guiding state legislative reform. In its current form, the ABA Model Act would require stepparents to assume a duty of support during the duration of the remarriage only if the child is not adequately supported by the custodial and noncustodial parent. The issue is ultimately left to the discretion of the family court, but the Model Act does not require that the stepparent would need to have a close relationship with a stepchild before a support duty is imposed. The Model Act, however, does not describe what the rule should be if the stepparent and the custodial parent divorce.

The proposed statute is rather more complete in its discussion of stepparent visitation or custody rights following divorce. It takes a two-tiered approach, first asking if the stepparent has standing (a legal basis) to seek visitation and then asking if the visitation would be in the best interests of the child. The standing question is to be resolved with reference to five factors, which essentially examine the role of the stepparent in the child's life (almost an *in loco parentis* question), the financial support offered by the stepparent, and the detriment to the child from denying visitation. The court, if it finds standing, then completes the analysis with the best interests standard of the jurisdiction. The Model Act's section on physical custody also requires a two-tiered test, requiring standing and increasing the burden on the stepparent to present clear and convincing proof that he or she is the better custodial parent.

The ABA Model Act is a worthwhile start, in my opinion, but it is little more than that. At most it moves away from a stranger model and provides a limited concept of mandatory stepparent support during a marriage, acknowledging that stepchildren are at least sometimes dependent. It also gives a stepparent a fighting chance for visitation or custody following a divorce. It fails to clarify stepparents' rights during the marriage, however, and does not deal with the issue of economic support at the period of maximum vulnerability, the termination of the marriage through death and divorce. Moreover, the Model Act, and, indeed, all the existing reform proposals, deal only with traditional legal concepts of parenthood defined by each state and do not consider the vast range of federal programs, or other public and private programs, that define the step parent-stepchild relationship for purposes of benefits, insurance, or other purposes.

I propose, instead, a new conceptualization of stepparent rights and responsibilities, a de facto parent model, that will cover all aspects of the stepparent-stepchild relationship and will extend to federal and private policy as well. My first concern in proposing a new framework is the welfare of the stepchildren, which is not adequately dealt with in either the stranger or the dependency model. The failure of state and, to a lesser extent, federal policy to address coherently the financial interdependencies of step relationships, described earlier in this [reading], means that children dependent upon a residential stepparent may not receive adequate support or benefits from that parent during the marriage, and they may not be protected economically in the event of divorce or parental death.

The longitudinal studies of families described earlier in this [reading] suggest that the most difficult periods for children are those of marital transition, for example, divorce and remarriage. Families with a residential stepfather have a much higher family income than mother-headed single families; indeed, their household incomes look much like nuclear families.[39] However, research demonstrates that stepfamilies are fragile and are more likely to terminate in divorce than biological families. The event of divorce can quite suddenly pull the resources available for the children back to the single-parent level. Currently children are at least financially cushioned by child support following the divorce of their biological parents, but have no protective support following the breakup of their stepfamily. Nor are they protected in the event of the death of the stepparent, which is certainly another period of vulnerability (as discussed earlier, only a small minority continue to receive support from noncustodial parents).

A second reason for proposing a new framework is to strengthen the relationship of the stepparent and stepchildren. While research generally finds that stepparents are less engaged in parenting than natural parents, research studies do not explain the causes; others must do so. In addition to the sociobiologists' claim for stingy, genetically driven behavior, sociologists have posited the explanation of "incomplete institutionalization."[40] This theory is based on the belief that, by and large, people act as they are expected to act by society. In the case of stepfamilies, there are unclear or absent societal norms and standards for how to define the remarried family, especially the role of the stepparent in relation to the stepchild.

Briefly, my new model requires, first of all, dividing stepparents into two subclasses: those who are de facto parents and those who are not. De facto parents would be defined as "those stepparents legally married to a natural parent who primarily reside with their stepchildren, or who provide at least 50 percent of the stepchild's financial support." Stepparents who do not meet the de facto parent requirements would, in all important respects, disappear from policy.

For the purposes of federal and state policy, under this scheme, a de facto parent would be treated virtually the same as a natural parent during the marriage. The same rights, obligations, and presumptions would attach vis-à-vis their stepchildren, including the obligation of support. These rights and duties would continue in some form, based on the length of the marriage, following the custodial parent's death or divorce from the stepparent, or the death of the stepparent. In the event of divorce the stepparent would have standing to seek custody or visitation but the stepparent could also be obligated for child support of a limited duration. Upon the death of a stepparent, a minor stepchild would be treated for purposes of inheritance and benefits as would a natural child.

So far this proposal resembles the common law doctrine of *in loco parentis*, described earlier, where the stepparent is treated for most purposes (except inheritance) as a parent on the condition that he or she voluntarily agrees to support the child. In the de facto model, however, support is mandatory, not voluntary, on the grounds both that it is not fair to stepchildren to be treated by the law in an unequal or arbitrary manner, and that child welfare considerations are best met by uniform support of stepchildren. Furthermore, in the traditional common law *in loco parentis* scenario, the noncustodial parent had died, and was not a factor to be reckoned with. Under this scheme, creating a de facto parent category for stepparents would not invalidate the existing rights and obligations of a noncustodial biological parent. Rather, this proposal would empower a stepparent as an additional parent.

Multiple parenting and the rights and obligations of the stepparent and children following divorce or death are controversial and difficult policy matters that require more detailed attention than the brief exposition that can be offered here. Multiple parenting is the barrier upon which many family law reform schemes, especially in custody and adoption, have foundered. It is also one of the reasons that there has been no consistent effort to reformulate the role of stepparents. Working out the details is critical. For instance, mandating stepparent support raises a central issue of fairness. If the stepparent is indeed required to support the child, there is a question about the support obligations of the noncustodial parent. Traditionally, most states have not recognized the stepparent contribution as an offset to child support.[41] While this policy promotes administrative efficiency, and may benefit some children, it may not be fair to the noncustodial parent. An important advance in recognizing the existence of multiple parents in the nonlinear family is to recognize multiple support obligations. The few states that require stepparent obligation have given limited attention to apportionment of child support obligations, offering no clear guidelines. I propose that state statutory requirements for stepparent obligation as de facto parents also include clear guidelines for apportionment of child support between the noncustodial natural parent and the stepparent.

Critics of this proposal may say that if the custodial parent's support is reduced, the child will have fewer resources. For some children, this may be true, but as discussed earlier in this [reading], only about 25 percent of all stepchildren, receive child support and the average amount is less than $2000 per year.[42] Therefore, a reduction of this small amount of support to a minority of stepchildren would not have a large overall effect compared with the increased resources of living with a stepparent that most stepchildren enjoy. And, certainly, the additional safety net of protection in the event of the death of the stepparent or divorce from the custodial parent would benefit all stepchildren. In addition, under the de facto scheme, the reduction of the support payment for the noncustodial parent may help to sweeten the multiple parenting relationship.

Let us apply this model to the Jones-Hutchins family introduced earlier. If Ray Jones, the noncustodial parent, were paying $6000 a year support for his two children (on the high end for noncustodial parents according to the National Survey for Children and Families), his payments could be reduced by as much as half, since Sam Hutchins's income is $50,000 per year and he has no other dependents. It should be emphasized, however, that in most stepfamilies there would be no reduction in support, because the noncustodial parent is paying no support. In the Jones-Hutchins family the $3000 relief would certainly be welcome to Ray, who is also now living with and helping to support his new wife's child. The relief would likely make him somewhat friendlier toward Sam, or at least more accepting of his role in his children's lives. It also might make him more likely to continue support past eighteen, since he would not feel as financially pinched over the years. More important, while the children would lose some support, they would have the security that if Sam died they would be legal heirs and default beneficiaries to his life insurance. They could also ask for damages if his death were caused by negligence or work-related events. And if he and their mother divorced, they could continue for a time to be considered dependents on his health and other benefits and to receive support from him.

Another facet of multiple parenting is legal authority. If stepparents are required to accept parental support obligations, equal protection and fairness concerns dictate that they must also be given parental rights. Currently, state laws, as noted earlier, recognize only natural or adoptive parents; a stepparent currently has no legal authority over a stepchild, even to authorize a field trip. If stepparents had full parental rights, in some cases, as when the parents have shared legal custody, the law would be recognizing the parental rights of three parents, rather than two. While this sounds unusual, it is an accurate reflection of how many families now raise their children. Most often, however, it would be only the custodial parent and his or her spouse, the de facto parent, who would have authority to make decisions for the children in their home.

In the Jones-Hutchins family this policy would give Sam more recognition as a parent. Schools, camps, hospitals, and other institutions that require parental consent or involvement would now automatically include him in their consideration of the children's interests. Since Sam is the more day-to-day parent, their biological father, Ray, may not mind at all. If he did mind, the three of them would have to work it out (or in an extreme event, take it to mediation or family court). In fact, since only a minority of noncustodial dads see their children on a regular basis, three-parent decision making would be unusual.

Critics of this scheme may argue that adoption, not the creation of the legal status of de facto parent, is the appropriate vehicle for granting a stepparent full parental rights and responsibilities.[43] If, as discussed earlier, nearly three-quarters of stepchildren are not being supported by their noncustodial parents, policy initiatives could be directed to terminating the nonpaying parents' rights and promoting stepparent adoption. Adoption is not possible, however, unless the parental rights of the absent natural parent have been terminated—a difficult procedure against a reluctant parent. Normally, the rights of a parent who maintains contact with his or her child cannot be terminated even if that parent is not contributing child support. And when parental rights are terminated, visitation rights are terminated as well in most states. It is by no means clear that it is in the best interests of children to terminate contact with a natural parent, even if the parent is not meeting his or her obligation to support.[44] As discussed earlier, a large percentage (another 25 percent or so), of noncustodial parents continue some contact with their children, even when not paying support.[45] And while stepparent adoption should be strongly encouraged when it is possible, this solution will not resolve the problem of defining the role of stepparents who have not adopted.

Extending, in some form, the rights and obligations following the termination of the marriage by divorce or death is equally problematical. Currently, only a few courts have ruled in favor of support payments following divorce, and these have been decided on an individual basis. Only one state, Missouri, statutorily continues stepparent support obligations following divorce.[46] It would clearly be in the best interests of the child to experience continued support, since a significant number of children may sink below the poverty line upon the dissolution of their stepfamily.[47]

Since the de facto model is based on dependency, not blood, a fair basis for support following divorce or the death of the custodial parent might be to require that a stepparent who qualified as a de facto parent for at least one year must contribute child support for half the number of years of dependency until the child reached majority. If a child resided with the stepparent for four years, the stepparent would be liable for support for two years. If the biological noncustodial parent were still paying support payments, the amount could be apportioned. While it may be said that this policy would discourage people from becoming stepparents by marrying, it could also be said to discourage divorce once one has become a stepparent. Stepparents might consider working harder at maintaining a marriage if divorce had some real costs.

Conversely, stepparents should have rights as well as responsibilities following divorce or the death of the custodial parent. Divorced or widowed stepparents should be able to pursue visitation or custody if they have lived with and supported the child for at least one year. Once again, multiple parent claims might sometimes be an issue, but these could be resolved, as they are now, under a primary caretaker, or a best interest standard.

The death of a stepparent is a particular period of vulnerability for stepchildren for which they are unprotected by inheritance law. While Social Security and other federal survivor benefits are based on the premise that a stepchild relies on the support of the residential stepparent and will suffer the same hardship as natural children if the stepparent dies, state inheritance laws, notoriously archaic, decree that only biology, not dependency, counts. State laws should assume that a de facto parent would wish to have all his dependents receive a share of his estate if he died without a will. If the stepchildren are no longer dependent, that assumption would not necessarily prevail. The same assumption should prevail for insurance policies and compensation claims following an accidental death. A dependent stepchild, just as a natural child, should have the right to sue for loss of support.

On the federal front, a clear definition of stepparents as de facto parents would eliminate the inconsistencies regarding stepparents which plague current federal policies and would clarify the role of the residential stepparent. For the duration of the marriage, a stepchild would be treated as a natural child for purposes of support and the receipt of federal benefits. This treatment would persist in the event of the death of the stepparent. The stepchild would receive all the survivor and death benefits that would accrue to a natural child.[48]

In the case of divorce, the issue of federal benefits is more complicated. Stepchildren and natural children should not have identical coverage for federal benefits following divorce, again, but neither is it good policy to summarily cut off children who have been dependent, sometimes for many years, on the de facto parent. A better policy is to extend federal benefits for a period following divorce, based on a formula that matches half the number of years of dependency, as earlier suggested for child support. For instance, if the stepparent resided with the stepchild for four years, the child would be covered by Social Security survivor benefits and other federal benefits, including federal employee benefits, for a period of two years following the divorce. This solution would serve children by at least providing a transitional cushion. It would also be relatively easy to administer. In the case of the death of the biological custodial parent, benefits could be similarly extended, or continued indefinitely if the child remains in the custody of the stepparent.

All other private benefits programs would similarly gain from the application of a clear definition of the rights and obligations of residential stepparents. While these nongovernmental programs, ranging from eligibility for private health and life insurance and annuities to access to employee child care, are not reviewed in this [reading], they almost surely reflect the same inconsistencies or silences evident in federal and state policies.

Ultimately, state law defines most of these stepfamily relationships, and it is difficult, if not impossible to achieve uniform reform on a state-by-state basis. In England it is possible to pass a single piece of national legislation, such as the Children Act of 1989, which completely redefines parental roles. In America, the process of reform is slower and less sure. Probably the first step in promoting a new policy would be for the federal government to insist all states pass stepparent general support obligation laws requiring stepparents acting as de facto parents (by my definition) to support their stepchildren as they do their natural children. This goal could be accomplished by making stepparent general support obligation laws a prerequisite for receiving federal welfare grants. Federal policy already assumes this support in figuring eligibility in many programs, but it has not insisted that states change their laws. Precedent for this strategy has been set by the Family Support Acts of 1988 in which the federal government mandated that states set up strict child support enforcement laws for divorced parents and unwed fathers at TANF levels in order to secure AFDC funding.[49] The second, larger step would be to require limited stepparent support following divorce, as described previously. Once the basic obligations were asserted, an articulation of basic rights would presumably follow.

CONCLUSION

Stepfamilies compose a large and growing sector of American families that is largely ignored by public policy. Social scientists tell us that these families have problems. Stepparent-stepchildren relationships, poorly defined by law and social norms, are not as strong or nurturing as those in nondivorced families, and stepchildren do not do as well in school and in other outside settings. Still, stepfamily relationships are important in lifting single-parent families out of poverty. When single or divorced mothers marry, the household income increases by more than threefold, rising to roughly the same level as nuclear families. A substantial portion of these families experiences divorce, however, placing the stepchildren at risk of falling back into poverty. It makes good public policy sense then, both to strengthen these stepfamily relationships and to cushion the transition for stepchildren should the relationship end.

Notes

1. Mary Ann Mason and David Simon, "The Ambiguous Stepparent: Federal Legislation in Search of a Model," *Family Law Quarterly* 29:446–448, 1995.

2. E. Mavis Heatherington and Kathleen M. Jodl, "Stepfamilies as Settings for Child Development," in Alan Booth and Judy Dunn (eds.), *Stepfamilies: Who Benefits? Who Does Not?* (Hillsdale, N.J.: L. Erlbaum 1994), 55; E. Mavis Heatherington, "An Overview of the Virginia Longitudinal Study of Divorce and Remarriage: A Focus on Early Adolescence," *Journal of Family Psychology* 7:39–56, 1993.

3. David Popenoe, "Evolution of Marriage and Stepfamily Problems," in Booth and Dunn (eds.), *Stepfamilies*, 3–28.

4. Mason and Simon, "The Ambiguous Stepparent," 467–482; Mary Ann Mason and Jane Mauldon, "The New Stepfamily Needs a New Public Policy," *Journal of Social Issues* 52(3), Fall 1996.

5. U.S. Bureau of Census, 1989.

6. Divorce is not always the background event. An increasing, but still relatively small number of custodial mothers have not previously wed.

7. Mason and Mauldon, "The New Stepfamily," 5.

8. Ibid., 6.

9. Heatherington and Jodl, "Stepfamilies," 55–81.

10. Ibid., 76.

11. E. Mavis Heatherington and William Clingempeel, "Coping with Marital Transitions: A Family Systems Perspective," *Monographs of the Society for Research in Child Development* 57:2–3, Serial No. 227, New York: 1992; E. Thomson, Sara McLanahan, and R. B. Curtin, "Family Structure, Gender, and Parental Socialization," *Journal of Marriage and the Family* 54:368–378, 1992.

12. Heatherington and Jodl, "Stepfamilies," 69.

13. Ibid., 64–65.

14. Thomson, McLanahan, and Curtin, "Family Structure," 368–378.

15. L. Bumpass and J. Sweet, *American Families and Households* (New York: Russell Sage Foundation, 1987), 23.

16. Paul Amato, "The Implications of Research Findings on Children in Stepfamilies," in Booth and Dunn (eds.), *Stepfamilies*, 84.

17. Nicholas Zill, "Understanding Why Children in Stepfamilies Have More Learning and Behavior Problems Than Children in Nuclear Families," in Booth and Dunn (eds.), *Stepfamilies*, 89–97.

18. Mason and Mauldon, "The New Stepfamily Needs a New Public Policy," 7.

19. Ibid., 8.

20. Ibid.

21. Lynn White, "Stepfamilies over the Lifecourse: Social Support," in Booth and Dunn (eds.), *Stepfamilies*, 109–139.

22. Ibid., 130.

23. A. S. Rossi and P. H. Rossi, *Of Human Bonding: Parent-Child Relations Across the Life Course* (New York: A. de Gruyter, 1990).

24. Utah Code Ann. 78-45-4.1.

25. Margaret Mahoney, *Stepfamilies and the Law* (Ann Arbor: University of Michigan Press, 1994), 13–47.

26. Miller v. United States, 123 F.2d 715, 717 (8th Cir, 1941).

27. Niesen v. Niesen, 157 N. W.2d 660 664(Wis. 1968).

28. Hawaii Revised Stat. Ann., Title 31, Sec. 577–4.

29. David Chambers, "Stepparents, Biologic Parents, and the Law's Perceptions of 'Family' after Divorce," in S. Sugarman and H. H. Kay (eds.), *Divorce Reform at the Crossroads* (New Haven: Yale University Press, 1990), 102–129.

30. Henrickson v. Gable.

31. Cal. Prob. Code, Sec. 6408.

32. Mason and Simon, "The Ambiguous Stepparent: Federal Legislation in Search of a Model," 449.

33. Ibid., p. 460–466.

34. 42 U.S.C. sec. 416(e), 1994.

35. M. Daly and M. Wilson, *Homicide* (New York: Aldine de Gruyter, 1988), 230.

36. Barbara Whitehead, "A New Familism?" *Family Affairs* Summer, 1992.

37. Chambers, "Stepparents, Biologic Parents, and the Law's Perceptions of 'Family' after Divorce," 26.

38. Mark A. Fine, "Social Policy Pertaining to Stepfamilies: Should Stepparents and Stepchildren Have the Option of Establishing a Legal Relationship?" in Booth and Dunn (eds.), *Stepfamilies*, 199.

39. Mason and Mauldon, "The New Stepfamily," 5.

40. Andrew Cherlin, "Remarriage as an Incomplete Institution," *American Journal of Sociology* 84:634–649, 1978.

41. S. Ramsey and J. Masson, "Stepparent Support of Stepchildren: A Comparative Analysis of Policies and Problems in the American and British Experience," *Syracuse Law Review* 36:649–666, 1985.

42. Mason and Mauldon, "The New Stepfamily," 7.

43. Joan Hollinger (ed.) et al., *Adoption Law and Practice* (New York: Matthew Bender, 1988).

44. Katherine Bartlett, "Re-thinking Parenthood as an Exclusive Status: The Need for Alternatives When the Premise of the Nuclear Family Has Failed," *Virginia Law Review* 70:879–903, 1984.

45. Mason and Mauldon, "The New Stepfamily," 5.

46. Vernon's Ann. Missouri Stats. 453.400, 1994.

47. Mason and Mauldon, "The New Stepfamily," 5.

48. Mason and Simon, "The Ambiguous Stepparent," 471.

49. 100 P.L. 485; 102 Stat. 2343 (1988).

III Parents and Children

No aspect of childhood seems more natural, universal, and changeless than the relationship between parents and children. Yet historical and crosscultural evidence reveal major changes in conceptions of childhood and adulthood and in the psychological relationships between children and parents. For example, the shift from an agrarian to an industrial society over the past 200 years has revolutionized parent–child relations and the conditions of child development.

Among the changes associated with this transformation of childhood are: the decline of agriculture as a way of life; the elimination of child labor; the fall in infant mortality; the spread of literacy and mass schooling; and a focus on childhood as a distinct and valuable stage of life. As a result of these changes, modern parents bear fewer children, make greater emotional and economic investments in them, and expect less in return than their agrarian counterparts. Agrarian parents were not expected to emphasize emotional bonds or the value of children as unique individuals. Parents and children were bound together by economic necessity: children were an essential source of labor in the family economy and a source of support in an old age. Today, almost all children are economic liabilities. But they now have profound emotional significance. Parents hope offspring will provide intimacy, even genetic immortality. Although today's children have become economically worthless, they have become emotionally "priceless" (Zelizer, 1985).

No matter how eagerly an emotionally priceless child is awaited, becoming a parent is usually experienced as one of life's major "normal" crises. In a classic article, Alice Rossi (1968) was one of the first to point out that the transition to parenthood is often one of life's difficult passages. Since Rossi's article first appeared more than three decades ago, a large body of research literature has developed, most of which supports her view that the early years of parenting can be a period of stress and change as well as joy.

Parenthood itself has changed since Rossi wrote. As Philip and Carolyn Cowan observe, becoming a parent may be more difficult now than it used to be. The Cowans studied couples before and after the births of their first children. Because of the rapid and dramatic social changes of the past decades, young parents today are like pioneers in a new, uncharted territory. For example, the vast majority of today's couples come to parenthood with both husband and wife in the workforce, and most have expectations of a more egalitarian relationship than their own parents had. But the balance in their lives and their relationship has to shift dramatically after the baby is born. Most couples cannot afford the traditional pattern of the wife staying home full time; nor is this arrangement free of strain for those who try it. Young families thus face more burdens than in the past, yet they lack the supportive services for new parents, such as visiting nurses, paid parental leave, and other family policies widely available in other countries. The Cowans suggest some newly developed ways to assist couples through this difficult transition.

After the earliest stage of parenthood, U.S. parents still struggle to find and afford even mediocre child care. In their article here, Dan Clawson and Naomi Gerstel describe child care in Europe. Most countries provide publicly supported high quality care. But these countries do not all follow the same model of child care. For example, some emphasize education, while others emphasize play; some rely more on professionals, while others rely on parents. These and other variations suggest that if and when the United States decides to fund child care, it will have a variety of models to choose from.

Of all the family changes of the past several decades, the adoption revolution is one of the most dramatic, yet least discussed. Lawrence Friedman reviews the surprising history of adoption. The unwritten traditional law of England—the common law—which is the foundation of American law, did not recognize anything like adoption. Of course people could always take a child into a family without any legal formalities, and this kind of informal adoption has always been common. In America, adoption laws were passed in the middle of the nineteenth century so that adopted children could inherit from their adoptive parents. This practice has continued to evolve. For example, older children who could help on the farm or around the house were preferred for adoption. In the twentieth century, adoptive parents strongly preferred newborn babies. The idea was to make adoptive family as much like a "natural" family as possible. Since the 1970s, however, adoption has become more open in many ways, and large numbers of parents are adopting children across ethnic, racial, and religious lines. Friedman discusses the ethical problems that have shadowed the practice of adoption.

In recent years, the role of fathers in children's lives—especially their absence—has become a hot-button political issue. But what are the everyday realities of life with a father in today's families? Of course, there is enormous diversity among fathers and families—in income, ethnicity, education, personality, and so on. But Nicholas Townsend has done an in-depth ethnographic study of the meaning of fatherhood to men in one community. In his article, he reports that fatherhood to these men is part of a "package deal." Along with the emotional relationship between father and child, it includes the father's relationship with the mother and his job as a major source of support for the family, as well as a home to shelter it. If the father is having trouble with any aspect of this relationship, it is likely to affect the whole "package."

Worry about working mothers is only part of the more general anxiety many Americans feel about children in today's families. Usually, we compare a troubled image of children now with rosy images of growing up in past times. But as historian Steven Mintz explains here, public thinking about the history of American childhood is clouded by a series of myths. One is the myth of a carefree childhood. We cling to a fantasy that once upon a time childhood and youth were years of carefree adventure, yet for most children in the past, growing up was anything but easy. Disease, family disruption, and entering into the world of work at an early age were typical aspects of family life. The notion of a long, secure childhood, devoted to education and free from adult-like responsibilities, is a very recent invention, one that only became a reality for a majority of children after World War II.

In her article, Ellen Galinsky addresses the issue of work and parenting through a research method that is remarkably rare in studies of family life—going to the children and asking them. Among her many findings, perhaps the most surprising is a discrepancy between the opinions of working parents and their children as to whether they are spending too little time together. Most people assume that the issue of time spent with children is about mothers. But although a majority of working mothers feel they are spending too little time with their offspring, the children themselves have a different view. A majority feel they have enough time with their mothers, but not enough with their fathers. These findings, Galinsky argues, show why it is so important to ask children directly about how family issues affect them, rather than rely on our own assumptions.

Vern L. Bengston and his colleagues also cast doubt on the conventional wisdom about the decline of the family. They draw their findings from the University of Southern California's long-running study of families across three generations. What they discovered about Generation X—the roughly 50 million or so Americans born between 1965 and 1980—will surprise many readers. The stereotype of this post–baby boom generation portrays them as slackers and drifters, alienated from their parents. In contrast, Bengston found that Generation X youth showed higher levels of education, career success, and self-esteem than their own parents when they were the same age. Moreover, all three generations in the study shared similar values. The researchers conclude that despite the massive family and social changes since the 1960s, family bonds across generations remain resilient.

References

Rossi, A. 1968. Transition to parenthood. *Journal of Marriage and the Family* 30, 26–39.
Zelizer, V. A. 1985. *Pricing the Priceless Child.* New York: Basic Books.

7 *Parenthood*

■ READING 19

New Families: Modern Couples as New Pioneers

Philip Cowan and Carolyn Pape Cowan

Mark and Abby met when they went to work for a young, ambitious candidate who was campaigning in a presidential primary. Over the course of an exhilarating summer, they debated endlessly about values and tactics. At summer's end they parted, returned to college, and proceeded to forge their individual academic and work careers. When they met again several years later at a political function, Mark was employed in the public relations department of a large company and Abby was about to graduate from law school. Their argumentative, passionate discussions about the need for political and social change gradually expanded to the more personal, intimate discussions that lovers have.

They began to plan a future together. Mark moved into Abby's apartment. Abby secured a job in a small law firm. Excited about their jobs and their flourishing relationship, they talked about making a long-term commitment and soon decided to marry. After the wedding, although their future plans were based on a strong desire to have children, they were uncertain about when to start a family. Mark raised the issue tentatively, but felt he did not have enough job security to take the big step. Abby was fearful of not being taken seriously if she became a mother too soon after joining her law firm.

Several years passed. Mark was now eager to have children. Abby, struggling with competing desires to have a baby *and* to move ahead in her professional life, was still hesitant. Their conversations about having a baby seemed to go nowhere but were dramatically interrupted when they suddenly discovered that their birth control method had failed: Abby was unmistakably pregnant. Somewhat surprised by their own reactions, Mark and Abby found that they were relieved to have the timing decision taken out of their hands. Feeling readier than they anticipated, they became increasingly excited as they shared the news with their parents, friends, and coworkers.

Most chapters [in the book from which this reading is taken] focus on high-risk families, a category in which some observers include all families that deviate from the traditional two-parent, nonteenage, father-at-work–mother-at-home "norm." The in-

244

creasing prevalence of these families has been cited by David Popenoe, David Blanken-horn, and others[1] as strong evidence that American families are currently in a state of de-cline. In the debate over the state of contemporary family life, the family decline theorists imply that traditional families are faring well. This view ignores clear evidence of the per-vasive stresses and vulnerabilities that are affecting most families these days—even those with two mature, relatively advantaged parents.

In the absence of this evidence, it appears as if children and parents in traditional two-parent families do not face the kinds of problems that require the attention of fam-ily policymakers. We will show that Abby and Mark's life, along with those of many mod-ern couples forming new families, is less ideal and more subject to distress than family observers and policymakers realize. Using data from our own and others' studies of part-ners becoming parents, we will illustrate how the normal process of becoming a family *in this culture, at this time* sets in motion a chain of potential stressors that function as risks that stimulate moderate to severe distress for a substantial number of parents. Results of a number of recent longitudinal studies make clear that if the parents' distress is not ad-dressed, the quality of their marriages and their relationships with their children are more likely to be compromised. In turn, conflictful or disengaged family relationships during the family's formative years foreshadow later problems for the children when they reach the preschool and elementary school years. This means that substantial numbers of new two-parent families in the United States do not fit the picture of the ideal family por-trayed in the family decline debate.

In what follows we: (1) summarize the changing historical context that makes life for many modern parents more difficult than it used to be; (2) explore the premises un-derlying the current debate about family decline; (3) describe how conditions associated with the transition to parenthood create risks that increase the probability of individual, marital, and family distress; and (4) discuss the implications of this family strain for Amer-ican family policy. We argue that systematic information about the early years of family life is critical to social policy debates in two ways: first, to show how existing laws and regulations can be harmful to young families, and second, to provide information about promising interventions with the potential to strengthen family relationships during the early childrearing years.

HISTORICAL CONTEXT: CHANGING FAMILIES IN A CHANGING WORLD

From the historical perspective of the past two centuries, couples like Mark and Abby are unprecedented. They are a modern, middle-class couple attempting to create a different kind of family than those of their parents and grandparents. Strained economic condi-tions and the shifting ideology about appropriate roles for mothers and fathers pose new challenges for these new pioneers whose journey will lead them through unfamiliar ter-rain. With no maps to pinpoint the risks and hardships, contemporary men and women must forge new trails on their own.

Based on our work with couples starting families over the past twenty years, we be-lieve that the process of becoming a family is more difficult now than it used to be. Be-cause of the dearth of systematic study of these issues, it is impossible to locate hard evidence that modern parents face more challenges than parents of the past. Nonetheless, a brief survey of the changing context of family life in North America suggests that the transition to parenthood presents different and more confusing challenges for modern couples creating families than it did for parents in earlier times.

Less Support = More Isolation

While 75 percent of American families lived in rural settings in 1850, 80 percent were living in urban or suburban environments in the year 2000. Increasingly, new families are created far from grandparents, kin, and friends with babies the same age, leaving parents without the support of those who could share their experiences of the ups and downs of parenthood. Most modern parents bring babies home to isolated dwellings where their neighbors are strangers. Many women who stay home to care for their babies find themselves virtually alone in the neighborhood during this major transition, a time when we know that inadequate social support poses a risk to their own and their babies' well-being.[2]

More Choice = More Ambiguity

Compared with the experiences of their parents and grandparents, couples today have more choice about whether and when to bring children into their lives. In addition to the fact that about 4.5 percent of women now voluntarily remain forever childless (up from 2.2 percent in 1980), partners who do become parents are older and have smaller families—only one or two children, compared to the average of three, forty years ago. The reduction in family size tends to make each child seem especially precious, and the decision about whether and when to become parents even more momentous. Modern birth control methods give couples more control over the timing of a pregnancy, in spite of the fact that many methods fail with some regularity, as they did for Mark and Abby. Although the legal and moral issues surrounding abortion are hotly debated, modern couples have a choice about whether to become parents, even after conception begins.

Once the baby is born, there are more choices for modern couples. Will the mother return to work or school, which most were involved in before giving birth, and if so, how soon and for how many hours? Whereas only 18 percent of women with a child under six were employed outside the home in 1960, according to the 2000 census, approximately 55 percent of women with a child *under one* now work at least part time. Will the father take an active role in daily child care, and if so, how much? Although having these new choices is regarded by many as a benefit of modern life, choosing from among alternatives with such far-reaching consequences creates confusion and uncertainty for both men and women—which itself can lead to tension within the couple.

New Expectations for Marriage = New Emotional Burdens

Mark and Abby, like many other modern couples, have different expectations for marriage than their forebears. In earlier decades, couples expected marriage to be a working partnership in which men and women played unequal but clearly defined roles in terms of family and work, especially once they had children. Many modern couples are trying to create more egalitarian relationships in which men and women have more similar and often interchangeable family and work roles.

The dramatic increase of women in the labor force has challenged old definitions of what men and women are expected to do inside and outside the family. As women have taken on a major role of contributing to family income, there has been a shift in *ideology* about fathers' greater participation in housework and child care, although the *realities* of men's and women's division of family labor have lagged behind. Despite the fact that modern fathers are a little more involved in daily family activities than their fathers were, studies in every industrialized country reveal that women continue to carry the major share of the burden of family work and care of the children, even when both partners are employed full time.[3] In a detailed qualitative study, Arlie Hochschild notes that working mothers come home to a "second shift." She describes vividly couples' struggle with contradictions between the values of egalitarianism and traditionalism, and between egalitarian ideology and the constraints of modern family life.

As husbands and wives struggle with these issues, they often become adversaries. At the same time, they expect their partners to be their major suppliers of emotional warmth and support.[4] These demanding expectations for marriage as a haven from the stresses of the larger world come naturally to modern partners, but this comfort zone is difficult to create, given current economic and psychological realities and the absence of helpful models from the past. The difficulty of the task is further compounded by the fact that when contemporary couples feel stressed by trying to work and nurture their children, they feel torn by what they hear from advocates of a "simpler," more traditional version of family life. In sum, we see Abby and Mark as new pioneers because they are creating a new version of family life in an era of greater challenges and fewer supports, increased and confusing choices about work and family arrangements, ambiguities about men's and women's proper roles, and demanding expectations of themselves to be both knowledgeable and nurturing partners and parents.

POLITICAL CONTEXT: DOES FAMILY CHANGE MEAN FAMILY DECLINE?

A number of writers have concluded that the historical family changes we described have weakened the institution of the family. One of the main spokespersons for this point of view, David Popenoe,[5] interprets the trends as documenting a "retreat from the traditional nuclear family in terms of a lifelong, sexually exclusive unit, with a separate-sphere division of labor between husbands and wives." He asserts, "Nuclear units are losing ground to single-parent families, serial and stepfamilies, and unmarried and homosexual couples."[6] The main problem in contemporary family life, he argues, is a shift in which familism as a cultural value has lost ground to other values such as individualism, self-focus, and egalitarianism.[7]

Family decline theorists are especially critical of single-parent families whether created by divorce or out-of-wedlock childbirth.[8] They assume that two-parent families of the past functioned with a central concern for children that led to putting children's needs first. They characterize parents who have children under other arrangements as putting themselves first, and they claim that children are suffering as a result.

The primary index for evaluating the family decline is the well-being of children. Family decline theorists repeatedly cite statistics suggesting that fewer children are being born, and that a higher proportion of them are living with permissive, disengaged, self-focused parents who ignore their physical and emotional needs. Increasing numbers of children show signs of mental illness, behavior problems, and social deviance. The remedy suggested? A social movement and social policies to promote "family values" that emphasize nuclear families with two married, monogamous parents who want to have children and are willing to devote themselves to caring for them. These are the families we have been studying.

Based on the work of following couples starting families over the past twenty years, we suggest that there is a serious problem with the suggested remedy, which ignores the extent of distress and dysfunction in this idealized family form. We will show that in a surprisingly high proportion of couples, the arrival of the first child is accompanied by increased levels of tension, conflict, distress, and divorce, not because the parents are self-centered but because it is inherently difficult in today's world to juggle the economic and emotional needs of all family members, even for couples in relatively "low-risk" circumstances. The need to pay more attention to the underside of the traditional family myth is heightened by the fact that we can now (1) identify in advance those couples most likely to have problems as they make the transition to parenthood, and (2) intervene to reduce the prevalence and intensity of these problems. Our concern with the state of contemporary families leads us to suggest remedies that would involve active support to enable parents to provide nurturance and stability for their children, rather than exhortations that they change their values about family life.

REAL LIFE CONTEXT: NORMAL RISKS ASSOCIATED WITH BECOMING A FAMILY

To illustrate the short-term impact of becoming parents, let us take a brief look at Mark and Abby four days after they bring their daughter, Lizzie, home from the hospital.

It is 3 A.M. Lizzie is crying lustily. Mark had promised that he would get up and bring the baby to Abby when she woke, but he hasn't stirred. After nudging him several times, Abby gives up and pads across the room to Lizzie's cradle. She carries her daughter to a rocking chair and starts to feed her. Abby's nipples are sore and she hasn't yet been able to relax while nursing. Lizzie soon stops sucking and falls asleep. Abby broods silently, the quiet broken only by the rhythmic squeak of the rocker. She is angry at Mark for objecting to her suggestion that her parents come to help. She fumes, thinking about his romantic image of the three of them as a cozy family. "Well, Lizzie and I are cozy all right, but where is Mr. Romantic now?" Abby is also preoccupied with worry. She is intrigued and drawn to Lizzie but because she hasn't experienced the "powerful surge of love" that she thinks "all mothers" feel, she worries that something is wrong with her. She is also anxious because she told her boss that she'd be back to work shortly, but she simply doesn't know how she will manage. She considers talking to her best friend, Adrienne, but Adrienne probably wouldn't understand because she doesn't have a child.

Hearing what he interprets as Abby's angry rocking, Mark groggily prepares his defense about why he failed to wake up when the baby did. Rather than engaging in conversation, recalling that Abby "barked" at him when he hadn't remembered to stop at the market and pharmacy on the way home from work, he pretends to be asleep. He becomes preoccupied with thoughts about the pile of work he will face at the office in the morning.

We can see how two well-meaning, thoughtful people have been caught up in changes and reactions that neither has anticipated or feels able to control. Based on our experience with many new parent couples, we imagine that, if asked, Abby and Mark would say that these issues arousing their resentment are minor; in fact, they feel foolish about being so upset about them. Yet studies of new parents suggest that the stage is set for a snowball effect in which these minor discontents can grow into more troubling distress in the next year or two. What are the consequences of this early disenchantment? Will Mark and Abby be able to prevent it from triggering more serious negative outcomes for them or for the baby?

To answer these questions about the millions of couples who become first-time parents each year, we draw on the results of our own longitudinal study of the transition to parenthood and those of several other investigators who also followed men and women from late pregnancy into the early years of life with a first child.[9] The samples in these studies were remarkably similar: the average age of first-time expectant fathers was about thirty years, of expectant mothers approximately one year younger. Most investigators studied urban couples, but a few included rural families. Although the participants' economic level varied from study to study, most fell on the continuum from working class, through lower-middle, to upper-middle class. In 1995 we reviewed more than twenty longitudinal studies of this period of family life; we included two in Germany by Engfer and Schneewind[10] and one in England by Clulow,[11] and found that results in all but two reveal an elevated risk for the marriages of couples becoming parents.[12] A more recent study and review comes to the same conclusion.[13]

We talk about this major normative transition in the life of a couple in terms of risk, conflict, and distress for the relationship because we find that the effects of the transition to parenthood create disequilibrium in each of five major domains of family life: (1) the parents' sense of self; (2) parent-grandparent relationships; (3) the parent-child relationships; (4) relationships with friends and work; and (5) the state of the marriage. We find that "fault lines" in any of these domains before the baby arrives amplify marital tensions during the transition to parenthood. Although it is difficult to determine precisely when the transition to parenthood begins and ends, our findings suggest that it encompasses a period of more than three years, from before conception until at least two years after the first child is born. Since different couples experience the transition in different ways, we rely here not only on Mark and Abby but also on a number of other couples in our study to illustrate what happens in each domain when partners become parents.

Parents' Sense of Self

Henry, aged 32, was doing well in his job at a large computer store. Along with Mei-Lin, his wife of four years, he was looking forward to the birth of his first child. Indeed, the first week or two found Henry lost in a euphoric haze. But as he came out of the clouds and went back to work, Henry began to be distracted by new worries. As his coworkers kept reminding him, he's a father now. He certainly feels like a different person, though he's not quite sure what a new father is supposed to be doing. Rather hesitantly, he confessed his sense of confusion to Mei-Lin, who appeared visibly relieved. "I've been feeling so fragmented," she told him. "It's been difficult to hold on to my sense of *me*. I'm a wife, a daughter, a friend, and a teacher, but the Mother part seems to have taken over my whole being."

Having a child forces a redistribution of the energy directed to various aspects of parents' identity. We asked expectant parents to describe themselves by making a list of the main aspects of themselves, such as son, daughter, friend, worker, and to divide a circle we called *The Pie* into pieces representing how large each aspect of self feels. Men and women filled out *The Pie* again six and eighteen months after their babies were born. As partners became parents, the size of the slice labeled *parent* increased markedly until it occupied almost one-third of the identity of mothers of eighteen-month-olds. Although men's *parent* slice also expanded, their sense of self as father occupied only one-third the "space" of their wives'. For both women and men, the *partner* or *lover* part of their identities got "squeezed" as the *parent* aspect of self expanded.

It is curious that in the early writing about the transition to parenthood, which E. E. LeMasters claimed constituted a crisis for a couple,[14] none of the investigators gathered or cited data on postpartum depression—diagnosed when disabling symptoms of depression occur within the first few months after giving birth. Accurate epidemiological estimates of risk for postpartum depression are difficult to come by. Claims about the incidence in women range from .01 percent for serious postpartum psychosis to 50 percent for the "baby blues." Results of a study by Campbell and her colleagues suggest that approximately 10 percent of new mothers develop serious clinical depressions that interfere with their daily functioning in the postpartum period.[15] There are no epidemiological estimates of the incidence of postpartum depression in new fathers. In our study of 100 couples, one new mother and one new father required medical treatment for disabling postpartum depression. What we know, then, is that many new parents like Henry and Mei-Lin experience a profound change in their view of themselves after they have a baby, and some feel so inadequate and critical of themselves that their predominant mood can be described as depressed.

Relationships with Parents and In-Laws

Sandra, one of the younger mothers in our study, talked with us about her fear of repeating the pattern from her mother's life. Her mother gave birth at sixteen, and told her children repeatedly that she was too young to raise a family. "Here I am with a beautiful little girl, and I'm worrying about whether I'm really grown up enough to raise her." At the same time, Sandra's husband, Daryl, who was beaten by his stepfather, is having flashbacks about how helpless he felt at those times: "I'm trying to maintain the confidence I felt when Sandra and I decided to start our family, but sometimes I get scared that I'm not going to be able to avoid being the kind of father I grew up with."

Psychoanalytically oriented writers[16] focusing on the transition to parenthood emphasize the potential disequilibration that is stimulated by a reawakening of intrapsychic conflicts from new parents' earlier relationships. There is considerable evidence that having a baby stimulates men's and women's feelings of vulnerability and loss associated with their own childhoods, and that these issues play a role in their emerging sense of self as parents. There is also evidence that negative relationship patterns tend to be repeated across the generations, despite parents' efforts to avoid them,[17] so Sandra and Daryl have good reason to be concerned. However, studies showing that a strong, positive couple relationship can provide a buffer against negative parent-child interactions suggest that the repetition of negative cycles is not inevitable.[18]

We found that the birth of a first child increases the likelihood of contact between the generations, often with unanticipated consequences. Occasionally, renewed contact allows the expectant parents to put years of estrangement behind them if their parents are receptive to renewed contact. More often, increased contact between the generations stimulates old and new conflicts—within each partner, between the partners, and between the generations. To take one example: Abby wants her mother to come once the baby is born but Mark has a picture of beginning family life on their own. Tensions between them around this issue can escalate regardless of which decision they make. If Abby's parents do visit, Mark may have difficulty establishing his place with the baby. Even if Abby's parents come to help, she and Mark may find that the grandparents need looking after too. It may be weeks before Mark and Abby have a private conversation. If the grandparents do not respond or are not invited, painful feelings between the generations are likely to ensue.

The Parent-Child Relationship

Few parents have had adequate experience in looking after children to feel confident immediately about coping with the needs of a first baby.

> Tyson and Martha have been arguing, it seems, for days. Eddie, their six-month-old, has long crying spells every day and into the night. As soon as she hears him, Martha moves to pick him up. When he is home, Tyson objects, reasoning that this just spoils Eddie and doesn't let him learn how to soothe himself. Martha responds that Eddie wouldn't be crying if something weren't wrong, but she worries that Tyson may be right; after all, she's never looked after a six-month-old for more than an evening of baby-sitting. Although Tyson continues to voice his objections, he worries that if Martha is right, *his* plan may not be the best for his son either.

To make matters more complicated, just as couples develop strategies that seem effective, their baby enters a new developmental phase that calls for new reactions and routines. What makes these new challenges difficult to resolve is that each parent has a set of ideas and expectations about how parents should respond to a child, most based on experience in their families of origin. Meshing both parents' views of how to resolve basic questions about child rearing proves to be a more complex and emotionally draining task than most couples had anticipated.

Work and Friends

Dilemmas about partners' work outside the home are particularly salient during a couple's transition to parenthood.

> Both Hector and Isabel have decided that Isabel should stay home for at least the first year after having the baby. One morning, as Isabel is washing out José's diapers and hoping the phone will ring, she breaks into tears. Life is not as she imagined it. She misses her friends at work. She misses Hector, who is working harder now to provide for his family than he was before José was born. She misses her parents and sisters who live far away in Mexico. She feels strongly that she wants to be with her child full time, and that she should be grateful that Hector's income makes this possible, but she feels so unhappy right now. This feeling adds to her realization that she has always contributed half of their family income, but now she has to ask Hector for household money, which leaves her feeling vulnerable and dependent.
>
> Maria is highly invested in her budding career as an investment counselor, making more money than her husband, Emilio. One morning, as she faces the mountain of unread files on her desk and thinks of Lara at the child care center almost ready to take her first steps, Maria bursts into tears. She feels confident that she and Emilio have found excellent child care for Lara, and reminds herself that research has suggested that when mothers work outside the home, their daughters develop more competence than daughters of mothers who stay home. Nevertheless, she feels bereft, missing milestones that happen only once in a child's life.

We have focused on the women in both families because, given current societal arrangements, the initial impact of the struggle to balance work and family falls more heavily on mothers. If the couple decides that one parent will stay home to be the primary caretaker of the child, it is almost always the mother who does so. As we have noted, in contemporary America, about 50 percent of mothers of very young children remain at home after having a baby and more than half return to work within the first year. Both alternatives have some costs and some benefits. If mothers like Isabel want to be home with their young children, and the family can afford this arrangement, they have the opportunity to participate fully in the early day-to-day life of their children. This usually has benefits for parents and children. Nevertheless, most mothers who stay home face limited opportunities to accomplish work that leads them to feel competent, and staying home deprives them of emotional support that coworkers and friends can provide, the kinds of support that play a significant role in how parents fare in the early postpartum years. This leaves women like Isabel at risk for feeling lonely and isolated from friends and family.[19] By contrast, women like Maria who return to work are able to maintain a network of adults to work with and talk with. They may feel better about themselves and "on track" as far as their work is concerned, but many become preoccupied with worry about their children's well-being, particularly in this age of costly but less than ideal child care. Furthermore, once they get home, they enter a "second shift" in which they do the bulk of the housework and child care.[20]

We do not mean to imply that all the work-family conflicts surrounding the transition to parenthood are experienced by women. Many modern fathers feel torn about how to juggle work and family life, move ahead on the job, and be more involved with their children than their fathers were with them. Rather than receive a reduction in workload, men tend to work longer hours once they become fathers, mainly because they take their role as provider even more seriously now that they have a child.[21] In talking to more than 100 fathers in our ongoing studies, we have become convinced that the common picture of men as resisting the responsibilities and workload involved in family life is seriously in error. We have become painfully aware of the formidable obstacles that bar men from assuming more active roles as fathers and husbands.

First, parents, bosses, and friends often discourage men's active involvement in the care of their children ("How come you're home in the middle of the day?" "Are you really serious about your work here?" "She's got you baby-sitting again, huh?"). Second, the economic realities in which men's pay exceeds women's, make it less viable for men to take family time off. Third, by virtue of the way males and females are socialized, men rarely get practice in looking after children and are given very little support for learning by trial and error with their new babies.

> In the groups that we conducted for expectant and new parents, to which parents brought their babies after they were born, we saw and heard many versions of the following: we are discussing wives' tendency to reach for the baby, on the assumption that their husbands will not respond. Cindi describes an incident last week when little Samantha began to cry. Cindi waited. Her husband, Martin, picked up Samantha gingerly, groped for a bottle, and awkwardly started to feed her. Then, according to Martin, within about sixty seconds, Cindi suggested that Martin give Samantha's head more support and prop the bottle in a different way so that the milk would flow without creating air bubbles. Martin quickly decided to hand the baby back to "the expert" and slipped into the next room "to get some work done."

The challenge to juggle the demands of work, family, and friendship presents different kinds of stressors for men and women, which propels the spouses even farther into separate worlds. When wives stay at home, they wait eagerly for their husbands to return, hoping the men will go "on duty" with the child, especially on difficult days. This leaves tired husbands who need to unwind facing tired wives who long to talk to an adult who will respond intelligibly to them. When both parents work outside the family, they must coordinate schedules, arrange child care, and decide how to manage when their child is ill. Parents' stress from these dilemmas about child care and lack of rest often spill over into the workday—and their work stress, in turn, gets carried back into the family atmosphere.[22]

The Marriage

It should be clearer now why we say that the normal changes associated with becoming a family increase the risk that husbands and wives will experience increased marital dissatisfaction and strain after they become parents. Mark and Abby, and the other couples we have described briefly, have been through changes in their sense of themselves and in their relationships with their parents. They have struggled with uncertainties and disagreements about how to provide the best care for their child. Regardless of whether one parent stays home full or part time or both work full days outside the home, they have limited time and energy to meet conflicting demands from their parents, bosses, friends, child, and each other, and little support from outside the family to guide them on this complex journey into uncharted territory. In almost every published study of the transition conducted over the last four decades, men's and women's marital satisfaction declined. Belsky and Rovine found that from 30 percent to 59 percent of the participants in their Pennsylvania study showed a decline between pregnancy and nine months postpartum, depending on which measure of the marriage they examined.[23] In our study of California parents, 45 percent of the men and 58 percent of the women showed declining satisfaction with marriage between pregnancy and eighteen months postpartum. The scores of approximately 15 percent of the new parents moved from below to above the clinical cutoff that indicates serious marital problems, whereas only 4 percent moved from above to below the cutoff.

Why should this optimistic time of life pose so many challenges for couples? One key issue for couples becoming parents has been treated as a surefire formula for humor in situation comedies—husband-wife battles over the "who does what?" of housework, child care, and decision making. Our own study shows clearly that, regardless of how equally family work is divided before having a baby, or of how equally husbands and wives *expect* to divide the care of the baby, the roles men and women assume tend to be gender-linked, with wives doing more family work than they had done before becoming a parent and substantially more housework and baby care than their husbands do. Furthermore, the greater the discrepancy between women's predicted and actual division of family tasks with their spouses, the more symptoms of depression they report. The more traditional the arrangements—that is, the less husbands are responsible for family work—the greater fathers' *and* mothers' postpartum dissatisfaction with their overall marriage.

Although theories of life stress generally assume that *any* change is stressful, we found no correlation between sheer *amount* of change in the five aspects of family life and parents' difficulties adapting to parenthood. In general, parenthood was followed by increasing discrepancies between husbands' and wives' perceptions of family life and their descriptions of their actual family and work roles. Couples in which the partners showed the greatest increase in those discrepancies—more often those with increasingly traditional role arrangements—described increasing conflict as a couple and greater declines in marital satisfaction.

These findings suggest that whereas family decline theorists are looking at statistics about contemporary families through 1950 lenses, actual families are responding to the realities of life in the twenty-first century. Given historical shifts in men's and women's ideas about family roles and present economic realities, it is not realistic to expect them to simply reverse trends by adopting more traditional values and practices. Contemporary families in which the parents' arrangements are at the more traditional end of the spectrum are *less* satisfied with themselves, with their relationships as couples, and with their role as parents, than those at the more egalitarian end.

DO WE KNOW WHICH FAMILIES WILL BE AT RISK?

The message for policymakers from research on the transition to parenthood is not only that it is a time of stress and change. We and others have found that there is predictability to couples' patterns of change: this means that it is possible to know whether a couple is at risk for more serious problems before they have a baby and whether their child will be at risk for compromised development. This information is also essential for purposes of designing *preventive* intervention. Couples most at risk for difficulties and troubling outcomes in the early postpartum years are those who were in the greatest individual and marital distress before they became parents. Children most at risk are those whose parents are having the most difficulty maintaining a positive, rewarding relationship as a couple.

The "Baby-Maybe" Decision

Interviews with expectant parents about their process of making the decision to have a baby provide one source of information about continuity of adaptation in the family-making period. By analyzing partners' responses to the question, "How did the two of you come to be having a baby at this time?" we found four fairly distinct types of decision making in our sample of lower-middle- to upper-middle-class couples, none of whom had identified themselves as having serious relationship difficulties during pregnancy: (1) The *Planners*—50 percent of the couples—agreed about whether and when to have a baby. The other 50 percent were roughly evenly divided into three patterns: (2) The *Acceptance of fate couples*—15 percent—had unplanned conceptions but were pleased to learn that they were about to become parents; (3) The *Ambivalent couples*—another 15 percent—continually went back and forth about their readiness to have a baby, even late in pregnancy; and (4) The *Yes-No couples*—the remaining 15 percent—claimed not to be having relationship difficulties but nonetheless had strong disagreements about whether to complete their unplanned pregnancy.

> Alice, thirty-four, became pregnant when she and Andy, twenty-seven, had been living together only four months. She was determined to have a child, regardless of whether Andy stayed in the picture. He did not feel ready to become a father, and though he dearly loved Alice, he was struggling to come to terms with the pregnancy. "It was the hardest thing I ever had to deal with," he said. "I had this idea that I wasn't even going to have to think about being a father until I was over thirty, but here it was, and I had to decide now. I was concerned about my soul. I didn't want, under any circumstances, to compromise myself, but I knew it would be very hard on Alice if I took action that would result in her being a single parent. It would've meant that I'm the kind of person who turns his back on someone I care about, and that would destroy me as well as her." And so he stayed.[24]

The *Planners* and *Acceptance of fate couples* experienced minimal decline in marital satisfaction, whereas the *Ambivalent couples* tended to have lower satisfaction to begin with and to decline even further between pregnancy and two years later. The greatest risk was for couples who had serious disagreement—more than ambivalence—about having a first baby. In these cases, one partner gave in to the other's wishes in order to remain in the relationship. The startling outcome provides a strong statement about the wisdom of this strategy: all of the *Yes-No couples* like Alice and Andy were divorced by the time their first child entered kindergarten, and the two *Yes-No couples* in which the wife was the reluctant partner reported severe marital distress at every postpartum assessment. This finding suggests that partners' unresolved conflict in making the decision to have a child is mirrored by their inability to cope with conflict to both partners' satisfaction once they become parents. Couples' styles of making this far-reaching decision seem to be a telling indicator of whether their overall relationship is at risk for instability, a finding that contradicts the folk wisdom that having a baby will mend serious marital rifts.

Additional Risk Factors for Couples

Not surprisingly, when couples reported high levels of outside-the-family life stress during pregnancy, they are more likely to be unhappy in their marriages and stressed in their parenting roles during the early years of parenthood. When there are serious problems in the relationships between new parents and their own parents the couples are more likely to experience more postpartum distress.[25] Belsky and colleagues showed that new parents who recalled strained relationships with their own parents were more likely to experience more marital distress in the first year of parenthood.[26] In our study, parents who reported early childhoods clouded by their parents' problem drinking had a more stressful time on every indicator of adjustment in the first two years of parenthood—more conflict, less effective problem solving, less effective parenting styles, and greater parenting stress.[27] Although the transmission of maladaptive patterns across generations is not inevitable, these data suggest that without intervention, troubled relationships in the family of origin constitute a risk factor for relationships in the next generation.

Although it is never possible to make perfect predictions for purposes of creating family policies to help reduce the risks associated with family formation, we have been able to identify expectant parents at risk for later individual, marital, and parenting difficulties based on information they provided during pregnancy. Recall that the participants in the studies we are describing are the two-parent intact families portrayed as ideal in the family decline debate. The problems they face have little to do with their family values. The difficulties appear to stem from the fact that the visible fault lines in couple relationships leave their marriages more vulnerable to the shake-up of the transition-to-parenthood process.

Risks for Children

We are concerned about the impact of the transition to parenthood not only because it increases the risk of distress in marriage but also because the parents' early distress can have far-reaching consequences for their children. Longitudinal studies make it clear that parents' early difficulties affect their children's later intellectual and social adjustment. For example, parents' well-being or distress as individuals and as couples during pregnancy predicts the quality of their relationships with their children in the preschool period.[28] In turn, the quality of both parent-child relationships in the preschool years is related to the child's academic and social competence during the early elementary school years.[29] Preschoolers whose mothers and fathers had more responsive, effective parenting styles had higher scores on academic achievement and fewer acting out, aggressive, or withdrawn behavior problems with peers in kindergarten and Grade 1.[30] When we receive teachers' reports, we see that overall, five-year-olds whose parents reported making the most positive adaptations to parenthood were the ones with the most successful adjustments to elementary school.

Alexander and Entwisle[31] suggested that in kindergarten and first grade, children are "launched into achievement trajectories that they follow the rest of their school years." Longitudinal studies of children's academic and social competence[32] support this hypothesis about the importance of students' early adaptation to school: children who are socially rejected by peers in the early elementary grades are more likely to have academic problems or drop out of school, to develop antisocial and delinquent behaviors, and to have difficulty in intimate relationships with partners in late adolescence and early adulthood. Without support or intervention early in a family's development, the children with early academic, emotional, and social problems are at greater risk for later, even more serious problems.

POLICY IMPLICATIONS

What social scientists have learned about families during the transition to parenthood is relevant to policy discussions about how families with young children can be strengthened.

We return briefly to the family values debate to examine the policy implications of promoting traditional family arrangements, of altering workplace policies, and of providing preventive interventions to strengthen families during the early childrearing years.

The Potential Consequences of Promoting Traditional Family Arrangements

What are the implications of the argument that families and children would benefit by a return to traditional family arrangements? We are aware that existing data are not adequate to provide a full test of the family values argument, but we believe that some systematic information on this point is better than none. At first glance, it may seem as if studies support the arguments of those proposing that "the family" is in decline. We have documented the fact that a substantial number of new two-parent families are experiencing problems of adjustment—parents' depression, troubled marriages, intergenerational strain, and stress in juggling the demands of work and family. Nevertheless, there is little in the transition to parenthood research to support the idea that parents' distress is attributable to a decline in their family-oriented *values.* First, the populations studied here are two-parent, married, nonteenage, lower-middle- to upper-middle-class families, who do not represent the "variants" in family form that most writers associate with declining quality of family life.

Second, threaded throughout the writings on family decline is the erroneous assumption that because these changes in the family have been occurring at the same time as increases in negative outcomes for children, the changes are the *cause* of the problems. These claims are not buttressed by systematic data establishing the direction of causal influence. For example, it is well accepted (but still debated) that children's adaptation is poorer in the period after their parents' divorce.[33] Nevertheless, some studies suggest that it is the unresolved conflict between parents prior to and after the divorce, rather than the divorce itself, that accounts for most of the debilitating effects on the children.[34]

Third, we find the attack on family egalitarianism puzzling when the fact is that, despite the increase in egalitarian ideology, modern couples move toward more traditional family role arrangements as they become parents—despite their intention to do otherwise. Our key point here is that traditional family and work roles in families of the last three decades tend to be associated with *more* individual and marital distress for parents. Furthermore, we find that when fathers have little involvement in household and child care tasks, both parents are less responsive and less able to provide the structure necessary for their children to accomplish new and challenging tasks in our project playroom. Finally, when we ask teachers how all of the children in their classrooms are faring at school, it is the children of these parents who are less academically competent and more socially isolated. There is, then, a body of evidence suggesting that a return to strictly traditional family arrangements may not have the positive consequences that the proponents of "family values" claim they will.

Family and Workplace Policy

Current discussions about policies for reducing the tensions experienced by parents of young children tend to be polarized around two alternatives: (1) Encourage more mothers to stay home and thereby reduce their stress in juggling family and work; (2) Make the workplace more flexible and "family friendly" for both parents through parental leave policies, flextime, and child care provided or subsidized by the workplace. There is no body of systematic empirical research that supports the conclusion that when mothers work outside the home, their children or husbands suffer negative consequences.[35] In fact, our own data and others' suggest that (1) children, especially girls, benefit from the model their working mothers provide as productive workers, and (2) mothers of young children who return to work are less depressed than mothers who stay home full time. Thus it is not at all clear that a policy designed to persuade contemporary mothers of young children to stay at home would have the desired effects, particularly given the potential for depression and the loss of one parent's wages in single paycheck families. Unless governments are prepared, as they are in Sweden and Germany, for example, to hold parents' jobs and provide *paid* leave to replace lost wages, a stay-at-home *policy* seems too costly for the family on both economic and psychological grounds.

We believe that the issue should not be framed in terms of policies to support single-worker *or* dual-worker families, but rather in terms of support for the well-being of all family members. This goal could entail financial support for families with very young children so that parents could choose to do full-time or substantial part-time child care themselves *or* to have support to return to work.

What about the alternative of increasing workplace flexibility? Studies of families making the transition to parenthood suggest that this alternative may be especially attractive and helpful when children are young, if it is accompanied by substantial increases in the availability of high-quality child care to reduce the stress of locating adequate care or making do with less than ideal caretakers. Adults and children tend to adapt well when both parents work *if both parents support that alternative*. Therefore, policies that support paid family leave along with flexible work arrangements could enable families to choose arrangements that make most sense for their particular situation.

Preventive Services to Address Family Risk Points

According to our analysis of the risks associated with the formation of new families, many two-parent families are having difficulty coping on their own with the normal challenges of becoming a family. If a priority in our society is to strengthen new families, it seems reasonable to consider offering preventive programs to reduce risks and distress and enhance the potential for healthy and satisfying family relationships, which we know lead to more optimal levels of adjustment in children. What we are advocating is analogous to the concept of Lamaze and other forms of childbirth preparation, which are now commonly sought by many expectant parents. A logical context for these programs would be existing public and private health and mental health delivery systems in which services could be provided for families who wish assistance or are already in difficulty. We recognize that there is skepticism in a substantial segment of the population about psychological services in general, and about services provided for families by government in particular. Nonetheless, the fact is that many modern families are finding parenthood unexpectedly stressful and they typically have no access to assistance. Evidence from intervention trials suggests that when preventive programs help parents move their family relationships in more positive directions, their children have fewer academic, behavioral, and emotional problems in their first years of schooling.[36]

Parent-Focused Interventions.
Elsewhere, we reviewed the literature on interventions designed to improve parenting skills and parent-child relationship quality in families at different points on the spectrum from low-risk to high-distress.[37] For parents of children already identified as having serious problems, home visiting programs and preschool and early school interventions, some of which include a broader family focus, have demonstrated positive effects on parents' behavior and self-esteem and on children's academic and social competence, particularly when the intervention staff are health or mental health professionals. However, with the exception of occasional classes, books, or tapes for parents, there are few resources for parents who need to learn more about how to manage small problems before they spiral out of their control.

Couple-Focused Interventions.
Our conceptual model of family transitions and results of studies of partners who become parents suggest that family-based interventions might go beyond enhancing parent-child relationships to strengthen the relationship *between* the parents. We have seen that the couple relationship is vulnerable in its own right around the decision to have a baby and increasingly after the birth of a child. We know of only

one pilot program that provided couples an opportunity to explore mixed feelings about the "Baby-Maybe" decision.[38] Surely, services designed to help couples resolve their conflict about whether and when to become a family—especially "Yes-No" couples—might reduce the risks of later marital and family distress, just as genetic counseling helps couples make decisions when they are facing the risk of serious genetic problems.

In our own work, we have been systematically evaluating two preventive interventions for couples who have not been identified as being in a high-risk category. Both projects involved work with small groups of couples who met weekly over many months, in one case expectant couples, in the other, couples whose first child is about to make the transition to elementary school.[39] In both studies, staff couples who are mental health professionals worked with *both parents* in small groups of four or five couples. Ongoing discussion over the months of regular meetings addressed participants' individual, marital, parenting, and three-generational dilemmas and problems. In both cases we found promising results when we compared adjustment in families with and without the intervention.

By two years after the Becoming a Family project intervention, new parents had avoided the typical declines in role satisfaction and the increases in marital disenchantment reported in almost every longitudinal study of new parents. There were no separations or divorces in couples who participated in the intervention for the first three years of parenthood, whereas 15 percent of comparable couples with no intervention had already divorced. The positive impact of this intervention was still apparent five years after it had ended.

In the Schoolchildren and Their Families project intervention, professional staff engaged couples in group discussions of marital, parenting, and three-generational problems and dilemmas during their first child's transition to school. Two years after the intervention ended, fathers and mothers showed fewer symptoms of depression and less conflict in front of their child, and fathers were more effective in helping their children with difficult tasks than comparable parents with no intervention. These positive effects on the parents' lives and relationships had benefits for the children as well: children of parents who worked with the professionals in an ongoing couples group showed greater academic improvement and fewer emotional and behavior problems in the first five years of elementary school than children whose parents had no group intervention.[40]

These results suggest that preventive interventions in which clinically trained staff work with "low-risk" couples have the potential to buffer some of the parents' strain, slow down or stop the spillover of negative and unrewarding patterns from one relationship to another, enhance fathers' responsiveness to their children, and foster the children's ability both to concentrate on their school work and to develop more rewarding relationships with their peers. The findings suggest that *without intervention*, there is increased risk of spillover from parents' distress to the quality of the parent-child relationships. This means that preventive services to help parents cope more effectively with their problems have the potential to enhance their responsiveness to their children *and* to their partners, which, in turn, optimizes their children's chances of making more successful adjustments to school. Such programs have the potential to reduce the long-term negative consequences of children's early school difficulties by setting them on more positive developmental trajectories as they face the challenges of middle childhood.

CONCLUSION

The transition to parenthood has been made by men and women for centuries. In the past three decades, the notion that this transition poses risks for the well-being of adults and, thus, potentially for their children's development, has been greeted by some with surprise, disbelief, or skepticism. Our goal has been to bring recent social science findings about the processes involved in becoming a family to the attention of social scientists, family policymakers, and parents themselves. We have shown that this often-joyous time is normally accompanied by changes and stressors that increase risks of relationship difficulty and compromise the ability of men and women to create the kinds of families they dream of when they set out on their journey to parenthood. We conclude that there is cause for concern about the health of "the family"—even those considered advantaged by virtue of their material and psychological resources.

Most chapters in this book focus on policies for families in more high-risk situations. We have argued that contemporary couples and their children in two-parent lower- to upper-middle-class families deserve the attention of policymakers as well. We view these couples as new pioneers, because, despite the fact that partners have been having babies for millennia, contemporary parents are journeying into uncharted terrain, which appears to hold unexpected risks to their own and their children's development.

Like writers describing "family decline," we are concerned about the strength and hardiness of two-parent families. Unlike those who advocate that parents adopt more traditional family values, we recommend that policies to address family health and well-being allow for the creation of programs and services for families in diverse family arrangements, with the goal of enhancing the development and well-being of all children. We recognize that with economic resources already stretched very thin, this is not an auspicious time to recommend additional collective funding of family services. Yet research suggests that without intervention, there is a risk that the vulnerabilities and problems of the parents will spill over into the lives of their children, thus increasing the probability of the transmission of the kinds of intergenerational problems that erode the quality of family life and compromise children's chances of optimal development. This will be very costly in the long run.

We left Mark and Abby, and a number of other couples, in a state of animated suspension. Many of them were feeling somewhat irritable and disappointed, though not ready to give up on their dreams of creating nurturing families. These couples provide a challenge—that the information they have offered through their participation in scores of systematic family studies in many locales will be taken seriously, and that their voices will play a role in helping our society decide how to allocate limited economic and social resources for the families that need them.

*Notes*_____

    1. D. Blankenhorn, S. Bayme, and J. B. Elshtain (eds.), *Rebuilding the Nest: A New Commitment to the American Family* (Milwaukee, WI: Family Service America, 1990), 3–26; D. Popenoe, "American Family Decline, 1960–1990," *Journal of Marriage and the Family* 55:527–541, 1993.

    2. S. B. Crockenberg, "Infant Irritability, Mother Responsiveness, and Social Support Influences on Security of Infant-Mother Attachment," *Child Development* 52:857–865, 1981; C. Cutrona,

"Nonpsychotic Postpartum Depression: A Review of Recent Research," *Clinical Psychology Review* 2:487–503, 1982.

3. A. Hochschild, *The Second Shift: Working Parents and the Revolution at Home* (New York: Viking Penguin, 1989); J. H. Pleck, "Fathers and Infant Care Leave," in E. F. Zigler and M. Frank (eds.), *The Parental Leave Crisis: Toward a National Policy* (New Haven, CT: Yale University Press, 1988).

4. A. Skolnick, *Embattled Paradise: The American Family in an Age of Uncertainty* (New York: Basic Books, 1991).

5. D. Popenoe, *Disturbing the Nest: Family Change and Decline in Modern Societies* (New York: Aldine de Gruyter, 1988); Popenoe, "American Family Decline."

6. Popenoe, "American Family Decline." 41–42. Smaller two-parent families and larger one-parent families are both attributed to the same mechanism: parental self-focus and selfishness.

7. D. Blankenhorn, "American Family Dilemmas," in D. Blankenhorn, S. Bayme, and J. B. Elshtain (eds.), *Rebuilding the Nest. A New Commitment to the American Family* (Milwaukee, WI: Family Service America, 1990), 3–26.

8. Although the proportion of single-parent families is increasing, the concern about departure from the two-parent form may be overstated. Approximately 70 percent of American babies born in the 1990s come home to two parents who are married. If we include couples with long-term commitments who are not legally married, the proportion of modern families that *begins* with two parents is even higher. The prevalence of two-parent families has declined since 1956, when 94 percent of newborns had married parents, but, by far, the predominant family form in the nonteenage population continues to be two parents and a baby.

9. J. Belsky, M. Lang, and M. Rovine, "Stability and Change across the Transition to Parenthood: A Second Study," *Journal of Personality and Social Psychology* 50:517–522, 1985; C. P. Cowan, P. A. Cowan, G. Heming, E. Garrett, W. S. Coysh, H. Curtis-Boles, and A. J. Boles, "Transitions to Parenthood: His, Hers, and Theirs," *Journal of Family Issues* 6:451–481, 1985; M. J. Cox, M. T. Owen, J. M. Lewis, and V. K. Henderson, "Marriage, Adult Adjustment, and Early Parenting," *Child Development* 60:1015–1024, 1989; F. Grossman, L. Eiehler, and S. Winickoff, *Pregnancy, Birth, and Parenthood* (San Francisco: Jossey-Bass, 1980); C. M. Heinicke, S. D. Diskin, D. M. Ramsay-Klee, and D. S. Oates, "Pre- and Postbirth Antecedents of 2-year-old Attention, Capacity for Relationships and Verbal Expressiveness," *Developmental Psychology* 22:777–787, 1986; R. Levy-Shiff, "Individual and Contextual Correlates of Marital Change Across the Transition to Parenthood," *Developmental Psychology* 30:591–601, 1994.

10. A. Engfer, "The Interrelatedness of Marriage and the Mother-Child Relationship," in R. A. Hinde and J. Stevenson-Hinde (eds.), *Relationships within Families: Mutual Influences* (Cambridge UK: Cambridge University Press, 1988), 104–118; K. A. Schneewind, "Konsequenzen der Ersteltelternschaft" [Consequences of the Transition to Parenthood: An Overview], *Psychologie in Erziehung und Unterricht* 30:161–172, 1983.

11. C. F. Clulow, *To Have and to Hold: Marriage, the First Baby and Preparing Couples for Parenthood* (Aberdeen, Scotland: Aberdeen University Press, 1982).

12. C. P. Cowan and P. A. Cowan, "Interventions to Ease the Transition to Parenthood: Why They Are Needed and What They Can Do," *Family Relations* 44:412–423, 1995.

13. A. F. Shapiro, J. M. Gottman, and S. Carrere, "The Baby and the Marriage. Identifying Factors that Buffer against Decline in Marital Satisfaction after the First Baby Arrives. *Journal of Family Psychology*, 14:59–70, 2000.

14. E. E. LeMasters, "Parenthood as Crisis," *Marriage and Family Living* 19:352–365,1957.

15. S. B. Campbell, J. F. Cohn, C. Flanagan, S. Popper, and T. Myers, "Course and Correlates of Postpartum Depression during the Transition to Parenthood," *Development and Psychopathology* 4:29–48, 1992.

16. T. Benedek, "Parenthood during the Life Cycle," in E. J. Anthony and T. Benedek (eds.), *Parenthood: Its Psychology and Psychopathology* (Boston: Little, Brown, 1970); J. D. Osofsky and H. J. Osofsky, "Psychological and Developmental Perspectives on Expectant and New Parenthood," in R. D. Parke (ed.), *Review of Child Development Research 7: The Family* (Chicago: University of Chicago Press, 1984), 372–397.

17. A. Caspi and G. H. Elder, Jr. "Emergent Family Patterns: The Intergenerational Construction of Problem Behavior and Relationships," in R. A. Hinde and J. Stevenson-Hinde (eds.), *Relationships Within Families: Mutual Influences* (Oxford: Clarendon Press, 1988), 218–241; M. H. van Ijzendoorn, F. Juffer, M. G. Duyvesteyn, "Breaking the Intergenerational Cycle of Insecure Attachment: A Review of the Ef-

fects of Attachment-based Interventions on Maternal Sensitivity and Infant Security," *Journal of Child Psychology & Psychiatry & Allied Disciplines* 36:225–248, 1995.

18. D. A. Cohn, P. A. Cowan, C. P. Cowan, and J. Pearson, "Mothers' and Fathers' Working Models of Childhood Attachment Relationships, Parenting Styles, and Child Behavior," *Development and Psychopathology* 4:417–431, 1992.

19. Crockenberg, "Infant Irritability."

20. Hochsehild, *The Second Shift*.

21. C. P. Cowan and P. A. Cowan, *When Partners Become Parents: The Big Life Change for Couples* (Mahwah, NJ: Lawrence Erlbaum, 2000).

22. M. S. Schulz, "Coping with Negative Emotional Arousal: The Daily Spillover of Work Stress into Marital Interactions," Unpublished doctoral dissertation. University of California, Berkeley, 1994; R. Repetti and J. Wood, "Effects of Daily Stress at Work on Mothers' Interactions with Preschoolers," *Journal of Family Psychology*, 11:90–108, 1997.

23. J. Belsky and M. Rovine, "Patterns of Marital Change across the Transition to Parenthood," *Journal of Marriage and the Family* 52:109–123, 1990.

24. We interviewed the couples in the mid-to-late stages of pregnancy. We were not, therefore, privy to the early phases of decision making of these couples, whether wives became pregnant on purpose, or whether husbands were coercive about the baby decision. What we saw in the Yes-No couples, in contrast with the Ambivalent couples, was that the decision to go ahead with the pregnancy, an accomplished fact, was still an unresolved emotional struggle.

25. M. Kline, P. A. Cowan, and C. P. Cowan, "The Origins of Parenting Stress during the Transition to Parenthood: A New Family Model," *Early Education and Development* 2:287–305, 1991.

26. J. Belsky and R. A. Isabella, "Marital and Parent-Child Relationships in Family of Origin and Marital Change Following the Birth of a Baby: A Retrospective Analysis," *Child Development* 56:342–349, 1985; C. P. Cowan, P. A. Cowan, and G. Heming, "Adult Children of Alcoholics: Adaptation during the Transition to Parenthood." Paper presented to the National Council on Family Relations, 1988.

27. Cowan, Cowan, and Heming; "Adult Children of Alcoholics."

28. Belsky, Lang, and Rovine, "Stability and Change across the Transition to Parenthood; Cowan and Cowan, *When Partners Become Parents*, Cox, Owen, Lewis, and Henderson, "Marriage, Adult Adjustment, and Early Parenting"; Heinicke, Diskin, Ramsay-Klee, and Oates, "Pre- and Postbirth Antecedents of 2-Year-Old Attention, Capacity for Relationships and Verbal Expressiveness."

29. D. Baumrind, "The Development of Instrumental Competence through Socialization," in A. D. Pick (ed.), *Minnesota Symposia on Child Psychology*, vol. 7, (Minneapolis: University of Minnesota Press, 1979); J. H. Block and J. Block, "The Role of Ego-Control and Ego-Resiliency in the Organization of Behavior," In W. A. Collins (ed.) *Minnesota Symposia on Child Psychology*, vol. 13 (Hillsdale, NJ: Erlbaum, 1980).

30. P. A. Cowan, C. P. Cowan, M. Schulz, and G. Heming, "Prebirth to Preschool Family Factors Predicting Children's Adaptation to Kindergarten," in R. Parke and S. Kellam (eds.), *Exploring Family Relationships with Other Social Contexts: Advances in Family Research*, vol. 4 (Hillsdale, NJ: Erlbaum, 1994). 75–114.

31. K. L. Alexander and D. Entwisle, "Achievement in the First 2 Years of School: Patterns and Processes," *Monographs of the Society for Research in Child Development* 53:2, Serial No. 218, 1988.

32. S. Asher and J. D. Coie, (eds.), *Peer Rejection in Childhood* (Cambridge: Cambridge University Press, 1990); S. G. Kellam, M. B. Simon, and M. E. Ensminger, "Antecedents in First Grade of Teenage Drug Use and Psychological Well-Being: A Ten-Year Community-wide Prospective Study," In D. Ricks and B. Dohrenwend (eds.), *Origins of Psychopathology: Research and Public Policy* (New York: Cambridge, 1982); N. Lambert, "Adolescent Outcomes for Hyperactive Children: Perspectives on General and Specific Patterns of Childhood Risk for Adolescent Educational, Social, and Mental Health Problems," *American Psychologist* 43:786–799, 1988; E. A. Carlson, L. A. Sroufe et al. "Early Environment Support and Elementary School Adjustment as Predictors of School Adjustment in Middle Adolescence," *Journal of Adolescent Research* 14:72–94, 1999.

33. E. M. Hetherington and J. Kelly, *For Better or for Worse: Divorce Reconsidered* (New York: W. W. Norton, 2002). J. Wallerstein and J. Kelly, *Surviving the Breakup* (New York: Basic Books, 1980).

34. E. M. Cummings and P. T. Davies, *Children and Marital Conflict: The Impact of Family Dispute and Resolution* (New York: Guilford Press, 1994).

35. M. Moorehouse, "Work and Family Dynamics," in P. A. Cowan, D. Field, D. A. Hansen, A. Skolnick, and G. E. Swanson (eds.), *Family, Self, and Society: Toward a New Agenda for Family Research* (Hillsdale, NJ: Erlbaum,1993).

36. P. A. Cowan and C. P. Cowan, "What an Intervention Design Reveals about How Parents Affect Their Children's Academic Achievement and Behavior Problems," in J. G. Borkowski, S. Ramey, and M. Bristol-Power (eds.), *Parenting and the Child's World: Influences on Intellectual, Academic, and Social-Emotional Development* (Mahwah, NJ: Lawrence Erlbaum, 2002).

37. P. A. Cowan, D. Powell, and C. P. Cowan, "Parenting Interventions: A Family Systems View of Enhancing Children's Development," in I. E. Sigel and K. A. Renninger (eds.), *Handbook of Child Psychology*, 5th ed. vol. 4: *Child Psychology in Practice* (New York: Wiley, 1997).

38. L. Potts, "Considering Parenthood: Group Support for a Critical Life Decision," *American Journal of Orthopsychiatry* 50:629–638, 1980.

39. P. A. Cowan, C. P. Cowan, and T. Heming. "Two Variations of a Preventive Intervention for Couples: Effects on Parents and Children during the Transition to Elementary School," in P. A. Cowan, C. P. Cowan, J. Ablow, V. K. Johnson, and J. Measelle (eds.), *The Family Context of Parenting in Children's Adaptation to Elementary School* (Mahwah, NJ: Lawrence Erlbaum Associates, in press).

40. Ibid.

■READING 20

Caring for Our Young: Child Care in Europe and the United States

Dan Clawson and Naomi Gerstel

When a delegation of American child care experts visited France, they were amazed by the full-day, free *écoles maternelles* that enroll almost 100 percent of French three-, four- and five-year-olds:

> Libraries better stocked than those in many U.S. elementary schools. Three-year-olds serving one another radicchio salad, then using cloth napkins, knives, forks and real glasses of milk to wash down their bread and chicken. Young children asked whether dragons exist [as] a lesson in developing vocabulary and creative thinking.

In the United States, by contrast, working parents struggle to arrange and pay for private care. Publicly-funded child care programs are restricted to the poor. Although most U.S. parents believe (or want to believe) that their children receive quality care, standardized ratings find most of the care mediocre and much of it seriously inadequate.

Looking at child care in comparative perspective offers us an opportunity—almost requires us—to think about our goals and hopes for children, parents, education and levels of social inequality. Any child care program or funding system has social and political assumptions with far-reaching consequences. National systems vary in their emphasis on education; for three- to five-year-olds, some stress child care as preparation for school, while others take a more playful view of childhood. Systems vary in the extent to which they stress that children's early development depends on interaction with peers or some version of intensive mothering. They also vary in the extent to which they support policies promoting center-based care as opposed to time for parents to stay at home with their very young children. Each of these emphases entails different national assumptions, if only implicit, about children and parents, education, teachers, peers and societies as a whole.

What do we want, why and what are the implications? Rethinking these questions is timely because with changing welfare, employment, and family patterns, more U.S. parents have come to believe they want and need a place for their children in child care centers. Even parents who are not in the labor force want their children to spend time in preschool. In the United States almost half of children less than one year old now spend a good portion of their day in some form of non-parental care. Experts increasingly emphasize the potential benefits of child care. A recent National Academy of Sciences report summarizes the views of experts: "Higher quality care is associated with outcomes that all parents want to see in their children." The word in Congress these days, especially in discussions of welfare reform, is that child care is good—it saves money later on by helping kids through school (which keeps them out of jail), and it helps keep mothers on the job and families together. A generation ago, by contrast, Nixon vetoed a child care bill as a "radical piece of social legislation" designed to deliver children to "communal approaches to child rearing over and against the family-centered approach." While today's vision is clearly different, most attempts to improve U.S. child care are incremental, efforts to get a little more money here or there, with little consideration for what kind of system is being created.

The U.S. and French systems offer sharp contrasts. Although many hold up the French system as a model for children three or older, it is only one alternative. Other European countries provide thought-provoking alternatives, but the U.S.-French contrast is a good place to begin.

FRANCE AND THE UNITED STATES: PRIVATE VERSUS PUBLIC CARE

Until their children start school, most U.S. parents struggle to find child care, endure long waiting lists, and frequently change locations. They must weave a complex, often unreliable patchwork in which their children move among relatives, informal settings and formal center care, sometimes all in one day. Among three- to four-year-old children with employed mothers, more than one out of eight are in three or more child care arrangements, and almost half are in two or more arrangements. A very small number of the wealthy hire nannies, often immigrants; more parents place their youngest children with relatives, especially grandmothers, or work alternate shifts so fathers can share child care with mothers (these alternating shifters now include almost one-third of families with infants and toddlers). Many pay kin to provide child care—sometimes not because they prefer it, but because they cannot afford other care, and it is a way to provide jobs and income to struggling family members. For children three and older, however, the fastest-growing setting in the United States is child care centers—almost half of three-year-olds (46 percent) and almost two-thirds of four-year-olds (64 percent) now spend much of their time there.

In France, participation in the *école maternelle* system is voluntary, but a place is guaranteed to every child three to six years old. Almost 100 percent of parents enroll their three-year-olds. Even non-employed parents enroll their children, because they believe it is best for the children. Schools are open from 8:30 a.m. to 4:30 p.m. with an extended lunch break, but care is available at modest cost before and after school and during the lunch break.

Integrated with the school system, French child care is intended primarily as early education. All children, rich and poor, immigrant or not, are part of the same national system, with the same curriculum, staffed by teachers paid good wages by the same national ministry. No major political party or group opposes the system.

When extra assistance is offered, rather than targeting poor children (or families), additional resources are provided to geographic areas. Schools in some zones, mostly in urban areas, receive extra funding to reduce class size, give teachers extra training and a bonus, provide extra materials and employ special teachers. By targeting an entire area, poor children are not singled out (as they are in U.S. free lunch programs).

Staff in the French *écoles maternelles* have master's degrees and are paid teachers' wages; in 1998, U.S. preschool teachers earned an average of $8.32 an hour, and child care workers earned $6.61, not only considerably less than (underpaid) teachers but also less than parking lot attendants. As a consequence employee turnover averages 30 percent a year, with predictably harmful effects on children.

What are the costs of these two very different systems? In almost every community across the United States, a year of child care costs more than a year at a public university—in some cases twice as much. Subsidy systems favor the poor, but subsidies (unlike tax breaks) depend on the level of appropriations. Congress does not appropriate enough money and, therefore, most of the children who qualify for subsidies do not receive them. In 1999, under federal rules 15 million children were eligible to receive benefits, but only 1.8 million actually received them. Middle- and working-class families can receive neither kind of subsidy. An Urban Institute study suggests that some parents place their children in care they consider unsatisfactory because other arrangements are just too expensive. The quality of care thus differs drastically depending on the parents' income, geographic location, diligence in searching out alternatives and luck.

The French system is not cheap. According to French government figures, the cost for a child in Paris was about $5,500 per year in 1999. That is only slightly more than the average U.S. parent paid for the care of a four-year-old in a center ($5,242 in 2000). But in France child care is a social responsibility, and thus free to parents, while in the United States parents pay the cost. Put another way, France spends about 1 percent of its Gross Domestic Product (GDP) on government-funded early education and care programs. If the United States devoted the same share of its GDP to preschools, the government would spend about $100 billion a year. Current U.S. government spending is less than $20 billion a year ($15 billion federal, $4 billion state).

OTHER EUROPEAN ALTERNATIVES

When the American child care community thinks about European models, the French model is often what they have in mind. With its emphasis on education, the French system has an obvious appeal to U.S. politicians, educators and child care advocates. Politicians' central concern in the United States appears to be raising children's test scores; in popular and academic literature, this standard is often cited as the major indicator of program success. But such an educational model is by no means the only alternative. Indeed, the U.S. focus on the French system may itself be a telling indicator of U.S. experts' values as well as their assessments of political realities. Many advocates insist that a substantial expansion of the U.S. system will be possible only if the system is presented as improving children's education. These advocates are no longer willing to use the term "child care," insisting on "early education" instead. The French model fits these priorities: it begins quasi-school about three years earlier than in the United States. Although the French obviously assist employed parents and children's center activities are said to be fun, the system is primarily touted and understood as educational—intended to treat children as pupils, to prepare them to do better in school.

The 11 European nations included in a recent Organization for Economic Cooperation and Development study (while quite different from one another) all have significantly better child care and paid leave than the United States. Each also differs significantly from France. Offering alternatives, these models challenge us to think even more broadly about childhood, parenting and the kind of society we value.

NON-SCHOOL MODEL: DENMARK

From birth to age six most Danish children go to child care, but most find that care in non-school settings. Overseen by the Ministry of Social Affairs (rather than the Ministry of Education), the Danish system stresses "relatively unstructured curricula" that give children time to "hang out." Lead staff are pedagogues, not teachers. Although pedagogues have college degrees and are paid teachers' wages, their role is "equally important but different" from that of the school-based teacher. "Listening to children" is one of the government's five principles, and centers emphasize "looking at everything from the child's perspective."

The Danish model differs from the French system in two additional ways that clarify its non-school character. First, in the Danish system, pedagogues care for very young children (from birth to age three as well as older children ages three to six). The French preschool (*école maternelle*) model applies only to children three and older. Before that, children of working parents can attend *crèches*. *Crèche* staff, however, have only high school educations and are paid substantially less than the (master's degree-trained) *écoles maternelles* teachers. Second, while the *écoles maternelles* are available to all children, the Danish system (like the French *crèches*) is only available to children with working parents because it is intended to aid working parents, not to educate children.

The Danish system is decentralized, with each individual center required to have a management board with a parent majority. But the system receives most of its money from public funding, and parents contribute only about one-fifth of total costs.

Given its non-school emphasis, age integration, and the importance it assigns to local autonomy, the Danish system might be appealing to U.S. parents, especially some people of color. To be sure, many U.S. parents—across race and class—are ambivalent about child care for their youngest children. Especially given the growing emphasis on testing, they believe that preschool might give them an edge, but they also want their children to have fun and play—to have, in short, what most Americans still consider a childhood. Some research suggests that Latina mothers are especially likely to feel that center-based care, with its emphasis on academic learning, does not provide the warmth and moral guidance they seek. They are, therefore, less likely to select center based care than either white or African-American parents, relying instead on kin or family child care providers whom they know and trust. U.S. experts' emphasis on the French model may speak not only to political realities but also to the particular class and even more clearly race preferences framing those realities.

MOTHERS OR PEERS

The United States, if only implicitly, operates on a mother-substitute model of child care. Because of a widespread assumption in the United States that all women naturally have maternal feelings and capacities, child care staff, who are almost all women (about 98 percent), are not required to have special training (and do not need to be well paid). Even for regulated providers, 41 out of 50 states require no pre-service training beyond orientation. Consequently, in the United States the child-staff ratio is one of the most prominent measures used to assess quality and is central to most state licensing systems. The assumption, based on the mother-substitute model, is that emotional support can be given and learning can take place only with such low ratios.

Considering the high quality and ample funding of many European systems, it comes as a surprise that most have much higher child-staff ratios than the United States. In the French *écoles maternelles*, for example, there is one teacher and one half-time aide for every 25 children. In Italy, in a center with one adult for every eight children (ages one to three years) the early childhood workers see no need for additional adults and think the existing ratios are appropriate. Leading researchers Sheila Kamerman and Alfred Kahn report that in Denmark, "what is particularly impressive is that children are pretty much on their own in playing with their peers. An adult is present all the time but does not lead or play with the children." In a similar vein, a cross-national study of academic literature found substantial focus on adult-child ratios in the United States, but very little literature on the topic in German-, French- or Spanish-language publications. Why not? These systems have a different view of children and learning. Outside the United States systems often center around the peer group. In Denmark the role of staff is to work "alongside children, rather than [to be] experts or leaders who teach children." Similarly, the first director of the early child-hood services in Reggio, Italy, argues that children learn through conflict and that placing children in groups facilitates learning through "attractive," "advantageous," and "constructive" conflict "because among children there are not strong relationships of authority and dependence." In a non-European example, Joseph Tobin, David Wu, and Dana Davidson argue that in Japan the aim is ratios that "keep teachers from being too mother-like in their interactions with students . . . Large class sizes and large ratios have become increasingly important strategies for promoting the Japanese values of groupism and selflessness." Such practices contrast with the individualistic focus in U.S. child care.

FAMILY LEAVES AND WORK TIME

When we ask how to care for children, especially those younger than three, one answer is for parents to stay home. Policy that promotes such leaves is what one would expect from a society such as the United States, which emphasizes a mothering model of child care. It is, however, European countries that provide extensive paid family leave, usually universal, with not only job protection but also substantial income replacement. In Sweden, for example, parents receive a full year and a half of paid parental leave (with 12 months at 80 percent of prior earnings) for each child. Because so many parents (mostly mothers) use family leave, fewer than 200 children under one year old in the entire country are in public care. Generous programs are common throughout Europe (although the length, flexibility and level of payment they provide vary).

The United States provides far less in the way of family leaves. Since its passage in 1993, the Family and Medical Leave Act (FMLA) has guaranteed a 12-week job-protected leave to workers of covered employers. Most employers (95 percent) and many workers (45 percent), however, are not covered. And all federally mandated leaves are unpaid.

The unpaid leaves provided by the FMLA, like the private system of child care, accentuate the inequality between those who can afford them and those who can't. Although the FMLA was touted as a "gender neutral" piece of legislation, men (especially white men) are unlikely to take leaves; it is overwhelmingly women (especially those who are married) who take them. As a result, such women pay a wage penalty when they interrupt their careers. To address such inequities, Sweden and Norway have introduced a "use it or lose it" policy. For each child, parents may divide up to a year of paid leave (say nine months for the mother, three for the father), *except* that the mother may not use more than eleven months total. One month is reserved for the father; if he does not use the leave, the family loses the month.

Finally, although not usually discussed as child care policy in the United States, policy makers in many European countries now emphasize that the number of hours parents work clearly shapes the ways young children are cared for and by whom. Workers in the United States, on average, put in 300 hours more per year than workers in France (and 400 more than those in Sweden).

2002–2003 Fee Schedule

(Prices effective until July 1, 2003)

Application Free	$50.00
(nonrefundable/annual fee)	
Materials Fee	$30.00 Full-time Enrollment
(nonrefundable)	$20.00 Part-time Enrollment

Tuition Deposit* *amount equal to one month's tuition*
(due in two installments)
a. Space guarantee Fee** $150.00
   (due upon acceptance to the school)
b. Balance due two months prior to starting date.
**See enrollment contract for refund conditions.

Full-time	$859.00/month

Morning Preschool (9:00 a.m.–1.00 p.m.)

three mornings	$321.00/month
four mornings	$397.00/month
five mornings	$462.00/month

Afternoon Preschool (1:00 p.m.–5.00 p.m.)

three afternoons	$285.00/month
four afternoons	$350.00/month
five afternoons	$404.00/month

Kindergarten Program (11:25 a.m.–5.00 p.m.)

three days	$339.00/month
four days	$416.00/month
five days	$486.00/month

—Extended Care (hour before 9:00 a.m. and the hour after
5.00 p.m.) $5.25/hour
—Unscheduled Drop-in $6.25/hour

Participating Parents (P.P.) & Board Members receive tuition
credit. P.P. credit is $25.00 per day of participation. Board
credits vary with position.

Tuition and fees for the U.S. preschool illustrated here, a
non-profit, parent-run cooperative that costs almost $1,000 per
month.

CONCLUSION

The child care system in the United States is a fragmentary patchwork, both at the level
of the individual child and at the level of the overall system. Recent research suggests that
the quality of care for young children is poor or fair in well over half of child care settings.
This low quality of care, in concert with a model of intensive mothering, means that many
anxious mothers privately hunt for high-quality substitutes while trying to ensure they are

not being really replaced. System administrators need to patch together a variety of funding streams, each with its own regulations and paperwork. Because the current system was fashioned primarily for the affluent at one end and those being pushed off welfare at the other, it poorly serves most of the working class and much of the middle class.

Most efforts at reform are equally piecemeal, seeking a little extra money here or there in ways that reinforce the existing fragmentation. Although increasing numbers of advocates are pushing for a better system of child care in the United States, they rarely step back to think about the characteristics of the system as a whole. If they did, what lessons could be learned from Europe?

The features that are common to our peer nations in Europe would presumably be a part of a new U.S. system. The programs would be publicly funded and universal, available to all, either at no cost or at a modest cost with subsidies for low-income participants. The staff would be paid about the same as public school teachers. The core programs would cover at least as many hours as the school day, and "wrap-around" care would be available before and after this time. Participation in the programs would be voluntary, but the programs would be of such a high quality that a majority of children would enroll. Because the quality of the programs would be high, parents would feel much less ambivalence about their children's participation, and the system would enjoy strong public support. In addition to child care centers, parents would be universally offered a significant period of paid parental leave. Of course, this system is expensive. But as the National Academy of Science Report makes clear, not caring for our children is in the long term, and probably even in the short term, even more expensive.

Centers in all nations emphasize education, peer group dynamics, and emotional support to some extent. But the balance varies. The varieties of European experience pose a set of issues to be considered if and when reform of the U.S. system is on the agenda:

- To what degree should organized care approximate school and at what age, and to what extent is the purpose of such systems primarily educational?
- To what extent should we focus on adult-child interactions that sustain or substitute for mother care as opposed to fostering child-child interactions and the development of peer groups?
- To what extent should policies promote parental time with children versus high-quality organized care, and what are the implications for gender equity of either choice?

These are fundamental questions because they address issues of social equality and force us to rethink deep-seated images of children and parents.

Recommended Resources

Cooper, Candy J. *Ready to Learn: The French System of Early Education and Care Offers Lessons for the United States.* New York: French American Foundation, 1999.

Gornick, Janet, and Marcia Meyers. "Support for Working Families: What the United States Can Learn from Europe." *The American Prospect* (January 1–15, 2001): 3–7.

Helburn, Suzanne W., and Barbara R. Bergmann. *America's Childcare Problem: The Way Out.* New York: Palgrave/St. Martin's, 2002.

Kamerman, Sheila B., and Alfred J. Kahn. *Starting Right: How America Neglects Its Youngest Children and What We Can Do About It.* New York: Oxford University Press, 1995.

Moss, Peter. "Workforce Issues in Early Childhood Education and Care Staff." Paper prepared for consultative meeting on International Developments in Early Childhood Education and Care, The Institute for Child and Family Policy, Columbia University, May 11–12, 2000.

Organization for Economic Co-operation and Development. *Starting Strong—Early Education and Care: Report on an OECD Thematic Review.* Online. www.oecd.org.

Shonkoff, Jack P., and Deborah Phillips, eds. *From Neurons to Neighborhoods: The Science of Early Childhood Development.* Washington, DC: National Academy of Sciences, 2000.

▪ R E A D I N G   2 1

Who Are Our Children? Adoption, Past and Present

Lawrence Friedman

In English, "children" is a word with two meanings. First of all, it refers to very young people; everybody in a kindergarten class is a child. But it also refers to offspring: the seventy-five-year-old son of a hundred-year-old woman is the woman's child. This double meaning is also found in many other languages (for example, *das Kind* in German). At one time, parental control over children continued as long as the children lived; for example, . . . parents arranged their children's marriages. In those aspects of law that deal with children, there has been a strong, long-term trend toward emancipating the child from its father and from the family in general. The emancipation is absolute for adult children. Adults are under no duty to obey their parents or to take account of them in any way; even the duty to support aged and infirm parents has been evaporating. The state has largely taken over that duty. Older people, retired people, get government pensions in Western countries (in the United States, this is called Social Security). More and more, elderly people tend to live alone or, at any rate, not with their grown children. Adult children also more and more tend to leave the nest. In the United States (though not in many other countries) if an adult male of, say, thirty still lives at home with his mother and father, people consider it somewhat unusual or even peculiar.

 Obviously, babies and young children cannot be emancipated. Their parents must manage their lives—feed them, watch them, train them. But even here the law more and more recognizes the child as a distinct individual. It punishes abusive or neglectful parents. It can take children away from a bad family and give them to a good family. It has the ability to act "in loco parentis," as the phrase goes—in place of the parents. In effect, children have legal rights as against their own mothers and fathers. If the children are too young to do it themselves, the state enforces these rights. Also—and this is a critical point—the state has taken over education. It teaches children what they need to know, at state expense. Laws make school mandatory up to a certain age.[1] The state, not the parents, decide what the child will learn, and how the child will learn it. Even for those few children who are home schooled—that is, children whose parents teach them and who do not go to state or private schools—many states require parents to cover certain material, or to file reports with some state or local agency. It also provides curriculum for private and religious schools. What children learn is, to be sure, often a source of conflict.

The general changes in family life we have seen over the past century are relative changes. The, authority of the family is weaker than it was, but it is still extremely strong. The state can take a child away from the family; but it does so for the most part reluctantly, and only in extreme cases. This reluctance is, if anything, growing: the days when children could be snatched from the homes of members of Native Americans and given to white families are over. Law and society clearly recognize that in general the rights of parents are sacred. The government has no right to tell parents how to raise their children; the parents, not the state, decide what church to attend or not attend, whom their kids can play with, what clothes they wear, what food they eat. Parental rights are constitutionally protected.[2] Family life and family relations are still, as they always were, central to most people. Modern times have revolutionized the family and changed its shape. New forms of family life have emerged. But nothing has actually replaced the family. Parents have less control over their children (parents of teenagers often feel they have none at all); but parents are still at the center of their young children's lives. Even for millions of older children, parents are a powerful influence on their lives; and for many parents, children (and grandchildren) are the very core of their existence.

The law that deals with children is complex and has many facets. . . .

ADOPTION

The English common law did not recognize any such thing as adoption. Essentially, in fact, no child could be legally adopted in England; the situation changed only in 1926, when Parliament enacted the Adoption of Children Act.[3] In English law, "children" meant children of the blood, and nothing else. In this regard, the common law stood apart from many other legal systems. In many systems, adoption was recognized as a way to guarantee that a family with no blood children would not die out. Adoption was a well-known feature of ancient Roman society. French law recognizes two forms of adoption. "Simple" (or limited) adoption allows a family to adopt even adults, in order to carry on the family name or for some similar purpose—uncles can adopt nephews, cousins can adopt cousins. Besides limited adoption, there is another kind of adoption: full adoption, or *adoption plénière*, the more familiar kind. Under full adoption, it is always young children who are taken into the family, and the adopting parents are usually childless. Indeed, until 1923 adults were not adoptable in this way at all; and until 1976 parents with children were not allowed to adopt (this was also once the rule in other countries—for example, Switzerland). In Brazil, too, under the 1916 Civil Code, couples with children were not eligible to adopt legally, nor were people under the age of fifty (presumably because they just possibly might have children of their own).[4] Rates of adoption vary from country to country. Adoption is still rather uncommon in France. French society—like English society at one time—seems to place enormous emphasis on actual blood lines.

The United States, by contrast, has four times the population of France but ten times as many adoptions.[5]

Adoption in the United States was altogether lacking throughout the colonial period and into the nineteenth century, just as it was lacking in England. The first true American adoption law, it is often said, was passed in the state of Massachusetts in 1851. But if we look carefully, we can find traces of adoption even before 1851. Certainly, the terms "adopt" and "adoption" were known; and arrangements that were functionally very similar to adoption existed even in the colonial period.[6] Children were commonly bound out as apprentices, for example, which meant that from a fairly early age they were living in somebody else's household.

Other practices came closer to the modern idea of adoption. A number of state legislatures passed private laws that were in effect adoption laws—laws making this or that child someone's heir, or changing the name of a child. Often these were illegitimate children whose father was acknowledging them and taking them into his home; sometimes they were orphaned relatives.[7] There were about 100 of these private laws passed in Massachusetts between 1781 and 1851; in Vermont, a small state, there were over 300 petitions for adoption between 1804 and 1864.[8] The statutes were brief and to the point. To take one example: in Kentucky, the legislature passed a law in 1845 permitting Nancy Lowry to "adopt . . . her step son, Robert W. Lowry, Jr. . . . as her own child, who, in all respects, shall stand in the same legal relation to her as if she were his mother in fact." Robert could inherit from her if she died, "as if he were her own personal issue, born in lawful wedlock." A few states apparently began to generalize the practice. A Mississippi statute of 1846 empowered local courts to change names and also, "upon application of any person, to make legitimate any of their offspring, not born in wedlock." After the court order, the child would be "legitimate and heir or joint heir of the person petitioning." The courts could also, for "sufficient reasons shown," make "any other person the heir" of the person petitioning. This was, in short, a general adoption law in everything but name—the word "adoption" never appears in the statute. A Texas statute of 1850 provided that anybody who wished to "adopt another" and make that person an "heir" could do so by filing a statement in the "office of the clerk of the county court," stating that he or she was adopting this person as a legal heir. Once this was done, the child was a legal heir.[9] But the Massachusetts law was a more elaborate statute, and the first one that required some sort of formal procedure for adoption.

After 1851, there was a strong movement to create adoption laws, more or less on the model of Massachusetts. State after state enacted its own adoption statute. By the end of the century, adoption was universally recognized in the United States; and this is of course still the case. Adoption laws reject the classic common law understanding that blood relationship is crucial, and that people are joined by blood or marriage or not at all. The laws reflect a more fluid and contractual notion of the family. Some of the early statutes were almost nakedly contractual. Under the first Missouri law (1857), the procedure for adopting a child was not much different from procedures for buying or selling a cornfield. Under the statute, if any person "shall desire to adopt a child, as his or her heir" it was to be done by a deed, "executed, acknowledged, and recorded . . . as in the case of conveyance of real estate."[10] In 1917, Missouri enacted a more modern adoption law; instead of a deed, adoption now required a court proceeding; the judge was to decide, "after due hearing," whether the adoptive parents were "of good character" and "of sufficient ability to properly care for, maintain and educate said child," and if the "welfare of said child would be promoted" by the adoption.[11]

This was the trend in the law. More and more, the rules and procedures expressed the idea that the welfare of the child was the paramount interest that these statutes protected. But not entirely. The adoptive parents had rights and interests as well. The same Missouri statute just mentioned, echoing considerations found in marriage and divorce laws, gave the adoptive parents the right to back out. They were entitled to annul the adoption if, within five years, the child developed "feeble mindedness or epilepsy or venereal infection as the result of conditions existing prior to the time such child was adopted." Other states had similar provisions in their laws.

What accounts for the flowering of adoption laws? Adoption, as a legal status, had a definite economic meaning. Adoption was important in American society (and, later, in other societies) because of its relationship to inheritance and property rights. Adoption was useful for that vast army of American families that owned a farm, a house, a plot of land in town, and maybe other assets. This is similar to the point made earlier about common law marriage and about divorce. The private adoption laws of the early nineteenth century often mentioned specifically the right to inherit. The pioneer Massachusetts statute stressed this point. The statute created a legal procedure for adoption and provided the adopted child with the right to inherit. It was, however, a rather narrow right. The child inherited from the adopting parents. Beyond this, the statute was silent. In some states the issue was resolved rather differently. New York's adoption statute of 1873 specifically provided that the adopted child did *not* inherit from the adopting parents. But this provision was sliced out of the statute in 1887.[12]

In general, under all adoption statutes, the adopted child inherits from the adoptive mother and father. In early statutes, the child also inherited from birth parents; gradually, adoption came to represent a sharper break with the past. Law and practice have vacillated, however, on whether the child also inherits from other relatives in the adoptive family. If a grandfather—the adoptive father's father, say—dies without a will and the adoptive father is dead, does the adopted daughter of the grandfather's son inherit? If the "natural born" son of the adoptive parent dies, does the adopted child inherit from the brother? The answer at first was maybe. Some states allowed rather broad inheritance rights; others did not.[13] Also, does the adopted child inherit from its own blood relatives? In a number of states, the answer to this question was yes. Under a Texas statute of 1931, when a child was adopted, even though "all legal rights and duties between such child and its natural parents" were to "cease and determine," this did not "prevent such adopted children from inheriting from its natural parent." An adopted child "shall inherit from the adopted as well as its natural parents."[14] But in other states adoption, as the California statute puts it, "severs the relationship of parent and child between an adopted person and a natural parent," and for all purposes.[15]

Suppose a person was the beneficiary of a trust, enjoying its income for life; after the beneficiary died, the property was to go to his or her "children" or "issue" or "heirs." Would this include an adopted child? Strictly speaking, this is a question of interpretation: What was in the mind of the person who set up the trust? If the text gave no clear answer, courts generally refused to include adopted children. This was the thrust of statutes and case law alike. This question, and other questions of inheritance, were contested well into the twentieth century.[16] As of about 1930, there was still considerable vacillation in the laws of the various states: In a number of states, the adopted child still could not [inherit] from adoptive uncles, aunts, or grandparents; and if the statutes were silent on this point, courts tended to hold against inheritance.[17] But more recent law is quite different. Unless a will, trust, or other document specifically excludes adopted children, these children inherit as if they were children of the physical body. In other words, the law now tends strongly to treat adopted children and "natural" children exactly the same—at least with regard to property and inheritance.

It must be remembered that adoption is a legal status. Nobody needs a court decision or a formal document to take a child into a family, feed it, raise it, and love it. Informal "adoption" was the norm in England and the United States before adoption laws were passed. (In upper-class families, guardianship was one way to provide for orphans.) Informal adoption is still very common in third world countries. In Brazil, for example, in the vast slums of the big cities, children often move from household to household—raised now by a relative, now by a neighbor, particularly when a mother or father is too poor to give them what they need. In these cases, the original family does not really "abandon" the child, no matter how the situation looks to middle-class professionals.[18]

Demographic change has had an important effect on adoption and adoption practices. In the nineteenth century, divorce rates were low, but families disintegrated at a high rate nonetheless. It was the angel of death, not the divorce courts, that produced "broken homes." Orphans were in plentiful supply. Women died giving birth; plagues and accidents carried off fathers and mothers alike. The children left behind were often raised by aunts, uncles, or grandparents. Those who had no relatives to take them in were often sent to orphanages. In the nineteenth century in the United States, many children were sent out of the big city (chiefly New York) into the countryside, to be taken in by farm families. This would be better for these children, it was thought, than life on the mean streets of the city, or in institutions. The farm families rarely adopted these children legally; in many cases, they were little better than servants, cheap labor for the farm. And not all of these children were orphans; some were the children of destitute, often immigrant, parents. In the second half of the nineteenth century, some 90,000 children were placed out by the Children's Aid Society, an organization founded by Charles Loring Brace. Brace's activities were not universally applauded. Many of the children came from Catholic families; the farms they were sent to, and the agencies that sent them, were resolutely Protestant.[19]

This brings up the dark side of adoption. In theory, adoption is an arrangement in which nobody loses: the child gets a good home, the birth parents get rid of a burden or an embarrassment, the adopting parents get the child they want so badly. The guiding principle, as in the law of child custody generally, is the best interests of the child. But it is not always easy to decide what these "best interests" demand. In practice, custody decisions have often been open to serious abuse. These decisions, like so many others in the legal system; are strongly influenced by social norms and prejudices. Courts and social workers tend to define a child's "best interests" in terms of middle-class notions and values. In most situations, there is no conflict: nobody would argue that children who are beaten, tortured, burned with cigarettes, or left to starve are not better off with somebody other than the parents who treated them this way. But there are many marginal situations; and the poor, the socially deviant, and the culturally distinct tended to lose out, in ways that we would now define as unfair, or worse. Charles Loring Brace thought of himself as a noble humanitarian; today we are not so sure he was. The problem has been particularly acute, and the abuses particularly blatant, in the case of children of native tribes, or black children whose parents are poor. Mothers who cannot afford to raise their children, single mothers, women in trouble, have in effect often been forced to give up their babies, who are given to "better" homes.[20] Whatever the legal theory, the best interests of middle-class adopting parents have often trumped the best interests of the birth parents, or perhaps even the best interests of the child.

Adoption laws generally claim to protect the rights of the birth parents, and especially the birth mother. Her consent is necessary for ordinary adoptions. The weak point is the reality of this consent. Social and family pressures can be intense. Families often badgered unmarried mothers to give up the babies and avoid the shame of a bastard child. Poverty and destitution could drive a mother to the same decision. In the United States, as well as in other countries—Australia is a prime example—possibly the worst historical scandal was the way the state dealt with children of native peoples. They were often removed—sometimes kidnapped—from their homes. They were then delivered to boarding schools or foster homes and, eventually, to respectable white families. The point of the boarding schools in the United States was to "civilize" the natives—to teach them how to be, in effect, white, and to get them to unlearn their own languages, religions, and customs.[21] A congressional report estimated that between a quarter and a third of all Native American children were adopted as babies, and almost all of them were given to non-Native families.[22] (Congress passed a law in 1978 that was designed to prevent this from happening.[23]) In Australia, between 1910 and 1970, somewhere between one in three and one in ten indigenous children were removed by force from their homes and families. Even as late as 1973, a native boy was kidnapped and sent a thousand miles away to live with a white family.[24] A 2002 movie, *Rabbit-Proof Fence*, told the story of some Australian children, whose fathers were white, who were forcibly removed from their native mothers and sent to boarding schools. The movie was based on actual incidents. Another sad and powerful movie, *The Official Story* (1985), dealt with the children born to political prisoners ("los desaparecidos") in Argentina. These children were given to families of the politically powerful, to be adopted. What all these tragedies have in common is devaluation of the birth parents. In the case of Australia and the United States, in the days before plural equality, no doubt many people honestly believed they were doing these children a favor. They were taking them out of "primitive" conditions and uncivilized homes and giving them a chance for a better life among people who could give them advantages beyond the reach of their birth parents. These policies were part of a more general policy of assimilation, which meant in practice the destruction of native customs, religions, and languages.

Mainstream adoption in the middle of the twentieth century was quite different from nineteenth-century adoption. Middle-class people were living longer. Death in childbirth had become a rare event. In the age of antibiotics, plagues and epidemics took a . . . smaller bite out of the population. The supply of orphans dried up. Adoption at one time primarily involved children whose parents were dead or too poor or desperate to keep them. In the twentieth century, adoption became more and more the destiny of children whose parents, for whatever reason, did not want them or were unable to resist social and legal pressures to give up their children. It was frequently the destiny of babies born to teenage, unmarried mothers. And the adopting parents, in many cases, were strangers, not relatives or neighbors. They were childless couples who wanted a baby and could not produce one themselves.[25] A study of adoption in Washington state documents the changes in the practice of adoption. In the 1930s, of birth parents who gave up their babies, 22 percent did so because the babies were illegitimate, 19 percent because the family was breaking up, 13 percent because the parents were poor; by 1970, illegitimacy accounted for 89 percent of the relinquishments of children, and the other motives were insignificant. In the 1930s, 9 percent of the birth parents were widows who could not support the children and 14 percent were widowers who had no way of taking care of the children. In the 1970s, the widowers had disappeared entirely, and the widows had almost disappeared; 85 percent of the birth parents were single women.[26]

More recently, the nature of adoption has changed again, in response to changes in social norms and in demography. For one thing, the birthrate has continued to spiral downward—especially in Western Europe, but generally in all developed countries. Many countries—Italy, Germany, France—face the prospect of shrinking populations. There are fewer babies generally, so there are fewer babies available for adoption. Moreover, by the late twentieth century illegitimacy had lost most of its stigma. A young middle-class woman who found herself pregnant would in an earlier time have been desperate to get rid of the baby; many hid their pregnancies, gave birth secretly and quietly, disposed of the baby to some agency or a private party, and then tried to get on with their lives. There are still women who feel this way; and in France, women have the right to give birth anonymously (the mother will be listed on the birth certificate as "X").[27] In most Western countries, however, this prime source of adoption babies—young mothers giving birth secretly—has all but vanished. In 1970, in the United States, some 89,000 babies were adopted by strangers. By 1975, this figure had dropped to 48,000. For many years thereafter, it remained more or less constant.[28] In the late 1990s, the figure began to balloon; and the number of adoptions doubled between 1995 and 2001, partly because the government offered money to help move children out of foster care and into adoptive homes.[29] Today, childless middle-class couples who wish to adopt are fairly desperate; they are willing to pay good money to get a baby. It would probably surprise these couples to learn that at one time the flow of money often went the other way: mothers paid people to take their babies off their hands. A study in Chicago in 1917, carried out by the Juvenile Protective Association, unmasked the scandalous behavior of the "baby farms." These organizations were charging money to take babies; the babies were supposed to be resold to adoptive parents. The study found "shocking abuses." Unscrupulous doctors and hospitals "took advantage of the unmarried mother willing to pay any amount of money to dispose of her child."[30] These baby farms made a profit from a "grisly calculus": most babies, in the days before reliable bottle-feeding, simply died when separated from their mothers. Add to this filthy conditions and poor care, and it is no surprise that most babies in baby farms did not survive. Allegedly, up to 80 percent of all babies admitted to one Baltimore baby farm died within weeks. Basically, nobody cared.[31]

All this seems like ancient history. As the demand for adoption increased, these newborn babies became valuable commodities. The adoption rate swelled in the twentieth century, then crested, and began to fall in the latter part of the century. Not that fewer couples wanted to adopt. It was the shortage of babies: particularly, in the United States, a shortage of the most desirable babies—white, middle-class, and newborn. In adoption practice, the ideal is to "match" children to their adoptive parents in race, background, and religion (as if babies have a religion). But all this is not so easily managed nowadays. Parents consequently are more willing to consider adoption across race and ethnic lines—even across national boundaries. In a fluid society, a society committed to plural equality, and a society that no longer punishes interracial marriage; white folks with black children no longer seem quite so extraordinary. The global market in babies is also flourishing. Desperate couples cast about for places with a better supply. After the Second World War, Americans found children to adopt in countries devastated by the war—Greece, for example, or Germany. After the Korean War in the early 1950s, Americans adopted flocks of Korean children.[32] Parents also turned to other poor countries. Latin America was a prime source in the 1970s. Russia and China are important sources today. American parents now commonly fly off to Bolivia, Romania, or China, bringing home children from these countries—legally or otherwise. It is estimated that there are between 15,000 and 20,000 such adoptions each year.[33] Some of these children are orphans; others come from very poor families. A study of Latin American birth mothers who gave up their children found that they were typically young (fourteen to eighteen years old), jobless (or beggars or prostitutes), with no education, and from bad homes themselves. In China, some parents were giving up excess daughters. Some Korean birth mothers were unmarried women, facing the stigma of illegitimacy. Many of these women were destitute; and some of the Korean children were mixed-blood children left behind by American soldiers.[34] The United States, of course, is not the only country where childless couples go abroad to find a supply of children. The leader in the field, in fact, is Sweden; it has the highest ratio of international adoptions to population of any country.[35]

By the 1970s, some white couples were choosing a once unthinkable answer to the problem of the shortage of babies. They were taking children of other races, mostly black, mostly American born. The practice became embroiled in controversy. Originally the objection came from other whites. Race mixing was taboo in many states. Under Texas law, for example, no white child could be adopted by a "negro person, nor can a negro child be adopted by a white person."[36] There were also some biased white judges who simply refused to allow such adoptions to take place.[37] A related issue arose in custody cases when, for example, a divorced white woman awarded custody of her children marries a black man or has a relationship with a black man and the father tries to get custody, claiming that an interracial household is unsuitable.[38] Generally speaking, in the late twentieth century the courts have rejected this notion; race could not be taken into account in this way. The Supreme Court also weighed in on the question. Linda Sidoti and her husband, Anthony Sidoti, were divorced in Florida in 1980; Linda got custody of their little daughter, Melanie. A year later, Anthony tried to get custody; Linda was "cohabiting with a Negro, Clarence Palmore, Jr., whom she married two months later." The trial court gave custody to the father. Despite "strides" in race relations, the judge said, little Melanie was sure to "suffer from . . . social stigmatization." The Supreme Court reversed this decision unanimously: "Private biases may be outside the reach of the law, but the law cannot, directly or indirectly, give them effect."[39]

The Sidoti case was decided in 1984. By this time, the situation had reversed itself. Objections to adoption across race line were coming from blacks, not from whites. The

National Association of Black Social Workers condemned transracial adoption in 1972; they labeled it a kind of cultural genocide.[40] To put black children in white homes would cut them off totally from black culture. Sometimes this was true; sometimes not. Some white parents of black children tried hard to expose their children to the world of black America. Whether these attempts were successful—or useful—is another question. These adopted children live lives quite different from the lives of children growing up in a black community. Two authors who studied the problem found it was just "not realistic for a black child in the United States to have two racial identities." Identifying "with the human race" was simply no substitute.[41]

Many of these children surely feel ambiguity, imbalance; many feel that they vacillate between two worlds and do not quite fit into either.[42] Yet on the whole, children adopted across race lines claimed to be happy with their adoptive parents. They were surely better off economically than with their birth parents. Most did not show much interest in finding their biological parents. The overwhelming majority criticized the attitude of the black social workers: one black female called the statement "a crock—it's just ridiculous . . . I am fully comfortable with who I am."[43] Of course, this woman had grown up in a white family; the damage (if it was damage) had already been done.

There were other arguments, too, against transracial adoption—for example, that it reinforced stereotypes. It perpetuated the idea that black mothers were bad mothers and that white mothers were better. In this way, the argument went, black-white adoption propped up white supremacy.[44] The furor over black-white adoption more or less died down after a while. Perhaps it was simply the pressing need for homes for black children that overcame the objections. The Multiethnic Placement Act of the 1990s, a federal statute, waffled a bit on the issue; but it did state that an agency that "receives Federal assistance" was not to discriminate in placement decisions "on the basis of the race, color, or national origin of the adoptive or foster parent, or the child"; the statute was, however, repealed a short time later.[45]

The black social workers were asserting racial pride—and, perhaps, the right of black children to *their* racial pride. That pride would be hard to maintain if black children were to grow up in a white neighborhood with a white family, white friends, and whiteness all around. These children would be lost to the black community. Yet (so the argument went) these children had a right to align themselves with the black community, black culture, black heritage. Native American tribes have taken much the same attitude. And so have many ethnic whites, and religious groups as well.

The argument assumes a distinct black culture in America—and a distinct Navajo culture, a Jewish culture, an Irish Catholic culture. To a certain extent, this is surely true. The *experience of* growing up black, or Jewish, or Navajo, is surely different from the experience of growing up white, or Catholic, or Italian-American. But exactly how different is it? The unspoken premise is that the differences are deep-seated, precious, and fundamental. Another premise is that there are such things as cultural rights. Identity groups have a right to perpetuate themselves, to foster their cultures, to fight against assimilation.

No one can deny some of the cultural differences. There is a Navajo language, and it is totally different from English. There are also native religions and native customs. In the age of plural equality, these differences get far more respect than they once did. In the Indian Child Welfare Act (1978),[46] Congress tried to make amends for the scandalous and tragic events of the past. Native American children were not to be torn from their families and homes. Tribes had the right to transmit language, religion, and culture to their young. The preamble to the act mentioned the "alarmingly high percentage of Indian families" who had lost their children in the past. Children were a "resource," vital "to the continued existence and integrity of Indian tribes." It was official policy, according to the law, to promote "the stability and security of Indian tribes and families" (though the statute also aimed to protect "the best interests of Indian children"). Rules for placement of children were to "reflect the unique values of Indian culture." The act gave Indian tribes "exclusive" jurisdiction of custody cases involving children living on the reservation. Tribes also had the right to intervene—subject to the objection of birth parents—in cases of termination of parental rights or of foster-care placement that took place off the reservation, if the parents were Indians.[47]

There has been a fair amount of litigation under this act, and one rather prominent Supreme Court case. In this case, a Choctaw woman, pregnant with twins, left the reservation in Mississippi and gave birth to the children elsewhere. The father was a Choctaw man. They had never married. Both parents signed a consent form in state court, authorizing the adoption of their children by non-Indians. The Choctaw tribe objected; and the Supreme Court, reading the Indian Child Welfare Act quite broadly, decided in favor of the tribe. The statute, said the Court, gave the tribe a right superior to the state of Mississippi to decide where the twins should live, and with whom.[48]

This was clearly a decision steeped in the ethos of plural equality—as, indeed, was the statute. The statute spoke of the "integrity" of tribal culture—an idea that would have astounded most people in the nineteenth century. This culture included, or could include, what Rachel Moran has called "alternative definitions of family."[49] Case and statute are evidence that official culture (and to a good extent, popular culture) has embraced a multicultural ideal and has decisively rejected the ethos of assimilation. The melting pot is gone. Or rather, it is a different sort of melting pot. There is no longer the belief that, say, Chinese-Americans, blacks, Jews, and Armenian-Americans have to learn to conform to the culture and norms of, say, white Presbyterians of British descent. Also, in a culture of choice, there is more and more a right to choose your roots, your heritage, and to insist on your own uniqueness and the uniqueness of your culture.

But what is culture? It is not something genetic. It is far more malleable than most people imagine. The great-grandchildren of slaves—or Africans—and the great-grandchildren of Jews from Polish villages, or Chinese workers on Western railroads, descend from cultures that were vastly different from each other, and from "American" culture as well. But today, these great-grandchildren are thoroughly American. They dress American, talk American, act American, listen to American music, watch American TV. However much they value their "roots," they are part of a single, overwhelming, pervasive American culture, an almost suffocating presence that surrounds them, influences them, and makes them what they are.

Editors' Note: *Notes and references for this reading can be found in the original source.*

■READING 22

The Four Facets of Fatherhood

Nicholas Townsend

> Especially in this area, it's a lifestyle not to have children. Alot of people don't. They'll be old and gray and I'll have my children around Christmas day. I don't determine success in life as financial or monetary or anything like that. My success in life is when my kids leave and go out and make their own lives; they'll come back and say, "Dad, you did the best job you could. Thanks." And they'll come back and see me. And to be a good husband to my wife. I consider that a successful life.—*Howard*

Fatherhood is one of the four elements that make up the package deal (fatherhood, marriage, employment, and home ownership). The elements are interconnected and mutually dependent. As a complex whole, they can be viewed from a number of different perspectives. An analysis of men's lives from the perspective of employment, for instance, would examine how fatherhood, marriage, and housing are affected by the structure of work and the employment opportunities available to men. It would also examine how men's employment prospects, experiences, and histories are affected by being (or not being) fathers, husbands, and home owners. In this book, I examine the elements of the package deal through the prism of fatherhood. My primary interest in men's employment is in its impact on their fatherhood, and my primary interest in their marriages is in the connections between marriage and fatherhood. This approach illuminates the tensions and complications within the package deal that have implications for fatherhood.

The fathers I talked to recognized that fathering was a complex activity with no guarantee of success. They were all concerned with ensuring their children's current well-being and future life chances. "Life chances" is used to describe the fact that the ability to obtain goods, living conditions, and life experiences differs between people according to their social position (Weber 1978). The idea of life chances is at the forefront of my descriptions of men and their lives. For me it captures simultaneously (1) the real possibilities and limits to what they can achieve, (2) their subjective perspective that life unfolds by presenting opportunities, (3) the fact that life outcomes depend on both the existence of opportunities and the availability of the resources to take advantage of them, and (4) the notion that social position or class is about consumption or "lifestyle" as well as production or income (Bourdieu 1984).

Most fathers saw successful parenting as doing the right thing but avoiding extremes. They wanted their children to be disciplined but still to have fun, to have opportunities but not to be forced into particular directions, to respect their parents but not to be afraid of them, and to make their own choices but not to make too many mistakes. Even though they saw no unquestioned rules or role models to follow, they were sure that the kind of relationship fathers have with their children was vitally important.

Knowing that the stakes were high but that there was no guarantee of success, the fathers repeatedly returned to the question of why some people turned out well and others did not, and of what fathers could do to make a difference in their children's lives. These discussions inevitably involved comparison with their peers who were also fathers and with their own experience of being fathered. Men talked a great deal about their own fathers and about the fathers of their friends.

Ralph drew on his memories of his friends' childhoods to muse on the importance of fathers, but also on the unpredictability of growing up. He was sure that social background made a difference, but not an automatic one. Surely a boy's father could help him to turn out to become a good man, he thought, but this was not guaranteed. Character seemed to count also, but he wondered where it came from. Ralph's high school companions and their parents served as a reference group for him as he considered what good fathering was, and what he should do as a father:

> When I was a kid, I remember I was a real hard worker. Always had two paper routes and always hustling to make a buck because I never had money. So I was determined to have money when I got older. I envied a lot of my friends whose parents were well off. They had motorcycles and they had the nicest bike. We had a ten-year reunion in high school and when I went to it, I saw some of these guys that had all the breaks in the world. They had everything given to them and now they had mediocre jobs and weren't going anywhere in life. It was just unbelievable. . . . But there was another friend of ours, Tom, his dad was really a great dad. He had four kids and two of them turned out OK and one didn't. I wonder about that often. With my kids, am I giving them too much? What can you do to make them better?

Part of the reason Ralph paid particular attention to his friends' fathers was that his own childhood had not given him direct examples of effective parenting. His parents had separated when he started high school and his father had moved out of state. Ralph did not want to live with either his father, who had married a woman who was "an alcoholic," or with his mother, who "drank too much," so he had lived with friends in an apartment of their own for the last two years of high school. Years later, a high school counselor who had helped him at the time told Ralph, "I thought you'd either be dead or doing time by now." Remembering his own high school years, Ralph said,

> That was tough, but it made me tougher down the road because I was having to worry about bills and rent, everything. I was that much more prepared when I got into my early twenties than other guys in their early twenties. . . .

Ralph was proud of himself for having worked hard and risen to a responsible position, for being married to a popular girl from his high school, and for having two children for whom he could provide a good life. Ralph's account was typical of those I heard from other men in the way it paired hardships and benefits, transforming, in retrospect, obstacles and disappointments into challenges and opportunities. The men's transformation and reinterpretation of their own life-story complicated their task of deciding on what was important for children. Since indulgence might make children lazy, and hardship could build character, it was never clear that doing the right thing by children was not simultaneously depriving them of important lessons.

Under these conditions, the men from Meadowview construct their accounts of their own fatherhood within the context of culture expectations and in comparison with, imitation of, or reaction against their own fathers. Judging their fathers and themselves by the standards of their culture, they took one or more of three positions: "He did well, and I do as he did"; "He did not do well, so I do differently"; "He did badly, but I don't know how to do differently." In every case there was a striving to meet a culturally approved and personally acceptable level of parenting. In their accounts, men talked about fathering, about what they did for their children, what they wanted to do for their children, what they wanted their children to be, and what they feared for them, and thus illuminated what fatherhood meant to them. As they talked about the similarities and differences between their own and their children's childhoods and about the things they did or wished to do differently or the same as their own fathers, they drew a picture of fatherhood as multifaceted.

Fatherhood, as one element of the package deal, is itself composed of four facets: emotional closeness, provision, protection, and endowment. Of these four, men said the most important thing they did for their children was to provide for them. This identification of fatherhood and providing is crucial, reflecting the central place of employment in men's sense of self-worth and helping to explain many of the apparent anomalies in men's accounts. But there are other things, not directly material, that fathers want: to be emotionally close with their children; to protect their children from threats, fears, and dangers; and to endow their children with opportunities and attributes that contribute to their life chances. As I describe what I was told about each of these facets of fatherhood, it will be clear that they merge and overlap, that no one of them can be achieved in isolation, and that protection and endowment depend on being a good provider. It will also become apparent that being close to one's children and being a good provider are in tension and that fathers have to do cultural work to make the case that they are doing both.

EMOTIONAL CLOSENESS

. . . Emotional closeness—intimacy or the lack of it—was the dominant emotional theme in my conversations with fathers. That their concern is widespread is indicated by the amount of attention that advice books directed at fathers devote to connecting to their children. In a typical example, James Levine and Todd Pittinsky appeal to men's memories of the absence of expressions of affection:

> To understand how much a hug, and expressions of affection in general, can mean to your kids, think back to how much it meant (or would have meant) to you when you were a child. A study of 300 male executives and mid-level managers found that "when managers were asked what one thing they would like to change in their relationships with their own fathers, the majority indicated they wished their fathers would have expressed emotions and feelings." (1998: 173)

Some of the men from Meadowview spoke with deep feeling about the love they had known from their own fathers; others talked about the distance they had felt from them. Many of them spoke about their own difficulty expressing emotion and about the joyful and transforming effect of children, who brought love into their lives and opened the way to their expressions of affection. The men of Meadowview High were well aware of the multiple positive contributions fatherhood made to their own well-being and sense of themselves, as well as the contributions they could make to their children's happiness and success. Phil Marwick, who had married for the first time at thirty and had two young sons, expressed the optimistic sense in which becoming a father allows a man to make a fresh start emotionally, to overcome the experience of his own childhood, and to be a warm and loving presence in his children's lives:

Of all my friends growing up, I don't know anybody who really had a good friendship with their father or mother. I'm trying to think. I must have seen it because it appealed to me. I do remember that kids that had a household that's open and a lot of communication really appealed to me a lot. Love wasn't real big in my house, so I wanted to be around a lot of love. And I had so much love to give because I never gave it growing up. And it's funny, I had such a hard time growing up telling anybody that I loved them, I just could never do that. And even to this day, with my wife, it's difficult for me to show feelings towards her. . . .

Phil clearly expressed the anguish of distance and the joy of closeness but his comments were also significant for what he left unsaid. It is noteworthy that Phil attributed his delayed marriage, and the issues in his relationship with his wife, to his own upbringing. Explaining one's adult situation in terms of one's childhood experience is a common practice in the contemporary United States, but there are other possible explanations for Phil's predicament. We might, for instance, consider male privilege that allows self-absorption, the pressures on masculinity that militate against emotional expression, and defects of characters such as selfishness or lack of empathy. . . .

Levine and Pittinsky stress the importance for fathers to reconnect with their children when they return from work. Their advice assumes that the children are already at home when fathers arrive. This assumption is explicit in their example of Michael Johnson, a man who has

an extremely clever way of cutting "to the chase" and connecting with his son. Before he comes home, he calls to ask his wife what their five-year-old son, Will, is up to. When Johnson comes home, he's able to be specific: "I'll say, 'I hear you were running around with an eye patch playing pirate today.' It lets him know I have been thinking about him." (1998: 175)

This example is paradigmatic of what I call women's mediating position between fathers and children. . . .

The consistency with which men expressed their shared vision of what makes a good father—warmth, involvement, doing things with his children, playing with them, teaching them good values, taking pleasure in them—was accompanied by a very variable sense of their own success at realizing that vision. Emotional closeness was a crucial facet of their vision of good fathering, but it was not the only one. These fathers wanted to experience emotional closeness to their children for its own sake, but they also saw emotional closeness instrumentally, as something that would make it more possible for them to protect their children from harm and to endow them with opportunities and character.

PROTECTION

I don't like to think I'm overprotective and I don't want to be. They've got to go out and do their own thing. But I want to keep them out of harm's way as much as possible. I don't know. It's tough.—*Paul*

. . . Most men I talked to expressed the fear about the dangers of the world. Most of them also said it was important to live in a safe neighborhood and to protect their children, distancing them from dangers and bad influences.

The men who had themselves been children in Meadowview remembered playing in the fields and orchards that have since been paved and built over. The landscape of their childhood was not only physically different, it was also a different social landscape. They remembered playing, alone and with groups of their peers, far from home and without adult supervision. They told me how they rode their bikes over the neighborhood and the town and played baseball and other games in the public parks. None of this was part of their children's experience. In informal conversations many adults from a range of backgrounds have said that their own childhoods were less supervised than are their children's. Bicycle helmets, car seats, playgrounds that charge by the hour, careful checking of Halloween candy, suspicion of adults who interact with children, and keeping children indoors or under the eye of adults are some of the many ways in which childhood has become increasingly circumscribed. This change has made the work of parenting more labor intensive at the same time that public provisioning for families and children has been systematically dismantled. Public space for children has been replaced by privatized extra-curricular activities; children's sociability is organized by adults. It is not only privileged children who are supervised and protected from what is seen as a dangerous world. Parents living in inner-city neighborhoods also feel forced to restrict their children's freedom in order to protect them, though they find themselves without the resources to provide the alternatives they would like. . . .

Every father I spoke to was concerned about his children's exposure to potentially harmful outside influences. Losing interest in school, using drugs, being violent or the victim of violence, and, for daughters, being the object of sexual attention (even in this era of AIDS no man volunteered concerns about his own sons' sexual activity) were seen as influences from the larger society, from other people, and from "the media.". . .

Protecting children, as a facet of fatherhood, was very closely linked to emotional closeness. Protecting children meant, to the fathers I talked to, not only physical protection but also being able to talk to them about the dangers they faced and about the consequences of their actions. In teaching values these men were filling their children with good influences and inoculating them against bad. At this point the protective facet of fatherhood merges into the facet that I call endowment. While protection is directed against harm from the outside, endowment aims to give children encouragement and opportunities and the inner qualities of character necessary to take advantage of opportunities. As they talked about the opportunities they could give their children, the fathers I talked to again reflected on the shortcomings of their own fathers, and on the changed circumstances their children faced.

ENDOWING CHILDREN WITH OPPORTUNITIES AND CHARACTER

They never pushed me to do anything except leave. My mother pushed me to leave the house. That was it. "Don't cause any problems and be a good boy." And that was the extent of it. "Get good grades." But they never once sat down and helped me with my homework. I don't say that out of exaggeration; they never once did. They were too busy doing what they had to do. Maybe in the fifties that's the way things were. I don't know.—*Paul*

In both protecting and encouraging their children, fathers need to strike a balance. On the one hand they did not want anything bad to happen to their children, but on the other they did not want to be overprotective and deprive their children of the opportunities to learn from their mistakes. Several men claimed that they were better people for the hardship or adversity of their childhoods. Indeed, it is hard to know how they could claim otherwise, for the alternative seemed to be to admit that they were damaged, as very few did. Similarly, they said they wanted to support their children in doing what they wanted to do, but they did not want to force them in any particular direction.

Sometimes even the most self-assured men did not persuade me that they had managed to maintain this balance. Mark Baxter, for instance, expressed the strain between competing values that makes child rearing a process of negotiation, alteration, and concealment of contradiction. His explicit position was unambiguous: "I don't want to push them into anything. I feel they'll do whatever they want to do. I can guide them in certain areas, but whatever they decide is fine with me." But Mark's general attitude that his children should make their own decisions, follow their own aptitudes and preferences, was in tension with his aspirations for his children. He was able to reconcile the contradiction through this use of "guidance."

Just how firm his guidance could be came out in our discussion of his son's academic performance. Then in the eighth grade, his son was in a program for the gifted and talented. Mark said he had to keep him "geared in" to school, and that in Mark's judgment, if he got below a B grade he was not trying. Mark helped his son to achieve by reviewing and correcting his homework, setting times for study, and setting high standards. The strain that this put on his son became clear to me as Mark described what happened when his son got a D on a math test and became so distraught that his teacher sent him to the school counselor. There it came out that his son was terrified of Mark's reaction: "My dad's going to kill me." As it turned out, Mark's son received a D because he had inadvertently skipped one question, so each of his answers was recorded on the answer sheet against the previous question. Mark denied that his son's distress was evidence that he was "pushing" his son, but interpreted the entire incident as confirmation that the "parameters" of the parent–child relationship were intact.

In all aspects of his parental relationship, Mark, like so many of the men I talked to, said he was steering a course to avoid what he perceived as outmoded, rigid, and authoritarian fathering, while not abdicating his parental responsibilities. The difficulties of the distinction came out particularly when Mark was considering whether he wanted his children to look up to him: "Looking up to me is not important. If they respect me, that is important.". . .

The difference between "looking up to" and "respecting" one's father is slight at best, and not easily defined. Mark explained that he did not want fear or obedience just because he was the father, and would always try to explain his actions to his children: "I want them to know I gave it some sort of logical thought before I yell." Mark, in fact, wanted his children to obey and respect him because they recognized his greater experience and because they thought he was right, not simply because he was their father. The distinction was blurred because it did not occur to Mark that his essential values and orientation could be incorrect. Since he saw himself as both his children's father and as correct on the issues, the practical consequences of the distinction were minimal. Whether they obeyed him because he was their father or because they recognized that he was telling them the right thing to do, Mark expected his children to do what they were told. . . .

Education was the one area in which there was a very clear and definite and universal change in both attitudes and practices between the men I talked to and their fathers. The men from Meadowview High School all agreed that their children's success and happiness as adults depended on their education, and they were involved in making sure that their children were successful in school and had opportunities for higher education. Some of the men's parents had expected them to go on to college, but for many finishing high school had been the summit of their aspirations. Their higher goals for their own children reflected changes in the distribution of wages. Adjusted for inflation, the average entry wage for college graduates was 2 percent lower in 1997 than it was in 1979. For high school graduates, the entry wage had dropped by 24 percent. A declining real minimum wage, more workers earning the minimum wage or little more, declining union membership, and the shift from manufacturing to service jobs have all contributed to these changes. The growing differential between wages for college and high school graduates underlay the realization of the fathers I talked to that going to college was more important for their children's financial well-being than it had been for their own. In 1979, about 18 percent of young people obtained four year degrees, by 1999 the figure had grown to 27 percent (Mishel, Bernstein, and Schmitt 2001).

The job market in 1972 had been such that many high school graduates had been able to find jobs and earn promotions without any additional credentials. . . .

THE FACETS OF FATHERHOOD IN THE CONTEXT OF THE PACKAGE DEAL

All the men I talked to denied that establishing one's virility or masculinity was any reason for having children—at least in their own cases. Frank made the typical exception of himself from the general rule when he said, "I think everybody has a big ego trip with having children. I don't think that was really the case with me." These men did, however, explicitly value having children as an affirmation of who they were, of their purpose in life, and as representations of what they found truly important. Frank elaborated on his personal sense of accomplishment on becoming a father:

> I think the first time Carol got pregnant, with our first child, I felt a sense of accomplishment. But as far as changing my manhood, I didn't really feel any change. I just felt that positive feeling that we could have kids. Everybody has that question: "Can I have kids? Will I have kids?" Just made me feel a lot better. Didn't feel like I had any more power or anything, but I felt a lot better knowing that I did have children.

Becoming a father was a moral transformation in that it shifted men's priorities and sense of responsibility. Within their script, marriage marked the end of a period of fun and responsibility only for oneself, and having children marked the shift from couple time to family time. The responsibility for children found its focus in working to provide for them, but was also expressed through the other facets of fatherhood. . . .

In particular, the continuing cultural primacy of providing for children means that men's time and energy are devoted to, and consumed by, their paid work. In important ways employment and fatherhood are mutually reinforcing, for having children provides a motivation for dedication to employment, and supporting a family is crucial to successful fatherhood. But there is tension within the system. The tension between dedication to employment and the desire for emotional closeness to children is addressed, if not resolved, by the cultural work men and women perform within the confines of the package deal. . . . The men I talked to recognized that their employment took them away from intimate relationship with their children, but they defined their work as an expression of their paternal love. They also used their earnings, in conjunction with their marriages, to ensure that their children had a mother who was at home, or was at least represented as being at home. In many cases the trade-off was explicit: Men told me that they worked longer hours so that their wives could be home with the children. These men's employment did nothing to contribute to their own, direct, emotional relationship with their children, but it did make sure that the culturally appropriate person, their mother, was there for them.

Figure 1 illustrates how each element of the package deal is linked to all others. The elements are mutually reinforcing, but this is a not system that returns to a stable

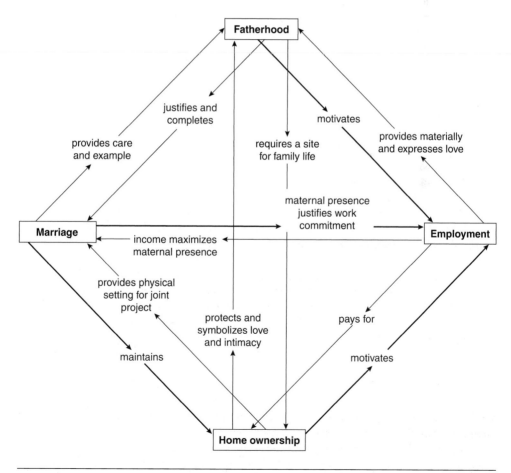

FIGURE 1   *The Interconnections and Tensions among the Elements of the Package Deal*

equilibrium. Men's employment, for instance, enables them to achieve appropriate housing, but also removes them physically from home and makes them more dependent on their wives to mediate their relationships with their children. The dark arrows emphasize that every other element motivates and reinforces the importance of employment, thus concentrating men's energies on the one element that does not contribute directly to emotional closeness to their children. Within the system, reducing the commitment to work in favor of any other element increases the tensions. Changing the experience of fatherhood involves transforming a cultural system, not just altering emphasis within it.

Editors' Note: *References for this reading can be found in the original source.*

8 Childhood

Beyond Sentimentality: American Childhood as a Social and Cultural Construct

Steven Mintz

Nowhere is it easier to romanticize childhood than in Mark Twain's hometown of Hannibal, Missouri. In this small Mississippi riverfront town, where Mark Twain lived, off and on, from the age of four until he was seventeen, many enduring American fantasies about childhood come to life. There is a historical marker next to a fence like the one that Tom's friends paid him for the privilege of whitewashing. There is another marker pointing to the spot where Huck's cabin supposedly stood. There is also the window where Huck hurled pebbles to wake the sleeping Tom. Gazing out across the raging waters of the Mississippi, now unfortunately hidden behind a floodwall, one can easily imagine the raft excursion that Huck and Jim took seeking freedom and adventure.

Hannibal occupies a special place in our collective imagination as the setting of two of fiction's most famous depictions of childhood. Our cherished myth about childhood as a bucolic time of freedom, untainted innocence, and self-discovery comes to life in this river town. But beyond the accounts of youthful wonder and small-town innocence, Twain's novels teem with grim and unsettling details about childhood's underside. Huck's father Pap was an abusive drunkard who beat his son for learning how to read. When we idealize Mark Twain's Hannibal and its eternally youthful residents, we suppress his novels' more sinister aspects.[1]

Twain's real-life mid-nineteenth-century Hannibal was anything but a haven of stability and security. It was a place where a quarter of the children died before their first birthday, half before they reached the age of twenty-one. Twain himself experienced the death of two siblings. Although he was not physically abused like the fictional Huck, his father was emotionally cold and aloof. There were few open displays of affection in his boyhood home. Only once did he remember seeing his father and mother kiss, and that was at the deathbed of his brother Ben. Nor was his home a haven of economic security.

291

His boyhood ended before his twelfth birthday when his father's death forced him to take up a series of odd jobs. Before he left home permanently at seventeen, he had already worked as a printer's apprentice; clerked in a grocery store, a bookshop, and a drug store; tried his hand at blacksmithing; and delivered newspapers. Childhood ended early in Twain's hometown, though full adulthood came no more quickly than it does today.[2]

A series of myths cloud public thinking about the history of American childhood. One is the myth of a carefree childhood. We cling to a fantasy that once upon a time childhood and youth were years of carefree adventure, despite the fact that for most children in the past, growing up was anything but easy. Disease, family disruption, and early entry into the world of work were integral parts of family life. The notion of a long childhood devoted to education and free from adult-like responsibilities is a very recent invention, a product of the past century and a half, and one that only became a reality for a majority of children after World War II.

Another myth is that of the home as a haven and bastion of stability in an ever-changing world. Throughout American history, family stability has been the exception, not the norm. At the beginning of the twentieth century, fully a third of all American children spent at least a portion of their childhood in a single-parent home, and as recently as 1940, one child in ten did not live with either parent—compared to one in twenty-five today.[3]

A third myth is that childhood is the same for all children, a status transcending class, ethnicity, and gender. In fact, every aspect of childhood is shaped by class—as well as by ethnicity, gender, geography, religion, and historical era. We may think of childhood as a biological phenomenon, but it is better understood as a life stage whose contours are shaped by a particular time and place. Childrearing practices, schooling, and the age at which young people leave home are all the products of particular social and cultural circumstances.

A fourth myth is that the United States is a peculiarly child-friendly society when, in actuality, Americans are deeply ambivalent about children. Adults envy young people their youth, vitality, and physical attractiveness, but they also resent children's intrusions on their time and resources and frequently fear their passions and drives. Many of the reforms that nominally have been designed to protect and assist the young were also instituted to insulate adults from children.

Lastly, the myth that is perhaps the most difficult to overcome is the myth of progress and its inverse, the myth of decline. There is a tendency to conceive of the history of childhood as a story of steps forward over time: of parental engagement replacing emotional distance, of kindness and leniency supplanting strict and stern punishment, of scientific enlightenment superceding superstition and misguided moralism. This progressivism is sometimes seen in reverse, that is, that childhood is disappearing: children are growing up too quickly and wildly and losing their innocence, playfulness, and malleability.

Various myths and misconceptions have contributed to this undue pessimism about the young. There has never been a golden age of childhood when the overwhelming majority of American children were well cared for and their experiences were idyllic. Nor has childhood ever been an age of innocence, at least not for the overwhelming majority of children. Childhood has never been insulated from the pressures and demands of the surrounding society and each generation of children has had to wrestle with the particular social, political, and economic constraints of its own historical period. In our own time, the young have had to struggle with high rates of family instability, a deepening disconnection from adults, and the expectation that all children should pursue the same academic path at the same pace, even as the attainment of full adulthood recedes ever further into the future.

THE SOCIAL AND CULTURAL CONSTRUCTION OF CHILDHOOD

The history of children is often treated as a marginal subject, and there is no question that the history of children is especially difficult to write. Children are rarely obvious historical actors. Compared to adults, they leave fewer historical sources, and their powerlessness makes them less visible than other social groups. Nevertheless, the history of childhood is inextricably bound up with the broader political and social events in the life of the nation—including colonization, revolution, slavery, industrialization, urbanization, immigration, and war—and children's experience embodies many of the key themes in American history, such as the rise of modern bureaucratic institutions, the growth of a consumer economy, and the elaboration of a welfare state. Equally important, childhood's history underscores certain long-term transformations in American life, such as an intensifying consciousness about age, a clearer delineation of distinct life stages, and the increasing tendency to organize institutions by age.

Childhood is not an unchanging, biological stage of life, and children are not just "grow'd," like Topsy in Harriet Beecher Stowe's *Uncle Tom's Cabin*. Rather, childhood is a social and cultural construct. Every aspect of childhood—including children's relationships with their parents and peers, their proportion of the population, and their paths through childhood to adulthood—has changed dramatically over the past four centuries. Methods of child rearing, the duration of schooling, the nature of children's play, young people's participation in work, and the points of demarcation between childhood, adolescence, and adulthood are products of culture, class, and historical era.[4]

Childhood in the past was experienced and conceived of in quite a different way than today. Just two centuries ago, there was far less age segregation than there is today and less concern with organizing experience by chronological age. There was also far less sentimentalization of children as special beings who were more innocent and vulnerable than adults. This does not mean that adults failed to recognize childhood as a stage of life, with its own special needs and characteristics, nor does it imply that parents were unconcerned about their children and failed to love them and mourn their deaths. Rather, it means that the experience of young people was organized and valued very differently than it is today.

Language itself illustrates shifts in the construction of childhood. Two hundred years ago, the words used to describe childhood were far less precise than those we use today. The word *infancy* referred not to the months after birth, but to the period in which children were under their mother's control, typically from birth to the age of 5 or 6. The word *childhood* might refer to someone as young as the age of 5 or 6 or as old as the late teens or early twenties. Instead of using our term adolescent or teenager, Americans two centuries ago used a broader and more expansive term *youth*, which stretched from the pre-teen years until the early or mid-20s. The vagueness of this term reflected the amorphousness of the life stages; chronological age was less important than physical strength, size, and maturity. A young person did not achieve full adult status until marriage and establishment of an independent farm or entrance into a full-time trade or profession. Full adulthood might be attained as early as the mid- or late teens, but usually did not occur until the late twenties or early thirties.[5]

How, then, has childhood changed over the past two hundred years? The transformations that have taken place might be grouped into three broad categories. The first involves shifts in the timing, sequence, and stages of growing up. Over the past two centuries, the stages of childhood have grown much more precise, uniform, and prescriptive. Before the Civil War, children and teens moved sporadically in and out of the parental home, schools, and jobs, in an irregular, episodic pattern that the historian Joseph F. Kett termed "semi-dependence.". . .

Beginning in the mid-nineteenth century, however, there were growing efforts to regularize and systematize childhood experiences. Unable to transmit their status position directly to their children, through bequests of family lands, transmission of craft skills, or selection of a marriage partner, middle-class parents adopted new strategies to assist their children, emphasizing birth control, maternal nurture, and prolonged schooling. Less formal methods of childrearing and education were replaced by intensive forms of childrearing and prescribed curricula in schools. Unstructured contacts with adults were supplanted by carefully age-graded institutions. Activities organized by young people themselves were succeeded by adult sponsored, adult-organized organization. Lying behind these developments was a belief that childhood should be devoted to education, play, and character-building activities; that children needed time to mature inside a loving home and segregated from adult affairs; and that precocious behavior needed to be suppressed.[6]

Demography is a second force for change. A sharp reduction in the birth rate substantially reduced the proportion of children in the general population, from half the population in the mid-nineteenth century to a third by 1900. A declining birth rate divided families into more distinct generations and allowed parents to lavish more time, attention, and resources on each child; it also made society less dependent on children's labor and allowed adult society to impose new institutional structures on young peoples' lives reflecting shifting notions about children's proper chronological development.

The third category is attitudinal. Adult conceptions of childhood have shifted profoundly over time, from the seventeenth-century Puritan image of the child as a depraved being who needed to be restrained; to the Enlightened notion of children as blank slates who could be shaped by environmental influences; to the Romantic conception of children as creatures with innocent souls and redeemable, docile wills; to the Darwinian emphasis on highly differentiated stages of children's cognitive, physiological, and emotional development; to the Freudian conception of children as seething cauldrons of instinctual drives; and to the contemporary notions that emphasize children's competence and capacity for early learning.

The history of childhood might be conceptualized in terms of three overlapping phases. The first, pre-modern childhood, which roughly coincides with the colonial era, was a period in which the young were viewed as adults in training. Religious and secular authorities regarded childhood as a time of deficiency and incompleteness, and adults rarely referred to their childhood with nostalgia or fondness. Infants were viewed as unformed and even animalistic due to their inability to speak or stand upright. A parent's duty was to hurry a child toward adult status, especially through early engagement in work responsibilities, both inside the parental home and outside it, as servants and apprentices.

The middle of the eighteenth century saw the emergence of a new set of attitudes, which came to define modern childhood. A growing number of parents began to regard children as innocent, malleable, and fragile creatures who needed to be sheltered from contamination. Childhood was increasingly viewed as a separate stage of life that required special care and institutions to protect it. During the nineteenth century, the growing acceptance of this new ideal among the middle class was evident in prolonged residence of young people within the parental home; longer periods of formal schooling; and an increasing consciousness about the stages of young peoples' development, culminating in the "discovery" (or, more accurately, the invention) of adolescence around the turn of the twentieth century.

Universalizing the modern ideal of a sheltered childhood was a highly uneven process and one that has never encompassed all American children. Indeed, it was not until the 1950s that the norms of modern childhood defined the modal experience of young people in the United States. But developments were already under way that would bring modern childhood to an end and replace it with something quite different, a new phase that might be called postmodern childhood. This term refers to the breakdown of dominant norms about the family, gender roles, age, and even reproduction, as they were subjected to radical change and revision. Age norms that many considered "natural" were thrown into question. Even the bedrock biological process of sexual maturation accelerated. Today's children are much more likely than the Baby Boomers to experience their parents' divorce; to have a working mother; to spend significant amounts of time unsupervised by adults; to grow up without siblings; and to hold a job during high school. Adolescent girls are much more likely to have sexual relations during their mid-teens.[7]

Superficially, postmodern childhood resembles premodern childhood. As in the seventeenth century, children are no longer regarded as the binary opposites of adults, nor are they considered naïve and innocent creatures. Today, adults quite rightly assume that even preadolescents are knowledgeable about the realities of the adult world. But unlike premodern children, postmodern children are independent consumers and participants in a separate, semi-autonomous youth culture. We still assume that the young are fundamentally different from adults; that they should spend their first eighteen years in the parents' home; and devote their time to education in age-graded schools. But it is also clear that basic aspects of the ideal of a protected childhood, in which the young are kept isolated from adult realities, have broken down.[8]

DIVERSITY

Diversity has always been the hallmark of American childhood. In seventeenth-century America, demographic, economic, religious, and social factors made geographical subcultures the most important markers of diversity in children's experience. In the early period of settlement, colonial childhood took profoundly different forms in New England, the Middle Colonies, and the Chesapeake and southernmost colonies. In seventeenth century New England, hierarchical, patriarchal Calvinist families shaped children's experiences. In the Chesapeake colonies of Maryland and Virginia, in contrast, families were highly unstable and indentured servitude shaped children's experience. Only in the Middle Colonies, from New York to Delaware, did a childhood emphasizing maternal nurture and an acceptance of early autonomy emerge, yet even here, large numbers of children experienced various forms of dependence, as household and indentured servants, apprentices, or slaves.[9]

In the nineteenth century, a highly uneven process of capitalist expansion made social class, gender, and race more salient contributors to childhood diversity. The children of the urban middle class, prosperous commercial farmers, and southern planters enjoyed increasingly longer childhoods, free from major household or work responsibilities until their late teens or twenties, whereas the offspring of urban workers, frontier farmers, and blacks, both slave and free, had briefer childhoods and became involved in work inside or outside the home before they reached their teens. Many urban working-class children contributed to the family economy through scavenging in the streets, vacant lots, or back alleys, collecting coal, wood, and other items that could be used at home or sold. Others took part in the street trades, selling gum, peanuts, and crackers. In industrial towns, young people under the age of 15 contributed on average about 20 percent of their family's income. In mining areas, boys as young as 10 or 12 worked as breakers, separating coal from pieces of slate and wood, before becoming miners in their mid- or late teens. On farms, children as young as 5 or 6 might pull weeds or chase birds and cattle away from crops. By the time they reached the age of 8, many tended livestock, and as they grew older they milked cows, churned butter, fed chickens, collected eggs, hauled water, scrubbed laundry, and harvested crops. A blurring of gender roles among children and youth was especially common on frontier farms. Schooling varied as widely as did work routines. In the rural North, the Midwest, and the Far West, most mid- and late-nineteenth-century students attended one-room schools for 3 to 6 months a year. In contrast, city children attended age-graded classes taught by professional teachers 9 months a year. In both rural and urban areas, girls tended to receive more schooling than boys.[10]

Late in the nineteenth century, self-described child-savers launched a concerted campaign to overcome diversity and universalize a middle-class childhood. This was a slow and bitterly resisted process. Not until the 1930s was child labor finally outlawed and not until the 1950s did high school attendance become a universal experience. Yet for all the success in advancing this middle-class ideal, even today, social class remains a primary determinant of children's well-being.[11]

In recent years, social conservatives have tended to fixate on family structure as a source of diversity in children's well-being, while political liberals have tended to focus on ethnicity, race, and gender. In fact, it is poverty that is the most powerful predictor of children's welfare. Economic stress contributes to family instability, inadequate health care, high degrees of mobility, poor parenting, and elevated levels of stress and depression. As in the nineteenth century, social class significantly differentiates contemporary American childhoods. There is a vast difference between the highly pressured, hyper-organized, fast-track childhoods of affluent children and the highly stressed childhoods of the one-third of children who live in poverty at some point before the age of eighteen. In many affluent families, the boundaries between work and family life have diminished, and parents manage by tightly organizing their children's lives. Yet, contradictorily, most affluent children have their own television and computer and therefore unmediated access to information and are unsupervised by their parents for large portions of the day. In many affluent families there are drastic swings between parental distance from children and parental indulgence, when fathers and mothers try to compensate for parenting too little. Yet at the same time, one-sixth of all children live in poverty at any one time, including 36 percent of black children and 34 percent of Hispanic children. This generally entails limited adult supervision, inferior schooling, and a lack of easy access to productive diversions and activities.

THE POLITICS OF CHILDHOOD

In recent years, two contrasting visions of childhood have collided. One is a vision of a protected childhood, in which children are to be sheltered from adult realities, especially from sex, obscenity, and death. The opposing vision is of a prepared childhood, of children who are exposed from a relatively early age to the realities of contemporary society, such as sexuality and diverse family patterns. Proponents of a prepared childhood argue that in a violent, highly commercialized, and hypersexualized society, a naïve child is a vulnerable child.

Clashes between conflicting conceptions of childhood are not new. For four hundred years, childhood has been a highly contested category. The late twentieth-century culture war—pitting advocates of a "protected" childhood, who sought to shield children from adult realities, against proponents of a "prepared" childhood—was only the most recent in a long series of conflicts over the definition of a proper childhood. In the seventeenth century, there were bitter struggles between Puritans who regarded even newborn infants as sinful, humanistic educators who emphasized children's malleability, and Anglican traditionalists who considered children as symbols of values (including the value of deference and respect for social hierarchy) that were breaking down as England underwent the wrenching economic transformations that accompanied the rise of modern capitalist enterprise. In the late eighteenth century, battles raged over infant depravity and patriarchal authority, conflicts that gave added resonance to the American revolutionaries' struggle against royal authority. At the turn of the twentieth century, conflict erupted between the proponents of a useful childhood, which expected children to reciprocate for their parents' sacrifices, and advocates of a sheltered childhood, free from labor and devoted to play and education.[12]

PARENTING

Anxiety is the hallmark of modern parenthood. Today's parents agonize incessantly about their children's physical health, personality development, psychological well-being, and academic performance. From birth, parenthood is colored by apprehension. Contemporary parents worry about sudden infant death syndrome, stranger abductions, and physical and sexual abuse, as well as more mundane problems, such as sleep disorders and hyperactivity.

Parental anxiety about children's well-being is not a new development, but parents' concerns have taken dramatically different forms over time. Until the mid-nineteenth century, parents were primarily concerned about their children's health, religious piety, and moral development. In the late nineteenth century, parents became increasingly attentive to their children's emotional and psychological well-being, and during the twentieth century, parental anxieties dwelt on children's personality development, gender identity, and their ability to interact with peers. Today, much more than in the past, guilt-ridden, uncertain parents worry that their children not suffer from boredom, low self-esteem, or excessive school pressures.[13]

Today, we consider early childhood life's formative stage and believe that children's experiences during the first two or three years of life mold their personality, lay the foundation for future cognitive and psychological development, and leave a lasting imprint on their emotional life. We also assume that children's development proceeds through a series of physiological, psychological, social, and cognitive stages; that even very young children have a capacity to learn; that play serves valuable developmental functions; and that growing up requires children to separate emotionally and psychologically from their parents. These assumptions differ markedly from those held three centuries ago. Before the mid-eighteenth century, most adults betrayed surprisingly little interest in the very first years of life and autobiographies revealed little nostalgia for childhood. Also, adults tended to dismiss children's play as trivial and insignificant.

Parenting has evolved through a series of successive and overlapping phases, from a seventeenth-century view of children as "adults-in-training" to the early nineteenth-century emphasis on character formation; the late-nineteenth century notion of scientific childrearing, stressing regularity and systematization; the mid-twentieth century emphasis on fulfilling children's emotional and psychological needs; and the late twentieth century stress on maximizing children's intellectual and social development. Seventeenth-century colonists recognized that children differed from adults in their mental, moral, and physical capabilities and drew a distinction between childhood, an intermediate stage they called youth, and adulthood. But they did not rigidly segregate children by age. Parents wanted children to speak, read, reason, and contribute to their family's economic well-being as soon as possible. Infancy was regarded as a state of deficiency. Unable to speak or stand, infants lacked two essential attributes of full humanity. Parents discouraged infants from crawling and placed them in "walking stools," similar to today's walkers. To ensure proper adult posture, young girls wore leather corsets and parents placed rods along the spines of very young children of both sexes.

During the eighteenth century, a shift in parental attitudes took place. Fewer parents expected children to bow or doff their hats in their presence or stand during meals. Instead of addressing parents as "sir" and "madam," children called them "papa" and "mama." By the end of the eighteenth century, furniture specifically designed for children, painted in pastel colors and decorated with pictures of animals or figures from nursery rhymes, began to be widely produced, reflecting the popular notion of childhood as a time of innocence and playfulness. There was a growing stress on implanting virtue and a capacity for self-government.

By the early nineteenth century, mothers in the rapidly expanding Northeastern middle class increasingly embraced an amalgam of earlier childrearing ideas. From John Locke, they absorbed the notion that children were highly malleable creatures and that a republican form of government required parents to instill a capacity for self-government in their children. From Jean-Jacques Rousseau and the Romantic poets, middle-class parents acquired the idea of childhood as a special stage of life, intimately connected with nature and purer and morally superior to adulthood. From the evangelicals, the middle class adopted the idea that the primary task of parenthood was to implant proper moral character in children and to insulate children from the corruptions of the adult world.

Toward the end of the nineteenth century, middle-class parents began to embrace the idea that childrearing needed to become more scientific. The Child Study movement, through which teachers and mothers under the direction of psychologists identified a series of stages of childhood development, culminating with the "discovery" of adolescence as a psychologically turbulent period that followed puberty. The belief that scientific principles had not been properly applied to childrearing produced new kinds of child-rearing manuals, of which the most influential was Dr. Luther Emmett Holt's *The Care and Feeding of Children*, first published in 1894. Holt emphasized rigid scheduling of feeding, bathing, sleeping, and bowel movements and advised mothers to guard vigilantly against germs and undue stimulation of infants. At a time when a well-adjusted adult was viewed as a creature of habit and self-control, he stressed the importance of imposing regular habits on infants. He discouraged mothers from kissing their babies and told them to ignore their crying and to break such habits as thumb-sucking.[14]

During the 1920s and 1930s, the field of child psychology exerted a growing influence on middle-class parenting. It provided a new language to describe children's emotional problems, such as sibling rivalry, phobias, maladjustment, and inferiority and Oedipus complexes; it also offered new insights into forms of parenting (based on such variables as demandingness or permissiveness), the stages and milestones of children's development, and the characteristics of children at particular ages (such as the "terrible twos," which was identified by Arnold Gesell, Frances L. Ilg, and Louise Bates Ames). The growing prosperity of the 1920s made the earlier emphasis on regularity and rigid self-control seem outmoded. A well-adjusted adult was now regarded as a more easygoing figure, capable of enjoying leisure. Rejecting the mechanistic and behaviorist notion that children's behavior could be molded by scientific control, popular dispensers of advice favored a more relaxed approach to childrearing, emphasizing the importance of meeting babies' emotional needs. The title of a 1936 book by pediatrician C. Anderson Aldrich—*Babies Are Human Beings*—summed up the new attitude.[15]

The Great Depression of the 1930s and World War II greatly intensified parental anxieties about childrearing. During the postwar era, there was an intense fear that faulty mothering caused lasting psychological problems in children. Leading psychologists such as Theodore Lidz, Irving Bieber, and Erik Erikson linked schizophrenia, homosexuality, and identity diffusion to mothers who displaced their frustrations and needs for independence onto their children. A major concern was that many boys, raised almost exclusively by women, failed to develop an appropriate sex role identity. In retrospect, it seems clear that an underlying source of anxiety lay in the fact that mothers were raising their children with an exclusivity and in an isolation unparalleled in American history.[16]

Since the early 1970s, parental anxieties have greatly increased both in scope and intensity. Many parents sought to protect children from every imaginable harm by baby-proofing their homes, using car seats, and requiring bicycle helmets. Meanwhile, as more mothers joined the labor force, parents arranged more structured, supervised activities for their children. A variety of factors contributed to a surge in anxiety. As parents had fewer children, they invested more emotion in each child. An increase in professional expertise about children, coupled with a proliferation of research and advocacy organizations, media outlets, and government agencies responsible for children's health and safety made parents increasingly aware of threats to children's well-being and of ways to maximize their children's physical, social, and intellectual development. Unlike postwar parents, who wanted to produce normal children who fit in, middle-class parents now wanted to give their child a competitive edge. For many middle-class parents, fears of downward mobility and anxiety that they would not be able to pass on their status and class to their children, made them worry that their offspring would underperform academically, athletically, or socially. . . .

MORAL PANICS OVER CHILDREN'S WELL-BEING

Americans are great believers in progress in all areas but one. For more than three centuries, Americans have feared that the younger generation is going to hell in a handbasket. Today, many adults mistakenly believe that compared to their predecessors, kids today are less respectful and knowledgeable, and more alienated, sexually promiscuous, and violent. They fear that contemporary children are growing up too fast and losing their sense of innocent wonder at too young an age. Prematurely exposed to the pressures, stresses, and responsibilities of adult life, they fear that the young mimic adult sophistication, dress inappropriately, and experiment with alcohol, drugs, sex, and tobacco before they are emotionally and psychologically ready.

A belief in the decline of the younger generation is one of this country's oldest convictions. In 1657, a Puritan minister, Ezekiel Rogers, admitted: "I find the greatest trouble and grief about the rising generation. . . . Much ado I have with my own family . . . the young breed doth much afflict me." For more than three centuries, American adults have worried that children are growing ever more disobedient and disrespectful. But wistfulness about a golden age of childhood is invariably misleading. Nostalgia almost always represents a yearning not for the past as it really was but rather for fantasies about the past. In 1820, children constituted about half of the workers in early factories. As recently as the 1940s, one child in ten lived apart from both parents and fewer than half of all high school students graduated. We forget that over the past century, the introduction of every new form of entertainment has generated intense controversy over its impact on children, and that the anxiety over video games and the Internet are only the latest in a long line of supposed threats to children that includes movies, radio, and even comic books. The danger of nostalgia is that it creates unrealistic expectations, guilt, and anger.[17]

Ever since the Pilgrims departed for Plymouth in 1620, fearful that "their posterity would be in danger to degenerate and be corrupted" in the Old World, Americans have experienced repeated panics over the younger generation. Sometimes these panics were indeed about children, such as the worries over polio in the early 1950s. More often, however, children stand in for some other issue, and the panics are more metaphorical than representational, such as the panic over teenage pregnancy, youth violence, and declining academic achievement in the late 1970s and 1980s, which reflected pervasive fears about family breakdown, crime, drugs, and America's declining competitiveness in the world.[18]

ABUSE OF CHILDREN

Concern about the abuse of children has waxed and waned over the course of American history. The seventeenth-century Puritans were the first people in the Western world to make the physical abuse of a children a criminal offense, though their concern with family privacy and patriarchal authority meant that these statutes were rarely enforced. During the pre-Civil War decades, temperance reformers argued that curbs on alcohol would reduce wife beating and child abuse. The first organizations to combat child abuse, which appeared in the 1870s, were especially concerned about abuse in immigrant, destitute, and foster families.[19]

Over half a century ago, Alfred Kinsey's studies found rates of sexual abuse similar to those reported today. His interviews indicated that exhibitionists had exposed themselves in front of 12 percent of preadolescent girls and that 9 percent of the girls had had their genitals fondled. But it was his findings about premarital and extramarital sex that grabbed the public's attention, not the sexual abuse of its children. Not until the publication of an influential article on "The Battered Child Syndrome" in 1962 was child abuse finally identified as a social problem demanding a significant governmental response. Even in succeeding years, however, public consciousness about abuse has fluctuated widely. In 1986, nearly a third of adults identified abuse as one of the most serious problems facing children and youth; in a survey a decade later abuse went unmentioned.[20]

We quite rightly focus on the way that young people are physically at risk, whether through physical or sexual abuse, neglect, or economic vulnerability. But across American history, some of the gravest threats to the young have involved their psychological vulnerability. Even worse than the physical sufferings under slavery were the psychological scars enslavement left. Worse than toiling in factories was the hidden curriculum that working class children were inferior to their supposed social betters, suited for little more than routine, repetitious labor. As the historian Daniel Kline has persuasively argued, contemporary American society subjects the young to three forms of psychological violence that we tend to ignore. First, there is the violence of expectations in which children are pushed beyond their social, physical, and academic capabilities, largely as an expression of their parents' needs. Then there is the violence of labeling that diagnoses normal childish behavior (for example, normal childhood exuberance or interest in sex) as pathological. Further, there is the violence of representation, the exploitation of children and adolescents by advertisers, marketers, purveyors of popular culture, and politicians, who exploit parental anxieties as well as young peoples' desire to be stylish, independent, and defiant, and eroticize teenage and preadolescent girls.

There is a fourth form of psychological abuse that is perhaps the most unsettling of all: the objectification of childhood. This involves viewing children as objects to be shaped and molded for their own good. Compared to its predecessors, contemporary American society is much more controlling in an institutional and ideological sense. We expect children to conform to standards that few adults could meet. Meanwhile, as the baby boom generation ages, we inhabit an increasingly adult-oriented society, a society

302 Part III • *Parents and Children*

that has fewer "free" spaces for the young, a society that values youth primarily as service workers and consumers and gawks at them as sex objects.

For more than three centuries, America has considered itself to be a particularly child-centered society despite massive evidence to the contrary. Today, no other advanced country allows as many young people to grow up in poverty or without health care, nor does any other western society make so poor a provision for child care or for paid parental leave. Still, Americans think of themselves as a child-centered nation. This paradox is not new. Beginning in the early nineteenth century, the United States developed a host of institutions for the young, ranging from the common school to the Sunday school, the orphanage, the house of refuge, and the reformatory, and eventually expanding to include the children's hospital, the juvenile court, and a wide variety of youth organizations. It was assumed that these institutions served children's interests, that they were caring, developmental, and educational. In practice, however, these institutions frequently proved to be primarily custodial and disciplinary. Indeed, many of the reforms that were supposed to help children were adopted partly because they served the adults' needs, interests, and convenience. The abolition of child labor removed competition from an overcrowded labor market. Age-grading not only made it much easier to control children within schools, it also divided the young into convenient market segments. One of the most serious challenges American society faces is to act on behalf of children's welfare rather than adults'.

The most important lesson that grows out of an understanding of the history of childhood is the simplest. While many fear that American society has changed too much, the sad fact is that it has changed too little. Americans have failed to adapt social institutions to the fact that the young mature more rapidly than they did in the past; that most mothers of preschoolers now participate in the paid workforce; and that a near majority of children will spend substantial parts of their childhood in a single-parent, cohabitating-parent, or stepparent household. How can we provide better care for the young, especially the one-sixth who are growing up in poverty? How can we better connect the worlds of adults and the young? How can we give the young more ways to demonstrate their growing competence and maturity? How can we tame a violence-laced, sex-saturated popular culture without undercutting a commitment to freedom and a respect for the free-floating world of fantasy? These are the questions we must confront as we navigate a new century of childhood.

Notes

1. Ron Powers, *Dangerous Water: A Biography of the Boy Who Became Mark Twain* (New York: Da Capo Press, 1999); Powers, *Tom and Huck Don't Live Here Anymore: Childhood and Murder in the Heart of America* (New York: St. Martin's Press, 2001), 2, 32–34, 40, 131; Shelley Fisher Fishkin, *Lighting Out for the Territories: Reflections on Mark Twain and American Culture* (New York: Oxford University Press, 1997).

2. Powers, *Dangerous Water*, 26, 84, 167; Powers, *Tom and Huck Don't Live Here Anymore*, 78.

3. Richard Weissbourd, *The Vulnerable Child: What Really Hurts America's Children and What We Can Do About It* (Reading, MA: Addison-Wesley, 1996), 48.

4. Colin Heywood, *A History of Childhood: Children and Childhood in the West from Medieval to Modern Times* (Cambridge, UK: Polity, 2001); Joseph Illick, *American Childhood* (Philadelphia: University of Pennsylvania Press, 2002); James A. Schultz, *The Knowledge of Childhood in the German Middle Ages, 1100–1350* (Philadelphia: University of Pennsylvania Press, 1995), 11.

5. Howard P. Chudacoff, *How Old Are You? Age Consciousness in American Society* (Princeton: Princeton University Press, 1989); Joseph F. Kett, *Rites of Passage: Adolescence in America* (New York: Basic, 1977).

6. Kett, *Rites of Passage, passim.*

7. On changes in the onset of sexual maturation, see Marcia E. Herman-Giddens and others, "Secondary Sexual Characteristics and Menses in Young Girls Seen in Office Practice: A Study from the Pediatric Research in Office Settings Network," *Pediatrics*, Vol. 99, No. 4 (April 1997), 505–512. In 1890, the average age of menarche in the United States was estimated to be 14.8 years; by the 1990s, the average age had fallen to 12.5 (12.1 for African American girls and 12.8 for girls of northern European ancestry). According to the study, which tracked 17,000 girls to find out when they hit different markers of puberty, 15 percent of white girls and 48 percent of African American girls showed signs of breast development or pubic hair by age 8. For conflicting views on whether the age of menarche has fallen, see Lisa Belkin, "The Making of an 8-Year-Old Woman," *New York Times*, December 24, 2000; Gina Kolata, "Doubters Fault Theory Finding Earlier Puberty, *New York Times*," February 20, 2001; and "2 Endocrinology Groups Raise Doubt on Earlier Onset of Girls' Puberty," *New York Times*, March 3, 2001.

8. Stephen Robertson, "The Disappearance of Childhood," http://teaching.arts.usyd.edu.au/history/2044/.

9. Gerald F. Moran, "Colonial America, Adolescence in," *Encyclopedia of Adolescence*, edited by Richard Lerner, Anne C. Petersen, Jeanne Brooks-Gunn (New York: Garland Pub., 1991), I, 159–167.

10. Priscilla Clement, *Growing Pains: Children in the Industrial Age* (New York: Twayne, 1997); David Nasaw, *Children in the City: At Work and at Play* (Garden City, NY: Anchor Press/Doubleday, 1985); Christine Stansell, *City of Women: Sex and Class in New York, 1789–1860* (New York: Knopf, 1986).

11. David I. Macleod, *The Age of the Child: Children in America, 1890–1912* (New York: Twayne, 1998).

12. Viviana Zelizer, *Pricing the Priceless Child: The Changing Social Value of Children* (Princeton: Princeton University Press).

13. Peter N. Stearns, *Anxious Parents: A History of Modern Childrearing in America* (New York: New York University Press, 2002).

14. Ann Hulbert, *Raising America: Experts, Parents, and a Century of Advice about Children* (New York: Knopf, 2003); Julia Grant, *Raising Baby by the Book: The Education of American Mothers* (New Haven: Yale University Press, 1998).

15. Kathleen W. Jones, *Taming the Troublesome Child* (Cambridge, MA: Harvard University Press, 1999).

16. Steven Mintz and Susan Kellogg, *Domestic Revolutions: A Social History of American Family Life* (New York: Free Press, 1988), 189.

17. Rogers quoted in James Axtell, *School Upon a Hill: Education and Society in Colonial New England* (New Haven: Yale University Press, 1974), 28. Hard as it is to believe, in 1951 a leading television critic decried the quality of children's television. Jack Gould, radio and TV critic for *The New York Times* from the late 1940s to 1972, complained that there was "nothing on science, seldom anything on the country's cultural heritage, no introduction to fine books, scant emphasis on the people of other lands, and little concern over hobbies and other things for children to do themselves besides watch television." *Chicago Sun Times*, Aug. 9, 1998, 35; Phil Scraton, ed., *Childhood in "Crisis"* (London; Bristol, Penn.: UCL Press, 1997), 161, 164.

18. William Bradford, *Of Plymouth Plantation*, edited by Samuel Elliot Morrison (New York: Modern Library, 1952), 25; Moran, "Colonial America, Adolescence in," 159.

19. Linda Gordon, *Heroes of their Own Lives: The Politics and History of Family Violence* (New York: Viking, 1988); Elizabeth Pleck, *Domestic Tyranny: the Making of Social Policy against Family Violence from Colonial Times to the Present* (New York: Oxford University Press, 1987).

20. William Feldman et al., "Is Childhood Sexual Abuse Really Increasing in Prevalence? An Analysis of the Evidence," *Pediatrics*, July 1991, Vol. 88 Issue 1, 29–34; Males, *Framing Youth*, 257. In 1998, government agencies substantiated over a million cases of child maltreatment, including approximately 101,000 cases of sexual abuse. About 51 percent of lifetime rapes occur prior to age 18 and 29 percent of lifetime rapes occur prior to age 12. Coordinating Council on Juvenile Justice and Delinquency Prevention, *Combating Violence and Delinquency: The National Juvenile Justice Action Plan: Report* (Washington DC: Coordinating Council on Juvenile Justice and Delinquency Prevention, 1996), 75; National Criminal Justice Reference Service, www.ncjrs.org/html/ojjdp/action_plan_2001_10/page1.html. The 1994 Sex in America study of the sex lives of 3,400 men and women reported that 17 percent of the women and 12 percent of the men reported childhood sexual abuse. See Males, *Scapegoat Generation*, 74.

■ READING 24

What Children Think about Their Working Parents

Ellen Galinsky

Despite all they hear and read proclaiming that working is okay or even good for children, if parents feel there is a problem about work and family life, they define the solution as *simply* having more time with their child.

We asked parents in our Ask the Children survey, "If *you* were granted one wish to change the way that your work affects your child's life, what would that wish be?" The largest proportion of parents—22 percent—wished to "have more time with their child." An additional 16 percent wished to "work less time."

We also asked parents another open-ended question: "If *your child* were granted one wish to change the way that your work affects his/her life, what would that wish be?" The largest proportion of parents—21 percent—thought their child would want "more time with me." An additional 19 percent thought their child would want them to work less time, and 16 percent thought their children would want them "not to have to go to work." Taken together, 56 percent of parents mentioned time.

In this chapter, we explore the issue of time. Why does the debate about quality time versus quantity time persist? Does the amount of time that children say that they have with their parents affect how they feel about their parents' parenting? Do other aspects of time matter, such as the kinds of activities parents and children do together and whether children's time with parents is rushed or calm? What does the research say about the impact of time together on children's development? Is this another either/or debate—quality time *or* quantity time—as many have portrayed it? And finally and very importantly, do children and parents feel the same way about having time together?

WHY WON'T THE DEBATE ABOUT QUALITY TIME VERSUS QUANTITY TIME GO AWAY?

This debate reminds me of a punching bag that is slugged, even beaten down, but rebounds right back up. For four decades, this debate has had real staying power. Clearly it strikes a resonant cord.

In the 1960s, researchers looked at children in orphanages who failed to thrive and extrapolated this result to children who experienced daily separations from their employed mothers. Others countered that it is not the *quantity* of time that matters, but what happens in that time—the *quality* of time—that is important. And besides, they noted, the prolonged separations children experience from parents in orphanages are not the same as daily separations. The embers of this debate were fanned into flame again in the 1980s when findings from a few studies found that infants whose mothers were away from them for more than 20 hours a week were at risk for being insecurely attached.

Many parents don't seem to like the notion of quality time. In our one-on-one interviews, some described it as a rationalization for parents to spend less time with their children. A cellular phone advertisement that ran in the late 1990s became a symbol—in fact, a lightning rod—for the issue of quality versus quantity time. In this ad, a child approaches her mother just before the mother is to leave for work. She and her siblings want to go to the beach. When the mother refuses, the child asks when she can be a "client." The mother pauses—then tells her children that they have 3 minutes to get ready to go the beach. The last shot shows the mother sitting on the beach making a conference call on her cellular phone while her children play nearby in the sand.

A mother of a 9-week-old child, who has just returned to work from maternity leave, comments:

> I would say that in general this generation of children may be getting signals that my generation didn't get—that they come in second. It is in this ad about this woman on the phone and the kid wants to go to the beach [and says to her mother,] "When am I going to be a client?" [The mother] gives such a mixed message. Instead of saying, "You're right. We are going to the beach," it's "We are going to the beach and I'm doing my conference call while you play around. And I'll [at least] make sure that you don't cut your foot on shells."

It is clear to many parents that one shouldn't make a distinction between the amount of time one spends with his or her children and what happens in that time. Both the quality and quantity of the time that parents and child share are important. Yet, when asked about their *one* wish to change the way their work affects their child, parents emphasize the *quantity* of time per se: They wish for "more time." What is going on?

WHAT IS GOING ON ABOUT TIME IN TODAY'S FAMILIES?

How Much Time Are Employed Parents Spending with Their Children?

To answer the question of time employed parents spend, let's compare two studies that were conducted 20 years apart: the Families and Work Institute's 1997 National Study of the Changing Workforce and the U.S. Department of Labor's 1977 Quality of Employment Survey (QES).[1]

My colleagues Terry Bond and Jennifer Swanberg and I find—no surprise—that in dual-earner families[2] with children under 18, mothers spend more time doing things and caring for children than fathers on workdays (3.2 hours for mothers versus 2.3 hours for fathers). We also find—again no surprise—that mothers today spend more time than fathers with their children on days off work (8.3 hours for mothers versus 6.4 hours for fathers).

But we find—to the surprise of many—that the gap between mothers and fathers in dual-earner families has narrowed considerably in the past 20 years. Although the amount of time that mothers spend with their children on workdays has not changed in a statistically significant way, fathers have increased the amount of time they spend with children by a half hour.

The 1997 National Study of the Changing Workforce also found that over the past 20 years fathers have increased the time they spend with their children by slightly more than 1 hour on nonwork days, whereas mothers' time has again remained the same.

When the Families and Work Institute released these findings in 1998, the media and public reactions were swift and strong. A few women wrote prominent editorials skeptical of the veracity of the findings, stating, for example, in *The New York Times* that "super dads need a reality check,"[3] whereas many men, like Matt Lauer, host of the *Today* show, gave the findings a high five sign. At last, good news for dads, he said to me.

The public reaction echoes the private fault line between men and women on the subject of time with children. Women ask, "Is he really caring for the children or is he just 'Dad, the helper,' 'Dad, the babysitter?'" "Why does he always wait until I ask him to be with the kids?" "Why doesn't he know what they like to eat for lunch and who their friends are?" Men ask, "Why does she always criticize what I do? When I try to do more, all I get are complaints, complaints, complaints." Or, "I am doing more, but nobody seems to notice."

Are men exaggerating? Are they really spending more time with their children? The 1997 National Study of the Changing Workforce didn't ask parents to keep time diaries, but it did have a reality check, as *The New York Times* called it: We asked fathers and mothers how much time their *partners* spent with the children. Although of course our findings are estimates, we found—again a surprise to many—that mothers' estimates of their husbands parallel the amount of time fathers report spending with their children. So fathers do not seem to be exaggerating—at least according to wives.

Furthermore, because employed mothers have managed to keep constant the amount of time they spend with their children, because fathers have increased their time, and because families have fewer children today than they did 20 years ago, it appears that employed parents indeed are spending somewhat more time with their children than they were two decades ago.

Where do parents get more time? Certainly not from their workdays. For employed fathers with children under 18, the 40-hour workweek is a myth. On average, including paid and unpaid time and including part-time and full-time work, fathers work 50.9 hours per week and mothers work 41.4 hours. By our calculations, fathers' total work time has increased by 3.1 hours per week in the past 20 years, and mothers' time has increased by 5.2 hours.[4]

There has also been an increase in the amount of time that parents spend on their jobs while at home. Almost one in three parents spends time on a weekly basis doing work at home that is directly related to his or her job. The proportion of parents who take work home from the job once a week or more has increased 10 percent since 1977, while the proportion who never take work home from the job has decreased by 16 percent.

So if parents are spending more time at work and fathers are spending more time with their children, where has this increased time come from? Employed parents know the answer to that question. They are spending less time on themselves:

> I haven't set aside time for myself all these years. That's one thing I really need to start working on, just for my own sanity.

On average, fathers in dual-earner families report they have 1.2 hours for themselves on workdays. Mothers have about 18 minutes less—0.9 hour per workday. This figure has decreased quite significantly over the past 20 years. On average, fathers in dual-earner families in 1997 had 54 fewer minutes for themselves on workdays than fathers did in 1977, while mothers have 42 fewer minutes for themselves on workdays today than mothers did in 1977.[5]

Even on days off work, fathers' time for themselves has also decreased—from 5.1 hours to 3.3 hours, a change of 1.8 hours over the past 20 years. Mothers' time for themselves on days off work has also decreased from 3.3 hours to 2.5 hours, a change of 0.8 hour.[6] So while both parents are sacrificing "time for themselves" to spend more time with their children, fathers have done so more than mothers (who, granted, were spending more time with their children to begin with).

WHAT DID WE FIND ABOUT TIME, EMPLOYED PARENTS, AND CHILDREN?

How Much Time Are Employed Parents Spending with Individual Children?

In the Ask the Children study,[7] we looked at how much time employed parents spend with just one of their children, randomly selected. Overall, employed mothers report

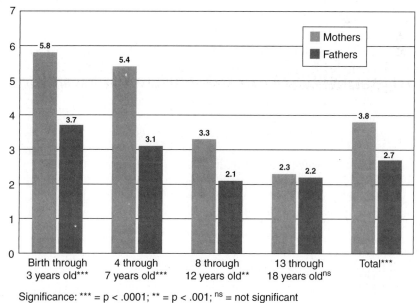

FIGURE 1 *Employed Parents: Hours Spent with Their Child on Workdays*

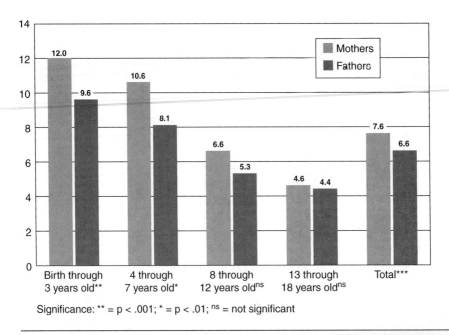

Significance: ** = p < .001; * = p < .01; ns = not significant

FIGURE 2 *Employed Parents: Hours Spent with Their Child on Nonworkdays*

spending about an hour more with their child than employed fathers on workdays (3.8 hours for mothers compared with 2.7 hours for fathers). On nonworkdays, mothers also report spending about an hour more with their child than employed fathers: 7.7 hours for mothers and 6.6 hours for fathers.[8]

When we look at the amount of time parents spend with children of different ages, there are shifts over time. Mothers spend more time with younger children than fathers do. By the teenage years, the amount of time that both parents spend declines—mothers' time more sharply than fathers'—to the point where there are no statistical differences in the amount of time mothers and fathers spend.

The same pattern applies to nonworkdays: Mothers reduce the amount of time they spend considerably as children age, dropping from 12 hours a day with a very young child to 4.6 hours with a teenager. Again, the difference in the amount of time mothers and fathers spend narrows and then disappears as the child grows up.[9] It is not simply that parents with an older child don't pay attention to that child; rather, children of these ages can be quite busy, doing their own thing. A mother with a teenage daughter says:

> I would like to be with my teenage daughter more, but she is so involved with schoolwork, activities, and her friends. Inevitably I will hang around the house weekend after weekend, and the one day that I make plans, she will come up to me and say, "Let's do something together today."

Since a few studies have found differences between how boys and girls are affected by their mothers' and fathers' work, I wondered whether there are gender differences here. I found that mothers spend more time with their daughters on workdays: 42.5 percent of mothers report spending 4.5 hours or more with their daughters on workdays compared with 24 percent who spend this much time with their sons. These differences occur during the teenage years, not when children are very young. In contrast, there is no difference in the amount of time mothers report spending with their daughters and their sons on nonworkdays. Moreover, there are no differences in the amount of time that fathers report spending with their sons and their daughters of all ages on workdays and nonworkdays.

How Much Time Do Children Say They Spend with Their Mothers and Fathers?

Now we turn full circle and look at children's estimates of the time they spend with their parents. Children in the third through twelfth grades were asked about how much time they spend with each of their parents—just the two of them or with other people—on a typical workday and on a typical nonworkday.[10]

Time Spent with Employed Parents on Workdays. The majority of children report spending considerable time with their mothers on workdays, although the amount of time fluctuates, depending on the age of the child. Twenty-nine percent of younger children (8 through 12 years old) say they spend 2 hours or less compared with 35 percent of older children (13 through 18 years old). At the other end of the spectrum, 47 percent

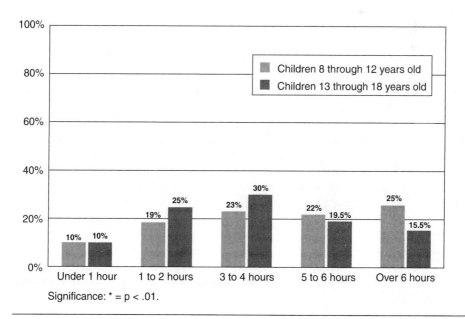

FIGURE 3 *Children Third through Twelfth Grades with Employed Mothers: Time Spent with Mother on Workdays*

of younger children and 35 percent of older children spend 5 hours or more with their mothers on workdays.

There is no difference in the amount of time that sons and daughters report spending with their mothers on workdays (although recall that mothers report spending more time with their teenage daughters than their teenage sons). It is not clear to me why there is a discrepancy between children's and parents' viewpoints, though children have less reason to overestimate than parents.

Children spend less time with their fathers than their mothers on workdays. Overall, 44 percent of children ages 8 through 18 years old report spending 2 hours or less with their fathers on workdays while 27 percent spend 5 hours or more. Interestingly, there is no significant difference in the amount of time younger and older children report spending with their fathers. Neither are there differences between boys and girls.

Time Spent with Parents on Nonworkdays.   An impressive 68.5 percent of both younger and older children say that they spend 5 hours or more with their mothers on nonworkdays. Although mothers do not report spending any more time with their daughters on nonworkdays than with their sons, children do report differences—girls say they spend more time with their mothers on nonworkdays than boys do. Here again, the discrepancy is hard to figure out.

Although children spend less time with their fathers than their mothers on nonworkdays, the amount of time they report spending with their fathers is still high: 66 per-

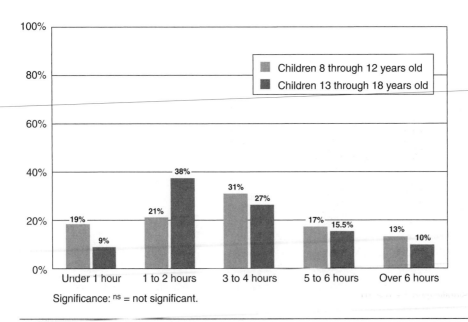

Significance: ns = not significant.

FIGURE 4   ***Children Third through Twelfth Grades with Employed Fathers: Time Spent with Father on Workdays***

cent of children—boys and girls alike—say that they spend 5 hours or more with their fathers on nonworkdays.

Do Parents and Children Feel They Have Enough Time Together?

Enough Time—According to Parents.   It is one thing to know the *amount* of time that parents and children report spending together, but it is another to know the *psychological meaning* of that time. Do parents feel they have enough time with their child? Do children concur? I especially wondered about fathers. Since fathers spend less time with their children—both by their own and by their children's estimates—are they more likely than mothers to want more time?

Overall, 50 percent of parents with children, birth through 18 years old, say that they have too little time with their child; however, beneath this overall figure *fathers*—much more so than mothers—seem to be yearning to be with their child: 56 percent of fathers versus 44 percent of mothers feel deprived of time with their child!

Because fathers work longer hours, they have less time for their lives off the job. One father of a 9-year-old boy reflects on the fleeting nature of time:

> Time is something, once it's gone, it's gone forever. So, you can look back and think, "Well, gee, I wish I would have spent more time with my kids when they were younger, I

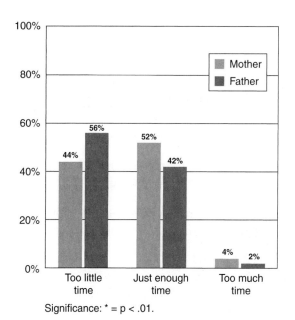

Significance: * = p < .01.

FIGURE 5   *Employed Parents with a Child Birth through 18: Enough Time with Their Child*

wish I would've spent more time with them when they were in high school," whatever. But once time is gone, that's it.

Mothers and fathers with a son or a daughter are equally likely to feel that they have too little time with this child. Moreover, parents of children of different ages—from infants to teenagers—are also equally likely to feel they have too little time.

Enough Time—According to Children.   The majority of children 8 through 18 years old feel that they have enough time with their employed mothers and fathers: 67 percent say that they have enough time with their mothers and 60 percent say they have enough time with their fathers. Paralleling the overall difference in the amount of time fathers and mothers spend with their children, children are more likely to feel that they have too little time with their *fathers* than with their mothers.

In our one-on-one interviews, a number of children talked about wanting more time with their fathers. One 12-year-old girl whose father takes frequent business trips says:

> I miss him. He's gone for short times. He calls from where he is. I'd rather have him at home during that time, but I know he has to do it because it's part of his job.

We heard a similar story from another girl whose father often works hard, including on weekends:

> I can't spend much time with him because he's working. Sometimes I go with him to work on the weekends. But I just wish that he wouldn't work so much.

Moreover, as has been the pattern thus far, children are far, far more likely to feel that they spend too little time with nonresident fathers (67 percent) than with resident fathers (35 percent).

These findings illustrate why it is so important to ask the children rather than to rely on our own assumptions. The issue of time with children has typically been framed in the public debate as mothers' issue. But when we ask the children, we see that fathers need to be front and center in this discussion as well.

Enough Time—Comparing Children's Views of Employed and Nonemployed Mothers.   All of the analyses in this chapter focus on employed mothers, but we also asked the question about having enough time with parents of children who have non-employed mothers. Children with employed mothers are no more likely to feel they have too little time with their mothers than children with nonemployed mothers. Stated differently, children with mothers at home and children with mothers who work are equally likely to feel they have enough time with their mother.

Enough Time—Comparing Children and Mothers.   What is also striking—and I must say unanticipated—is the discrepancy between the views of children and those of their mothers on whether they have enough time together. Almost half of mothers (49 percent) with a child 13 through 18 years old feel that they have too little time with their child, whereas less than one third of children (30 percent) this age concur. The results

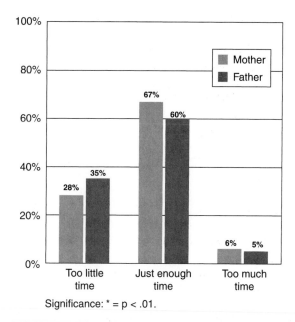

Significance: * = p < .01.

FIGURE 6 *Children Third through Twelfth Grades with Employed Parents: Enough Time with Mothers and Fathers*

comparing mothers and younger children do not reach statistical significance but follow the same pattern. Perhaps mothers of teenagers anticipate the soon-to-occur loss of everyday contact with their child as the child grows up, goes to college, moves out. So they often long for more time, whereas children may be more eager (though ambivalently so) to separate from their mothers.

Enough Time—Comparing Children and Fathers. Teenagers are more likely than their younger counterparts to want more time with their fathers. Thirty-nine percent of children 13 through 18 years old feel they have too little time with their fathers compared with 29 percent of children 8 through 12 years old. On the other hand, children do not feel as strongly about this issue as fathers. For example, almost two thirds of fathers (64 percent) with a child 13 through 18 years feel that they have too little time with this child, but only 39 percent of children this age feel the same way about time with their fathers.

Unexpected Findings about Employed Parents and Time

In sum, while 53 percent of employed parents with a child 8 through 18 feel they have too little time with their child, only 31 percent of children with employed parents feel the same way.

Typically, when issues of employed parents and time are discussed, the focus is on comparing children with employed versus nonemployed mothers. When we "ask the

TABLE 1   *Employed Mothers and Children with Employed Mothers: Enough Time Together*

	Children 8 through 12 years old	Children 13 through 18 years old
Too little time		
Mother	31%	49%
Child	24.5	30
Just enough time		
Mother	68%	50%
Child	69	65
Too much time		
Mother	1.5%	1%
Child	6.5	5
Significance:	*ns = not significant;*	**** = p < .0001.*

TABLE 2   *Employed Fathers and Children with Employed Fathers: Enough Time Together*

	Children 8 through 12 years old	Children 13 through 18 years old
Too little time		
Father	64%	64%
Child	29	39
Just enough time		
Father	35%	34%
Child	65	56
Too much time		
Father	1%	2%
Child	5.5	5
Significance:	**** = p < .0001;*	*** = p < .001.*

children," however, we find that there is no statistically significant difference between these two groups of children in feeling that they have too little time with their mothers.

Second, the public discussion has been more concerned with mothers than with fathers. When we turn to children, we find that children 8 through 18 years old are more likely to feel that they have too little time with their employed *fathers* than with their employed mothers. We also find that fathers—more so than mothers—feel they have too little time with their child.

Third, the public discussion about employed parents and time has centered on younger children, but we find that older children are more likely than younger children to feel that they have too little time with their fathers. Asking the children helps us see that the hidden story about working parents and time is about fathers and teenagers.

Editors' Note: *Notes for this reading can be found in the original source.*

■READING 25

How Families Still Matter: A Longitudinal Study of Youth in Two Generations

Vern L. Bengston, Timothy J. Biblarz, and Robert E. L. Roberts

How Families Still Matter casts doubt on much conventional wisdom about family decline during the last decades of the twentieth century. Generation X youth, who came of age in the 1990s, have been described as a "generation at risk" because they are the first cohort to have grown up in families with very high rates of divorce, "fatherlessness," and working mothers. There is concern that a decrease in family "togetherness" has spawned a generation of "slackers," because their achievements have appeared, at least in some studies, lower than that of previous generations. Authors Bengtson, Biblarz, and Roberts examine this claim and the evidence for and against the general proposition often advanced by politicians and pundits that the American family is at risk and declining in influence.

The authors draw from one of the longest-running longitudinal studies of families in the world—the Longitudinal Study of Generations, conducted at the University of Southern California—to discover whether parents are really less critical in shaping the life orientations and achievements of youth than they were a generation ago. Using survey data collected from as early as 1971, they compare the influence of parents (on self-confidence, values, and levels of achievement) on the Baby Boomer generation with that of Baby Boomer parents on their own Generation X children. The findings will be surprising to many readers.

The authors find, first, that the Generation X youth display higher, not lower, achievement orientations than did their Baby Boomer parents when they were young almost thirty years earlier. This is especially true for Generation X women, who have far outpaced their mothers' educational and occupational aspirations and are more ambitious than their male counterparts. Second, the strength of parents' influence on life choices and achievement is significant—and at about the same level—as that of the Baby Boomers' parents. Third, the negative effect of parental divorce on Generation X youths' achievement orientations has been small—certainly much lower than the "divorce is disaster" literature would predict. Maternal employment has had no impact on achievement orientations. Finally, while Generation X members' education and career aspirations and self-esteem are higher than that of their parents and youth, the data show similar values about individualism and humanism across generations. These findings indicate the resilience of family intergenerational bonds in the context of massive social changes since the 1960s. They suggest that in the twenty-first century, families and cross-generational connections will still be vitally important in influencing youths' values, choices, and their life course. The authors offer three new hypotheses about the processes that may be underlying their findings: (1) extended kin relations—particularly the role of grandparents—are more important than ever; (2) today's two-parent families may be more successful than ever before; and (3) through ups and downs, most mothers and fathers seem to continue to find ways to take good care of their children.

First, children's *feelings of solidarity and closeness* with their parents—particularly their mothers—were high in both generations, even though Generation Xers in childhood experienced rates of family disruption and maternal employment that were never experienced by their Baby Boomer parents. Solidarity with parents, in turn, was among the strongest positive predictors of youths' self-esteem and aspirations both today (Generation Xers) and in the previous generation (Baby Boomers).

Second, the effects of *parental divorce* on younger generations were not as significant as we had expected. Our evidence shows that three core dimensions of children's identity—aspirations, self-esteem, and values—are not strongly affected by the rise in divorce rate over the past thirty years. Most important, the experience of parental divorce did not erode the self-confidence of Generation X youth. Both Generation X youth who experienced parental divorce and those from traditional families had high and roughly equivalent levels of self-esteem. The late-adolescent Generation Xers who experienced their parents' divorce did have slightly lower aspirations than their Generation X counterparts whose parents did not divorce. While Generation X youth who experienced parental divorce were more materialistic than those who did not, they also held more collectivistic and less individualistic value orientations.

Third, the impact of *maternal employment* on child well-being was also not as significant as we had expected; in fact, it was negligible. One of our most important findings is that across two generations and twenty-six years, mothers' labor force participation did not harm children's status aspirations, self-esteem, or prosocial value orientations, and in some cases maternal employment proved beneficial to children (e.g., in the case of sons, maternal employment was associated with heightened self-esteem). Overall, it made little difference whether mothers worked or stayed home.

Fourth, when we examined parental influences on youths' aspirations, self-esteem, and values—the measure of the family's success in the socialization of its children—we found that *parents'* ability to *influence their children has not declined over recent generations.* Contrary to the hypothesis of family decline, our data indicate that the importance of parental influences for the self-esteem, aspirations, and values of their children has not diminished across generations.

Fifth, we found that *intergenerational transmission processes* are still working effectively to shape achievement orientations of youth. For one thing, these data indicate that *children learn from and model themselves after their parents* in occupational and educational aspirations and values. Children hold for themselves the values they learned from parents, such as high individualism or low materialism. For another, these data indicate the crucial role of *parental affirmation and intergenerational solidarity* in the transmission process. Children who are close to their parents have higher self-esteem and educational and occupational aspirations than those who are not close. Finally, *status inheritance* processes are important in achievement orientations. The social standing and resources of families continue to be crucial predictors of what youth come to aspire for themselves. Parental education and occupational status has a strong resemblance to the aspirations of youth in both generations—the Gen Xers as well as the Baby Boomers. Moreover, parental status and resources had the same effect on children from divorced families as they did in two-parent, long-married families.

In this study we compared the magnitude and direction of intergenerational influences on child outcomes, and the average child outcomes themselves, among families who were raising children in very different social milieus (the 1950s and 1960s in the case of our G2/G3 parent/child dyads, and the 1980s and 1990s in the case of our G3/G4 dyads), and in very different kinds of family structures and family divisions of labor over time. Our data indicate more continuity than contrast in the processes of intergenerational transmission and in the course of generational progress. With some exceptions, our families seem to be able to do well by their children, even under a variety of more or less taxing and challenging conditions. The contemporary families in our analysis, changed in many ways from their predecessors by high divorce rates and the shifting market and nonmarket responsibilities of parents, have been relatively successful in raising a generation of youth that appears well equipped to face the challenges of adulthood.

To sum up, our results demonstrate the continuing influence and enduring importance of families across recent generations, despite the effects of divorce, alternative family forms, and changing gender roles on family commitments and functions. The family is still fulfilling its basic task, the socialization of children, but in a world very different from that of the late 1950s. Its forms are more fluid, its relationship ties are both ascribed and chosen. Traditional "nuclear" family forms are no longer the norm in American society. Marriages, having evolved from "institutional" to "companionate" relationships based largely on bonds of affection, are more fragile. But despite this, family influences across generations are strong, and families still matter—much more than advocates of the family decline hypothesis would admit.

WHY FAMILIES STILL MATTER

These findings about *how* families are important raise the question of *why*. This is particularly relevant in light of other research and family decline theory predicting that recent social trends and changes in the family have significantly diminished intergenerational transmission processes and negatively affected child outcomes. Parental divorce, for example, has been shown to create emotional distress, behavioral or school difficulties and related problems for children in the short term (Dawson 1991; Kline, Johnson, and Tschann 1991) and over several decades (according to Wallerstein et al. 2000). The modal pattern is that children suffer substantial economic loss following divorce (since children most often reside with their mothers), and that children's relationships with nonresidential fathers decline over time following divorce. The effects of maternal employment on children should also be negative following the "family decline" hypothesis, because employment involves mothers' reallocation of time away from childrearing, and mothers' time investments in children have been shown to be central for many aspects of children's development.

Below we offer three propositions about why families still matter, why Generation X children have done well, and why divorce and maternal employment have not had (at least in our sample) the severe detrimental effects on children predicted by some commentators and researchers. We set forth these propositions as important issues to be tested in future research.

> **Proposition 1:** Families are adapting by expanding support across generations. There is increasing interdependence and exchange across several generations of family members; this expansion has protected and enhanced the well-being of new generations of children.

> **Proposition 2:** Nondivorced, two-parent families are more successful than their counterparts a generation ago. Relational processes within two-parent families are changing over time in ways that have enhanced the well-being of new generations of children.

> **Proposition 3:** Maternal investment in children has not declined over generations. Despite growth in the rate of labor force participation among mothers, maternal investment in children has remained high and constant over time, and this has assured a generally positive level of well-being among new generations of children.

In a sense, these propositions summarize our major findings. But our data are limited and the story they tell is incomplete. We present the propositions as issues to be tested in further research, using larger and nationally representative samples.

Proposition 1: Families Are Adapting by Expanding Support across Generations

The apparent resiliency of Generation X children who have experienced recent changes in family structure and roles may be accounted for by the adaptive and compensatory processes that their families have drawn on, particularly in times of need. These processes may often involve expanding the family to bring additional parent-like figures and family members into the lives of children. African American families, for example, have had a long history of adaptation to family disruption induced (in fact, often forced) by slavery, segregation, employment discrimination, and other manifestations of racism. Research like Hill's (1999) *The Strengths of African American Families* (also Johnson 1999; Oates 1999) has emphasized the resilient capacities of African American families to care and provide for children under difficult conditions (such as fatherlessness) by forming extended and fictive kin relations. In father-absent African American families historically, the "fatherly" role was often played by someone other than a biological father, and aunts, uncles, and grandparents (biologically or socially related) have been instrumental in the rearing of children.

An important direction for further family research and theory involves the application of this "families adapt by extending kin" concept to other kinds of families, particularly those who have experienced disruptive events such as divorce. The relationships that children and parents have with their grandparents following divorce, in particular, should be carefully explored (Bengtson 2001). Emotional closeness and support from grandparents have been shown to compensate for or mitigate divorce-related family processes and custodial-parent role overload that can have a negative impact on the well-being of both adult children and grandchildren (Johnson and Barer 1987; Silverstein, Giarrusso, and Bengtson 1998). For example, greater grandparental involvement with children could compensate for the temporary declines in mothers' attention and time with her children immediately following divorce. In this situation, children would continue to receive the adult-family-member time investment that is so essential to their development. This type of compensation may ameliorate the risk of negative outcomes for today's children in divorced families.

Grandparental involvement in postdivorce families is an especially important potential source of social support (Johnson 2000; Johnson and Barer 1987) because—unlike day-care centers, after-school programs, babysitters, or nannies—grandparents typically have a high level of concern for the interests of their children and grandchildren. Grandparents today bring other strengths to their family roles. Grandparents are considerably more financially secure than they were just twenty-five years ago; they have a higher standard of living (Treas 1995). At the same time, grandparents today are healthier and much more active, with many more years ahead of them after retirement. Grandparents today, as they age, can expect fewer years with chronic illnesses and limiting disabilities than previous generations (Hayward and Heron 1999). These positive trends may make grandparent/grandchildren relationships far more important and rewarding than ever before.

In the context of the diversity of family conditions that exist today, there are pressures and opportunities to shift more familial responsibility to members of the extended family (Bengtson 2001). Contemporary families may be moving beyond the confines of the shrinking nuclear family to encompass the broader support and emotional resources of multigenerational families, relationships that are both ascribed and created, where (as Robert Frost noted), ". . . when you have to go there . . . they have to take you in." And increasingly they do. This can be seen in the growing incidence of grandparents raising grandchildren, where the middle generations' marriages dissolve, or where there are other difficulties (such as drug addiction) that interfere with the younger adults' ability to parent. To the extent that traditional nuclear families weaken or transform themselves, the strengths and resources of the multigenerational family may take on new importance.

At the same time that exchange, dependence, and support among multiple generations of family members are becoming increasingly important, so, too, are patterns of intergenerational exchange, dependence, and support over the life course. In the new economic reality of postindustrialism, for example, many midlife parents still have their young adult children at home or at school. Generation X young adults will be in college far longer on average than their Baby Boomer parents were, extending the period of economic dependence on the resources of their parents. This extended period of intergenerational exchange and support tends to strengthen the bonds of solidarity between parents and children as well (Bengtson, Rosenthal, and Burton 1995; Elder 1994). In an unexpected way, these examples of "prolonged parenting" by those now at midlife (that is, Baby Boomers) may reflect, in practice, the shift that we found in this study toward more collectivistic values. Especially in light of the ways in which families are diversifying, we believe that multi- and intergenerational exchange and support among family members over the life course of children must become an important object of study in examining consequences for children of recent changes in the family.

Proposition 2: Today's Nondivorced, Two-Parent Families Are More Successful Than Their Counterparts a Generation Ago

A major finding in our study was the discovery of strengths in a family type that is typically used as a reference category but not as often explored in its own right: the two-biological parent family of the 1990s and beyond. The aspirations, self-esteem, and values of the Generation Xers from these families were significantly more positive than those of comparable two-parent families in the previous generation (Baby Boomer youth). In several respects, today's two-parent families seem to be more effective in the socialization of their children than yesterday's two-parent families.

It is likely these two-parent families are to some extent a select group, as less happily married or dysfunctional parents of Generation Xers would have already divorced (unlike similarly predisposed marital partners of earlier generations, who would have found divorce much more difficult to accomplish). Nevertheless, uncovering how today's two-parent families have been successful in navigating the postmodern social structure—balancing work and home, negotiating divisions of labor, and finding individual self-fulfillment while at the same time maintaining a high level of investment in children—may reveal family processes of adaptation that can be of use to all kinds of families. Once uncovered and described, these processes can also be compared—for similarity and difference—with those occurring in the new extended families that have accompanied family diversification.

There are several important questions that research on today's two-parent, long-married families should pursue. For example, are these families characterized by fairly traditional gender-based divisions of labor, or do these parents share a more equitable division of housework, childcare, paid employment, and decision-making? The uniquely high levels of humanistic and collectivistic values among Generation Xers from two-parent families in our study may be related to a greater egalitarianism between still-married mothers and fathers in the Baby Boom generation. Traditionally, women in the United States have married men who were better educated than themselves. Improvement in women's educational attainment over the past thirty years has, for the first time, reversed this trend. In fact, since 1980 marriages in which women were better educated than their husbands have become more likely than marriages in which men were better educated than their wives (Qian 1998). Women's greater education and economic power within marriage may mean that they participate in household decision-making about childrearing, consumption, and other life choices not only in their role as wives and mothers but as educational equals and breadwinners. This change within marriages may have served children well. We found, for example, that among two-biological-parent families, mother/child bonds enhanced the values and self-esteem of Generation X youth more than they did those of the previous generation.

The role of "absentee" fathers in a context of high divorce has been much investigated. We have found, consistent with other research (Amato 1994; Amato and Keith 1991), that divorced fathers have become increasingly disadvantaged in terms of their emotional bonds with their young adult children when compared with mothers. Parental divorce has reduced the ability of Baby Boomer fathers to influence their Generation X children's aspirations, self-esteem, and prosocial values, while mother/child affective bonds and maternal influence have tended to remain high. Perhaps this is a reflection of a broader cultural shift toward the "feminization of kinship" relations that has been observed by other family researchers (Fry 1995; Hagestad 1986; Rossi and Rossi 1990).

While evidence has accumulated showing decline in paternal investment in children among divorced dads, some striking evidence—particularly that assembled and analyzed by Bianchi (2000)—has also shown that today's married fathers are exhibiting an unprecedented, high level of involvement with their children. According to time diary studies between 1965 and 1998, fathers' time spent with children grew from about 25 percent to fully two-thirds the amount of time that mothers spent with children. The greater involvement of today's fathers within two-parent family contexts may be contributing to the high levels of self-esteem and ambition that we observed in the aggregate among Generation X youth. More generally, good parenting on the part of fathers—custodial or noncustodial—has been shown to enhance many dimensions of children's well-being (Lamb 1997).

We have suggested that recent demographic trends (e.g., increased longevity and active life expectancy) may have intersected with other demographic trends (growth in nonmarital fertility, divorce, remarriage, and the labor force participation of mothers) to facilitate the growth of new kinds of extended families in the United States. The numbers and kinds of multigenerational family members available to families and children have certainly increased (Bengtson 2001). The support functions served by multigenerational family members may also have increased, accordingly. This kind of family expansion appears adaptive; that is, under diverse and potentially disruptive conditions, it may be a way that families care for their children. It may also lie behind many of the findings of this study: that families of all kinds still matter for children.

We have also proposed that, over time, processes within two-biological-parent families have shifted in ways that benefit children. We believe that an intriguing and important next step is to explore potential similarities and differences in processes that occur in these new-form two-parent families, on the one hand, and these new-form extended families, on the other. For many families (probably an increasing number), close multigenerational ties are adaptive and very much needed in a fast-changing world. The adaptive strengths evolving from these family arrangements—including, perhaps, shared parenting, authoritative parenting practices (not just necessarily by parents, but also by additional parent-like figures), egalitarian household arrangements, more collectivistic and humanistic value orientations—may parallel to some extent what is occurring in today's two-parent families, including the Baby Boom parents with Generation X children in our study. It may be that through their intergenerational socialization processes and practices, both two-parent families and extended multigenerational families—though distinct in their relationship intensity or the immediacy of their responsibilities for children—engender similar patterns and strengths.

Proposition 3: Maternal Investment in Children Has Not Declined Over Time

Social critics became alarmed at the huge growth in the labor force participation of mothers over the past thirty years, for fear that the well-being of new generations of children would be compromised by a lack of attention given to them by their mothers. However, our study shows nonexistent, small, or ambiguous effects of mothers' labor force participation on children. This is similar to findings of other researchers (Parcel and Menaghan 1994).

The prognostications of negative consequences were not supported empirically, in part because they rested on a shaky foundation: that the stay-at-home moms of yesteryear surely spent more time with their children than working moms do today. Bianchi (2000) has questioned this assumption. She argues that the amount of nonmarket time that mothers invested in children in the past has been overestimated. While employment rates for mothers earlier in this century were much lower than today, mothers in the past also faced more time-consuming family work and domestic chores, relied on older children to spend time with the younger children, and had less education. Education is positively correlated with the amount of direct time mothers spend caring for children. Bianchi also suggests that the extent to which paid work takes mothers' time away from children today has been overestimated. The net result of these often offsetting trends, according to many of the studies Bianchi draws from, is a relatively constant level of maternal investment in children over time, and a conclusion, consistent with the findings of our study, that employment has generally not meant decline in mothers' time with and care for children.

This constancy in maternal investment may help explain why the consequences of family change for Generation X youth were not more evident. In terms of their actual time allocation to children, the mothers of our Baby Boomer and Generation X youth, respectively, may not have been that different. Generation X children who experienced divorce felt as close to their mothers as those who did not, suggesting again a kind of safety net provided by a generally high and stable average level of maternal investment. Other research has shown that in the context of divorce, mothers tend to sustain a high level of emotional investment in children amidst spousal conflict and marital disruption, whereas fathers' relations with children diminish as their relationship with spouses diminish (Belsky et al. 1991). This maternal investment (the parameters and variations of which need to be carefully explored) may be linked to the patterns borne out by our data showing how families—divorced or not, dual-employed or not—are bringing up children with high self-esteem on average and aspirations that exceed those of each generation before them.

High levels of paternal investment and involvement (among both residential and nonresidential fathers) also positively affect many aspects of children's lives, but evidence shows that, on average, levels of paternal involvement are relatively low (Simons et al.

1996). However, if upward trends have been occurring in the proportion of highly involved, "good dads" as described by Furstenberg (1988), this too may be linked to some of the findings reported here.

THE PARADOX OF CONTINUITY AND CHANGE ACROSS GENERATIONS

In concluding this examination of family functioning and change at the start of the twenty-first century, we return to a question raised by philosophers and playwrights (and more recently by social historians and social scientists) over six millennia of human experience: *How much is changing, and how much remains the same, across generations today?*

Karl Mannheim (1952) called this "the sociological problem of generations": the ongoing tension between continuity and change, affirmation and innovation, as each new generation comes into contact with the existing social order represented by their parents' generation, and how they attempt to adapt to or radically change this heritage.

Mannheim used this generational tension as a means to explain the development of social and political movements in Europe throughout the eighteenth and nineteenth centuries, from cultural changes in style and art to political revolution and warfare. While Mannheim's sweeping sociopolitical theory has not been supported by subsequent analyses, his central argument has become a central premise of life-course theory today.

The paradox of change and continuity is reflected in our data on family influences on younger generations during the past three decades. We have approached this issue from three analytic levels, each central to the life-course theoretical perspective in family sociology and family psychology.

At the *macrosocial* level of analysis, it is important to recognize the changing configurations of human demography reflected in the age structures of society, the social metabolism of changes in birth and death rates, immigration and emigration, longevity and morbidity. These trends are crucial for twenty-first-century societies, and particularly for cross-generational relationships (Bengtson and Putney 2000).

At the *mesosocial* level, the life-course perspective calls us to inquire about the interactive effects of maturation, historical placement, and emerging sociohistorical events on generational differences and continuities. And at the *microsocial* level, our focus is on the processes by which generations within a family pass on the knowledge and values, and the material and psychological resources that its members need to live successfully in society.

It is within the family—the *microsocial* level—that the paradox of continuity and change, the problem of balancing individuality and allegiance, is most immediate. It is a fluid, unending process and at times contentious. At times we think that surely a break from the past has occurred: Families aren't what they used to be; families are in trouble. Yet if we look closely, we can see threads of continuity and patterns of influence across generations. These patterns within families across historical time have been the focus of our study. How do they emerge? How are they sustained? What do they tell us about the structure and function of families and intergenerational relations in our now postindustrial world?

The family is the fulcrum balancing change and continuity over time in human society. It has been so in the past; we believe it will be so in the twenty-first century. We look to the family as the context for negotiating the problems of continuity and change, of individuality and integration, between and within the generations in ways that allow the continuous re-creation of society. Families still matter.

Editors' Note: *References for this reading can be found in the original source.*

IV Families in Society

During the 1950s and 1960s, family scholars and the mass media presented an image of the typical, normal, or model U.S. family. It included a father, a mother, and two or three children living a middle-class existence in a single-family home in an area neither rural nor urban. Father was the breadwinner, and mother was a full-time homemaker. Both were white, as were virtually all families portrayed in the mass media.

No one denied that many families and individuals fell outside the standard nuclear model. Single persons, one-parent families, two-parent families in which both parents worked, three-generation families, and childless couples abounded. Three- or four-parent families were not uncommon, as one or both divorced spouses often remarried. Many families, moreover, neither white nor well-off, also varied from the dominant image. The image scarcely reflected the increasing ratio of older people in the empty nest and retirement parts of the life cycle. But like poverty before its "discovery" in the mid-1960s, family complexity and variety existed on some dim fringe of semi-awareness.

When they were discussed, individuals or families who departed from the standard model were analyzed in a context of pathology. Studies of one-parent families or working mothers, for example, focused on the harmful effects to children of such "deviant" situations. Couples childless by choice were assumed to possess some basic personality inadequacy. Single persons were similarly interpreted, or else thought to be homosexual. Homosexuals symbolized evil, depravity, degradation, and mental illness.

Curiously, although social scientists have always emphasized the pluralism of U.S. society in terms of ethnic groups, religion, and geographic region, the concept of pluralism had rarely been applied to the family. In the wake of the social upheavals of the 1960s and 1970s, middle-class "mainstream" attitudes toward women's roles, sexuality, and the family were transformed. Despite the backlash that peaked in the 1980s, the "traditional" family did not return. U.S. families became increasingly diverse, and Americans were increasingly willing to extend the notion of pluralism to family life.

The selections in this part of the book discuss not only diversity in families, but also the reality that families are both embedded in and sensitive to changes in the social structure and economics of U.S. life. The economic pressures on families since the mid-1970s have done as much as feminism to draw women into the paid workforce. The two-parent family in which both parents work is the form that now comes closest to being the "typical American family." In the 1950s, the working mother was considered deviant, even though many women were employed in the labor force. It was taken for granted that maternal employment must be harmful to children; much current research on working mothers still takes this "social problem" approach to the subject.

Katherine S. Newman's article reports on her ethnographic studies of family life among the working poor in America's inner cities. She contrasts media images of "the underclass"—with its drug-addicted mothers and swaggering, criminal men who father children by as many different women as possible—with the realities she observed. She found that while there are families that unfortunately fit this description, they are a small minority. Moreover, such families are despised by the majority of inner-city residents and do not reflect the dominant family values of those communities. Nevertheless, despite their values, these families are not carbon copies of mainstream, middle-class ones. Newman shows how economic pressures at the bottom of the income scale affect the psychological and social functioning of people who are trying to "play by the rules."

What happens inside the family as women share the role of the family breadwinner with their husband? Arlie Hochschild and Anne Machung take a close look at the emotional dynamics inside the family when both parents work full-time and the "second shift"—the work of caring for children and maintaining the home—is not shared equitably. The selection from their book portrays a painful dilemma shared by many couples in their study: The men saw themselves as having equal marriages; they were doing more work around the house than their fathers had done and more than they thought other men did. The women, whose lives were different from their own mothers', saw their husbands' contributions as falling far short of true equality. They resented having to carry more than their share of the "second shift," yet stifled their angry feelings in order to preserve their marriages. Still, this strategy took its toll on love and intimacy.

In their article, Kathleen Gerson and Jerry A. Jacobs challenge widespread notions about families and work; first, the notion that the average person is putting in more time at work than earlier generations did, and second, that there has been a cultural shift in which people have come to prefer the workplace to the home. Gerson and Jacobs have found that average working time has not changed all that much, but that this average is misleading. Rather, the workforce has come to be divided; one group of workers is putting in very long work weeks, while another group is unable to find enough work to meet their needs. In fact, given a choice, both men and women, especially those with young children, would prefer more time at home and greater flexibility at work.

In addition to time pressures, as Lillian B. Rubin writes in "Families on the Fault Line," words such as *downsizing, restructuring,* and *reengineering* have become all too familiar and even terrifying to blue-collar workers and their families. Rubin had carried out a similar study of working-class families two decades earlier. In the 1970s, she found that while these families were never entirely secure, they felt they had a grasp of the American dream. Most owned their own homes, and expected that their children would do even better. In the more recent study, the people Rubin interviewed perceived a discontinuity between past and present, a sense that something had gone very wrong in the country.

Thirty-five percent of the men in the study were either unemployed at the time or had experienced bouts of unemployment. Parents and children had given up hope of upward mobility, or even that the children could own homes comparable to the one they had grown up in. The families, particularly the men, were angry, yet perplexed about who or what to blame—the government, high taxes, immigrants, minorities, women—for displacing men from the workplace.

About two out of five working Americans—40 percent of our labor force—face additional pressures from their nonstandard work schedules. As Harriet Presser explains, today's nonstop 24/7 economy makes it necessary for millions of people, mostly lower income, to work through the night, on weekends, or on shifts 12 or more hours long. This work pattern has some advantages for families, but it also puts a heavy burden of stress on them. Nonstandard schedules are particularly hard on single mothers and married parents with children.

Not even the solid middle class is immune from the stresses of the current economy. Millions of employed, educated, and homeowning Americans are in financial trouble, having mortgages foreclosed, even filing for bankruptcy. Indeed, in 2004, more families filed for bankruptcy than for divorce. In their article Elizabeth Warren and Amelia Warren Tyagi debunk what they call "the over-consumption myth"—the idea that Americans are spending themselves into financial ruin for luxuries they don't really need. Instead, the rising costs of housing, decent elementary schools, and college tuition have placed middle-class parents at greater risk than in earlier generations.

The next group of articles address family diversity along a number of dimensions— economic status, race, ethnicity, and sexual orientation. In recent years, family researchers have recognized that diversity is more complicated than previously thought. It's too simple to sort people into distinct categories—African Americans, Hispanics, Asians, European Americans, or gays. These aspects of diversity cross-cut one another, along with many other aspects of difference—such as social class, religion, region, family structure (e.g., stepfamilies), and many more.

There is also great diversity within groups. In his article Ronald L. Taylor explores diversity among African American families. He recalls being troubled that the stereotypes of black Americans that appeared in the media as well as in social science did not reflect the families he knew growing up in a small southern city. The dominant image of black families remains the low-income, single-parent family living in a crime-ridden inner-city neighborhood. Yet only a quarter of African American families fits that description. All African Americans share a common history of slavery and segregation, and they still face discrimination in housing and employment. Taylor discusses the impact of these past and present features on African American family life.

Latino families are now emerging as America's largest "minority." They are more diverse than other groups, as Maxine Baca Zinn and Barbara Wells show in their article. Mexican Americans are the largest group among Latinos and have been the most studied. But Puerto Ricans, Cubans, and Central and South Americans differ from those of Mexican background, and among themselves. These differences are not just cultural, but reflect the immigrants' social and economic status in their home country as well as the reasons for and the timing of their departure for the United States.

While family life in America has always been diverse, gay and lesbian families are a new addition to the mix. For some peple, homosexuality is immoral and unnatural. But as Judith Stacey makes clear in her article, families with same-sex parents are here to stay. Stacey traces the emergence of these families in the wake of the gay liberation movements of the 1970s, the growing willingness of courts and legislatures to grant legal recognition to gay families, and the fierce backlash against such efforts. Stacey argues that children in both gay and heterosexual families would benefit if both law and society would be more accepting of diversity in American family life.

While gay couples seek to be recognized as "normal American families," the same image of normality serves a framework for the grown children of Korean and Vietnamese immigrants trying to make sense of their own lives. They tend to see their own parents as deficient in comparison to the image; they seem too strict and emotionally distant. On the other hand, their own cultures seem superior when it comes to children taking care of their aging parents. Karen Pyke concludes that public images of the family serve as ideological templates that can shape the wishes and disappointments experienced by children of immigrants. Indeed, cultural images of families, such as the Cleavers and other TV sitcom families of the 1950s, can have similar emotional effects on all Americans, no matter what their background.

In the final section we look at three kinds of family trouble. First, we consider an issue that is rarely thought of as a family problem: the huge spike in the prison population in recent decades, due to the "war on drugs" and other get-tough-on-crime policies. The United States now locks up a higher proportion of its citizens than any other country in the world. Of course, people who commit violent crimes should go to prison, both as punishment and to protect the community. But about half those now in prison for long sentences are not there for violent acts. As Jeremy Travis points out here, prison places a huge burden on the families of prisoners, especially on their relationships with partners and children. He also spells out the ripple effects that high rates of imprisonment have on poor and minority communities—for example, creating a shortage of marriageable men.

Thus, Travis gives part of the answer to the questions that Katherine Edin and Maria Kefalas address in their article on poor unmarried young mothers. Why do they have babies when they know they will have to struggle to support them? Have they given up the marriage norm? The Bush administration is currently promoting marriage as a poverty policy, on the theory that if low-income people marry, they will no longer be poor. In contrast, Edin and Kefalas find that this kind of thinking has it backwards—their research shows that these women revere marriage, and about 70 percent will eventually marry. But in America's poor neighborhoods, plagued by joblessness, drug and alcohol abuse, as well as high rates of crime and imprisonment, a good man is hard to find. Edin and Kefalas conclude that the real cure for poverty and "too-early" motherhood is access to good jobs for both men and women.

The most dramatic and disturbing form of family trouble is violence between family members. The media regularly report on shocking cases of child abuse or wife battering. But as Denise Hines and Kathleen Malley-Morrison point out, not everyone agrees on what should be considered family violence in the first place. What about spanking, for example? Should any amount of physical punishment by a parent be considered child abuse? What about a couple of swats on a child's rear end to keep him or her from doing something dangerous? The authors discuss the controversies over these matters and suggest some ways to resolve them.

9 *Work and Family*

■ R E A D I N G   2 6

Family Values against the Odds

Katherine S. Newman

Rosa Lee Cunningham, the subject of Leon Dash's Pulitzer Prize–winning series in the *Washington Post*, is an epitome of poverty for the end of the twentieth century.[1] Born the eldest girl in a Washington, D.C., family that had been liberated from the privations of southern sharecropping only in the 1930s, Rosa Lee quickly spiraled down into oblivion. Rosa Lee's first child was born when she was a mere fourteen years old. By the time she was twenty-four, Rosa Lee's children numbered eight and their six fathers were nowhere to be seen. She raised her kids on her own by waitressing in nightclubs, selling drugs, and shoplifting. In the wake of her own disillusionment and the overwhelming burden of taking care of her children, Rosa Lee was drawn to heroin. When stealing to support her family and her habit proved unreliable, she sold herself on the street and then turned her own daughter into a hooker to maintain the needed cash flow.

Responses to Dash's series, and the book that followed, have taken a predictable path: reviewers have been as worried as they have been disgusted by the cultural disintegration Rosa Lee and her ilk represent. Rosa Lee, who could not stay away from men of questionable character, and then did disastrously poorly by the children that resulted, takes center stage as the prototypical underclass mother, the prime mover in her own despair. And the crime and degradation that follow are depicted as the inevitable result of a culture of poverty so deep that it defies remedy. No jobs program, no drug program, no heavenly social worker, can rescue someone like Rosa Lee Cunningham. She is a lost soul, with children condemned to repeat her mistakes,[2] while the rest of society suffers the consequences of predatory criminals in its midst.

Powerful portraits of this kind have shaped public impressions of inner-city families. They present implicit explanations for how poor people fall to the bottom of society's heap: by failing to control their impulses. American culture is predisposed to find such an explanation appealing, since it rests upon the view that people are masters of their own destinies, that they can, by dint of individual effort, control the circumstances of their lives. Those that fail fall to the ground where they belong, not because they have been denied opportunity, or are victims of forces larger than anyone could control, but because they have succumbed to temptation or lack the brains to do any better—the story told by Herrnstein and Murray's book *The Bell Curve.* It is a story as old as the Puritans and as resonant today as it was in the seventeenth century.

The inner city does indeed have more than its share of families like the Cunninghams. Their problems reflect the crushing personal costs of living in parts of our country where good jobs have gone the way of the dinosaurs, where schools can be hard to distinguish from penitentiaries, and where holding families together has become women's work, while the means to do so have become the object of a fierce competition. More than a few in central Harlem have found themselves in Rosa Lee's situation.

But they are a minority, and a despised one at that. . . . Journalists and scholars who write about the Rosa Lees of this world have focused their energies on those inner-city residents who are the most troubled and who inflict the greatest damage on their neighbors. Their passions are understandable, for in keeping with the spirit that animated the original War on Poverty, they want to reawaken America's conscience and persuade us that we have a cancer growing in the midst of our prosperity. That message worked effectively in the 1960s, when the country was bursting with economic growth, the middle class was secure in its comforts, and faith in the capacity of government to eradicate social ills had not yet been eviscerated.

The same message delivered in the 1990s has had the opposite impact. Focusing on the deviant cases, on the whoring mothers, the criminal fathers, the wilding teenagers, and the abandoned toddlers, merely confirms a knowing hopelessness or worse: a Darwinian conviction that perhaps we should just "let it burn," sacrificing the present generation in the hope of rehabilitating future ghetto dwellers. Attitudes have hardened in part as the litany of broken lives dominates the only "news" in print from the inner city.

It would be absurd to suggest that the downbeat reports are untrue. The "underclass" story is a persistent, intractable, and most of all depressing reality for those who cannot escape it. But there is a war for the soul of the ghetto, and it has two sides. On the other side of deviance lie the families who embrace mainstream values, even if they don't look like Ozzie and Harriet, who push their children to do better, even when they have not progressed far in life themselves. Indeed, these families—the working poor and many a "welfare family" as well—are the first to condemn Rosa Lees of their own neighborhood, to point to them as examples of what they don't want to be.

Who is winning this culture war? What are the *dominant* values of inner-city residents? The sociological emphasis on separated subcultures in the inner city has ignored the power of mainstream models and institutions like schools, the influence of the media, the convictions of poor parents, and the power of negative examples to shape the moral world of the ghetto poor. We must not confuse the irregular social structures of families—which do indeed depart from the canonical forms of middle-class society—with a separate set of values. Structure and culture can diverge in ghetto society as they do elsewhere in this country.

FAMILY VALUES

Latoya has a complicated family tree. Her mother, Ilene, who is on disability because of her diabetes, lives in the Bronx, far enough away to be in another world. Latoya's father,

Alvin, has had many jobs in the course of his adult life—working mainly as a truck driver—and has only recently, in his later years, become once again a constant presence in Latoya's life. His problems with alcohol have made him a nuisance at times, but he has been welcomed back into the extended family fold because "he's blood" and has, for now at least, made a sincere effort to leave the booze behind.

Many years ago, Latoya's father began living with Elizabeth, then a recent migrant from rural Georgia, from a sleepy little town where there was nothing much to do and nowhere to go. First chance she got, Lizzie had boarded a bus for New York and begun her lifelong career cleaning houses for wealthy whites on New York's Upper East Side. She has been doing domestic work now for about twenty-five years, during which she gave birth to two daughters, Natasha and Stephanie, Latoya's half sisters through the father they share.

Though Alvin has been only sporadically in the picture, Latoya, Natasha, and Stephanie became a devoted band of sisters who look to Lizzie as the spiritual and practical head of the family. Together they form an extended family of long standing. They live within a few blocks of one another; they attend church together, especially on the important holidays.

Latoya was the first of the sisters to land a job at Burger Barn, but she was able to get Natasha on the crew not long thereafter. The two half sisters have worked together, covering for one another, blowing off the steam generated by confrontational customers, and supporting one another in the face of problem-seeking managers for nearly five years now. Little sister Stephanie, a junior in high school who has also had a summer stint at the Barn, makes it possible for Latoya to maintain a steady presence at work. It falls to Stephanie to retrieve Latoya's children from their city-funded day care center and after-school programs on those days when Latoya has to work late. Stephanie is often the one who stays with her nieces and nephews when Latoya has to work the night shift. Natasha used to do the same for Latoya.

Without the support that Natasha and Stephanie provide, Latoya would have a very hard time holding on to her job. But if we reduced the role these sisters play in Latoya's life to the instrumental need for emergency child care, we would miss the true depth of their interdependence. This is really one family, spread over several physical households in a pattern that will be familiar to readers of Carol Stack's classic book *All Our Kin*. Stack describes the complex exchange relations that characterize the families of the "Flats," a poor community in southern Illinois where goods and people circulate in a never-ending swap system. Reciprocal relations provide mothers with an insurance system against scarcity, unpredictable landlords, jobs that come and go, AFDC checks that get cut off without warning, and men who give what they can but much of the time find they have little to contribute.

FAMILY CIRCLES—SUPPORT STRUCTURES AMONG THE WORKING POOR

No one in Latoya's extended family network is on welfare; the adults are working, even Alvin, drinking problem and all. The children are in school. Yet because they are poor as well, these folk live in clusters of households that are perpetually intertwined. Although Latoya and Lizzie are separate "heads of households" as the Census Bureau might define them, in a very real sense they are one social system with moving parts that cannot stand alone. The older sisters, Natasha and Latoya, go out to clubs together when they can get Stephanie to baby-sit; together they hatch surprise birthday celebrations for Lizzie. Joining forces with their cousins, aunts, and uncles, they haul turkeys and cranberries up the stairs to whichever apartment can hold the largest number of people when it is time to host the Thanksgiving feast. And when Christmas comes, Latoya's children, sisters, and cousins and Lizzie and Alvin dress up in their Sunday best and lay claim to nearly a whole pew in the Baptist church several blocks away. Lizzie complains that her children don't attend church in the regular way she does, a habit born of her southern origins. But like many American families, Latoya and her sisters honor their mother's attachment to the church and participate in this family ritual.

Latoya, Natasha, Stephanie, and Lizzie have deliberately stayed close to one another not only because they need one another for practical support but because they value family above all else. "Family are your best friends," Natasha explains. Latoya is Natasha's closest friend, the person she socializes with, the person she confides in, her defender at work, the woman she goes shopping with when they want to look their best after hours. Danielle, cousin to them both, is part of the same inner circle, and together with her children they all form a tightly knit extended family.

Indeed, Latoya's three children look upon their aunts, Natasha and Stephanie, as permanent members of their household, people they can depend on to braid their hair for church, answer the occasional homework question, and bring them home an illicit burger or two. It was rare to find Latoya and her children at home without one of her half sisters as well.

Public perceptions of America center around middle-class nuclear families as the norm, the goal toward which others should be striving. Yet in those suburban households, it would be rare to find the intensity of relations that knits these sisters and cousins together, keeping them in daily contact with one another. Middle-class Americans value autonomy, including autonomous relations between generations and siblings once they reach adulthood. And, of course, if they have a stable hold on a decent income, there is little forcing them together into the sort of private safety net that Latoya and her relatives maintain.

The same could be said, and then some, for the immigrant families who make up a significant part of Harlem's low-wage workforce. Dominicans, Haitians, Jamaicans, West Africans, and South Americans from various countries have settled in Harlem's outer pockets. Immigrant workers in the low-wage economy depend upon extensive family networks—composed of seasoned migrants who have lived in New York for some time and those newly arrived—to organize their housing, child care, and a pool of income that they can tap when the need arises. Streaming into New York in an age-old pattern of chain migration, immigrants are often faced with the need to support family members back home while they attempt to meet the far higher costs of living they encounter in their adopted city. Families that are ineligible for government benefits routinely provided to the native-born must work long hours, pack a large number of people into small apartments, and recruit as many wage earners into the network as possible.

Immigrants cluster into apartment buildings in much the same fashion as the African-American poor do, both because relatives have been instrumental in helping their family members find housing and because proximity makes it that much easier to organize collective child-minding or communal meals. In Carmen's building there are five households linked together by kinship connections. Their members move freely between them, opening the refrigerator door in one to see whether there's anything good to eat, watching television in another because it has a cable hookup, using the one phone that hasn't been cut off for nonpayment. Carmen's grandmother watches her grandchildren, a half-dozen in all now, so that their parents can go to work.

Yet to really understand the meaning of family in Carmen's life, one has to look back to the Dominican Republic, where her mother and one of her sisters still live. Carmen had to leave her mother behind to join her father and his kin, a transition necessitated both by her ambitions and by the declining purchasing power of her mother's paycheck. Carmen sends back money whenever she can, usually once a month, and that remittance spells the difference between a decent standard of living in *La Republica* and a slide into poverty.[3] For Carmen, though, this is a poor substitute for the intimacy she longs for, the daily love and affection of her mother. What she really wants, more than anything in this world, is to obtain a green card so that she can sponsor her mother and younger sister in New York. Now that she is a young parent herself, she wants her own mother close by so that she does not have to depend exclusively on her paternal relatives. That prospect is far off, though, and Carmen has to be content with the occasional trip back to her homeland, something she manages once every two or three years.

For immigrants, then, the meaning of family stretches over the seas and persists through long absences. It is organized into daisy chains of people who have followed each other, one by one, and then settled into pockets that turn into ethnic enclaves dense with interlocking ties. Families that lived next door to one another in Haiti land on adjacent blocks in Harlem. The same pattern organizes the native migrants from America's rural South, who also put down roots in Harlem neighborhoods. One can still find blocks dominated by people from particular towns in Georgia or the Carolinas and their descendants. In this respect, the native-born and the international migrant share common settlement patterns, which, in turn, provide the social structure that is so vital to the survival of the working poor.

Well-heeled families can buy the services they need to manage the demands of work and family. They can purchase child care, borrow from banks when they need to, pay their bills out of their salaries, and lean on health insurance when a doctor is needed. Affluence loosens the ties that remain tight, even oppressive at times, in poor communities. Yet there is an enduring uneasiness in our culture about the degree of independence generations and members of nuclear families maintain from one another, a sense that something has been lost. We look back with nostalgia at the close-knit family ties that were characteristic of the "immigrant generations" of the past and that still bind together newcomers to our shores, for the same reasons immigrants clung together at the turn of the century.[4]

What we fail to recognize is that many inner-city families, especially the majority who work to support themselves, maintain these close links with one another, preserving a form of social capital that has all but disappeared in many an American suburb.[5] These strong ties are the center of social life for the likes of Latoya and Natasha. It is true that these family values compete with other ambitions: the desire for a nice house and a picket fence in a suburb where graffiti doesn't mar the scenery and mothers needn't worry constantly about street violence. They dream about the prospect of owning a home and

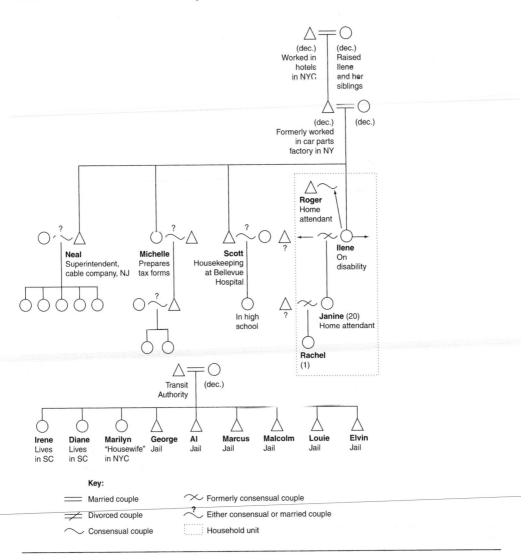

FIGURE 1A

garden somewhere far away from Harlem. Yet if that miracle day arrived, they would be faced with a serious dilemma: unless they could afford to take everyone near and dear to them along on the adventure, they would find it very hard to live with the distance such a move would put between them and their relatives.

Why do we assume that family values of this kind are a thing of the past in the ghetto? While the answer lies in part on the emphasis that writers have given to people like Rosa Lee, it is just as much an artifact of the way we confuse kinship structures with the moral culture of family life in the inner city. Very few of the people who work for Burger Barn live in households that resemble the Bill Cosby model. Most are adult chil-

ford air-conditioning and a Nintendo machine, items that sound like luxuries but turn out to be the key—or at least one key—to keeping her kids indoors and safe through the hot summer months. They must have something to play with and somewhere to cool off if she is to leave the teenagers to their own devices while she is working. At least equally important, however, is Patty's reliance upon her siblings and her mother as substitute supervisors of her kids, her adjunct eyes and ears, when she is at work. Without them, she would be faced with some unhappy choices.

While family support is critical for working parents, it is no less important in the lives of working youth. Teenagers at Burger Barn are often on the receiving end of the same kind of care from older relatives or "friends of the family" who are so close they constitute what anthropologists call "fictive kin," honorary aunts and uncles. Shaquena, who began working in a gym for little kids sponsored by a local church when she was just eleven, has had a difficult life. Her mother has been in and out of jail on drug convictions; one of her brothers was convicted of murder. Had her grandmother not been willing to take her in, Shaquena might have joined the thousands of New York City children shuffled into foster care.

As it is, she lives with her grandmother, who has raised her since she was ten years old. And Shaquena isn't the only one in the family who has sheltered under Grandma's wing. The household includes Shaquena's aunt, her aunt's two children, a cousin, two unmarried uncles, and an aunt and uncle who have a child as well. The grandmother has taken in her adult children and grandchildren, so that the household is a three-generation affair, albeit with several missing links (like Shaquena's own mother). Together the generations share the burden of supporting this extended household, relying on a combination of earned income and state aid: SSI for the grandmother, unemployment insurance for one of the aunts, the wages brought in by one of the uncles who works in a police station, the underground earnings of another who washes cars, and Shaquena's Burger Barn salary.

The Harlem neighborhood Shaquena calls home is jam-packed with people—kin and friends—who visit one another, eat together, and borrow from one another when the need arises.

> My aunt . . . lives right across the street from us. She, like last night, my grandmother ran out of sugar. My grandmother called my aunt and my aunt bought her the sugar. The guy down the hall, he real cool with us, he give us stuff, and my grandmother's cool with a lot of elderly on our floor. She will ask her daughter, my aunt, for things before she asks a friend, but she's got friends [to ask]. If I need something, I go right upstairs, because my best friend lives right upstairs. Her grandmother and my grandmother are friends and they keep a kitchen full of food.

Shaquena can depend upon this circle of friends and relatives to take care of her basic needs, so she can reserve her own earnings for the necessities of teenage life. But she is conscious of the dry periods when funds are tight and often uses her savings to buy toothpaste, soap, and little things for the baby in the house or for her godson who lives across the street with her aunt. It is important to her to pull her own weight and to contribute to the collective well-being of her family whenever she knows it's needed.

The practical side of this arrangement is important. Yet so too is the emotional value of having a big family, especially since Shaquena has had such a rocky relationship with her mother. With her grandmother, aunts, uncles, and cousins, she has a secure place in a situation that is as real and important to her as any nuclear family, suburban-style.

"ABSENT" MEN

Popular accounts of the ghetto world often lament the declining presence of men—especially fathers—in the life of the family. Men are in jail in record numbers; they have no interest in marrying the mothers of their children; they "hit" and run. That men cause grief to the women and children who need them is hardly news. As the divorce statistics remind us, this is a sad story repeated in every class. All over America there are children who need fathers but don't have them. We have developed a culture, both in the ghetto and outside it, that assigns to women the responsibility for raising children, leaving men peripheral to the task.

This is not to minimize the difference between a jailed father and a divorced father, a poor father who has never married the mother of his children and a more affluent father who fails to pay child support. There are differences, and they have consequences. Survey research tells us, for example, that single-parent children of never-married mothers are more likely than those of divorced parents to drop out of high school, and that daughters of never-married mothers are more likely than those of divorced parents to become teen mothers—though, it should be added, the differences are not as large as some pundits might claim.[9]

Yet it would be drawing too broad a brush stroke to suggest that men have absented themselves wholesale from the inner city. Uncles, fathers, brothers, sons, boyfriends—and husbands—are very much in evidence in the daily comings-and-goings of working poor families in Harlem. They help to support the households they live in and often provide regular infusions of cash, food, and time to the mothers of their children with whom they do not live.[10] The Bureau of the Census or a sociologist looking at a survey could easily miss the presence of men in Harlem households where they do not officially live, but to which they are nonetheless important as providers. Juan, father of Kyesha's son, is a case in point. He regularly gives part of his paycheck to his mother, who has several younger children and has been on AFDC for as long as he can remember. Juan also gives money to Kyesha to help take care of their son. Little of this check is left by the time he takes care of everyone who depends on him.

> It is a struggle to make ends meet. Like if I plan on buying something that week, then I got to hold back on that. 'Cause we got cable and you got to help out, you know. Or say the lights got to be paid. So I give a hundred dollars this week, fifty the next week. My mother has a bad habit sometimes. She doesn't think reasonably. So sometimes a lot of money has to come out of my pocket—I pay whole bills so I can get that off my back.

When the welfare authorities discovered that Juan was giving his mother money, they moved to take away some of her grant. He countered by finding a couch to sleep on in a friend's apartment so that his mother could report that he no longer lives in her home.

Reynaldo, whose mother is Puerto Rican and father from Ecuador, is a jack-of-all-trades who worked for a brief time at Burger Barn in between various hustles as a nonunion electrician, car repairman, carpenter, and cellular phone dealer for fellow Latinos in his Dominican neighborhood. A tall, stocky young man with a love of baggy pants and gold chains, Rey is a classic entrepreneur. He mixes and matches his job opportunities, picking up anything he can get on the side. For a time he had a job stocking shelves in a drugstore, but during his off-hours he made money fixing up broken-down cars for neighbors and rewiring a vacant apartment for his landlord. Rey works all the hours that are not consumed by school, his girlfriend, and hanging out with his younger brother.

No doubt he is influenced in his own brand of workaholism by the example of his father, Ernie, who taught him much of what he knows about electrical and machine repair. Ernie has never met a mechanical device he couldn't tear down to the foundation and rebuild just like new. Outside on the street curb sit the broken-down Fords, Dodges, and GM cars that await his attention. His auto repair shop is just the sidewalk in front of their apartment building, but everyone in the neighborhood knows that this is a business venue. Ernie is forever walking around with a cloth in his hands, wiping away the grease and oil from an old car he has torn apart and made whole again. The shelves of the family's back room are crammed with blowtorches, pliers, hammers, wrenches, reels of plastic-coated wiring—all the equipment needed to fix the long line of radios and TV sets that friends and friends of friends have left behind for repair.

As if he weren't busy enough, Ernie has a lively sideline as an off-the-books contractor, renovating apartments destined for immigrant families just like his own. Old apartment buildings in the Dominican neighborhoods have bad plumbing, plaster weeping off the walls, tiles missing, caulking cracked and flaking, windows shattered and taped. Landlords claim to have little money for keeping apartments up to code and in any case prefer to use local workers and avoid union labor. Their preferences keep Ernie in work as the apartments turn over. In turn, Ernie has kept Rey at his side and taught him everything he knows so he can turn over some of the work he has no time for, maintaining the opportunity "in the family."

Rey's mother is a student, working toward an Associate in Arts degree that will, she hopes, make it possible for her to work in computer administration someday. Most of her days are spent going to a community college that is a long subway ride from home. Until Mayor Giuliani canceled the policy, her education was subsidized by the city welfare system (in an effort to further the long-term career prospects of women on AFDC). After many years of working in a bra factory, she has come to understand the importance of credentials and is determined to accumulate them so that she can get a good job with decent pay.

Rey's younger brother, now sixteen, has staked his future on the prospect of going to college, for he seems to have the academic gifts. Where Rey coasts through school and sees little purpose in it, his brother would visit me at Columbia University and look eagerly at the college as heaven. He works during the summers and on the weekends for a print shop that is owned by a friend of the family.

In contrast to the households discussed earlier, whose earnings come mainly from the hard work of women, Rey's family relies largely on the income of the menfolk. While his mother has worked odd factory jobs now and again and hopes to find a real job when she finishes her studies, it is the entrepreneurial spirit of the men in the household that keeps the family going. Between them, father and sons earn enough in the (nontaxed) underground economy and the formal (wage-labor) system to keep the family at a lower-working-class standard of living. They have nothing to spare, they cannot do without any of these sources of income, but they are not starving. They can even hope that the youngest child will be able to get through high school and make it into a public college, something that will require heavy doses of financial aid, but is not an unthinkable goal.

It is tempting to look at Rey's family as an inner-city exception, an icon of middle-class virtue. The two-parent family, the loving brothers, and the entrepreneurial energy all add up to an admirable portrait of a stable, supportive circle of kin pulling together. And there is much truth to the view. Yet, Rey's parents are actually divorced. They broke up years ago in order to qualify the household for welfare. Rey's father maintains an official address elsewhere.

If we were to look at an official government census of Rey's household, we would find that the adults within it are classified as out of the labor force. Indeed, it would be deemed a single-parent household supported by the welfare system. Harlem is populated by thousands of families whose official profiles look just like this. Yet there is a steady income stream coming into Rey's home, because most of the adults are indeed working, often in the mostly unregulated economy of small-scale services and self-employment, including home-based seamstresses, food vendors, gypsy cab drivers, and carpenters.[11] Most of this income never sees the tax man.

Much of what has been written about this underground system focuses on the drug world. But for thousands of poor people in New York who cannot afford a unionized plumber or electrician, unlicensed craftsmen and informal service workers (who provide child care or personal services) are more important exemplars of the shadow economy. Men like Rey and his father provide reasonably priced services and products, making it possible for people who would otherwise have to do without to get their cars fixed, their leaking roofs patched, or their children looked after. Immigrants who lack legal papers find employment in this shadow world, and those who are legal take second jobs in the underground economy.

It has proved extremely hard to estimate the size of this alternative system,[12] but it is so widespread in poor communities that it often rivals the formal economy. The multipurpose shop Rey's father runs from the living room and the street corner is the mainstay of the family's income, and in this they are hardly alone. The thoroughfares of Harlem have, for many years, had an active sidewalk market trade that is largely invisible to the Internal Revenue Service.[13]

Whether we look at employment or "family structure," Rey's household departs from the normative model of the nuclear family. The statistical observer or census-taker might lump this family together with others as dissolved, or as one whose adult members have been out of the labor force for many years. But anyone who is paying closer attention will see that this makes no sense. These people do make up an actively functioning family, and in fact kinship means everything to them. Their values place work and family at the center of their own culture in a form that would be embraced even by conservative forces in American society. And the men of the family are at least as committed to these norms as the women.

Jamal is the only income-earner in his tiny household. His common-law wife, Kathy, once received SSA, a government support provided to her because her father died when she was just a child. But once she ran away to live with Jamal, these funds were appropriated by her mother. Nowadays Jamal spends hours on the bus to reach his job sweeping floors and cleaning toilets in a Burger Barn in another borough. In Jamal's opinion, a real man earns a living and supports his family, and he puts his dictum into practice daily in a job that most Americans wouldn't waste their time on. In this, he follows a path, a cultural definition of manhood, that continues to emphasize responsibility to family, responsibility that is sometimes expressed from a distance (as in Juan's case), while other times defined by coresidence (as is true for Ernie or Jamal).

Black men have been blanketed with negative publicity, excoriated as no good, irresponsible, swaggering in their masculinity, trapped in a swamp of "ghetto-related behavior."[14] Is this simply the force of stereotypes at work on a national psyche predisposed to believe the worst? Of course not. There are men in Harlem who have turned their backs on their mothers, wives, girlfriends, and children. Yet while we deplore the damage these males cause, we may overlook people like Jamal or Juan, or fifteen-year-old James, who brings his paycheck home to his parents to help with the rent, or Salvador, who works two jobs so that his wife, Carmen, and daughter will have a roof over their heads. We will not see the contributions that Latoya's common-law husband has made to the support of her children. And if we are to truly understand the role that men play in sustaining family values, we have to credit the existence of these honorable examples, while recognizing that many of their brethren have failed to follow through.

Some of those "failures" are young blacks who have irregular connections to family, who have no real place to live, whose seasonal labor is so poorly paid that there isn't much they can do to provide for their girlfriends even when they are so inclined.[15] Ron's mother died when he was a teenager. He now lives somewhat uneasily on the sufferance of his girlfriend while working at Burger Barn off and on. Since this relationship also is off and on, his living arrangements are precarious.

> You could say I work and pay my rent. I pay for where I stay at with my girl. My girl is my landlord, but nobody knows that. She does want money. I don't like to say this is my own bread, 'cause I don't like to be caught up in that "I'm gonna kick you out." So I always stay in contact with my family. That way, if something happens between me and her, my sister lives in Brooklyn and she always has the door open for me until I make me another power move. My sister's household is secure, but me, I'm on the edge when it comes to financial things. 'Cause if Burger Barn falls off, then I'm off.

Ron is so close to the edge that he cannot do anything more than contribute some of his wages to whatever household he lands in for the time being. People in his situation have nothing left over for anyone else, which is one of the reasons they don't behave like people with commitments. This is no excuse for siring children they can't support, but it does point to the importance of steady, reasonably paid employment in encouraging responsibility, a point William Julius Wilson has brought to national attention in *When Work Disappears*. Men who lack the wherewithal to be good fathers, often aren't.

FAMILY FLAWS

In pointing to the continuous importance of family as a set of values expressed in practice, I do not mean to paint the households of the working poor as indistinguishable from the "mainstream model." Seen through middle-class eyes, there is much to worry about. Parents who work at the bottom of the income pyramid are stressed, tired, and stretched to the limit of their ability to cope. The irregularity of the income they receive, whether from low-wage jobs, undependable partners, or both, subjects families like Latoya's to unpredictable shortages, gnawing insecurities. Welfare reform is blowing like an ill wind through many of these kin networks, and because the working poor and the AFDC recipients are interleaved, policy directives aimed at the latter are derailing many of the former. Lacking vacations, having little left over to pamper themselves with after a long day flipping burgers, and seeing so little advancement ahead of them, Burger Barn workers are often short-tempered at home. Economic pressures cannot descend upon families without showing their effects, especially on young kids.

Kyesha's two-year-old son, Anthony, spends much of his day in front of a television set tuned perpetually to soap operas and game shows. Sesame Street crosses the screen on occasion, but the purpose of the tube is not to educate little Anthony but to entertain his grandmother, stuck at home with him and several children of her own. Grandma Dana is not particularly attentive to Anthony's emotional needs, even though she keeps him fed and safe. He is never left alone, he does not run into the street, and his clothes are clean. But the focus stops there, and Anthony's behavior reflects the absence of sustained adult attention.

When Kyesha comes home, she wants to flop down on her bed and skim through movie star magazines. She lacks the energy to play with an active child.[16] She spends a lot of time figuring out how she is going to get to see her boyfriend and works on Dana in the hope that she will babysit Anthony for yet another evening so she can go out. The little boy is given to wandering into the tiny room they share and sounding off in an attempt to get Kyesha's attention. More often than not, she shoos him away so she can relax. If, like any normal two-year-old, he fails to obey, he is likely to be swatted.

Anthony will not start kindergarten knowing his colors and numbers, or the daily drill of communal "circle time" that is thoroughly familiar to any child who has spent time in a quality day care center. He will head down the road with a lack of basic experience that will weigh heavily when his teachers begin to assess his reading readiness or language fluency. There are consequences to growing up poor in a household of people who are pedaling hard just to stay afloat and have no time or reserve capacity left to provide the kind of enrichment that middle-class families can offer in abundance.

Shaquena has a rich array of people to turn to when she needs help. She has a web of kin and family friends living all around her, people who feed her and give her a place to hang out when all is not well at home. Yet her mother is a drug addict and her family broke up long ago under the strain. Had it not been for her grandmother, she would have found herself in foster care, her mother declared unfit. Hanging out with her girlfriends in the public housing project near her apartment in her younger years, she was known for getting into trouble. Fights, retaliation for insults, conflicts over boys—all have escalated to the point of serious violence. Shaquena's attachment to the work world is impressive because of this unlikely background, but the traces of her upbringing are visible enough in her temper, in the difficulty she has getting along with people at work from time to time.

Her family cares about her, but to say that they are just as loving and stable in their irregular configuration as any Bill Cosby family in the suburbs would be pure romanticism.

Latoya and her common-law husband have had an on-again-off-again relationship that has caused her no end of grief. He messes up and she kicks him out. Left behind is his ten-year-old daughter by a previous relationship, not to mention the son they have in common. Latoya dreams of having a house in the suburbs, something she could afford if she could get her man to settle down, for he has a well-paid job as a carpenter, a unionized position that gives him benefits and upward of $15 an hour. Together they could make a break for it, but the instability of their relationship renders this fantasy almost unattainable. Latoya's heart bears the scars of his irresponsibility, and her children miss their dad when he is not around. Latoya's salary from Burger Barn barely stretches to meet the mounting expenses of a family of five, even with Jason's contributions. When they are together, though, their joint income puts them well above the poverty line, straight into the blue-collar working class. Hence family stability and standard of living go hand in hand in Latoya's household: when the family is together, everything looks rosy, and when things fall apart, the struggle is monumental.

Middle-class families have their ups and downs too, of course. Television is a babysitter in many families. Suburban marriages break up, leaving children in serious economic straits, with divorced mothers facing a job market that will not allow them to keep a secure hold on the lives their children are accustomed to.[17] The poor have no lock on the pitfalls of modern family life. Yet the consequences of family instability in poor neighborhoods are clearly more devastating because the whole institutional structure that surrounds folks at the bottom—the schools, the low-wage work place, the overcrowded labor market, the potholed streets, the unsavory crack dealers on the front stoop—creates more vulnerability in families that have to deal with internal troubles. Support is more problematic, more likely to depend upon the resources of relatives and friends who are, in turn, also poor and troubled.

Editors' Note: *Notes for this reading can be found in the original source.*

■ READING 27

The Second Shift: Working Parents and the Revolution at Home

Arlie Hochschild, with Anne Machung

Between 8:05 A.M. and 6:05 P.M., both Nancy and Evan are away from home, working a "first shift" at full-time jobs. The rest of the time they deal with the varied tasks of the second shift: shopping, cooking, paying bills; taking care of the car, the garden, and yard; keeping harmony with Evan's mother who drops over quite a bit, "concerned" about Joey, with neighbors, their voluble babysitter, and each other. And Nancy's talk reflects a series of second-shift thoughts: "We're out of barbecue sauce. . . . Joey needs a Halloween costume. . . . The car needs a wash. . . . " and so on. She reflects a certain "second-shift sensibility," a continual attunement to the task of striking and restriking the right emotional balance between child, spouse, home, and outside job.

When I first met the Holts, Nancy was absorbing far more of the second shift than Evan. She said she was doing 80 percent of the housework and 90 percent of the childcare. Evan said she did 60 percent of the housework, 70 percent of the childcare. Joey said, "I vacuum the rug, and fold the dinner napkins," finally concluding, "Mom and I do it all." A neighbor agreed with Joey. Clearly, between Nancy and Evan, there was a "leisure gap": Evan had more than Nancy. I asked both of them, in separate interviews, to explain to me how they had dealt with housework and childcare since their marriage began.

One evening in the fifth year of their marriage, Nancy told me, when Joey was two months old and almost four years before I met the Holts, she first seriously raised the issue with Evan. "I told him: 'Look, Evan, it's not working. I do the housework, I take the major care of Joey, *and* I work a full-time job. I get pissed. This is *your* house too. Joey is *your* child too. It's not all *my* job to care for them.' When I cooled down I put to him, 'Look, how about this: I'll cook Mondays, Wednesdays, and Fridays. You cook Tuesdays, Thursdays, and, Saturdays. And we'll share or go out Sundays.' "

According to Nancy, Evan said he didn't like "rigid schedules." He said he didn't necessarily agree with her standards of housekeeping, and didn't like that standard "imposed" on him, especially if she was "sluffing off" tasks on him which from time to time he felt she was. But he went along with the idea in principle. Nancy said the first week of the new plan went as follows: On Monday, she cooked. For Tuesday, Evan planned a meal that required shopping for a few ingredients, but on his way home he forgot to shop for them. He came home, saw nothing he could use in the refrigerator or in the cupboard and suggested to Nancy that they go out for Chinese food. On Wednesday, Nancy cooked. On Thursday morning, Nancy reminded Evan, "Tonight it's your turn." That night Evan fixed hamburgers and french fries and Nancy was quick to praise him. On Friday, Nancy cooked. On Saturday, Evan forgot again.

As this pattern continued, Nancy's reminders became sharper. The sharper they became, the more actively Evan forgot—perhaps anticipating even sharper reprimands if he resisted more directly. This cycle of passive refusal followed by disappointment and anger gradually tightened, and before long the struggle had spread to the task of doing the laundry. Nancy said it was only fair that Evan share the laundry. He agreed in principle, but anxious that Evan would not share, Nancy wanted a clear, explicit agreement. "You ought to wash and fold every other load," she had told him. Evan experienced this "plan" as a yoke around his neck. On many weekdays, at this point, a huge pile of laundry sat like a disheveled guest on the living-room couch.

In her frustration, Nancy began to make subtle emotional jabs at Evan. "I don't know *what's* for dinner," she would say with a sigh. Or "I can't cook now, I've got to deal with this pile of laundry." She tensed at the slightest criticism about household disorder; if Evan wouldn't do the housework, he had absolutely *no* right to criticize how she did it. She would burst out angrily at Evan. She recalled telling him: "After work *my* feet are just as tired as *your* feet. I'm just as wound up as you are. I come home. I cook dinner. I wash and I clean. Here we are, planning a second child, and I can't cope with the one we have."

About two years after I first began visiting the Holts, I began to see the problem in a certain light: as a conflict between their two gender ideologies. Nancy wanted to be the sort of woman who was needed and appreciated both at home and at work—like Lacey, she told me, on the television show "Cagney and Lacey." She wanted Evan to appreciate her for being a caring social worker, a committed wife, and a wonderful mother. But she cared just as much that she be able to appreciate *Evan* for what *he* contributed at home, not just for how he supported the family. She would feel proud to explain to women friends that she was married to one of these rare "new men."

A gender ideology is often rooted in early experience, and fueled by motives formed early on and such motives can often be traced to some cautionary tale in early life. So it was for Nancy. Nancy described her mother:

> My mom was wonderful, a real aristocrat, but she was also terribly depressed being a house-wife. My dad treated her like a doormat. She didn't have any self-confidence. And growing up, I can remember her being really depressed. I grew up bound and determined not to be like her and not to marry a man like my father. As long as Evan doesn't do the housework, I feel it means he's going to be like my father—coming home, putting his feet up, and hol-lering at my mom to serve him. That's my biggest fear. I've had *bad* dreams about that.

Nancy thought that women friends her age, also in traditional marriages, had come to similarly bad ends. She described a high school friend: "Martha barely made it through City College. She had no interest in learning anything. She spent nine years trailing around behind her husband [a salesman]. It's a miserable marriage. She hand washes all his shirts. The high point of her life was when she was eighteen and the two of us were running around Miami Beach in a Mustang convertible. She's gained seventy pounds and she hates her life." To Nancy, Martha was a younger version of her mother, depressed, lacking in self-esteem, a cautionary tale whose moral was "if you want to be happy, de-velop a career and get your husband to share at home." Asking Evan to help again and again felt like "hard work" but it was essential to establishing her role as a career woman.

For his own reasons, Evan imagined things very differently. He loved Nancy and if Nancy loved being a social worker, he was happy and proud to support her in it. He knew that because she took her caseload so seriously, it was draining work. But at the same time, he did not see why, just because she chose this demanding career, *he* had to change *his own* life. Why should her personal decision to work outside the home require him to do more inside it? Nancy earned about two-thirds as much as Evan, and her salary was a big help, but as Nancy confided, "If push came to shove, we could do without it." Nancy was a so-cial worker because she loved it. Doing daily chores at home was thankless work, certainly not something Evan needed her to appreciate about him. Equality in the second shift meant a loss in his standard of living, and despite all the high-flown talk, he felt he hadn't *really* bargained for it. He was happy to help Nancy at home if she needed help; that was fine. That was only decent. But it was too risky a matter "committing" himself to sharing.

Two other beliefs probably fueled his resistance as well. The first was his suspicion that if he shared the second shift with Nancy, she would "dominate him." Nancy would ask him to do this, ask him to do that. It felt to Evan as if Nancy had won so many small victories that he had to draw the line somewhere. Nancy had a declarative personality; and as Nancy said, "Evan's mother sat me down and told me once that I was too forceful, that Evan needed to take more authority." Both Nancy and Evan agreed that Evan's sense of career and self was in fact shakier than Nancy's. He had been unemployed. She never had. He had had some bouts of drinking in the past. Drinking was foreign to her. Evan thought that sharing housework would upset a certain balance of power that felt culturally "right."

He held the purse strings and made the major decisions about large purchases (like their house) because he "knew more about finances" and because he'd chipped in more inheritance than she when they married. His job difficulties had lowered his self-respect, and now as a couple they had achieved some ineffable "balance"—tilted in his favor, she thought—which, if corrected to equalize the burden of chores, would result in his giving in "too much." A certain driving anxiety behind Nancy's strategy of actively renegotiating roles had made Evan see agreement as "giving in." When he wasn't feeling good about work, he dreaded the idea of being under his wife's thumb at home.

Underneath these feelings, Evan perhaps also feared that Nancy was avoiding taking care of *him*. His own mother, a mild-mannered alcoholic, had by imperceptible steps phased herself out of a mother's role, leaving him very much on his own. Perhaps a personal motive to prevent that happening in his marriage—a guess on my part, and unarticulated on his—underlay his strategies of passive resistance. And he wasn't altogether wrong to fear this. Meanwhile, he felt he was "offering" Nancy the chance to stay home, or cut back her hours, and that she was refusing his "gift;" while Nancy felt that, given her feelings about work, this offer was hardly a gift.

In the sixth year of her marriage, when Nancy again intensified her pressure on Evan to commit himself to equal sharing, Evan recalled saying, "Nancy, why don't you cut back to half time, that way you can fit everything in." At first Nancy was baffled: "We've been married all this time, and you *still* don't get it. Work is important to me. I worked *hard* to get my MSW. Why *should* I give it up?" Nancy also explained to Evan and later to me, "I think my degree and my job has been my way of reassuring myself that I won't end up like my mother." Yet she'd received little emotional support in getting her degree from either her parents or in-laws. (Her mother had avoided asking about her thesis, and her in-laws, though invited, did not attend her graduation, later claiming they'd never been invited.)

In addition, Nancy was more excited about seeing her elderly clients in tenderloin hotels than Evan was about selling couches to furniture salesmen with greased-back hair. Why shouldn't Evan make as many compromises with his career ambitions and his leisure as she'd made with hers? She couldn't see it Evan's way, and Evan couldn't see it hers.

In years of alternating struggle and compromise, Nancy had seen only fleeting mirages of cooperation, visions that appeared when she got sick or withdrew and disappeared when she got better or came forward.

After seven years of loving marriage, Nancy and Evan had finally come to a terrible impasse. Their emotional standard of living had drastically declined, they began to snap at each other, to criticize, to carp. Each felt taken advantage of. Evan, because his offering of a good arrangement was deemed unacceptable, and Nancy, because Evan wouldn't do what she deeply felt was "fair."

This struggle made its way into their sexual life—first through Nancy directly, and then through Joey. Nancy had always disdained any form of feminine wiliness or manipulation. Her family saw her as "a flaming feminist" and that was how she saw herself. As such, she felt above the underhanded ways traditional women used to get around men. She mused, "When I was a teenager, I vowed I would *never* use sex to get my way with a man. It is not self-respecting; it's demeaning. But when Evan refused to carry his load at home, I did, I used sex, I said, 'Look, Evan, I would not be this exhausted and asexual every night if I didn't have so much to face every morning.'" She felt reduced to an old "strategy," and her modern ideas made her ashamed of it. At the same time, she'd run out of other, modern ways.

The idea of a separation arose, and they became frightened. Nancy looked at the deteriorating marriages and fresh divorces of couples with young children around them. One unhappy husband they knew had become so uninvolved in family life (they didn't know whether his unhappiness made him uninvolved, or whether his lack of involvement had caused his wife to be unhappy) that his wife left him. In another case, Nancy felt the wife had "nagged" her husband so much that he abandoned her for another woman. In both cases, the couple was less happy after the divorce than before, and both wives took the children and struggled desperately to survive financially. Nancy took stock. She asked herself, "Why wreck a marriage over a dirty frying pan?" Is it really worth it?

UPSTAIRS-DOWNSTAIRS: A FAMILY MYTH AS "SOLUTION"

Not long after this crisis in the Holts' marriage, there was a dramatic lessening of tension over the issue of the second shift. It was as if the issue was closed. Evan had won. Nancy would do the second shift. Evan expressed vague guilt but beyond that he had nothing to say. Nancy had wearied of continually raising the topic, wearied of the lack of resolution. Now in the exhaustion of defeat, she wanted the struggle to be over too. Evan was "so good" in *other* ways, why debilitate their marriage by continual quarreling. Besides, she told me, "Women always adjust more, don't they?"

One day, when I asked Nancy to tell me who did which tasks from a long list household chores, she interrupted me with a broad wave of her hand and said, "I do the upstairs, Evan does the downstairs." What does that mean? I asked. Matter-of-factly, she explained that the upstairs included the living room, the dining room, the kitchen, two bedrooms, and two baths. The downstairs meant the garage, a place for storage and hobbies—Evan's hobbies. She explained this was a "sharing" arrangement, without humor or irony—just as Evan did later. Both said they had agreed it was the best solution to their dispute. Evan would take care of the car, the garage, and Max, the family dog. As Nancy explained, "the dog is all Evan's problem. I don't have to deal with the dog." Nancy took care of the rest.

For purposes of accommodating the second shift, then, the Holts' garage was elevated to the full moral and practical equivalent of the rest of the home. For Nancy and Evan, "upstairs and downstairs," "inside and outside," were vaguely described like "half and half," a fair division of labor based on a natural division of their house.

The Holts presented their upstairs-downstairs agreement as a perfectly equitable solution to a problem they "once had." This belief is what we might call "family myth," even a modest delusional system. Why did they believe it? I think they believed it because they needed to believe it, because it solved a terrible problem. It allowed Nancy to continue thinking of herself as the sort of woman whose husband didn't abuse her—a self-conception that mattered a great deal to her. And it avoided the hard truth that, in his stolid, passive way, Evan had refused to share. It avoided the truth, too, that in their showdown, Nancy was more afraid of divorce than Evan was. This outer cover to their family life, this family myth was jointly devised. It was an attempt to agree that there was no conflict over the second shift, no tension between their versions of manhood and womanhood, that the powerful crisis that had arisen was temporary and minor.

The wish to avoid such a conflict is natural enough. But their avoidance tacitly supported by the surrounding culture, especially the image of the woman with the flying hair. After all, this admirable woman also proudly does the "upstairs" each day without a husband's help and without conflict.

After Nancy and Evan reached their upstairs-downstairs agreement, the confrontations ended. They were nearly forgotten. Yet, as she described daily life months after the agreement, Nancy's resentment still seemed alive and well. For example, she said:

> Evan and I eventually divided the labor so that I do the upstairs and Evan does the downstairs and the dog. So the dog is my husband's problem. But when I was getting the dog outside and getting Joey ready for childcare, and cleaning up the mess, feeding the cat, and getting the lunches together, and having my son wipe his nose on my outfit so I would have to change—then I was pissed! I felt that I was doing *everything*. All Evan was doing was getting up, having coffee, reading the paper, saying, "Well, I have to go now," and often forgetting the lunch I'd bothered to make.

She also mentioned that she had fallen into the habit of putting Joey to bed in a certain way: he asked to be swung around by the arms, dropped on the bed and nuzzled and hugged, whispered to in his ear. Joey waited for her attention. He didn't go to sleep without it. But, increasingly, when Nancy tried it at eight and nine, the ritual didn't put Joey to sleep. On the contrary, it woke him up. It was then that Joey began to say he could only go to sleep in his parents' bed, that he began to sleep in their bed and to encroach on their sexual life.

Near the end of my visits, it struck me that Nancy was putting Joey to bed in an "exciting" way, later and later at night, in order to tell Evan something important: "You win, I'll go on doing all the work at home, but I'm angry about it and I'll make you pay." Evan had won the battle but lost the war. According to the family myth, all was well: the struggle had been resolved by the upstairs-downstairs agreement. But suppressed in one area of their marriage, this struggle lived on in another—as Joey's Problem, and as theirs.

NANCY'S "PROGRAM" TO SUSTAIN THE MYTH

There was a moment, I believe, when Nancy seemed to *decide* to give up on this one. She decided to try not to resent Evan. Whether or not other women face a moment just like this, at the very least they face the need to deal with all the feelings that naturally arise from a clash between a treasured ideal and an incompatible reality. In the age of a stalled revolution, it is a problem a great many women face.

Emotionally, Nancy's compromise from time to time slipped; she would forget and grow resentful again. Her new resolve needed maintenance. Only half aware that she was doing so, Nancy went to extraordinary lengths to maintain it. She could tell me now, a year or so after her "decision," in a matter-of-fact and noncritical way: "Evan likes to come home to a hot meal. He doesn't like to clear the table. He doesn't like to do the dishes. He likes to go watch TV. He likes to play with his son when he feels like it and not feel like he should be with him more." She seemed resigned.

Everything was "fine." But it had taken an extraordinary amount of complex "emotion work"—the work of *trying* to feel the "right" feeling, the feeling she wanted to feel—to make and keep everything "fine." Across the nation at this particular time in history, this emotion work is often all that stands between the stalled revolution on the one hand, and broken marriages on the other.

HOW MANY HOLTS?

In one key way the Holts were typical of the vast majority of two-job couples: their family life had become the shock absorber for a stalled revolution whose origin lay far outside it—in economic and cultural trends that bear very differently on men and women. Nancy was reading books, newspaper articles, and watching TV programs on the changing role of women. Evan wasn't. Nancy felt benefited by these changes; Evan didn't. In her ideals and in reality, Nancy was more different from her mother than Evan was from his father, for the culture and economy were in general pressing change faster upon women like her than upon men like Evan. Nancy had gone to college; her mother hadn't. Nancy had a professional job; her mother never had. Nancy had the idea that she should be equal with her husband; her mother hadn't been much exposed to that idea in her day. Nancy felt she should share the job of earning money, and that Evan should share the work at home; her mother hadn't imagined that was possible. Evan went to college, his father (and the other boys in his family, though not the girls) had gone too. Work was important to Evan's identity as a man as it had been for his father before him. Indeed, Evan felt the same way about family roles as his father had felt in his day. The new job opportunities and the feminist movement of the 1960s and '70s had transformed Nancy but left Evan pretty much the same. And the friction created by this difference between them moved to the issue of second shift as metal to a magnet. By the end, Evan did less housework and childcare than most men married to working women—but not much less. Evan and Nancy were also typical of nearly 40 percent of the marriages studied in their clash of gender ideologies and their corresponding difference is a notion about what constituted a "sacrifice" and what did not. By far the most common form of mismatch was like that between Nancy, an egalitarian, and Evan, a transitional.

But for most couples, the tensions between strategies did not move so quickly and powerfully to issues of housework and childcare. Nancy pushed harder than most women to get her husband to share the work at home, and she also lost more overwhelmingly than the few other women who fought that hard. Evan pursued his strategy of passive resistance with more quiet tenacity then most men, and he allowed himself to become far more marginal to his son's life than most other fathers. The myth of the Holts' "equal" arrangement seems slightly more odd than other family myths that encapsulated equally powerful conflicts.

Beyond their upstairs-downstairs myth, the Holts tell us a great deal about the subtle ways a couple can encapsulate the tension caused by a struggle over the second shift without resolving the problem or divorcing. Like Nancy Holt, many women struggle to avoid, suppress, obscure, or mystify a frightening conflict over the second shift. They do not struggle like this because they start off wanting to, or because such struggle is inevitable or because women inevitably lose, but because they are forced to choose between equality and marriage. And they choose marriage. When asked about "ideal" relations between men and women in general, about what they want for their daughters or about what "ideally" they'd like in their own marriage, most working mothers "wished" their men would share the work at home.

But many "wish" it instead of "want" it. Other goals—like keeping peace at home—come first. Nancy Holt did some extraordinary behind-the-scenes emotion work to prevent her ideals from clashing with her marriage. In the end she had confined and miniaturized her ideas of equality successfully enough to do two things she badly wanted to do: feel like a feminist, and live at peace with a man who was not. Her program had "worked." Evan won on the reality of the situation, because Nancy did the second shift. Nancy won on the cover story, they would talk about it as if they shared.

Nancy wore the upstairs-downstairs myth as an ideological cloak to protect her from the contradictions in her marriage and from the cultural and economic forces that press upon it. Nancy and Evan Holt were caught on opposite sides of the gender revolution occurring all around them. Through the 1960s, 1970s, and 1980s masses of women entered the public world of work—but went only so far up the occupational ladder. They tried for "equal" marriages, but got only so far in achieving it. They married men who liked them to work at the office and who wouldn't share the extra month a year at home. When confusion about the identity of the working woman created a cultural vacuum in the 1970s and 1980s, the image of the supermom quietly glided in. She made the "stall" seem normal and happy. But beneath the happy image of the woman with the flying hair are modern marriages like the Holts', reflecting intricate webs of tension, and the huge, hidden emotional cost to women, men, and children of having to "manage" inequality. Yet on the surface, all we might see would be Nancy Holt bounding confidently out the door at 8:30 A.M. briefcase in one hand, Joey in the other. All we might hear would be Nancy's and Evan's talk about their marriage as happy, normal, even "equal"—because equality was so important to Nancy.

■READING 28

The Work-Home Crunch

Kathleen Gerson and Jerry A. Jacobs

More than a decade has passed since the release of *The Overworked American*, a prominent 1991 book about the decline in Americans' leisure time, and the work pace in the United States only seems to have increased. From sleep-deprived parents to professionals who believe they must put in long hours to succeed at the office, the demands of work are colliding with family responsibilities and placing a tremendous time squeeze on many Americans.

Yet beyond the apparent growth in the time that many Americans spend on the job lies a more complex story. While many Americans are working more than ever, many others are working less. What is more, finding a balance between work and other obligations seems increasingly elusive to many workers—whether or not they are actually putting in more time at work than workers in earlier generations. The increase in harried workers and hurried families is a problem that demands solutions. But before we can resolve this increasingly difficult time squeeze we must first understand its root causes.

AVERAGE WORKING TIME AND BEYOND

"There aren't enough hours in the day" is an increasingly resonant refrain. To most observers, including many experts, the main culprit appears to be overwork—our jobs just take up too much of our time. Yet it is not clear that the average American is spending more time on the job. Although it may come as a surprise to those who feel overstressed, the average work week—that is, hours spent working for pay by the average employee—has hardly changed over the past 30 years. Census Bureau interviews show, for example, that the average male worked 43.5 hours a week in 1970 and 43.1 hours a week in 2000, while the average female worked 37.1 hours in 1970 and 37.0 hours in 2000.

Why, then, do more and more Americans feel so pressed for time? The answer is that averages can be misleading. Looking only at the average experience of American workers misses key parts of the story. From the perspective of individual workers, it turns out some Americans are working more than ever, while others are finding it harder to get as much work as they need or would like. To complicate matters further, American families are now more diverse than they were in the middle of the 20th century, when male-breadwinner households predominated. Many more Americans now live in dual-earner or single-parent families where all the adults work.

These two trends—the growing split of the labor force and the transformation of family life—lie at the heart of the new time dilemmas facing an increasing number of Americans. But they have not affected all workers and all families in the same way. Instead, these changes have divided Americans into those who feel squeezed between their work and the rest of their life, and those who have more time away from work than they need or would like. No one trend fits both groups.

So, who are the time-squeezed, and how do they differ from those with fewer time pressures but who may also have less work than they may want or need? To distinguish and describe the two sets of Americans, we need to look at the experiences of both individual workers and whole families. A focus on workers shows that they are increasingly divided between those who put in very long work weeks and who are concentrated in the better-paying jobs, and those who put in comparatively short work weeks, who are more likely to have fewer educational credentials and are more likely to be concentrated in the lower-paying jobs.

But the experiences of individuals does not tell the whole story. When we shift our focus to the family, it becomes clear that time squeezes are linked to the total working hours of family members in households. For this reason, two-job families and single parents face heightened challenges. Moreover, women continue to assume the lion's share of home and child care responsibilities and are thus especially likely to be squeezed for time. Changes in jobs and changes in families are putting overworked Americans and underemployed Americans on distinct paths, are separating the two-earner and single-parent households from the more traditional households, and are creating different futures for parents (especially mothers) than for workers without children at home. (On the issue of which specific schedules people work and the consequences of nonstandard shifts, see "The Economy that Never Sleeps," *Contexts*, Spring 2004.)

A GROWING DIVIDE IN INDIVIDUAL WORKING TIME

In 1970, almost half of all employed men and women reported working 40 hours a week. By 2000, just 2 in 5 worked these "average" hours. Instead, workers are now far more likely to put in either very long or fairly short work weeks. The share of working men putting in 50 hours or more rose from 21 percent in 1970 to almost 27 percent in 2000, while the share of working women putting in these long work weeks rose from 5 to 11 percent.

At the other end of the spectrum, more workers are also putting in shorter weeks. In 1970, for example, 5 percent of men were employed for 30 or fewer hours a week, while 9 percent worked these shortened weeks in 2000. The share of employed women spending 30 or fewer hours on the job also climbed from 16 percent to 20 percent (see Figure 1). In total, 13 million Americans in 2000 worked either shorter or longer work weeks than they would have if the 1970s pattern had continued.

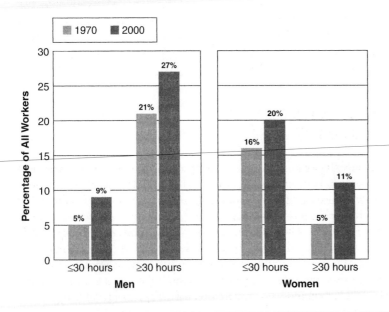

FIGURE 1   *The Percentage of Men and Women Who Put in 30 or Fewer Hours and Who Put in 50 or More Hours a Week in 1970 and 2000*

Source: Match Current Population Surveys; nonfarm wage and salary workers.

These changes in working time are not evenly distributed across occupations. Instead, they are strongly related to the kinds of jobs people hold. Managers and professionals, as one might expect, tend to put in the longest work weeks. More than 1 in 3 men in this category now work 50 hours or more per week, compared to only 1 in 5 for men in other occupations. For women, 1 in 6 professionals and managers work these long weeks, compared to fewer than 1 in 14 for women in all other occupations. And because jobs are closely linked to education, the gap in working time between the college educated and those with fewer educational credentials has also grown since 1970.

Thus, time at work is growing most among those Americans who are most likely to read articles and buy books about overwork in America. They may not be typical, but they are indeed working more than their peers in earlier generations. If leisure time once signaled an elite lifestyle, that no longer appears to be the case. Working relatively few hours is now more likely to be concentrated among those with less education and less elite jobs.

Workers do not necessarily prefer these new schedules. On the contrary, when workers are asked about their ideal amount of time at work, a very different picture emerges. For example, in a 1997 survey of workers conducted by the Families and Work Institute, 60 percent of both men and women responded that they would like to work less while 19 percent of men and women said that they would like to work more. Most workers—both women and men—aspire to work between 30 and 40 hours per week. Men generally express a desire to work about 38 hours a week while women would like to work about 32 hours. The small difference in the ideal working time of men and women is less significant than the shared preferences among them. However, whether their jobs require very long or comparatively short work weeks, this shared ideal does stand in sharp contrast to their job realities. As some workers are pressured to put in more time at work and others less, finding the right balance between work and the rest of life has become increasingly elusive.

OVERWORKED INDIVIDUALS OR OVERWORKED FAMILIES?

Fundamental shifts in family life exacerbate this growing division between the over- and under-worked. While most analyses of working time focus on individual workers, time squeezes are typically experienced by families, not isolated individuals. A 60-hour work week for a father means something different depending on whether the mother stays at home or also works a 60-hour week. Even a 40-hour work week can seem too long if both members of a married couple are juggling job demands with family responsibilities. And when a family depends on a single parent, the conflicts between home and work can be even greater. Even if the length of the work week had not changed at all, the rise of families that depend on either two incomes or one parent would suffice to explain why Americans feel so pressed for time.

To understand how families experience time squeezes, we need to look at the combined working time of all family members. For example, how do married couples with two earners compare with those anchored by a sole, typically male, breadwinner? For all married couples, the work week has indeed increased from an average of about 53 hours in 1970 to 63 hours in 2000. Given that the average work week for individuals did not change, it may seem strange that the couples' family total grew so markedly. The explanation for this apparent paradox is both straightforward and crucial: married women are now far more likely to work. In 1970, half of all married-couple families had only male breadwinners. By 2000, this group had shrunk to one quarter (see Figure 2). In 1970, one-third of all married-couple families had two wage-earners, but three-fifths did in 2000. In fact, two-earner families are more common today than male-breadwinner families were 30 years ago.

Each type of family is also working a little more each week, but this change is relatively modest and certainly not large enough to account for the larger shift in total household working time. Two-earner families put in close to 82 working hours in 2000 compared with 78 hours in 1970. Male-breadwinner couples worked 44 hours on average in 1970 and 45 hours in 2000. The vast majority of the change in working time over the past 30 years can thus be traced to changes in the kinds of families we live in rather than to changes in how much we work. Two-earner couples work about as much today as they did 30 years ago, but there are many more of them because more wives are working.

Single parents, who are overwhelmingly mothers, are another group who are truly caught in a time squeeze. They need to work as much as possible to support their fam-

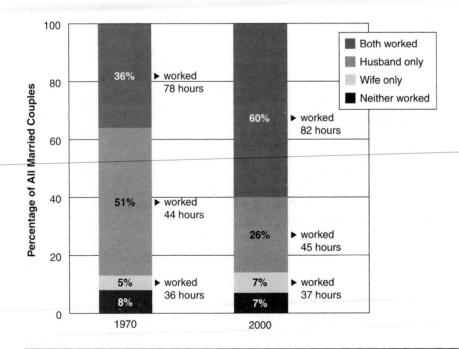

FIGURE 2   *Total Hours of Work per Week for Married Couples, 1970 and 2000*

Source: March Current Population Surveys; nonfarm married couples aged 18–64.

ily, and they are less likely to be able to count on a partner's help in meeting their children's daily needs. Although these households are not displayed in Figure 2, Census Bureau data show that women headed one-fifth of all families in 2000, twice the share of female-headed households in 1970. Even though their average work week remained unchanged at 39 hours, the lack of childcare and other support services leaves them facing time squeezes at least as sharp. Single fathers remain a much smaller group, but their ranks have also grown rapidly. Single dads work almost as much as single moms—37 hours per week in 2000. Even though this represents a drop of two hours since 1970, single fathers face time dilemmas as great as those facing single mothers. Being a single parent has always posed daunting challenges, and now there are more mothers and fathers than ever in this situation.

At the heart of these shifts is American families' growing reliance on a woman's earnings—whether or not they depend on a man's earnings as well. Women's strengthened commitment to paid employment has provided more economic resources to families and given couples more options for sharing the tasks of breadwinning and caretaking. Yet this revolution in women's work has not been complemented by an equal growth in the amount of time men spend away from the job or in the availability of organized childcare. This limited change at the workplace and in men's lives has intensified the time pressures facing women.

DUAL-EARNER PARENTS AND WORKING TIME

The expansion of working time is especially important for families with children, where work and family demands are most likely to conflict. Indeed, there is a persisting concern that in their desire for paid work, families with two earners are shortchanging their children in time and attention. A closer looks reveals that even though parents face increased time pressure, they cope with these dilemmas by cutting back on their combined joint working time when they have children at home. For example, U.S. Census data show that parents in two-income families worked 3.3 fewer hours per week than spouses in two-income families without children, a slightly wider difference than the 2.6 hours separating them in 1970. Working hours also decline as the number of children increase. Couples with one child under 18 jointly averaged 81 hours per week in 2000, while couples with three or more children averaged 78 hours. Rather than forsaking their children, employed parents are taking steps to adjust their work schedules to make more time for the rest of life.

However, it is mothers, not fathers, who are cutting back. Fathers actually work more hours when they have children at home, and their working hours increase with the number of children. Thus, the drop in joint working time among couples with children reflects less working time among mothers. Figure 3 shows that in 2000, mothers worked almost 4 fewer hours per week than married women without children. This gap is not substantially different than in 1970.

This pattern of mothers reducing their hours while fathers increase them creates a larger gender gap in work participation among couples with children compared to the gender gap for childless couples. However, these differences are much smaller than the

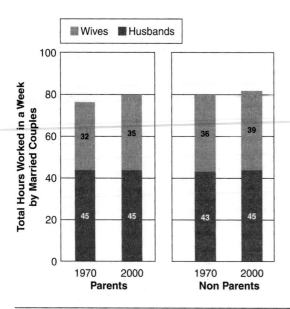

FIGURE 3 *Average Hours of Work per Week of Couples (Parents and Non-Parents)*
Source: March Current Population Surveys; nonfarm married couples aged 18–64.

once predominant pattern in which many women stopped working for pay altogether when they bore children. While the transition to raising children continues to have different consequences for women and men, the size of this difference is diminishing.

It is also important to remember that the rise in working time among couples is not concentrated among those with children at home. Though Americans continue to worry about the consequences for children when both parents go to work, the move toward more work involvement does not reflect neglect on the part of either mothers or fathers. On the contrary, employed mothers continue to spend less time at the workplace than their childless peers, while employed fathers today do not spend substantially more time at work than men who are not fathers.

SOLVING THE TIME PRESSURE PUZZLE

Even though changes in the average working time of American workers are modest, many American families have good reason to feel overworked and time-deprived. The last several decades have witnessed the emergence of a group of workers who face very long work weeks and live in families that depend on either two incomes or one parent. And while parents are putting in less time at work than their peers without children at home, they shoulder domestic responsibilities that leave them facing clashes between work demands and family needs.

The future of family well-being and gender equality will depend on developing policies to help workers resolve the time pressures created by the widespread and deeply rooted social changes discussed above. The first step toward developing effective policy responses requires accepting the social transformations that sent women into the workplace and left Americans wishing for a balance between work and family that is difficult to achieve. Unfortunately, these changes in the lives of women and men continue to evoke ambivalence.

For example, mothers continue to face strong pressures to devote intensive time and attention to child rearing. Indeed, generally they want to, despite the rising economic and social pressure to hold a paid job as well. Even though most contemporary mothers are counted on to help support their families financially, the United States has yet to develop the child care services and flexible jobs that can help workers meet their families' needs. Whether or not mothers work outside the home, they face conflicting expectations that are difficult to meet. These social contradictions can be seen in the political push to require poor, single mothers to work at a paid job while middle-class mothers continue to be chastised for spending too much time on their jobs and away from home.

To a lesser but still important extent, fathers also face intensifying and competing pressures. Despite American families' increasing reliance on women's earnings, men face significant barriers to family involvement. Resistance from employers and co-workers continues to greet individual fathers who would like to spend less time at work to care for their children. For all the concern and attention focused on employed mothers, social policies that would help bring men more fully into the work of parenting get limited notice or support. New time squeezes can thus be better understood by comparing the large changes in women's lives with the relative lack of changes in the situation for men. The family time bind is an unbalanced one.

Even as family time has become squeezed, workers are also contending with changes in the options and expectations they face at work, Competitive workplaces appear to be creating rising pressures for some workers, especially professionals and managers, to devote an excessive amount of time to their jobs, while not offering enough work to others. In contrast to these bifurcating options, American workers increasingly express a desire to balance the important work of earning a living and caring for a new generation.

Finding solutions to these new time dilemmas will depend on developing large scale policies that recognize and address the new needs of 21st century workers and their families. As we suggest in our book, *The Time Divide*, these policies need to address the basic organization of American work and community institutions. This includes revising regulations on hours of work and providing benefit protections to more workers, moving toward the norm of a shorter work week, creating more family-supportive workplaces that offer both job flexibility and protections for employed parents, and developing a wider array of high quality, affordable child care options.

Extending protections, such as proportional benefits and overtime pay, to workers in a wider range of jobs and occupations would reduce the built-in incentives employers have to extract as much work as possible from professionals and managers while offering less work to other employees. If professionals and managers were given overtime pay for overtime work, which wage workers are now guaranteed under the Fair Labor Standards Act, the pressures on these employees to put in endless workdays might lessen. Yet, the Bush administration recently revised these rules to move more employees into the category of those ineligible for overtime pay. Similarly, if part-time workers were offered fringe benefits proportional to the hours they work (such as partial pensions), there would be fewer reasons for employers to create jobs with work weeks so short that they do not provide the economic security all families need.

Reducing the average work week to 35 hours would also reduce the pressures on workers and help them find a better work-family balance. While this goal may seem utopian, it is important to remember that the 40-hour standard also seemed unimaginably idealistic before it was adopted in the early 20th century. Other countries, most notably France, have adopted this standard without sacrificing economic well-being. A shorter work week still would allow for variation in work styles and commitments, but it would also create a new cultural standard that better reflects the needs and aspirations of most contemporary workers. It would also help single parents meet their dual obligations and allow couples to fashion greater equality in their work and caretaking responsibilities.

Time at work is clearly important, but it is not the whole story. The organization of the workplace and the structure of jobs also matters, especially for those whose jobs and occupations require intensive time at work. Among those putting in very long work weeks, we find that having job flexibility and autonomy help ease the perceived strains and conflicts. The work environment, especially in the form of support from supervisors and co-workers, also makes a difference. In addition, we find that workers with access to such family-friendly options as flexible work schedules are likely to use them, while workers without such benefits would like to have them.

Flexibility and autonomy are only useful if workers feel able to use them. Women and men both express concern that making use of "family-friendly" policies, such as extended parental leaves or nonstandard working hours, may endanger their future work prospects. Social policies need to protect the rights of workers to be involved parents without incurring excessive penalties at the workplace. Most Americans spend a portion of their work lives simultaneously immersed in work for pay and in parenting. Providing greater flexibility at the workplace will help workers develop both short- and longer-term strategies for integrating work and family life. However, even basic changes in the organization of work will not suffice to meet the needs of 21st century families. We also need to join the ranks of virtually all other industrialized nations by creating widely available, high quality and affordable child care. In a world where mothers and fathers are at the workplace to stay, we need an expanded network of support to care for the next generation of workers.

These changes will not be easy to achieve. But in one form or another, they have been effectively adopted in other societies throughout the modern world. While no one policy is a cure-all, taken together they offer a comprehensive approach for creating genuine resolution to the time pressures that confront growing numbers of American workers and their families. Ultimately, these new time dilemmas cannot be resolved by chastising workers (and, most often, mothers) for working too much. Rather, the time has come to create more flexible, family-supportive, and gender-equal workplaces and communities that complement the 21st century forms of work and family life.

*Recommended Resources*_____

Bond, James T. *Highlights of the National Study of the Changing Workforce*. New York: Families and Work Institute, 2003. Bond reports findings from a major national survey of contemporary American workers, workplace conditions and work-family conflict.

Gornick, Janet, and Marcia Meyers. *Families that Work: Policies for Reconciling Parenthood and Employment*. New York: Russell Sage Foundation, 2003. This important study compares family-supportive policies in Europe and the United States.

Hays, Sharon. *The Cultural Contradictions of Motherhood*. New Haven, CT: Yale University Press, 1997. Hays examines how American mothers continue to face pressure to practice intensive parenting even as they increase their commitment to paid work.

Heymann, Jody. *The Widening Gap: Why America's Working Families Are in Jeopardy And What Can Be Done About It*. New York: Basic Books, 2000. Drawing from a wide range of data, this study makes a compelling case for more flexible work structures.

Hochschild, Arlie. *The Time Bind: When Home Becomes Work and Work Becomes Home*. New York: Metropolitan Books, 1997. This is a rich study of how employees in one company try to reconcile the tensions between spending time at work and caring for their families.

Jacobs, Jerry A., and Kathleen Gerson. *The Time Divide: Work, Family and Gender Inequality*. Cambridge, MA: Harvard University Press, 2004. An overview of trends in working time, our book shows why and how time pressures have emerged in America over the past three decades, how they are linked to gender inequality and family change and what we can do to alleviate them.

Robinson, John P., and Geoffrey Godbey. *Time For Life. The Surprising Ways Americans Use Their Time*. University Park, PA: Pennsylvania State University Press, 1999. Drawing on time diaries, Robinson and Godbey conclude that Americans' leisure time has increased.

Schor, Juliet. *The Overworked American: The Unexpected Decline of Leisure*. New York: Basic Books, 1991. This early and original analysis of how Americans are overworked sparked a national discussion on and concern for the problem.

10 *Family and the Economy*

■ **READING 29**

Families on the Fault Line

Lillian B. Rubin

THE BARDOLINOS

It has been more than three years since I first met the Bardolino family, three years in which to grow accustomed to words like *downsizing, restructuring,* or the most recent one, *reengineering;* three years in which to learn to integrate them into the language so that they now fall easily from our lips. But these are no ordinary words, at least not for Marianne and Tony Bardolino.

The last time we talked, Tony had been unemployed for about three months and Marianne was working nights at the telephone company and dreaming about the day they could afford a new kitchen. They seemed like a stable couple then—a house, two children doing well in school, Marianne working without complaint, Tony taking on a reasonable share of the family work. Tony, who had been laid off from the chemical plant where he had worked for ten years, was still hoping he'd be called back and trying to convince himself their lives were on a short hold, not on a catastrophic downhill slide. But instead of calling workers back, the company kept cutting its work force. Shortly after our first meeting, it became clear: There would be no recall. Now, as I sit in the little cottage Marianne shares with her seventeen-year-old daughter, she tells the story of these last three years.

"When we got the word that they wouldn't be calling Tony back, that's when we really panicked; I mean *really* panicked. We didn't know what to do. Where was Tony going to find another job, with the recession and all that? It was like the bottom really dropped out. Before that, we really hoped he'd be called back any day. It wasn't just crazy; they told the guys when they laid them off, you know, that it would be three, four months at most. So we hoped. I mean, sure we worried; in these times, you'd be crazy not to worry. But he'd been laid off for a couple of months before and called back, so we thought maybe it's the same thing. Besides, Tony's boss was so sure the guys would be coming back in a couple of months; so you tried to believe it was true."

She stops speaking, takes a few sips of coffee from the mug she holds in her hand, then says with a sigh, "I don't really know where to start. So much happened, and sometimes you can't even keep track. Mostly what I remember is how scared we were. Tony started to look for a job, but there was nowhere to look. The union couldn't help; there were no jobs in the industry. So he looked in the papers, and he made the rounds of all the places around here. He even went all the way to San Francisco and some of the places down near the airport there. But there was nothing.

"At first, I kept thinking, *Don't panic; he'll find something.* But after his unemployment ran out, we couldn't pay the bills, so then you can't help getting panicked, can you?"

She stops again, this time staring directly at me, as if wanting something. But I'm not sure what, so I sit quietly and wait for her to continue. Finally, she demands, "Well, can you?"

I understand now; she wants reassurance that her anxiety wasn't out of line, that it's not she who's responsible for the rupture in the family. So I say, "It sounds as if you feel guilty because you were anxious about how the family would manage."

"Yeah, that's right," she replies as she fights her tears. "I keep thinking maybe if I hadn't been so awful, I wouldn't have driven Tony away." But as soon as the words are spoken, she wants to take them back. "I mean, I don't know, maybe I wasn't that bad. We were both so depressed and scared, maybe there's nothing I could have done. But I think about it a lot, and I didn't have to blame him so much and keep nagging at him about how worried I was. It wasn't his fault; he was trying.

"It was just that we looked at it so different. I kept thinking he should take anything, but he only wanted a job like the one he had. We fought about that a lot. I mean, what difference does it make what kind of job it is? No, I don't mean that; I know it makes a difference. But when you have to support a family, that should come first, shouldn't it?"

As I listen, I recall my meeting with Tony a few days earlier and how guiltily he, too, spoke about his behavior during that time. "I wasn't thinking about her at all," he explained. "I was just so mad about what happened; it was like the world came crashing down on me. I did a little too much drinking, and then I'd just crawl into a hole, wouldn't even know whether Marianne or the kids were there or not. She kept saying it was like I wasn't there. I guess she was right, because I sure didn't want to be there, not if I couldn't support them."

"Is that the only thing you were good for in the family?" I asked him.

"Good point," he replied laughing. "Maybe not, but it's hard to know what else you're good for when you can't do that."

I push these thoughts aside and turn my attention back to Marianne. "Tony told me that he did get a job after about a year," I remark.

"Yeah, did he tell you what kind of job it was?"

"Not exactly, only that it didn't work out."

"Sure, he didn't tell you because he's still so ashamed about it. He was out of work so long that even he finally got it that he didn't have a choice. So he took this job as a dishwasher in this restaurant. It's one of those new kind of places with an open kitchen, so there he was, standing there washing dishes in front of everybody. I mean, we used to go there to eat sometimes, and now he's washing the dishes and the whole town sees him doing it. He felt so ashamed, like it was such a comedown, that he'd come home even worse than when he wasn't working.

"That's when the drinking really started heavy. Before that he'd drink, but it wasn't so bad. After he went to work there, he'd come home and drink himself into a coma. I was working days by then, and I'd try to wait up until he came home. But it didn't matter; all he wanted to do was go for that bottle. He drank a lot during the day, too, so sometimes I'd come home and find him passed out on the couch and he never got to work that day. That's when I was maddest of all. I mean, I felt sorry for him having to do that work. But I was afraid he'd get fired."

"Did he?"

"No, he quit after a couple of months. He heard there was a chemical plant down near L.A. where he might get a job. So he left. I mean, we didn't exactly separate, but we didn't exactly not. He didn't ask me and the kids to go with him; he just went. It didn't make any difference. I didn't trust him by then, so why would I leave my job and pick up the kids and move when we didn't even know if he'd find work down there?

"I think he went because he had to get away. Anyway, he never found any decent work there either. I know he had some jobs, but I never knew exactly what he was doing. He'd call once in awhile, but we didn't have much to say to each other then. I always figured he wasn't making out so well because he didn't send much money the whole time he was gone."

As Tony tells it, he was in Los Angeles for nearly a year, every day an agony of guilt and shame. "I lived like a bum when I was down there. I had a room in a place that wasn't much better than a flop house, but it was like I couldn't get it together to go find something else. I wasn't making much money, but I had enough to live decent. I felt like what difference did it make how I lived?"

He sighs—a deep, sad sound—then continues, "I couldn't believe what I did, I mean that I really walked out on my family. My folks were mad as hell at me. When I told them what I was going to do, my father went nuts, said I shouldn't come back to his house until I got some sense again. But I couldn't stay around with Marianne blaming me all the time."

He stops abruptly, withdraws to someplace inside himself for a few moments, then turns back to me. "That's not fair. She wasn't the only one doing the blaming. I kept beating myself up, too, you know, blaming myself, like I did something wrong.

"Anyhow, I hated to see what it was doing to the kids; they were like caught in the middle with us fighting and hollering, or else I was passed out drunk. I didn't want them to have to see me like that, and I couldn't help it. So I got out."

For Marianne, Tony's departure was both a relief and a source of anguish. "At first I was glad he left; at least there was some peace in the house. But then I got so scared; I didn't know if I could make it alone with the kids. That's when I sold the house. We were behind in our payments, and I knew we'd never catch up. The bank was okay; they said they'd give us a little more time. But there was no point.

"That was really hard. It was our home; we worked so hard to get it. God, I hated to give it up. We were lucky, though. We found this place here. It's near where we used to live, so the kids didn't have to change schools, or anything like that. It's small, but at least it's a separate little house, not one of those grungy apartments." She interrupts herself with a laugh, "Well, 'house' makes it sound a lot more than it is, doesn't it?"

"How did your children manage all this?"

"It was real hard on them. My son had just turned thirteen when it all happened, and he was really attached to his father. He couldn't understand why Tony left us, and he was real angry for a long time. At first, I thought he'd be okay, you know, that he'd get over it. But then he got into some bad company. I think he was doing some drugs, although he still won't admit that. Anyway, one night he and some of his friends stole a car. I think they just wanted to go for a joyride; they didn't mean to really steal it forever. But they got caught, and he got sent to juvenile hall.

"I called Tony down in L.A. and told him what happened. It really shocked him; he started to cry on the phone. I never saw him cry before, not with all our trouble. But he just cried and cried. When he got off the phone, he took the first plane he could get, and he's been back up here ever since.

"Jimmy's trouble really changed everything around. When Tony came back, he didn't want to do anything to get Jimmy out of juvy right away. He thought he ought to stay there for a while; you know, like to teach him a lesson. I was mad at first because Jimmy wanted to come home so bad; he was so scared. But now I see Tony was right.

"Anyhow, we let Jimmy stay there for five whole days, then Tony's parents lent us the money to bail him out and get him a lawyer. He made a deal so that if Jimmy pleaded guilty, he'd get a suspended sentence. And that's what happened. But the judge laid down the law, told him if he got in one little bit of trouble again, he'd go to jail. It put the fear of God into the boy."

For Tony, his son's brush with the law was like a shot in the arm. "It was like I had something really important to do, to get that kid back on track. We talked it over and Marianne agreed it would be better if Jimmy came to live with me. She's too soft with the kids; I've got better control. And I wanted to make it up to him, too, to show him he could count on me again. I figured the whole trouble came because I left them, and I wanted to set it right.

"So when he got out of juvy, he went with me to my folks' house where I was staying. We lived there for awhile until I got this job. It's no great shakes, a kind of general handyman. But it's a job, and right from the start I made enough so we could move into this here apartment. So things are going pretty good right now."

"Pretty good" means that Jimmy, now sixteen, has settled down and is doing well enough in school to talk about going to college. For Tony, too, things have turned around. He set up his own business as an independent handyman several months ago and, although the work isn't yet regular enough to allow him to quit his job, his reputation as a man who can fix just about anything is growing. Last month the business actually made enough money to pay his bills. "I'll hang onto the job for a while, even if the business gets going real good, because we've got a lot of catching up to do. I don't mind working hard; I like it. And being my own boss, boy, that's really great," he concludes exultantly.

"Do you think you and Marianne will get together again?"

"I sure hope so; it's what I'm working for right now. She says she's not sure, but she's never made a move to get a divorce. That's a good sign, isn't it?"

When I ask Marianne the same question, she says, "Tony wants to, but I still feel a little scared. You know, I never thought I could manage without him, but then when I was forced to, I did. Now, I don't know what would happen if we got together again. It wouldn't be like it was before. I just got promoted to supervisor, so I have a lot of responsibility on my job. I'm a different person, and I don't know how Tony would like that. He says he likes it fine, but I figure we should wait a while and see what happens. I mean, what if things get tough again for him? I don't ever want to live through anything like these last few years."

"Yet you've never considered divorce."

She laughs, "You sound like Tony." Then more seriously, "I don't want a divorce if I can help it. Right now, I figure if we got through these last few years and still kind of like each other, maybe we've got a chance."

* * *

When the economy falters, families tremble. The Bardolinos not only trembled, they cracked. Whether they can patch up the cracks and put the family back together again remains an open question. But the experience of families like those on the pages of this book provides undeniable evidence of the fundamental link between the public and private arenas of modern life.

No one has to tell the Bardolinos or their children about the many ways the structural changes in the economy affect family life. In the past, a worker like Tony Bardolino didn't need a high level of skill or literacy to hold down a well-paying semiskilled job in a steel mill or an automobile plant. A high school education, often even less, was enough. But an economy that relies most heavily on its service sector needs highly skilled and educated workers to fill its better-paying jobs, leaving people like Tony scrambling for jobs at the bottom of the economic order.

The shift from the manufacturing to the service sector, the restructuring of the corporate world, the competition from low-wage workers in underdeveloped countries that entices American corporations to produce their goods abroad, all have been going on for decades; all are expected to accelerate through the 1990s. The manufacturing sector, which employed just over 26 percent of American workers in 1970, already had fallen to nearly 18 percent by 1991. And experts predict a further drop to 12.5 percent by the year 2000. "This is the end of the post–World War boom era. We are never going back to what we knew," says employment analyst Dan Lacey, publisher of the newsletter *Workplace Trends*.

Yet the federal government has not only failed to offer the help working-class families need, but as a sponsor of a program to nurture capitalism elsewhere in the world it has become party to the exodus of American factories to foreign lands. Under the auspices of the U.S. Agency for International Development (AID), for example, Decaturville Sportswear, a company that used to be based in Tennessee, has moved to El Salvador. AID not only gave grants to trade organizations in El Salvador to recruit Decaturville but also subsidized the move by picking up the $5 million tab for the construction of a new plant, footing the bill for over $1 million worth of insurance, and providing low-interest loans for other expenses involved in the move.

It's a sweetheart deal for Decaturville Sportswear and the other companies that have been lured to move south of the border under this program. They build new factories at minimal cost to themselves, while their operating expenses drop dramatically. In El Salvador, Decaturville is exempted from corporate taxes and shipping duties. And best of all, the hourly wage for factory workers there is forty-five cents an hour; in the United States the minimum starting wage for workers doing the same job is $4.25.

True, like Tony Bardolino, many of the workers displaced by downsizing, restructuring, and corporate moves like these will eventually find other work. But like him also, they'll probably have to give up what little security they knew in the past. For the forty-hour-a-week steady job that pays a decent wage and provides good benefits is quickly becoming a thing of the past. Instead, as part of the new lean, clean, mean look of corporate America, we now have what the federal government and employment agencies call "contingent" workers—a more benign name for what some labor economists refer to as "disposable" or "throwaway" workers.

It's a labor strategy that comes in several forms. Generally, disposable workers are hired in part-time or temporary jobs to fill an organizational need and are released as soon as the work load lightens. But when union contracts call for employees to join the union after thirty days on the job, some unscrupulous employers fire contingent workers on the twenty-ninth day and bring in a new crew. However it's done, disposable workers earn less than those on the regular payroll and their jobs rarely come with benefits of any kind. Worse yet, they set off to work each morning fearful and uncertain, not knowing how the day will end, worrying that by nightfall they'll be out of a job.

The government's statistics on these workers are sketchy, but Labor Secretary Robert Reich estimates that they now make up nearly one-third of the existing work force. This means that about thirty-four million men and women, most of whom want steady, full-time work, start each day as contingent and/or part-time workers. Indeed, so widespread is this practice now that in some places temporary employment agencies are displacing the old ones that sought permanent placements for their clients.

Here again, class makes a difference. For while it's true that managers and professionals now also are finding themselves disposable, most of the workers who have become so easily expendable are in the lower reaches of the work order. And it's they who are likely to have the fewest options. These are the workers, the unskilled and the semiskilled—the welders, the forklift operators, the assemblers, the clerical workers, and the like—who are most likely to seem to management to be interchangeable. Their skills are limited; their job tasks are relatively simple and require little training. Therefore, they're able to move in and perform with reasonable efficiency soon after they come on the job. Whatever lost time or productivity a company may suffer by not having a steady crew of workers is compensated by the savings in wages and benefits the employment of throwaway workers permits. A resolution that brings short-term gains for the company at the long-term expense of both the workers and the nation. For when a person can't count on a permanent job, a critical element binding him or her to society is lost.

THE TOMALSONS

When I last met the Tomalsons, Gwen was working as a clerk in the office of a large Manhattan company and was also a student at a local college where she was studying nursing. George Tomalson, who had worked for three years in a furniture factory, where he laminated plastic to wooden frames, had been thrown out of a job when the company went bankrupt. He seemed a gentle man then, unhappy over the turn his life had taken but still wanting to believe that it would come out all right.

Now, as he sits before me in the still nearly bare apartment, George is angry. "If you're a black man in this country, you don't have a chance, that's all, not a chance. It's like no matter how hard you try, you're nothing but trash. I've been looking for work for over two years now, and there's nothing. White people are complaining all the time that black folks are getting a break. Yeah, well, I don't know who those people are, because it's not me or anybody else I know. People see a black man coming, they run the other way, that's what I know."

"You haven't found any work at all for two years?" I ask.

"Some temporary jobs, a few weeks sometimes, a couple of months once, mostly doing shit work for peanuts. Nothing I could count on."

"If you could do any kind of work you want, what would you do?"

He smiles, "That's easy; I'd be a carpenter. I'm good with my hands, and I know a lot about it," he says, holding his hands out, palms up, and looking at them proudly. But his mood shifts quickly; the smile disappears; his voice turns harsh. "But that's not going to happen. I tried to get into the union, but there's no room there for a black guy. And in this city, without being in the union, you don't have a chance at a construction job. They've got it all locked up, and they're making sure they keep it for themselves."

When I talk with Gwen later, she worries about the intensity of her husband's resentment. "It's not like George; he's always been a real even guy. But he's moody now, and he's so angry, I sometimes wonder what he might do. This place is a hell hole," she says, referring to the housing project they live in. "It's getting worse all the time; kids with guns, all the drugs, grown men out of work all around. I'll bet there's hardly a man in this whole place who's got a job, leave alone a good one."

"Just what is it you worry about?"

She hesitates, clearly wondering whether to speak, how much to tell me about her fears, then says with a shrug, "I don't know, everything, I guess. There's so much crime and drugs and stuff out there. You can't help wondering whether he'll get tempted." She stops herself, looks at me intently, and says, "Look, don't get me wrong; I know it's crazy to think like that. He's not that kind of person. But when you live in times like these, you can't help worrying about everything.

"We both worry a lot about the kids at school. Every time I hear about another kid shot while they're at school, I get like a raving lunatic. What's going on in this world that kids are killing kids? Doesn't anybody care that so many black kids are dying like that? It's like a black child's life doesn't count for anything. How do they expect our kids to grow up to be good citizens when nobody cares about them?

"It's one of the things that drives George crazy, worrying about the kids. There's no way you can keep them safe around here. Sometimes I wonder why we send them to school. They're not getting much of an education there. Michelle just started, but Julia's in the fifth grade, and believe me she's not learning much.

"We sit over her every night to make sure she does her homework and gets it right. But what good is it if the people at school aren't doing their job. Most of the teachers there don't give a damn. They just want the paycheck and the hell with the kids. Everybody knows it's not like that in the white schools; white people wouldn't stand for it.

"I keep thinking we've got to get out of here for the sake of the kids. I'd love to move someplace, anyplace out of the city where the schools aren't such a cesspool. But," she says dejectedly, "we'll never get out if George can't find a decent job. I'm just beginning my nursing career, and I know I've got a future now. But still, no matter what I do or how long I work at it, I can't make enough for that by myself."

George, too, has dreams of moving away, somewhere far from the city streets, away from the grime and the crime. "Look at this place," he says, his sweeping gesture taking in the whole landscape. "Is this any place to raise kids? Do you know what my little girls see every day they walk out the door? Filth, drugs, guys hanging on the corner waiting for trouble.

"If I could get any kind of a decent job, anything, we'd be out of here, far away, someplace outside the city where the kids could breathe clean and see a different life. It's so bad here, I take them over to my mother's a lot after school; it's a better neighborhood. Then we stay over there and eat sometimes. Mom likes it; she's lonely, and it helps us out. Not that she's got that much, but there's a little pension my father left."

"What about Gwen's family? Do they help out, too?"

"Her mother doesn't have anything to help with since her father died. He's long gone; he was killed by the cops when Gwen was a teenager," he says as calmly as if reporting the time of day.

"Killed by the cops." The words leap out at me and jangle my brain. But why do they startle me so? Surely with all the discussion of police violence in the black community in recent years, I can't be surprised to hear that a black man was "killed by the cops."

It's the calmness with which the news is relayed that gets to me. And it's the realization once again of the distance between the lives and experiences of blacks and others, even poor others. Not one white person in this study reported a violent death in the family. Nor did any of the Latino and Asian families, although the Latinos spoke of a difficult and often antagonistic relationship with Anglo authorities, especially the police. But four black families (13 percent) told of relatives who had been murdered, one of the families with two victims—a teenage son and a twenty-two-year-old daughter, both killed in violent street crimes.

But I'm also struck by the fact that Gwen never told me how her father died. True, I didn't ask. But I wonder now why she didn't offer the information. "Gwen didn't tell me," I say, as if trying to explain my surprise.

"She doesn't like to talk about it. Would you?" he replies somewhat curtly.

It's a moment or two before I can collect myself to speak again. Then I comment, "You talk about all this so calmly."

He leans forward, looks directly at me, and shakes his head. When he finally speaks, his voice is tight with the effort to control his rage. "What do you want? Should I rant and rave? You want me to say I want to go out and kill those mothers? Well, yeah, I do. They killed a good man just because he was black. He wasn't a criminal; he was a hard-working guy who just happened to be in the wrong place when the cops were looking for someone to shoot," he says, then sits back and stares stonily at the wall in front of him.

We both sit locked in silence until finally I break it. "How did it happen?"

He rouses himself at the sound of my voice. "They were after some dude who robbed a liquor store, and when they saw Gwen's dad, they didn't ask questions; they shot. The bastards. Then they said it was self-defense, that they saw a gun in his hand. That man never held a gun in his life, and nobody ever found one either. But nothing happens to them; it's no big deal, just another dead nigger," he concludes, his eyes blazing.

It's quiet again for a few moments, then, with a sardonic half smile, he says, "What would a nice, white middle-class lady like you know about any of that? You got all those degrees, writing books and all that. How are you going to write about people like us?"

"I was poor like you once, very poor," I say somewhat defensively.

He looks surprised, then retorts, "Poor and white; it's a big difference."

* * *

Thirty years before the beginning of the Civil War, Alexis de Tocqueville wrote: "If ever America undergoes great revolutions, they will be brought about by the presence of the black race on the soil of the United States; that is to say they will owe their origin, not to the equality, but to the inequality of condition." One hundred and sixty years later, relations between blacks and whites remain one of the great unresolved issues in American life, and "the inequality of condition" that de Tocqueville observed is still a primary part of the experience of black Americans.

I thought about de Tocqueville's words as I listened to George Tomalson and about how the years of unemployment had changed him from, as Gwen said, "a real even guy" to an angry and embittered one. And I was reminded, too, of de Tocqueville's observation that "the danger of conflict between the white and black inhabitants perpetually haunts the imagination of the [white] Americans, like a painful dream." Fifteen generations later we're still paying the cost of those years when Americans held slaves—whites still living in fear, blacks in rage. "People see a black man coming, they run the other way," says George Tomalson.

Yet however deep the cancer our racial history has left on the body of the nation, most Americans, including many blacks, believe that things are better today than they were a few decades ago—a belief that's both true and not true. There's no doubt that in ending the legal basis for discrimination and segregation, the nation took an important step toward fulfilling the promise of equality for all Americans. As more people meet as equals in the workplace, stereotypes begin to fall away and caricatures are transformed into real people. But it's also true that the economic problems of recent decades have raised the level of anxiety in American life to a new high. So although virtually all whites today give verbal assent to the need for racial justice and equality, they also find ways to resist the implementation of the belief when it seems to threaten their own status or economic well-being.

Our schizophrenia about race, our capacity to believe one thing and do another, is not new. Indeed, it is perhaps epitomized by Thomas Jefferson, the great liberator. For surely, as Gordon Wood writes in an essay in the *New York Review of Books*, "there is no greater irony in American history than the fact that America's supreme spokesman for liberty and equality was a lifelong aristocratic owner of slaves."

Jefferson spoke compellingly about the evils of slavery, but he bought, sold, bred, and flogged slaves. He wrote eloquently about equality but he was convinced that blacks were an inferior race and endorsed the racial stereotypes that have characterized African-Americans since their earliest days on this continent. He believed passionately in individual liberty, but he couldn't imagine free blacks living in America, maintaining instead that if the nation considered emancipating the slaves, it must also prepare for their expulsion.

No one talks seriously about expulsion anymore. Nor do many use the kind of language to describe African-Americans that was so common in Jefferson's day. But the duality he embodied—his belief in justice, liberty, and equality alongside his conviction of black inferiority—still lives.

THE RIVERAS

Once again Ana Rivera and I sit at the table in her bright and cheerful kitchen. She's sipping coffee; I'm drinking some bubbly water while we make small talk and get reacquainted. After a while, we begin to talk about the years since we last met. "I'm a grandmother now," she says, her face wreathed in a smile. "My daughter Karen got married and had a baby, and he's the sweetest little boy, smart, too. He's only two and a half, but you should hear him. He sounds like five."

"When I talked to her the last time I was here, Karen was planning to go to college. What happened?" I ask.

She flushes uncomfortably. "She got pregnant, so she had to get married. I was heartbroken at first. She was only nineteen, and I wanted her to get an education so bad. It was awful; she had been working for a whole year to save money for college, then she got pregnant and couldn't go."

"You say she had to get married. Did she ever consider an abortion?"

"I don't know; we never talked about it. We're Catholic," she says by way of explanation. "I mean, I don't believe in abortion." She hesitates, seeming uncertain about what more she wants to say, then adds, "I have to admit, at a time like that, you have to ask yourself what you really believe. I don't think anybody's got the right to take a child's life. But when I thought about what having that baby would do to Karen's life, I couldn't help thinking, *What if . . . ?*" She stops, unable to bring herself to finish the sentence.

"Did you ever say that to Karen?"

"No, I would *never* do that. I didn't even tell my husband I thought such things. But, you know," she adds, her voice dropping to nearly a whisper, "if she had done it, I don't think I would have said a word."

"What about the rest of the kids?"

"Paul's going to be nineteen soon; he's a problem," she sighs. "I mean, he's got a good head, but he won't use it. I don't know what's the matter with kids these days; it's like they want everything but they're not willing to work for anything. He hardly finished high school, so you can't talk to him about going to college. But what's he going to do? These days if you don't have a good education, you don't have a chance. No matter what we say, he doesn't listen, just goes on his smart-alecky way, hanging around the neighborhood with a bunch of no-good kids looking for trouble.

"Rick's so mad, he wants to throw him out of the house. But I say no, we can't do that because then what'll become of him? So we fight about that a lot, and I don't know what's going to happen."

"Does Paul work at all?"

"Sometimes, but mostly not. I'm afraid to think about where he gets money from. His father won't give him a dime. He borrows from me sometimes, but I don't have much to give him. And anyway, Rick would kill me if he knew."

I remember Paul as a gangly, shy sixteen-year-old, no macho posturing, none of the rage that shook his older brother, not a boy I would have thought would be heading for trouble. But then, Karen, too, had seemed so determined to grasp at a life that was different from the one her parents were living. What happens to these kids?

When I talk with Rick about these years, he, too, asks in bewilderment: What happened? "I don't know; we tried so hard to give the kids everything they needed. I mean, sure, we're not rich, and there's a lot of things we couldn't give them. But we were always here for them; we listened; we talked. What happened? First my daughter gets pregnant and has to get married; now my son is becoming a bum."

"Roberto—that's what we have to call him now," explains Rick, "he says it's what happens when people don't feel they've got respect. He says we'll keep losing our kids until they really believe they really have an equal chance. I don't know; I knew I had to *make* the Anglos respect me, and I had to make my chance. Why don't my kids see it like that?" he asks wearily, his shoulders seeming to sag lower with each sentence he speaks.

"I guess it's really different today, isn't it?" he sighs. "When I was coming up, you could still make your chance. I mean, I only went to high school, but I got a job and worked myself up. You can't do that anymore. Now you need to have some kind of special skills just to get a job that pays more than the minimum wage.

"And the schools, they don't teach kids anything anymore. I went to the same public schools my kids went to, but what a difference. It's like nobody cares anymore."

"How is Roberto doing?" I ask, remembering the hostile eighteen-year-old I interviewed several years earlier.

"He's still mad; he's always talking about injustice and things like that. But he's different than Paul. Roberto always had some goals. I used to worry about him because he's so angry all the time. But I see now that his anger helps him. He wants to fight for his people, to make things better for everybody. Paul, he's like the wind; nothing matters to him.

"Right now, Roberto has a job as an electrician's helper, learning the trade. He's been working there for a couple of years; he's pretty good at it. But I think—I hope—he's going to go to college. He heard that they're trying to get Chicano students to go to the university, so he applied. If he gets some aid, I think he'll go," Rick says, his face radiant at the thought that at least one of his children will fulfill his dream. "Ana and me, we tell him even if he doesn't get aid, he should go. We can't do a lot because we have to help Ana's parents and that takes a big hunk every month. But we'll help him, and he could work to make up the rest. I know it's hard to work and go to school, but people do it all the time, and he's smart; he could do it."

His gaze turns inward; then, as if talking to himself, he says, "I never thought I'd say this but I think Roberto's right. We've got something to learn from some of these kids. I told that to Roberto just the other day. He says Ana and me have been trying to pretend we're one of them all of our lives. I told him, 'I think you're right.' I kept thinking if I did everything right, I wouldn't be a 'greaser.' But after all these years, I'm still a 'greaser' in their eyes. It took my son to make me see it. Now I know. If I weren't I'd be head of the shipping department by now, not just one of the supervisors, and maybe Paul wouldn't be wasting his life on the corner."

* * *

We keep saying that family matters, that with a stable family and two caring parents children will grow to a satisfactory adulthood. But I've rarely met a family that's more constant or more concerned than the Riveras. Or one where both parents are so involved with their children. Ana was a full-time homemaker until Paul, their youngest, was twelve. Rick has been with the same company for more than twenty-five years, having worked his way up from clerk to shift supervisor in its shipping department. Whatever the conflicts in their marriage, theirs is clearly a warm, respectful, and caring relationship. Yet their daughter got pregnant and gave up her plans for college, and a son is idling his youth away on a street corner.

Obviously, then, something more than family matters. Growing up in a world where opportunities are available makes a difference. As does being able to afford to take advantage of an opportunity when it comes by. Getting an education that broadens horizons and prepares a child for a productive adulthood makes a difference. As does being able to find work that nourishes self-respect and pays a living wage. Living in a world that doesn't judge you by the color of your skin makes a difference. As does feeling the respect of the people around you.

This is not to suggest that there aren't also real problems inside American families that deserve our serious and sustained attention. But the constant focus on the failure of family life as the locus of both our personal and social difficulties has become a mindless litany, a dangerous diversion from the economic and social realities that make family life so difficult today and that so often destroy it.

THE KWANS

It's a rare sunny day in Seattle, so Andy Kwan and I are in his backyard, a lovely showcase for his talents as a landscape gardener. Although it has been only a few years since we first met, most of the people to whom I've returned in this round of interviews seem older, grayer, more careworn. Andy Kwan is no exception. The brilliant afternoon sunshine is cruel as it searches out every line of worry and age in his angular face. Since I interviewed his wife the day before, I already know that the recession has hurt his business. So I begin by saying, "Carol says that your business has been slow for the last couple of years."

"Yes," he sighs. "At first when the recession came, it didn't hurt me. I think Seattle didn't really get hit at the beginning. But the summer of 1991, that's when I began to feel it. It's as if everybody zipped up their wallets when it came to landscaping.

"A lot of my business has always been when people buy a new house. You know, they want to fix up the outside just like they like it. But nobody's been buying houses lately, and even if they do, they're not putting any money into landscaping. So it's been tight, real tight."

"How have you managed financially?"

"We get by, but it's hard. We have to cut back on a lot of stuff we used to take for granted, like going out to eat once in a while, or going to the movies, things like that. Clothes, nobody gets any new clothes anymore.

"I do a lot of regular gardening now—you know, the maintenance stuff. It helps; it takes up some of the slack, but it's not enough because it doesn't pay much. And the competition's pretty stiff, so you've got to keep your prices down. I mean, everybody knows that it's one of the things people can cut out when things get tough, so the gardeners around here try to hold on by cutting their prices. It gets pretty hairy, real cutthroat."

He gets up, walks over to a flower bed, and stands looking at it. Then, after a few quiet moments, he turns back to me and says, "It's a damned shame. I built my business like you build a house, brick by brick, and it was going real good. I finally got to the point where I wasn't doing much regular gardening anymore. I could concentrate on land-scaping, and I was making a pretty good living. With Carol working, too, we were doing all right. I even hired two people and was keeping them busy most of the time. Then all of a sudden, it all came tumbling down.

"I felt real bad when I had to lay off my workers. They have families to feed, too. But what could I do? Now it's like I'm back where I started, an ordinary gardener again and even worrying about how long that'll last," he says disconsolately.

He walks back to his seat, sits down, and continues somewhat more philosophically, "Carol says I shouldn't complain because, with all the problems, we're lucky. She still has her job, and I'm making out. I mean, it's not great, but it could be a lot worse." He pauses, looks around blankly for a moment, sighs, and says, "I guess she's right. Her sister worked at Boeing for seven years and she got laid off a couple of months ago. No notice, noth-ing; just the pink slip. I mean, everybody knew there'd be layoffs there, but you know how it is. You don't think it's really going to happen to you.

"I try not to let it get me down. But it's hard to be thankful for not having bigger trouble than you've already got," he says ruefully. Then, a smile brightening his face for the first time, he adds, "But there's one thing I can be thankful for, and that's the kids; they're doing fine. I worry a little bit about what's going to happen, though. I guess you can't help it if you're a parent. Eric's the oldest; he's fifteen now, and you never know. Kids get into all kinds of trouble these days. But so far, he's okay. The girls, they're good kids. Carol worries about what'll happen when they get to those teenage years. But I think they'll be okay. We teach them decent values; they go to church every week. I have to believe that makes a difference."

"You say that you worry about Eric but that the girls will be fine because of the val-ues of your family. Hasn't he been taught the same values?"

He thinks a moment, then says, "Did I say that? Yeah, I guess I did. I think maybe there's more ways for a boy to get in trouble than a girl." He laughs and says again, "Did I say *that?*" Then, more thoughtfully, "I don't know. I guess I worry about them all, but if you don't tell yourself that things'll work out okay, you go nuts. I mean, so much can go wrong with kids today.

"It used to be the Chinese family could really control the kids. When I was a kid, the family was law. My father was Chinese-born; he came here as a kid. My mother was born right here in this city. But the grandparents were all immigrants; everybody spoke Chinese at home; and we never lived more than a couple of blocks from both sides of the family. My parents were pretty Americanized everywhere but at home, at least while their parents were alive. My mother would go clean her mother's house for her because that's what a Chinese daughter did."

"Was that because your grandmother was old or sick?"

"No," he replies, shaking his head at the memory. "It's because that's what her mother expected her to do; that's the way Chinese families were then. We talk about that, Carol and me, and how things have changed. It's hard to imagine it, but that's the kind of control families had then.

"It's all changed now. Not that I'd want it that way. I want my kids to know respect for the family, but they shouldn't be servants. That's what my mother was, a servant for her mother.

"By the time my generation came along, things were already different. I couldn't wait to get away from all that family stuff. I mean, it was nice in some ways; there was always this big, noisy bunch of people around, and you knew you were part of something. That felt good. But Chinese families, boy, they don't let go. You felt like they were choking you.

"Now it's *really* different; it's like the kids aren't hardly Chinese any more. I mean, my kids are just like any other American kids. They never lived in a Chinese neighborhood like the one I grew up in, you know, the kind where the only Americans you see are the people who come to buy Chinese food or eat at the restaurants."

"You say they're ordinary American kids. What about the Chinese side? What kind of connection do they have to that?"

"It's funny," he muses. "We sent them to Chinese school because we wanted them to know about their history, and we thought they should know the language, at least a little bit. But they weren't really interested; they wanted to be like everybody else and eat peanut butter and jelly sandwiches. Lately it's a little different, but that's because they feel like they're picked on because they're Chinese. I mean, everybody's worrying about the Chinese kids being so smart and winning all the prizes at school, and the kids are angry about that, especially Eric. He says there's a lot of bad feelings about Chinese kids at school and that everybody's picking on them—the white kids and the black kids, all of them.

"So all of a sudden, he's becoming Chinese. It's like they're making him think about it because there's all this resentment about Asian kids all around. Until a couple of years ago, he had lots of white friends. Now he hangs out mostly with other Asian kids. I guess that's because they feel safer when they're together."

"How do you feel about this?"

The color rises in his face; his voice takes on an edge of agitation. "It's too bad. It's not the way I wanted it to be. I wanted my kids to know they're Chinese and be proud of it, but that's not what's going on now. It's more like . . . , " he stops, trying to find the words, then starts again. "It's like they have to defend themselves *because* they're Chinese. Know what I mean?" he asks. Then without waiting for an answer, he explains, "There's all this prejudice now, so then you can't forget you're Chinese.

"It makes me damn mad. You grow up here and they tell you everybody's equal and that any boy can grow up to be president. Not that I ever thought a Chinese kid could ever be president; any Chinese kid knows that's fairy tale. But I did believe the rest of it, you know, that if you're smart and work hard and do well, people will respect you and you'll be successful. Now, it looks like the smarter Chinese kids are, the more trouble they get."

"Do you think that prejudice against Chinese is different now than when you were growing up?"

"Yeah, I do. When I was a kid like Eric, nobody paid much attention to the Chinese. They left us alone, and we left them alone. But now all these Chinese kids are getting in the way of the white kids because there's so many of them, and they're getting better grades, and things like that. So then everybody gets mad because they think our kids are taking something from them."

He stops, weighs his last words, then says, "I guess they're right, too. When I was growing up, Chinese kids were lucky to graduate from high school, and we didn't get in anybody's way. Now so many Chinese kids are going to college that they're taking over places white kids used to have. I can understand that they don't like that. But that's not our problem; it's theirs. Why don't they work hard like Chinese kids do?

"It's not fair that they've got quotas for Asian kids because the people who run the colleges decided there's too many of them and not enough room for white kids. Nobody ever worried that there were too many white kids, did they?"

* * *

"It's not fair"— a cry from the heart, one I heard from nearly everyone in this study. For indeed, life has not been fair to the working-class people of America, no matter what their color or ethnic background. And it's precisely this sense that it's not fair, that there isn't enough to go around, that has stirred the racial and ethnic tensions that are so prevalent today.

In the face of such clear class disparities, how is it that our national discourse continues to focus on the middle class, denying the existence of a working class and rendering them invisible?

Whether a family or a nation, we all have myths that play tag with reality—myths that frame our thoughts, structure our beliefs, and organize our systems of denial. A myth encircles reality, encapsulates it, controls it. It allows us to know some things and to avoid knowing others, even when somewhere deep inside we really know what we don't want to know. Every parent has experienced this clash between myth and reality. We see signals that tell us a child is lying and explain them away. It isn't that we can't know; it's that we won't, that knowing is too difficult or painful, too discordant with the myth that defines the relationship, the one that says: *My child wouldn't lie to me.*

The same is true about a nation and its citizens. Myths are part of our national heritage, giving definition to the national character, offering guidance for both public and private behavior, comforting us in our moments of doubt. Not infrequently our myths trip over each other, providing a window into our often contradictory and ambivalently held beliefs. The myth that we are a nation of equals lives side-by-side in these United States with the belief in white supremacy. And, unlikely as it seems, it's quite possible to believe both at the same time. Sometimes we manage the conflict by shifting from one side to the other. More often, we simply redefine reality. The inequality of condition between whites and blacks isn't born in prejudice and discrimination, we insist; it's black inferiority that's the problem. Class distinctions have nothing to do with privilege, we say; it's merit that makes the difference.

It's not the outcome that counts, we maintain; it's the rules of the game. And since the rules say that everyone comes to the starting line equal, the different results are merely products of individual will and wit. The fact that working-class children usually grow up to be working-class parents doesn't make a dent in the belief system, nor does it lead to questions about why the written rule and the lived reality are at odds. Instead, with perfect circularity, the outcome reinforces the reasoning that says they're deficient, leaving those so labeled doubly wounded—first by the real problems in living they face, second by internalizing the blame for their estate.

Two decades ago, when I began the research for *Worlds of Pain*, we were living in the immediate aftermath of the civil rights revolution that had convulsed the nation since the mid-1950s. Significant gains had been won. And despite the tenacity with which this headway had been resisted by some, most white Americans were feeling good about themselves. No one expected the nation's racial problems and conflicts to dissolve easily or quickly. But there was also a sense that we were moving in the right direction, that there was a national commitment to redressing at least some of the worst aspects of black-white inequality.

In the intervening years, however, the national economy buckled under the weight of three recessions, while the nation's industrial base was undergoing a massive restructuring. At the same time, government policies requiring preferential treatment were enabling African-Americans and other minorities to make small but visible inroads into what had been, until then, largely white terrain. The sense of scarcity, always a part of American life but intensified sharply by the history of these economic upheavals, made minority gains seem particularly threatening to white working-class families.

It isn't, of course, just working-class whites who feel threatened by minority progress. Wherever racial minorities make inroads into formerly all-white territory, tensions increase. But it's working-class families who feel the fluctuations in the economy most quickly and most keenly. For them, these last decades have been like a bumpy roller coaster ride. "Every time we think we might be able to get ahead, it seems like we get knocked down again," declares Tom Ahmundsen, a forty-two-year-old white construction worker. "Things look a little better; there's a little more work; then all of a sudden, boom, the economy falls apart and it's gone. You can't count on anything; it really gets you down."

This is the story I heard repeatedly: Each small climb was followed by a fall, each glimmer of hope replaced by despair. As the economic vise tightened, despair turned to anger. But partly because we have so little concept of class resentment and conflict in America, this anger isn't directed so much at those above as at those below. And when whites at or near the bottom of the ladder look down in this nation, they generally see blacks and other minorities.

True, during all of the 1980s and into the 1990s, white ire was fostered by national administrations that fanned racial discord as a way of fending off white discontent—of diverting anger about the state of the economy and the declining quality of urban life to the foreigners and racial others in our midst. But our history of racial animosity coupled with our lack of class consciousness made this easier to accomplish than it might otherwise have been.

The difficult realities of white working-class life not withstanding, however, their whiteness has accorded them significant advantages—both materially and psychologically—over people of color. Racial discrimination and segregation in the workplace have kept competition for the best jobs at a minimum. They do, obviously, have to compete with each other for the resources available. But that's different. It's a competition among equals; they're all white. They don't think such things consciously, of course; they don't have to. It's understood, rooted in the culture and supported by the social contract that says they are the superior ones, the worthy ones. Indeed, this is precisely why, when the courts or the legislatures act in ways that seem to contravene that belief, whites experience themselves as victims.

From the earliest days of the republic, whiteness has been the ideal, and freedom and independence have been linked to being white. "Republicanism," writes labor historian

David Roediger, "had long emphasized that the strength, virtue and resolve of a people guarded them from enslavement." And it was whites who had these qualities in abundance, as was evident, in the peculiarly circuitous reasoning of the time, in the fact that they were not slaves.

By this logic, the enslavement of blacks could be seen as stemming from their "slavishness" rather than from the institution of slavery. Slavery is gone now, but the reasoning lingers on in white America, which still insists that the lowly estate of people of color is due to their deficits, whether personal or cultural, rather than to the prejudice, discrimination, and institutionalized racism that has barred them from full participation in the society.

This is not to say that culture is irrelevant, whether among black Americans or any other group in our society. The lifeways of a people develop out of their experiences—out of the daily events, large and small, that define their lives; out of the resources that are available to them to meet both individual and group needs; out of the place in the social, cultural, and political systems within which group life is embedded. In the case of a significant proportion of blacks in America's inner cities, centuries of racism and economic discrimination have produced a subculture that is both personally and socially destructive. But to fault culture or the failure of individual responsibility without understanding the larger context within which such behaviors occur is to miss a vital piece of the picture. Nor does acknowledging the existence of certain destructive subcultural forms among some African-Americans disavow or diminish the causal connections between the structural inequalities at the social, political, and economic levels and the serious social problems at the community level.

In his study of "working-class lads" in Birmingham, England, for example, Paul Willis observes that their very acts of resistance to middle-class norms—the defiance with which these young men express their anger at class inequalities—help to reinforce the class structure by further entrenching them in their working-class status. The same can be said for some of the young men in the African-American community, whose active rejection of white norms and "in your face" behavior consigns them to the bottom of the American economic order.

To understand this doesn't make such behavior, whether in England or the United States, any more palatable. But it helps to explain the structural sources of cultural forms and to apprehend the social processes that undergird them. Like Willis's white "working-class lads," the hip-hoppers and rappers in the black community who are so determinedly "not white" are not just making a statement about black culture. They're also expressing their rage at white society for offering a promise of equality, then refusing to fulfill it. In the process, they're finding their own way to some accommodation and to a place in the world they can call their own, albeit one that ultimately reinforces their outsider status.

But, some might argue, white immigrants also suffered prejudice and discrimination in the years after they first arrived, but they found more socially acceptable ways to accommodate. It's true—and so do most of today's people of color, both immigrant and native born. Nevertheless, there's another truth as well. For wrenching as their early experiences were for white ethnics, they had an out. Writing about the Irish, for example, Roediger shows how they were able to insist upon their whiteness and to prove it by adopting the racist attitudes and behaviors of other whites, in the process often becoming leaders in the assault against blacks. With time and their growing political power, they won the prize they sought—recognition as whites. "The imperative to define themselves as white," writes Roediger, "came from the particular 'public and psychological wages' whiteness offered to a desperate rural and often preindustrial Irish population coming to labor in industrializing American cities."

Thus does whiteness bestow its psychological as well as material blessings on even the most demeaned. For no matter how far down the socioeconomic ladder whites may fall, the one thing they can't lose is their whiteness. No small matter because, as W. E. B. DuBois observed decades ago, the compensation of white workers includes a psychological wage, a bonus that enables them to believe in their inherent superiority over nonwhites.

It's also true, however, that this same psychological bonus that white workers prize so highly has cost them dearly. For along with the importation of an immigrant population, the separation of black and white workers has given American capital a reserve labor force to call upon whenever white workers seemed to them to get too "uppity." Thus, while racist ideology enables white workers to maintain the belief in their superiority, they have paid for that conviction by becoming far more vulnerable in the struggle for decent wages and working conditions than they might otherwise have been. . . .

■ READING 30

The Economy That Never Sleeps

Harriet B. Presser

Forty percent of the American labor force works mostly during nonstandard times—in the evenings, overnight, on rotating or variable shifts, or on weekends. These schedules challenge American families, particularly those with children. Research suggests that such schedules undermine the stability of marriages, increase the amount of housework to be done, reduce family cohesiveness, and require elaborate child-care arrangements.

Nonstandard work schedules also have some benefits. Most notably, when fathers and mothers work different shifts, fathers and children typically spend more time together and child care costs less. Parents of school-aged children who work late shifts can see their children off to school and welcome them home. However, the advantages and disadvantages of nonstandard work hours are not evenly distributed. Some kinds of families and workers feel the downside more than others. And all off-hour workers and families need more attention than they are now getting.

Late and rotating work shifts are certainly not new. Some people have always worked at all hours of the day and night. While official data on which hours people work have only recently become available, in recent decades the number of people working nonstandard schedules seems to have increased. A central factor is the remarkable growth of the service economy—particularly in the food, recreation, travel and medical care industries—all of which require more round-the-clock employees than does manufacturing. Consumers are clamoring for continuously available services as well. We see these trends in the newly common phrase "24/7" and in the extension of store hours. Indeed, the 7-Eleven convenience stores, once considered unusual for opening at 7 a.m. and closing at 11 p.m., are anachronistically named: almost all of them are now open around the clock.

At the same time, families themselves are changing. With the growth of female employment, spouses increasingly both work. Also, increasingly many employed mothers are single parents. The "Ozzie and Harriet" family—in which the father works outside the home full time and the mother is a full-time homemaker—has become more and more of an exception. Although we have belatedly come to acknowledge this change, we still tend to think of employed parents as working in the daytime and home with their children in the evening and at night. This remains the case for most parents, but not for a substantial minority.

With more employed mothers—married or single—and more diverse work schedules, the rhythm of family life is changing for millions of Americans. We need to discuss whether employers and government can and should do more to ease the social and physical stresses that many families experience. Moreover, employees need to be aware of the risks of working late and rotating hours so that they can make more informed decisions before accepting such a job—assuming, of course, they have a genuine choice in the matter.

WHO WORKS NONSTANDARD SCHEDULES?

Nonstandard work schedules are surprisingly common. One out of five employed Americans work most of their hours outside the range of 8 a.m. to 4 p.m., or have a regularly rotating schedule. Many more work at least some of their hours in the evenings or at night. About one-third of employed Americans work Saturday, Sunday or both. Men are somewhat more likely than women to work nonstandard schedules, and minorities—particularly blacks—are more likely to do so than non-Hispanic whites. (These estimates are based on a large, representative national sample in 1997. More recent numbers, not yet fully analyzed, suggest little change since then.)

Dual-earner married couples are especially likely to have at least one spouse working late or rotating shifts. In 1997, this was so for 28 percent of all such couples, but even more so for those with children: 35 percent of dual-earner couples with a child under 5 had a parent with such a schedule. (Rarely did both spouses work such schedules.) These percentages are yet higher among low-income couples, the families most likely to be under financial stress while juggling a difficult work schedule.

Weekend work among dual-earner couples is also very common. In more than two-fifths of all dual-earner couples, at least one spouse worked on Saturday or Sunday. The ratio was closer to one-half of all dual-earner couples with children under five. And again, low-income couples had especially high rates of weekend work.

Single mothers are more likely than married mothers to work at nonstandard times and to work long hours. About one-fourth of single mothers with children worked late or rotating shifts and more than one-third worked weekends. For single mothers with children under age five, these ratios were one-fourth and two-fifths, respectively—and still higher for those with low incomes.

STRESS ON MARRIAGES

Late and rotating work schedules seem particularly damaging to marriages when the couples have children at home. The competing demands of children and spouses come through in intensive interviews with such couples. In *Families on the Fault Line*, Lillian Rubin writes about one couple working split shifts: "If the arriving spouse gets home early enough, there may be an hour when both are there together. But with the pressures of the workday fresh for one and awaiting for the other, and with children clamoring for parental attention, there isn't a promising moment for serious conversation" (p. 95). From similar interviews in *Halving It All*, Francine Deutsch reports that, although this arrangement allowed both spouses to care for their children themselves and contribute to family income, "the loss of time together was a bitter pill to swallow. The physical separation symbolized a spiritual separation as well" (p. 177).

Large survey studies confirm that dual-earner couples with children have a less satisfactory married life when one spouse works at nonstandard times. I found, in a sample of about 3,500 married couples, that those in which one spouse works a late shift report having substantially less quality time together and more marital unhappiness. Couples with children are also more likely to separate or divorce. Neither working the evening shift nor weekends seemed to endanger the marriages; only night work did. One might think that spouses who choose to work night shifts do so because their marriages have soured, but data suggest the opposite: the schedule is the cause and marital strain is the effect. Spouses who moved into night work after the first interviews were not any less happy with their marriages during those pre-change interviews than were other employed spouses.

FAMILY REACTIONS

When spouses work different shifts, housework expands. Spouses tend to fend for themselves more, adding to the total family work load. Each one may make dinner for him- or herself rather than one cooking for two (as well as for the children). The husbands also do more traditionally female tasks, such as cleaning house, washing, ironing and cooking. These changes emerge for couples both with and without children. Although wives typically still spend considerably more time than husbands doing housework, husbands shoulder a larger share when their wives are not available. Working late shifts may not be the ideal way of achieving gender equality in housework, but it may be considered a good change by many wives in this situation. However, men who have traditional expectations may see it differently, making housework a potential source of friction.

The family dinner is typically the only daily event that allows for meaningful family time. The dinnertime absence of parents who work evening shifts is clearly a cost. (Night shifts and weekend employment do not generally undercut the family dinner, although schedules that rotate around the clock can.) As [Figure 1] shows, among dual-earner couples with children ages 5 to 13, about 45 percent of the mothers and 59 percent of the fathers who worked evenings had dinner with their children fewer than five days a week. Many of their children at least had one parent available at dinnertime—but not children of single mothers. When single moms worked evenings, fewer than 40 percent ate with their children at least five days a week. Their children may have been eating with other adults, with siblings, or alone—we do not know. (Parents who miss dinner with their children because they work the evening shift do not compensate by having breakfast with them more often.)

Child care also must be negotiated differently. If mothers who work evenings or nights are married, their husbands who work during the day typically assume responsibility for child care during those hours. More than four-fifths of fathers with children under age 5 did so. Child care is also shared when the work schedules of spouses are reversed and the husband works nonstandard hours.

This tag-team arrangement increases father-child interaction. It also reduces the cost of child care. Holding down expenses is especially a concern when married mothers have low-paying jobs. But most married mothers who work evenings, nights or rotating shifts do not say they do it for this reason. Many say it is because the job demands it. Similarly, very few fathers of young children report that they work non-standard schedules

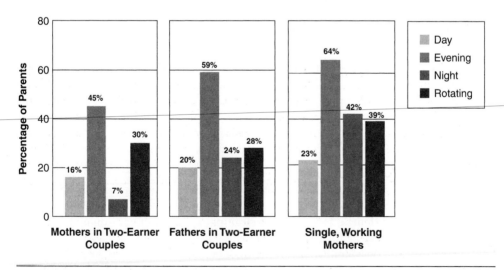

FIGURE 1   *Missing Dinner: Percentage of Parents Who Ate Dinner with Their Children Fewer than 5 Times in the Last Week, According to the Work Shift*

Source: 1987–88 National Survey of Families and Households.

for child care reasons, even though they are often caregivers. Many parents simply do not have a choice in their work schedules.

Child care studies show that off-hours workers also rely heavily on relatives, particularly grandparents. Single mothers are especially likely to rely on grandparents, particularly grandmothers, who often work jobs with hours different from their daughters', allowing them to care for their grandchildren in their "off time."

Both single and married mothers have to rely on relatives (as well as neighbors and other informal caregivers) because only a few child care centers are open evenings or nights and not many are open on weekends. Because relatives and neighbors may not be available or willing to babysit during all the mothers' work hours, mothers are often forced to rely on multiple child care providers. More than half of all American mothers with children under age five who work late or rotating schedules or weekends rely on two or more caregivers. Multiple child care arrangements can create multiple breakdowns. Single mothers are especially vulnerable to such problems, since given their usually low earnings, they have fewer child care options. A recent tragedy reported in the *New York Times* (October 19, 2003) illuminates the frustration many single mothers on the night shift must face, as well as the potential for calamity:

> [A]s her night shift neared, Kim Brathwaite faced a hard choice. Her baby sitter had not shown up, and to miss work might end her position as assistant manager at a McDonald's in downtown Brooklyn. So she left her two children, 9 and 1, alone, trying to stay in touch by phone. It turned out to be a disastrous decision. Someone, it seems, deliberately set fire to the apartment. Her children died. And within hours, Ms. Brathwaite was under arrest, charged with recklessly endangering her children . . . and now faces up to 16 years in prison. . . .

HEALTH

Several intensive studies suggest that sleep deprivation is a chronic problem for people who work late at night or rotate their hours around the clock on a regular basis. Parents who forego sleep in order to be available for their children when they are home from school aggravate the toll on their personal health. People with such schedules run higher risks of gastrointestinal disorders, cardiovascular disease and breast cancer. Late and changing work schedules affect our sleep cycles, which in turn are linked to such biological functions as body temperature and hormone levels. Also, being out of sync with the daily rhythms of other family members raises stress and further affects physiological and psychological health.

A PUBLIC DISCUSSION

Clearly, employment in a 24/7 economy challenges American families. Given what we already know—and there is more to learn—we need more public discussion on the role of employers and government. How can we help American workers and families who are feeling the pinch of nonstandard work shifts either to change to day schedules or cope with the odd hours? Low-income parents merit special attention, because they have the fewest work options and suffer the worst financial and emotional stress.

There are several policy options. For instance, we could require higher wages for late shifts to compensate workers for the social and health costs of their schedules, or reduce work hours on late shifts (without a reduction in pay) to minimize the stress on individuals and families. Such reforms could make a major difference for 24/7 workers. Although employment at nonstandard times is pervasive from the worst to the best jobs, one-third of the nonstandard jobs are concentrated in just 10 service-sector occupations, most of which are low paying: cashiers; truck drivers; sales people; waiters and waitresses; cooks; janitors and cleaners; sales supervisors and proprietors; registered nurses; food service and lodging managers; and nursing aides, orderlies, and attendants. Except for registered nurses, the median hourly pay for those in the same occupations who work at nonstandard times is about the same as or less than the pay for people who work daytimes and weekdays only. On the other hand, a financial premium for taking late shifts might tempt more nonparents to compete for those jobs or more low-income parents to take them.

Efforts to enact workshift reforms are constrained by a lack of legal guidelines for adult workers. The Fair Labor Standards Act deals with overtime compensation for working more than 40 hours a week, but does not deal explicitly with work shifts. Pay premiums for shift work are generally negotiated by unions, but only a small minority of American workers are union members. Some unions have negotiated reduced hours at full-time pay for people working late shifts, but this is rare and the pay premiums generally are not large.

Policy could also address the particular difficulties of nonstandard shifts for parents with children by expanding the availability, flexibility and affordability of child care. Little child care is available in the evening and overnight. (Ironically, the people who would provide the care would themselves become part of the problem.) Extra compensation from public sources to providers may be needed. On-site care by employers, as some hospitals provide, and near-site care, as some airports provide, may also help. But many neighborhoods resist the late-night traffic of parents dropping off and picking up their children.

Alternatively, child care subsidies would give more low-income mothers the option of working standard hours while using day care for their young children. As noted earlier, parents who work late shifts rely heavily on multiple child-care arrangements with spouses, relatives and others. Such arrangements for late-hour home care may be financially cheaper than center care, but they may be more costly socially for everyone involved.

Finally, a policy option is to regulate night work, as many other highly industrialized countries do. For example, Belgium has highly restrictive legislation, which generally prohibits work between 8 p.m. and 6 a.m. (exceptions allow for emergency services) and all night workers are entitled by law to substantial pay premiums. However, while European unions fought for such legislation, the restriction of late work shifts does not seem to be high on the agenda of American organized labor. Some voices call for reducing the work week from 40 to 35 hours without reducing pay, but these suggestions treat all hours alike.

If new regulations are pursued, they must avoid discouraging employers from hiring parents of young children. Janet Gornick and Marcia Meyers have proposed the adoption of gender-egalitarian protections that would prevent employers from forcing parents into nonstandard shifts. These protections would expand child care as well, so that parents could switch out of those shifts if they so desire (and presumably not lose their jobs). This is clearly a complex social issue, especially in light of the increasing wariness of protective legislation amid concerns about who is protected by it. In 1990, the International Labor Organization decided to drop its recommended restrictions on women working at night after realizing that the rule had a discriminatory effect: to save those jobs for men. Similarly, in the United States, legislation protective of women was declared by the courts to be invalid under the 1964 Civil Rights Act, which outlawed sex discrimination.

Americans may not be debating these matters because, as consumers, we like stores to be open around the clock, medical services to be available continuously, and people to answer the phone when we make travel reservations late at night. Also, as employees, we may benefit from the expansion of job opportunities in a 24/7 economy. But, again, the economy that never sleeps poses risks to the workers who staff it, and to their families. Given that difficult work schedules are currently a fact of life in our economy, it is obvious that we need to think about how to mitigate their harm. Some employers have tried out shift rotation systems that minimize employee fatigue; others have investigated the use of light to control or change the circadian rhythms of people working late hours. There is also talk about medications that could reset the body's clock. We must consider as well the ethical issues that underlie these manipulations, insofar as they put workers out of sync with family and friends.

When 2 of every 5 working Americans are on nonstandard shifts, employment in a 24/7 economy and its effects on them and their families clearly need to be put higher on the public agenda. The underlying trends that have brought about the great diversity in work schedules among Americans will surely continue, and we need to confront the challenges they pose for American families.

Recommended Resources

Casper, Lynne M. "My Daddy Takes Care of Me!: Fathers as Care Providers." *Current Population Reports.* Washington, D.C.: U.S. Government Printing Office for the U.S. Bureau of the Census, 1997. Casper describes in detail the extent to which American fathers provide child care when mothers are employed.

Deutsch, Francine. *Halving It All: How Equally Shared Parenting Works.* Cambridge, MA: Harvard University Press, 1999. This interview-based study includes a chapter on how some dual-earner couples work different shifts to manage child care.

Presser, Harriet B. *Working in a 24/7 Economy: Challenges for American Families.* New York: Russell Sage Foundation, 2003. This book describes what we know about work shifts in the United States and their consequences for American families.

Presser, Harriet B. "Race-Ethnic and Gender Differences in Nonstandard Work Shifts." *Work and Occupations* 30 (2003): 412–439. I examine how work shifts differ by race, ethnicity and gender.

Wedderburn, Alexander, ed. "Shiftwork and Health." Special issue of *Bulletin of Studies on Time, Vol. 1.* Luxembourg: Office for Official Publications of the European Communities, 2001. Online. http://www.eurofound.ie. This report provides a comprehensive analysis of the relationship between shift work and health.

■ READING 31

Why Middle-Class Mothers and Fathers Are Going Broke

Elizabeth Warren and Amelia Warren Tyagi

During the past generation, a great myth has swept through America. Like all good myths, the Over-Consumption Myth tells a tale to explain a confusing world. Why are so many Americans in financial trouble? Why are credit card debts up and savings down? Why are millions of mothers heading into the labor force and working overtime? The myth is so deeply embedded in our collective understanding that it resists even elementary questioning: Families have spent too much money buying things they don't need. Americans have a new character flaw—"the urge to splurge"[1]—and it is driving them to spend, spend, spend like never before.

The drive for all that spending is almost mystical in origin. John de Graaf and his coauthors explain in *Affluenza: The All-Consuming Epidemic,* "It's as if we Americans, despite our intentions, suffer from some kind of Willpower Deficiency Syndrome, a breakdown in affluenza immunity."[2] Economist Juliet Schor blames "the never consumerism," but the results are the same. She points to "mass 'overspending' within the middle class [in which] large numbers of Americans spend more than they say they would like to, and more than they have. That they spend more than they realize they are spending, and more than is fiscally prudent.[3]

Many maladies are explained away by the Over-Consumptive Myth. Why are Americans in debt? Sociologist Robert Frank claims that America's newfound "Luxury Fever" forces middle-class families "to finance their consumption increases largely by reduced savings and increased debt."[4] Why are schools failing and streets unsafe? Juliet Schor cites "competitive spending" as a major contributor to "the deterioration of public goods" such as "education, social services, public safety, recreation, and culture."[5] Why are Americans unhappy? *Affluenza* sums it up: "The dogged pursuit for more" accounts for Americans' "overload, debt, anxiety, and waste."[6] Everywhere we turn, it seems that over-consumption is tearing at the very fabric of society.

The Over-Consumption Myth rests on the premise that families spend their money on things they don't really need. Over-consumption is not about medical care or basic housing; it is, in the words of Juliet Schor, about "designer clothes, a microwave, restaurant meals, home and automobile air conditioning, and, of course, Michael Jordan's ubiquitous athletic shoes, about which children and adults both display near-obsession."[7] And it isn't about buying a few goodies with extra income; it is about going deep into debt to finance consumer purchases that sensible people could do without.

The beauty of the Over-Consumption Myth is that it squares neatly with our own intuitions. We see the malls packed with shoppers. We receive catalogs filled with outrageously expensive gadgets. We think of that overpriced summer dress that hangs in the back of the closet or those power tools gathering dust in the garage. The conclusion seems indisputable: The "urge to splurge" is driving folks into economic ruin.

But is it true? Intuitions and anecdotes are no substitute for hard data, so we searched deep in the recesses of federal archives, where we found detailed information on Americans' spending patterns since the early 1970s, carefully sorted by spending categories and family size.[9] If families really are blowing their paychecks on designer clothes and restaurant meals, then the expenditure data should show that today's families are spending more on these frivolous items than ever before. (Throughout our discussion, in this [reading] . . . all figures will be adjusted for the effects of inflation.[9]) But we found that the numbers pointed in a very different direction, demonstrating that the over-consumption explanation is just a myth.

Consider clothing. *Newsweek* recently ran a multipage cover story about Americans drowning in debt. The reason for widespread financial distress and high bankruptcy rates? "Frivolous shopping is part of the problem: many debtors blame their woes squarely on Tommy, Ralph, Gucci, and Prada."[10] That certainly sounds reasonable. After all, Banana Republic is so crowded with shoppers we can barely find an empty fitting room, Adidas and Nike clad the feet of every teenager we meet, and designer shops rake in profits selling nothing but underwear or sunglasses. Even little children's clothes now carry hip brand names, and babies sport "GAP" or "YSL" on their T-shirts and sleepers.

And yet, when it is all added up, including the Tommy sweatshirts and Ray-Ban sunglasses, the average family of four today spends 21 percent *less* (inflation adjusted) on clothing than a similar family did in the early 1970s. How can this be? What the finger-waggers have forgotten are the things families *don't* spend money on anymore. I (Elizabeth) recall the days of rushing off to Stride Rite to buy two new pairs of sensible leather shoes for each of my children every three months (one for church and one for everyday) plus a pair of sneakers for play. Today, Amelia's toddler owns nothing but a pair of $5 sandals from Wal-Mart. Suits, ties, and pantyhose have been replaced by cotton trousers and knit tops, as "business casual" has swept the nation. New fabrics, new technology, and cheap labor have lowered prices. And discounters like Target and Marshall's have popped up across the country, providing reasonable, low-cost clothes for today's families. The differences add up. In 1973, Sunday dresses, wool jackets, and the other clothes for a family of four claimed nearly $750 more a year from the family budget than all the name-brand sneakers and hip T-shirts today's families are buying.[11]

OK, so if Americans aren't blowing their paychecks on clothes, then they must be overspending on food. Designer brands have hit the grocery shelves as well, with far more prepared foods, high-end ice creams, and exotic juices. Families even buy bottles of *water*, a purchase that would have shocked their grandparents. Besides, who cooks at home any-more? With Mom and Dad both tied up at work, Americans are eating out (or ordering in) more than ever before. The authors of *Affluenza* grumble, "City streets and even suburban malls sport a United Nations of restaurants. . . . Eating out used to be a special occasion. Now we spend more money on restaurant food than on the food we cook ourselves.[12]

They are right, but only to a point. The average family of four spends more at restaurants than it used to, but it spends less at the grocery store—a lot less. Families are saving big bucks by skipping the T-bone steaks, buying their cereal in bulk at Costco, and opting for generic paper towels and canned vegetables. Those savings more than compensate for all that restaurant eating—so much so that today's family of four is actually spending 22 percent *less* on food (at-home and restaurant eating combined) than its counterpart of a generation ago.[13]

Outfitting the home? *Affluenza* rails against appliances "that were deemed luxuries as recently as 1970, but are now found in well over half of U.S. homes, and thought of by a majority of Americans as necessities: dishwashers, clothes dryers, central heating and air conditioning, color and cable TV."[14] These handy gadgets may have captured a new place in Americans' hearts, but they aren't taking up much space in our wallets. Manufacturing costs are down, and durability is up. When the microwave oven, dishwasher, and clothes dryer are combined with the refrigerator, washing machine, and stove, families are actually spending 44 percent *less* on major appliances today than they were a generation ago.[15]

Vacation homes are another big target. A financial columnist for *Money* magazine explains how life has changed. A generation ago, the dream vacation was a modest affair: "Come summer, the family piled into its Ford country wagon (with imitation wood-panel doors) and tooled off to Lake Watchamasakee for a couple of weeks." Now, laments the columnist, things have changed. "The rented cabin on the lake gave way to a second home high on an ocean dune."[16] But the world he describes does not exist, at least not for the middle-class family. Despite the rhetoric, summer homes remain the fairly exclusive privilege of the well-to-do. In 1973, 32 percent of families reported expenses associated with owning a vacation home; by 2000, the proportion had inched up to 4 percent.[17]

That is not to say that middle-class families never fritter away any money. A generation ago no one had cable, big-screen televisions were a novelty reserved for the very rich, and DVD and TiVo were meaningless strings of letters. So how much more do families spend on "home entertainment," premium channels included? They spend 23 percent more—a whopping extra $170 annually. Computers add another $300 to the annual family budget.[18] But even that increase looks a little different in the context of other spending. The extra money spent on cable, electronics, and computers is more than offset by families' savings on major appliances and household furnishings.

The same balancing act holds true in other areas. The average family spends more on airline travel than it did a generation ago, but it spends less on dry cleaning. More on telephone services, but less on tobacco. More on pets, but less on carpets.[19] And, when we add it all up, increases in one category are offset by decreases in another. In other words, there seems to be about as much frivolous spending today as there was a generation ago.

Yet the myth remains rock solid: Middle-class families are rushing headlong into financial ruin because they are squandering too much money on Red Lobster, Gucci, and trips to the Bahamas. Americans cling so tightly to the myth not because it is supported by hard evidence, but because it is a comforting way to explain away some very bad news. If families are in trouble because they squander their money, then those of us who shop at Costco and cook our own pasta have nothing to worry about. Moreover, if families are to blame for their own failures, then the rest of us bear no responsibility for helping those who are in trouble. Their fault, their problem. We can join the chorus of experts advising the financial failures to "simplify"—stay away from Perrier and Rolex. Follow this sensible advice, and credit card balances will vanish, bankruptcy filings will disappear, and mortgage foreclosures will cease to plague America.

Reality is not nearly so neat. Sure, there are some families who buy too much stuff, but there is no evidence of any "epidemic" in overspending—certainly nothing that could explain a 255 percent increase in the foreclosure rate, a 430 percent increase in the bankruptcy rolls, and a 570 percent increase in credit card debt.[20] A growing number of families are in terrible financial trouble, but no matter how many times the accusation is hurled, Prada and HBO are not the reason.

WHERE DID THE MONEY GO?

If they aren't spending themselves into oblivion on designer water and DVDs, how did middle-class families get into so much financial trouble? The answer starts, quite literally, at home.

We could pile cliché on cliché about the home, but we will settle for this observation: The home is the most important purchase for the average middle-class family. To the overwhelming majority of Americans, home ownership stands out as the single most important component of "the good life."[21] Homes mark the lives of their children, setting out the parameters of their universe. The luck of location will determine whether there are computers in their classrooms, whether there are sidewalks for them to ride bikes on, and whether the front yard is a safe place to play. And a home will consume more of the family's income than any other purchase—more than food, more than cars, more than health insurance, more than child care.

As anyone who has read the newspapers or purchased a home knows, it costs a lot more to buy a house than it used to.[22] (Since the overwhelming majority of middle-class parents are homeowners, we focus this discussion on the costs of owning, rather than renting.[23]) What most of us have forgotten, however, is that today's home prices are not the product of some inevitable demographic force that has simply rolled its way across America. Quite the opposite. In the late 1980s, several commentators predicted a spectacular collapse in the housing market. Economists reasoned that the baby boomers were about to become empty nesters, so pressure on the housing market would undergo a sharp reversal. According to these experts, housing prices would reverse their forty-year upward trend and drop during the 1990s and 2000s—anywhere from 10 to 47 percent.[24]

Of course, the over-consumption critics have a ready explanation for why housing prices shot up despite expert predictions: Americans are bankrupting themselves to buy over-gadgeted, oversized "McMansions." *Money* magazine captures this view: "A generation or so ago . . . a basic, 800-square-foot, $8,000 Levittown box with a carport was heaven. . . . By the 1980s, the dream had gone yupscale. Home had become a 6,000-square-foot contemporary on three acres or a gutted and rehabbed townhouse in a gentrified ghetto."[25]

Where did so many people get this impression? Perhaps from the much ballyhooed fact that the average size of a new home has increased by nearly 40 percent over the past generation (though it is still less than 2,200 square feet).[26] But before the over-consumption camp declares victory, there are a few more details to consider. The overwhelming majority of middle-income families don't live in one of those spacious new homes. Indeed, the proportion of families living in older homes has increased by nearly 50 percent over the past generation, leaving a growing number of homeowners grappling with deteriorating roofs, peeling paint, and old wiring. Today, nearly six out of ten families own a home that is more than twenty-five years old, and nearly a quarter own a house that is more than fifty years old.[27]

Despite all the hoopla over the highly visible status symbols of the well-to-do, the size and amenities of the average middle-class family home have increased only modestly. The median owner-occupied home grew from 5.7 rooms in 1975 to 6.1 rooms in the late 1990s—an increase of less than half of a room in more than two decades.[28] What was this half a room used for? Was it an "exercise room," a "media room," or any of the other exotic uses of space that critics have so widely mocked? No. The data show that most often that extra room was a second bathroom or a third bedroom.[28] These are meaningful improvements, to be sure, but the average middle-class family in a six-room house has hardly rocketed to McMansion status.

FOR THE CHILDREN

The finger-waggers missed another vital fact: The rise in housing costs has become a *family* problem. Home prices have grown across the board, but the brunt of the price increases has fallen on families with children. Data from the Federal Reserve show that the median home value for the average childless individual increased by 23 percent between 1983 and 1998—an impressive rise in just fifteen years.[30] (Again, these and all other figures are adjusted for inflation.) For married couples with children, however, housing prices shot up 79 percent—*more than three times faster.*[31] To put this in dollar terms, compare the single person without children to a married couple with children. In 1983 the average childless individual bought a $73,000 house, compared with a $90,000 house today (adjusted for inflation). In 1983 the average married couple with children owned a house worth $98,000. Just fifteen years later, a similar family with children bought a house worth $175,000. The growing costs made a big dent in the family budget, as monthly mortgage costs made a similar jump, despite falling interest rates.[32] No matter how the data are cut, couples with children are spending more than ever on housing.

Why would the average parent spend so much money on a home? The overconsumption theory doesn't offer many insights. We doubt very much that families with children have a particular love affair with "bathroom spas" and "professional kitchens" while the swinging singles are perfectly content to live in Spartan apartments with outdated kitchens and closet sized bathrooms.

No, the real reason lies elsewhere. For many parents, the answer came down to two words so powerful that families would pursue them to the brink of bankruptcy: *safety* and *education.* Families put Mom to work, used up the family's economic reserves, and took on crushing debt loads in sacrifice to these twin gods, all in the hope of offering their children the best possible start in life.

The best possible start begins with good schools, but parents are scrambling to find those schools. Even politicians who can't agree on much of anything agree that there is a major problem in America's public schools. In the 2000 election campaign, for example, presidential candidates from both political parties were tripping over each other to promote their policies for new educational programs. And they had good reason. According to a recent poll, education now ranks as voters' single highest priority for increased federal spending—higher than health care, research on AIDS, environmental protection, and fighting crime.[33]

Everyone has heard the all-too-familiar news stories about kids who can't read, gang violence in the schools, classrooms without textbooks, and drug dealers at the school doors. For the most part, the problems aren't just about flawed educational policies; they are also depicted as the evils associated with poverty.[34] Even President Bush (who didn't exactly run on a Help-the-Poor platform) focused on helping "failing" schools, which, by and large, translates into help for schools in the poorest neighborhoods.

So what does all this have to do with educating middle-class children, most of whom have been lucky enough to avoid the worst failings of the public school system? The answer is simple—money. Failing schools impose an enormous cost on those children who are forced to attend them, but they also inflict an enormous cost on those who don't.

Talk with an average middle-class parent in any major metropolitan area, and she'll describe the time, money, and effort she devoted to finding a slot for her offspring in a decent school. In some cases, the story will be about mastering the system: "we put Joshua on the wait-list for the Science Magnet School the day he was born." In other cases, it will be one of leaving the public school system altogether, as middle-class parents increasingly opt for private, parochial, or home schooling. "My husband and I both went to public schools, but we just couldn't see sending Erin to the [local] junior high." But private schools and strategic maneuvering go only so far. For most middle-class parents, ensuring that their children get a decent education translates into one thing: snatching up a home in the small subset of school districts that have managed to hold on to a reputation of high quality and parent confidence.

Homes can command a premium for all sorts of amenities, such as a two-car garage, proximity to work or shopping, or a low crime rate. A study conducted in Fresno (a mid-sized California metropolis with 400,000 residents) found that, for similar homes, school quality was *the single most important determinant of neighborhood prices*—more important than racial composition of the neighborhood, commute distance, crime rate, or proximity to a hazardous waste site.[35] A study in suburban Boston showed the impact of school boundary lines. Two homes located less than half a mile apart and similar in nearly every aspect, will command significantly different prices if they are in different elementary school zones.[36] Schools that scored just 5 percent higher on fourth-grade math and reading tests added a premium of nearly $4,000 to nearby homes, even though these homes were virtually the same in terms of neighborhood character, school spending, racial composition, tax burden, and crime rate.

By way of example, consider University City, the West Philadelphia neighborhood surrounding the University of Pennsylvania. In an effort to improve the area, the university committed funds for a new elementary school. The results? At the time of the announcement, the median home value in the area was less than $60,000. Five years later, "homes within the boundaries go for about $200,000, even if they need to be totally renovated."[37] The neighborhood is otherwise pretty much the same: the same commute to work, the same distance from the freeways, the same old houses. And yet, in five years families are willing to pay more than *triple* the price for a home, just so they can send their kids to a better public elementary school. Real estate agents have long joked that the three things that matter in determining the price of a house are "location, location, location." Today, that mantra could be updated to "schools, schools, schools."

This phenomenon isn't new, but the pressure has intensified considerably. In the early 1970s, not only did most Americans believe that the public schools were functioning reasonably well, a sizable majority of adults thought that public education had actually *improved* since they were kids. Today, only a small minority of Americans share this optimistic view. Instead, the majority now believes that schools have gotten significantly worse.[38] Fully half of all Americans are dissatisfied with America's public education system, a deep concern shared by black and white parents alike.[39]

Even Juliet Schor, a leading critic of over-consumption, acknowledges the growing pressure on parents. For all that she criticizes America's love affair with granite countertops and microwave ovens, she recognizes that parents can find themselves trapped by the needs of their children:

> Within the middle class, and even the upper middle class, many families experience an almost threatening pressure to keep up, both for themselves and their children. They are deeply concerned about the rigors of the global economy, and the need to have their children attend "good" schools. This means living in a community with relatively high housing costs.[40]

In other words, the only way to ensure that a beloved youngster gets a solid education is to spring for a three-bedroom Colonial with an hour-long commute to a job in the city.

Today's parents must also confront another frightening prospect as they consider where their children will attend school: the threat of school violence. The widely publicized rise in shootings, gangs, and dangerous drugs at public schools sent many parents in search of a safe haven for their sons and daughters: Violent incidents can happen anywhere, as the shootings at lovely suburban Columbine High School in Colorado revealed to a horrified nation. But the statistics show that school violence is not as random as it might seem. According to one study, the incidence of serious violent crime—such as robbery, rape, or attack with a weapon—is more than three times higher in schools characterized by high poverty levels than those with predominantly middle- and upper-income children.[41] Similarly, urban children are more than twice as likely as suburban children to fear being attacked on the way to or from school.[42] The data expose a harsh reality: Parents who can get their kids into a more *economically* segregated neighborhood really improve the odds that their sons and daughters will make it through school safely.

Newer, more isolated suburbs with restrictive zoning also promise a refuge from the random crimes that tarnish urban living.[43] It may seem odd that families would devote so much attention to personal safety—or the lack thereof—when the crime rate in the United States has fallen sharply over the past decade.[44] But national statistics mask differences among communities, and disparities have grown over time. In many cities, the urban centers have grown more dangerous while outlying areas have gotten safer—further intensifying the pressure parents feel to squeeze into a suburban refuge.[45] In Baltimore and Philadelphia, for example, the crime rate fell in the surrounding suburbs just as it increased in the center city. The disparities are greatest for the most frightening violent crimes. Today a person is *ten times* more likely to be murdered in center city Philadelphia than in its surrounding suburbs, and twelve times more likely to be killed in central Baltimore.[46]

Dyed-in-the-wool urbanites would be quick to remind us that although the crime rate may have climbed in many urban areas, the average family faces only minuscule odds of being killed in a random act of violence in downtown Baltimore or any other city. That may be true, but it is beside the point, because it ignores a basic fact of parental psychology—worry. Parents are constantly mindful of the vulnerability of their children, and no amount of statistical reasoning can persuade them to stop worrying.

Emily Cheung tells a story that resonates with millions of parents. A psychotherapist and longtime city dweller, Emily had rented an apartment in a working-class neighborhood. For years, she sang the praises of city living. But as her boys got older, her views began to change. "We were close to The Corner and I was scared for [my sons]. I didn't want them to grow up there." After a series of break-ins on her block, Emily started looking for a new place for her family to live. "I wasn't looking to buy a house, but I wanted to rent something away from [this neighborhood] to get my boys out to better schools and a safer place." It wasn't as easy as she had hoped. Emily couldn't find any apartments in the neighborhood she wanted to live in. When her real estate agent convinced her that she could qualify for a mortgage, she jumped at the chance to move to the suburbs.

> The first night in the house, I just walked around in the dark and was so grateful. . . . At this house, it was so nice and quiet. [My sons] could go outdoors and they didn't need to be afraid. [She starts crying.] I thought that if I could do this for them, get them to a better place, what a wonderful gift to give my boys. I mean, this place was three thousand times better. It is safe with a huge front yard and a back yard and a driveway. It is wonderful. I had wanted this my whole life.

Emily took a huge financial gamble buying a house that claimed nearly half of her monthly income, but she had made up her mind to do whatever she could to keep her boys safe.

Families like Emily's have long acknowledged crime as an unfortunate fact of life, but the effect on parents has changed. A generation ago, there just wasn't much that average parents could do to escape these hazards. A family could buy a guard dog or leave the lights on, but if the suburbs were about as troubled as the cities—or if crime wasn't framed as a *city* problem—then the impetus to move wasn't very compelling. Today, however, cities and suburbs seem to present two very distinct alternatives. When the car is stolen or the news features a frightening murder on a nearby street, families are more inclined to believe that the suburbs will offer them a safer alternative. According to one study, more than one-third of families who had left central Baltimore and over half of families who had considered leaving "were moved to do so by their fear of crime."[47]

Ultimately, however, it did not matter whether there was a meaningful gap between the schools in the center cities and those in the surrounding suburbs, or whether the streets really were safer far away from the big city. It didn't even matter whether there really was a crisis in public education, as the politicians and the local news might insist. What mattered was that parents *believed* that there was an important difference—and that the difference was growing.[48] The only answer for millions of loving parents was to buy their way into a decent school district in a safe neighborhood—whatever the cost.

BIDDING WAR IN THE SUBURBS

And so it was that middle-class families across America have been quietly drawn into an all-out war. Not the war on drugs, the war about creationism, or the war over sex education. Their war has received little coverage in the press and no attention from politicians, but it has profoundly altered the lives of parents everywhere, shaping every economic decision they make. Their war is a bidding war. The opening shots in this war were fired in the most ordinary circumstances. Individual parents sought out homes they thought were good places to bring up kids, just as their parents had done before them. But as families saw urban centers as increasingly unattractive places to live, the range of desirable housing options began to shrink and parents' desire to escape from failing schools began to take on new urgency. Millions of parents joined in the search for a house on a safe street with a good school nearby. Over time, demand heated up for an increasingly narrow slice of the housing stock.

This in itself would have been enough to trigger a bidding war for suburban homes in good school districts. But a growing number of families brought new artillery to the war: a second income. In an era when the overwhelming majority of mothers are bringing home a paycheck and covering a big part of the family's bills, it is easy to forget that just one generation ago most middle-class mothers—including those in the workforce—made only modest contributions to the family's regular expenses. A generation ago, the average working wife contributed just one-quarter of the family's total income.[49] In many families, Mom's earnings were treated as "pin money" to cover treats and extras, not mortgages and car payments. Unenlightened husbands weren't the only ones to foster this attitude. Banks and loan companies routinely ignored women's earnings in calculating whether to approve a mortgage, on the theory that a wife might leave the workforce at any moment to pursue full-time homemaking.[50]

In 1975 Congress passed an important law with far-reaching consequences for families' housing choices. The Equal Craft Opportunity Act stipulated, among other things, that lenders could no longer ignore a wife's income when judging whether a family earned enough to qualify for a mortgage.[51] By the early 1980s, women's participation in the labor force had become a significant factor in whether a married couple could buy a home.[52] Both families and banks had started down the path of counting Mom's income as an essential part of the monthly budget.

This change may not sound revolutionary today, but it represents a seismic shift in family economics. No longer were families constrained by Dad's earning capacity. When Mom wanted a bigger yard or Dad wanted a better school for the kids, families had a new answer: Send Mom to work and use her paycheck to buy that nice house in the suburbs.

The women's movement contributed to this trend, opening up new employment possibilities and calling on mothers to reconsider their lifetime goals. For some women, the decision to head into the workplace meant personal fulfillment and expanded opportunities to engage in interesting, challenging occupations. For many more, the sense of independence that accompanied a job and a paycheck provided a powerful incentive. But for most middle-class women, the decision to get up early, drop the children off at day care, and head to the office or factory was driven, at least in part, by more prosaic reasons. Millions of women went to work in a calculated attempt to give their families an economic edge.[53]

The transformation happened gradually, as hundreds of thousands of mothers marched into the workforce year after year. But over the course of a few decades, the change has been nothing short of revolutionary. As recently as 1976 a married mother was more than twice as likely to stay home with her children as to work full-time. By 2000, those figures had almost reversed: The modern married mother is now nearly twice as likely to have a full-time job as to stay home.[54] The transformation can be felt in other ways. In 1965 only 21 percent of working women were back at their jobs within 6 months of giving birth to their first child. Today, that figure is higher than 70 percent. Similarly, a modern mother with a three-month-old infant is more likely to be working outside the home than was a 1960s woman with a five-year-old child.[55] As a claims adjuster with two children told us, "It never even occurred to me not to work, even after Zachary was born. All the women I know have a job."

Even these statistics understate the magnitude of change among middle-class mothers. Before the 1970s, large numbers of older women, lower-income women, and childless women were in the workforce.[56] But middle-class mothers were far more likely to stay behind, holding on to the more traditional role of full-time homemaker long after many of their sisters had given it up. Over the past generation, middle-class mothers flooded into offices, shops, and factories, undergoing a greater increase in workforce participation than either their poor or their well-to do sisters.[57] Attitudes changed as well. In 1970, when the women's revolution was well under way, 78 percent of younger married women thought that it was "better for wives to be homemakers and husbands to do the breadwinning."[58] Today, only 38 percent of women believe that it is "ideal" for one parent to be home full-time, and nearly 70 percent of Americans believe it doesn't matter whether it is the husband or the wife who stays home with the children.[59]

It is also the middle-class family whose finances have been most profoundly affected by women's entry into the workforce. Poorer, less educated women have seen small gains in real wages over the past generation. Wealthy women have enjoyed considerable increases, but those gains were complemented by similar increases in their husbands' rapidly rising incomes.[60] For the middle class, however, women's growing paychecks have made all the difference, compensating for the painful fact that their husbands' earnings have stagnated over the past generation.[61]

For millions of middle-class families hoping to hold on to a more traditional mother-at-home lifestyle, the bidding wars crushed those dreams. A group of solidly middle-class Americans—our nation's police officers—illustrate the point. A recent study showed that the average police officer could not afford a median priced home in *two-thirds* of the nation's metropolitan areas on the officer's income alone.[62] The same is true for elementary school teachers. Nor is this phenomenon limited to high-cast cities such as New York and San Francisco. Without a working spouse, the family of a police officer or teacher is forced to rent an apartment or buy in a marginal neighborhood even in more modestly priced cities such as Nashville, Kansas City, and Charlotte. These families have found that in order to hold on to all the benefits of a stay-at-home mom . . . , they will be shoved to the bottom rungs of the middle class.

What about those families with middle-class aspirations who earned a little less than average or those who lived in a particularly expensive city? Even with both parents in the workforce, they have fallen behind. Rather than drop out of the bidding war and resign themselves to sending their kids to weaker schools, many middle-class couples have seized on another way to fund their dream home: take on a bigger mortgage. In 1980, the mortgage lending industry was effectively deregulated. . . . As a result, average families could find plenty of banks willing to issue them larger mortgages relative to their incomes. As the bidding war heated up, families took on larger and larger mortgages just to keep up, committing themselves to debt loads that were unimaginable just a generation earlier.

With extra income from Mom's paycheck and extra mortgage money from the bank, the usual supply and demand in the market for homes in desirable areas exploded into an all-out bidding war. As millions of families sent a second earner into the workforce, one might expect that they would spend *less* on housing as a proportion of total income. Instead, just the opposite occurred. A growing number of middle-class families now spend *more* on housing relative to family income.[63] As demand for the limited stock of desirable family housing continued to grow, prices did not reach the natural limit that would have been imposed by the purchasing power of the single-income family confined to a conventional 80 percent mortgage. Instead, monthly mortgage expenses took a leap of *69 percent* at a time that other family expenditures—food, clothing, home furnishings, and the like—remained steady or fell.[64]

Parents were caught. It may have been their collective demand for housing in family neighborhoods that drove prices up, but each individual family that wanted one of those houses had no choice but to join in the bidding war. If one family refused to pay, some other family would snatch up the property. No single family could overcome the effects of millions of other families wanting what it wanted.

Each year, a growing number of stay-at-home mothers made the move into the workforce, hoping to put their families into solidly middle-class neighborhoods. But the rules quietly changed. Today's mothers are no longer working to get ahead; now they must work just to keep up. Somewhere along the way, they fell into a terrible trap.

. . . Short of buying a new home, parents currently have only one way to escape a failing public school: Send the kids to private school. But there is another alternative, one that would keep much-needed tax dollars inside the public school system while still reaping the advantages offered by a voucher program. Local governments could enact meaningful reform by enabling parents to choose from among *all* the public schools in a locale, with no presumptive assignment based on neighborhood. Under a public school voucher program, parents, not bureaucrats, would have the power to pick schools for their children—and to choose which schools would get their children's vouchers. Students would be admitted to a particular public school on the basis of their talents, their interests, or even their lottery numbers; their zip codes would be irrelevant. Tax dollars would follow the children, not the parents' home addresses, and children who live in a $50,000 house would have the same educational opportunities as those who live in a $250,000 house.

Children who required extra resources, such as those with physical or learning disabilities, could be assigned proportionately larger vouchers, which would make it more attractive for schools to take on the more challenging (and expensive) task of educating these children. It might tales some re-jiggering to settle on the right amount for a public school voucher, but eventually every child would have a valuable funding ticket to be used in any school in the area. To collect those tickets, schools would have to provide the education parents want. And parents would have a meaningful set of choices, *without* the need to buy a new home or pay private school tuition. Ultimately, an all-voucher system would diminish the distinction between public and private schools, as parents were able to exert more direct control over their children's schools.[65]

Of course, public school vouchers would not entirely eliminate the pressure parents feel to move into better family neighborhoods. Some areas would continue to have higher crime rates or better parks, and many parents might still prefer to live close to their children's schools. But a fundamental revision of school assignment policies would broaden the range of housing choices families would consider. Instead of limiting themselves to homes within one or two miles of a school, parents could choose a home five or even ten miles away—enough distance to give them several neighborhoods to choose from, with a broad range of price alternatives.

School change, like any other change, would entail some costs. More children might need to take a bus to school, pushing up school transportation expenses. On the other hand many parents might actually shorten their own commutes, since they would no longer be forced to live in far-flung suburbs for the sake of their children. The net costs could be positive or negative.

An all-voucher system would be a shock to the educational system, but the shake-out might be just what the system needs. In the short run, a large number of parents would likely chase a limited number of spots in a few excellent schools. But over time, the whole concept of "the Beverly Hills schools" or "Newton schools" would die out, replaced in the hierarchy by schools that offer a variety of programs that parents want for their children, regardless of the geographic boundaries. By selecting where to send their children (and where to spend their vouchers), parents would take control over schools' tax dollars, making them the de facto owners of those schools. Parents, not administrators, would decide on programs, student-teacher ratios, and whether to spend money on art or sports. Parents' competitive energies could be channeled toward signing up early or improving their children's qualifications for a certain school, not bankrupting themselves to buy homes they cannot afford.

If a meaningful public school voucher system were instituted, the U.S. housing market would change forever. These changes might dampen, and perhaps even depress, housing prices in some of today's most competitive neighborhoods. But these losses would be offset by other gains. Owners of older homes in urban centers might find more willing buyers, and the urge to flee the cities might abate. Urban sprawl might slow down as families recalculate the costs of living so far from work. At any rate, the change would cause a one-time readjustment. The housing market would normalize, with supply and demand more balanced and families freed from ruinous mortgages.

THE PRICE OF EDUCATION

Even with that perfect house in a swanky school district parents still are not covered when it comes to educating their kids—not by a long shot. The notion that taxpayers foot the bill for educating middle-class children has become a myth in yet another way. The two ends of the spectrum—everything that happens before a child shows up for his first day of kindergarten and after he is handed his high-school diploma—fall directly on the parents. Preschool and college, which now account for one-third (or more) of the years a typical middle-class kid spends in school, are paid for almost exclusively by the child's family.

Preschool has always been a privately funded affair, at least for most middle-class families. What has changed is its role for middle-class children. Over the past generation, the image of preschool has transformed from an optional stopover for little kids to a "prerequisite" for elementary school. Parents have been barraged with articles telling them that early education is important for everything from "pre-reading" skills to social development. As one expert in early childhood education observes, "In many communities around the country, kindergarten is no longer aimed at the entry level. And the only way Mom and Dad feel they can get their child prepared is through a pre-kindergarten program."[66]

Middle-class parents have stepped into line with the experts' recommendations. Today, nearly two-thirds of America's three- and four-year-olds attend preschool, compared with just 4 percent in the mid-1960s.[67] This isn't just the by-product of more mothers entering the workforce; nearly half of all stay-at-home moms now send their kids to a prekindergarten program.[68] As *Newsweek* put it, "The science says it all: preschool programs are neither a luxury nor a fad, but a real necessity."[69]

As demand has heated up, many families have found it increasingly difficult to *find* a prekindergarten program with an empty slot. Author Vicki Iovine describes the struggle she experienced trying to get her children into preschool in southern California:

> Just trying to get an application to any old preschool can be met with more attitude than the maitre d' at Le Cirque. If you should be naïve enough to ask if there will be openings in the next session, you may be reminded that there are always more applicants than openings, or the person might just laugh at you and hang up.[70]

Ms. Iovine's remarks are tongue-in-cheek, and pundits love to mock the parent who subscribes to the theory that "if little Susie doesn't get into the right preschool she'll never make it into the right medical school." But the shortage of quality preschool programs is very real. Child development experts have rated day-care centers, and the news is not good. The majority are lumped in the "poor to mediocre" range.[71] Not surprisingly, preschools with strong reputations often have long waiting lists.[72]

Once again, today's parents find themselves caught in a trap. A generation ago, when nursery school was regarded as little more than a chance for Mom to take a break, parents could consider the economics in a fairly detached way, committing to pay no more than what they could afford. And when only a modest number of parents were shopping for those preschool slots, the prices had to remain low to attract a full class. Today, when scores of experts routinely proclaim that preschool is decisive in a child's development, but a slot in a preschool—any preschool—can be hard to come by, parents are in a poor position to shop around for lower prices.

The laws of supply and demand take hold in the opposite direction, eliminating the pressure for preschool programs to keep prices low as they discover that they can increase fees without losing pupils. A full-day program in a prekindergarten offered by the Chicago *public* school district costs $6,500 a year—more than the cost of a year's tuition at the University of Illinois.[73] High? Yes, but that hasn't deterred parents: At just one Chicago public school, there are ninety-five kids on a waiting list for twenty slots. That situation is fairly typical. According to one study, the annual cost for a four-year-old to attend a child care center in an urban area is more than *double* the price of college tuition in fifteen states.[74] And so today's middle-class families simply spend and spend, stretching their budgets to give their child the fundamentals of a modern education.

Editors' Note: *Notes and references for this reading can be found in the original source.*

Diversity within African American Families

Ronald L. Taylor

PERSONAL REFLECTIONS

My interest in African American families as a topic of research was inspired more than two decades ago by my observation and growing dismay over the stereotypical portrayal of these families presented by the media and in much of the social science literature. Most of the African American families I knew in the large southern city in which I grew up were barely represented in the various "authoritative" accounts I read and other scholars frequently referred to in their characterizations and analyses of such families. Few such accounts have acknowledged the regional, ethnic, class, and behavioral diversity within the African American community and among families. As a result, a highly fragmented and distorted public image of African American family life has been perpetuated that encourages perceptions of African American families as a monolith. The 1986 television documentary *A CBS Report: The Vanishing Family: Crisis in Black America*, hosted by Bill Moyers, was fairly typical of this emphasis. It focused almost exclusively on low-income, single-parent households in inner cities, characterized them as "vanishing" non-families, and implied that such families represented the majority of African American families in urban America. It mattered little that poor, single-parent households in the inner cities made up less than a quarter of all African American families at the time the documentary was aired.

As an African American reared in the segregated South, I was keenly aware of the tremendous variety of African American families in composition, lifestyle, and socio-economic status. Racial segregation ensured that African American families, regardless of means or circumstances, were constrained to live and work in close proximity to one another. Travel outside the South made me aware of important regional differences among African American families as well. For example, African American families in the Northeast appeared far more segregated by socioeconomic status than did families in many parts of the South with which I was familiar. As a graduate student at Boston University during the late 1960s, I recall the shock I experienced upon seeing the level of concentrated poverty among African American families in Roxbury, Massachusetts, an experience duplicated in travels to New York, Philadelphia, and Newark. To be sure, poverty of a similar magnitude was prevalent throughout the South, but was far less concentrated and, from my perception, far less pernicious.

As I became more familiar with the growing body of research on African American families, it became increasingly clear to me that the source of a major distortion in the portrayal of African American families in the social science literature and the media was the overwhelming concentration on impoverished inner-city communities of the Northeast and Midwest to the near exclusion of the South, where more than half the African American families are found and differences among them in family patterns, lifestyles, and socioeconomic characteristics are more apparent.

In approaching the study of African American families in my work, I have adopted a *holistic* perspective. This perspective, outlined first by DuBois (1898) and more recently by Billingsley (1992) and Hill (1993), emphasizes the influence of historical, cultural, social, economic, and political forces in shaping contemporary patterns of family life among African Americans of all socioeconomic backgrounds. Although the impact of these external forces is routinely taken into account in assessing stability and change among white families, their effects on the structure and functioning of African American families are often minimized. In short, a holistic approach undertakes to study African American families *in context*. My definition of the *family*, akin to the definition offered by Billingsley (1992), views it as an intimate association of two or more persons related to each other by blood, marriage, formal or informal adoption, or appropriation. The latter term refers to the incorporation of persons in the family who are unrelated by blood or marital ties but are treated as though they are family. This definition is broader than other dominant definitions of families that emphasize biological or marital ties as defining characteristics.

This [reading] is divided into three parts. The first part reviews the treatment of African American families in the historical and social sciences literatures. It provides a historical overview of African American families, informed by recent historical scholarship, that corrects many of the misconceptions about the nature and quality of family life during and following the experience of slavery. The second part examines contemporary patterns of marriage, family, and household composition among African Americans in response to recent social, economic, and political developments in the larger society. The third part explores some of the long-term implications of current trends in marriage and family behavior for community functioning and individual well-being, together with implications for social policy.

THE TREATMENT OF AFRICAN AMERICAN FAMILIES IN AMERICAN SCHOLARSHIP

As an area of scientific investigation, the study of African American family life is of recent vintage. As recently as 1968, Billingsley, in his classic work *Black Families in White America*, observed that African American family life had been virtually ignored in family studies and studies of race and ethnic relations. He attributed the general lack of interest among white social scientists, in part, to their "ethnocentrism and intellectual commitment to peoples and values transplanted from Europe" (p. 214). Content analyses of key journals in sociology, social work, and family studies during the period supported Billingsley's contention. For example, a content analysis of 10 leading journals in sociology and social work by Johnson (1981) disclosed that articles on African American families constituted only 3% of 3,547 empirical studies of American families published between 1965 and 1975. Moreover, in the two major journals in social work, only one article on African American families was published from 1965 to 1978. In fact, a 1978 special issue of the *Journal of Marriage and the Family* devoted to African American families accounted for 40% of all articles on these families published in the 10 major journals between 1965 and 1978.

Although the past two decades have seen a significant increase in the quantity and quality of research on the family lives of African Americans, certain features and limitations associated with earlier studies in this area persist (Taylor, Chatters, Tucker, & Lewis, 1990). In a review of recent research on African American families, Hill (1993) concluded that many studies continue to treat such families in superficial terms; that is, African American families are not considered to be an important unit of focus and, consequently, are treated peripherally or omitted altogether. The assumption is that African American families are automatically treated in all analyses that focus on African Americans as individuals; thus, they are not treated in their own right. Hill noted that a major impediment to understanding the functioning of African American families has been the failure of most analysts to use a theoretical or conceptual framework that took account of the totality of African American family life. Overall, he found that the preponderance of recent studies of African American families are

> (a) fragmented, in that they exclude the bulk of Black families by focusing on only a subgroup; (b) ad hoc, in that they apply arbitrary explanations that are not derived from systematic theoretical formulations that have been empirically substantiated; (c) negative, in that they focus exclusively on the perceived weaknesses of Black families; and (d) internally oriented, in that they exclude any systematic consideration of the role of forces in the wider society on Black family life. (p. 5)

THEORETICAL APPROACHES

The study of African American families, like the study of American families in general, has evolved through successive theoretical formulations. Using white family structure as the norm, the earliest studies characterized African American families as impoverished versions of white families in which the experiences of slavery, economic deprivation, and racial discrimination had induced pathogenic and dysfunctional features (Billingsley, 1968). The classic statement of this perspective was presented by Frazier, whose study, *The Negro Family in the United States* (1939), was the first comprehensive analysis of African American family life and its transformation under various historical conditions—slavery, emancipation, and urbanization (Edwards, 1968).

It was Frazier's contention that slavery destroyed African familial structures and cultures and gave rise to a host of dysfunctional family features that continued to undermine the stability and well-being of African American families well into the 20th century. Foremost among these features was the supposed emergence of the African American "matriarchal" or maternal family system, which weakened the economic position of African American men and their authority in the family. In his view, this family form was inherently unstable and produced pathological outcomes in the family unit, including high rates of poverty, illegitimacy, crime, delinquency, and other problems associated with the socialization of children. Frazier concluded that the female-headed family had become a common tradition among large segments of lower-class African American migrants to the North during the early 20th century. The two-parent male-headed household represented a second tradition among a minority of African Americans who enjoyed some of the freedoms during slavery, had independent artisan skills, and owned property.

Frazier saw an inextricable connection between economic resources and African American family structure and concluded that as the economic position of African Americans improved, their conformity to normative family patterns would increase. However, his important insight regarding the link between family structure and economic resources was obscured by the inordinate emphasis he placed on the instability and "self-perpetuating pathologies" of lower-class African American families, an emphasis that powerfully contributed to the pejorative tradition of scholarship that emerged in this area. Nonetheless, Frazier recognized the diversity of African American families and in his analyses, "consistently attributed the primary sources of family instability to external forces (such as racism, urbanization, technological changes and recession) and not to internal characteristics of Black families" (Hill, 1993, pp. 7–8).

During the 1960s, Frazier's characterization of African American families gained wider currency with the publication of Moynihan's *The Negro Family: The Case for National Action* (1965), in which weaknesses in family structure were identified as a major source of social problems in African American communities. Moynihan attributed high rates of welfare dependence, out-of-wedlock births, educational failure, and other problems to the "unnatural" dominance of women in African American families. Relying largely on the work of Frazier as a source of reference, Moynihan traced the alleged "tangle of pathology" that characterized urban African American families to the experience of slavery and 300 years of racial oppression, which, he concluded, had caused "deep-seated structural distortions" in the family and community life of African Americans.

Although much of the Moynihan report, as the book was called, largely restated what had become conventional academic wisdom on African American families during the 1960s, its generalized indictment of all African American families ignited a firestorm of criticism and debate and inspired a wealth of new research and writings on the nature and quality of African American family life in the United States (Staples & Mirande, 1980). In fact, the 1970s saw the beginning of the most prolific period of research on African American families, with more than 50 books and 500 articles published during that decade alone, representing a fivefold increase over the literature produced in all the years since the publication of DuBois's (1909) pioneering study of African American family life (Staples & Mirande, 1980). To be sure, some of this work was polemical and defensively apologetic, but much of it sought to replace ideology with research and to provide alternative perspectives for interpreting observed differences in the characteristics of African American and white families (Allen, 1978).

Critics of the deficit or pathology approach to African American family life (Scanzoni, 1977; Staples, 1971) called attention to the tendency in the literature to ignore family patterns among the majority of African Americans and to overemphasize findings derived from studies of low-income and typically problem-ridden families. Such findings were often generalized and accepted as descriptive of the family life of all African American families, with the result that popular but erroneous images of African American family life were perpetuated. Scrutinizing the research literature of the 1960s, Billingsley (1968) concluded that when the majority of African American families was considered, evidence refuted the characterization of African American family life as unstable, dependent on welfare, and matriarchal. In his view, and in the view of a growing number of scholars in the late 1960s and early 1970s, observed differences between white and African American families were largely the result of differences in socioeconomic position and of differential access to economic resources (Allen, 1978; Scanzoni, 1977).

Thus, the 1970s witnessed not only a significant increase in the diversity, breadth, and quantity of research on African American families, but a shift away from a social pathology perspective to one emphasizing the resilience and adaptiveness of African American families under a variety of social and economic conditions. The new emphasis reflected what Allen (1978) referred to as the "cultural variant" perspective, which treats African American families as different but legitimate functional forms. From this perspective, "Black and White family differences [are] taken as given, without the presumption of one family form as normative and the other as deviant." (Farley & Allen, 1987, p. 162). In accounting for observed racial differences in family patterns, some researchers have taken a *structural perspective*, emphasizing poverty and other socioeconomic factors as key processes (Billingsley, 1968). Other scholars have taken a *cultural approach*, stressing elements of the West African cultural heritage, together with distinctive experiences, values, and behavioral modes of adaptation developed in this country, as major determinants (Nobles, 1978; Young, 1970). Still others (Collins, 1990; Sudarkasa, 1988) have pointed to evidence supporting both interpretations and have argued for a more comprehensive approach.

Efforts to demythologize negative images of African American families have continued during the past two decades, marked by the development of the first national sample of adult African Americans, drawn to reflect their distribution throughout the United States (Jackson, 1991), and by the use of a variety of conceptualizations, approaches, and methodologies in the study of African American family life (Collins, 1990; McAdoo, 1997). Moreover, the emphasis in much of the recent work

> has not been the defense of African American family forms, but rather the identification of forces that have altered long-standing traditions. The ideological paradigms identified by Allen (1978) to describe the earlier thrust of Black family research—cultural equivalence, cultural deviance, and cultural variation—do not fully capture the foci of this new genre of work as a whole. (Tucker & Mitchell-Kernan, 1995, p. 17)

Researchers have sought to stress balance in their analyses, that is, to assess the strengths and weaknesses of African American family organizations at various socioeconomic levels, and the need for solution-oriented studies (Hill, 1993). At the same time, recent historical scholarship has shed new light on the relationship of changing historical circumstances to characteristics of African American family organization and has underscored the relevance of historical experiences to contemporary patterns of family life.

AFRICAN AMERICAN FAMILIES IN HISTORICAL PERSPECTIVE

Until the 1970s, it was conventional academic wisdom that the experience of slavery decimated African American culture and created the foundation for unstable female-dominated households and other familial aberrations that continued into the 20th century. This thesis, advanced by Frazier (1939) and restated by Moynihan (1965), was seriously challenged by the pioneering historical research of Blassingame (1972), Furstenberg, Hershberg, and Modell (1975), and Gutman (1976), among others. These works provide compelling documentation of the centrality of family and kinship among African Americans during the long years of bondage and how African Americans created and sustained a rich cultural and family life despite the brutal reality of slavery.

In his examination of more than two centuries of slave letters, autobiographies, plantation records, and other materials, Blassingame (1972) meticulously documented the nature of community, family organization, and culture among American slaves. He concluded that slavery was not "an all-powerful, monolithic institution which strip[ped] the slave of any meaningful and distinctive culture, family life, religion or manhood" (p. vii). To the contrary, the relative freedom from white control that slaves enjoyed in their quarters enabled them to create and sustain a complex social organization that incorporated "norms of conduct, defined roles and behavioral patterns" and provided for the traditional functions of group solidarity, defense, mutual assistance, and family organization. Although the family had no legal standing in slavery and was frequently disrupted, Blassingame noted its major role as a source of survival for slaves and as a mechanism of social control for slaveholders, many of whom encouraged "monogamous mating arrangements" as insurance against runaways and rebellion. In fashioning familial and community organization, slaves drew upon the many remnants of their African heritage (e.g., courtship rituals, kinship networks, and religious beliefs), merging those elements with American forms to create a distinctive culture, features of which persist in the contemporary social organization of African American family life and community.

Genovese's (1974) analysis of plantation records and slave testimony led him to similar conclusions regarding the nature of family life and community among African Americans under slavery. Genovese noted that, although chattel bondage played havoc with the domestic lives of slaves and imposed severe constraints on their ability to enact and sustain normative family roles and functions, the slaves "created impressive norms of family, including as much of a nuclear family norm as conditions permitted and . . . entered the postwar social system with a remarkably stable base" (p. 452). He attributed this stability to the extraordinary resourcefulness and commitment of slaves to marital relations and to what he called a "paternalistic compromise," or bargain between masters and slaves that recognized certain reciprocal obligations and rights, including recognition of slaves' marital and family ties. Although slavery undermined the role of African

American men as husbands and fathers, their function as role models for their children and as providers for their families was considerably greater than has generally been supposed. Nonetheless, the tenuous position of male slaves as husbands and fathers and the more visible and nontraditional roles assumed by female slaves gave rise to legends of matriarchy and emasculated men. However, Genovese contended that the relationship between slave men and women came closer to approximating gender equality than was possible for white families.

Perhaps the most significant historical work that forced revisions in scholarship on African American family life and culture during slavery was Gutman's (1976) landmark study, *The Black Family in Slavery and Freedom.* Inspired by the controversy surrounding the Moynihan report and its thesis that African American family disorganization was a legacy of slavery, Gutman made ingenious use of quantifiable data derived from plantation birth registers and marriage applications to re-create family and kinship structures among African Americans during slavery and after emancipation. Moreover, he marshaled compelling evidence to explain how African Americans developed an autonomous and complex culture that enabled them to cope with the harshness of enslavement, the massive relocation from relatively small economic units in the upper South to vast plantations in the lower South between 1790 and 1860, the experience of legal freedom in the rural and urban South, and the transition to northern urban communities before 1930.

Gutman reasoned that, if family disorganization (fatherless, matrifocal families) among African Americans was a legacy of slavery, then such a condition should have been more common among urban African Americans closer in time to slavery—in 1850 and 1860—than in 1950 and 1960. Through careful examination of census data, marriage licenses, and personal documents for the period after 1860, he found that stable, two-parent households predominated during slavery and after emancipation and that families headed by African American women at the turn of the century were hardly more prevalent than among comparable white families. Thus "[a]t all moments in time between 1860 and 1925 . . . the typical Afro-American family was lower class in status and headed by two parents. That was so in the urban and rural South in 1880 and 1900 and in New York City in 1905 and 1925" (p. 456). Gutman found that the two-parent family was just as common among the poor as among the more advantaged, and as common among southerners as those in the Northeast. For Gutman, the key to understanding the durability of African American families during and after slavery lay in the distinctive African American culture that evolved from the cumulative slave experiences that provided a defense against some of the more destructive and dehumanizing aspects of that system. Among the more enduring and important aspects of that culture are the enlarged kinship network and certain domestic arrangements (e.g., the sharing of family households with nonrelatives and the informal adoption of children) that, during slavery, formed the core of evolving African American communities and the collective sense of interdependence.

Additional support for the conclusion that the two-parent household was the norm among slaves and their descendants was provided by Furstenberg et al. (1975) from their study of the family composition of African Americans, native-born whites, and immigrants to Philadelphia from 1850 to 1880. From their analysis of census data, Furstenberg et al. found that most African American families, like those of other ethnic groups, were headed by two parents (75% for African Americans versus 73% for native whites). Similar results are reported by Pleck (1973) from her study of African American family structure in late 19th-century Boston. As these and other studies (Jones, 1985; White, 1985) have shown, although female-headed households were common among African Americans during and following slavery, such households were by no means typical. In fact, as late as the 1960s, three fourths of African American households were headed by married couples (Jaynes & Williams, 1989; Moynihan, 1965).

However, more recent historical research would appear to modify, if not challenge, several of the contentions of the revisionist scholars of slavery. Manfra and Dykstra (1985) and Stevenson (1995), among others, found evidence of considerably greater variability in slave family structure and in household composition than was reported in previous works. In her study of Virginia slave families from 1830 to 1860, Stevenson (1995) discovered evidence of widespread matrifocality, as well as other marital and household arrangements, among antebellum slaves. Her analysis of the family histories of slaves in colonial and antebellum Virginia revealed that many slaves did not have a nuclear "core" in their families. Rather, the "most discernible ideal for their principal kinship organization was a malleable extended family that provided its members with nurture, education, socialization, material support, and recreation in the face of the potential social chaos the slavemasters' power imposed" (1995, p. 36).

A variety of conditions affected the family configurations of slaves, including cultural differences among the slaves themselves, the state or territory in which they lived, and the size of the plantation on which they resided. Thus, Stevenson concluded that

> the slave family was not a static, imitative institution that necessarily favored one form of family organization over another. Rather, it was a diverse phenomenon, sometimes assuming several forms even among the slaves of one community. . . . Far from having a negative impact, the diversity of slave marriage and family norms, as a measure of the slave family's enormous adaptive potential, allowed the slave and the slave family to survive. (p. 29)

Hence, "postrevisionist" historiography emphasizes the great diversity of familial arrangements among African Americans during slavery. Although nuclear, matrifocal, and extended families were prevalent, none dominated slave family forms. These postrevisionist amendments notwithstanding, there is compelling historical evidence that African American nuclear families and kin-related households remained relatively intact and survived the experiences of slavery, Reconstruction, the Great Depression, and the transition to northern urban communities. Such evidence underscores the importance of considering recent developments and conditions in accounting for changes in family patterns among African Americans in the contemporary period.

CONTEMPORARY AFRICAN AMERICAN FAMILY PATTERNS

Substantial changes have occurred in patterns of marriage, family, and household composition in the United States during the past three decades, accompanied by significant alterations in the family lives of men, women, and children. During this period, divorce rates have more than doubled, marriage rates have declined, fertility rates have fallen to record levels, the proportion of "traditional" families (nuclear families in which children live with both biological parents) as a percentage of all family groups has declined, and the proportion of children reared in single-parent households has risen dramatically (Taylor, 1997).

Some of the changes in family patterns have been more rapid and dramatic among African Americans than among the population as a whole. For example, while declining rates of marriage and remarriage, high levels of separation and divorce, and higher proportions of children living in single-parent households are trends that have characterized the U.S. population as a whole during the past 30 years, these trends have been more pronounced among African Americans and, in some respects, represent marked departures from earlier African American family patterns. A growing body of research has implicated demographic and economic factors as causes of the divergent marital and family experiences of African Americans and other populations.

In the following section, I examine diverse patterns and evolving trends in family structure and household composition among African Americans, together with those demographic, economic, and social factors that have been identified as sources of change in patterns of family formation.

Diversity of Family Structure

Since 1960, the number of African American households has increased at more than twice the rate of white households. By 1995, African American households numbered 11.6 million, compared with 83.7 million white households. Of these households, 58.4 million white and 8.0 million African American ones were classified as family households by the U.S. Bureau of the Census (1996), which defines a *household* as the person or persons occupying a housing unit and a *family* as consisting of two or more persons who live in the same household and are related by birth, marriage, or adoption. Thus, family households are households maintained by individuals who share their residence with one or more relatives, whereas nonfamily households are maintained by individuals with no relatives in the housing unit. In 1995, 70% of the 11.6 million African American households were family households, the same proportion as among white households (U.S. Bureau of the Census, 1996). However, nonfamily households have been increasing at a faster rate than family households among African Americans because of delayed marriages among young adults, higher rates of family disruption (divorce and separation), and sharp increases in the number of unmarried cohabiting couples (Cherlin, 1995; Glick, 1997).

Family households vary by type and composition. Although the U.S. Bureau of the Census recognizes the wide diversity of families in this country, it differentiates between three broad and basic types of family households: married-couple or husband-wife families, families with female householders (no husband present), and families with male householders (no wife present). Family composition refers to whether the household is *nuclear*, that is, contains parents and children only, or extended, that is, nuclear plus other relatives.

To take account of the diversity in types and composition of African American families, Billingsley (1968; 1992) added to these conventional categories *augmented* families (nuclear plus nonrelated persons), and modified the definition of nuclear family to include *incipient* (a married couple without children), *simple* (a couple with children), and *attenuated* (a single parent with children) families. He also added three combinations of augmented families: *incipient extended augmented* (a couple with relatives and nonrelatives), *nuclear extended augmented* (a couple with children, relatives, and nonrelatives), and *attenuated extended augmented* (a single parent with children, relatives, and nonrelatives). With these modifications, Billingsley identified 32 different kinds of nuclear, extended, and augmented family households among African Americans. His typology has been widely used and modified by other scholars (see, for example, Shimkin, Shimkin, & Frate, 1978; Stack, 1974). For example, on the basis of Billingsley's typology, Dressler, Haworth-Hoeppner, and Pitts (1985) developed a four-way typology with 12 subtypes for their study of household structures in a southern African American community and found a variety of types of female-headed households, less than a fourth of them consisting of a mother and her children or grandchildren.

However, as Staples (1971) pointed out, Billingsley's typology emphasized the household and ignored an important characteristic of such families—their "extendedness." African Americans are significantly more likely than whites to live in extended families that "transcend and link several different households, each containing a separate . . . family" (Farley & Allen, 1987, p. 168). In 1992, approximately 1 in 5 African American families was extended, compared to 1 in 10 white families (Glick, 1997). The greater proportion of extended households among African Americans has been linked to the extended family tradition of West African cultures (Nobles, 1978; Sudarkasa, 1988) and to the economic marginality of many African American families, which has encouraged the sharing and exchange of resources, services, and emotional support among family units spread across a number of households (Stack, 1974).

In comparative research on West African, Caribbean, and African American family patterns some anthropologists (Herskovits, 1958; Sudarkasa, 1997) found evidence of cultural continuities in the significance attached to coresidence, formal kinship relations, and nuclear families among black populations in these areas. Summarizing this work, Hill (1993, pp. 104–105) observed that, with respect to

> co-residence, the African concept of family is not restricted to persons living in the same household, but includes key persons living in separate households. . . . As for defining kin relationships, the African concept of family is not confined to relations between formal kin, but includes networks of unrelated [i.e., "fictive kin"] as well as related persons living in separate households. . . . [According to] Herskovits (1941), the African nuclear family unit is not as central to its family organization as is the case for European nuclear families: "The African immediate family, consisting of a father, his wives, and their children, is but a part of a larger unit. This immediate family is generally recognized by Africanists as belonging to a local relationship group termed the 'extended family.'"

Similarly, Sudarkasa (1988) found that unlike the European extended family, in which primacy is given to the conjugal unit (husband, wife, and children) as the basic building block, the African extended family is organized around blood ties (consanguineous relations).

In their analysis of data from the National Survey of Black Americans (NSBA) on household composition and family structure, Hatchett, Cochran, and Jackson (1991) noted that the extended family perspective, especially kin networks, was valuable in describing the nature and functioning of African American families. They suggested that the "extended family can be viewed both as a family network in the physical-spatial sense and in terms of family relations or contact and exchanges. In this view of extendedness, family structure and function are interdependent concepts" (p. 49). Their examination of the composition of the 2,107 households in the NSBA resulted in the identification of 12 categories, 8 of which roughly captured the "dimensions of household family structure identified in Billingsley's typology of Black families (1968)—the incipient nuclear family, the incipient nuclear extended and/or augmented nuclear family, the simple nuclear family, the simple extended and/or augmented nuclear family, the attenuated nuclear family, and the attenuated extended and/or augmented family, respectively" (p. 51). These households were examined with respect to their *actual kin networks*, defined as subjective feelings of emotional closeness to family members, frequency of contact, and patterns of mutual assistance, and their *potential kin networks*, defined as the availability or proximity of immediate family members and the density or concentration of family members within a given range.

Hatchett et al. (1991) found that approximately 1 in 5 African American households in the NSBA was an extended household (included other relatives—parents and siblings of the household head, grandchildren, grandparents, and nieces and nephews). Nearly 20% of the extended households with children contained minors who were not the head's; most of these children were grandchildren, nieces, and nephews of the head. The authors suggested that "[t]hese are instances of informal fostering or adoption—absorption of minor children by the kin network" (p. 58).

In this sample, female-headed households were as likely to be extended as male-headed households. Hatchett et al. (1991) found little support for the possibility that economic hardship may account for the propensity among African Americans to incorporate other relatives in their households. That is, the inclusion of other relatives in the households did not substantially improve the overall economic situation of the households because the majority of other relatives were minor children, primarily grandchildren of heads who coresided with the household heads' own minor and adult children. Moreover, they stated, "household extendedness at both the household and extra-household levels appears to be a characteristic of black families, regardless of socioeconomic level" (p. 81), and regardless of region of the country or rural or urban residence.

The households in the NSBA were also compared in terms of their potential and actual kin networks. The availability of potential kin networks varied by the age of the respondent, by the region and degree of urban development of the respondent's place of residence, and by the type of household in which the respondent resided (Hatchett et al., 1991). For example, households with older heads and spouses were more isolated from kin than were younger households headed by single mothers, and female-headed households tended to have greater potential kin networks than did individuals in nuclear households. With respect to region and urbanicity, the respondents in the Southern and North Central regions and those in rural areas had a greater concentration of relatives closer at hand than did the respondents in other regions and those in urban areas. However, proximity to relatives and their concentration nearby did not translate directly into actual kin networks or extended family functioning:

> Complex relationships were found across age, income, and type of household. From these data came a picture of the Black elderly with high psychological connectedness to family in

the midst of relative geographical and interactional isolation from them. The image of female single-parent households is, on the other hand, the reverse or negative of this picture. Female heads were geographically closer to kin, had more contact with them, and received more help from family but did not perceive as much family solidarity or psychological connectedness. (Hatchett et al., 1991, p. 81)

The nature and frequency of mutual aid among kin were also assessed in this survey. More than two thirds of the respondents reported receiving some assistance from family members, including financial support, child care, goods and services, and help during sickness and at death. Financial assistance and child care were the two most frequent types of support reported by the younger respondents, whereas goods and services were the major types reported by older family members. The type of support the respondents received from their families was determined, to some extent, by needs defined by the family life cycle.

In sum, the results of the NSBA document the wide variety of family configurations and households in which African Americans reside and suggest, along with other studies, that the diversity of structures represents adaptive responses to the variety of social, economic, and demographic conditions that African Americans have encountered over time (Billingsley, 1968; Farley & Allen, 1987).

Although Hatchett et al. (1991) focused on extended or augmented African American families in their analysis of the NSBA data, only 1 in 5 households in this survey contained persons outside the nuclear family. The majority of households was nuclear, containing one or both parents with their own children.

Between 1970 and 1990, the number of all U.S. married-couple families with children dropped by almost 1 million, and their share of all family households declined from 40% to 26% (U.S. Bureau of the Census, 1995). The proportion of married-couple families with children among African Americans also declined during this period, from 41% to 26% of all African American families. In addition, the percentage of African American families headed by women more than doubled, increasing from 33% in 1970 to 57% in 1990. By 1995, married-couple families with children constituted 36% of all African American families, while single-parent families represented 64% (U.S. Bureau of the Census, 1996). The year 1980 was the first time in history that African American female-headed families with children outnumbered married-couple families. This shift in the distribution of African American families by type is associated with a number of complex, interrelated social and economic developments, including increases in age at first marriage, high rates of separation and divorce, male joblessness, and out-of-wedlock births.

Marriage, Divorce, and Separation

In a reversal of a long-time trend, African Americans are now marrying at a much later age than are persons of other races. Thirty years ago, African American men and women were far more likely to have married by ages 20–24 than were white Americans. In 1960, 56% of African American men and 36% of African American women aged 20–24 were never married; by 1993, 90% of all African American men and 81% of African American women in this age cohort were never married (U.S. Bureau of the Census, 1994).

The trend toward later marriages among African Americans has contributed to changes in the distribution of African American families by type. Delayed marriage tends to increase the risk of out-of-wedlock childbearing and single parenting (Hernandez, 1993). In fact, a large proportion of the increase in single-parent households in recent years is accounted for by never-married women maintaining families (U.S. Bureau of the Census, 1990).

The growing proportion of never-married young African American adults is partly a result of a combination of factors, including continuing high rates of unemployment, especially among young men; college attendance; military service; and an extended period of cohabitation prior to marriage (Glick, 1997; Testa & Krogh, 1995; Wilson, 1987). In their investigation of the effect of employment on marriage among African American men in the inner city of Chicago, Testa and Krogh (1995) found that men in stable jobs were twice as likely to marry as were men who were unemployed, not in school, or in the military. Hence, it has been argued that the feasibility of marriage among African Americans in recent decades has decreased because the precarious economic position of African American men has made them less attractive as potential husbands and less interested in becoming husbands, given the difficulties they are likely to encounter in performing the provider role in marriage (Tucker & Mitchell-Kernan, 1995).

However, other research has indicated that economic factors are only part of the story. Using census data from 1940 through the mid-1980s, Mare and Winship (1991) sought to determine the impact of declining employment opportunities on marriage rates among African Americans and found that although men who were employed were more likely to marry, recent declines in employment rates among young African American men were not large enough to account for a substantial part of the declining trend in their marriage rates. Similarly, in their analysis of data from a national survey of young African American adults, Lichter, McLaughlin, Kephart, and Landry (1992) found that lower employment rates among African American men were an important contributing factor to delayed marriage—and perhaps to nonmarriage—among African American women. However, even when marital opportunities were taken into account, the researchers found that the rate of marriage among young African American women in the survey was only 50% to 60% the rate of white women of similar ages.

In addition to recent declines in employment rates, an unbalanced sex ratio has been identified as an important contributing factor to declining marriage rates among African Americans. This shortage of men is due partly to high rates of mortality and incarceration of African American men (Kiecolt & Fossett, 1995; Wilson & Neckerman, 1986). Guttentag and Secord (1983) identified a number of major consequences of the shortage of men over time: higher rates of singlehood, out-of-wedlock births, divorce, and infidelity and less commitment among men to relationships. Among African Americans, they found that in 1980 the ratio of men to women was unusually low; in fact, few populations in the United States had sex ratios as low as those of African Americans. Because African American women outnumber men in each of the age categories 20 to 49, the resulting "marriage squeeze" puts African American women at a significant disadvantage in the marriage market, causing an unusually large proportion of them to remain unmarried. However, Glick (1997) observed a reversal of the marriage squeeze among African Americans in the age categories 18 to 27 during the past decade: In 1995, there were 102 African American men for every 100 African American women in this age range. Thus, "[w]hereas the earlier marriage squeeze made it difficult for Black women to marry, the future marriage squeeze will make it harder for Black men" (Glick, 1997, p. 126). But, as Kiecolt and Fossett (1995) observed, the impact of the sex ratio on marital outcomes for African Americans may vary, depending on the nature of the local marriage market. Indeed, "marriage markets are local, as opposed to national, phenomena which may have different implications for different genders . . . [for example,] men and women residing near a military base face a different sex ratio than their counterparts attending a large university" (Smith, 1995, p. 137).

African American men and women are not only delaying marriage, but are spending fewer years in their first marriages and are slower to remarry than in decades past. Since 1960, a sharp decline has occurred in the number of years African American women spend with their first husbands and a corresponding rise in the interval of separation and divorce between the first and second marriages (Espenshade, 1985; Jaynes & Williams, 1989). Data from the National Fertility Surveys of 1965 and 1970 disclosed that twice as many African American couples as white couples (10% versus 5%) who reached their 5th wedding anniversaries ended their marriages before their 10th anniversaries (Thornton, 1978), and about half the African American and a quarter of the white marriages were dissolved within the first 15 years of marriage (McCarthy, 1978). Similarly, a comparison of the prevalence of marital disruption (defined as separation or divorce) among 13 racial-ethnic groups in the United States based on the 1980 census revealed that of the women who had married for the first time 10 to 14 years before 1980, 53% of the African American women, 48% of the Native American women, and 37% of the non-Hispanic white women were separated or divorced by the 1980 census (Sweet & Bumpass, 1987).

Although African American women have a higher likelihood of separating from their husbands than do non-Hispanic white women, they are slower to obtain legal divorces (Chertin, 1996). According to data from the 1980 census, within three years of separating from their husbands, only 55% of the African American women had obtained divorces, compared to 91% of the non-Hispanic white women (Sweet & Bumpass, 1987). Cherlin speculated that, because of their lower expectations of remarrying, African American women may be less motivated to obtain legal divorces. Indeed, given the shortage of African American men in each of the age categories from 20 to 49, it is not surprising that the proportion of divorced women who remarry is lower among African American than among non-Hispanic white women (Glick, 1997). Overall, the remarriage rate among African Americans is about one fourth the rate of whites (Staples & Johnson, 1993).

Cherlin (1996) identified lower educational levels, high rates of unemployment, and low income as importance sources of differences in African American and white rates of marital dissolution. However, as he pointed out, these factors alone are insufficient to account for all the observed difference. At every level of educational attainment, African American women are more likely to be separated or divorced from their husbands than are non-Hispanic white women. Using data from the 1980 census, Jaynes and Williams (1989) compared the actual marital-status distributions of African Americans and whites, controlling for differences in educational attainment for men and women and for income distribution for men. They found that when differences in educational attainment were taken into account, African American women were more likely to be "formerly married than White women and much less likely to be living with a husband" (p. 529). Moreover, income was an important factor in accounting for differences in the marital status of African American and white men. Overall, Jaynes and Williams found that socio-economic differences explained a significant amount of the variance in marital status differences between African Americans and whites, although Bumpass, Sweet, and Martin (1990) noted that such differences rapidly diminish as income increases, especially for men. As Glick (1997) reported, African American men with high income levels are more likely to be in intact first marriages by middle age than are African American women with high earnings. This relationship between income and marital status, he stated, is strongest at the lower end of the income distribution, suggesting that marital permanence for men is less dependent on their being well-to-do than on their having the income to support a family.

As a result of sharp increases in marital disruption and relatively low remarriage rates, less than half (43%) the African American adults aged 18 and older were currently married in 1995, down from 64% in 1970 (U.S. Bureau of the Census, 1996). Moreover, although the vast majority of the 11.6 million African Americans households in 1995 were family households, less than half (47%) were headed by married couples, down from 56% in 1980. Some analysts expect the decline in marriage among African Americans to continue for some time, consistent with the movement away from marriage as a consequence of modernization and urbanization (Espenshade, 1985) and in response to continuing economic marginalization. But African American culture may also play a role. As a number of writers have noted (Billingsley, 1992; Cherlin, 1996), blood ties and extended families have traditionally been given primacy over other types of relationships, including marriage, among African Americans, and this emphasis may have influenced the way many African Americans responded to recent shifts in values in the larger society and the restructuring of the economy that struck the African American community especially hard.

Such is the interpretation of Cherlin (1992, p. 112), who argued that the institution of marriage has been weakened during the past few decades by the increasing economic independence of women and men and by a cultural drift "toward a more individualistic ethos, one which emphasized self-fulfillment in personal relations." In addition, Wilson (1987) and others described structural shifts in the economy (from manufacturing to service industries as a source of the growth in employment) that have benefited African American women more than men, eroding men's earning potential and their ability to support families. According to Cherlin, the way African Americans responded to such broad sociocultural and economic changes was conditioned by their history and culture:

> Faced with difficult times economically, many Blacks responded by drawing upon a model of social support that was in their cultural repertoire. . . . This response relied heavily on extended kinship networks and deemphasized marriage. It is a response that taps a traditional source of strength in African-American society: cooperation and sharing among a large network of kin. (p. 113)

Thus, it seems likely that economic developments and cultural values have contributed independently and jointly to the explanation of declining rates of marriage among African Americans in recent years (Farley & Allen, 1987).

Single-Parent Families

Just as rates of divorce, separation, and out-of-wedlock childbearing have increased over the past few decades, so has the number of children living in single-parent households. For example, between 1970 and 1990, the number and proportion of all U.S. single-parent households increased threefold, from 1 in 10 to 3 in 10. There were 3.8 million single-parent families with children under 18 in 1970, compared to 11.4 million in 1994. The vast majority of single-parent households are maintained by women (86% in 1994), but the number of single-parent households headed by men has more than tripled: from 393,000 in 1970 to 1.5 million in 1994 (U.S. Bureau of the Census, 1995).

Among the 58% of African American families with children at home in 1995, more were one-parent families (34%) than married-couple families (24%). In 1994, single-parent families accounted for 25% of all white family groups with children under age 18, 65% of all African American family groups, and 36% of Hispanic family groups (U.S. Bureau of the Census, 1995).

Single-parent families are created in a number of ways: through divorce, marital separation, out-of-wedlock births, or death of a parent. Among adult African American women aged 25–44, increases in the percentage of never-married women and disrupted marriages are significant contributors to the rise in female-headed households; for white women of the same age group, marital dissolution or divorce is the most important factor (Demo, 1992; Jaynes & Williams, 1989). Moreover, changes in the living arrangements of women who give birth outside marriage or experience marital disruption have also been significant factors in the rise of female-headed households among African American and white women. In the past, women who experienced separation or divorce, or bore children out of wedlock were more likely to move in with their parents or other relatives, creating subfamilies; as a result, they were not classified as female headed. In recent decades, however, more and more of these women have established their own households (Parish, Hao, & Hogan, 1991).

An increasing proportion of female-headed householders are unmarried teenage mothers with young children. In 1990, for example, 96% of all births to African American teenagers occurred outside marriage; for white teenagers, the figure was 55% (National Center for Health Statistics, 1991). Although overall fertility rates among teenage women declined steadily from the 1950s through the end of the 1980s, the share of births to unmarried women has risen sharply over time. In 1970, the proportion of all births to unmarried teenage women aged 15–19 was less than 1 in 3; by 1991, it had increased to 2 in 3.

Differences in fertility and births outside marriage among young African American and white women are accounted for, in part, by differences in sexual activity, use of contraceptives, the selection of adoption as an option, and the proportion of premarital pregnancies that are legitimized by marriage before the children's births (Trusell, 1988). Compared to their white counterparts, African American teenagers are more likely to be sexually active and less likely to use contraceptives, to have abortions when pregnant, and to marry before the babies are born. In consequence, young African American women constitute a larger share of single mothers than they did in past decades. This development has serious social and economic consequences for children and adults because female-headed households have much higher rates of poverty and deprivation than do other families (Taylor, 1991b).

Family Structure and Family Dynamics

As a number of studies have shown, there is a strong correspondence between organization and economic status of families, regardless of race (Farley & Allen, 1987). For both African Americans and whites, the higher the income, the greater the percentage of families headed by married couples. In their analysis of 1980 census data on family income and structure, Farley and Allen (1987) found that "there were near linear decreases in the proportions of households headed by women, households where children reside with a single parent, and extended households with increases in economic status" (p. 185). Yet, socioeconomic factors, they concluded, explained only part of the observed differences in family organization between African Americans and whites. "Cultural factors—that is, family preferences, notions of the appropriate and established habits—also help explain race differences in family organization" (p. 186).

One such difference is the egalitarian mode of family functioning in African American families, characterized by complementarity and flexibility in family roles (Billingsley, 1992; Hill, 1971). Egalitarian modes of family functioning are common even among low-income African American families, where one might expect the more traditional patriarchal pattern of authority to prevail. Until recently, such modes of family functioning were interpreted as signs of weakness or pathology because they were counternormative to the gender-role division of labor in majority families (Collins, 1990). Some scholars have suggested that role reciprocity in African American families is a legacy of slavery, in which the traditional gender division of labor was largely ignored by slaveholders, and Black men and women were "equal in the sense that neither sex wielded economic power over the other" (Jones, 1985, p. 14). As a result of historical experiences and economic conditions, traditional gender distinctions in the homemaker and provider roles have been less rigid in African American families than in white families (Beckett & Smith, 1981). Moreover, since African American women have historically been involved in the paid labor force in greater numbers than have white women and because they have had a more significant economic role in families than their white counterparts, Scott-Jones and Nelson-LeGall (1986, p. 95) argued that African Americans "have not experienced as strong an economic basis for the subordination of women, either in marital roles or in the preparation of girls for schooling, jobs, and careers."

In her analysis of data from the NSBA, Hatchett (1991) found strong support for an egalitarian division of family responsibilities and tasks. With respect to attitudes toward the sharing of familial roles, 88% of the African American adults agreed that women and men should share child care and housework equally, and 73% agreed that both men and women should have jobs to support their families. For African American men, support for an egalitarian division of labor in the family did not differ by education or socioeconomic level, but education was related to attitudes toward the sharing of family responsibilities and roles among African American women. College-educated women were more likely than were women with less education to support the flexibility and interchangeability of family roles and tasks.

Egalitarian attitudes toward familial roles among African Americans are also reflected in child-rearing attitudes and practices (Taylor, 1991a). Studies have indicated that African American families tend to place less emphasis on differential gender-role socialization than do other families (Blau, 1981). In her analysis of gender-role socialization among southern African American families, Lewis (1975) found few patterned differences in parental attitudes toward male and female roles. Rather, age and relative birth order were found to be more important than gender as determinants of differential treatment and behavioral expectations for children. Through their socialization practices, African American parents seek to inculcate in both genders traits of assertiveness, independence, and self-confidence (Boykin & Toms, 1985; Lewis, 1975). However, as children mature, socialization practices are adapted to reflect "more closely the structure of expectations and opportunities provided for Black men and women by the dominant society" (Lewis, 1975, p. 237)—that is, geared to the macrostructural conditions that constrain familial role options for African American men and women.

However, such shifts in emphasis and expectations often lead to complications in the socialization process by inculcating in men and women components of gender-role definitions that are incompatible or noncomplementary, thereby engendering a potential source of conflict in their relationships. Franklin (1986) suggested that young African American men and women are frequently confronted with contradictory messages and dilemmas as a result of familial socialization. On the one hand, men are socialized to embrace an androgynous gender role within the African American community, but, on the other hand, they are expected to perform according to the white masculine gender-role paradigm in some contexts. According to Franklin, this dual orientation tends to foster confusion in some young men and difficulties developing an appropriate gender identity. Likewise, some young African American women may receive two different and contradictory messages: "One message states, 'Because you will be a Black woman, it is imperative that you learn to take care of yourself because it is hard to find a Black man who will take care of you.' A second message . . . that conflicts with the first . . . is 'your ultimate achievement will occur when you have snared a Black man who will take care of you' " (Franklin, 1986, p. 109). Franklin contended that such contradictory expectations and mixed messages frequently lead to incompatible gender-based behaviors among African American men and women and conflicts in their relationships.

Despite the apparently greater acceptance of role flexibility and power sharing in African American families, conflict around these issues figures prominently in marital instability. In their study of marital instability among African American and white couples in early marriages, Hatchett, Veroff, and Douvan (1995) found young African American couples at odds over gender roles in the family. Anxiety over their ability to function in the provider role was found to be an important source of instability in the marriages for African American husbands, but not for white husbands. Hatchett (1991) observed that marital instability tended to be more common among young African American couples if the husbands felt that their wives had equal power in the family and if the wives felt there was not enough sharing of family tasks and responsibilities. Hatchett et al. (1991) suggested that African American men's feelings of economic anxiety and self-doubt may be expressed in conflicts over decisional power and in the men's more tenuous commitment to their marriages vis-à-vis African American women. Although the results of their study relate to African American couples in the early stages of marriage, the findings may be predictive of major marital difficulties in the long term. These and other findings (see, for example, Tucker & Mitchell-Kernan, 1995) indicate that changing attitudes and definitions of familial roles among young African American couples are tied to social and economic trends (such as new and increased employment opportunities for women and new value orientations toward marriage and family) in the larger society.

African American Families, Social Change, and Public Policy

Over the past three decades, no change in the African American community has been more fundamental and dramatic than the restructuring of families and family relationships. Since the 1960s, unprecedented changes have occurred in rates of marriage, divorce, and separation; in the proportion of single and two-parent households and births to unmarried mothers; and in the number of children living in poverty. To be sure, these changes are consistent with trends for the U.S. population as a whole, but they are more pronounced among African Americans, largely because of a conflux of demographic and economic factors that are peculiar to the African American community.

In their summary of findings from a series of empirical studies that investigated the causes and correlates of recent changes in patterns of African American family formation, Tucker and Mitchell-Kernan (1995) came to several conclusions that have implications for future research and social policy. One consistent finding is the critical role that sex ratios–the availability of mates play in the formation of African American families. Analyzing aggregate-level data on African American sex ratios in 171 U.S. cities, Sampson (1995) found that these sex ratios were highly predictive of female headship, the percentage of married couples among families with school-age children, and the percentage of African American women who were single. In assessing the causal effect of sex ratios on the family structure of African Americans and whites, he showed that the effect is five times greater for the former than the latter. Similarly, Kiecolt and Fossett's (1995) analysis of African American sex ratios in Louisiana cities and counties disclosed that they had strong positive effects on the percentage of African American women who were married and had husbands present, the rate of marital births per thousand African American women aged 20–29, the percentage of married-couple families, and the percentage of children living in two-parent households.

Another consistent finding is the substantial and critical impact of economic factors on African American family formation, especially men's employment status. Analyses by Sampson (1995) and Darity and Myers (1995) provided persuasive evidence that economic factors play a major and unique role in the development and maintenance of African American families. Using aggregate data, Sampson found that low employment rates for African American men in cities across the United States were predictive of female headship, the percentage of women who were single, and the percentage of married-couple families among family households with school-age children. Moreover, comparing the effect of men's employment on the family structure of African American and white families, he found that the effect was 20 times greater for African Americans than for whites. Similar results are reported by Darity and Myers, who investigated the effects of sex ratio and economic marriageability—Wilson and Neckerman's (1986) Male Marriageability Pool Index—on African American family structure. They found that, although both measures were independently predictive of female headship among African Americans, a composite measure of economic and demographic factors was a more stable and effective predictor. Moreover, Sampson found that the strongest independent effect of these factors on family structure was observed among African American families in poverty. That is, "the lower the sex ratio and the lower the male employment rate the higher the rate of female-headed families with children and in poverty" (p. 250). It should be noted that neither rates of white men's employment nor white sex ratios was found to have much influence on white family structure in these analyses, lending support to Wilson's (1987) hypothesis regarding the structural sources of family disruption among African Americans.

Although the findings reported here are not definitive, they substantiate the unique and powerful effects of sex ratios and men's employment on the marital behavior and family structure of African Americans and point to other problems related to the economic marginalization of men and family poverty in African American communities. Some analysts have predicted far-reaching consequences for African Americans and for society at large should current trends in marital disruption continue unabated. Darity and Myers (1996) predicted that the majority of African American families will be headed by women by the beginning of the next decade if violent crime, homicide, incarceration, and other problems associated with the economic marginalization of African American men are allowed to rob the next generation of fathers and husbands. Moreover, they contended, a large number of such families are likely to be poor and isolated from the mainstream of American society.

The growing economic marginalization of African American men and their ability to provide economic support to families have contributed to their increasing estrangement from family life (Bowman, 1989; Tucker & Mitchell-Kernan, 1995) and are identified as pivotal factors in the development of other social problems, including drug abuse, crime, homicide, and imprisonment, which further erode their prospects as marriageable mates for African American women.

In addressing the structural sources of the disruption of African American families, researchers have advanced a number of short- and long-term proposals. There is considerable agreement that increasing the rate of marriage alone will not significantly improve the economic prospects of many poor African American families. As Ehrenreich (1986) observed, given the marginal economic position of poor African American men, impoverished African American women would have to be married to three such men—simultaneously—to achieve an average family income! Thus, for many African American women, increasing the prevalence of marriage will not address many of the problems they experience as single parents.

With respect to short-term policies designed to address some of the more deleterious effects of structural forces on African American families, Darity and Myers (1996) proposed three policy initiatives that are likely to produce significant results for African American communities. First, because research has indicated that reductions in welfare benefits have failed to stem the rise in female-headed households, welfare policy should reinstate its earlier objective of lifting the poor out of poverty. In Darity and Myers's view, concerns about the alleged disincentives of transfer payments are "moot in light of the long-term evidence that Black families will sink deeper into a crisis of female headship with or without welfare. Better a world of welfare-dependent, near-poor families than one of welfare-free but desolate and permanently poor families" (p. 288). Second, programs are needed to improve the health care of poor women and their children. One major potential benefit of such a strategy is an improvement in the sex ratio because the quality of prenatal and child care is one of the determinants of sex ratios. "By assuring quality health care now, we may help stem the tide toward further depletion of young Black males in the future" (p. 288). A third strategy involves improvements in the quality of education provided to the poor, which are key to employment gains.

Although these are important initiatives with obvious benefits to African American communities, in the long term, the best strategy for addressing marital disruptions and other family-related issues is an economic-labor market strategy. Because much of current social policy is ideologically driven, rather than formulated on the basis of empirical evidence, it has failed to acknowledge or address the extent to which global and national changes in the economy have conspired to marginalize significant segments of the African American population, both male and female, and deprive them of the resources to form or support families. Although social policy analysts have repeatedly substantiated the link between the decline in marriages among African Americans and fundamental changes in the U.S. postindustrial economy, their insights have yet to be formulated into a meaningful and responsive policy agenda. Until these structural realities are incorporated into governmental policy, it is unlikely that marital disruption and other adverse trends associated with this development will be reversed.

There is no magic bullet for addressing the causes and consequences of marital decline among African Americans, but public policies that are designed to improve the economic and employment prospects of men and women at all socioeconomic levels have the greatest potential for improving the lot of African American families. Key elements of such policies would include raising the level of education and employment training among African American youth, and more vigorous enforcement of antidiscrimination laws, which would raise the level of employment and earnings and contribute to higher rates of marriage among African Americans (Burbridge, 1995). To be sure, many of the federally sponsored employment and training programs that were launched during the 1960s and 1970s were plagued by a variety of administrative and organizational problems, but the effectiveness of some of these programs in improving the long-term employment prospects and life chances of disadvantaged youth and adults has been well documented (Taylor et al., 1990).

African American families, like all families, exist not in a social vacuum but in communities, and programs that are designed to strengthen community institutions and provide social support to families are likely to have a significant impact on family functioning. Although the extended family and community institutions, such as the church, have been important sources of support to African American families in the past, these community support systems have been overwhelmed by widespread joblessness, poverty, and a plethora of other problems that beset many African American communities. Thus, national efforts to rebuild the social and economic infrastructures of inner-city communities would make a major contribution toward improving the overall health and well-being of African American families and could encourage more young people to marry in the future.

Winning support for these and other policy initiatives will not be easy in a political environment that de-emphasizes the role of government in social policy and human welfare. But without such national efforts, it is difficult to see how many of the social conditions that adversely affect the structure and functioning of African American families will be eliminated or how the causes and consequences of marital decline can be ameliorated. If policy makers are serious about addressing conditions that destabilize families, undermine communities, and contribute to a host of other socially undesirable outcomes, new policy initiatives, such as those just outlined, must be given higher priority.

References

Allen, W. (1978). The search for applicable theories of black family life. *Journal of Marriage and the Family, 40*, 117–129.

Beckett, J., & Smith, A. (1981). Work and family roles: Egalitarian marriage in black and white families. *Social Service Review, 55*, 314–326.

Billingsley, A. (1968). *Black families in white America.* Englewood Cliffs, NJ: Prentice Hall.

Billingsley, A. (1992). *Climbing Jacob's ladder: The enduring legacy of African American families.* New York: Simon & Schuster.

Blassingame, J. (1972). *The slave community.* New York: Oxford University Press.

Blau, Zena. (1981). *Black children/white socialization.* New York: Free Press.

Bowman, P. J. (1989). Research perspectives on black men: Role strain and adaptation across the life cycle. In R. L. Jones (Ed.), *Black adult development and aging* (pp. 117–150). Berkeley, CA: Cobb & Henry.

Bowman, P. J. (1995). Commentary. In M. B. Tucker & C. Mitchell-Kernan (Eds.), *The decline in marriage among African Americans* (pp. 309–321). New York: Russell Sage Foundation.

Boykin, A. W., & Toms, F. D. (1985). Black child socialization: A conceptual framework. In H. P. McAdoo & J. L. McAdoo (Eds.), *Black children* (pp. 33–54). Beverly Hills, CA: Sage.

Bumpass, L., Sweet, J., & Martin, T. C. (1990). Changing patterns of remarriage. *Journal of Marriage and the Family, 52*, 747–756.

Burbridge, L. C. (1995). Policy implications of a decline in marriage among African Americans. In M. B. Tucker & C. Mitchell-Kernan (Eds.), *The decline in marriage among African Americans* (pp. 323–344). New York: Russell Sage Foundation.

Cherlin, A. (1992). *Marriage, divorce, remarriage* (rev. ed.). Cambridge, MA: Harvard University Press.

Cherlin, A. (1995). Policy issues of child care. In P. Chase-Lansdale & J. Brooks-Gunn (Eds.), *Escape from poverty* (pp. 121–137). New York: Cambridge University Press.

Cherlin, A. (1996). *Public and private families.* New York: McGraw-Hill.

Collins, P. (1990). *Black feminist thought.* Boston, MA: Unwin Hyman.

Darity, W., & Myers, S. (1995). Family structure and the marginalization of black men: Policy implications. In M. B. Tucker & C. Mitchell-Kernan (Eds.), *The decline in marriage among African Americans* (pp. 263–308). New York: Russell Sage Foundation.

Demo, D. (1992). Parent-child relations: Assessing recent changes. *Journal of Marriage and the Family, 54*, 104–117.

Dressler, W., Haworth-Hoeppner, S., & Pitts, B. (1985). Household structure in a southern black community. *American Anthropologist, 87*, 853–862.

DuBois, W. E. B. (1898). The study of the Negro problem. *Annals, 1*, 1–23.

DuBois, W. E. B. (1909). *The Negro American family.* Atlanta: Atlanta University Press.

Edwards, G. F. (1968). *E. Franklin Frazier on race relations.* Chicago: University of Chicago Press.

Ehrenreich, B. (1986, July-August). Two, three, many husbands. *Mother Jones*, 8–9.

Espenshade, T. (1985). Marriage trends in America: Estimates, implications, and underlying causes. *Population and Development Review, 11*, 193–245.

Farley, R., & Allen, W. (1987). *The color line and the quality of life in America.* New York: Oxford University Press.

Franklin, C. (1986). Black male-Black female conflict: Individually caused and culturally nurtured. In R. Staples (Ed.), *The black family* (3rd ed., pp. 106–113). Belmont, CA: Wadsworth.

Frazier, E. F. (1939). *The Negro family in the United States.* Chicago: University of Chicago Press.

Furstenberg, F., Hershberg, T., & Modell, J. (1975). The origins of the female-headed black family: The impact of the urban experience. *Journal of Interdisciplinary History, 6,* 211–233.

Genovese, E. (1974). *Roll Jordan roll: The world slaves made.* New York: Pantheon.

Glick, P. (1997). Demographic pictures of African American families. In H. McAdoo (Ed.), *Black families* (3rd ed., pp. 118–138). Thousand Oaks, CA: Sage.

Gutman, H. (1976). *The black family in slavery and freedom, 1750–1925.* New York: Pantheon.

Guttentag, M., & Secord, P. F. (1983). *Too many women.* Beverly Hills, CA: Sage.

Hatchett, S. (1991). Women and men. In J. Jackson (Ed.), *Life in black America* (pp. 84–104). Newbury Park, CA: Sage.

Hatchett, S., Cochran, D., & Jackson, J. (1991). In J. Jackson (Ed.), *Life in black America* (pp. 46–83). Newbury Park, CA: Sage.

Hatchett, S., Veroff, J., & Douvan, E. (1995). Marital instability among black and white couples in early marriage. In M. B. Tucker & C. Mitchell-Kernan (Eds.), *The decline in marriage among African Americans* (pp. 177–218). New York: Russell Sage Foundation.

Hernandez, D. J. (1993). *America's children.* New York: Russell Sage.

Herskovits, M. J. (1958). *The myth of the Negro past* (Beacon Paperback No. 69). Boston: Beacon Press.

Hill, R. (1971). *The strengths of black families.* New York: Emerson Hall.

Hill, R. (1993). *Research on the African American family: A holistic perspective.* Westport, CT: Auburn House.

Jackson, J. (Ed.). (1991). *Life in black America.* Newbury Park, CA: Sage.

Jaynes, G., & Williams, R. (1989). *A common destiny: Blacks and American society.* Washington, DC: National Academy Press.

Johnson, L. B. (1981). Perspectives on black family empirical research: 1965–1978. In H. P. McAdoo (Ed.), *Black families* (pp. 252–263). Beverly Hills, CA: Sage.

Jones, J. (1985). *Labor of love, labor of sorrow: Black women, work, and the family from slavery to the present.* New York: Basic Books.

Kiecolt, K., & Fossett, M. (1995). Mate availability and marriage among African Americans: Aggregate- and individual-level analysis. In M. B. Tucker & C. Mitchell-Kernan (Eds.), *The decline in marriage among African Americans* (pp. 121–135). New York: Russell Sage Foundation.

Lewis, D. (1975). The black family: Socialization and sex roles. *Phylon, 36,* 221–237.

Lichter, D. T., McLaughlin, D. K., Kephart, G., & Landry, G. (1992). Race and the retreat from marriage: A shortage of marriageable men? *American Sociological Review, 57,* 781–799.

Manfra, J. A. & Dykstra, R. P. (1985). Serial marriage and the origins of the black stepfamily: The Rowanty evidence. *Journal of American History, 7,* 18–44.

Mare, R., & Winship, C. (1991). Socioeconomic change and the decline of marriage for blacks and whites. In C. Jencks & P. E. Peterson (Eds.), *The urban underclass* (pp. 175–204). Washington, DC: Brookings Institute.

McAdoo, H. P. (Ed.). (1997). *Black families* (3rd ed.). Thousand Oaks, CA: Sage.

McCarthy, J. (1978). A comparison of the probability of the dissolution of first and second marriages. *Demography, 15,* 345–359.

Moynihan, D. P. (1965). *The Negro family: The case for national action.* Washington, DC: U.S. Government Printing Office.

National Center for Health Statistics. (1991). *Monthly Vital Statistics Report* (Vol. 35, No. 4, Suppl.). Washington, DC: U.S. Department of Health and Human Services.

Nobles, W. (1978). Toward an empirical and theoretical framework for defining black families. *Journal of Marriage and the Family, 40,* 679–688.

Parish, W. L., Hao, L., & Hogan, D. P. (1991). Family support networks, welfare, and work among young mothers. *Journal of Marriage and the Family, 53,* 203–215.

Pleck, E. (1973). The two-parent household: Black family structure in late nineteenth-century Boston. In M. Gordon (Ed.), *The American family in socio-historical perspective* (pp. 152–178). New York: St. Martin's Press.

Sampson, R. J. (1995). Unemployment and unbalanced sex ratios: Race-specific consequences for family structure and crime. In M. B. Tucker & C. Mitchell-Keman (Eds.), *The decline in marriage among African Americans* (pp. 229–254). New York: Russell Sage Foundation.

Scanzoni, J. (1977). *The black family in modern society.* Chicago: University of Chicago Press.

Scott-Jones, D., & Nelson-LeGall, S. (1986). Defining black families: Past and present. In E. Seidman & J. Rappaport (Eds.), *Redefining social problems* (pp. 83–100). New York: Plenum.

Shimkin, D., Shimkin, E. M., & Frate, D. A. (Eds.). (1978). *The extended family in black societies.* The Hague, the Netherlands: Mouton.

Smith, A. W. (1995). Commentary. In M. B. Tucker & C. Mitchell-Kernan (Eds.), *The decline in marriage among African Americans* (pp. 136–141). New York: Russell Sage Foundation.

Stack, C. (1974). *All our kin.* New York: Harper & Row.

Staples, R. (1971). Toward a sociology of the black family: A decade of theory and research. *Journal of Marriage and the Family, 33,* 19–38.

Staples, R., & Johnson, L. B. (1993). *Black families at the crossroads.* San Francisco: Jossey-Bass.

Staples, R., & Mirande, A. (1980). Racial and cultural variations among American families: A decennial review of the literature on minority families. *Journal of Marriage and the Family, 42,* 157–173.

Stevenson, B. (1995). Black family structure in colonial and antebellum Virginia: Amending the revisionist perspective. In M. B. Tucker & C. Mitchell-Kernan (Eds.), *The decline in marriage among African Americans* (pp. 27–56). New York: Russell Sage Foundation.

Sudarkasa, N. (1988). Interpreting the African heritage in Afro-American family organization. In H. P. McAdoo (Ed.), *Black families* (pp. 27–42). Newbury Park, CA: Sage.

Sudarkasa, N. (1997). African American families and family values. In H. P. McAdoo (Ed.), *Black families* (pp. 9–40). Thousand Oaks, CA: Sage.

Sweet, J., & Bumpass, L. (1987). *American families and households.* New York: Russell Sage Foundation.

Taylor, R. L. (1991a). Child rearing in African American families. In J. Everett, S. Chipungu, & B. Leashore (Eds.), *Child welfare: An Africentric perspective* (pp. 119–155). New Brunswick, NJ: Rutgers University Press.

Taylor, R. L. (1991b). Poverty and adolescent black males: The subculture of disengagement. In P. Edelman & J. Ladner (Eds.), *Adolescence and poverty: Challenge for the 1990s* (pp. 139–162). Washington, DC: Center for National Policy Press.

Taylor, R. L. (1997). Who's parenting? Trends and Patterns. In T. Arendell (Ed.), *Contemporary parenting: Challenges and issues* (pp. 68–91). Thousand Oaks, CA: Sage.

Taylor, R. J., Chatters, L., Tucker, M. B., & Lewis, E. (1990). Developments in research on black families: A decade review. *Journal of Marriage and the Family, 52,* 993–1014.

Testa, M., & Krogh, M. (1995). The effect of employment on marriage among black males in inner-city Chicago. In M. B. Tucker & C. Mitchell-Kernan (Eds.), *The decline in marriage among African Americans* (pp. 59–95). New York: Russell Sage Foundation.

Thornton, A. (1978). Marital instability differentials and interactions: Insights from multivariate contingency table analysis. *Sociology and Social Research, 62,* 572–595.

Trusell, J. (1988). Teenage pregnancy in the United States. *Family Planning Perspectives, 20,* 262–272.

Tucker, M. B., & Mitchell-Kernan, C. (1995). Trends in African American family formation: A theoretical and statistical overview. In M. B. Tucker & C. Mitchell Kernan (Eds.), *The decline in marriage among African Americans* (pp. 3–26). New York: Russell Sage Foundation.

U.S. Bureau of the Census. (1990). Marital status and living arrangements: March 1989. *Current Population Reports* (Series P-20, No. 445). Washington, DC: U.S. Government Printing Office.

U.S. Bureau of the Census. (1994). Marital status and living arrangements: March 1993. *Current Population Reports* (Series P-20, No. 478). Washington, DC: U.S. Government Printing Office.

U.S. Bureau of the Census. (1995). Household and family characteristics: March 1994. *Current Population Reports* (Series P-20, No. 483). Washington, DC: U.S. Government Printing Office.

U.S. Bureau of the Census. (1996). *Statistical abstract of the United States: 1996.* Washington, DC: U.S. Government Printing Office.

White, D. G. (1985). *Ain't I a woman? Female slaves in the plantation South.* New York: W. W. Norton.

Wilson, W. J. (1987). *The truly disadvantaged: The inner city, the underclass and public policy.* Chicago: University of Chicago Press.

Wilson, W. J., & Neckerman K. (1986). Poverty and family structure: The widening gap between evidence and public policy issues. In S. Danziger & D. Weinberg (Eds.), *Fighting poverty: What works and what doesn't* (pp. 232–259). Cambridge, MA: Harvard University Press.

Young, V. H. (1970). Family and childhood in a southern Negro community. *American Anthropologist, 72,* 269–288.

■READING 33

Diversity within Latino Families: New Lessons for Family Social Science

Maxine Baca Zinn and Barbara Wells

Who are Latinos? How will their growing presence in U.S. society affect the family field? These are vital questions for scholars who are seeking to understand the current social and demographic shifts that are reshaping society and its knowledge base. Understanding family diversity is a formidable task, not only because the field is poorly equipped to deal with differences at the theoretical level, but because many decentering efforts are themselves problematic. Even when diverse groups are included, family scholarship can distort and misrepresent by faulty emphasis and false generalizations.

Latinos are a population that can be understood only in terms of increasing heterogeneity. Latino families are unprecedented in terms of their diversity. In this [reading], we examine the ramifications of such diversity on the history, boundaries, and dynamics of family life. We begin with a brief look at the intellectual trends shaping Latino family research. We then place different Latino groups at center stage by providing a framework that situates them in specific and changing political and economic settings. Next, we apply our framework to each national origin group to draw out their different family experiences, especially as they are altered by global restructuring. We turn, then, to examine family structure issues and the interior dynamics of family living as they vary by gender and generation. We conclude with our reflections on studying Latino families and remaking family social science. In this [reading], we use interchangeably terms that are commonly used to describe Latino national-origin groups. For example, the terms Mexican American, Mexican, and Mexican-origin population will be used to refer to the same segment of the Latino population. Mexican-origin people may also be referred to as Chicanos.

INTELLECTUAL TRENDS, CRITIQUES, AND CHALLENGES

Origins

The formal academic study of Latino families originated in the late 19th and early 20th centuries with studies of Mexican immigrant families. As the new social scientists of the times focused their concerns on immigration and social disorganization, Mexican-origin and other ethnic families were the source of great concern. The influential Chicago School of Sociology led scholars to believe that Mexican immigration, settlement, and poverty created problems in developing urban centers. During this period, family study was emerging as a new field that sought to document, as well as ameliorate, social problems in urban settings (Thomas & Wilcox, 1987). Immigrant families became major targets of social reform.

Interwoven themes from race relations and family studies gave rise to the view of Mexicans as particularly disorganized. Furthermore, the family was implicated in their plight. As transplants from traditional societies, the immigrants and their children were thought to be at odds with social requirements in the new settings. Their family arrangements were treated as cultural exceptions to the rule of standard family development. Their slowness to acculturate and take on Western patterns of family development left them behind as other families modernized (Baca Zinn, 1995).

Dominant paradigms of assimilation and modernization guided and shaped research. Notions of "traditional" and "modern" forms of social organization joined the new family social science's preoccupation with a standard family form. Compared to mainstream families, Mexican immigrant families were analyzed as traditional cultural forms. Studies of Mexican immigrants highlighted certain ethnic lifestyles that were said to produce social disorganization. Structural conditions that constrained families in the new society were rarely a concern. Instead, researchers examined (1) the families' foreign patterns and habits, (2) the moral quality of family relationships, and (3) the prospects for their Americanization (Bogardus, 1934).

Cultural Preoccupations

Ideas drawn from early social science produced cultural caricatures of Mexican families that became more exaggerated during the 1950s, when structural functionalist theories took hold in American sociology. Like the previous theories, structural functionalism's strategy for analyzing family life was to posit one family type (by no means the only family form, even then) and define it as "the normal family" (Boss & Thorne, 1989). With an emphasis on fixed family boundaries and a fixed division of roles, structural functionalists focused their attention on the group-specific characteristics that deviated from the normal or standard family and predisposed Mexican-origin families to deficiency. Mexican-origin families were analyzed in isolation from the rest of social life, described in simplistic terms of rigid male dominance and pathological clannishness. Although the earliest works on Mexican immigrant families reflected a concern for their eventual adjustment to American society, the new studies virtually abandoned the social realm. They dealt with families as if they existed in a vacuum of backward Mexican traditionalism. Structural functionalism led scholars along a path of cultural reductionism in which differences became deficiencies.

The Mexican family of social science research (Heller, 1966; Madsen, 1964; Rubel, 1966) presented a stark contrast with the mythical "standard family." Although some studies found that Mexican family traditionalism was fading as Mexicans became acculturated, Mexican families were stereotypically and inaccurately depicted as the chief cause of Mexican subordination in the United States.

New Directions

In the past 25 years, efforts to challenge myths and erroneous assumptions have produced important changes in the view of Mexican-origin families. Beginning with a critique of structural functionalist accounts of Mexican families, new studies have successfully challenged the old notions of family life as deviant, deficient, and disorganized.

The conceptual tools of Latino studies, women's studies, and social history have infused the new scholarship to produce a notable shift away from cultural preoccupations. Like the family field in general, research on Mexican-origin families has begun to devote greater attention to the "social situations and contexts that affect Mexican families" (Vega, 1990, p. 1015). This "revisionist" strategy has moved much Latino family research to a different plane—one in which racial-ethnic families are understood to be constructed by powerful social forces and as settings in which different family members adapt in a variety of ways to changing social conditions.

Current Challenges

Despite important advances, notable problems and limitations remain in the study of Latino families. A significant portion of scholarship includes only Mexican-origin groups (Massey, Zambrana, & Bell, 1995) and claims to generalize the findings to other Latinos. This practice constructs a false social reality because there is no Latino population in the same sense that there is an African American population. However useful the terms *Latino* and *Hispanic* may be as political and census identifiers, they mask extraordinary diversity. The category Hispanic was created by federal statisticians to provide data on people of Mexican, Cuban, Puerto Rican, and other Hispanic origins in the United States. There is no precise definition of group membership, and Latinos do not agree among themselves on an appropriate group label (Massey, 1993). While many prefer the term *Latino*, they may use it interchangeably with *Hispanic* to identify themselves (Romero, 1996). These terms are certainly useful for charting broad demographic changes in the United States, but when used as panethnic terms, they can contribute to misunderstandings about family life.

The labels Hispanic or Latino conceal variation in the family characteristics of Latino groups whose differences are often greater than the overall differences between Latinos and non-Latinos (Solis, 1995). To date, little comparative research has been conducted on Latino subgroups. The systematic disaggregation of family characteristics by national-origin groups remains a challenge, a necessary next step in the development of Latino family research.

We believe that the lack of a comprehensive knowledge base should not stand in the way of building a framework to analyze family life. We can use the burgeoning research on Latinos in U.S. social life to develop an analytical, rather than just a descriptive, account of families. The very complexity of Latino family arrangements begs for a unified (but not unitary) analysis. We believe that we can make good generalizations about Latino family diversity. In the sections that follow, we use a structural perspective grounded in intergroup differences. We make no pretense that this is an exhaustive review of research. Instead, our intent is to examine how Latino family experiences differ in relation to socially constructed conditions.

CONCEPTUAL FRAMEWORK

Conventional family frameworks, which have never applied well to racial-ethnic families, are even less useful in the current world of diversity and change. Incorporating multiplicity into family studies requires new approaches. A fundamental assumption guiding our analysis is that Latino families are not merely an expression of ethnic differences but, like all families, are the products of social forces.

Family diversity is an outgrowth of distinctive patterns in the way families and their members are embedded in environments with varying opportunities, resources, and rewards. Economic conditions and social inequalities associated with race, ethnicity, class, and gender place families in different "social locations." These differences are the key to understanding family variation. They determine labor market status, education, marital relations, and other factors that are crucial to family formation.

Studying Latino family diversity means exposing the structural forces that impinge differently on families in specific social, material, and historical contexts. In other words, it means unpacking the structural arrangements that produce and often require a range of family configurations. It also requires analyzing the cross-cutting forms of difference that permeate society and penetrate families to produce divergent family experiences. Several macrostructural conditions produce widespread family variations across Latino groups: (1) the sociohistorical context; (2) the structure of economic opportunity; and (3) global reorganization, including economic restructuring and immigration.

The Sociohistorical Context

Mexicans, Puerto Ricans, Cubans, and other Latino groups have varied histories that distinguish them from each other. The timing and conditions of their arrival in the United States produced distinctive patterns of settlement that continue to affect their prospects for success. Cubans arrived largely between 1960 and 1980; a group of Mexicans indigenous to the Southwest was forcibly annexed into the United States in 1848, and another has been migrating continually since around 1890; Puerto Ricans came under U.S. control in 1898 and obtained citizenship in 1917; Salvadorans and Guatemalans began to migrate to the United States in substantial numbers during the past two decades.

The Structure of Economic Opportunity

Various forms of labor are needed to sustain family life. Labor status has always been the key factor in distinguishing the experiences of Latinos. Mexicans, Puerto Ricans, Cubans, and others are located in different regions of the country where particular labor markets and a group's placement within them determine the kind of legal, political, and social supports available to families. Different levels of structural supports affect family life, often producing various domestic and household arrangements. Additional complexity stems from gendered labor markets. In a society in which men are still assumed to be the primary breadwinners, jobs generally held by women pay less than jobs usually held by men. Women's and men's differential labor market placement, rewards, and roles create contradictory work and family experiences.

Global Reorganization, Including Economic Restructuring and Immigration

Economic and demographic upheavals are redefining families throughout the world. Four factors are at work here: new technologies based primarily on the computer chip, global economic interdependence, the flight of capital, and the dominance of the information and service sectors over basic manufacturing industries (Baca Zinn & Eitzen, 1998). Latino families are profoundly affected as the environments in which they live are reshaped and they face economic and social marginalization because of underemployment and unemployment. Included in economic globalization are new demands for immigrant labor and the dramatic demographic transformations that are "Hispanicizing" the United States. Family flexibility has long been an important feature of the immigrant saga. Today, "Latino immigration is adding many varieties to family structure" (Moore & Vigil, 1993, p. 36).

The macrostructural conditions described earlier provide the context within which to examine the family experiences of different Latino groups. They set the foundation for comparing family life across Latino groups. These material and economic forces help explain the different family profiles of Mexicans, Puerto Ricans, Cubans, and others. In other words, they enable sociologists to understand how families are bound up with the unequal distribution of social opportunities and how the various national-origin groups develop broad differences in work opportunities, marital patterns, and household structures. However, they do not explain other important differences in family life that cut across national-origin groups. People of the same national origin may experience family differently, depending on their location in the class structure as unemployed, poor, working class or professional; their location in the gender structure as female or male; and their location in the sexual orientation system as heterosexual, gay, lesbian, or bisexual (Baca Zinn & Dill, 1996). In addition to these differences, family life for Latinos is shaped by age, generation living in the United States, citizenship status, and even skin color. All these differences intersect to influence the shape and character of family and household relations.

While our framework emphasizes the social context and social forces that construct families, we do not conclude that families are molded from the "outside in." What happens on a daily basis in family relations and domestic settings also constructs families. Latinos themselves—women, men, and children—have the ability actively to shape their family and household arrangements. Families should be seen as settings in which people are agents and actors, coping with, adapting to, and changing social structures to meet their needs (Baca Zinn & Eitzen, 1996).

Sociohistorical Context for Family Diversity among Mexicans

Families of Mexican descent have been incorporated into the United States by both conquest and migration. In 1848, at the end of the Mexican War, the United States acquired a large section of Mexico, which is now the southwestern United States. With the signing of the Treaty of Guadalupe Hidalgo, the Mexican population in that region became residents of U.S. territory. Following the U.S. conquest, rapid economic growth in that region resulted in a shortage of labor that was resolved by recruiting workers from Mexico. So began the pattern of Mexican labor migration that continues to the present (Portes & Rumbaut, 1990). Some workers settled permanently in the United States, and others continued in cycles of migration, but migration from Mexico has been continuous since around 1890 (Massey et al., 1995).

Dramatic increases in the Mexican-origin population have been an important part of the trend toward greater racial and ethnic diversity in the United States. The Mexican population tripled in size in 20 years, from an estimated 4.5 million in 1970 to 8.7 million in 1980 to 13.5 million in 1990 (Rumbaut, 1995; Wilkinson, 1993). At present, approximately two thirds of Mexicans are native born, and the remainder are foreign born (Rumbaut, 1995). Important differences are consistently found between the social experiences and economic prospects of the native born and the foreign born (Morales & Ong, 1993; Ortiz, 1996). While some variation exists, the typical Mexican migrant to the United States has low socioeconomic status and rural origins (Ortiz, 1995; Portes & Rumbaut, 1990). Recent immigrants have a distinct disadvantage in the labor market because of a combination of low educational attainment, limited work skills, and limited English language proficiency. Social networks are vital for integrating immigrants into U.S. society and in placing them in the social class system (Fernandez-Kelly & Schauffler, 1994). Mexicans are concentrated in barrios that have social networks in which vital information is shared, contacts are made, and job referrals are given. But the social-class context of these Mexican communities is overwhelmingly poor and working class. Mexicans remain overrepresented in low-wage occupations, especially service, manual labor, and low-end manufacturing. These homogeneous lower-class communities lack the high-quality resources that could facilitate upward mobility for either new immigrants or second- and later-generation Mexicans.

The common assumption that immigrants are assimilated economically by taking entry-level positions and advancing to better jobs has not been supported by the Mexican experience (Morales & Ong, 1993; Ortiz, 1996). Today's Mexican workers are as likely as ever to be trapped in low-wage unstable employment situations (Ortiz, 1996; Sassen, 1993). Studies (Aponte, 1993; Morales & Ong, 1993; Ortiz, 1996) have found that high labor force participation and low wages among Mexicans have created a large group of working poor. Households adapt by holding multiple jobs and pooling wages (Velez-Ibañez & Greenberg, 1992).

Mexicans are the largest Latino group in the United States; 6 of 10 Latinos have Mexican origins. This group has low family incomes, but high labor force participation for men and increasing rates for women. Mexicans have the lowest educational attainments and the largest average household size of all Latino groups. (See Table 1 and Figure 1 for between-group comparisons.)

Puerto Ricans

The fortunes of Puerto Rico and the United States were joined in 1899 when Puerto Rico became a U.S. possession in the aftermath of Spain's defeat in the Spanish-American War. Puerto Ricans are U.S. citizens and, as such, have the right to migrate to the mainland without regulation. A small stream of migrants increased dramatically after World War II for three primary reasons: high unemployment in Puerto Rico, the availability of inexpensive air travel between Puerto Rico and the United States, and labor recruitment by U.S. companies (Portes & Rumbaut, 1990). Puerto Ricans were concentrated in or near their arrival point—New York City—although migrant laborers were scattered throughout the Northeast and parts of the Midwest. They engaged in a variety of blue-collar occupations; in New York City, they were particularly drawn into the textile and garment industries (Torres & Bonilla, 1993). The unique status of Puerto Rico as a commonwealth of the United States allows Puerto Ricans to engage in a circulating migration between Puerto Rico and the mainland (Feagin & Feagin, 1996).

TABLE 1 *Social and Economic Population Characteristics*

	Median Income	Poverty	% Female Head of Household	Labor Force Participation Male	Female	High School Graduate	Average Household
Mexican	23,609	29.6	19.9	80.9	51.8	46.5	3.86
Puerto Rican	20,929	33.2	41.2	70.6	47.4	61.3	2.91
Cuban	30,584	13.6	21.3	69.9	50.8	64.7	2.56
Central/ South American	28,558	23.9	25.4	79.5	57.5	64.2	3.54
Other Hispanic	28,658	21.4	29.5			68.4	
All Hispanic	24,313	27.8	24	79.1	52.6	53.4	2.99
All U.S.	38,782	11.6	12	75	58.9	81.7	2.65
	1994	1994	1995	1995	1995	1995	1995

Source: U.S. Bureau of the Census, Statistical Abstract of the United States: 1996 (116th ed.), Washington, D.C.: U.S. Government Printing Office, 1996, Tables 53, 68, 241, 615, 622, 723, 738.

Puerto Ricans are the most economically disadvantaged of all major Latino groups. The particular context of Puerto Ricans' entry into the U.S. labor market helps explain this group's low economic status. Puerto Ricans with limited education and low occupational skills migrated to the eastern seaboard to fill manufacturing jobs (Ortiz, 1995); their economic well-being was dependent on opportunities for low-skill employment (Aponte, 1993). The region in which Puerto Ricans settled has experienced a major decline in its manufacturing base since the early 1970s. The restructuring of the economy means that, in essence, the jobs that Puerto Ricans came to the mainland to fill have largely disappeared. Latinos who have been displaced from manufacturing have generally been unable to gain access to higher-wage service sector employment (Carnoy, Daly, & Ojeda, 1993).

Compared to Mexicans and Cubans, Puerto Ricans have the lowest median family incomes and the highest unemployment and poverty rates. Puerto Ricans also have a high rate of female-headed households.

Cubans

The primary event that precipitated the migration of hundreds of thousands of Cubans to the United States was the revolution that brought Fidel Castro to power in 1959. This revolution set off several waves of immigration, beginning with the former economic and political elite and working progressively downward through the class structure. Early

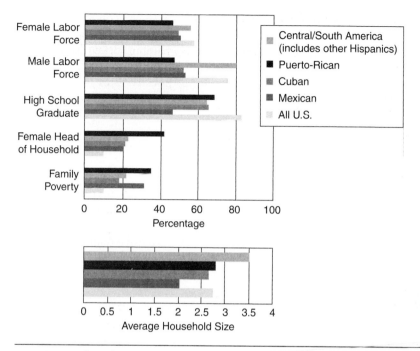

FIGURE 1 *Social and Economic Population Characteristics*

Cuban immigrants entered the United States in a highly politicized cold-war context as political refugees from communism. The U.S. government sponsored the Cuban Refugee Program, which provided massive supports to Cuban immigrants, including resettlement assistance, job training, small-business loans, welfare payments, and health care (Dominguez, 1992; Perez-Stable & Uriarte, 1993). By the time this program was phased out after the mid-1970s, the United States had invested nearly $1 billion in assistance to Cubans fleeing from communism (Perez-Stable & Uriarte, 1993, p. 155). Between 1960 and 1980, nearly 800,000 Cubans immigrated to the United States (Dominguez, 1992).

The Cuban population is concentrated in south Florida, primarily in the Miami area, where they have established a true ethnic enclave in which they own businesses; provide professional services; and control institutions, such as banks and newspapers (Perez, 1994). The unique circumstances surrounding their immigration help explain the experience of Cubans. U.S. government supports facilitated the economic successes of early Cuban immigrants (Aponte, 1993; Fernandez-Kelley & Schauffler, 1994). High rates of entrepreneurship resulted in the eventual consolidation of an enclave economy (Portes & Truelove, 1987).

Immigrants, women, and minorities have generally supplied the low-wage, flexible labor on which the restructured economy depends (Morales & Bonilla, 1993). However, Cubans "embody a privileged migration" in comparison to other Latino groups (Morales & Bonilla, 1993, p. 17). Their social-class positions, occupational attainments, and public supports have insulated them from the effects of restructuring. Yet Cubans in Miami are not completely protected from the displacements of the new economic order. As Perez-Stable and Uriarte (1993) noted, the Cuban workforce is polarized, with one segment moving into higher-wage work and the other remaining locked in low-wage employment.

Cuban families have higher incomes and far lower poverty rates than do other major Latino groups. Cubans are the most educated major Latino group and have the smallest average household size.

Other Latinos

In each national-origin group discussed earlier, one finds unique socioeconomic, political and historical circumstances. But the diversity of Latinos extends beyond the differences between Mexican Americans, Cuban Americans, and mainland Puerto Ricans. One finds further variation when one considers the experiences of other Latino national-origin groups. Although research on "other Latinos" is less extensive than the literature cited earlier, we consider briefly contexts for diversity in Central American and Dominican families.

Central Americans.   Political repression, civil war, and their accompanying economic dislocations have fueled the immigration of a substantial number of Salvadorans, Guatemalans, and Nicaraguans since the mid-1970s (Hamilton & Chinchilla, 1997). The U.S. population of Central Americans more than doubled between the 1980 and 1990 censuses and now outnumbers Cubans (U.S. Bureau of the Census, 1993). These Latinos migrated under difficult circumstances and face a set of serious challenges in the United States (Dorrington, 1995). Three factors render this population highly vulnerable: (1) a high percentage are undocumented (an estimated 49% of Salvadorans and 40% of Guatemalans), (2) they have marginal employment and high poverty rates, and (3) the U.S. government does not recognize them as political refugees (Lopez, Popkin, & Telles, 1996).

The two largest groups of Central Americans are Salvadorans and Guatemalans, the majority of whom live in the Los Angeles area. Lopez et al.'s (1996) study of Central Americans in Los Angeles illumined the social and economic contexts in which these Latinos construct their family lives. In general, the women and men have little formal education and know little English, but have high rates of labor force participation. Salvadorans and Guatemalans are overrepresented in low-paying service and blue-collar occupations. Salvadoran and Guatemalan women occupy a low-wage niche in private service (as domestic workers in private homes). Central Americans, especially the undocumented who fear deportation and usually have no access to public support, are desperate enough to accept the poorest-quality, lowest-paying work that Los Angeles has to offer. These immigrants hold the most disadvantageous position in the regional economy (Scott, 1996). Lopez et al. predicted that in the current restructured economy, Central Americans will continue to do the worst of the "dirty work" necessary to support the lifestyles of the high-wage workforce.

Dominicans.   A significant number of Dominicans began migrating to the U.S. in the mid-1960s. What Grasmuck and Pessar (1996) called the "massive displacement" of Dominicans from their homeland began with the end of Trujillo's 30-year dictatorship and the political uncertainties that ensued. Dominican immigrant families did not fit the conventional image of the unskilled, underemployed peasant. They generally had employed breadwinners who were relatively well educated by Dominican standards; the majority described themselves as having urban middle-class origins (Mitchell, 1992).

The Dominican population is heavily concentrated in New York City. They entered a hostile labor market in which their middle class aspirations were to remain largely unfulfilled because the restructured New York economy offers low-wage, marginal, mostly dead-end employment for individuals without advanced education (Torres & Bonilla, 1993). Dominicans lacked the English language competence and educational credentials that might have facilitated their upward mobility (Grasmuck & Pessar, 1996). More than two thirds of the Dominican-origin population in the United States is Dominican born. As a group, Dominicans have high rates of poverty and female-headed families. Approximately 4 in 10 family households are headed by women.

THE STRUCTURE OF ECONOMIC OPPORTUNITY

Latino families remain outside the economic mainstream of U.S. society. Their median family income stands at less than two thirds the median family income of all U.S. families (U.S. Bureau of the Census, 1996). But the broad designation of "Latino" obscures important differences among national-origin groups. In this section, we explore variations in the structure of economic opportunity and consider how particular economic contexts shape the lives of different groups of Latino families.

Class, Work, and Family Life

A number of studies (see, for example, Cardenas, Chapa, & Burek, 1993; Grasmuck & Pessar, 1996; Lopez et al., 1996; Ortiz, 1995; Perez, 1994) have documented that diverse social and economic contexts produce multiple labor market outcomes for Latino families. The quality, availability, and stability of wage labor create a socioeconomic context in which family life is constructed and maintained. Cuban American families have fared far better socioeconomically than have other Latino families. Scholars consistently cite the role of the Cuban enclave in providing a favorable economic context with advantages that other groups have not enjoyed (Morales & Bonilla, 1993; Perez, 1994; Perez-Stable & Uriarte, 1993). Cuban families have the highest incomes, educational attainments, and levels of upper-white-collar employment. Puerto Rican, Mexican, and Central American families cluster below Cubans on these socioeconomic indicators, with Puerto Ricans the most disadvantaged group.

The structure of Mexican American economic opportunity stands in sharp contrast to that of Cubans. Betancur, Cordova, and Torres (1993) documented the systematic exclusion of Mexicans from upward-mobility ladders, tracing the incorporation of Mexican Americans into the Chicago economy to illustrate the historic roots of the concentration of Mexicans in unstable, poor-quality work. Throughout the 20th century Mexican migrants have constituted a transient workforce that has been continually vulnerable to fluctuations in the labor market and cycles of recruitment and deportation.

Betancur et al.'s study highlighted the significance of the bracero program of contract labor migration in institutionalizing a segmented market for labor. The bracero program limited Mexican workers to specific low-status jobs and industries that prohibited promotion to skilled occupational categories. Mexicans were not allowed to compete for higher-status jobs, but were contracted to fill only the most undesirable jobs. Although formal bracero-era regulations have ended, similar occupational concentrations continue to be reproduced among Mexican American workers.

The effects of these diverging social-class and employment contexts on families are well illustrated by Fernandez-Kelly's (1990) study of female garment workers—Cubans in Miami and Mexicans in Los Angeles—both of whom placed a high value on marriage and family; however, contextual factors shaped differently their abilities to sustain marital relationships over time. Fernandez-Kelly contended that the conditions necessary for maintaining long-term stable unions were present in middle-class families but were absent in poor families. That is, the marriages of the poor women were threatened by unemployment and underemployment. Among these Mexican women, there was a high rate of poor female-headed households, and among the Cuban women, many were members of upwardly mobile families.

Women's Work

Several studies (Chavira-Prado, 1992; Grasmuck & Pessar, 1991; Lamphere, Zavella, Gonzales, & Evans, 1993; Stier & Tienda, 1992; Zavella, 1987) that have explored the intersection of work and family for Latinas have found that Latinas are increasingly likely to be employed. Labor force participation is the highest among Central American women and the lowest among Puerto Rican women, with Mexican and Cuban women equally likely to be employed. Not only do labor force participation rates differ by national origin, but the meaning of women's work varies as well. For example, Fernandez-Kelly's (1990) study demonstrated that for Cuban women, employment was part of a broad family objective to reestablish middle-class status. Many Cuban immigrants initially experienced downward mobility, and the women took temporary jobs to generate income while their husbands cultivated fledgling businesses. These women often withdrew from the workforce when their families' economic positions had been secured. In contrast, Mexican women in Los Angeles worked because of dire economic necessity. They were drawn into employment to augment the earnings of partners who were confined to secondary-sector work that paid less than subsistence wages or worse, to provide the primary support for their households. Thus, whereas the Cuban women expected to work temporarily until their husbands could resume the role of middle-class breadwinner, the Mexican women worked either because their partners could not earn a family wage or because of the breakdown of family relationships by divorce or abandonment.

GLOBAL REORGANIZATION

Economic Restructuring

The economic challenges that Latinos face are enormous. A workforce that has always been vulnerable to exploitation can anticipate the decline of already limited mobility prospects. A recent body of scholarship (see, for example, Lopez et al., 1996; Morales & Bonilla, 1993; Ortiz, 1996) has demonstrated that the restructuring of the U.S. economy has reshaped economic opportunities for Latinos.

Torres and Bonilla's (1993) study of the restructuring of New York City's economy is particularly illustrative because it focused on Puerto Ricans, the Latino group hit hardest by economic transformations. That study found that restructuring in New York City is based on two processes that negatively affect Puerto Ricans. First, stable jobs in both the public and private sectors have eroded since the 1960s because many large corporations that had provided long-term, union jobs for minorities left the New York area and New York City's fiscal difficulties restricted the opportunities for municipal employment. Second, the reorganization of light manufacturing has meant that new jobs offer low wages and poor working conditions; new immigrants who are vulnerable to exploitation by employers generally fill these jobs. The restructuring of the economy has resulted in the exclusion or withdrawal of a substantial proportion of Puerto Ricans from the labor market (Morales & Bonilla, 1993).

Families are not insulated from the effects of social and economic dislocations. Research that has tracked this major social transformation has considered how such changes affect family processes and household composition (Grasmuck & Pessar, 1996; Lopez et al., 1996; Rodriguez & Hagan, 1997). What Sassen (1993) called the "informalization" and "casualization" of urban labor markets will, in the end, shape families in ways that deviate from the nuclear ideal. The marginalization of the Puerto Rican workforce is related not only to high unemployment and poverty rates, but to high rates of nonmarital births and female-headed households (Fernandez-Kelly, 1990; Morrissey, 1987).

Contrasting the experience of Dominicans to that of Puerto Ricans indicates that it is impossible to generalize a unitary "Latino experience" even within a single labor market—New York City. Torres and Bonilla (1993) found that as Puerto Ricans were displaced from manufacturing jobs in the 1970s and 1980s, new Dominican immigrants came into the restructured manufacturing sector to fill low-wage jobs. Dominicans were part of a pool of immigrant labor that entered a depressed economy, was largely ineligible for public assistance, and was willing to accept exploitative employment. Grasmuck and Pessar (1991, 1996) showed how the incorporation of Dominicans into the restructured New York economy has affected families. Although the rate of divorce among early immigrants was high, relationships have become increasingly precarious as employment opportunities have become even more constrained. Currently, rates of poverty and female-headed households for Dominicans approximate those of Puerto Ricans (Rumbaut, 1995).

A Latino Underclass? Rising poverty rates among Latinos, together with the alarmist treatment of female-headed households among "minorities," have led many policy makers and media analysts to conclude that Latinos have joined inner-city African Americans to form part of the "underclass." According to the underclass model, inner-city men's joblessness has encouraged nonmarital childbearing and undermined the economic foundations of the African American family (Wilson, 1987, 1996). Researchers have also been debating for some time whether increases in the incidence of female-headed households and poverty among Puerto Ricans are irreversible (Tienda, 1989). Recent thinking, however, suggests that applying the underclass theory to Latinos obscures more than it reveals and that a different analytical model is needed to understand poverty and family issues in each Latino group (Massey et al., 1995). Not only do the causes of poverty differ across Latino communities, but patterns of social organization at the community and family levels produce a wide range of responses to poverty. According to Moore and Pinderhughes (1993), the dynamics of poverty even in the poorest Latino barrios differ in fundamental ways from the conventional portrait of the under-class. Both African Americans and Puerto Ricans have high rates of female-headed households. However, Sullivan's (1993) research in Brooklyn indicated that Puerto Ricans have high rates of cohabitation and that the family formation processes that lead to these household patterns are different from those of African Americans. Other case studies have underscored the importance of family organization. For example, Velez-Ibañez (1993) described a distinctive family form among poor Mexicans of South Tucson—cross-class household clusters surrounded by kinship networks that stretch beyond neighborhood boundaries and provide resources for coping with poverty.

Immigration

Families migrate for economic reasons, political reasons, or some combination of the two. Immigration offers potential and promise, but one of the costs is the need for families to adapt to their receiving community contexts. A growing body of scholarship has focused on two areas of family change: household composition and gender relations.

Household Composition.   Immigration contributes to the proliferation of family forms and a variety of household arrangements among Latinos (Vega, 1995). Numerous studies have highlighted the flexibility of Latino family households. Chavez (1990, 1992) identified transnational families, binational families, extended families, multiple-family households, and other arrangements among Mexican and Central American immigrants. Landale and Fennelly (1992) found informal unions that resemble marriage more than cohabitation among mainland Puerto Ricans, and Guarnizo (1997) found binational households among Dominicans who live and work in both the United States and the Dominican Republic. Two processes are at work as families adapt their household structures. First, family change reflects, for many, desperate economic circumstances (Vega, 1995), which bring some families to the breaking point and lead others to expand their household boundaries. Second, the transnationalization of economies and labor has created new opportunities for successful Latino families; for example, Guarnizo noted that Dominican entrepreneurs sometimes live in binational households and have "de facto binational citizenship" (p. 171).

Immigration and Gender.   Several important studies have considered the relationship between immigration and gender (Boyd, 1989; Grasmuck & Pessar, 1991; Hondagneu-Sotelo, 1994). In her study of undocumented Mexican immigrants, Hondagneu-Sotelo (1994) demonstrated that gender shapes migration and immigration shapes gender relations. She found that family stage migration, in which husbands migrate first and wives and children follow later, does not fit the household-strategy model. Often implied in this model is the assumption that migration reflects the unanimous and rational collective decision of all household members. However, as Hondagneu-Sotelo observed, gender hierarchies determined when and under what circumstances migration occurred; that is, men often decided spontaneously, independently, and unilaterally to migrate north to seek employment. When Mexican couples were finally reunited in the United States, they generally reconstructed more egalitarian gender relations. Variation in the form of gender relations in the United States is partially explained by the circumstances surrounding migration, such as the type and timing of migration, access to social networks, and U.S. immigration policy.

FAMILY DYNAMICS ACROSS LATINO GROUPS

Familism

Collectivist family arrangements are thought to be a defining feature of the Latino population. Presumably, a strong orientation and obligation to the family produces a kinship structure that is qualitatively different from that of all other groups. Latino familism, which is said to emphasize the family as opposed to the individual, "is linked to many of the pejorative images that have beset discussions of the Hispanic family" (Vega, 1990, p. 1018). Although themes of Latino familism figure prominently in the social science literature, this topic remains problematic owing to empirical limitations and conceptual confusion.

Popular and social science writing contain repeated descriptions of what amounts to a generic Latino kinship form. In reality, a Mexican-origin bias pervades the research on this topic. Not only is there a lack of comparative research on extended kinship structures among different national-origin groups, but there is little empirical evidence for all but Mexican-origin families. For Mexican-origin groups, studies are plentiful (for reviews, see Baca Zinn, 1983; Vega, 1990, 1995), although they have yielded inconsistent evidence about the prevalence of familism, the forms it takes, and the kinds of supportive relationships it serves.

Among the difficulties in assessing the evidence on extended family life are the inconsistent uses of terms like *familism* and *extended family system*. Seeking to clarify the multiple meanings of familism, Ramirez and Arce (1981) treated familism as a multidimensional concept comprised of such distinct aspects as structure, behavior, norms and attitudes, and social identity, each of which requires separate measurement and analysis. They proposed that familism contains four key components: (1) demographic familism, which involves such characteristics as family size; (2) structural familism, which measures the incidence of multigenerational (or extended) households; (3) normative families, which taps the value that Mexican-origin people place on family unity and solidarity; and (4) behavioral familism, which has to do with the level of interaction between family and kin networks.

Changes in regional and local economies and the resulting dislocations of Latinos have prompted questions about the ongoing viability of kinship networks. Analyzing a national sample of minority families, Rochelle (1997) argued that extended kinship networks are declining among Chicanos, Puerto Ricans, and African Americans. On the other hand, a large body of research has documented various forms of network participation by Latinos. For three decades, studies have found that kinship networks are an important survival strategy in poor Mexican communities (Alvirez & Bean, 1976; Hoppe & Heller, 1975; Velez-Ibañez, 1996) and that these networks operate as a system of cultural, emotional, and mental support (Keefe, 1984; Mindel, 1980; Ramirez, 1980), as well as a system for coping with socioeconomic marginality (Angel & Tienda, 1982; Lamphere et al., 1993).

Research has suggested, however, that kinship networks are not maintained for socioeconomic reasons alone (Buriel & De Ment, 1997). Familistic orientation among Mexican-origin adults has been associated with high levels of education and income (Griffith & Villavicienco, 1985). Familism has been viewed as a form of social capital that is linked with academic success among Mexican-heritage adolescents (Valenzuela & Dornbusch, 1994).

The research on the involvement of extended families in the migration and settlement of Mexicans discussed earlier (Chavez, 1992; Hondagneu-Sotelo, 1994; Hondagneu-Sotelo & Avila, 1997) is profoundly important. In contrast to the prevailing view that family extension is an artifact of culture, this research helps one understand that the structural flexibility of families is a social construction. Transnational families and their networks of kin are extended in space, time, and across national borders. They are quintessential adaptations—alternative arrangements for solving problems associated with immigration.

Despite the conceptual and empirical ambiguities surrounding the topic of familism, there is evidence that kinship networks are far from monolithic. Studies have revealed that variations are rooted in distinctive social conditions, such as immigrant versus non-immigrant status and generational status. Thus, even though immigrants use kin for assistance, they have smaller social networks than do second-generation Mexican Americans who have broader social networks consisting of multigenerational kin (Vega, 1990). Studies have shown that regardless of class, Mexican extended families in the United States become stronger and more extensive with generational advancement, acculturation, and socioeconomic mobility (Velez-Ibañez, 1996). Although an assimilationist perspective suggests that familism fades in succeeding generations, Velez-Ibañez found that highly elaborated second- and third-generation extended family networks are actively maintained through frequent visits, ritual celebrations, and the exchange of goods and services. These networks are differentiated by the functions they perform, depending on the circumstances of the people involved.

Gender

Latino families are commonly viewed as settings of traditional patriarchy and as different from other families because of machismo, the cult of masculinity. In the past two decades, this cultural stereotype has been the impetus for corrective scholarship on Latino families. The flourishing of Latina feminist thought has shifted the focus from the determinism of culture to questions about how gender and power in families are connected with other structures and institutions in society. Although male dominance remains a central theme, it is understood as part of the ubiquitous social ordering of women and men. In the context of other forms of difference, gender exerts a powerful influence on Latino families.

New research is discovering gender dynamics among Latino families that are both similar to and different from those found in other groups. Similarities stem from social changes that are reshaping all families, whereas differences emerge from the varied locations of Latino families and the women and men in them. Like other branches of scholarship on Latino families, most studies have been conducted with Mexican-origin populations. The past two decades of research have shown that family life among all Latino groups is deeply gendered. Yet no simple generalizations sum up the essence of power relations.

Research has examined two interrelated areas: (1) family decision making and (2) the allocation of household labor. Since the first wave of "revisionist works" (Zavella, 1987) conducted in the 1970s and 1980s (Baca Zinn, 1980; Ybarra, 1982), researchers have found variation in these activities, ranging from patriarchal role-segregated patterns to egalitarian patterns, with many combinations in between. Studies have suggested that Latinas' employment patterns, like those of women around the world, provide them with resources and autonomy that alter the balance of family power (Baca Zinn, 1980; Coltrane & Valdez, 1993; Pesquera, 1993; Repack, 1997; Williams, 1990; Ybarra, 1982; Zavella, 1987). But, as we discussed earlier, employment opportunities vary widely, and the variation produces multiple work and family patterns for Latinas. Furthermore, women's employment, by itself, does not eradicate male dominance. This is one of the main lessons of Zavella's (1987) study of Chicana cannery workers in California's Santa Clara Valley. Women's cannery work was circumscribed by inequalities of class, race, and gender. As seasonal, part-time workers, the women gained some leverage in the home, thereby creating temporary shifts in their day-to-day family lives, but this leverage did not alter the balance of family power. Fernandez-Kelly and Garcia's (1990) comparative study of women's work and family patterns among Cubans and Mexican Americans found strikingly different configurations of power. Employed women's newfound rights are often contradictory. As Repack's study (1997) of Central American immigrants revealed, numerous costs and strains accompany women's new roles in a new landscape. Family relations often became contentious when women pressed partners to share domestic responsibilities. Migration produced a situation in which women worked longer and harder than in their countries of origin.

Other conditions associated with varying patterns in the division of domestic labor are women's and men's occupational statuses and relative economic contributions to their families. Studies by Pesquera (1993), Coltrane and Valdez (1993), and Coltrane (1996) found a general "inside/outside" dichotomy (wives doing most housework, husbands doing outside work and sharing some child care), but women in middle-class jobs received more "help" from their husbands than did women with lower earnings.

"Family power" research should not be limited to women's roles, but should study the social relations between women and men. Recent works on Latino men's family lives have made important strides in this regard (Coltrane & Valdez, 1993; Shelton & John, 1993). Still, there is little information about the range and variety of Latino men's family experiences (Mirande, 1997) or of their interplay with larger structural conditions. In a rare study of Mexican immigrant men, Hondagneu-Sotelo and

Messner (1994) discussed the diminution of patriarchy that comes with settling in the United States. They showed that the key to gender equality in immigrant families is women's and men's relative positions of power and status in the larger society. Mexican immigrant men's status is low owing to racism, economic marginality, and possible undocumented status. Meanwhile, as immigrant women move into wage labor, they develop autonomy and economic skills. These conditions combine to erode patriarchal authority.

The research discussed earlier suggested some convergences between Latinos and other groups in family power arrangements. But intertwined with the shape of domestic power are strongly held ideals about women's and men's family roles. Ethnic gender identities, values, and beliefs contribute to gender relations and constitute an important but little understood dimension of families. Gender may also be influenced by Latinos' extended family networks. As Lamphere et al. (1993) discovered, Hispanas in Albuquerque were living in a world made up largely of Hispana mothers, sisters, and other relatives. Social scientists have posited a relationship between dense social networks and gender segregation. If this relationship holds, familism could well impede egalitarian relations in Latino families (Coltrane, 1996; Hurtado, 1995).

Compulsory heterosexuality is an important component of both gender and family systems. By enforcing the dichotomy of opposite sexes, it is also a form of inequality in its own right, hence an important marker of social location. A growing literature on lesbian and gay identity among Latinas and Latinos has examined the conflicting challenges involved in negotiating a multiple minority status (Alarcon, Castillo, & Moraga, 1989; Almaguer, 1991; Anzaldúa, 1987; Carrier, 1992; Moraga, 1983; Morales, 1990). Unfortunately, family scholarship on Latinos has not pursued the implications of lesbian and gay identities for understanding family diversity. In fact, there have been no studies in the social sciences in the area of sexual orientation and Latino families (Hurtado, 1995). But although the empirical base is virtually nonexistent and making *families* the unit of analysis no doubt introduces new questions (Demo & Allen, 1996), we can glean useful insights from the discourse on sexual identity. Writing about Chicanos, Almaguer (1991) identified the following obstacles to developing a safe space for forming a gay or lesbian identity: racial and class subordination and a context in which ethnicity remains a primary basis of group identity and survival. "Moreover Chicano *family life* [italics added] requires allegiance to patriarchal gender relations and to a system of sexual meanings that directly mitigate against the emergence of this alternative basis of self identity" (Almaguer, p. 88). Such repeated references to the constraints of ethnicity, gender, and sexual orientation imposed by Chicano families (Almaguer, 1991; Moraga, 1983) raise important questions. How do varied family contexts shape and differentiate the development of gay identities among Latinos? How do they affect the formation of lesbian and gay families among Latinas and Latinos? This area is wide open for research.

Children and Their Parents

Latinos have the highest concentration of children and adolescents of all major racial and ethnic groups. Nearly 40% of Latinos are aged 20 or younger, compared to about 26% of non-Hispanic whites (U.S. Bureau of the Census, 1996). Among Latino subgroups, the highest proportions of children and adolescents are among Mexicans and Puerto Ricans and the lowest among Cubans (Solis, 1995).

Latino socialization patterns have long held the interest of family scholars (Martinez, 1993). Most studies have focused on the child-rearing practices of Mexican families. Researchers have questioned whether Mexican families have permissive or authoritarian styles of child rearing and the relationship of childrearing styles to social class and cultural factors (Martinez, 1993). Patterns of child rearing were expected to reveal the level of acculturation to U.S. norms and the degree of modernization among traditional immigrant families. The results of research spanning the 1970s and 1980s were mixed and sometimes contradictory.

Buriel's (1993) study brought some clarity to the subject of child-rearing practices by situating it in the broad social context in which such practices occur. This study of Mexican families found that child-rearing practices differ by generation. Parents who were born in Mexico had a "responsibility-oriented" style that was compatible with their own life experience as struggling immigrants. U.S.-born Mexican parents had a "concern-oriented" style of parenting that was associated with the higher levels of education and income found among this group and that may also indicate that parents compensate for their children's disadvantaged standing in U.S. schools.

Mainstream theorizing has generally assumed a middle-class European-American model for the socialization of the next generation (Segura & Pierce, 1993). But the diverse contexts in which Latino children are raised suggest that family studies must take into account multiple models of socialization. Latino children are less likely than Anglo children to live in isolated nuclear units in which parents have almost exclusive responsibility for rearing children and the mothers' role is primary. Segura and Pierce contended that the pattern of nonexclusive mothering found in some Latino families shapes the gender identities of Latinos in ways that conventional thinking does not consider. Velez-Ibañez & Greenberg (1992) discussed how the extensive kinship networks of Mexican families influence child rearing and considered the ramifications for educational outcomes. Mexican children are socialized into a context of "thick" social relations. From infancy onward, these children experience far more social interaction than do children who are raised in more isolated contexts. The institution of education—second only to the family as an agent of socialization—is, in the United States, modeled after the dominant society and characterized by competition and individual achievement. Latino students who have been socialized into a more cooperative model of social relations often experience a disjuncture between their upbringing and the expectations of their schools (Velez-Ibañez & Greenberg, 1992).

Social location shapes the range of choices that parents have as they decide how best to provide for their children. Latino parents, who are disproportionately likely to occupy subordinate social locations in U.S. society, encounter severe obstacles to providing adequate material resources for their children. To date, little research has focused on Latino fathers (Powell, 1995). Hondagneu-Sotelo and Avila's (1997) study documented a broad range of mothering arrangements among Latinas. One such arrangement is transnational mothering, in which mothers work in the United States while their children remain in Mexico or Central America; it is accompanied by tremendous costs and undertaken when options are extremely limited. The researchers found that transnational mothering occurred among domestic workers, many of whom were live-in maids or child care providers who could not live with their children, as well as mothers who could better provide for their children in their countries of origin because U.S. dollars stretched further in Central America than in the United States. Other mothering arrangements chosen by Latinas in the study included migrating with their children, migrating alone and later sending for their children, and migrating alone and returning to their children after a period of work.

Intrafamily Diversity

Family scholars have increasingly recognized that family experience is differentiated along the lines of age and gender (Baca Zinn & Eitzen, 1996; Thorne, 1992). Members of particular families—parents and children, women and men—experience family life differently. Scholarship that considers the internal differentiation of Latino families is focused on the conditions surrounding and adaptations following immigration.

While immigration requires tremendous change of all family members, family adaptation to the new context is not a unitary phenomenon. Research has found patterns of differential adjustment as family members adapt unevenly to an unfamiliar social environment (Gold, 1989). Gil and Vega's (1996) study of acculturative stress in Cuban and Nicaraguan families in the Miami area identified significant differences in the adjustment of parents and their children. For example, Nicaraguan adolescents reported more initial language conflicts than did their parents, but their conflicts diminished over time, whereas their parents' language conflicts increased over time. This difference occurred because the adolescents were immediately confronted with their English language deficiency in school, but their parents could initially manage well in the Miami area without a facility with English. The authors concluded that family members experience "the aversive impacts of culture change at different times and at variable levels of intensity" (p. 451).

Differential adjustment creates new contexts for parent-child relations. Immigrant children who are school-aged generally become competent in English more quickly than do their parents. Dorrington (1995) found that Salvadoran and Guatemalan children often assume adult roles as they help their parents negotiate the bureaucratic structure of their new social environment; for example, a young child may accompany her parents to a local utility company to act as their translator.

Immigration may also create formal legal distinctions among members of Latino families. Frequently, family members do not share the same immigration status. That is, undocumented Mexican and Central American couples are likely, over time, to have children born in the United States and hence are U.S. citizens; the presence of these children then renders the "undocumented family" label inaccurate. Chavez (1992, p. 129) used the term *binational family* to refer to a family with both members who are undocumented and those who are citizens or legal residents.

Not only do family members experience family life differently, but age and gender often produce diverging and even conflicting interests among them (Baca Zinn & Eitzen, 1996). Both Hondagneu-Sotelo's (1994) and Grasmuck and Pessar's (1991) studies of family immigration found that Latinas were generally far more interested in settling permanently in the United States than were their husbands. In both studies, the women had enhanced their status by migration, while the men had lost theirs. Hondagneu-Sotelo noted that Mexican women advanced the permanent settlement of their families by taking regular, nonseasonal employment; negotiating the use of public and private assistance; and forging strong community ties. Grasmuck and Pessar observed that Dominican women tried to postpone their families' return to the Dominican Republic by extravagantly spending money that would otherwise be saved for their return and by establishing roots in the United States.

DISCUSSION AND CONCLUSION

The key to understanding diversity in Latino families is the uneven distribution of constraints and opportunities among families, which affects the behaviors of family members and ultimately the forms that family units take (Baca Zinn & Eitzen, 1996). Our goal in this review was to call into question assumptions, beliefs, and false generalizations about the way "Latino families are." We examined Latino families not as if they had some essential characteristics that set them apart from others, but as they are affected by a complex mix of structural features.

Our framework enabled us to see how diverse living arrangements among Latinos are situated and structured in the larger social world. Although this framework embraces the interplay of macro- and microlevels of analysis, we are mindful that this review devoted far too little attention to family experience, resistance, and voice. We do not mean to underestimate the importance of human agency in the social construction of Latino families, but we could not devote as much attention as we would have liked to the various ways in which women, men, and children actively produce their family worlds. Given the sheer size of the literature, the "non-comparability of most contemporary findings and the lack of a consistent conceptual groundwork" (Vega, 1990, p. 102), we decided that what is most needed is a coherent framework within which to view and interpret diversity. Therefore, we chose to focus on the impact of social forces on family life.

The basic insights of our perspective are sociological. Yet a paradox of family sociology is that the field has tended to misrepresent Latino families and those of other racial-ethnic groups. Sociology has distorted Latino families by generalizing from the experience of dominant groups and ignoring the differences that make a difference. This is a great irony. Family sociology, the specialty whose task it is to describe and understand social diversity, has marginalized diversity, rather than treated it as a central feature of social life (Baca Zinn & Eitzen, 1993).

As sociologists, we wrote this [reading] fully aware of the directions in our discipline that hinder the ability to explain diversity. At the same time, we think the core insight of sociology should be applied to challenge conventional thinking about families. Reviewing the literature for this [reading] did not diminish our sociological convictions, but it did present us with some unforeseen challenges. We found a vast gulf between mainstream family sociology and the extraordinary amount of high-quality scholarship on Latino families. Our review took us far beyond the boundaries of our discipline, making us "cross disciplinary migrants" (Stacey, 1995). We found the new literature in diverse and unlikely locations, with important breakthroughs emerging in the "borderlands" between social science disciplines. We also found the project to be infinitely more complex than we anticipated. The extensive scholarship on three national-origin groups and "others" was complicated by widely varying analytic snapshots. We were, in short, confronted with a kaleidoscope of family diversity. Our shared perspective served us well in managing the task at hand. Although we have different family specializations and contrasting family experiences, we both seek to understand multiple family and household forms that emanate from structural arrangements.

What are the most important lessons our sociological analysis holds for the family field? Three themes offer new directions for building a better, more inclusive, family social science. First, understanding Latino family diversity does not mean simply appreciating the ways in which families are different; rather, it means analyzing how the formation of diverse families is based on and reproduces social inequalities. At the heart of many of the differences between Latino families and mainstream families and the different aggregate family patterns among Latino groups are structural forces that place families in different social environments. What is not often acknowledged is that the same social structures—race, class, and other hierarchies—affect *all* families, albeit in different ways. Instead of treating family variation as the property of group difference, recent sociological theorizing (Baca Zinn, 1994; Dill, 1994; Glenn, 1992; Hill Collins, 1990, 1997) has conceptualized diverse family arrangements in *relational* terms, that is, mutually dependent and sustained through interaction across racial and class boundaries. The point is not that family differences based on race, class, and gender simply coexist. Instead, many differences in family life involve relationships of domination and subordination and differential access to material resources. Patterns of privilege and subordination characterize the historical relationships between Anglo families and Mexican families in the Southwest (Dill, 1994). Contemporary diversity among Latino families reveals *new* interdependences and inequalities. Emergent middle-class and professional lifestyles among Anglos and even some Latinos are interconnected with a new Latino servant class whose family arrangements, in turn, must accommodate to the demands of their labor.

Second, family diversity plays a part in different economic orders and the shifts that accompany them. Scholars have suggested that the multiplicity of household types is one of the chief props of the world economy (Smith, Wallerstein, & Evers, 1985). The example of U.S.-Mexican cross-border households brings this point into full view. This household arrangement constitutes an important "part of the emerging and dynamic economic and technological transformations in the region" (Velez-Ibañez, 1996, p. 143). The structural reordering required by such families is central to regional economic change.

Finally, the incredible array of immigrant family forms and their enormous capacity for adaptation offer new departures for the study of postmodern families. "Binational," "transnational," and "multinational" families, together with "border balanced households" and "generational hopscotching," are arrangements that remain invisible even in Stacey's (1996) compelling analysis of U.S. family life at the century's end. And yet the experiences of Latino families—flexible and plastic—as far back as the late 1800s (Griswold del Castillo, 1984), give resonance to the image of long-standing family fluidity and of contemporary families lurching backward and forward into the postmodern age (Stacey, 1990). The shift to a postindustrial economy is not the only social transformation affecting families. Demographic and political changes sweeping the world are engendering family configurations that are yet unimagined in family social science.

These trends offer new angles of vision for thinking about family diversity. They pose new opportunities for us to remake family studies as we uncover the mechanisms that construct multiple household and family arrangements.

References

Alarcon, N., Castillo, A., & Moraga, C. (Eds.). (1989). *Third woman: The sexuality of Latinas.* Berkeley, CA: Third Woman.

Almaguer, T. (1991). Chicano men: A cartography of homosexual identity and behavior. *Differences: A Journal of Feminist Cultural Studies, 3,* 75–100.

Alvirez, D., & Bean, F. (1976). The Mexican American family. In C. Mindel & R. Habenstein (Eds.), *Ethnic families in America* (pp. 271–292). New York: Elsevier.

Angel, R., & Tienda, M. (1982). Determinants of extended household structure: Cultural pattern or economic need? *American Journal of Sociology, 87,* 1360–1383.

Anzaldúa, G. (1987). *Borderlands/La Frontera: The new meztiza.* San Francisco: Spinsters, Aunt Lute Press.

Aponte, R. (1993). Hispanic families in poverty: Diversity, context, and interpretation. *Families in Society: The Journal of Contemporary Human Services, 36,* 527–537.

Baca Zinn, M. (1980). Employment and education of Mexican American women: The interplay of modernity and ethnicity in eight families. *Harvard Educational Review, 50,* 47–62.

Baca Zinn, M. (1983). Familism among Chicanos: A theoretical review. *Humboldt Journal of Social Relations, 10,* 224–238.

Baca Zinn, M. (1994). Feminist rethinking from racial-ethnic families. In M. Baca Zinn & B. T. Dill (Eds.), *Women of color in U.S. society* (pp. 303–312). Philadelphia: Temple University Press.

Baca Zinn, M. (1995). Social science theorizing for Latino families in the age of diversity. In R. E. Zambrana (Ed.), *Understanding Latino families* (pp. 177–187). Thousand Oaks, CA: Sage.

Baca Zinn, M., & Dill, B. T. (1996). Theorizing difference from multiracial feminism. *Feminist Studies, 22,* 321–332.

Baca Zinn, M., & Eitzen, D. S. (1993). The demographic transformation and the sociological enterprise. *American Sociologist, 24,* 5–12.

Baca Zinn, M., & Eitzen, D. S. (1996). *Diversity in families* (4th ed.). New York: HarperCollins.

Baca Zinn, M., & Eitzen, D. S. (1998). Economic restructuring and systems in inequality. In M. L. Andersen & P. H. Collins (Eds.), *Race, class and gender* (3rd ed., pp. 233–237). Belmont, CA: Wadsworth.

Betancur, J. J., Cordova, T., & Torres, M. L. A. (1993). Economic restructuring and the process of incorporation of Latinos into the Chicago economy. In R. Morales & F. Bonilla (Eds.), *Latinos in a changing U.S. economy: Comparative perspectives on growing inequality* (pp. 109–132). Newbury Park, CA: Sage.

Bogardus, A. (1934). *The Mexican in the United States.* Los Angeles: University of Southern California Press.

Boss, P., & Thorne, B. (1989). Family sociology and family therapy. In M. McGoldrick, C. M. Anderson, & F. Walsh (Eds.), *Women in families* (pp. 78–96). New York: W. W. Norton.

Boyd, M. (1989). Family and personal networks in international migration: Recent developments and new agendas. *International Migration Review, 23,* 638–670.

Buriel, R. (1993). Childrearing orientations in Mexican American families: The influence of generation and sociocultural factors. *Journal of Marriage and the Family, 55,* 987–1000.

Buriel, R., & De Ment, T. (1997). Immigration and sociocultural change in Mexican, Chinese, and Vietnamese American families. In A. Booth, A. C. Crouter, & N. Landale (Eds.), *Immigration and the family: Research and policy on U.S. immigrants* (pp. 165–200). Mahway, NJ: Lawrence Erlbaum.

Cardenas, G., Chapa, J., & Burek, S. (1993). The changing economic position of Mexican Americans in San Antonio. In R. Morales & F. Bonilla (Eds.), *Latinos in a changing U.S. economy: Comparative perspectives on growing inequality* (pp. 160–183). Newbury Park, CA: Sage.

Carnoy, M., Daley, H. M., & Ojeda, R. H. (1993). The changing economic position of Latinos in the U.S. labor market since 1939. In R. Morales & F. Bonilla (Eds.), *Latinos in a changing U.S. economy: Comparative perspectives on growing inequality* (pp. 28–54). Newbury Park, CA: Sage.

Carrier, J. (1992). Miguel: Sexual life history of a gay Mexican American. In G. Herdt (Ed.), *Gay culture in America* (pp. 202–224). Boston: Beacon Press.

Chavez, L. R. (1990). Coresidence and resistance: Strategies for survival among undocumented Mexicans and Central Americans in the United States. *Urban Anthropology, 19,* 31–61.

Chavez, L. R. (1992). *Shadowed lives: Undocumented immigrants in American society.* Forth Worth, TX: Holt, Rinehart, & Winston.

Chavira-Prado, A. (1992). Work, health, and the family: Gender structure and women's status in an undocumented migrant population. *Human Organization, 51,* 53–64.

Coltrane, S. (1996). *Family man.* New York: Oxford University Press.

Coltrane, S., & Valdez, E. O. (1993). Reluctant compliance: Work-family role allocation in dual earner Chicano families. In J. Hood (Ed.), *Men, work, and family* (pp. 151–175). Newbury Park, CA: Sage.

Demo, D. H., & Allen, K. R. (1996). Diversity within gay and lesbian families: Challenges and implications for family theory and research. *Journal of Social and Personal Relationships, 13,* 415–434.

Dill, B. T. (1994). Fictive kin, paper sons, and compadrazgo: Women of color and the struggle for survival. In M. Baca Zinn & B. T. Dill (Eds.), *Women of color in U.S. society* (pp. 149–169). Philadelphia: Temple University Press.

Dominguez, J. I. (1992). Cooperating with the enemy? U.S. immigration policies toward Cuba. In C. Mitchell (Ed.), *Western hemisphere immigration and United States foreign policy* (pp. 31–88). University Park, PA: Pennsylvania State University Press.

Dorrington, C. (1995). Central American refugees in Los Angeles: Adjustment of children and families. In R. Zambrana (Ed.), *Understanding Latino families: Scholarship, policy, and practice* (pp. 107–129). Thousand Oaks, CA: Sage.

Feagin, J. R., & Feagin, C. B. (1996). *Racial and ethnic relations.* Upper Saddle River, NJ: Prentice Hall.

Fernandez-Kelly, M. P. (1990). Delicate transactions: Gender, home, and employment among Hispanic women. In F. Ginsberg & A. L. Tsing (Eds.), *Uncertain terms* (pp. 183–195). Boston: Beacon Press.

Fernandez-Kelly, M. P., & Garcia, A. (1990). Power surrendered and power restored: The politics of home and work among Hispanic women in southern California and southern Florida. In L. Tilly & P. Gurin (Eds.), *Women and politics in America* (pp. 130–149). New York: Russell Sage Foundation.

Fernandez-Kelly, M. P., & Schauffler, R. (1994). Divided fates: Immigrant children in a restructured U.S. economy. *International Migration Review, 28,* 662–689.

Gil, A. G., & Vega, W. A. (1996). Two different worlds: Acculturation stress and adaptation among Cuban and Nicaraguan families. *Journal of Social and Personal Relationships, 13,* 435–456.

Glenn, E. N. (1992). From servitude to service work: Historical continuities in the racial division of paid reproductive labor. *Signs: Journal of Women in Culture and Society, 18,* 1–43.

Gold, S. J. (1989). Differential adjustment among new immigrant family members. *Journal of Contemporary Ethnography, 17,* 408–434.

Grasmuck, S., & Pessar, P. R. (1991). *Between two islands: Dominican international migration.* Berkeley: University of California Press.

Grasmuck, S., & Pessar, P. R. (1996). Dominicans in the United States: First- and second-generation settlement, 1960–1990. In S. Pedraza & R. G. Rumbaut (Eds.), *Origins and destinies: Immigration, race, and ethnicity in America* (pp. 280–292). Belmont, CA: Wadsworth.

Griffith, J., & Villavicienco, S. (1985). Relationships among culturation, sociodemographic characteristics, and social supports in Mexican American adults. *Hispanic Journal of Behavioral Science, 7,* 75–92.

Griswold del Castillo, R. (1984). *La familia.* Notre Dame, IN: University of Notre Dame Press.

Guarnizo, L. E. (1997). Los Dominicanyorks: The making of a binational society. In M. Romero, P. Hondagneu-Sotelo, & V. Ortiz (Eds.), *Challenging fronteras: Structuring Latina and Latino lives in the U.S.* (pp. 161–174). New York: Routledge.

Hamilton, N., & Chinchilla, N. S. (1997). Central American migration: A framework for analysis. In M. Romero, P. Hondagneu-Sotelo, & V. Ortiz (Eds.), *Challenging fronteras: Structuring Latina and Latino lives in the U.S.* (pp. 81–100). New York: Routledge.

Heller, C. (1996). *Mexican American youth: Forgotten youth at the crossroads.* New York: Random House.

Hill Collins, P. (1990). *Black feminist thought: Knowledge, consciousness and the politics of empowerment.* Boston: Unwin Hyman.

Hill Collins, P. (1997). African-American women and economic justice: A preliminary analysis of wealth, family, and black social class. Unpublished manuscript, Department of African American Studies. University of Cincinnati.

Hondagneu-Sotelo, P. (1994). *Gendered transitions: Mexican experiences of migration.* Berkeley: University of California Press.

Hondagneu-Sotelo, P., & Avila, E. (1997). "I'm here, but I'm there": The meanings of transnational motherhood. *Gender and Society, 11,* 548–571.

Hondagneu-Sotelo, P., & Messner, M. A. (1994). Gender displays and men's power: The "new man" and the Mexican immigrant man. In H. Brod & M. Kaufman (Eds.), *Theorizing masculinities* (pp. 200–218). Newbury Park, CA: Sage.

Hoppe, S. K., & Heller, P. L. (1975). Alienation, familism and the utilization of health services by Mexican-Americans. *Journal of Health and Social Behavior, 16,* 304–314.

Hurtado, A. (1995). Variations, combinations, and evolutions: Latino families in the United States. In R. E. Zambrana (Ed.), *Understanding Latino families* (pp. 40–61). Thousand Oaks, CA: Sage.

Keefe, S. (1984). Deal and ideal extended familism among Mexican Americans and Anglo Americans: On the meaning of "close" family ties. *Human Organization, 43,* 65–70.

Lamphere, L., Zavella, P., & Gonzales F., with Evans, P. B. (1993). *Sunbelt working mothers: Reconciling family and factory.* Ithaca, NY: Cornell University Press.

Landale, N. S., & Fennelly, K. (1992). Informal unions among mainland Puerto Ricans: Cohabitation or an alternative to legal marriage? *Journal of Marriage and the Family, 54,* 269–280.

Lopez, D. E., Popkin, E., & Telles, E. (1996). Central Americans: At the bottom, struggling to get ahead. In R. Waldinger & M. Bozorgmehr (Eds.), *Ethnic Los Angeles* (pp. 279–304). New York: Russell Sage Foundation.

Madsen, W. (1973). *The Mexican-Americans of south Texas.* New York: Holt, Rinehart & Winston.

Martinez, E. A. (1993). Parenting young children in Mexican American/Chicago families. In H. P. McAdoo (Ed.), *Family ethnicity: Strength in diversity* (pp. 184–194). Newbury Park, CA: Sage.

Massey, D. S. (1993). Latino poverty research: An agenda for the 1990s. Items, *Social Science Research Council Newsletter, 47*(l), 7–11.

Massey, D. S., Zambrana, R. E., & Bell, S. A. (1995). Contemporary issues for Latino families: Future directions for research, policy, and practice. In R. E. Zambrana (Ed.), *Understanding Latino families* (pp. 190–204). Thousand Oaks, CA: Sage.

Mindel, C. H. (1980). Extended familism among urban Mexican-Americans, Anglos and blacks. *Hispanic Journal of Behavioral Sciences, 2,* 21–34.

Mirande, A. (1997). *Hombres y machos: Masculinity and Latino culture.* Boulder, CO: Westview Press.

Mitchell, C. (1992). U.S. foreign policy and Dominican migration to the United States. In C. Mitchell (Ed.), *Western hemisphere immigration and United States foreign policy* (pp. 89–123). University Park: Pennsylvania State University Press.

Moore, J. W., & Pinderhughes, R. (Eds.). (1993). *In the barrios: Latinos and the underclass debate.* New York: Russell Sage Foundation.

Moore, J. W., & Vigil, J. D. (1993). Barrios in transition. In J. W. Moore & R. Pinderhughes (Eds.), *In the barrios: Latinos and the underclass debate* (pp. 27–50). New York: Russell Sage Foundation.

Moraga, C. (1983). *Loving in the war years: Lo que nunca paso por sus labios.* Boston: South End Press.

Morales, E. S. (1990). Ethnic minority families and minority gays and lesbians. In F. W. Bozett & M. B. Sussman (Eds.), *Homosexuality and family relations* (pp. 217–239). New York: Harrington Park Press.

Morales, R., & Ong, P. M. (1993). The illusion of progress: Latinos in Los Angeles. In R. Morales & F. Bonilla (Eds.), *Latinos in a changing U.S. economy: Comparative perspectives on growing inequality* (pp. 55–84). Newbury Park, CA: Sage.

Morales, R., & Bonilla, F. (1993). Restructuring and the new inequality. In R. Morales & F. Bonilla (Eds.), *Latinos in a changing U.S. economy: Comparative perspectives on growing inequality* (pp. 1–27). Newbury Park, CA: Sage.

Morrissey, M. (1987). Female-headed families: Poor women and choice. In N. Gerstel & H. Gross (Eds.), *Families and work* (pp. 302–314). Philadelphia: Temple University Press.

Ortiz, V. (1995). The diversity of Latino families. In R. Zambrana (Ed.), *Understanding Latino families: Scholarship, policy, and practice* (pp. 18–30). Thousand Oaks, CA: Sage.

Ortiz, V. (1996). The Mexican-origin population: Permanent working class or emerging middle class? In R. Waldinger & M. Bozorgmehr (Eds.), *Ethnic Los Angeles* (pp. 247–277). New York: Russell Sage Foundation.

Perez, L. (1994). Cuban families in the United States. In R. L. Taylor (Ed.), *Minority families in the United States: A multicultural perspective*. Englewood Cliffs, NJ: Prentice Hall.

Perez-Stable, M., & Uriarte, M. (1993). Cubans and the changing economy of Miami. In R. Morales & F. Bonilla (Eds.), *Latinos in a changing U.S. economy: Comparative perspectives on growing inequality* (pp. 133–159). Newbury Park, CA: Sage.

Pesquera, B. M. (1993). In the beginning he wouldn't lift even a spoon: The division of household labor. In A. de la Torre & B. M. Pesquera (Eds.), *Building with our hands* (pp. 181–198). Berkeley: University of California Press.

Portes, A., & Rumbaut, R. G. (1990). *Immigrant America: A portrait*. Berkeley: University of California Press.

Portes, A., & Truelove, C. (1987). Making sense of diversity: Recent research on Hispanic minorities in the United States. *Annual Review of Sociology, 13*, 357–385.

Powell, D. R. (1995). Including Latino fathers in parent education and support programs: Development of a program model. In R. E. Zambrana (Ed.), *Understanding Latino families* (pp. 85–106). Thousand Oaks, CA: Sage.

Ramirez, O. (1980, March). Extended family support and mental health status among Mexicans in Detroit. *Micro, Onda, LaRed, Monthly Newsletter of the National Chicano Research Network*, p. 2.

Ramirez, O., & Arce, C. H. (1981). The contemporary Chicano family: An empirically based review. In A. Baron, Jr. (Ed.), *Explorations in Chicano Psychology* (pp. 3–28). New York: Praeger.

Repack, T. A. (1997). New rules in a new landscape. In M. Romero, P. Hondagneu-Sotelo, & V. Ortiz (Eds.), *Challenging fronteras: Structuring Latina and Latino lives in the U.S.* (pp. 247–257). New York: Routledge.

Rochelle, A. (1997). *No more kin: Exploring race, class, and gender in family networks*. Thousand Oaks, CA: Sage.

Rodriguez, N. P., & Hagan, J. M. (1997). Apartment restructuring and Latino immigrant tenant struggles: A case study of human agency. In M. Romero, P. Hondagneu-Sotelo, & V. Ortiz (Eds.), *Challenging fronteras: Structuring Latina and Latina lives in the U.S.* (pp. 297–309). New York: Routledge.

Romero, M. (1997). Introduction. In M. Romero, P. Hondagneu-Sotelo, & V. Ortiz (Eds.), *Challenging fronteras: Structuring Latina and Latino lives in the U.S.* (pp. xiii-xix). New York: Routledge.

Rubel, A. J. (1966). *Across the tracks: Mexican Americans in a Texas city*. Austin: University of Texas Press.

Rumbaut, R. G. (1995). *Immigrants from Latin America and the Caribbean: A socioeconomic profile* (Statistical Brief No. 6). East Lansing: Julian Samora Research Institute, Michigan State University.

Sassen, S. (1993). Urban transformation and employment. In R. Morales & F. Bonilla (Eds.), *Latinos in a changing U.S. economy: Comparative perspectives on growing inequality* (pp. 194–206). Newbury Park, CA: Sage.

Scott, A. J. (1996). The manufacturing economy: Ethnic and gender divisions of labor. In R. Waldinger & M. Bozorgmehr (Eds.), *Ethnic Los Angeles*. New York: Russell Sage Foundation.

Segura, D. A., & Pierce, J. L. (1993). Chicana/o family structure and gender personality: Chodorow, familism, and psychoanalytic sociology revisited. *Signs, 19*, 62–91.

Shelton, B. A., & John, D. (1993). Ethnicity, race, and difference: A comparison of white, black, and Hispanic men's household labor time. In J. Hood (Ed.), *Men, work, and family* (pp. 1–22). Newbury Park, CA: Sage.

Smith, J., Wallerstein, I., & Evers, H. D. (1985). *The household and the world economy.* Beverly Hills, CA: Sage.

Solis, J. (1995). The status of Latino children and youth: Challenges and prospects. In R. E. Zambrana (Ed.), *Understanding Latino families* (pp. 62–84). Thousand Oaks, CA: Sage.

Stacey, J. (1990). *Brave new families: Stories of domestic upheaval in late twentieth century America.* New York: Basic Books.

Stacey, J. (1995). Disloyal to the disciplines: A feminist trajectory in the border lands. In D. C. Stanton & A. Stewart (Eds.), *Feminisms in the academy* (pp. 311–330). Ann Arbor: University of Michigan Press.

Stacey, J. (1996). *In the name of the family: Rethinking family values in the postmodern age.* Boston: Beacon Press.

Stier, H., & Tienda, M. (1992). Family, work, and women: The labor supply of Hispanic immigrant wives. *International Migration Review, 26,* 1291–1313.

Sullivan, M. L. (1993). Puerto Ricans in Sunset Park, Brooklyn: Poverty amidst ethnic and economic diversity. In J. W. Moore & R. Pinderhughes (Eds.), *In the barrios: Latinos and the underclass debate* (pp. 1–26). New York: Russell Sage Foundation.

Thomas, D., & Wilcox, J. E. (1987). The rise of family theory. In M. B. Sussman & S. Steinmetz (Eds.), *Handbook of marriage and the family* (pp. 81–102). New York: Plenum.

Thorne, B. (1992). Feminism and the family: Two decades of thought. In B. Thorne & M. Yalom (Eds.), *Rethinking the family: Some feminist questions* (pp. 3–30). Boston: Northeastern University Press.

Tienda, M. (1989). Puerto Ricans and the underclass debate. *Annals of the American Association of Political and Social Sciences, 501,* 105–119.

Torres, A., & Bonilla, F. (1993). Decline within decline: The New York perspective. In R. Morales & F. Bonilla (Eds.), *Latinos in a changing U.S. economy: Comparative perspectives on growing inequality* (pp. 85–108). Newbury Park, CA: Sage.

U.S. Bureau of the Census. (1993). *1990 census of the population: Persons of Hispanic origin in the United States.* Washington, DC: U.S. Government Printing Office.

U.S. Bureau of the Census. (1996). *Statistical abstract Of the United States: 1996.* Washington DC: U.S. Government Printing Office.

Valenzuela, A., & Dombusch, S. (1994). Familism and social capital in the academic achievement of Mexican origin and Anglo adolescents. *Social Science Quarterly, 75,* 18–36.

Vega, W. (1990). Hispanic families in the 1980s: A decade of research. *Journal of Marriage and the Family, 52,* 1015–1024.

Vega, W. A. (1995). The study of Latino families: A point of departure. In R. E. Zambrana (Ed.), *Understanding Latino families* (pp. 3–17). Thousand Oaks, CA: Sage.

Velez-Ibañez, C. (1993). U.S. Mexicans in the borderlands: Being poor without the underclass. In J. Moore & R. Pinderhughes (Eds.), *In the barrios: Latinos and the underclass debate* (pp. 195–220). New York: Russell Sage Foundation.

Velez-Ibañez, C. (1996). *Border visions.* Tucson: University of Arizona Press.

Velez-Ibañez, C. G., & Greenberg, J. B. (1992). Formation and transformation of funds of knowledge among U.S.-Mexican households. *Anthropology and Education Quarterly, 23,* 313–335.

Williams, N. (1990). *The Mexican American family: Tradition and change.* Dix Hills, NY: General Hall.

Wilkinson, D. (1993). Family ethnicity in America. In H. P. McAdoo (Ed.), *Family ethnicity: Strength in diversity* (pp. 15–59). Newbury Park, CA: Sage.

Wilson, W. J. (1987). *The truly disadvantaged. The inner city, the underclass, and public policy.* Chicago: University of Chicago Press.

Wilson, W. J. (1996). *When work disappears: The world of the new urban poor.* New York: Alfred A. Knopf.

Ybarra, L. (1982). When wives work: The impact on the Chicano family. *Journal of Marriage and the Family, 44,* 169–178.

Zavella, P. (1987). *Women's work and Chicano families: Cannery workers of the Santa Clara Valley.* Ithaca, NY: Cornell University Press.

■ **READING 34**

Gay and Lesbian Families: Queer Like Us

Judith Stacey

Until recently, gay and lesbian families seemed quite a queer concept, if not oxymoronic, not only to scholars and the general public but even to most lesbians and gay men. The grass roots movement for gay liberation of the late 1960s and early 1970s struggled along with the militant feminist movement of that period to liberate gays and women *from* perceived evils and injustices represented by "the family," rather than *for* access to its blessings and privileges. Early marches for gay pride and women's liberation flaunted provocative, countercultural banners, like "Smash the Family" and "Smash Monogamy." Their legacy is a lasting public association of gay liberation and feminism with family subversion. Today, however, gays and lesbians are in the thick of a vigorous profamily movement of their own.

Gay and lesbian families are indisputably here. By the late 1980s an astonishing "gay-by" boom had swelled the ranks of children living with at least one gay or lesbian parent.[1] *Family Values*, the title of a popular 1993 book by and about a lesbian's successful struggle to become a legal second mother to the son she and his biological mother have coparented since his birth,[2] is also among the most popular themes of contemporary Gay Pride marches. In 1989, Denmark became the first nation in the world to legalize a form of gay marriage, termed "registered partnerships," and its Nordic neighbors, Norway and Sweden, soon followed suit. In April 2001, the Netherlands leap-frogged ahead to become the first nation in the world to grant full legal marriage rights to same-sex couples. Meanwhile, in 1993, thousands of gay and lesbian couples participated in a mass wedding ceremony on the Washington Mall during the largest demonstration for gay rights in U.S. history. That same year, the Hawaiian state supreme court issued a ruling that raised the prospect that Hawaii would become the first state in the United States to legalize same-sex marriage. As a result, controversies over gay and lesbian families began to receive center stage billing in U.S. electoral politics.

Gay and lesbian families come in different sizes, shapes, ethnicities, races, religions, resources, creeds, and quirks, and even engage in diverse sexual practices.[3] The gay and lesbian family label primarily marks the cognitive dissonance, and even emotional threat, that much of the nongay public experiences upon recognizing that gays can participate in family life at all. What unifies such families is their need to contend with the particular array of psychic, social, legal, practical, and even physical challenges to their very existence that institutionalized hostility to homosexuality produces. Paradoxically, the label "gay and lesbian family" might become irrelevant if the nongay population could only "get used to it."

In this [reading] I hope to facilitate such a process of normalization, ironically, perhaps, to make using the marker "gay and lesbian" to depict a family category seem queer—as queer, that is, as it now seems to identify a *family*, rather than an individual or a desire, as heterosexual.[4] I will suggest that this historically novel category of family crystallizes widespread processes of family diversification and change that characterize the postmodern family conditions.[5] Gay and lesbian families represent such a new, embattled, visible, and, necessarily, self-conscious genre of kinship, that they help to expose the widening gap between the complex reality of contemporary family forms and the dated family ideology that still undergirds most public rhetoric, policy, and law concerning families. Nongay families, family scholars, and policymakers alike can learn a great deal from examining the experience, struggles, conflicts, needs, and achievements of contemporary gay and lesbian families.

BRAVE NEW FAMILY PLANNING

History rarely affords a social scientist an opportunity to witness during her own lifetime the origins and evolution of a dramatic and significant cultural phenomenon in her field. For a family scholar, it is particularly rare to be able to witness the birth of a historically unprecedented variety of family life. Yet the emergence of the "genus" gay and lesbian family as a distinct social category, and the rapid development and diversification of its living species, have occurred during the past three decades, less than my lifetime. Same-sex desire and behavior, on the other hand, have appeared in most human societies, including all Western ones, as well as among most mammalian species; homosexual relationships, identities, and communities have much longer histories than most Western heterosexuals imagine; and historical evidence documents the practice of sanctioned and/or socially visible same-sex unions in the West, as well as elsewhere, since ancient times.[6] Nonetheless, the notion of a gay or lesbian family is decidedly a late-twentieth-century development, and several particular forms of gay and lesbian families were literally "inconceivable" prior to recent developments in reproductive technology.

Indeed, before the Stonewall rebellion in 1969, the family lives of gays and lesbians were so invisible, both legally and socially, that one can actually date the appearance of the first identifiable species of gay family life—a unit that includes at least one self-identified gay or lesbian parent and children from a former heterosexual marriage. Only one U.S. child custody case reported before 1950 involved a gay or lesbian parent, and only five more gays or lesbians dared to sue for custody of their children between 1950 and 1969. Then, immediately after Stonewall, despite the predominantly antifamily ethos of the early gay liberation period, gay custody conflicts jumped dramatically, with fifty occurring during the 1970s and many more since then.[7] Courts consistently denied parental rights to these early pioneers, rendering them martyrs to a cause made visible by their losses. Both historically and numerically, formerly married lesbian and gay parents who "came out" after marriage and secured at least shared custody of their children represent the most significant genre of gay families. Such gay parents were the first to level a public challenge against the reigning cultural presumption that the two terms, "gay" and "parent" are antithetical. Their family units continue to comprise the vast majority of contemporary gay families and to manifest greater income and ethnic diversity than newer categories of lesbian and gay parents. Moreover, studies of these families provide the primary data base of the extant research on the effects of gay parenting on child development.

It was novel, incongruous, and plain brave for lesbian and gay parents to struggle for legitimate family status during the height of the antinatalist, antimaternalist, anti-family fervor of grass roots feminism and gay liberation in the early 1970s. Fortunately for their successors, such fervor proved to be quite short-lived. Within very few years many feminist theorists began to celebrate women's historically developed nurturing capacities, not coincidentally at a time when aging, feminist baby-boomers had begun producing a late-life boomlet of their own.[8] During the middle to late seventies, the legacy of sexual revolution and feminist assertions of female autonomy combined with the popularization of alternative reproductive technologies and strategies to embolden a first wave of "out" lesbians to join the burgeoning ranks of women actively choosing to have children outside of marriage.

Fully intentional childbearing outside of heterosexual unions represents one of the only new, truly original, and decidedly controversial genres of family formation and structure to have emerged in the West during many centuries. While lesbian variations on this cultural theme include some particularly creative reproductive strategies, they nonetheless represent not deviant, but vanguard manifestations of much broader late-twentieth-century trends in Western family life. Under postmodern conditions, processes of sexuality, conception, gestation, marriage, and parenthood, which once appeared to follow a natural, inevitable progression of gendered behaviors and relationships, have come unhinged, hurtling the basic definitions of our most taken-for-granted familial categories—like mother, father, parent, offspring, sibling, and, of course, "family" itself—into cultural confusion and contention.

The conservative turn toward profamily and postfeminist sensibilities of the Reagan-Bush era, combined with the increased visibility and confidence of gay and lesbian communities, helped to fuel the "gay-by" boom that escalated rapidly during the 1980s. It seems more accurate to call this a "lesbaby" boom, because lesbians vastly outnumber the gay men who can, or have chosen to, become parents out of the closet. Lesbian "planned parenthood" strategies have spread and diversified rapidly during the past two decades. With access to customary means to parenthood denied or severely limited, lesbians necessarily construct their chosen family forms with an exceptional degree of reflection and intentionality. They have been choosing motherhood within a broad array of kinship structures. Some become single mothers, but many lesbians choose to share responsibility for rearing children with a lover and/or with other coparents, such as sperm donors, gay men, and other friends and relatives. Several states expressly prohibit adoptions and/or foster care by lesbians and gay men, and many states and adoption agencies actively discriminate against them. Consequently, independent adoption provided the first, and still traveled, route to planned lesbian maternity, but increasing numbers of lesbians have been choosing to bear children of their own. In pursuit of sperm, some lesbians resort quite instrumentally to heterosexual intercourse—with or without the knowledge of the man involved—but most prefer alternative insemination strategies, locating known or anonymous donors through personal networks or through private physicians or sperm banks.

Institutionalized heterosexism and married-couple biases pervade the medically controlled fertility market. Many private physicians and many sperm banks in the United

States, as well as the Canadian and most European health services, refuse to inseminate unmarried women in general, and lesbians particularly. More than 90 percent of U.S. physicians surveyed in 1979 denied insemination to unmarried women, and a 1988 federal government survey of doctors and clinics reported that homosexuality was one of their top four reasons for refusing to provide this service.[9] Thus, initially, planned lesbian pregnancies depended primarily upon donors located through personal networks, very frequently involving gay men or male relatives who might also agree to participate in child rearing, in varying degrees. Numerous lesbian couples solicit sperm from a brother or male relative of one woman to impregnate her partner, hoping to buttress their tenuous legal, symbolic, and social claims for shared parental status over their "turkey-baster babies."

Despite its apparent novelty, "turkey-baster" insemination for infertility dates back to the late eighteenth century, and, as the nickname implies, is far from a high-tech procedure requiring medical expertise.[10] Nonetheless, because the AIDS epidemic and the emergence of child custody conflicts between lesbians and known sperm donors led many lesbians to prefer the legally sanitized, medical route to anonymous donors, feminist health care activists mobilized to meet this need. In 1975 the Vermont Women's Health Center added donor insemination to its services, and in 1980 the Northern California Sperm Bank opened in Oakland expressly to serve the needs of unmarried, disabled, or nonheterosexual women who want to become pregnant. The clinic ships frozen semen throughout North America, and more than two-thirds of the clinic's clients are not married.[11]

The absence of a national health system in the United States commercializes access to sperm and fertility services. This introduces an obvious class bias into the practice of alternative insemination. Far more high-tech, innovative, expensive, and, therefore, uncommon is a procreative strategy some lesbian couples now are adopting in which an ovum from one woman is fertilized with donor sperm and then extracted and implanted in her lover's uterus. In June 2000, one such couple in San Francisco became the first to receive joint recognition as the biological and legal co-mothers of their infant. The irony of deploying technology to assert a biological, and thereby a legal, social, and emotional claim to maternal and family status throws the contemporary instability of all the relevant categories—biology, technology, nature, culture, maternity, family—into bold relief.

While the advent of AIDS inhibited joint procreative ventures between lesbians and gay men, the epidemic also fostered stronger social and political solidarity between the two populations and stimulated gay men to keener interest in forming families. Their ranks are smaller and newer than those of lesbian mothers, but by the late eighties gay men were also visibly engaged in efforts to become parents, despite far more limited opportunities to do so. Not only do men still lack the biological capacity to derive personal benefits from most alternative reproductive technologies, but social prejudice also severely restricts gay male access to children placed for adoption, or even into foster care. Ever since Anita Bryant's "Save the Children" campaign against gay rights in 1977, right-wing mobilizations in diverse states, including Florida, Utah, New Hampshire, and Massachusetts, have successfully cast gay men, in particular, as threats to children and families and denied them the right to adopt or foster the young. In response, some wishful gay fathers have resorted to private adoption and surrogacy arrangements, accepting the most difficult-to-place adoptees and foster children, or entering into shared social parenting arrangements with lesbian couples or single women. During the 1990s, "Growing Generations," the world's first gay and lesbian-owned surrogacy agency, opened in Los Angeles to serve an international constituency of prospective gay parents.

Compelled to proceed outside conventional channels, lesbian and gay male planned parenthood has become an increasingly complex, creative, and politicized, self-help enterprise. Because gays forge kin ties without established legal protections or norms, relationships between gay parents and their children suffer heightened risks. By the mideighties many lesbians and gays found themselves battling each other, as custody conflicts between lesbian coparents or between lesbian parents and sperm donors and/or other relatives began to reach the dockets and to profoundly challenge family courts.[12] Despite a putative "best interests of the child" standard, a bias favoring the heterosexual family guided virtually all the judges who heard these early cases. Biological claims of kinship nearly always trumped those of social parenting, even in heartrending circumstances of custody challenges to bereaved lesbian "widows" who, with their deceased lovers, had jointly planned for, reared, loved, and supported children since their birth.[13] Likewise, judges routinely honored fathers' rights arguments by favoring parental claims of donors who had contributed nothing more than sperm to their offspring over those of lesbians who had coparented from the outset, *even when these men had expressly agreed to abdicate paternal rights or responsibilities.* The first, and still rare, exception to this rule involved a donor who did not bring his paternity suit until the child was ten years old.[14] While numerous sperm donors have reneged on their prenatal custody agreements with lesbian parents, thus far no lesbian mother has sued a donor to attain parental terms different from those to which he first agreed. On the other hand, in the first case in which a lesbian biological mother sought financial support from her former lesbian partner, a New York court found the nonbiological coparent to be a parent. Here, the state's fiduciary interest rather than gay rights governed the decision.[15]

Perhaps the most poignant paradox in gay and lesbian family history concerns how fervently many lesbians and gay men have had to struggle for family status precisely when forces mobilized in *the name of The Family* conspire to deny this to them. The widely publicized saga of the Sharon Kowalski case, in which the natal family of a lesbian who had been severely disabled in a car crash successfully opposed her guardianship by her chosen life-companion, proved particularly galvanizing in this cause, perhaps because all of the contestants were adults. After eight years of legal and political struggle, Sharon's lover, Karen Thompson, finally won a reversal, in a belated, but highly visible, landmark victory for gay family rights.[16]

Gay family struggles rapidly achieved other significant victories, like the 1989 *Braschi* decision by New York State's top court, which granted protection against eviction to a gay man by explicitly defining family in inclusive, social terms, to rest upon

> the exclusivity and longevity of the relationship, the level of emotional and financial commitment, the manner in which the parties have conducted their everyday lives and held themselves out to society, and the reliance placed upon one another for daily family services . . . it is the totality of the relationship as evidenced by the dedication, caring and self-sacrifice of the parties which should, in the final analysis, control.[17]

More recently, in 2000, Vermont became the first state in the United States to grant same-sex couples the right to enter a civil union, a status that confers all of the legal benefits of marriage except those denied by federal law, and numerous state legislatures will be considering similar proposals. The struggle for second-parent adoption rights, which enable a lesbian or gay man to adopt a lover's children without removing the lover's custody rights, represents one of the most active, turbulent fronts in the struggle for gay family rights. In more than half of the 50 states, individual lesbian and gay male couples have won petitions for second-parent adoptions at the trial court level. However, many trial judges deny such petitions, and only a handful of states have granted this right at the appeals court level. In 2000, a Pennsylvania appeals court decision denied such an appeal, thereby setting back the drive for gay parental rights in that state. Even the Nordic countries explicitly excluded adoption rights when they first legalized gay registered partnerships, but since then the Netherlands, Denmark, and Iceland have granted these rights, and other European and Commonwealth countries are beginning to follow suit.

The highly politicized character of family change in the United States renders struggles for gay parenting rights painfully vulnerable to unfavorable political winds. For example, state barriers to lesbian and gay second-parent adoptions in California rise and fall with the fortunes of Republican and Democratic gubernatorial campaigns. The National Center for Lesbian Rights considers second-parent adoptions right to be so crucial to the lesbian "profamily" cause that it revoked its former policy of abstaining from legal conflicts between lesbians over this issue. Convinced that the long-term, best interests of lesbian parents and their children depend upon defining parenthood in social rather than biological terms, the center decided to represent lesbian parents who are denied custody of their jointly reared children when their former lovers exploit the biological and homophobic prejudices of the judiciary.[18]

Here again, gay family politics crystallize, rather than diverge from, pervasive cultural trends. Gay second-parent adoptions, for example, trek a kin trail blazed by court responses to families reconstituted after divorce and remarriage. Courts first allowed some stepparents to adopt their new spouses' children without terminating the custody rights of the children's former parents. Gay family rights law also bears a kind of second cousin tie to racial kin case law. Gay and lesbian custody victories rely heavily on a milestone race custody case, *Palmore v. Sidoti* (1984), which restored the custody rights of a divorced, white mother who lost her children after she married a black man. Even though *Palmore* was decided on legal principles governing race discrimination, which do not yet apply to gender or sexual discrimination, several successful gay and lesbian custody decisions rely on its logic. The first successful second-parent adoption award to a lesbian couple actually was a "third-parent" adoption on the new model of stepparent adoption after divorce, which Mary Ann Mason discusses in [Reading 18]. The court granted coparent status to the nonbiological mother without withdrawing it from the sperm donor father, a Native American, in order to honor the shared desires of all three parents to preserve the child's bicultural inheritance.[19]

As U.S. tabloid and talk show fare testify daily, culturally divisive struggles over babies secured or lost through alternative insemination, in vitro fertilization, ovum extraction, frozen embryos, surrogacy, transracial adoption, not to mention mundane processes of divorce and remarriage are not the special province of a fringe gay and lesbian minority. We now inhabit a world in which technology has upended the basic premises of the old nature-nurture debate by rendering human biology more amenable to intervention than human society. Inevitably, therefore, contests between biological and social definitions of kinship, such as depicted in the chapters on adoption and stepfamilies, will continue to proliferate and to rub social nerves raw.

Thus while one can discern a gradual political and judicial trend toward granting parental and family rights to gays, the legal situation in the fifty states remains uneven, volatile, and replete with major setbacks for gay and lesbian parents.[20] Forces opposed to gay parenting continue to introduce statewide initiatives and regulations to rescind such rights. The crucial fact remains that numerous states still criminalize sodomy, supported by the 1986 U.S. Supreme Court decision in *Bowers* v. *Hardwick*, which upheld the constitutionality of this most basic impediment to civil rights for gay relationships. One decade later, however, in May 1996, the court struck down a Colorado antigay rights initiative in *Romer* v. *Evans*, raising the hopes of gays and lesbians that it might soon reconsider the detested *Bowers* ruling. As of 2002, however, such wishes remain unfulfilled.

A MORE, OR LESS, PERFECT UNION?

Much nearer at hand, however, than most ever dared to imagine is the momentous prospect of legal gay marriage. The idea of same-sex marriage used to draw nearly as many jeers from gays and lesbians as from nongays. As one lesbian couple recalls,

> In 1981, we were a very, very small handful of lesbians who got married. We took a lot of flak from other lesbians, as well as heterosexuals. In 1981, we didn't know any other lesbians, not a single one, who had had a ceremony in Santa Cruz, and a lot of lesbians live in that city. Everybody was on our case about it. They said, What are you doing, How heterosexual. We really had to sell it.[21]

Less than a decade later, gay and lesbian couples would proudly announce their weddings and anniversaries, not only in the gay press, which now includes specialized magazines for gay and lesbian couples and parents, like *Partners Magazine,* but even in such mainstream, midwestern newspapers as the Minneapolis *Star Tribune.*[22] Jewish rabbis, Protestant ministers, Quaker meetings, and even some Catholic priests regularly perform gay and lesbian wedding or commitment ceremonies, and the phenomenon has become a fashionable pop culture motif. In December 1995, the long-running, provocative TV sitcom program *Roseanne* featured a gay male wedding, and one month later, the popular sitcom *Friends* aired a lesbian wedding on primetime television. A few years later, a high profile made-for-TV HBO movie starring Vanessa Redgrave, Michelle Williams, Ellen DeGeneres, and Sharon Stone, *If These Walls Could Talk 2,* expanded on the theme by highlighting difficulties experienced by lesbian couples who cannot be legally married. Such popular culture breakthroughs have helped normalize what once seemed inconceivable to gay and straight audiences alike.

Gradually, major corporations, universities, and nonprofit organizations are providing spousal benefits to the domestic mates of their gay and lesbian employees, and a small but growing number of U.S. municipalities, states, and increasing numbers of European and Commonwealth nations have legalized domestic partnerships, which grant legal status and varying rights and responsibilities to cohabiting couples, irrespective of gender or sexual identity.

When the very first social science research collection about gay parents was published in 1987, its editor concluded that however desirable such unions might be, "it is highly unlikely that marriages between same-sex individuals will be legalized in any state in the foreseeable future."[23] Yet, almost immediately thereafter, precisely this specter began to exercise imaginations across the political spectrum. A national poll reported by the *San Francisco Examiner* in 1989 found that 86 percent of lesbians and gay men supported legalizing same-sex marriage.[24] A few years later, the Hawaiian supreme court issued a ruling that made such a prospect seem imminent. Amidst rampant rumors that thousands of mainland gay and lesbian couples were stocking their hope chests with Hawaiian excursion fares, posed to fly to tropical altars the instant the first gay matrimonial bans falter, right-wing Christian groups began actively to mobilize resistance. Utah became the first state to pass legislation refusing recognition to same-sex marriages if they were performed in other states. Soon a majority of states were considering similar bills.

On May 8, 1996, gay marriage galloped onto the nation's center political stage when Republicans introduced the Defense of Marriage Act (DOMA) to define marriage in exclusively heterosexual terms as "a legal union between one man and one woman as husband and wife." Introduced primarily as a "wedge" issue in the Republican 1996 electoral strategy, DOMA passed both houses of Congress in a landslide vote, and President Clinton promptly signed it, despite his personal support for gay rights.

As with child custody, the campaign for gay marriage clings to legal footholds planted by racial justice pioneers. It is startling to recall how recent it was that the Supreme Court finally struck down antimiscegenation laws. Not until 1967, that is only two years before the Stonewall rebellion, did the high court, in *Loving* v. *Virginia*, find state restrictions on interracial marriages to be unconstitutional. (Twenty states still had such restrictions on the books in 1967, a greater number than currently prohibit sodomy.) A handful of gay couples quickly sought to marry in the 1970s through appeals to this precedent, but until three lesbian and gay male couples sued Hawaii in *Baehr* v. *Lewin* for equal rights to choose marriage partners without restrictions on gender, all U.S. courts had dismissed the analogy. In a historic ruling in 1993, the Hawaii Supreme Court remanded this suit to the trial court, requiring the state to demonstrate a "compelling interest" in prohibiting same-sex marriage, a strict scrutiny standard that the state was unable to meet when the case was retried. Significantly, the case was neither argued nor adjudicated as a gay rights issue. Rather, just as ERA opponents once had warned and advocates had denied, passage of an equal rights amendment to Hawaii's state constitution in 1972 paved the legal foundation for *Baehr*.[25]

Although backlash forces succeeded in preventing the legalization of gay marriage in Hawaii, this global struggle keeps achieving milestone victories at a breathless pace. Marriage rights in all but name are now available throughout most of Western Europe and Canada, as well as in Vermont. In 2001, the Netherlands assumed world leadership in fully legalizing same-sex marriage at the national level, and similar developments appear imminent in the Nordic nations, Canada, and perhaps in South Africa. Clearly this issue is on the historical agenda for the twenty-first century. Not all gay activists or legal scholars embrace this prospect with enthusiasm. Although most of their constituents desire the right to marry, gay activists and theorists continue to debate vigorously the politics and effects of this campaign. An articulate, vocal minority seeks not to extend the right to marry, but to dismantle an institution they regard as inherently, and irredeemably, hierarchical, unequal, conservative, and repressive.[26] A second perspective supports legal marriage as one long-term goal of the gay rights movement but voices serious strategic objections to making this a priority before there is sufficient public support to sustain a favorable ruling in any state or the nation. Such critics fear that a premature victory will prove pyrrhic, because efforts to defend it against the vehement backlash it has already begun to incite are apt to fail, after sapping resources and time better devoted to other urgent struggles for gay rights. Rather than risk a major setback for the gay movement, some leaders advocate an incremental approach to establishing legal family status for gay and lesbian kin ties through a multifaceted struggle for "family diversity."[27]

However, the largest, and most diverse, contingent of gay activist voices now supports the marriage rights campaign, perhaps because gay marriage can be perceived as harmonizing with virtually every hue on the gay ideological spectrum. Progay marriage arguments range from profoundly conservative to liberal humanist to radical and deconstructive. Conservatives, like those radicals who still oppose marriage, view it as an institution that promotes monogamy, commitment, and social stability, along with interests in private property, social conformity, and mainstream values.[28] Liberal gays support legal marriage, of course, not only to affirm the legitimacy of their relationships and help sustain them in a hostile world but as a straightforward matter of equal civil rights. They also recognize the social advantages of divorce law. "I used to say, 'Why do we want to get married? It doesn't work for straight people,'" one gay lawyer comments. "But now I say we should care: They have the privilege of divorce and we don't. We're left out there to twirl around in pain."[29]

Some feminist and other critical gay legal theorists craft more radical defenses of gay marriage. Nan Hunter, for example, rejects feminist colleague Nancy Polikoff's belief that marriage is an unalterably sexist and heterosexist institution. Hunter argues that legalized same-sex marriage would have "enormous potential to destabilize the gendered definition of marriage for everyone."[30] Likewise, Evan Wolfson, director of the Marriage Project of the gay legal rights organization Lambda Legal Defense, who served as co-counsel in *Baehr*, argues that marriage is neither inherently equal nor unequal, but depends upon an ever-changing cultural and political context.[31] (Anyone who doubts this need only consider such examples as polygamy, arranged marriage, or the same-sex unions in early Western history documented by the late Princeton historian John Boswell.)

Support for gay marriage, not long ago anathema to radicals and conservatives, gays and nongays alike, now issues forth from ethical and political perspectives as diverse, and even incompatible, as these. The cultural and political context has changed so dramatically since Stonewall that it now seems easier to understand why marriage has come to enjoy overwhelming support in the gay community than to grasp the depth of resistance to the institution that characterized the early movement.

Gay marriage, despite its apparent compatibility with mainstream "family values" sentiment, raises far more threatening questions than does military service about gender relations, sexuality, and family life. Few contemporary politicians, irrespective of their personal convictions, display the courage to confront this contradiction, even when urged to do so by gay conservatives. Gay marriage would strengthen the ranks of those endangered two-parent, "intact," married-couples families whose praises conservative, "pro-family" enthusiasts tirelessly sing. Unsurprisingly, however, this case has won few nongay conservative converts to the cause. After all, homophobia is a matter of passion, politics, and prejudice, not logic.

Surveys suggest, however, that while a majority of citizens still oppose legalizing gay marriage, the margin of opposition is declining slowly but surely. In a 1994 *Time* magazine/CNN poll, 64 percent of respondents did not want to legalize gay marriages.[32] A *Newsweek* poll conducted right after the DOMA was introduced in May 1996 reported that public opposition to gay marriage had declined to 58 percent, and a Gallup poll conducted June 2001 indicated a further drop to 52 percent.[33]

Despite the paucity of mainstream political enthusiasm for legalizing gay marriage, there are good reasons to believe that gays and lesbians will eventually win this right and to support their struggle to do so. Legitimizing gay and lesbian marriages would promote a democratic, pluralist expansion of the meaning, practice, and politics of family life in the United States, helping to supplant the destructive sanctity of *The Family* with respect for diverse and vibrant *families*. To begin with, the liberal implications of legal gay marriage are far from trivial, as the rush to nullify them should confirm. For example, legal gay marriage in one state could begin to threaten antisodomy laws in all the others. Policing marital sex would be difficult to legitimate, and differential prosecution of conjugal sex among same-sex couples could violate equal protection legislation. Likewise, if gay marriage were legalized, the myriad of state barriers to child custody, adoption, fertility services, inheritance, and other family rights that lesbians and gay men currently suffer could also become subject to legal challenge. Moreover, it seems hard to overestimate the profound cultural implications for the struggle against the injurious effects of legally condoned homophobia that would ensue were lesbian and gay relationships to be admitted into the ranks of legitimate kinship. In a society that forbids most public school teachers and counselors even the merest expression of tolerance for homosexuality, while lesbian and gay youth attempt suicide at rates estimated to be at least three times greater than other youth,[34] granting full legal recognition to lesbian and gay relationships could have dramatic, and salutary, consequences.

Moreover, while it is unlikely that same-sex marriage can in itself dismantle the patterned gender and sexual injustices of the institution, I believe it could make a potent contribution to those projects, as the research on gay relationships I discuss later seems to indicate. Admitting gays to the wedding banquet invites gays and nongays alike to consider the kinds of place settings that could best accommodate the diverse needs of all contemporary families. Subjecting the conjugal institution to this sort of heightened democratic scrutiny could help it to assume varied, creative, and adaptive contours. If we begin to value the meaning and quality of intimate bonds over their customary forms, people might devise marriage and kinship patterns to serve diverse needs. For example, the "companionate marriage," a much celebrated, but less often realized, ideal of modern sociological lore, could take on new life. Two friends might decide to "marry" without basing their bond on erotic or romantic attachment, as Dorthe, a prominent Danish lesbian activist who had initially opposed the campaign for gay marriage, fantasized after her nation's parliament approved gay "registered partnerships": If I am going to marry it will be with one of my oldest friends in order to share pensions and things like that. But

I'd never marry a lover. That is the advantage of being married to a close friend. Then, you never have to marry a lover![35]

While conservative advocates of gay marriage scoff at such radical visions, they correctly realize that putative champions of committed relationships and children who oppose gay marriage can be charged with gross hypocrisy on this score. For access to legal marriage not only would promote long-term, committed intimacy and economic security among gay couples but also would afford invaluable protection to the children of gay parents. Public legitimacy for gay relationships would also provide indirect protection to closeted gay youth who reside with nongay parents. Clearly, only through a process of massive denial of the fact that millions of children living in gay and lesbian families are here, and here to stay, can anyone genuinely concerned with the best interests of children deny their parents the right to marry.

IN THE BEST INTERESTS OF WHOSE CHILDREN?

The most cursory survey of the existing empirical research on gay and lesbian families reveals the depth of sanctioned discrimination they continue to suffer and the absence of evidence to justify this iniquity. To be sure, substantial limitations mar the social science research on this subject, which is barely past its infancy. Mainstream journals, even those specializing in family research, warmed to this subject startlingly late and little, relegating the domain primarily to sexologists, clinicians, and a handful of movement scholars and their sympathizers and opponents. In 1995, a survey of the three leading journals of family research in the United States found only 12 of the 2598 articles published between 1980 and 1993, that is less than .05 percent, focused on the families of lesbians and gay men, which, even by conservative estimates make up at least 3 percent of U.S. families.[36] The research that does exist, moreover, has deficiencies that skew results so as to exaggerate rather than understate any defects of gay and lesbian families. Until very recently, most investigators began with a deviance perspective, seeking, whether homophobically or defensively, to "test" the validity of the popular prejudice that gay parenting is harmful to children. In other words, the reigning premise has been that gay and lesbian families are dangerously, and *prima facie*, "queer" in the pejorative sense, unless proven otherwise. Taking children reared by nongay parents as the unquestioned norm, most studies asymmetrically ask whether lesbian and gay parents hinder their children's emotional, cognitive, gender, or sexual development. Because lesbian and gay "planned parenthood" is so new, and its progeny so young, nearly all of the studies to date sample the ranks of formerly married parents who had children before they divorced and came out of the closet. The studies are generally small-scale and draw disproportionately from urban, white, middle-class populations. Frequently they make misleading comparisons between divorced lesbian and nongay, single-mother households by ignoring the presence or absence of lesbian life partners or other caretakers in the former.[37]

Despite such limitations, psychologists, social psychologists, and sociologists have by now conducted dozens of studies which provide overwhelming support for the "proven otherwise" thesis. Almost without exception they conclude, albeit in defensive tones, that lesbian and gay parents do not produce inferior, nor even particularly different kinds of children than do other parents. Generally they find no significant differences in school achievement, social adjustment, mental health, gender identity, or sexual orientation between the two groups of children. As Joan Laird's overview of research on lesbian and gay parents summarizes:

> a generation of research has failed to demonstrate that gays or lesbians are any less fit to parent than their heterosexual counterparts. Furthermore, a substantial number of studies on the psychological and social development of children of lesbian and gay parents have failed to produce any evidence that children of lesbian or gay parents are harmed or compromised or even differ from, in any significant ways along a host of psychosocial developmental measures, children raised in heterosexual families.[38]

The rare small differences between gay and nongay parents reported tend to favor gay parents, portraying them as somewhat more nurturant and tolerant, and their children, in turn, more tolerant and empathic, and less aggressive than those reared by nongay parents.[39] In April 1995, British researchers published the results of their unusual sixteen-year-long study which followed twenty-five children brought up by lesbian mothers and twenty-one brought up by heterosexual mothers from youth to adulthood. They found that the young adults raised in lesbian households had better relationships with their mothers' lesbian partners than the young adults brought up by heterosexual single mothers had with their mothers' male partners.[40] Published research to date seems to vindicate one ten-year-old girl who, rather apologetically, deems herself privileged to be the daughter of two lesbian parents: "But I think you get more love with two moms. I know other kids have a mom and a dad, but I think that moms give more love than dads. This may not be true, but it's what I think." Her opinion is shared by a six-year-old girl from another lesbian family: "I don't tell other kids at school about my mothers because I think they would be jealous of me. Two mothers is better than one."[41]

In light of the inhospitable, often outrightly hostile climate which gay families typically encounter, this seems a remarkable achievement. One sign that mainstream social scientists have begun to recognize the achievement is the inclusion of Laird's chapter, "Lesbian and Gay Families," in the 1993 edition of a compendium of research, *Normal Family Processes*, whose first edition, in 1982, ignored the subject.[42] Researchers have begun to call for, and to initiate, a mature, creative, undefensive approach to studying the full range of gay and lesbian families. Coming to terms with the realities of the postmodern family condition, such studies begin with a pluralist premise concerning the legitimacy and dignity of diverse family structures. They ask whether and how gay and lesbian families differ, rather than deviate, from nongay families; they attend as much to the differences among such families as to those dividing them from nongays; and they explore the particular benefits as well as the burdens such families bestow on their members.[43]

This kind of research has begun to discover more advantages of gay and lesbian family life for participants and our society than have yet been explored. Most obvious, certainly, are mental health rewards for gay and lesbian youth fortunate enough to come of age in such families. Currently most youth who experience homosexual inclinations either conceal their desires from their immediate kin or risk serious forms of rejection.

State hostility to gay parents can have tragic results. In 1994, for example, the Nebraska Department of Social Services adopted a policy forbidding lesbian or gay foster homes, and the next day a seventeen-year-old openly gay foster child committed suicide, because he feared he would be removed from the supportive home of his gay foster parents.[44]

Of course, this speaks precisely to the heart of what homophobes most fear, that public acceptance of lesbian and gay families will spawn an "epidemic" of gay youth. As Pat Robertson so crudely explained to a Florida audience: "That gang of idiots running the ACLU, the National Education Association, the National Organization of Women, they don't want religious principles in our schools. Instead of teaching the Ten Commandments, they want to teach kids how to be homosexuals."[45] Attempting to respond to such anxieties, most defenders of gay families have stressed the irrelevance of parental sexual identity to that of their children. Sympathetic researchers repeatedly, and in my view misguidedly, maintain that lesbian and gay parents are no more likely than nongay parents to rear lesbian and gay children. Laird, for example, laments:

> One of the most prevalent myths is that children of gay parents will themselves grow up gay; another that daughters will be more masculine and sons more feminine than "normal" children. A number of researchers have concluded that the sexual orientations/preferences of children of gay or lesbian parents do not differ from those whose parents are heterosexual.[46]

Increasingly this claim appears illogical, unlikely, and unwittingly anti-gay. Ironically, it presumes the very sort of fixed definition of sexuality that the best contemporary gay and lesbian scholarship has challenged. Although it is clearly true that, until now, nearly all "homosexuals," like almost everyone else, have been reared by nongays, it is equally clear that sexual desire and identity do not represent a singular fixed "trait" that expresses itself free of cultural context. However irresolvable eternal feuds over the relative weight of nature and nurture may forever prove to be, historical and anthropological data leave no doubt that culture profoundly influences sexual meanings and practices. Homophobes are quite correct to believe that environmental conditions incite or inhibit expressions of homosexual desire, no matter its primary source. If culture had no influence on sexual identity, there would not have emerged the movement for gay and lesbian family rights that inspired me to write this [reading].

Contrary to what most current researchers claim, public acceptance of gay and lesbian families should, in fact, slightly expand the percentage of youth who would dare to explore their same-sex desires. In fact, a careful reading of the studies does suggest just this.[47] Children reared by lesbian or gay parents feel greater openness to homosexuality or bisexuality. In January 1996, the researchers who conducted the long-term British study conceded this point, after issuing the obligatory reassurance that, "the commonly held assumption that children brought up by lesbian mothers will themselves grow up to be lesbian or gay is not supported by the findings." Two of the twenty-five young adults in the study who were reared by lesbians grew up to identify as lesbians, but none of the twenty-one who were reared in the comparison group of heterosexual mothers identify as lesbian or gay. More pertinent, in my view, five daughters and one son of lesbian mothers, but none of the children of heterosexual mothers, reported having had a same-sex erotic experience of some sort, prompting the researchers to acknowledge that, "It seems that growing up in an accepting atmosphere enables individuals who are attracted to same-sex partners to pursue these relationships."[48] This prospect should disturb only those whose antipathy to homosexuality derives from deeply held religious convictions or irrational prejudice.

The rest of us could benefit from permission to explore and develop sexually free from the rigid prescriptions of what Adrienne Rich memorably termed "compulsory heterosexuality."[49] Currently, lesbian and gay parents grant their children such permission much more generously than do other parents. Not only do they tend to be less doctrinaire or phobic about sexual diversity than heterosexual parents, but, wishing to spare their children the burdens of stigma, some gay parents actually prefer that their youngsters do not become gay. Indeed, despite the ubiquity of Pat Robertson's sort of alarmist, propagandistic warnings, "advice on how to help your kids turn out gay," as cultural critic Eve Sedgwick sardonically puts it, "not to mention your students, your parishioners, your therapy clients, or your military subordinates, is less ubiquitous than you might think."[50]

Heterosexual indoctrination is far more pervasive and far the greater danger. Contemporary adolescent culture is even more mercilessly homophobic, or perhaps less hypocritically so, than most mainstream adult prejudices countenance. Verbal harassment, ridicule, hazing, and ostracism of "faggots," "bull-dykes," and "queers"—quotidien features of our popular culture—are particularly blatant among teens. "Sometimes I feel like no one really knows what I'm going through," one fifteen-year-old daughter of a lesbian laments: "Don't get me wrong. I really do love my mom and all her friends, but being gay is just not acceptable to other people. Like at school, people make jokes about dykes and fags, and it really bothers me. I mean I bite my tongue, because if I say anything, they wonder, Why is she sticking up for them?"[51] In a 1995 survey, nearly half the teen victims of reported violent physical assaults identified their sexual orientation as a precipitating factor. Tragically, family members inflicted 61 percent of these assaults on gay youth.[52]

Little wonder such disproportionate numbers of gay youth commit suicide. Studies claim that gay youth commit one-third of all teenage suicide attempts.[53] To evade harassment, most of the survivors suffer their clandestine difference in silent isolation, often at great cost to their self-esteem, social relationships, and to their very experience of adolescence itself. One gay man bought his life partner a Father's Day card, because he "realized that in a lot of ways we've been brother and father to each other since we've had to grow up as adults. Because of homophobia, gay people don't have the same opportunity as heterosexuals to be ourselves when we are teenagers. A lot of times you have to postpone the experiences until you're older, until you come out."[54]

The increased social visibility and community-building of gays and lesbians have vastly improved the quality of life for gay adults. Ironically, however, Linnea Due, author of a book about growing up gay in the nineties, was disappointed to find that this improvement has had contradictory consequences for gay teens. Due expected to find conditions much better for gay youth than when she grew up in the silent sixties. Instead, many teens thought their circumstances had become more difficult, because, as one young man put it, "now they know we're here."[55]

While most youth with homosexual desires will continue to come of age closeted in nongay families into the foreseeable future, they would surely gain some comfort from greater public acceptance of gay and lesbian families. Yet in 1992, when the New York City Board of Education tried to introduce the Rainbow multicultural curriculum guide which advocated respect for lesbian and gay families in an effort "to help increase the tolerance and acceptance of the lesbian/gay community and to decrease the staggering number of hate crimes perpetrated against them," public opposition became so vehement that it contributed to the dismissal of Schools Chancellor Joseph Fernandez.[56]

Indeed, the major documented special difficulties that children in gay families experience derive directly from legal discrimination and social prejudice. As one, otherwise well-adjusted, sixteen-year-old son of a lesbian puts it: "If I came out and said my mom was gay, I'd be treated like an alien."[57] Children of gay parents are vicarious victims of homophobia and institutionalized heterosexism. They suffer all of the considerable economic, legal, and social disadvantages imposed on their parents, sometimes even more harshly. They risk losing a beloved parent or coparent at the whim of a judge. They can be denied access to friends by the parents of playmates. Living in families that are culturally invisible or despised, the children suffer ostracism by proxy, forced continually to negotiate conflicts between loyalty to home, mainstream authorities, and peers.

However, as the Supreme Court belatedly concluded in 1984, when it repudiated discrimination against interracial families in *Palmore* v. *Sidoti*, and as should be plain good sense, the fact that children of stigmatized parents bear an unfair burden provides no critique of their families. The sad *social* fact of prejudice and discrimination indicts the "family values" of the bigoted society, not the stigmatized family. In the words of the Court: "private biases may be outside the reach of the law, but the law cannot, directly or indirectly, give them effect."[58] Although the strict scrutiny standards that now govern race discrimination do not apply to sexual discrimination, several courts in recent years have relied on the logic of *Palmore* in gay custody cases. These decisions have approved lesbian and gay custody awards while explicitly acknowledging that community disapproval of their parents' sexual identity would require "greater than ordinary fortitude" from the children, but that in return they might more readily learn that, "people of integrity do not shrink from bigots." The potential benefits that children might derive from being raised by lesbian or gay parents which a New Jersey court enumerated could serve as child-rearing ideals for a democracy:

> emerge better equipped to search out their own standards of right and wrong, better able to perceive that the majority is not always correct in its moral judgments, and better able to understand the importance of conforming their beliefs to the requirements of reason and tested knowledge, not the constraints of currently popular sentiment or prejudice.[59]

The testimony of one fifteen-year-old daughter of a lesbian mother and gay father indicates just this sort of outcome:

> I think I am more open-minded than if I had straight parents. Sometimes kids at school make a big deal out of being gay. They say it's stupid and stuff like that. But they don't really know, because they are not around it. I don't say anything to them, but I know they are wrong. I get kind of mad, because they don't know what they are talking about.[60]

However, literature suggests that parents and children alike who live in fully closeted lesbian and gay families tend to suffer more than members of "out" gay families who contend with stigma directly.[61] Of course, gay parents who shroud their families in closets do so for compelling cause. Some judges still make the closet an explicit condition for awarding custody or visitation rights to gay or lesbian parents, at times imposing direct restrictions on their participation in gay social or political activity.[62] Or, fearing judicial homophobia, some parents live in mortal terror of losing their children, like one divorced lesbian in Kansas City whose former, violent husband has threatened an ugly custody battle if anyone finds out about her lesbianism.[63]

Heroically, more and more brave new "queer" families are refusing the clandestine life. If the survey article, "The Families of Lesbians and Gay Men: A New Frontier in Family Research,"[64] is correctly titled, then research on fully planned lesbian and gay families is its vanguard outpost. Researchers estimate that by 1990, between five thousand and ten thousand lesbians in the United States had given birth to chosen children, and the trend has been increasing ever since.[65] Although this represents a small fraction of the biological and adopted children who live with lesbian parents, planned lesbian births, as Kath Weston suggests, soon, "began to overshadow these other kinds of dependents, assuming a symbolic significance for lesbians and gay men disproportionate to their numbers."[66] Lesbian "turkey-baster" babies are equally symbolic to those who abhor the practice. "National Fatherhood Initiative" organizer David Blankenhorn, for example, calls for restricting sperm bank services to infertile married couples in order to inhibit the production of such "radically fatherless children," and similar concerns have been expressed in such popular publications as *U.S. News and World Report* and *Atlantic Monthly*.[67] (Interestingly, restrictions that limit access to donor sperm exclusively to married women remain widespread in Europe, even in most of the liberal Nordic nations.) Because discrimination against prospective gay and lesbian adoptive parents leads most to conceal their sexual identity, it is impossible to estimate how many have succeeded in adopting or fostering children, but this, too, has become a visible form of gay planned parenthood.[68]

Research on planned gay parenting is too young to be more than suggestive, but initial findings give more cause for gay pride than alarm. Parental relationships tend to be more cooperative and egalitarian than among heterosexual parents, child rearing more nurturant, children more affectionate.[69] On the other hand, lesbian mothers do encounter some particular burdens. Like straight women who bear children through insemination, they confront the vexing question of how to negotiate their children's knowledge of and relationship to sperm donors. Some progeny of unknown donors, like many adopted children, quest for contact with their genetic fathers. One ten-year-old girl, conceived by private donor insemination, explains why she was relieved to find her biological father: "I wanted to find my dad because it was hard knowing I had a dad but not knowing who he was. It was like there was a missing piece."[70]

Lesbian couples planning a pregnancy contend with some unique decisions and challenges concerning the relationship between biological and social maternity. They must decide which woman will try to become pregnant and how to negotiate feelings of jealousy, invisibility, and displacement that may be more likely to arise between the two than between a biological mother and father. Struggling to equalize maternal emotional stakes and claims, some couples decide to alternate the childbearing role, others attempt simultaneous pregnancies, and some, as we have seen, employ reproductive technology to divide the genetic and gestational components of procreation. Some nongestational lesbian mothers stimulate lactation, so that they can jointly breastfeed the babies their partners bear, some assume disproportionate responsibility for child care to compensate for their biological "disadvantage," and others give their surnames to their partners' offspring.

Planned lesbian and gay families, however, most fully realize the early planned Parenthood goal, "every child a wanted child," as one twelve-year-old son of a lesbian recognized: "I think that if you are a child of a gay or lesbian, you have a better chance of having a great parent. If you are a lesbian, you have to go through a lot of trouble to get a child, so that child is really wanted."[71] Disproportionately "queer" families choose to reside in and construct communities that support family and social diversity. Partly because fertility and adoption services are expensive and often difficult to attain, intentional gay parents are disproportionately white, better educated, and more mature than other parents. Preliminary research indicates that these advantages more than offset whatever problems their special burdens cause their children.[72] Clearly, it is in the interest of all our children to afford their families social dignity and respect.

If we exploit the research with this aim in mind, deducing a rational wish list for public policy is quite a simple matter. A straightforward, liberal, equal rights agenda for lesbians and gays would seem the obvious and humane course. In the best interests of all children, we would provide lesbian and gay parents equal access to marriage, child custody, adoption, foster placements, fertility services, inheritance, employment, and all social benefits. We would adopt "rainbow" curricula within our schools and our public media that promote the kind of tolerance and respect for family and sexual diversity that Laura Sebastian, an eighteen-year-old reared by her divorced mother and her mother's lesbian lover, advocates:

> A happy child has happy parents, and gay people can be as happy as straight ones. It doesn't matter what kids have—fathers, mothers, or both—they just need love and support. It doesn't matter if you are raised by a pack of dogs, just as long as they love you! It's about time lesbians and gays can have children. It's everybody's right as a human being.[73]

OUR QUEER POSTMODERN FAMILIES

Far from esoteric, the experiences of diverse genres of gay and lesbian "families we choose" bear on many of the most feverishly contested issues in contemporary family politics. They can speak to our mounting cultural paranoia over whether fathers are expendable, to nature-nurture controversies over sexual and gender identities and the gender division of labor, to the meaning and purpose of voluntary marriage, and, most broadly, to those ubiquitous "family values" contests over the relative importance for children of family structure or process, of biological or "psychological" parents.

From the African-American "Million Man March" in October 1995, the stadium rallies of Christian male "Promise Keepers" that popularized the subject of responsible fatherhood in evangelical churches across the nation, and the National Fatherhood Initiative, to congressional hearings on the Father's Responsibility Act in 2001, the nation seems to be gripped by cultural obsession over the decline of dependable dads. Here research on lesbian families, particularly on planned lesbian couple families, could prove of no small import. Thus far, as we have seen, such research offers no brief for Blankenhorn's angst over "radically fatherless children." Also challenging to those who claim that the mere presence of a father in a family confers significant benefits on his children are surprising data reported in a study of youth and violence commissioned by Kaiser Permanente and Children Now. The study of 1000 eleven to seventeen-year-olds and of 150 seven to ten-year-olds found that, contrary to popular belief, 68 percent of the "young people exposed to higher levels of health and safety threats" were from conventional two-parent families. Moreover, poignantly, fathers were among the last people these troubled teens would turn to for help, even when they lived in such families. Only 10 percent of the young people in these two-parent families said they would seek their fathers' advice first, compared with 44 percent who claimed they would turn first to their mothers, and 26 percent who would first seek help from friends. Many more youth were willing to discuss concerns over their health, safety, and sexuality with nurses or doctors.[74] Thus, empirical social science to date, like the historical record, gives us impeccable cause to regard fathers and mothers alike as "expendable." The quality, not the gender, of parenting is what truly matters.

Similarly, research on the relationships of gay male and lesbian couples depicts diverse models for intimacy from which others could profit. "Freed" from normative conventions and institutions that govern heterosexual gender and family relationships, self-consciously "queer" couples and families, by necessity, have had to reflect much more seriously on the meaning and purpose of their intimate commitments. Studies that compare lesbian, gay male, and heterosexual couples find intriguing contrasts in their characteristic patterns of intimacy. Gender seems to shape domestic values and practices more powerfully than sexual identity, so that same-sex couples tend to be more compatible than heterosexual couples. For example, both lesbian and straight women are more likely than either gay or straight men to value their relationships over their work. Yet both lesbian and gay male couples agree that both parties should be employed, while married men are less likely to agree with wives who wish to work. Predictably, same-sex couples share more interests and time together than married couples. Also unsurprising, lesbian couples have the most egalitarian relationships, and married heterosexual couples the least. Lesbian and gay male couples both share household chores more equally and with less conflict than married couples, but they share them differently. Lesbian couples tend to share most tasks equally, while gay males more frequently assign tasks "to each according to his abilities," schedules, and preferences.[75] Each of these modal patterns for intimacy has its particular strengths and vulnerabilities. Gender conventions and gender fluidity alike have advantages and limitations, as Blumstein and Schwartz and other researchers have discussed. Accepting queer families does not mean converting to any characteristic patterns of intimacy, but coming to terms with the collapse of a monolithic cultural regime governing our intimate bonds. It would mean embracing a genuinely pluralist understanding that there are diverse, valid ways to form and sustain these.

Perhaps what is truly distinctive about lesbian and gay families is how unambiguously the substance of their relationships takes precedence over their form, emotional and social commitments over genetic claims. Compelled to exercise "good, old-fashioned American" ingenuity to fulfill familial desires, gays and lesbians improvisationally assemble a patchwork of "blood" and intentional relations—gay, straight, and other—into creative, extended kin bonds."[76] Gay communities more adeptly integrate singles into their social worlds than does mainstream heterosexual society, a social "skill" quite valuable in a world in which divorce, widowhood, and singlehood are increasingly normative.

Because "queer" families must continually, self-consciously migrate in and out of the closet, they hone bicultural skills particularly suitable for life in a multicultural society.[77] Self-identified queer families serve on the front lines of the postmodern family condition, commanded directly by its regime of improvisation, ambiguity, diversity, contradiction, self-reflection, and flux.

Even the distinctive, indeed the definitional, burden that pervasive homophobia imposes on lesbian and gay families does not fully distinguish them from other contemporary families. Unfortunately, prejudice, intolerance, and disrespect for "different" or "other" families is all too commonplace in the contemporary world. Ethnocentric familism afflicts the families of many immigrants, interracial couples, single mothers (be they unwed or divorced, impoverished or affluent), remarried couples, childless "yuppie" couples, bachelors and "spinsters," househusbands, working mothers, and the homeless. It even places that vanishing, once-hallowed breed of full-time homemakers on the ("I'm-just-a-housewife") defensive.

Gay and lesbian families simply brave intensified versions of ubiquitous contemporary challenges. Both their plight and their pluck expose the dangerous disjuncture between our family rhetoric and policy, on the one hand, and our family and social realties, on the other. In stubborn denial of the complex, pluralist array of contemporary families and kinship, most of our legal and social policies atavistically presume to serve a singular, "normal" family structure—the conventional, heterosexual, married-couple, nuclear family. In the name of children, politicians justify decisions that endanger children, and in the name of *The Family*, they cause grave harm to our families. It is time to get used to the queer, post-modern family condition we all now inhabit.

Notes

1. An estimate that at least six million children would have a gay parent by 1985 appeared in J. Schulenberg, *Gay Parenting* (New York: Doubleday, 1985) and has been accepted or revised upwards by most scholars since then. See, for example, F. W. Bozett (ed.), *Gay and Lesbian Parents* (New York: Praeger, 1987), 39; C. Patterson, "Children of Lesbian and Gay Parents," *Child Development* 63:1025–1042; K. R. Allen and D. H. Demo, "The Families of Lesbians and Gay Men: A New Frontier in Family Research," *Journal of Marriage and the Family* 57 (February 1995):111–127. Nevertheless, these estimates are based upon problematic assumptions and calculations, so the actual number could be considerably lower—especially if we exclude children whose parents have not acknowledged to anyone else in the family that they are gay or lesbian. Still, even a conservative estimate would exceed one million.

2. P. Burke, *Family Values: A Lesbian Mother's Fight for Her Son.* (New York: Random House, 1993).

3. For a sensitive discussion of the definitional difficulties involved in research on gay and lesbian families, see Allen and Demo, "Families of Lesbians and Gay Men," 112–113.

4. Many gay activist groups and scholars, however, have begun to reclaim the term "queer" as a badge of pride, in much the same way that the black power movement of the 1960s reclaimed the formerly derogatory term for blacks.

5. In J. Stacey, *Brave New Families* (New York: Basic Books, 1990). I provide a book-length, ethnographic treatment of postmodern family life in the Silicon Valley.

6. For historical and cross-cultural treatments of same-sex marriages, relationships, and practices in the West and elsewhere, see J. Boswell, *Same-Sex Unions in Premodern Europe* (New York: Villard Books, 1994) and W. N. Eskridge Jr., "A History of Same-Sex Marriage," *Virginia Law Review* 79:1419–1451, 1993.

7. R. R. Rivera, "Legal Issues in Gay and Lesbian Parenting," in Bozett, ed., *Gay and Lesbian Parents.*

8. Among the influential feminist works of this genre were: N. Chodorow, *The Reproduction of Mothering* (Berkeley and Los Angeles: University of California Press, 1978); C. Gilligan, *In a Different Voice*

(Cambridge: Harvard University Press, 1982); and S. Ruddick, *Maternal Thinking* (Boston: Beacon Press, 1989).

9. See R. Rosenbloom (ed.), *Unspoken Rules: Sexual Orientation and Women's Human Rights* (San Francisco: International Gay and Lesbian Human Right Commission, 1995), 226 (fn22); and L. Benkov, *Reinventing the Family* (New York: Crown, 1994), 117.

10. D. Wikler and N. J. Wikler, "Turkey-baster Babies: The Demedicalization of Artificial Insemination," *Milbank Quarterly* 69(1):10, 1991.

11. Ibid.

12. The first known custody battle involving a lesbian couple and a sperm donor was *Loftin* v. *Flournoy* in California. For a superb discussion of the relevant case law, see N. Polikoff, "This Child Does Have Two Mothers," *Georgetown Law Journal* 78(1990):459–575.

13. Polikoff, "Two Mothers" provides detailed discussion of the most significant legal cases of custody contests after death of the biological lesbian comother. In both the most prominent cases, higher courts eventually reversed decisions that had denied custody to the surviving lesbian parent, but only after serious emotional harm had been inflicted on the children and parents alike. See pp. 527–532.

14. V. L. Henry, "A Tale of Three Women," *American Journal of Law & Medicine* XIX, 3:297, 1993.

15. Ibid., 300; Polikoff, "This Child Does Have Two Mothers," 492.

16. J. Griscom, "The Case of Sharon Kowalski and Karen Thompson," in P. S. Rothenberg (ed.), *Race, Class, and Gender in the United States* (New York: St. Martin's Press, 1992).

17. See W. B. Rubenstein (ed.), *Lesbians, Gay Men, and the Law* (New York: New Press, 1993), 452.

18. National Center for Lesbian Rights, "Our Day in Court—Against Each Other," in Rubenstein, 561–562.

19. M. Gil de Lamadrid, "Expanding the Definition of Family: A Universal Issue," *Berkeley Women's Law Journal* v. 8:178, 1993.

20. The Sharon Bottoms case in Virginia is the most prominent of current setbacks. In 1994, Sharon Bottoms lost custody of her two-year-old son because the trial court judge deemed her lesbianism to be immoral and illegal. In April 1995, the Virginia state supreme court upheld the ruling, which at this writing is being appealed to the U.S. Supreme Court.

21. Quoted in S. Sherman (ed.), *Lesbian and Gay Marriage* (Philadelphia: Temple University Press, 1992), 191.

22. Ibid., 173.

23. Bozett, epilogue to *Gay and Lesbian Parents*, 232.

24. Cited in Sherman, *Lesbian and Gay Marriage*, 9 (fn. 6). A more recent poll conducted by *The Advocate* suggests that the trend of support for gay marriage is increasing. See E. Wolfson, "Crossing the Threshhold," *Review of Law & Social Change* XXI, 3:583, 1994–95.

25. The decision stated that the sexual orientation of the parties was irrelevant because same-sex spouses could be of any sexual orientation. It was the gender discrimination involved in limiting one's choice of spouse that violated the state constitution. See Wolfson, "Crossing the Threshold," 573.

26. See, for example, Nancy Polikoff, "We Will Get What We Ask For: Why Legalizing Gay and Lesbian Marriage Will Not 'Dismantle the Legal Structure of Gender in Every Marriage.'" *Virginia Law Review* 79:1549–1550, 1993.

27. Law professor Thomas Coleman, executive director of the "Family Diversity Project" in California, expresses these views in Sherman, 128–129. Likewise, Bob Hattoy, a gay White House aide in the Clinton administration, believed that "to support same-sex marriage at this particular cultural moment in America is a loser." Quoted in Francis X. Clines, "In Gay-Marriage Storm, Weary Clinton Aide Is Buffeted on All Sides." *New York Times*, May 29, 1996, A16.

28. A. Sullivan, "Here Comes the Groom: A Conservative Case for Gay Marriage," *New Republic* 201 (9):20–22, August 28, 1989; J. Rauch, "A Pro-Gay, Pro-Family Policy," *Wall Street Journal*, November 29, 1995, A22.

29. Kirk Johnson, quoted in Wolfson, 567.

30. N. D. Hunter, "Marriage, Law and Gender: A Feminist Inquiry," *Law & Sexuality* 1(1):12, 1991.

31. Wolfson, "Crossing the Threshhold."

32. "Some Progress Found in Poll on Gay Rights," *San Francisco Chronicle*, June 20, 1994.

33. Support for Clinton's Stand on Gay Marriage," *San Francisco Chronicle*, May 25, 1996, A6; Available online at www.gallup.com/poll/releases/ pr010604.asp.

34. G. Remafedi (ed.), *Death by Denial* (Boston: Alyson Publications, 1994).

35. Quoted in Miller, *Out in the World*, 350.

36. The three journals were *Journal of Marriage and the Family, Family Relations*, and *Journal of Family Issues*; Allen and Demo, "Families of Lesbians and Gay Men," 119.

37. For overviews of the research, see Patterson, "Children of Lesbian and Gay Parents"; J. Laird, "Lesbian and Gay Families," in Walsh (ed.), *Normal Family Processes* 2nd ed. (New York: Guilford Press, 1993), 282–328; Allen and Demo, "Families of Lesbians and Gay Men."

38. Laird, "Lesbian and Gay Families," 316–317.

39. Ibid., 317; D. H. Demo and K. Allen, "Diversity within Lesbian and Gay Families," *Journal of Social and Personal Relationships* 13 (3):26, 1996; F. Tasker and S. Golombok, "Adults Raised as Children in Lesbian Families," *American Journal of Orthopsychiatry*, 65:203–215, 1998.

40. Tasker and Golombok, "Adults Raised as Children in Lesbian Families."

41. Quoted in L. Rafkin, *Different Mothers* (Pittsburgh: Cleis Press, 1990), 34.

42. Laird, "Lesbian and Gay Families."

43. See, for example, Patterson; Demo and Allen; Benkov; K. Weston, *Families We Choose* (New York: Columbia University Press, 1991); and L. Peplau, "Research on Homosexual Couples: An Overview," in J. P. De Cecco (ed.), *Gay Relationships* (New York: Hayworth Press, 1988).

44. S. Minter, "U.S.A.," in Rosenbloom (ed.), *Unspoken Rules*, 219.

45. Quoted in Maralee Schwartz & Kenneth J. Cooper, "Equal Rights Initiative in Iowa Attacked," *Washington Post*, Aug 23, 1992, A15.

46. Laird, 315–316.

47. See, for example, Judith Stacey and Timothy Biblarz, "Does the Sexual Orientation of Parents Matter?" *American Sociological Review* 66(2):159–183, April 2001.

48. As Tasker and Golombok concede, "Young adults from lesbian homes tended to be more willing to have a sexual relationship with someone of the same gender if they felt physically attracted to them. They were also more likely to have considered the possibility of developing same-gender sexual attractions or relationships. Having a lesbian mother, therefore, appeared to widen the adolescent's view of what constituted acceptable sexual behavior to include same-gender sexual relationships," 212.

49. A. Rich, "Compulsory Heterosexuality and the Lesbian Continuum," *Signs* 5(4):Summer 1980:631–660.

50. Eve Sedgwick, "How to Bring Your Kids Up Gay," in Warner (ed.), *Fear of a Queer Planet* (Minneapolis: University of Minnesota Press, 1993), 76.

51. Quoted in Rafkin, *Different Mothers*, 64–65.

52. Minter, "U.S.A.," 222.

53. Remafedi, *Death by Denial*.

54. Quoted in Sherman, 70.

55. L. Due, *Joining the Tribe* (New York: Doubleday, 1996).

56. See J. M. Irvine, "A Place in the Rainbow: Theorizing Lesbian and Gay Culture," *Sociological Theory* 12(2):232, July 1994.

57. Quoted in Rafkin, *Different Mothers*, 24.

58. Quoted in Polikoff, "This Child Does Have Two Mothers," 569–570.

59. Quoted in Polikoff, 570.

60. Quoted in Rafkin, 81.

61. Benkov, *Reinventing the Family*, chap. 8.

62. L. Kurdek and J. P. Schmitt, "Relationship Quality of Gay Men in Closed or Open Relationships," *Journal of Homosexuality* 12(2):85–99, 1985; and F. R. Lynch, "Nonghetto Gays: An Ethnography of Suburban Homosexuals," In Herdt (ed.), *Gay Culture in America* (Boston: Beacon Press, 1992), 165–201.

63. Rafkin, 39.

64. Allen and Demo.

65. Polikoff, "This Child Does Have Two Mothers," 461 (fn.2).

66. Weston, "Parenting in the Age of AIDs," 159.

67. D. Blankenhorn, *Fatherless America* (New York: Basic Books, 1995), 233; J. Leo, "Promoting no-dad families," *U.S. News and World Report*, May 15, 1995:26; and S. Seligson, "Seeds of Doubt," *Atlantic Monthly*, March 1995:28.

68. Bozett, p. 4 discusses gay male parenthood strategies. Also, available on-line at www.growing generations.com.

69. Stacey and Biblarz, "Does the Sexual Orientation of Parents Matter?"; Maureen Sullivan, "Rozzie and Harriet?: Gender and Family Patterns of Lesbian Coparents," *Gender & Society* 10(6):747–767, December 1996.

70. Quoted in Rafkin, 33.
71. Ibid., 53.
72. Stacey and Biblarz "Does the Sexual Orientation of Parents Matter?" 176.
73. Rafkin, 174.
74. T. Moore, "Fear of Violence Rising among 1990s Youth," *San Francisco Chronicle*, December 7, 1995, A1, A15.
75. L. Kurdek, "The Allocation of Household Labor in Gay, Lesbian, and Heterosexual Married Couples," *Journal of Social Issues* 49 (3):127–139, 1993; P. Blumstein and P. Schwartz, *American Couples* (New York: William Morrow, 1983); Peplau, 193; Stacey and Biblarz, "Does the Sexual Orientation of Parents Matter," 173–174; Sullivan, "Rozzie and Harriet?"; Gillian Dunne, "Opting into Motherhood: Lesbians Blurring the Boundaries and Transforming the Meaning of Parenthood and Kinship," *Gender & Society* 14(1):11–35, 2000.
76. See Weston, *Families We Choose,* for an ethnographic treatment of these chosen kin ties.
77. As Allen and Demo suggest, "An aspect of biculturalism is resilience and creative adaptation in the context of minority group oppression and stigma," and this "offers a potential link to other oppressed groups in American society." "Families of Lesbians and Gay Men," 122.

▪READING 35

"The Normal American Family" as an Interpretive Structure of Family Life among Grown Children of Korean and Vietnamese Immigrants

Karen Pyke

This article examines the ways that children of Korean and Vietnamese immigrants describe growing up in their families and their plans for filial care. Based on an analysis of 73 in-depth interviews, this study finds that respondents repeatedly invoked a monolithic image of the "Normal American Family" as an interpretive framework in giving meaning to their own family life. The Family served as a contrast structure in respondents' accounts of parents— and Asian parents in general—as overly strict, emotionally distant, and deficient. However, when discussing plans for filial care, respondents relied on favorable images of the close family ties associated with Asian immigrants, such as those depicted in "model minority" stereotypes. In so doing they generated positive descriptions of their families, particularly in contrast to mainstream American families. The findings suggest that narrow and ethnocentric images of the Family promulgated throughout mainstream culture compose an ideological template that can shape the desires, disappointments, and subjective realities of children of immigrant minorities.

The use of monolithic images of the "Normal American Family" as a stick against which all families are measured is pervasive in the family wars currently raging in political and scholarly discourses (Holstein & Gubrium, 1995). The hotly contested nature of these images—consisting almost exclusively of White middle-class heterosexuals—attests to their importance as resources in national debates. Many scholars express concern that hegemonic images of the Normal American Family are ethnocentric and that they denigrate the styles and beliefs of racial–ethnic, immigrant, gay–lesbian, and single-parent families while encouraging negative self-images among those who do not come from the ideal family type (Bernades, 1993; Dilworth-Anderson, Burton, & Turner, 1993; Smith, 1993; Stacey, 1998; Zinn, 1994). Yet we still know little about how the Family ideology shapes the consciousness and expectations of those growing up in the margins of the mainstream. This study examines the accounts that grown children of Korean and Vietnamese immigrants provide of their family life and filial obligations. The findings suggest that public images of the Normal American Family constitute an ideological template that shapes respondents' familial perspectives and desires as new racial–ethnic Americans.

FAMILY IDEOLOGY AS AN INTERPRETIVE STRUCTURE

Images of the Normal American Family (also referred to as the Family) are pervasive in the dominant culture—part of a " 'large-scale' public rhetoric" (Holstein & Miller, 1993, p. 152). They are found in the discourse of politicians, social commentators, and moral leaders; in the talk of everyday interactions; and in movies, television shows, and books. Smith (1993, p. 63) describes these ubiquitous images as an "ideological code" that subtly "inserts an implicit evaluation into accounts of ways of living together." Such images serve as instruments of control, prescribing how families ought to look and behave (Bernades, 1985). Most scholarly concern centers on how this ideology glorifies and presents as normative that family headed by a breadwinning husband with a wife who, even if she works for pay, is devoted primarily to the care of the home and children. The concern is that families of diverse structural forms, most notably divorced and female-headed families, are comparatively viewed as deficient and dysfunctional (Fineman, 1995; Kurz, 1995; Stacey, 1998). Scholars concerned about the impact of such images point to those who blame family structures that deviate from this norm for many of society's problems and who suggest policies that ignore or punish families that don't fit the construct (e.g., Blankenhorn, 1995; Popenoe, 1993, 1996).

In addition to prescribing the structure of families, the Family ideal contains notions about the appropriate values, norms, and beliefs that guide the way family members relate to one another. The cultural values of "other" families, such as racial–ethnic families, are largely excluded. For example, prevailing family images emphasize sensitivity, open honest communication, flexibility, and forgiveness (Greeley, 1987). Such traits are less important in many cultures that stress duty, responsibility, obedience, and a commitment to the family collective that supercedes self-interests (Chung, 1992; Freeman, 1989). In further contrast to the traditional family systems of many cultures, contemporary American family ideals stress democratic rather than authoritarian relations, individual autonomy, psychological well-being, and emotional expressiveness (Bellah, Madsen, Sullivan, Swidler, & Tipton, 1985; Bernades, 1985; Cancian, 1987; Coontz, 1992; Skolnick, 1991). Family affection, intimacy, and sentimentality have grown in importance in the United States over time (Coontz, 1992), as evident in new ideals of fatherhood that stress emotional involvement (Coltrane, 1996).

These mainstream family values are evident in the therapeutic ethic, guiding the ways that those who seek professional advice are counseled and creating particular therapeutic barriers in treating immigrant Asian Americans (Bellah et al., 1985; Cancian, 1987; Tsui & Schultz, 1985). Family values are also widely disseminated and glorified in the popular culture, as in television shows like *Ozzie and Harriet, Leave It To Beaver, The Brady Bunch, Family Ties,* and *The Cosby Show,* many of which are rerun on local stations and cable networks (Coontz, 1992). Parents in these middle-class, mostly White, television families are emotionally nurturing and supportive, understanding, and forgiving (Shaner, 1982; Skill, 1994). Indeed, such shows tend to focus on the successful resolution of relatively minor family problems, which the characters accomplish through open communication and the expression of loving concern. Children in the United States grow up vicariously experiencing life in these television families, including children of immigrants who rely on television to learn about American culture. With 98% of all U.S. households having at least one television set, Rumbaut (1997, p. 949) views TV as an immense "assimilative" force for today's children of immigrants. Yet, he continues, it remains to be studied how their world views are shaped by such "cultural propaganda." The images seen on television serve as powerful symbols of the "normal" family or the "good" parent—and they often eclipse our appreciation of diverse family types (Brown & Bryant, 1990; Greenberg, Hines, Buerkel-Rothfuss, & Atkin, 1980). As the authors of one study on media images note, "The seductively realistic portrayals of family life in the media may be the basis for our most common and pervasive conceptions and beliefs about what is natural and what is right" (Gerbner, Gross, Morgan, & Signorielli, 1980, p. 3). Family scholars have rarely displayed analytic concern about the emphasis on emotional expressiveness and affective sentimentality that pervades much of the Family ideology, probably because the majority—who as middle-class, well-educated Whites live in the heartland of such values—do not regard them as problematic. As a result, this Western value orientation can seep imperceptibly into the interpretive framework of family research (Bernades, 1993; Dilworth-Anderson et al., 1993; Fineman, 1995; Smith, 1993; Thorne & Yalom, 1992).

The theoretical literature on the social construction of experience is an orienting framework for this study (Berger & Luckmann, 1966; Holstein & Gubrium, 1995). According to this view, cultural ideologies and symbols are integral components of the way individuals subjectively experience their lives and construct reality. The images we carry in our heads of how family life is supposed to be frame our interpretation of our own domestic relations. This is evident in the different ways that Korean and Korean American children perceived their parents' childrearing behavior in a series of studies. In Korea, children were found to associate parental strictness with warmth and concern and its absence as a sign of neglect (Rohner & Pettengill, 1985). These children were drawing on Korean family ideology, which emphasizes strong parental control and parental responsibility for children's failings. In this interpretive framework, parental strictness is a positive characteristic of family life and signifies love and concern. Children of Korean immigrants living in the United States, on the other hand, viewed their parents' strictness in negative terms and associated it with a lack of warmth—as did American children in general (Pettengill & Rohner, 1985). Korean American children drew on American family ideology, with its emphasis on independence and autonomy, and this cast a negative shadow on their parents' strict practices.

Although pervasive images of the Normal American Family subtly construct Asian family patterns of interaction as "deviant," countervailing images of Asians as a "model minority" are also widely disseminated. News stories and scholarly accounts that profile the tremendous academic success among some immigrant Asian children or describe the upward economic mobility observed among segments of the Asian immigrant population credit the cultural traditions of collectivist family values, hard work, and a strong emphasis on education. Such images exaggerate the success of Asian immigrants and mask intraethnic diversity (Caplan, Choy, & Whitmore, 1991; Kibria, 1993; Min, 1995; Zhou & Bankston, 1998). Meanwhile, conservative leaders use model minority images as evidence of the need to return to more traditional family structures and values, and they blame the cultural deficiency of other racial minority groups for their lack of similar success, particularly African Americans and Latinos (Kibria, 1993; Min, 1995; Zhou & Bankston, 1998). The model minority construct thus diverts attention from racism and poverty while reaffirming the Family ideology. In the analysis of the accounts that children of immigrants provided of their family life, references to such cultural images and values emerged repeatedly as a mechanism by which respondents gave meaning to their own family lives.

KOREAN AND VIETNAMESE IMMIGRANT FAMILIES

This study focuses on children of Vietnamese and Korean immigrants because both groups constitute relatively new ethnic groups in the United States. Few Vietnamese and Koreans immigrated to the United States before 1965. However, from 1981 to 1990, Korea and Vietnam were two of the top five countries from which immigrants arrived (*Statistical Yearbook*, 1995, table 2, pp. 29–30). Thus adaptation to the United States is a relatively new process for large groups of Koreans and Vietnamese, one that is unassisted by earlier generations of coethnic immigrants. The children of these immigrants, located at the crossroads of two cultural worlds, offer a good opportunity to examine the familial perspectives and desires of new racial–ethnic Americans.

Most in-depth study of children of immigrants examines only one ethnic group, which makes it difficult to know which aspects of adaptation are shared with other ethnic groups and which are distinct. Studying only one Asian ethnic group also contributes to a tendency to over-generalize the findings to all Asian ethnic groups. Thus this study was designed to compare two Asian ethnicities so that ethnic differences and similarities could be noted. The author selected Koreans and Vietnamese because, in addition to being new American ethnic groups, their economic status and pathways to immigration differ. Whereas Koreans have immigrated voluntarily, in search of better economic opportunities and educations for their children, most Vietnamese arrived as political refugees or to rejoin family members, some doing so after spending time in Vietnam's prisons or "reeducation camps" (Gold, 1993; Hurh, 1998; Kibria, 1993; Min, 1998). Vietnamese immigrants have been, overall, less educated and from more rural and poorer backgrounds than Korean immigrants. Only 12% of first-generation Vietnamese heads of household have a college degree, compared with 45% for Koreans (Oropesa & Landale, 1995). Family socioeconomic status is important to the study of adaptation because it affects the kinds of neighborhoods where immigrant children grow up and attend school (Zhou, 1997). However, equally important are the cultural practices that organize family relationships, including parental values and childrearing practices, and the expectations that parents have of their children. It is here that ethnic differences among Koreans and Vietnamese appear more subtle.

Due to the relatively short history of massive Asian immigration, Asian American family research has been fragmented and limited. As Uba (1994) points out, most of the research has been descriptive rather than explanatory, has focused on Chinese Americans and Japanese Americans, and has given little attention to between-group differences. Thus the empirical picture of Korean and Vietnamese family systems is incomplete. What we do know is that the philosophical values of Chinese Confucianism have influenced the traditional family systems of Korea and Vietnam. These values emphasize solidarity, hierarchal relations, and filial piety (Kibria, 1993; Hurh, 1998; Min, 1998; Sue & Morishima, 1982). Confucianism provides a firm set of rules about how family members are supposed to behave toward one another (Cha, 1994; Chung, 1992; Kim & Choi, 1994; Min, 1998; Zhou & Bankston, 1998). Priority is placed on family interests over individual desires and needs in order to maintain stability and harmony. Status distinctions guide the way in which members are to interact with one another. Younger members are expected to display respect, deference, and obedience to elders (including to older siblings, especially brothers), and wives are expected to show the same to their husbands and parents-in-law. Children—including adult offspring—are forbidden from expressing dissenting opinions or confronting parents, which is viewed as disrespectful (Chung, 1992; Kibria, 1993; Min, 1998; Pettengill & Rohner, 1985). Emotional expressiveness, including displays of affection, is discouraged, while self-control is emphasized (Hurh, 1998; Uba, 1994). Family ties and roles are central from birth until death, with a strong emphasis on family devotion. In general, parents are expected to rely on their children's support in later life. Confucianism assigns the care and financial support of aging parents to the eldest son and his wife, who are expected to live under the same roof as the parents. Korean and Vietnamese cultures also derive from Confucianism a respect for the well educated, and education is considered the primary means for social mobility. This undergirds the great importance that many Asian parents place on their children's education (Min, 1998; Zhou & Bankston, 1998). The economic hardships of many immigrant parents strengthen their emphasis on the education of their children, whom they expect to forge success in the United States (Kibria, 1993; Min, 1998).

There are, of course, ethnic differences between Korean and Vietnamese families, as well as differences in the degree to which they conform to traditional family practices. Although the comparative research is scant, Confucianism appears to have a stronger influence on the traditional family system in Korea than in Vietnam. For example, in Vietnamese families there is a greater tendency for siblings to pool resources in providing filial care rather than relying on the elder son alone, which might be related to their poorer economic circumstances. Additionally, Vietnamese women are permitted stronger kinship ties to their family of origin upon marriage than are Korean women, who are expected to live with their in-laws if they marry an elder son (Hurh, 1998; Kibria, 1993).

Although more research is needed that closely examines Asian ethnic differences in family practices, the existing literature reveals patterns of similarities among the family systems of Koreans and Vietnamese that differentiate them from American family patterns. The role prescriptions, family obligations, hierarchal relations, lack of emotional expressiveness, and collectivist values associated with the traditional family systems of Korea and Vietnam contrast sharply with the emphasis on individualism, self-sufficiency, egalitarianism, expressiveness, and self-development in mainstream U.S. culture (Bellah et al., 1985; Cancian, 1987; Chung, 1992; Hurh, 1998; Kim & Choi, 1994; Min, 1998; Pyke & Bengtson, 1996; Tran, 1988; Uba, 1994). Immigrant children tend to quickly adopt American values and standards, creating generational schisms and challenges to parental control and authority. That parent–child conflict and cultural gaps exist in many Asian immigrant families is well documented (Gold, 1993; Freeman, 1989; Kibria, 1993; Min, 1998; Rumbaut, 1994; Zhou & Bankston, 1998; Wolfe, 1997). However, no study to date has closely examined the cultural mechanisms at play in this process. This study begins that task.

METHOD

The data are from an interview study of the family and social experiences of grown children of Korean and Vietnamese immigrants. Respondents were either located at a California university where 47% of all undergraduates are of Asian descent (Maharaj, 1997) or were referred by students from that university. In-depth interviews were conducted with 73 respondents consisting of 34 Korean Americans (24 women, 10 men) and 39 Vietnamese Americans (23 women, 16 men). Both parents of each respondent were Korean or Vietnamese, except for one respondent, whose parents were both Sino-Vietnamese. Respondents ranged in age from 18–26 and averaged 21 years. Only one respondent was married, and none had children.

Respondents were either born in the United States (second generation) or immigrated prior to the age of 15 (1.5 generation), except for one Vietnamese American woman who immigrated at 17. The foreign born accounted for 77% of the sample and immigrated at an average age of 5 years. The remaining 23% were born in the United States. Most respondents in this sample spent their entire adolescence in the United States, and a majority lived in the United States for most, if not all, of their childhood. Eight percent of the Vietnamese American respondents were born in the United States, compared to 38 percent of Korean American respondents (see Table 1 for gender and ethnic differences). All study participants were college graduates or students and all resided in California, where one-third of U.S. legal immigrants arrive and 45% of the nation's immigrant student population lives (Zhou, 1997). Thus the sample over-represents those who are academically successful. Because the respondents have endured sustained exposure to assimilation pressures from the educational system, higher levels of assimilation were expected in this sample than in the larger immigrant population. As a result, these respondents were perhaps more likely to invoke American cultural ideals in describing their family life than a more representative sample that included the less educated and those who immigrated at older ages.

TABLE 1 *Sample Characteristics*

Ethnicity	n	Average Age (years)	Foreign Born (%)	Average Age at Immigration (years)
Korean American women	24	21	62	5
Korean American men	10	21	60	7
Vietnamese American women	23	21	96	5
Vietnamese American men	16	22	81	5
Total for sample	73	21	77	5

The author gathered the 73 individual interviews analyzed here in the preliminary phase of data collection for a larger ongoing project sponsored by the National Science Foundation (#SBR-9810725). The larger study includes a sample of 184 who participated in individual and focus group interviews. Only the initial phase of data collection was designed to prompt respondents' extensive descriptions of family life. The purpose of the larger study is to compare the dynamic complexities and structural contexts of adaptation and ethnic identity among children of immigrants, with special attention to their subjective experiences in mediating different cultural worlds. Because ethnic identity development differs for males and females (Espiritu, 1997; Waters, 1996), I also stratified the sample by gender.

As previously discussed, I stratified the sample by ethnicity, as well, in order to compare the effects of structural and cultural factors on adaptation processes. Despite Korean and Vietnamese distinctions in socioeconomic status, pathways to immigration, and cultural practices, I did not observe ethnic differences relevant to the central focus of this analysis. Although this is surprising, ethnic differences in the specific areas of family life that I was investigating are probably relatively subtle, particularly from the viewpoint of American children of Asian immigrant parents. More specifically, because respondents relied on American family ideology in giving meaning to their domestic relations, their focus was on how immigrant family life differs from the American ideal rather than from other Asian ethnic groups. This can blur ethnic distinctions and serve as a basis for shared personal experiences across ethnic groups. In fact, the rise of an Asian American ethnic identity among Asian-origin individuals is believed to result, in part, from the shared experiences of growing up American in an Asian home (Kibria, 1997).

Gender differences observed in these data focused on the nature of respondents' criticisms of parents, with females complaining that parents grant more freedom and respect to sons. Males also complained of strict parents, but when asked, acknowledged receiving more respect and freedom than sisters. These observed differences are not central to this analysis and are presented elsewhere (Pyke & Johnson, 1999).

A five-page interview guide with open-ended questions and follow-up probes concerning the familial and social experiences of respondents directed the intensive interview process. All respondents were asked what being a child of immigrants was like, how they think immigration affected their family, what their parents were like when the respondent was growing up, what communication was like with their parents, what their parents' marriage was like, how close they feel to their parents, whether they ever felt embarrassed by their parents, whether they ever deceived their parents, what kinds of things their parents would do to get them to obey, whether they have ever disappointed their parents in any way, how they would change their parents if they could change anything about them they wanted, what kinds of assistance they plan to provide for their parents, and how they feel about providing assistance. The author conducted about one-third of the interviews, and several trained student assistants conducted the remainder. The student assistants took a qualitative methods course with the author, in which they learned interviewing skills and conducted practice interviews. They also received extensive training and practice with the interview guide prior to collecting project data. Most trained student interviewers were children of Asian immigrants near in age to the respondents. They were therefore able to establish rapport with respondents, and they typically received candid responses, as revealed by respondents' frequent use of colloquialisms and profanity in interviews. Interviews were conducted in 1996 and 1997 and lasted between 1½ and 3 hours. They were tape-recorded and transcribed for analysis.

This research began with the general goal of learning about the subjective family experiences of children of Asian immigrants. I used a grounded research approach that emphasized an inductive method of generating explanation from the data (Glaser & Strauss, 1967; Strauss & Corbin, 1990). Except for the general assumption that respondents are active agents in the construction of their family experiences, I imposed no a priori assumptions, hypotheses, or specific theoretical frames on the research process. This allowed unanticipated data to emerge. Interviews focusing on family dynamics were conducted until a point of saturation was reached, as indicated by the recurring nature of the data and the emergence of clear trends (Ambert, Adler, Adler, & Detzner, 1995; Glaser & Strauss, 1967).

The overwhelming majority of respondents provided negative descriptions of their parents and upbringing in at least one domain, such as discipline, emotional closeness, or communication; only a small minority provided wholly positive accounts. Despite such intergenerational strain or distance, most respondents were strongly committed to caring for their parents in later life. In order to more closely examine the interview data, and thus to uncover deeper layers of understanding to these prominent patterns, two research assistants coded data into topical categories that corresponded with the questions asked. These coded segments were extracted for ease in theoretical sorting. I then analyzed the data, moving back and forth between emerging theoretical categories of the extracted data and the full interviews in order to check the validity of the findings. Because I am a native-born White American and wanted both to guard against the introduction of personal bias in the analysis and to acquire greater awareness of ethnic meanings, I shared my interpretive understandings of the data with Asian American students and student assistants. I then incorporated their insights into the analysis.

During the analysis, I noted recurring references in one form or another to notions about so-called normal families. Respondents used such references for one purpose only—as a point of contrast to life in their families. Three categorical expressions of this theme emerged in the data: (a) comparisons with television families; (b) comparisons with families of non-Asian friends; and (c) contrasts with specific family behavior or characteristics described as normal or American. I did not anticipate the importance of such family imagery when I devised the interview guide; thus I never asked respondents about family life on TV or among friends, or what they regarded as a normal or ideal family. Rather this theme emerged unexpectedly in the interviews. The unprompted and recurring nature of these references indicates their importance as resources in respondents' construction of their family experiences. In the following discussion, I present a sample of the qualitative data, in the form of quotes, to illustrate the observed patterns (Ambert et al., 1995). Respondents chose the pseudonyms used here.

RESULTS

I examine two ways in which respondents commonly used the typification of American family life as a contrast structure against which behavior in immigrant Asian families was juxtaposed and interpreted (Gubrium & Holstein, 1997). When describing relations with their parents, most respondents provided negative accounts of at least one aspect of their relationship, and they criticized their parents for lacking American values that emphasize psychological well-being and expressive love. Recurring references to a narrow Americanized notion of what families ought to look like were woven throughout many such accounts. However, when respondents described the kinds of filial care they planned to provide for their parents, the respondents switched to an interpretive lens that values ethnic family solidarity. In this context, respondents' references to notions of the Normal American Family became a negative point of comparison that cast their own immigrant families, and Asian families in general, in positive terms.

Viewing Parental Relations Through an Americanized Lens

Respondents were asked to fantasize about how they would change their parents if they could change anything about them that they wanted to change. The three areas of desired change that respondents mentioned most often reveal their adoption of many mainstream American values. They wished for parents who: (a) were less strict and gave them more freedom; (b) were more liberal, more open-minded, more Americanized, and less traditional; (c) were emotionally closer, more communicative, more expressive, and more affectionate. These three areas are interrelated. For example, being more Americanized and less traditional translates into being more lenient and expressive. A small minority of respondents presented a striking contrast to the dominant pattern by describing, in terms both positive and grateful, parents who had liberal attitudes or Americanized values and parenting styles.

    The communication most respondents described with parents focused on day-to-day practical concerns, such as whether the child had eaten, and about performance in school and college, a major area of concern among parents. Conversations were often limited to parental directives or lectures. For the most part, respondents were critical of the emotional distance and heavy emphasis on obedience that marked their relations with their parents. Chang-Hee, an 18-year-old who immigrated from Korea at 8, provided a typical case. When asked about communication, she disparaged her parents for not talking more openly, which she attributed to their being Asian. Respondents typically linked parental styles with race and not with other factors such as age or personality. Like many other respondents, Chang-Hee constructed an account not only of her family relations, but also of Asian families in general.

> To tell you the truth, in Asian families you don't have conversations. You just are told to do something and you do it. . . . You never talk about problems, even in the home. You just kind of forget about it and you kind of go on like nothing happened. Problems never really get solved. That's why I think people in my generation, I consider myself 1.5 generation, we have such a hard time because I like to verbalize my emotions. . . . [My parents] never allowed themselves to verbalize their emotions. They've been repressed so much [that] they expect the same out of me, which is the hardest thing to do because I have so many different things to say and I'm just not allowed.

Some respondents volunteered that their parents never asked them about their well-being, even when their distress was apparent. Chang-Hee observed, "If I'm sad, [my mom] doesn't want to hear it. She doesn't want to know why. . . . She's never asked me, 'So what do you feel?' " This lack of expressed interest in children's emotional well-being, along with the mundane level of communication, was especially upsetting to respondents because, interpreted through the lens of American family ideology, it defined their parents as emotionally uncaring and distant.

Several respondents longed for closer, more caring relationships with their parents that included expressive displays of affection. Thanh, a married 22-year-old college student who left Vietnam when she was 6, said, "I'd probably make them more loving and understanding, showing a bit more affection. . . . A lot of times I just want to go up and hug my parents, but no, you don't do that sort of thing."

Research indicates that the desire for greater intimacy is more common among women than men (Cancian, 1987). Thus it was surprising that many male respondents also expressed strong desires for more caring and close talk—especially from their fathers, who were often described as harsh and judgmental. Ralph, 20, a Korean American man born in the United States, said:

> My dad, he's not open. He is not the emotional type. So he talks . . . and I would listen and do it. It's a one-way conversation, rather than asking for my opinions. . . . I would think it'd be nicer if he was . . . much more compassionate, caring, because it seems like he doesn't care.

Similarly, Dat, a 22-year-old biology major who left Vietnam when he was 5, said:

> I would fantasize about sitting down with my dad and shooting the breeze. Talk about anything and he would smile and he would say, "Okay, that's fine, Dat." Instead of, you know, judge you and tell me I'm a loser. . . .

A definition of love that emphasizes emotional expression and close talk predominates in U.S. culture (Cancian, 1986). Instrumental aspects of love, like practical help, are ignored or devalued in this definition. In Korean and Vietnamese cultures, on the other hand, the predominant definitions of love emphasize instrumental help and support. The great divide between immigrant parents who emphasize instrumental forms of love and children who crave open displays of affection was evident in the following conversation, which occurred between Dat and his father when Dat was 7 or 8 years old. Dat recalled, "I tried saying 'I love you' one time and he looked at me and said, 'Are you American now? You think this is *The Brady Bunch?* You don't love me. You love me when you can support me.'" These different cultural definitions of love contributed to respondents' constructions of immigrant parents as unloving and cold.

The Family as a Contrast Structure in the Negative Accounts of Family Life

Many of the images of normal family life that respondents brought to their descriptions came in the form of references to television families or the families of non–Asian American friends. Although these monolithic images do not reflect the reality of American family life, they nevertheless provided the basis by which respondents learned how to be American, and they served as the interpretive frame of their own family experiences. By contrasting behavior in their immigrant families with mainstream images of normalcy, the respondents interpreted Asian family life as lacking or deficient. Dat referred to images of normal family life in America, as revealed on television and among friends, as the basis for his desire for more affection and closeness with his father:

> Sometimes when I had problems in school, all I wanted was my dad to listen to me, of all people. I guess that's the American way and I was raised American. . . . That's what I see on TV and in my friends' family. And I expected him to be that way too. But it didn't happen. . . . I would like to talk to him or, you know, say "I love you," and he would look at me and say, "Okay." That's my ultimate goal, to say, "I love you." It's real hard. Sometimes when I'm in a good mood, the way I show him love is to put my hands over his shoulders and squeeze it a little bit. That would already irritate him a little. . . . You could tell. He's like, "What the fuck's he doing?" But I do it because I want to show him love somehow. Affection. I'm an affectionate person.

Similarly, Hoa, a 23-year-old Vietnamese American man who immigrated at age 2, referred to television in describing his own family: "We aren't as close as I would like . . . We aren't as close as the dream family, you know, what you see on TV. Kind of like. . . . *Leave It To Beaver.* You know, stuff I grew up on."

Paul, a 21-year-old Korean American born in the United States, also criticizes his father, and Asian fathers in general, in relation to the fathers of friends and those on television:

> I think there is somewhat of a culture clash between myself and my parents. They are very set on rules—at least my father is. He is very strict and demanding and very much falls into that typical Asian father standard. I don't like that too much and I think it is because . . . as a child, I was always watching television and watching other friends' fathers. All the relationships seemed so much different from me and my father's relationship. . . . I guess it's pretty cheesy but I can remember watching *The Brady Bunch* reruns and thinking Mike Brady would be a wonderful dad to have. He was always so supportive. He always

knew when something was wrong with one of his boys. Whenever one of his sons had a problem, they would have no problem telling their dad anything and the dad would always be nice and give them advice and stuff. Basically I used what I saw on television as a picture of what a typical family should be like in the United States. I only wished that my family could be like that. And friends too—I used to see how my friends in school would be in Little League Baseball and their dad would be like their coaches or go to their games to cheer their sons on and give them support. I could not picture my father to be like that kind of man that I saw on TV, or like my friends' fathers.

Respondents did not refer to non–Asian American friends who had distant, conflict-ridden family relationships. Yet many respondents likely did have contact with such individuals. It appears as though respondents see only in ways permitted by the Family ideology. That is, as Bernades argued, "the image or idol of 'The Family' rather than the reality of people's lives is taken as the object of attention" (1985, p. 288). Looking at "American" families through this ideological lens determines which families are "seen." Those that do not fit the cultural imagery are not seen or are viewed as atypical. "Atypical" families are not referenced in these accounts, even though, in actuality, they are probably closer to the empirical reality of American family life. Friends whose families do comply, on the other hand, loom large as symbols that verify the existence of the Family ideal.

In comparison to this ideal, even parents who had adopted more American parenting practices fell short. For example, the parents of Mike, 22, who had immigrated to the United States from Vietnam as an infant, were less strict than the parents of most respondents. Nevertheless, Mike said:

> My parents were really easy. They let me hang out with my friends, they had no problem with me sleeping over or other people sleeping over. So having friends in high school wasn't hard at all, and going out wasn't a problem at all. It was just, you know, you go over to your friend's house and he just talks to his parents about everything. So I got a little bit jealous. You know, I wished I could talk to my parents about stuff like that but I couldn't.

Sometimes respondents simply made assumptive references to normal or American families, against which they critically juxtaposed Asian immigrant families. Being American meant that one was a member of the Normal American Family and enjoyed family relations that were warm, close, and harmonious. Being Asian, on the other hand, meant living outside such normality. Thuy, a 20-year-old Vietnamese American woman who had immigrated when 13, said:

> If I could, I would have a more emotional relationship with my parents. I know they love me, but they never tell me they love me. They also are not very affectionate. This is how I've always grown up. It wasn't really until we came to the United States that I really noticed what a lack of love my parents show. *American* kids are so lucky. They don't know what it's like to not really feel that you can show emotion with your own parents.

Similarly, Cora, 20, a Korean American woman born in the United States, remarked:

> I would probably want [my parents] to be more open, more understanding so I could be more open with them, 'cause there's a lot of things that I can't share with them because

they're not as open-minded as *American* parents. . . . 'Cause I have friends and stuff. They talk to their parents about everything, you know?

When asked how he was raised, Josh, 21, a Vietnamese American man who immigrated when 2, responded by calling up a construction of the "good" American Family and the "deficient" Asian Family. He said, "I'm sure that for all *Asian* people, if they think back to [their] childhood, they'll remember a time they got hit. *American* people, they don't get hit."

Respondents repeatedly constructed American families as loving, harmonious, egalitarian, and normal. Using this ideal as their measuring stick, Asian families were constructed as distant, overly strict, uncaring, and not normal. In fact, respondents sometimes used the word "normal" in place of "American." For example, Hoa, who previously contrasted his family with the one depicted in *Leave It To Beaver*, said, "I love my dad but we never got to play catch. He didn't teach me how to play football. All the stuff a *normal* dad does for their kids. We missed out on that." Thomas, 20, a Korean American who arrived in the United States at age 8, said, "I always felt like maybe we are not so normal. Like in the real America, like Brady Bunch normal. . . . I always felt like . . . there was something irregular about me." Similarly, after describing a childhood where she spoke very little to her parents, Van, 24, who immigrated to the United States from Vietnam at 10, began crying and noted, "I guess I didn't have a *normal* childhood." To be a normal parent is to be an American parent. Asian immigrant parents are by this definition deficient. Such constructions ignore diversity within family types, and they selectively bypass the social problems, such as child abuse, that plague many non–Asian American families. It is interesting, for example, that respondents did not refer to the high divorce rate of non–Asian Americans (Sweet & Bumpass, 1987) to construct positive images of family stability among Asian Americans. This may be because, applying an Americanized definition of love, many respondents described their parents' marriage as unloving and some thought their parents ought to divorce.

Respondents relied on the Family not only as an interpretive framework, but also as a contrast structure by which to differentiate Asian and American families. This juxtaposition of American and Asian ignores that most of the respondents and the coethnics they describe are Americans. "American" is used to refer to non–Asian Americans, particularly Whites. The words "White" and "Caucasian" were sometimes used interchangeably with "American." Indeed, the Normal American Family *is* White. This Eurocentric imagery excludes from view other racial minority families such as African Americans and Latino Americans. It is therefore not surprising that racial–ethnic families were not referenced as American in these interviews. In fact, respondents appeared to use the term "American" as a code word denoting not only cultural differences but also racial differences. For example, Paul, who was born in the United States, noted, "I look Korean but I think I associate myself more with the *American race*." The oppositional constructions of Asian and American families as monolithic and without internal variation imply that these family types are racialized. That is, the differences are constructed as not only cultural but also racially essential and therefore immutable (Omi & Winant, 1994). By defining American as White, respondents revealed the deep-seated notion that, as Asian Americans, they can never truly be American. Such notions dominate in mainstream depictions of Asian Americans as perpetual foreigners. For example, in a speech about foreign donations, Ross Perot read the names of several Asian American political donors and commented, "So far we haven't found an American name" (Nakao, 1996). When respondents centered Whites as a point of reference in these accounts, they re-affirmed the marginalized position of racial–ethnic minorities in the Family ideology and in U.S. culture writ large.

These data illustrate how Eurocentric images of normal family relationships promulgated in the larger society served as an ideological template in the negative accounts that respondents provided of their immigrant parents. However, as described next, when respondents discussed their plans for filial care, they presented positive accounts of their immigrant families.

Maintaining Ethnic Values of Filial Obligation

Respondents were not consistent in their individual constructions of Asian and American families as revealed in their interviews. When discussing future plans for filial care, most respondents positively evaluated their family's collectivist commitment to care. Such an interpretation is supported by model minority stereotypes in mainstream U.S. culture that attribute the success enjoyed by some Asian immigrants to their strong family values and collectivist practices (Kibria, 1993; Zhou & Bankston, 1998).

The majority of respondents valued and planned to maintain their ethnic tradition of filial care. For example, Josh, who criticized his parents (and Asian parents in general) for using physical forms of punishment, nonetheless plans to care for his parents in their old age. He said, "I'm the oldest son, and in Vietnamese culture the oldest son cares for the parents. That is one of the things that I carry from my culture. I would not put my parents in a [nursing] home. That's terrible." In contrast to White Americans who condition their level of filial commitment on intergenerational compatibility (Pyke, 1999), respondents displayed a strong desire to fulfill their filial obligation and—especially among daughters—were often undeterred by distant and even conflict-ridden relations with parents. For example, after describing a strained relationship with her parents, Kimberly, 20, who came to this country from Vietnam when 7, added, "I would still take care of them whether I could talk to them or not. It doesn't matter as long as I could take care of them." Similarly, in Wolf's study of 22 grown children of Filipino immigrants, respondents who complained of tension and emotional distance with parents nonetheless experienced family ties and responsibilities as a central component of their daily lives and identities (1997).

Most respondents expected to begin financially supporting their parents prior to their elderly years, with parents in their 50s often regarded as old. A few respondents had already begun to help out their parents financially. Many planned on living with parents. Others spoke of living near their parents, often as neighbors, rather than in the same house, as a means of maintaining some autonomy. The tradition of assigning responsibility for the care of parents to the eldest son was not automatically anticipated for many of these families, especially those from Vietnam. Respondents most often indicated that responsibility would be pooled among siblings or would fall exclusively to the daughters. Several said that parents preferred such arrangements, because they felt closer to daughters. Although the tendency for daughters to assume responsibility for aging parents is similar to the pattern of caregiving common in mainstream American families (Pyke &

Bengtson, 1996), several respondents noted that such patterns are also emerging among relatives in their ethnic homeland.

The Importance of Collectivism as an Expression of Love

Respondents typically attributed their future caregiving to reciprocation for parental care in the past and a cultural emphasis on filial respect and support. Yet the enthusiasm and strong commitment that pervades their accounts suggests that they are motivated by more than obligation. For example, Vinh, 26, a graduate student who immigrated from Vietnam at age 5, said about his parents:

> They are my life. They will never be alone. I will always be with them. When I was growing [up] as a child, my parents were always with me. And I believe . . . when you grow up, you should be with them; meaning, I will take care of them, in my house, everything. Your parents didn't abandon you when you were a kid. They did not abandon you when you [were] pooping in your diaper. Then when they do, I will not abandon them. . . . Whatever it takes to make them comfortable, I will provide it. There is no limit.

Unable to express love via open displays of affection and close talk, filial assistance becomes a very important way for adult children to symbolically demonstrate their affection for their parents and to reaffirm family bonds. Blossom, 21, who immigrated to the United States from Korea when 6, described the symbolic value of the financial assistance her father expects. She said, "Money is not really important, but it's more about our heart that [my dad] looks at. Through money, my dad will know how we feel and how we appreciate him." Remember that Dat's father told him, "You love me when you can support me." Because instrumental assistance is the primary venue for expressing love and affection in these immigrant families, adult children often placed no limits on what they were willing to do. For example, John, 20, who immigrated from Vietnam when 3, remarked "I'm willing to do anything (for my parents), that's how much I care."

Parental financial independence was not always welcomed by those children who gave great weight to their role of parental caregivers. For example, it was very important to Sean, 19, an only child, to care for his Sino-Vietnamese parents. Sean, who planned to become a doctor, commuted from his home to a local university. He said, "I want my parents to stay with me. I want to support them. . . . I'll always have room for my parents. . . . When I get my first paycheck, I want to support them financially." As reflected in the following exchange with the interviewer, Sean viewed his parents' retirement plan with some hurt.

> **Sean:** They have their own retirement plan, and they keep track of it themselves, so they're all prepared for me to be the disobedient son and run away.
>
> **Interviewer:** Is that how you feel?
>
> **Sean:** Yes I do. . . . Or if I don't succeed in life, they'll be taken care of by themselves.
>
> **Interviewer:** So is that how you see their retirement plan, as a kind of symbol that they're . . . ?
>
> **Sean:** They're ready for me to mess up.

The emotional centrality of family ties is also apparent in Sean's description of his hurt when his father—who worries that the time Sean spends away from home studying or at his job is pulling him away from the family—occasionally tests his son's commitment by suggesting that he leave the family home and "fly away." With tear-filled eyes, Sean explained:

> It hurts me because I've never had that idea to fly away. . . . I don't want to go and that's what hurts me so bad. I mean, I could cry over things like that. And this is a 19-year-old kid that's crying in front of you. How seldom do you get that?

The Family as a Contrast Structure in the Positive Accounts of Filial Obligation

Many respondents distinguished their ethnic collectivist tradition of filial obligation from practices in mainstream American families, which they described as abandoning elderly parents in retirement or nursing homes. The belief that the elderly are abandoned by their families is widespread in U.S. society and very much a part of everyday discourse. Media accounts of nursing home atrocities bolster such views. Yet most eldercare in this country is not provided in formal caregiving settings but by family members (Abel, 1991). Nonetheless, respondents used this tenacious myth as a point of contrast in constructing Asian American families as more instrumentally caring. For example, Thuy, who previously described wanting a "more emotional relationship" with her parents, like "American kids" have, explained:

> With the American culture, it's . . . not much frowned upon to put your parents in a home when they grow old. In our culture, it is a definite no-no. To do anything like that would be disrespectful. . . . If they need help, my brother and I will take care of them, just like my mom is taking care of her parents right now.

Similarly, Hien, 21, a Vietnamese American woman who arrived in this country as an infant, noted, "I know a lot of non-Asians have their parents go to the nursing homes . . . but I personally prefer to find a way of trying to keep them at home."

Mike, who wished he could talk to his parents the way his friends do to theirs, plans to care for his Americanized parents even though they have told him they do not want him to. He was not alone in remaining more committed to filial care than his parents required him to be. He said:

> They tell me to just succeed for yourself and take care of your own family. But [referring to filial care] that's just how the Vietnamese culture is. Here in America, once your parents are old, you put them in a retirement home. But not in my family. When the parents get old you take care of them. It doesn't matter if they can't walk, if they can't function anymore. You still take care of them.

When discussing relationships with their parents, respondents used the Family as the ideological raw material out of which they negatively constructed their parents as unloving and distant. However, when the topic changed to filial care, respondents switched to an ethnic definition of love that emphasizes instrumental support and that casts a positive and loving light on their families. As Katie, 21, a Korean American woman born in the United States, observed:

> When you say that you are close to your parents here in America, I think most people would take that as you are affectionate with your parents, you hang out with them, you can talk to them about anything . . . more of a friendship thing. But Korean families are not like that. . . . They do not get close to their children like that. They are not friends with them. The kids of Korea do not open up with their parents. Their parents are really their *parents*. . . . But still, no matter what, they are very close. Here in America . . . Caucasians don't take care of their parents like we do. They just put them in an old people's home and that's it. It's like they say, "You are too old for me. I don't need you anymore and I'm just going to put you here 'cause it's convenient for me and you'd be in the way anyway. . . ." And in that way, Americans are *not* close to their parents. So it really depends on how you define the word "close"—the answer changes. [Note that the words "Caucasian" and "American" are used synonymously here, as previously discussed.]

In describing their plans for parental care, respondents turned their previous construction of Asian and American families on its head. In this context the Family was constructed as deficient and uncaring, while the families of respondents—and Asian families in general—were described as more instrumentally caring and closer. Respondents' view of American families as uncaring should not be interpreted as a departure from mainstream family ideology. There has been much concern in the public discourse that today's families lack a commitment to the care of their elders and children (e.g., Popenoe, 1993; see Coontz, 1992, pp. 189–191). Indeed, the pervasive criticism that "individualism has gone haywire" in mainstream families—bolstered by references to the solidarity of model minority families—provides ideological support for ethnic traditions of filial care. That is, children of immigrants do not face ideological pressure from the dominant society to alter such practices; rather, they are given an interpretive template by which to view such practices as evidence of love and care in their families. In fact, U.S. legislative attempts to withdraw social services from legal immigrants without citizenship, with the expectation that family sponsors will provide such support, structurally mandate collectivist systems of caregiving in immigrant families (Huber & Espenshade, 1997). In other words, the dominant society ideologically endorses and, in some ways, structurally requires ethnic immigrant practices of filial care. Filial obligation thus serves as a site where children of Korean and Vietnamese immigrants can maintain their ethnic identity and family ties without countervailing pressure from the mainstream.

DISCUSSION

Interweaving respondents' accounts with an analysis of the interpretive structure from which those accounts are constructed suggests that the Family ideology subtly yet powerfully influences the children of immigrants, infiltrating their subjective understandings of and desires for family life. Respondents relied on American family images in two ways. When discussing their relations with parents and their upbringing, respondents used the

Family ideology as a standard of normal families and good parents, leading them to view their immigrant parents as unloving, deficient, and not normal. However, when respondents discussed filial care, a complete reversal occurred. Respondents referred to negative images of rampant individualism among mainstream American families, specifically in regard to eldercare, to bolster their positive portrayals of the instrumental care and filial piety associated with their ethnic families. Thus the Family ideology was called upon in contradictory ways in these accounts—in the denigration of traditional ethnic parenting practices and in the glorification of ethnic practices of filial obligation.

Findings from this study illustrate how a narrow, ethnocentric family ideology that is widely promulgated throughout the larger culture and quickly internalized by children of immigrants creates an interpretive framework that derogates many of the ethnic practices of immigrant families. As others have argued, the cultural imposition of dominant group values in this form of "controlling images" can lead minorities to internalize negative self-images (Espiritu, 1997). That is, racial–ethnic immigrants can adopt a sense of inferiority and a desire to conform with those values and expectations that are glorified in the mainstream society as normal. Indeed, many respondents explicitly expressed a desire to have families that were like White or so-called American families, and they criticized their own family dynamics for being different. Rather than resist and challenge the ethnocentric family imagery of the mainstream, respondents' accounts reaffirmed the Normal American Family and the centrality of White native-born Americans in this imagery. This research thus reveals a subtle yet powerful mechanism of internalized oppression by which the racial–ethnic power dynamics in the larger society are reproduced. This is a particularly important finding in that racial–ethnic families will soon constitute a majority in several states, causing scholars to ponder the challenge of such a demographic transformation of the cultural and political hegemony of White native-born Americans (Maharidge, 1996). This study describes an ideological mechanism that could undermine challenges to that hegemony.

This research also uncovered an uncontested site of ethnic pride among the second-generation respondents who drew on mainstream images of elder neglect in their positive interpretation of ethnic filial commitment. As previously discussed, the belief that mainstream American families abandon their elders is tenacious and widespread in the dominant society, despite its empirical inaccuracy. This negative myth has been widely used in popular discourse as an example of the breakdown of American family commitment, and it sometimes serves as a rallying cry for stronger "family values." Such cries are often accompanied by references to the family solidarity and filial piety celebrated in the model minority stereotype. Thus the mainstream glorification of ethnic filial obligation, as contrasted with negative images of abandoned White American elders, provided respondents with a positive template for giving meaning to ethnic practices of filial care. The mainstream endorsement of filial obligation marks it as a locale where respondents can maintain family ties and simultaneously produce a positive self-identity in both cultural worlds. This might explain why some respondents were steadfastly committed to filial care despite parental requests to the contrary.

It remains to be seen, however, whether these young adults will be able to carry out their plans of filial obligation. It is likely that many will confront barriers in the form of demanding jobs, childrearing obligations, geographic moves, unsupportive spouses, competing demands from elderly in-laws, and financial difficulties. Furthermore, parents' access to alternative sources of support such as Social Security and retirement funds could diminish the need for their children's assistance. Some research already finds that elderly Korean immigrants prefer to live on their own and are moving out of the homes of their immigrant children despite the protests of children, who see it as a public accusation that they did not care for their parents (Hurh, 1998). Although this research examined first-generation immigrant adults and their aging parents, it suggests a rapid breakdown in traditional patterns of coresidential filial care that will likely be reiterated in the next generation. Future research is needed to examine these dynamics among second-generation immigrants, to look at how they will cope with inabilities to fulfill ethnic and model minority expectations of filial obligation, and to assess the impact of any such inabilities on their ethnic identity.

This study makes a unique contribution to the small and largely descriptive literature on Asian immigrant families. Rather than simply reiterating as descriptive data the accounts of family life offered by respondents, I examined the ideological underpinnings of those accounts. In so doing, I uncovered a subtle process by which White hegemonic images of the Family infiltrate the ways that children of immigrants think about their own family lives. Although scholars have often assumed that the prescriptive and moralistic characteristics of the Family are hurtful to those whose families do not comply, the findings presented here provide an empirical description of how such ideology negatively biases the family accounts of children of immigrants. It must be noted, however, that because the sample in the study was demographically predisposed to higher levels of assimilation, the respondents are probably more likely than a less assimilated sample to view their families through an Americanized lens. This suggests the need for further study of how variations in acculturation levels affect the accounts that children of immigrants provide of their family lives.

A broader sample of families that do not conform with images of the Normal American Family also needs to be investigated. This sample should include native-born racial minorities and children of single parents, as well as immigrants. Studying a broader sample will allow greater understanding of whether narrow cultural notions of a normal family life influence the subjective experience of diverse groups of children growing up in the margins of the mainstream. It is particularly important, as family scholars begin to respond to the burgeoning numbers of ethnically and structurally diverse family forms, that researchers generate culturally sensitive interpretive frameworks that do not automatically and unconsciously perpetuate existing notions that certain family types and practices are inferior. The effort to develop such frameworks requires researchers to examine not only the values and assumptions they bring to their analyses (Dilworth-Anderson et al., 1993), but also the values and assumptions that respondents bring to their accounts. To summarize, this study suggests the need for family researchers to analytically bracket as problematic the ideological structures that shape the empirical accounts of family life we rely upon in our research.

Note

I am grateful to Katherine Allen, Susan Blank, Francesca Cancian, Tran Dang, Yen Le Espiritu, Joe Feagin, Jaber Gubrium, Nazli Kibria, Pyong Gap Min, Karen Seccombe, Darin Weinberg, Min Zhou, and the reviewers for their suggestions. I also thank Van-Dzung Nguyen and Mumtaz Mohammedi for their research assistance, the Department of Sociology at University of California-Irvine for its support of this research, and the many students who eagerly participated as research assistants or respondents.

References

Abel, E. K. (1991). *Who cares for the elderly?* Philadelphia: Temple University Press.

Ambert, A., Adler, P. Adler, P. & Detzner, D. (1995). Understanding and evaluating qualitative research. *Journal of Marriage and the Family, 57,* 879–893.

Bellah, R. N., Madsen, R., Sullivan, W. M., Swidler, A., & Tipton, S. (1985). *Habits of the heart.* San Francisco: Harper & Row.

Berger, P. L., & Luckmann, T. (1966). *The social construction of reality.* New York: Doubleday.

Bernades, J. (1985). "Family ideology": Identification and exploration. *Sociological Review, 33,* 275–297.

Bernades, J. (1993). Responsibilities in studying postmodern families. *Journal of Family Issues, 14,* 35–49.

Blankenhorn, D. (1995). *Fatherless America.* New York: Basic Books.

Brown, D., & Bryant, J. (1990). Effects of television on family values and selected attitudes and behaviors. In J. Bryant (Ed.), *Television and the American family* (pp. 253–274). Hillsdale, NJ: Erlbaum.

Cancian, E. M. (1986). The feminization of love. *Signs, 11,* 692–708.

Cancian, E. M. (1987). *Love in America.* New York: Cambridge University Press.

Caplan, N., Choy, M. H., & Whitmore, J. K. (1991). *Children of the boat people: A study of educational success.* Ann Arbor: University of Michigan Press.

Cha, J. (1994). Aspects of individualism and collectivism in Korea. In U. Kim, H. C. Triandis, Ç. Kâğitçibaşi, S. Choi, & G. Yoon (Eds.), *Individualism and collectivism: Theory, methods, and applications* (pp. 157–174). Thousand Oaks, CA: Sage.

Chung, D. K. (1992). Asian cultural commonalities: A comparison with mainstream American culture. In S. Furuto, R. Biswas, D. Chung, K. Murase, R. Ross-Sheriff (Eds.), *Social work practice with Asian Americans* (pp. 27–44). Newbury Park, CA: Sage.

Coltrane, S. (1996). *Family man.* New York: Oxford University Press.

Coontz, S. (1992). *The way we never were.* New York: Basic Books.

Dilworth-Anderson, P., Burton, L. M., & Turner, W. L. (1993). The importance of values in the study of culturally diverse families. *Family Relations, 42,* 238–242.

Espiritu, Y. L. (1997). *Asian American women and men.* Thousand Oaks, CA: Sage.

Fineman, M. A. (1995). *The neutered mother, the sexual family, and other twentieth century tragedies.* New York: Routledge.

Freeman, J. M. (1989). *Hearts of sorrow: Vietnamese-American lives.* Stanford, CA: Stanford University Press.

Gerbner, G., Gross, L., Morgan, M., & Signorielli, N. (1980). *Media and the family: Images and impact.* Washington, DC: White House Conference on the Family, National Research Forum on Family Issues. (ERIC Document Reproduction Service No. ED 198 919).

Glaser, B. G., & Strauss, A. L. (1967). *The discovery of grounded theory.* New York: Aldine.

Gold, S. J. (1993). Migration and family adjustment: Continuity and change among Vietnamese in the United States. In H. P. McAdoo (Ed.), *Family ethnicity* (pp. 300–314). Newbury Park, CA: Sage.

Greeley, A. (1987, May 17). Today's morality play: The sitcom. *New York Times,* p. H1.

Greenberg, B. S., Hines, M., Buerkel-Rothfuss, N., & Atkin, C. K. (1980). Family role structures and interactions on commercial television. In B. S. Greenberg (Ed.), *Life on television: Content analyses of U.S. TV drama* (pp. 149–160). Norwood, NJ: Ablex.

Gubrium, J. F. & Holstein, J. A. (1997). *The new language of qualitative method.* New York: Oxford University Press.

Holstein, J. A., & Gubrium, J. F. (1995). Deprivatization and the construction of domestic life. *Journal of Marriage and the Family, 57,* 894–908.

Holstein, J. A., & Miller, G. (1993). Social constructionism and social problems work. In J. A. Holstein & G. Miller (Eds.), *Reconsidering social constructionism* (pp. 151–172). New York: Aldine De Gruyter.

Huber, G. A., & Espenshade, T. J. (1997). Neo-isolationism, balanced-budget conservatism, and the fiscal impacts of immigrants. *International Migration Review, 31,* 1031–1054.

Hurh, W. M. (1998). *The Korean Americans.* Westport, CN: Greenwood Press.

Kibria, N. (1993). *The family tightrope: The changing lives of Vietnamese Americans.* Princeton, NJ: Princeton University Press.

Kibria, N. (1997). The construction of 'Asian American': Reflections on intermarriage and ethnic identity among second-generation Chinese and Korean Americans. *Ethnic and Racial Studies, 20,* 523–544.

Kim, U., & Choi, S. (1994). Individualism, collectivism, and child development: A Korean perspective. In P. Greenfield & R. Cocking (Eds.), *Cross-cultural roots of minority child development* (pp. 227–257). Hillsdale, NJ: Erlbaum.

Kurz, D. (1995). *For richer, for poorer.* New York: Routledge.

Maharaj, D. (1997, July 8). E-mail hate case tests free speech protections. *Los Angeles Times,* pp. Al, A16.

Maharidge, D. (1996). *The coming white minority: California erupts and America's future.* New York: New York Times Books.

Min, P. G. (1995). Major issues relating to Asian American experiences. In P. G. Min (Ed.), *Asian Americans* (pp. 38–57). Thousand Oaks, CA: Sage.

Min, P. G. (1998). *Changes and conflicts: Korean immigrant families in New York.* New York: Allyn and Bacon.

Nakao, A. (1996, November 17). Asians' political image marred: Fundraising probes' timing "unfortunate." *The San Francisco Examiner,* p. Al.

Omi, M., & Winant, H. (1994). *Racial formation in the United States.* New York: Routledge.

Oropesa, R. S., & Landale, N. S. (1995). *Immigrant legacies: The socioeconomic circumstances of children by ethnicity and generation in the United States.* (Working Paper 95–01R). Population Research Institute, The Pennsylvania State University, State College.

Pettengill, S. M., & Rohner, R. P. (1985). Korean-American adolescents' perceptions of parental control, parental acceptance–rejection and parent–adolescent conflict. In I. R. Lagunes & Y. H. Poortinga (Eds.), *From a different perspective: Studies of behavior across culture* (pp. 241–249). Berwyn, IL: Sweets North America.

Popenoe, D. (1993). American family decline, 1960–1990: A review and appraisal. *Journal of Marriage and the Family, 55,* 527–555.

Popenoe, D. (1996). *Life without father: Compelling new evidence that fatherhood and marriage are indispensable and for the good of the children and society.* New York: Martin Kessler/Free Press.

Pyke, K. D. (1999). The micropolitics of care in relationships between aging parents and adult children Individualism, collectivism, and power. *Journal of Marriage and the Family, 61,* 661–672.

Pyke, K. D., & Bengtson, V. L. (1996). Caring more of less: Individualistic and collectivist systems of family eldercare. *Journal of Marriage and the Family, 58,* 379–392.

Pyke, K. D., & Johnson, D. (1999, November). *Between: two faces of gender: The incongruity of home and mainstream cultures among sons and daughters of Asian immigrants.* Paper presented at the Annual Meeting of the National Council of Family Relations, Irvine, CA.

Rohner, R. P., & Pettengill, S. M. (1985). Perceived parental acceptance–rejection and parental control among Korean adolescents. *Child Development, 56,* 524–528.

Rumbaut, R. G. (1994). The crucible within: Ethnic identity, self-esteem and segmented assimilation among children of immigrants. *International Migration Review, 28,* 748–794.

Rumbaut, R. G. (1997). Assimilation and its discontents: Between rhetoric and reality. *International Migration Review, 31,* 923–960.

Shaner, J. (1982). Parental empathy and family role interactions as portrayed on commercial television. *Dissertation Abstracts International, 42,* 3473A.

Skill, T. (1994). Family images and family actions as presented in the media: Where we've been and what we've found. In D. Zillmann, J. Bryant, & A. C. Huston (Eds.), *Media, children, and the family* (pp. 37–50). Hillsdale, NJ: Erlbaum.

Skolnick, A. (1991). *Embattled paradise: The American family in an age of uncertainty.* New York: Basic Books.

Smith, D. E. (1993). The standard North American family: SNAF as an ideological code. *Journal of Family Issues, 14,* 50–65.

Stacey, J. (1998). The right family values. In K. Hansen & A. Garey (Eds.), *Families in the U.S.* (pp. 859–880). Philadelphia: Temple University Press.

Strauss, A., & Corbin, J. (1990). *Basics of qualitative research.* Newbury Park, CA: Sage.

Sue, S., & Morishima, J. K. (1982). *The mental health of Asian Americans.* San Francisco: Jossey-Bass.

Sweet, J. A., & Bumpass, L. (1987). *American families and households*. New York: Russell Sage Foundation.

Thorne, B., & Yalom, M. (1992). *Rethinking the family: Some feminist questions*. Boston: Northeastern University.

Tran, T. V. (1988). The Vietnamese American family. In C. H. Mindel, R. W. Habenstein, & R. Wright, Jr. (Eds.), *Ethnic families in America: Patterns and variations* (pp. 276–299). New York: Elsevier.

Tsui, P., & Schultz, G. (1985). Failure of rapport: Why psychotherapeutic engagement fails in the treatment of Asian clients. *American Journal of Orthopsychiatry*, *55*, 561–569.

Uba, L. (1994). *Asian Americans: Personality patterns, identity, and mental health*. New York: The Guilford Press.

U.S. Immigration and Naturalization Service (1997). *Statistical yearbook of the immigration and naturalization service, 1995*. Washington, DC: U.S. Government Printing Office.

Waters, M. C. (1996). The intersection of gender, race, and ethnicity in identity development of Caribbean American teens. In M. C. Waters (Ed.), *Urban girls: Resisting stereotypes, creating identities* (pp. 65–81) New York: New York University Press.

Wolf, D. (1997). Family secrets: Transnational struggles among children of Filipino immigrants. *Sociological Perspectives*, *40*, 457–482.

Zhou, M. (1997). Growing up American: The challenge confronting immigrant children and children of immigrants. *Annual Review of Sociology*, *23*, 63–95.

Zhou, M., & Bankston, III, C. (1998). *Growing up American: How Vietnamese children adapt to life in the United States*. New York: Russell Sage Foundation.

Zinn, M. B. (1994). Feminist rethinking of racial–ethnic families. In M. B. Zinn & B. T. Dill (Eds.), *Women of color in U.S. society* (pp. 303–314). Philadelphia: Temple University Press.

12 *Trouble in the Family*

Prisoners' Families and Children

Jeremy Travis

As the nation debates the wisdom of a fourfold increase in our incarceration rate over the past generation, one fact is clear: Prisons separate prisoners from their families. Every individual sent to prison leaves behind a network of family relationships. Prisoners are the children, parents, siblings, and kin to untold numbers of relatives who are each affected differently by a family member's arrest, incarceration, and ultimate homecoming.

Little is known about imprisonment's impact on these family networks. Descriptive data about the children of incarcerated parents only begin to tell the story. During the 1990s, as the nation's prison population increased by half, the number of children who had a parent in prison also increased by half—from 1 million to 1.5 million. By the end of 2002, 1 in 45 minor children had a parent in prison (Mumola 2004).[1] These children represent 2 percent of all minor children in America, and a sobering 7 percent of all African-American children (Mumola 2000). With little if any public debate, we have extended prison's reach to include hundreds of thousands of young people who were not the prime target of the criminal justice policies that put their parents behind bars.

In the simplest human terms, prison places an indescribable burden on the relationships between these parents and their children. Incarcerated fathers and mothers must learn to cope with the loss of normal contact with their children, infrequent visits in inhospitable surroundings, and lost opportunities to contribute to their children's development. Their children must come to terms with the reality of an absent parent, the stigma of parental imprisonment, and an altered support system that may include grandparents, foster care, or a new adult in the home. In addition, in those communities where incarceration rates are high, the experience of having a mother or father in prison is now quite commonplace, with untold consequences for foster care systems, multigenerational households, social services delivery, community norms, childhood development, and parenting patterns.

Imprisonment profoundly affects families in another, less tangible way. When young men and women are sent to prison, they are removed from the traditional rhythms of dating, courtship, marriage, and family formation. Because far more men than women are sent to prison each year, our criminal justice policies have created a "gender imbalance" (Braman 2002), a disparity in the number of available single men and women in many communities. In neighborhoods where incarceration and reentry have hit hardest, the gender imbalance is particularly striking. Young women complain about the shortage of men who are suitable marriage prospects because so many of the young men cycle in and out of the criminal justice system. The results are an increase in female-headed households and narrowed roles for fathers in the lives of their children and men in the lives of women and families in general. As more young men grow up with fewer stable attachments to girl-friends, spouses, and intimate partners, the masculine identity is redefined.

The family is often depicted as the bedrock of American society. Over the years, we have witnessed wave after wave of social policy initiatives designed to strengthen, reunite, or simply create families. Liberals and conservatives have accused each other of espous-ing policies that undermine "family values." In recent years, policymakers, foundation of-ficers, and opinion leaders have also decried the absence of fathers from the lives of their children. These concerns have translated into a variety of programs, governmental ini-tiatives, and foundation strategies that constitute a "fatherhood movement." Given the iconic stature of the family in our vision of American life and the widespread consensus that the absence of father figures harms future generations, our national experiment with mass incarceration seems, at the very least, incongruent with the rhetoric behind pre-vailing social policies. At worst, the imprisonment of millions of individuals and the dis-ruption of their family relationships has significantly undermined the role that families could play in promoting our social well-being.

The institution of family plays a particularly important role in the crime policy arena. Families are an integral part of the mechanisms of informal social control that con-strain antisocial behavior. The quality of family life (e.g., the presence of supportive parent-child relationships) is significant in predicting criminal delinquency (Loeber and Farrington 1998, 2001). Thus, if families suffer adverse effects from our incarceration policies, we would expect these harmful effects to be felt in the next generation, as chil-dren grow up at greater risk of engaging in delinquent and criminal behavior. The insti-tution of marriage is another important link in the mechanism of informal social control. Marriage reduces the likelihood that ex-offenders will associate with peers involved in crime, and generally inhibits a return to crime (Laub, Nagin, and Sampson 1998). In fact, marriage is a stronger predictor of desistance from criminal activity than simple cohabi-tation, and a "quality" marriage—one based on a strong mutual commitment—is an even stronger predictor (Homey, Osgood, and Marshall 1995). Thus, criminal justice policies that weaken marriage and inhibit spousal commitments are likely to undermine the nat-ural processes of desistance, thereby causing more crime. In short, in developing crime policies, families matter. If our crime policies have harmful consequences for families, we risk undermining the role families can play in controlling criminal behavior.

This [reading] examines the impact of incarceration and reentry on families. We begin by viewing the antecedents to the creation of families—the relationships between young men and young women—in communities where the rates of arrest, removal, in-carceration, and reentry are particularly high. Then we discuss imprisonment's impact on relationships between an incarcerated parent and his or her children. Next we examine the effects of parental incarceration on the early childhood and adolescent development of children left behind. We then observe the family's role in reentry. We close with reflections on the impact of imprisonment on prisoners' family life, ways to mitigate incarceration's harmful effects, and ways to promote constructive connections between prisoners and their families.

THE "GENDER IMBALANCE"

To understand the magnitude of the criminal justice system's impact on the establishment of intimate partner relationships, we draw upon the work of Donald Braman (2002, 2004), an anthropologist who conducted a three-year ethnographic study of incarceration's impact on communities in Washington, D.C. In the District of Columbia, 7 percent of the adult African-American male population returns to the community from jail or prison each year. According to Braman's estimates, more than 75 percent of African-American men in the District of Columbia can expect to be incarcerated at some point during their lifetime. One consequence of these high rates of incarceration is what Braman calls a "gender imbalance," meaning simply that there are fewer men than women in the hardest hit communities. Half of the women in the nation's capital live in communities with low incarceration rates. In these communities, there are about 94 men for every 100 women. For the rest of the women in D.C.—whose neighborhoods have higher incarceration rates—the ratio is about 80 men for every 100 women. Furthermore, 10 percent of the District's women live in neighborhoods with the highest incarceration rates, where more than 12 percent of men are behind bars. In these neighborhoods, there are fewer than 62 men for every 100 women.

This gender imbalance translates into large numbers of fatherless families in communities with high rates of incarceration. In neighborhoods with a 2 percent male incarceration rate, Braman (2002) found that fathers were absent from more than one-half of the families. But in the communities with the highest male incarceration rates—about 12 percent—more than three-quarters of the families had a father absent. This phenomenon is not unique to Washington, D.C., however. In a national study, Sabol and Lynch (1998) also found larger numbers of female-headed families in counties receiving large numbers of returning prisoners.

Clearly, mass incarceration results in the substantial depletion in the sheer numbers of men in communities with high rates of imprisonment. For those men who are arrested, removed, and sent to prison, life in prison has profound and long-lasting consequences for their roles as intimate partners, spouses, and fathers. In the following sections, we will document those effects. Viewing this issue from a community perspective, however, reminds us that incarceration also alters the relationships between the men and women who are not incarcerated. In her research on the marriage patterns of low-income mothers, Edin (2000) found that the decision to marry (or remarry) depends, in part, on the economic prospects, social respectability, and reliability of potential husbands—attributes that are adversely affected by imprisonment. Low marriage rates, in turn, affect the life courses of men who have been imprisoned, reducing their likelihood of desistance from criminal activity. Thus, the communities with the highest rates of incarceration are caught in what Western, Lopoo, and McLanahan (2004, 21) call the "high-crime/low-marriage equilibrium." In these communities, women "will be understandably averse to marriage because their potential partners bring few social or economic benefits to the table. Men, who remain unmarried or unattached to stable households, are likely to continue their criminal involvement."

Braman quotes two of his community informants to illustrate these ripple effects of the gender imbalance. "David" described how the shortage of men affected dating patterns:

> Oh, yeah, everybody is aware of [the male shortage]. . . . And the fact that [men] know the ratio, and they feel that the ratio allows them to take advantage of just that statistic. 'Well, this woman I don't want to deal with, really because there are six to seven women to every man.' (2002,166)

The former wife of a prisoner commented that women were less discerning in their choices of partners because there were so few men:

> Women will settle for whatever it is that their man [wants], even though you know that man probably has about two or three women. Just to be wanted, or just to be held, or just to go out and have a date makes her feel good, so she's willing to accept. I think now women accept a lot of things—the fact that he might have another woman or the fact that they can't clearly get as much time as they want to. The person doesn't spend as much time as you would [like] him to spend. The little bit of time that you get you cherish. (2002, 167)

The reach of our incarceration policies thus extends deep into community life. Even those men and women who are never arrested pay a price. As they are looking for potential partners in marriage and parenting, they find that the simple rituals of dating are darkened by the long shadow of imprisonment.

THE IMPACT OF INCARCERATION ON PARENT-CHILD RELATIONSHIPS

The Family Profile of the Prisoner Population

Before turning to a closer examination of the effects of imprisonment on the relationships between incarcerated parents and their children, we should first describe the family circumstances of the nation's prisoners. In 1997, about half (47 percent) of state prisoners reported they had never been married. Only 23 percent reported they were married at the time of their incarceration, while 28 percent said they were divorced or separated (Figure 1). Yet most prisoners are parents. More than half (55 percent) of all state prisoners reported having at least one minor child. Because the overwhelming majority of state prisoners are men, incarcerated parents are predominantly male (93 percent). The number of incarcerated mothers, however, has grown dramatically in the past decade. Between 1991 and 2000, the number of incarcerated mothers increased by 87 percent, compared with a 60 percent increase in the number of incarcerated fathers. Of the men in state prison, 55 percent have children—a total of about 1.2 million—under

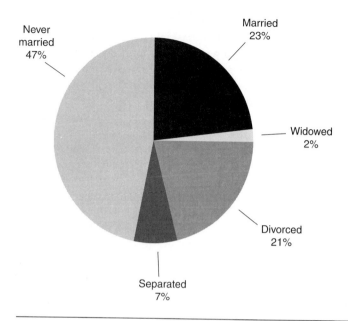

FIGURE 1   *Marital Status of Parents in State Prison, 1997*
Source: Mumola (2000).

the age of 18. About 65 percent of women in state prison are mothers to children younger than 18; their children number about 115,500 (Mumola 2000).

A mother's incarceration has a different impact on living arrangements than does that of a father. Close to two-thirds (64 percent) of mothers reported living with their children before incarceration, compared with slightly less than half (44 percent) of fathers in 1997. Therefore, as the percentage of women in prison increases, more children experience a more substantial disruption. We should not conclude, however, that the imprisonment of a nonresident father has little impact on his children. Research has shown that nonresident fathers can make considerable contributions to the development and well-being of their children (Amato and Rivera 1999; Furstenberg 1993). They contribute to their children's financial support, care, and social support even when they are not living in the children's home (Edin and Lein 1997; Hairston 1998; Western and McLanahan 2000). Therefore, a depiction of families' living arrangements only begins to describe the nature of the parenting roles played by fathers before they were sent to prison.

The national data on incarcerated parents also fail to capture the diversity of parent-child relationships. According to research conducted by Denise Johnston (2001) at the Center for Children of Incarcerated Parents, it is not uncommon for both incarcerated fathers and mothers to have children by more than one partner. Furthermore, these parents may have lived with some but not all of their children prior to their incarceration. This perspective leads to another conclusion: Individuals who are incarcerated may also have served as parent figures to children not their own—as stepparents or surrogate parents in families that blend children into one household.

We know little about the nature of these parent-child relationships. As was noted above, even absent fathers can provide emotional and financial support prior to their incarceration. However, the profiles of incarcerated parents also point to indicia of stress and dysfunction within these families. More than three-quarters of parents in state prison reported a prior conviction and, of those, more than half had been previously incarcerated. During the time leading up to their most current arrest and incarceration, nearly half were out of prison on some type of conditional release, such as probation or parole, in 1997. Nearly half (46 percent) of incarcerated fathers were imprisoned for a violent crime, as were one-quarter (26 percent) of the mothers. Mothers in prison were much more likely than fathers to be serving time for drug offenses (35 percent versus 23 percent). Nearly one-third of the mothers reported committing their crime to get either drugs or money for drugs, compared with 19 percent of fathers. More than half of all parents in prison reported using drugs in the month before they were arrested, and more than a third were under the influence of alcohol when they committed the crime. Nearly a quarter of incarcerated mothers (23 percent) and about a tenth (13 percent) of incarcerated fathers reported a history of mental illness (Mumola 2000). Clearly, these individuals were struggling with multiple stressors that, at a minimum, complicated their role as parents.

The portrait of prisoners' extended family networks is also sobering. According to findings from the Urban Institute's *Returning Home* (Visher, La Vigne, and Travis 2004) study in Maryland, these networks exhibit high rates of criminal involvement, substance abuse, and family violence (La Vigne, Kachnowski, et al. 2003). In interviews conducted with a sample of men and women just prior to their release from prison and return to homes in Baltimore, the Institute's researchers found that about 40 percent of the prisoners reported having at least one relative currently serving a prison sentence. Nine percent of the women said they had been threatened, harassed, or physically hurt by their husband, and 65 percent of those who reported domestic violence also reported being victimized by a nonspouse intimate partner. No male respondents reported this kind of abuse. The women reported that, other than their partners, the highest level of abuse came from other women in their families—their mothers, stepmothers, or aunts. Nearly two-thirds of inmates (62 percent) reported at least one family member with a substance abuse or alcohol problem and more than 16 percent listed four or more family members with histories of substance abuse. These characteristics highlight the high levels of risks and challenges in the families prisoners leave behind.

The Strain of Incarceration on Families

We turn next to a discussion of the impact of parental incarceration on the families left behind. One obvious consequence is that the families have fewer financial resources. According to the Bureau of Justice Statistics, in 1997 most parents in state prison (71 percent) reported either full-time or part-time employment in the month preceding their current arrest (Mumola 2002). Wages or salary was the most common source of income among incarcerated fathers before imprisonment, 60 percent of whom reported having a full-time job. Mothers, on the other hand, were less likely to have a full-time job (39 percent). For them, the most common sources of income were wages (44 percent) or public assistance (42 percent). Very few mothers reported receiving formal child support payments (6 percent) (Mumola 2000). During incarceration, the flow of financial support from the incarcerated parent's job stops, leaving the family to either make do with less or make up the difference, thereby placing added strains on the new caregivers. Eligibility for welfare payments under the TANF (Temporary Assistance for Needy Families) program ceases as soon as an individual is no longer a custodial parent—i.e., upon incarceration. In some cases, a caregiver may continue to receive TANF payments when the incarcerated parent loses eligibility, but because these benefits are now "child-only," they are lower than full TANF benefits. Food stamps are also unavailable to incarcerated individuals.

New caregivers often struggle to make ends meet during the period of parental incarceration. Bloom and Steinhart (1993) found that in 1992 nearly half (44 percent) of families caring for the children of an incarcerated parent were receiving welfare payments under TANF's predecessor program, AFDC (Aid to Families with Dependent Children). Under the recent welfare reform laws, however, TANF support is more limited than in the past, as lifetime eligibility has been capped at 60 months, work requirements have been implemented, and restrictions have been placed on TANF funds for those who have violated probation or parole, or have been convicted of certain drug crimes (Phillips and Bloom 1998). Even under the old AFDC program, most caregivers reported that they did not have sufficient resources to meet basic needs (Bloom and Steinhart 1993). Moreover, these economic strains affect more than the family's budget. According to several studies, financial stress can produce negative consequences for caretakers' behavior, including harsh and inconsistent parenting patterns, which, in turn, cause emotional and behavioral problems for the children (McLoyd 1998).

Other adjustments are required as well. Because most prisoners are men, and 55 percent of them are fathers, the first wave of impact is felt by the mothers of their children. Some mothers struggle to maintain contact with the absent father, on behalf of their children as well as themselves. Others decide that the incarceration of their children's father is a turning point, enabling them to start a new life and cut off ties with the father. More fundamentally, Furstenberg (1995) found that a partner left behind often becomes more independent and self-sufficient during the period of incarceration, changes that may ultimately benefit the family unit or lead to the dissolution of the relationship. At a minimum, however, these changes augur a significant adjustment in roles when the incarcerated partner eventually returns home.

In some cases, the incarceration period can have another, longer-lasting effect on the legal relationships between parents and children. In 1997, Congress enacted the Adoption and Safe Families Act (ASFA) to improve the safety and well-being of children in the foster care system as well as to remove barriers to the permanent placement, particularly adoption, of these children.[2] The ASFA stipulates that "permanency" decisions (determinations about a child's ultimate placement) should be made within 12 months of the initial removal of the child from the home. With limited exceptions, foster care placements can last no longer than 15 months, and if a child has been in foster care for 15 out of the previous 22 months, petitions must be filed in court to terminate parental rights. At least half the states now include incarceration as a reason to terminate parental rights (Genty 2001).

This new legislation has far-reaching consequences for the children of incarcerated parents. According to BJS, 10 percent of mothers in prison, and 2 percent of fathers, have at least one child in foster care (Mumola 2000). Because the average length of time served for prisoners released in 1997 was 28 months (Sabol and Lynch 2001), the short time-lines set forth in ASFA establish a legal predicate that could lead to increases in the termination of parental rights for parents in prison (Lynch and Sabol 2001). Philip Genty (2001), a professor at Columbia University Law School, made some rough calculations of ASFA's impact. Looking only at reported cases discoverable through a Lexis search, he found, in the five years following ASFA's enactment, a 250 percent increase in cases terminating parental rights due to parental incarceration, from 260 to 909 cases.

In addition to those legal burdens placed on incarcerated parents, the new family caregivers face challenges in forging relationships with the children left behind. Some of these new caregivers may not have had much contact with the children before the parent's incarceration, so they must establish themselves as de facto parents and develop relationships with the children. Contributing to the trauma of this changing family structure, prisoners' children are sometimes separated from their siblings during incarceration because the new network of caregivers cannot care for the entire sibling group (Hairston 1995).

In short, when the prison gates close and parents are separated from their children, the network of care undergoes a profound realignment. Even two-parent families experience the strain of lost income, feel the remaining parent's sudden sole responsibility for the children and the household, and suffer the stigma associated with imprisonment. However, prisoners' family structures rarely conform to the two-parent model and are more often characterized by nonresident fathers, children living with different parents, and female-headed households. In these circumstances, the ripple effects of a mother or father going to prison reach much farther, and grandparents, aunts and uncles, and the foster care system must step into the breach. In addition, these extended networks feel the financial, emotional, and familial weight of their new responsibilities.

Incarceration has yet one more effect on the structure of prisoners' families. One of the important functions that families perform is to create assets that are passed along to the next generation. These assets are sometimes quite tangible: Money is saved, real estate appreciates in value, and businesses are built. These tangible assets can typically be transferred to one's children. Sometimes the assets are intangible: Social status is achieved, professional networks are cultivated, and educational milestones are reached. These intangible assets can also translate into economic advantage by opening doors for the next generation. Braman asks whether the minimal intergenerational transfer of wealth in black families is related to the high rates of incarceration among black men. Taking a historical view, he concludes:

> The disproportionate incarceration of black men . . . helps to explain why black families are less able to save money and why each successive generation inherits less wealth than their white counterparts. Incarceration acts like a hidden tax, one that is visited disproportionately on poor and minority families; and while its costs are most directly felt by the adults closest to the incarcerated family member, the full effect is eventually felt by the next generation as well. (2004, 156)

The ripple effects of incarceration on the family are far-reaching. The gender imbalance disturbs the development of intimate relationships that might support healthy families. Families' financial resources and relationship capabilities are strained at the same time they are scrambling for more assets to support their incarcerated loved one. Yet, despite the hardships of incarceration, families can play an important role in improving outcomes for prisoners and prisoners' children. Several studies have shown that the "quality of care children receive following separation and their ongoing relationships with parents" are "instrumental forces in shaping outcomes for children" (Hairston 1999, 205). According to one study (Sack 1977), the behavioral problems displayed by children of incarcerated fathers diminished once the children got to spend time with their fathers.

On the other hand, in a small percentage of cases, continued parental involvement may not be in the child's best interests. For example, BJS (Greenfeld et al. 1998) reports that 7 percent of prisoners convicted of violent crimes were convicted of intimate partner violence. Even more disturbing are those cases involving child abuse and neglect, where the child's best interests argue against parental involvement. According to BJS, among inmates who were in prison for a sex crime against a child, the child was the prisoner's own child or stepchild in a third of the cases (Langan, Schmitt, and Durose 2003). Yet there has been very little research on the nexus between this form of family violence, incarceration, and reentry.

Discussion of prisoners convicted of violence within the family only raises larger questions—questions not answered by current research—about whether some parent-child relationships are so troubled and so characterized by the patterns of parental substance abuse, criminal involvement, mental illness, and the intrusions of criminal justice supervision that parental removal is a net benefit for the child. It is undoubtedly true that removing a parent involved in certain types of child abuse is better for the child. But we know little about the critical characteristics of the preprison relationships between children and their incarcerated parents, especially as to what kind of parents they were, and how their removal affects their children.

Even without a deeper understanding of the parenting roles played by America's prisoners, we still must face several incontrovertible, troubling facts. First, expanding the use of prison to respond to crime has put more parents in prison. Between 1991 and 1999, a short eight-year period, the number of parents in state and federal prisons increased by 60 percent, from 452,500 to 721,500 (Mumola 2000). By the end of 2002, 3.7 million parents were under some form of correctional supervision (Mumola 2004). Second, many children are left behind when parents are incarcerated. By 1999, *2* percent of all minor children in the United States—about 1.5 million—had a parent in state or federal prison. (If we include parents who are in jail, on probation or parole, or recently released from prison, the estimate of children with a parent involved in the criminal justice system reaches 7 million, or nearly 10 percent of all minor children in America [Mumola 2000].) Third, the racial disparities in America's prison population translate into substantial, disturbing racial inequities in the population of children affected by our current levels of imprisonment. About 7 percent of all African-American minor children and nearly 3 percent of all Hispanic minor children in America have a parent in prison. In comparison, barely 1 percent of all Caucasian minor children have a parent in prison (Mumola 2000). Finally, most of the children left behind are quite young. Sixty percent are under age 10, while the average child left behind is 8 years old.

In this era of mass incarceration, our criminal justice system casts a wide net that has altered the lives of millions of children, disrupting their relationships with their parents, altering the networks of familial support, and placing new burdens on such governmental services as schools, foster care, adoption agencies, and youth-serving organizations. As Phillips and Bloom succinctly concluded, "by getting tough on crime, the United States has gotten tough on children" (1998, 539). These costs are rarely included in our calculations of the costs of justice.

Parent-Child Relationships during Imprisonment

When a parent is arrested and later incarcerated, the child's world undergoes significant, sometimes traumatic, disruption. Most children are not present at the time of their parent's arrest, and arrested parents typically do not tell the police that they have minor children (ABA 1993). Family members are often reluctant to tell the children that their parent has been incarcerated because of social stigma (Braman 2003). Therefore, the immediate impact of an arrest can be quite traumatizing—a child is abruptly separated from his or her parent, with little information about what happened, why it happened, or what to expect.

The arrest and subsequent imprisonment of a parent frequently results in a significant realignment of the family's arrangements for caring for the child, depicted in Figure 2. Not surprisingly, the nature of the new living arrangements depends heavily on which parent is sent to prison. Recall that about two-thirds of incarcerated mothers in state prison lived with their children before they were imprisoned. Following the mother's incarceration, about a quarter (28 percent) of their children remain with their fathers. Most children of incarcerated mothers, however, are cared for by an extended family that is suddenly responsible for another mouth to feed and child to raise. More than half of these children (53 percent) will live with a grandparent, adding burdens to a generation that supposedly has already completed its child-rearing responsibilities. Another quarter of these children (26 percent) will live with another relative, placing new duties on the extended family. Some children have no familial safety net: almost 10 percent of incarcerated mothers reported that their child was placed in foster care (Mumola 2000).[3]

The story for incarcerated fathers is quite different. Less than half (44 percent) lived with their children before prison; once they are sent to prison, most of their children (85 percent) will live with the children's mother. Grandparents (16 percent) and other relatives (6 percent) play a much smaller role in assuming child care responsibilities when a father is incarcerated. Only 2 percent of the children of incarcerated men enter the foster care system. In sum, a child whose father is sent to prison is significantly less likely to experience a life disruption, such as moving in with another family member or placement in a foster home.

The nation's foster care system has become a child care system of last resort for many children with parents in prison. Research by the Center for Children of Incarcerated Parents (Johnston 1999) found that, at any given time, 10 percent of children in foster care currently have a mother—and 33 percent have a father—behind bars. Even more striking, 70 percent of foster children have had a parent incarcerated at one time or another during their time in foster care.

When a parent goes to prison, the separation between parent and child is experienced at many levels. First, there is the simple fact of distance. The majority of state prisoners (62 percent) are held in facilities located more than 100 miles from their homes

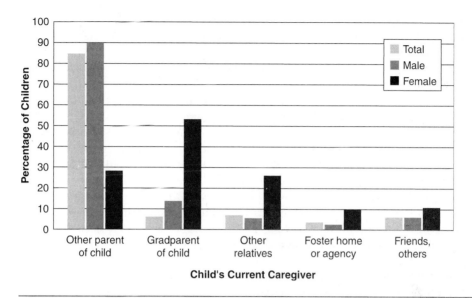

FIGURE 2 *Living Arrangements of Minor Children of State Inmates prior to Incarceration*
Figures do not total 100 percent because some prisoners had children living with multiple caregivers.
Source: Mumola (2000).

(Mumola 2000). Because prison facilities for women are scarce, mothers are incarcerated an average of 160 miles away from their children (Hagan and Coleman 2001). The distance between prisoners and their families is most pronounced for District of Columbia residents. As a result of the federal takeover of the District's prison system, defendants sentenced to serve felony time are now housed in facilities that are part of the far-flung network of federal prisons. In 2000, 12 percent of the District's inmates were held in federal prisons more than 500 miles from Washington. By 2002, that proportion had risen to 30 percent. Nineteen percent are in prisons as far away as Texas and California (Santana 2003). Not surprisingly, in an analysis of BJS data, Hairston and Rollin (2003, 68) found a relationship between this distance and family visits: "The distance prisoners were from their homes influenced the extent to which they saw families and friends. The farther prisoners were from their homes, the higher the percentage of prisoners who had no visitors in the month preceding the survey. . . . Those whose homes were closest to the prison had the most visits."

Geographic distance inhibits families from making visits and, for those who make the effort, imposes an additional financial burden on already strained family budgets. Donald Braman tells the story of Lilly, a District resident whose son Anthony is incarcerated in Ohio (Braman 2002). When Anthony was held in Lorton, a prison in Virginia that formerly housed prisoners from the District, she visited him once a week. Since the federal takeover, she manages to make only monthly visits, bringing her daughter, Anthony's sister. For each two-day trip, she spends between $150 and $200 for car rental, food, and a motel. Added to these costs are her money orders to supplement his inmate account and the care packages that she is allowed to send twice a year. She also pays about $100 a month for the collect calls he places. She lives on a fixed income of $530 a month.

Given these realities, the extent of parent-child contact during incarceration is noteworthy. Mothers in prison stay in closer contact with their children than do fathers. According to BJS, nearly 80 percent of mothers have monthly contact and 60 percent have at least weekly contact. Roughly 60 percent of fathers, by contrast, have monthly contact, and 40 percent have weekly contact with their children (Mumola 2000). These contacts take the form of letters, phone calls, and prison visits. Yet, a large percentage of prisoners serve their entire prison sentence without ever seeing their children. More than half of all mothers, and 57 percent of all fathers, never receive a personal visit from their children while in prison.

Particularly disturbing is Lynch and Sabol's finding (2001) that the frequency of contact decreases as prison terms get longer. Between 1991 and 1997, as the length of prison sentences increased, the level of contact of all kinds—calls, letters, and visits—decreased (Figure 3). This is especially troubling in light of research showing that the average length of prison sentences is increasing in America, reflecting more stringent sentencing policies. Thus, prisoners coming home in the future are likely to have had fewer interactions with their children, a situation that further weakens family ties and makes family reunification even more difficult.

In addition to the significant burden imposed by the great distances between prisoners and their families, corrections policies often hamper efforts to maintain family ties across the prison walls. The Women's Prison Association (1996) has identified several obstacles to constructive family contacts, some of which could easy be solved. The association found that it is difficult to get simple information on visiting procedures, and correctional administrators provide little help in making visiting arrangements. The visiting procedures themselves are often uncomfortable or humiliating. Furthermore, little attention is paid to mitigating the impact on the children of visiting a parent in prison.

Elizabeth Gaynes, director of the Osborne Association in New York City, tells a story that captures the emotional and psychological impact of a particular correctional policy upon a young girl who had come to visit her father. Because inmates were not allowed to handle money, the prison had drawn a yellow line three feet in front of the soda vending machines. Only visitors could cross that line. The father could not perform the simple act of getting his daughter a soda. If he wanted one, he had to ask his daughter to get it. According to Ms. Gaynes, this interaction represented an unnecessary and damaging role transformation; the child had become the provider, the parent had become the child.[4]

Family Contact during Imprisonment: Obstacles and Opportunities

For a number of reasons, it is difficult to maintain parent-child contact during a period of incarceration. For one thing, many prisons narrowly define the family members who are granted visiting privileges. The State of Michigan's corrections department, for example, promulgated regulations in 1995 restricting the categories of individuals who are

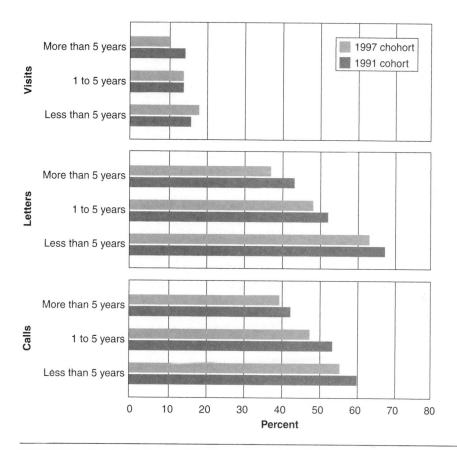

FIGURE 3 *Level of Prisoners' Weekly Contact with Children, by Method and Length of Stay, 1991 and 1997*

Prisoners to be released in the next 12 months.

Source: Lynch and Sabol (2001).

allowed to visit a prisoner. The approved visiting list may include minor children under the age of 18, but only if they are the prisoner's children, stepchildren, grandchildren, or siblings. Prisoners who are neither the biological parents nor legal stepparents of the children they were raising do not have this privilege. Finally, a child authorized to visit must be accompanied by either an adult who is an immediate family member of the child or of the inmate, or who is the child's legal guardians.[5] Many prisoners' extended family networks, including girlfriends and boyfriends who are raising prisoners' children, are not recognized in these narrow definitions of "family." Limitations on visiting privileges are commonly justified on security or management grounds, but fail to recognize the complexity of the prisoner's familial networks. Rather than allowing the prisoner to define the "family" relationships that matter most, the arbitrary distinctions of biology or legal status are superimposed on the reality of familial networks, limiting meaningful contact that could make a difference to both prisoner and child.

Telephone contact is also burdened by prison regulations and by controversial relationships between phone companies and corrections departments. Prisoners are typically limited in the number of calls they can make. Their calls can also be monitored. The California Department of Corrections interrupts each call every 20 seconds with a recorded message: "This is a call from a California prison inmate." Most prisons allow prisoners to make only collect calls, and those calls typically cost between $1 and $3 per minute, even though most phone companies now charge less than 10 cents per minute for phone calls in the free society (Petersilia 2003). Telephone companies also charge between $1.50 and $4 just to place the collect call, while a fee is not charged for collect calls outside of prison.

The high price of collect calls reflects sweetheart arrangements between the phone companies and corrections agencies, under which the prisons receive kickbacks for every collect call, about 40 to 60 cents of every dollar. This arrangement translates into a substantial revenue source for corrections budgets. In 2001, for example, California garnered $35 million, based on $85 million of total revenue generated from prison calls. Some states require, by statute or policy, that these revenues pay for programs for inmates. Most states simply deposit this money into the general budget for their department of corrections.

Yet who bears these additional costs for maintaining phone contact with prisoners? The families of prisoners do, of course. In a study conducted by the Florida House of Representatives Corrections Committee (1998), family members reported spending an average amount of $69.19 per month accepting collect phone calls. According to this report, "Several family members surveyed stated that, although they wanted to continue to maintain contact with the inmate, they were forced to remove their names from the inmate's approved calling list because they simply could not afford to accept the calls" (1998, 23).

This monopolistic arrangement between phone companies and prisons makes families the unwitting funders of the prisons holding their loved ones. In essence, the states have off-loaded upwards of hundreds of millions of dollars of prison costs on to prisoners' families. Subsequently, families are placed in the unacceptable position of either agreeing to accept the calls, thereby making contributions to prison budgets, or ceasing phone contact with their loved ones. Of course, there are other, deeper costs attached to this practice. If a family chooses to limit (or stop) these phone calls, then family ties are weakened and the support system that could sustain the prisoner's reintegration is damaged. If the family chooses to pay the phone charges, then those financial resources are not available for other purposes, thereby adding to the strain the household experiences. In recent years, efforts to reform prison telephone policies have been successful in several states.[7] Yet, while these reform efforts are under way, tens of thousands of families are setting aside large portions of their budgets to pay inflated phone bills to stay in touch with their imprisoned family members.

Fortunately, a number of communities have implemented programs designed to overcome the barriers of distance, cost, and correctional practices that reduce contact between prisoners and their families. For example, Hope House, an organization in Washington, D.C., that connects incarcerated fathers with their children in the District, hosts summer camps at federal prisons in North Carolina and Maryland where children spend several hours a day for a week visiting with their fathers in prison. Hope House has also created a teleconference hookup with federal prisons in North Carolina, Ohio, and New Mexico so that children can go to a neighborhood site to talk to their fathers in prison. In another instance, a Florida program called "Reading and Family Ties—Face to Face" also uses technology to overcome distance. Incarcerated mothers and their children transmit live video recordings via the Internet. These sessions occur each week, last an hour, and are available at no cost to the families. In addition, the U.S. Department of Justice in 1992 initiated the Girl Scouts Beyond Bars program, the first mother-daughter visitation program of its kind. Twice a month, more than 500 girls across the country, much like other girls their age, participate in Girl Scout programs, but in this program these Girl Scouts meet their mothers in prison. Finally, in Washington State, the McNeil Island Correction Center has launched a program that teaches incarcerated fathers the skills of active and involved parenting, encourages them to provide financial support for their children, and facilitates events to bring prisoners together with their families.

These programs—and many others like them—demonstrate that, with a little creativity and a fair amount of commitment, corrections agencies can find ways to foster ongoing, constructive relationships between incarcerated parents and their children. It seems particularly appropriate, in an era when technology has overcome geographical boundaries, to harness the Internet to bridge the divide between prisons and families. Yet the precondition for undertaking such initiatives is the recognition that corrections agencies must acknowledge responsibility for maintaining their prisoners' familial relationships. If these agencies embraced this challenge for all inmates—and were held accountable to the public and elected officials for the results of these efforts—the quality of family life for prisoners and their extended family networks would be demonstrably improved.

Editors' Note: *Notes and references for this reading can be found in the original source.*

■READING 37

Unmarried with Children

Kathryn Edin and Maria Kefalas

Jen Burke, a white tenth-grade dropout who is 17 years old, lives with her stepmother, her sister, and her 16-month-old son in a cramped but tidy row home in Philadelphia's beleaguered Kensington neighborhood. She is broke, on welfare, and struggling to complete her GED. Wouldn't she and her son have been better off if she had finished high school, found a job, and married her son's father first?

In 1950, when Jen's grandmother came of age, only 1 in 20 American children was born to an unmarried mother. Today, that rate is 1 in 3—and they are usually born to those least likely to be able to support a child on their own. In our book, *Promises I Can*

Keep: Why Poor Women Put Motherhood Before Marriage, we discuss the lives of 162 white, African American, and Puerto Rican low-income single mothers living in eight destitute neighborhoods across Philadelphia and its poorest industrial suburb, Camden. We spent five years chatting over kitchen tables and on front stoops, giving mothers like Jen the opportunity to speak to the question so many affluent Americans ask about them: Why do they have children while still young and unmarried when they will face such an uphill struggle to support them?

ROMANCE AT LIGHTNING SPEED

Jen started having sex with her 20-year-old boyfriend Rick just before her 15th birthday. A month and a half later, she was pregnant. "I didn't want to get pregnant," she claims. "He wanted me to get pregnant." "As soon as he met me, he wanted to have a kid with me," she explains. Though Jen's college-bound suburban peers would be appalled by such a declaration, on the streets of Jen's neighborhood, it is something of a badge of honor. "All those other girls he was with, he didn't want to have a baby with any of them," Jen boasts. "I asked him, 'Why did you choose me to have a kid when you could have a kid with any one of them?' He was like, 'I want to have a kid with you.'" Looking back, Jen says she now believes that the reason "he wanted me to have a kid that early is so that I didn't leave him."

In inner-city neighborhoods like Kensington, where child-bearing within marriage has become rare, romantic relationships like Jen and Rick's proceed at lightning speed. A young man's avowal, "I want to have a baby by you," is often part of the courtship ritual from the beginning. This is more than idle talk, as their first child is typically conceived within a year from the time a couple begins "kicking it." Yet while poor couples' pillow talk often revolves around dreams of shared children, the news of a pregnancy—the first indelible sign of the huge changes to come—puts these still-new relationships into overdrive. Suddenly, the would-be mother begins to scrutinize her mate as never before, wondering whether he can "get himself together"—find a job, settle down, and become a family man—in time. Jen began pestering Rick to get a real job instead of picking up day-labor jobs at nearby construction sites. She also wanted him to stop hanging out with his ne'er-do-well friends, who had been getting him into serious trouble for more than a decade. Most of all, she wanted Rick to shed what she calls his "kiddie mentality"—his habit of spending money on alcohol and drugs rather than recognizing his growing financial obligations at home.

Rick did not try to deny paternity, as many would-be fathers do. Nor did he abandon or mistreat Jen, at least intentionally. But Rick, who had been in and out of juvenile detention since he was 8 years old for everything from stealing cars to selling drugs, proved unable to stay away from his unsavory friends. At the beginning of her seventh month of pregnancy, an escapade that began as a drunken lark landed Rick in jail on a carjacking charge. Jen moved back home with her stepmother, applied for welfare, and spent the last two-and-a-half months of her pregnancy without Rick.

Rick sent penitent letters from jail. "I thought he changed by the letters he wrote me. I thought he changed a lot," she says. "He used to tell me that he loved me when he was in jail. . . . It was always gonna be me and the baby when he got out." Thus, when Rick's alleged victim failed to appear to testify and he was released just days before Colin's birth, the couple's reunion was a happy one. Often, the magic moment of childbirth calms the troubled waters of such relationships. New parents typically make amends and resolve to stay together for the sake of their child. When surveyed just after a child's birth, eight in ten unmarried parents say they are still together, and most plan to stay together and raise the child.

Promoting marriage among the poor has become the new war on poverty, Bush style. And it is true that the correlation between marital status and child poverty is strong. But poor single mothers already believe in marriage. Jen insists that she will walk down the aisle one day, though she admits it might not be with Rick. And demographers still project that more than seven in ten women who had a child outside of marriage will eventually wed someone. First, though, Jen wants to get a good job, finish school, and get her son out of Kensington.

Most poor, unmarried mothers and fathers readily admit that bearing children while poor and unmarried is not the ideal way to do things. Jen believes the best time to become a mother is "after you're out of school and you got a job, at least, when you're like 21. . . .When you're ready to have kids, you should have everything ready, have your house, have a job, so when that baby comes, the baby can have its own room." Yet given their already limited economic prospects, the poor have little motivation to time their births as precisely as their middle-class counterparts do. The dreams of young people like Jen and Rick center on children at a time of life when their more affluent peers plan for college and careers. Poor girls coming of age in the inner city value children highly, anticipate them eagerly, and believe strongly that they are up to the job of mothering—even in difficult circumstances. Jen, for example, tells us, "People outside the neighborhood, they're like, 'You're 15! You're pregnant?' I'm like, it's not none of their business. I'm gonna be able to take care of my kid. They have nothing to worry about." Jen says she has concluded that "some people . . . are better at having kids at a younger age. . . . I think it's better for some people to have kids younger."

WHEN I BECAME A MOM

When we asked mothers like Jen what their lives would be like if they had not had children, we expected them to express regret over foregone opportunities for school and careers. Instead, most believe their children "saved" them. They describe their lives as spinning out of control before becoming pregnant—struggles with parents and peers, "wild," risky behavior, depression, and school failure. Jen speaks to this poignantly. "I was just real bad. I hung with a real bad crowd. I was doing pills. I was really depressed. . . . I was drinking. That was before I was pregnant." "I think," she reflects, "if I never had a baby or anything, . . . I would still be doing the things I was doing. I would probably still be doing drugs. I'd probably still be drinking." Jen admits that when she first became pregnant, she was angry that she "couldn't be out no more. Couldn't be out with my friends. Couldn't do nothing." Now, though, she says, "I'm glad I have a son . . . because I would still be doing all that stuff."

Children offer poor youth like Jen a compelling sense of purpose. Jen paints a before-and-after picture of her life that was common among the mothers we interviewed. "Before, I didn't have nobody to take care of. I didn't have nothing left to go home for . . . Now I have my son to take care of. I have him to go home for. . . . I don't have to go buy weed or drugs with my money. I could buy my son stuff with my money! . . . I have something to look up to now." Children also are a crucial source of relational intimacy, a self-made community of care. After a nasty fight with Rick, Jen recalls, "I was crying. My son came in the room. He was hugging me. He's 16 months and he was hugging me with his little arms. He was really cute and happy, so I got happy. That's one of the good things. When you're sad, the baby's always gonna be there for you no matter what." Lately she has been thinking a lot about what her life was like back then, before the baby. "I thought about the stuff before I became a mom, what my life was like back then. I used to see pictures of me, and I would hide in every picture. This baby did so much for me. My son did a lot for me. He helped me a lot. I'm thankful that I had my baby."

Around the time of the birth, most unmarried parents claim they plan to get married eventually. Rick did not propose marriage when Jen's first child was born, but when she conceived a second time, at 17, Rick informed his dad, "It's time for me to get married. It's time for me to straighten up. This is the one I wanna be with. I had a baby with her, I'm gonna have another baby with her." Yet despite their intentions, few of these couples actually marry. Indeed, most break up well before their child enters preschool.

I'D LIKE TO GET MARRIED, BUT . . .

The sharp decline in marriage in impoverished urban areas has led some to charge that the poor have abandoned the marriage norm. Yet we found few who had given up on the idea of marriage. But like their elite counterparts, disadvantaged women set a high financial bar for marriage. For the poor, marriage has become an elusive goal—one they feel ought to be reserved for those who can support a "white picket fence" lifestyle: a mortgage on a modest row home, a car and some furniture, some savings in the bank, and enough money left over to pay for a "decent" wedding. Jen's views on marriage provide a perfect case in point. "If I was gonna get married, I would want to be married like my Aunt Nancy and my Uncle Pat. They live in the mountains. She has a job. My Uncle Pat is a state trooper; he has lots of money. They live in the [Poconos]. It's real nice out there. Her kids go to Catholic school. . . .That's the kind of life I would want to have. If I get married, I would have a life like [theirs]." She adds, "And I would wanna have a big wedding, a real nice wedding."

Unlike the women of their mothers' and grandmothers' generations, young women like Jen are not merely content to rely on a man's earnings. Instead, they insist on being economically "set" in their own right before taking marriage vows. This is partly because they want a partnership of equals and they believe money buys say-so in a relationship. Jen explains, "I'm not gonna just get into marrying him and not have my own house! Not have a job! I still wanna do a lot of things before I get married. He [already] tells me I can't do nothing. I can't go out. What's gonna happen when I marry him? He's gonna say he owns me!"

Economic independence is also insurance against a marriage gone bad. Jen explains, "I want to have everything ready, in case something goes wrong. . . . If we got a divorce, that would be my house. I bought that house, he can't kick me out or he can't take my kids from me." "That's what I want in case that ever happens. I know a lot of people that happened to. I don't want it to happen to me." These statements reveal that despite her desire to marry, Rick's role in the family's future is provisional at best. "We get along, but we fight a lot. If he's there, he's there, but if he's not, that's why I want a job . . . a job with computers . . . so I could afford my kids, could afford the house. . . . I don't want to be living off him. I want my kids to be living off me."

Why is Jen, who describes Rick as "the love of my life," so insistent on planning an exit strategy before she is willing to take the vows she firmly believes ought to last "forever?" If love is so sure, why does mistrust seem so palpable and strong? In relationships among poor couples like Jen and Rick, mistrust is often spawned by chronic violence and infidelity, drug and alcohol abuse, criminal activity, and the threat of imprisonment. In these tarnished corners of urban America, the stigma of a failed marriage is far worse than an out-of-wedlock birth. New mothers like Jen feel they must test the relationship over three, four, even five years' time. This is the only way, they believe, to insure that their marriages will last.

Trust has been an enormous issue in Jen's relationship with Rick. "My son was born December 23rd, and [Rick] started cheating on me again . . . in March. He started cheating on me with some girl—Amanda. . . . Then it was another girl, another girl, another girl after. I didn't wanna believe it. My friends would come up to me and be like, 'Oh yeah, your boyfriend's cheating on you with this person.' I wouldn't believe it. . . . I would see him with them. He used to have hickies. He used to make up some excuse that he was drunk—that was always his excuse for everything." Things finally came to a head when Rick got another girl pregnant. "For a while, I forgave him for everything. Now, I don't forgive him for nothing." Now we begin to understand the source of Jen's hesitancy. "He wants me to marry him, [but] I'm not really sure. . . . If I can't trust him, I can't marry him, 'cause we would get a divorce. If you're gonna get married, you're supposed to be faithful!" she insists. To Jen and her peers, the worst thing that could happen is "to get married just to get divorced."

Given the economic challenges and often perilously low quality of the romantic relationships among unmarried parents, poor women may be right to be cautious about marriage. Five years after we first spoke with her, we met with Jen again. We learned that Jen's second pregnancy ended in a miscarriage. We also learned that Rick was out of the picture—apparently for good. "You know that bar [down the street?] It happened in that bar. . . . They were in the bar, and this guy was like bad-mouthing [Rick's friend] Mikey, talking stuff to him or whatever. So Rick had to go get involved in it and start with this guy. . . . Then he goes outside and fights the guy [and] the guy dies of head trauma. They were all on drugs, they were all drinking, and things just got out of control, and that's what happened. He got fourteen to thirty years."

THESE ARE CARDS I DEALT MYSELF

Jen stuck with Rick for the first two and a half years of his prison sentence, but when another girl's name replaced her own on the visitors' list, Jen decided she was finished with him once and for all. Readers might be asking what Jen ever saw in a man like Rick. But Jen and Rick operate in a partner market where the better-off men go to the better-off women. The only way for someone like Jen to forge a satisfying relationship with a man is to find a diamond in the rough or improve her own economic position so that she can realistically compete for more upwardly mobile partners, which is what Jen is trying to do now. "There's this kid, Donny, he works at my job. He works on C shift. He's a supervisor! He's funny, three years older, and he's not a geek or anything, but he's not a real preppy good boy either. But he's not [a player like Rick] and them. He has a job, you know, so that's good. He doesn't do drugs or anything. And he asked my dad if he could take me out!"

These days, there is a new air of determination, even pride, about Jen. The aimless high school dropout pulls ten-hour shifts entering data at a warehouse distribution center Monday through Thursday. She has held the job for three years, and her aptitude and hard work have earned her a series of raises. Her current salary is higher than anyone in her household commands—$10.25 per hour, and she now gets two weeks of paid vacation, four personal days, 60 hours of sick time, and medical benefits. She has saved up the necessary $400 in tuition for a high school completion program that offers evening and weekend classes. Now all that stands between her and a diploma is a passing grade in mathematics, her least favorite subject. "My plan is to start college in January. [This month] I take my math test . . . so I can get my diploma," she confides.

Jen clearly sees how her life has improved since Rick's dramatic exit from the scene. "That's when I really started [to get better] because I didn't have to worry about what he was doing, didn't have to worry about him cheating on me, all this stuff. [It was] then I realized that I had to do what I had to do to take care of my son. . . .When he was there, I think that my whole life revolved around him, you know, so I always messed up somehow because I was so busy worrying about what he was doing. Like I would leave the [GED] programs I was in just to go home and see what he was doing. My mind was never concentrating." Now, she says, "a lot of people in my family look up to me now, because all my sisters dropped out from school, you know, nobody went back to school. I went back to school, you know? . . . I went back to school, and I plan to go to college, and a lot of people look up to me for that, you know? So that makes me happy . . . because five years ago nobody looked up to me. I was just like everybody else."

Yet the journey has not been easy. "Being a young mom, being 15, it's hard, hard, hard, you know." She says, "I have no life. . . . I work from 6:30 in the morning until 5:00 at night. I leave here at 5:30 in the morning. I don't get home until about 6:00 at night." Yet she measures her worth as a mother by the fact that she has managed to provide for her son largely on her own. "I don't depend on nobody. I might live with my dad and them, but I don't depend on them, you know." She continues, "There [used to] be days when I'd be so stressed out, like, 'I can't do this!' And I would just cry and cry and cry. . . . Then I look at Colin, and he'll be sleeping, and I'll just look at him and think I don't have no [reason to feel sorry for myself]. The cards I have I've dealt myself so I have to deal with it now. I'm older. I can't change anything. He's my responsibility—he's nobody else's but mine—so I have to deal with that."

Becoming a mother transformed Jen's point of view on just about everything. She says, "I thought hanging on the corner drinking, getting high—I thought that was a good life, and I thought I could live that way for eternity, like sitting out with my friends. But it's not as fun once you have your own kid. . . . I think it changes [you]. I think, 'Would I want Colin to do that? Would I want my son to be like that . . . ?' It was fun to me but it's not fun anymore. Half the people I hung with are either . . . Some have died from drug overdoses, some are in jail, and some people are just out there living the same life that they always lived, and they don't look really good. They look really bad." In the end, Jen believes, Colin's birth has brought far more good into her life than bad. "I know 1 could have waited [to have a child], but in a way I think Colin's the best thing that could have happened to me. . . . So I think I had my son for a purpose because I think Colin changed my life. He saved my life, really. My whole life revolves around Colin!"

PROMISES I CAN KEEP

There are unique themes in Jen's story—most fathers are only one or two, not five years older than the mothers of their children, and few fathers have as many glaring problems as Rick—but we heard most of these themes repeatedly in the stories of the 161 other poor, single mothers we came to know. Notably, poor women do not reject marriage; they revere it. Indeed, it is the conviction that marriage is forever that makes them think that divorce is worse than having a baby outside of marriage. Their children, far from being liabilities, provide crucial social-psychological resources—a strong sense of purpose and a profound source of intimacy. Jen and the other mothers we came to know are coming of age in an America that is profoundly unequal—where the gap between rich and poor continues to grow. This economic reality has convinced them that they have little to lose and, perhaps, something to gain by a seemingly "ill-timed" birth.

The lesson one draws from stories like Jen's is quite simple: Until poor young women have more access to jobs that lead to financial independence—until there is reason to hope for the rewarding life pathways that their privileged peers pursue—the poor will continue to have children far sooner than most Americans think they should, while still deferring marriage. Marital standards have risen for all Americans, and the poor want the same things that everyone now wants out of marriage. The poor want to marry too, but they insist on marrying well. This, in their view, is the only way to avoid an almost certain divorce. Like Jen, they are simply not willing to make promises they are not sure they can keep.

*Recommended Resources*_____

Kathryn Edin and Maria Kefalas. *Promises I Can Keep: Why Poor Women Put Motherhood Before Marriage* (University of California Press, 2005). An account of how low-income women make sense of their choices about marriage and motherhood.

Christina Gibson, Kathryn Edin, and Sara McLanahan. "High Hopes but Even Higher Expectations: A Qualitative and Quantitative Analysis of the Marriage Plans of Unmarried Couples Who Are New

Parents." Working Paper 03-06-FF, Center for Research on Child Wellbeing, Princeton University, 2004. Online at http://crcw.princeton.edu/workingpapers/WP03-06-FF-Gibson.pdf. The authors examine the rising expectations for marriage among unmarried parents.

Sharon Hays. *Flat Broke with Children: Women in the Age of Welfare Reform* (Oxford University Press, 2003). How welfare reform has affected the lives of poor moms.

Annette Lareau. *Unequal Childhoods: Class, Race, and Family Life* (University of California Press, 2003). A fascinating discussion of different childrearing strategies among low-income, working-class, and middle-class parents.

Timothy J. Nelson, Susan Clampet-Lundquist, and Kathryn Edin. "Fragile Fatherhood: How Low-Income, Non-Custodial Fathers in Philadelphia Talk About Their Families." In *The Handbook of Father Involvement: Multidisciplinary Perspectives*, ed. Catherine Tamis-LeMonda and Natasha Cabrera (Lawrence Earlbaum Associates, 2002). What poor, single men think about fatherhood.

READING 38

Issues in the Definition of Family Violence and Abuse

Denise A. Hines and Kathleen Malley-Morrison

Women can verbally abuse you. They can rip your clothes off without even touching you, the way women know how to talk, converse. But men . . . weren't brought up to talk as much as women do . . . So it was a resort to violence, if I couldn't get through to her by words . . . On some occasions she was the provoker. It didn't call for physical abuse . . . [but] it did call for something. You know, you're married for that long, if somebody gets antagonistic, you want to defend yourself. (Ptacek, 1998, p. 188)

What are your views on this case? If this man struck his wife when she antagonized him, has he been abusive? How about his wife? If she verbally attacked him, put him down, tried to antagonize him with her words, was she also guilty of spousal abuse? Is one form of abuse (e.g., physical aggression) more abusive than another form (e.g., verbal aggression)? What is the basis for your judgment? Does abusive behavior by one spouse justify retaliatory aggression?

He always wanted to have sex. He was jealous and if he didn't have sex with me every single day that means that I was with another guy and that was his theory. From the time I was 18, I had sex every single day for the first year we were married . . . [We] did it every day because he wanted to and I thought I had to. (Bergen, 1998, pp. 240–241)

Is the woman who reported this experience a victim of domestic violence, wife abuse, or maltreatment? Apparently she did not resist his advances even if she was often unhappy with his insistence on daily sex. If she did not resist, can his behavior be called "marital rape"?

His hand on my throat, pressing me into the bed . . . I never called it . . . rape. I called it rough sex. Forcing himself on me. Being selfish and inconsiderate, a beast, a monster. He called it getting what he wanted. What he was entitled to. (Letellier, 1999, p. 10)

Does this appear to be a more obvious case of marital rape? A definite case of domestic assault? The victim in this case is a gay male. Does that affect your judgment of the case in any way? If so, how? How likely is it that the victim in this case will be able to find appropriate support services to help him deal with this relationship and its effects on him?

When my son was a toddler . . . he would often attempt to squeeze past the front door where stone steps awaited his fall. Verbal reprimands and redirecting his attention elsewhere were fruitless, as he attempted time and again to get out . . . Rather than allow him to experience for himself the consequences of wandering too close to those steps, I swatted him smartly a couple of times on his diapered behind . . . ! It took two more swattings before he became convinced of the certain connection between trying to get out the front door and the painful consequences, but after that, he needed no more reminders! (Newberger, 1999, p. 79)

The woman who told this story did so proudly, pleased with her ability to discipline her son. What is your view? Is corporal punishment an appropriate response to self-endangering behaviors in a toddler? Is it appropriate in other circumstances? Or, is it possible that there are always better methods for dealing with child behavior that is considered undesirable?

After being hospitalized with a broken hip, 80-year-old Mr. Jaffin began living with his daughter and son-in-law. His daughter repeatedly berated him for not being able to clean his room and began referring to him as their third child. Reminding him what an avid golfer he'd been before the accident, she ridiculed him for now being unable to go to the mailbox without his walker and assistance from a family member. Within a month, Mr. Jaffin began to feel worthless and withdrew from his family and friends. He spent the day in his room sleeping or watching television, no longer socializing with or even phoning old friends. (Humphries Lynch, 1997)

What are your views of Mr. Jaffin's situation? His daughter and son-in-law have taken him in, provided him with his own room and television, presumably keep him warm, safe, and well fed, and try to motivate him to be the active man he once was. Given these circumstances, would you say he is being maltreated in any way? Should the medical personnel who are overseeing his recovery from the broken hip intervene in the family situation? If so, how?

In the United States, one can expect considerable disagreement on the answers to these questions. Consider the first case. The problem of wife abuse has received a great deal of attention as an important social problem in recent years, but many people argue that husband abuse is not a social problem in need of a societal response, however painful it may be for its victims (e.g., Kurz, 1993; Walker, 1990). The Violence Against Women Act (VAWA) of 1994, expanded in 1998 and 2002, was designed to provide women with broad protections against violence not only in their communities but also in their homes, but society has been slower to provide protections for male victims of intimate abuse. As recently as July 2003, a Los Angeles man filed a sex discrimination lawsuit against ten local battered women's shelters because none of them would provide him with a bed (Zwerling, 2003). Some people assume that cases where women abuse their partners are so rare there is no need to provide shelters for their victims. Others assume that shelters for men are unnecessary because most women, like the one in Case 1, are only verbally abusive, or that verbal aggression such as name-calling is in poor taste but calling it abusive is a misuse of the term. What do you think of these arguments?

Consider the other cases. Does marriage—or cohabitation, for that matter—entitle individuals to engage in sexual behavior with their partners whenever and however they want? Although most readers would probably say "No," when the second author of this book submitted an article on dating aggression to a major interpersonal violence journal, one reviewer criticized the article for including the item, "pressured you to have sex in a way you didn't like or didn't want," in the (previously published) measure of interpersonal abuse completed by the participants. According to that reviewer, pressuring someone to have unwanted sex is abusive only in the context of prior physical assault. What is your view of this?

Battered women who have also experienced sexual abuse often find that shelters provide very little assistance with the aftermath of their sexually abusive experiences. Historically, many shelters did not consider cases of marital rape to fall within their domain because it is not life threatening, and many rape crisis centers did not want to deal with wife abuse victims; consequently, battered women who had also been sexually assaulted were sometimes shuffled back and forth, unaided, between facilities (see Malley-Morrison & Hines, 2004, Chapter 15). This situation appears to be changing, with efforts being made to promote greater responsiveness to wife rape victims by domestic violence shelters (Wellesley Center for Women, 1998).

For many decades after the public recognition of child abuse and wife abuse as serious social problems, members of the gay/lesbian community, fearing additional stigmatization, were reluctant to admit that abuse took place within their relationships. Only recently have victims of intimate violence in those communities begun to speak out, although services are still limited. There are now some states that legally recognize gay/lesbian unions (e.g., Vermont, Massachusetts), and many gay/lesbian couples are raising children. In response to these developments, many researchers have begun studying violence in gay/lesbian relationships.

The extent to which corporal punishment should be considered abusive is very controversial. Although the percentages of adults who approve of corporal punishment may be declining, a majority of parents in the U.S. spank their children and consider spanking appropriate and necessary (Straus, 1994), despite the fact that many professional organizations, such as the American Psychological Association and the American Academy of Pediatrics, have issued statements recommending that children not be subjected to corporal punishment.

Finally, should we view Mr. Jaffin's feelings and behavior simply as inevitable outcomes of the medical and other problems associated with aging, or is he a victim of elder maltreatment? He is not being physically abused. Nobody is trying to hurt or exploit him. But is he being emotionally abused? If so, how should he be helped? When he went to his orthopedist for a follow-up on his hip, he was referred to a psychologist who diagnosed him as clinically depressed. This psychologist began seeing him and his overwhelmed daughter regularly and helped them both work out a better way of dealing with their circumstances (Humphries Lynch, 1997). Given that elder abuse is a reportable offense, should the hospital personnel have notified Adult Protective Services rather than privately initiating the counseling program?

DEFINITIONAL ISSUES

At the heart of many of the debates concerning whether particular behaviors are abusive are inconsistencies in the definitions of terms. Definitions of abuse, for example, have varied in the extent to which they incorporate assumptions about causes (e.g., people who hurt the ones they love are "sick"); effects (e.g., abusive behaviors are those that cause harm); motivations (e.g., abusive behaviors are intended to hurt rather than discipline); frequency (e.g., slapping is abusive only if it is chronic); and intensity (e.g., hitting is abusive if it is hard enough to cause injury). Such definitions, which vary in their inclusiveness and differ within and across fields, influence the likelihood that individuals subjected to unwanted behaviors within domestic settings will receive interventions from the legal, medical, and/or social service communities.

Efforts to distinguish among terms such as violence, abuse, and maltreatment have not led to any consensus. Definitions continue to vary in their inclusiveness (how broadly the construct is defined) and their abstractness (the extent to which they focus on specific behaviors or define one abstract construct in terms of another). For example, Levesque (2001) held that "family violence includes family members' acts of omission or commission *resulting in* physical abuse, sexual abuse, emotional abuse, neglect, or other forms of maltreatment that hamper individuals' healthy development" (p. 13, italics added). Emery and Laumann-Billings (1998) distinguished between two levels of *abuse— maltreatment* (i.e., minimal or moderate forms of abuse, such as hitting, pushing, and name-calling) and *violence* (i.e., more violent abuse involving serious endangerment, physical injury, and sexual violation). Here, *abuse* is the broader term, and *maltreatment* and *violence* are considered subtypes of abuse, varying in level of intensity. According to the American Academy of Family Physicians (2004), "Family violence can be defined as the intentional intimidation or abuse of children, adults, or elders by a family member, intimate partner or caretaker to gain power and control over the victim. Abuse has many forms, including physical and sexual assault, emotional or psychological mistreatment, threats and intimidation, economic abuse and violation of individual rights" (paragraph 7). Thus, the Academy defined family violence as abuse, emphasized the intention of power and control, and included "mistreatment" as a form of abuse. Finally, Straus, in his early work (Straus, Gelles, & Steinmetz, 1980), distinguished between *socially accepted violence* (e.g., spanking) and *abusive violence*, defined as an "act which has a high potential for injuring the person being hit" (pp. 21–22).

One of the biggest debates in the field is whether corporal punishment should be considered inherently abusive. Straus and Yodanis (1996) defines corporal punishment as "the use of physical force with the intention of causing pain but not injury for purposes of coercion and control" (p. 826)—thus emphasizing both intent and expectations concerning outcomes. Straus and Runyan (1997) noted that most cases of physical abuse happen when corporal punishment gets out of control, and that ordinary corporal punishment of adolescents is associated with a heightened risk for many social and psychological problems. If child abuse is defined as behaviors that put children at risk for injury, and both psychological and physical injuries are considered, then there is a basis for considering corporal punishment abusive because of the demonstrated negative effects of corporal punishment. Straus (1994) has made this argument in his efforts to ban corporal punishment in the United States, as it is in many European countries. There has been considerable resistance to a ban among professionals as well as laypeople. Box 1 provides a sampling of major social science perspectives on the issue. Each of these authorities presents empirical data in support of his or her position, yet there are no signs that the differences will be resolved soon.

Another perspective comes from Emery (1989), who holds that "calling an act 'abusive' or 'violent' is not an objective decision but a social judgment, a judgment that is outside of the realm of responsibility of social scientists" (p. 322). Similarly, Zuriff (1988) argued that "the definition of psychological maltreatment is not a task appropriate for psychologists as scientists or researchers . . . [The] problem of defining 'maltreatment' is one of determining a point on a set of continua at which the psychological effects of parental behavior are to be designated 'harmful.' I suggest this is not an empirical question . . . [Psychologists] should leave the determination of good and evil, benefit and harm, to the law, ethics, and religion" (p. 201).

BOX 1 • *Is Corporal Punishment Abusive?*

Corporal punishment of children is essentially a legalized form of assault. Acts of "minor violence" that would be crimes if committed on an adult are legal when they occur as "discipline." (Berliner, 1988, p. 222)

In the toddler years, parents should fast respond with the least aversive discipline they think will stop the misbehavior. If that does not elicit compliance, they should then turn to more aversive responses . . . If the child still fails to comply. . . , such noncompliance should result in a mild prescribed spanking. (Larzelere, 1994, p. 205)

Almost without exception, when harsh punishment is mentioned and has [negative] long-term consequences . . . what is being referred to is corporal punishment. (Casey, 1994, p. 1007)

Authoritative parents endorse the judicious use of aversive consequences, which may (but certainly need not) include spanking . . . The prudent use of punishment within the context of a responsive, supportive parent-child relationship is a necessary tool in the disciplinary encounter. (Baumrind, 1997, p. 330)

Regardless of the numerous factors . . . that might provoke the use of spanking in a given instance, even the most abusive parent believes he or she is spanking as a response to some child behavior that requires discipline. (Benjet & Kazdin, 2003, p. 220)

In our opinion, motivating parents to change from corporal punishment to alternative methods of discipline would seem to be the most productive public mental health program known. (Ontario Consultants on Religious Tolerance, 2003, paragraph 4)

While agreeing that terms like maltreatment represent social constructions and value judgments, we disagree that psychologists and other social scientists cannot aid in the definitional process by means of scientific data and scientific thinking. Social and medical scientists are in some ways uniquely qualified to provide evidence concerning the harmfulness of particular behaviors for the well-being of their recipients, others with whom those recipients interact, and even the larger community within which the recipients of those behaviors must function. Indeed, in considering the kinds of behaviors and interactions that may be harmful to members of families (broadly defined to include gay/lesbian relationships and cohabiting couples), we prefer the term *maltreatment* to the other commonly used terms, in part because of the explicit value judgment built into the prefix "mal."

Our term *maltreatment* embraces *corporal punishment* as well as *abuse, family violence, wife beating, domestic violence, spousal abuse,* and *elder abuse,* as these are commonly defined. We acknowledge that some forms of maltreatment are more serious than others. Children who receive a single slap on the hand or the buttocks during childhood are not being maltreated to the same degree as a child who is raped, or beaten every day, or constantly criticized and humiliated. However, we view all these behaviors as forms of maltreatment, and not beneficial ways for individuals to treat each other, inside or outside of families. As Straus has repeatedly pointed out, even acts that seem like relatively minor forms of maltreatment (e.g., spanking, name-calling) are risk factors for negative outcomes for individuals and society (Straus, 2001; Vissing, Straus, Gelles, & Harrop, 1991). Although our conceptual preference is for the term *maltreatment,* most researchers in family violence study the more extreme forms of maltreatment, and therefore, throughout this book, we generally use the term that the researchers used to describe the particular form of maltreatment of interest to them.

Definitions of terms such as maltreatment are embedded in broader perspectives on human beings, families, and intimate relationships. During the second half of the 20th century, new perspectives emerged within the international community, including the view that the more vulnerable members of the human race (particularly women, children, the elderly, and people with mental and physical disabilities) have an inherent right to freedom from exploitation and abuse. Concurrent with the evolution of that perspective, many countries criminalized forms of family aggression that had a long history of normative acceptance—for example, the beating and rape of wives and children. Accompanying the criminalization of such behaviors has been a *medicalization* of their effects (Newberger & Bourne, 1978). *Medicalization* refers to perceiving a behavior, such as child maltreatment, as a medical problem or illness, and expecting the medical profession to treat the problem. The medical communities in many countries, including the United States, have increasingly been given and/or have assumed the responsibility not just to heal intentional burns, set broken bones, and mend bruised and battered skin, but to alert legal and social service agencies about behaviors now deemed abusive.

Just as the concept of "family" has been broadened to include nonmarital cohabiting relationships and same-sex intimate relationships, legal protections against spousal abuse have increasingly been expanded to include nonmarital relationships. Also, because most definitions of abuse emphasize negative outcomes, the social science community has directed intensive efforts at providing a scientific basis for defining, studying, and intervening in situations of family violence and abuse. In the next sections, we provide a brief introduction to major perspectives on maltreatment in family settings. Many of these perspectives reflect assumptions held before individuals selected a profession or developed as part of their professional training and experience. These perspectives, which may guide important decisions concerning the current or future well-being of victims of family maltreatment, may or may not have a solid theoretical or empirical basis. This section is followed by an overview of several theories of familial maltreatment. During the past several decades, increasing work has been done to empirically test such theories in order to improve our understanding of the predictors and consequences of maltreatment and to provide a foundation for intervention and prevention efforts.

PERSPECTIVES ON MALTREATMENT

The Human Rights Perspective

One major view on human rights is that they are privileges granted by people in power to those who are less powerful. For much of human history, women and children were seen as having no rights separate from those that men offered them—and such rights were generally extremely limited. A second major view is that human rights are *inherent* in being human. From this latter perspective, human rights are, in the words of Amartya Sen (1998), "entitlements of every human being" (paragraph 1). This second view that is embodied in the United States Declaration of Independence: "We hold these truths to be self-evident, that all men are created equal, that they are endowed by their Creator with certain unalienable Rights, that among these are Life, Liberty and the pursuit of Happiness." It is also embodied in international human rights agreements promulgated by the United Nations and other nongovernmental organizations (NGOs).

Emerging from the horrors of World War II, wherein "disregard and contempt for human rights have resulted in barbarous acts which have outraged the conscience of mankind," the newly born United Nations adopted the task of establishing a lasting peace. One of its first accomplishments (1948) was the Universal Declaration of Human Rights, which proclaimed "all members of the human family" have "equal and inalienable rights" and that recognition of these rights is "the foundation of freedom, justice and peace in the world" (Universal Declaration, Preamble, paragraph 1). Article 5, which is most relevant to family maltreatment, states, "No one shall be subjected to torture or to cruel, inhuman or degrading treatment or punishment."

Since the passage of the Universal Declaration, the United Nations has promulgated other international treaties addressing the rights of individuals to freedom from maltreatment even within their own families. The Convention on the Rights of the Child (1989) specifies that member states "shall take all appropriate legislative, administrative, social and educational measures to protect the child from all forms of physical or mental violence, injury or abuse, neglect or negligent treatment, maltreatment or exploitation, including sexual abuse, while in the care of parent(s), legal guardian(s) or any other person who has the care of the child" (Article 19). According to this Convention, assuring such rights to children is necessary in order to rear them "in the spirit of the ideals proclaimed in the Charter of the United Nations, and in particular in the spirit of peace, dignity, tolerance, freedom, equality and solidarity." Thus, the international promulgators of this document, like many social scientists in the United States, recognize a connection between eschewing violence in the home and promoting international peace.

Child advocates in many countries have argued that corporal punishment violates the United Nations Convention on the Rights of the Child. The European Network of Ombudsmen for Children (ENOC; 2001) urged the governments of all European countries as well as NGOs concerned with children to work to end all corporal punishment. In their view, "eliminating violent and humiliating forms of discipline is a vital strategy for improving children's status as people, and reducing child abuse and all other forms of violence in European societies." ENOC concurred that no level of corporal punishment is compatible with the Convention on the Rights of the Child and that legal and educational steps should be taken to eliminate it. The United States is one of only two countries (the other being Somalia, which has no central government) that have not ratified the Convention on the Rights of the Child, and parents in the United States appear to be very resistant to the notion that corporal punishment may violate a child's rights.

Another important declaration adopted by the United Nations General Assembly was the Declaration on the Elimination of Violence Against Women, endorsed by all member states of the United Nations. According to this Declaration, "violence against women means any act of gender-based violence that results in, or is likely to result in, physical, sexual or psychological harm or suffering to women, including threats of such acts, coercion or arbitrary deprivation of liberty, whether occurring in public or in private life" (Declaration on the Elimination of Violence against Women, 1993, Article 1). Other NGOs taking a stand against maltreatment in domestic settings include Amnesty International, which in 2001 released a statement asserting that violence against women is a human rights issue, and that if a government fails to "prevent, prosecute and punish" acts of violence, those acts should be considered forms of torture—and therefore a violation of the United Nations Declaration on Human Rights.

The international human rights perspective emphasizes the relationship between social justice and individual rights to freedom from abuse, and between peaceful resolution of conflict in the home and peaceful resolution of conflict in the international community. Proponents of a human rights perspective are often critical of systemic or structural abuse—that is, abuse of individuals by the very systems or structures responsible for protecting them (e.g., Hearn, 1988). One human rights advocate has argued that attention to international human rights principles can help Americans "move away from practices and assumptions that condone, encourage, and improperly respond to family violence" (Levesque, 2001, p. 17).

Legal/Criminal Justice Perspectives

Although the United Nations Convention on the Rights of the Child has some legal status in international law, it has functioned not so much to enforce children's rights judicially or to criminalize violation of those rights, as to establish a universal standard that the international community has agreed to adopt. To our knowledge, the World Court has not tried any cases of family maltreatment. However, the European Court of Human

Rights, established by the European Convention On Human Rights and Its Five Proto-
cols, has addressed cases of family violence originating in a number of different European countries.

In general, the legal approach to family maltreatment in the United States has been
to criminalize it. The focus is on both punishment and deterrence. Criminalization has
involved mandating members of medical and social service professions to report sus-
pected cases of abuse and imposing criminal penalties on perpetrators of acts identified
as abusive. Although the United States has not ratified the Convention on the Rights of
the Child, it has ratified the Declaration on the Elimination of Violence Against Women
and has criminalized abuse of children, domestic partners; and the elderly. According to
the federal Child Abuse Prevention and Treatment Act (CAPTA), "child abuse and neglect is, at a minimum, any recent act or failure to act on the part of a parent or caretaker
which results in death, serious physical or emotional harm, sexual abuse or exploitation
of a child (individual under the age of 18) and any act or failure to act which presents an
imminent risk of serious harm" (42 U.S.C. 5106g). However, each state has its own set
of laws, and, in contrast to the stance taken in many European countries, corporal punishment by parents is legal in every state.

The Violence Against Women Act (VAWA), passed in 1994 as part of an Omnibus
Crime Bill, and modified in 2002, was revolutionary in its provisions for addressing violence against women, including wife abuse. The federal Older Americans Act provides
definitions of elder abuse and authorizes expenditure of federal funds for a National Center on Elder Abuse but does not fund adult protective services or shelters for abused older
persons. Every state has its own set of statutes criminalizing abuse of women and elders
and its own procedures for investigating complaints and prosecuting violators. Actual
practices often fall far short of the intent of the law; however, there has been enormous
change since the days when the criminal justice system saw itself as not concerned with
any violence short of murder when it took place behind the closed doors of the family
home (Iovanni & Miller, 2001). Nevertheless, although there are laws addressing family
violence against children, wives, and the elderly, no legislation deals specifically with family violence against siblings or husbands, who are also frequent victims of maltreatment
in the family.

Although physical assault of wives has received increasing attention over the years,
marital rape has been a virtual oxymoron until very recently. The so-called "marital rape
exemption," mandating that forced sex of a wife by a husband could not be considered a
form of rape, had its basis in English common law, according to which wives, by virtue
of the marital contract, gave themselves willingly and irrevocably to their husbands. The
nature of the marital contract was interpreted as negating the possibility of marital rape
and ensuring the husband's right to have his desires satisfied by his wife (Bergen, 1998).
Consistent with this perspective, rape was traditionally defined as a male's "sexual intercourse with a female, not his wife, by force and against her will" (Finkelhor & Yllo, 1985,
p. 1). It was not until July 5, 1993 that all states had enacted legislation to criminalize the
rape of wives; however, many laypeople are unaware that wife rape is now considered a
crime, and still others do not believe it can or should be a crime (Malley-Morrison &
Hines, 2004). There are still no laws against sexual assault of husbands, although we
know that this form of sexual aggression takes place.

Although the principal legislation relating to domestic maltreatment provides funding for educational and social service programs, the legal perspective emphasizes the criminal justice system response to violation of federal and state statutes. Studies using legal definitions of abuse typically report the number of cases of identified child, spouse, or elder abuse reported to protective service agencies. Such reports provide a vast underestimation of the actual frequency of maltreatment in families because many cases are never reported to any agency. Moreover, many statutes related to maltreatment have exemptions. For example, in every state, the child abuse statutes have exemptions allowing parents to use "reasonable force" for purposes of child discipline and control. Legal definitions of physical abuse reflect cultural norms concerning what exceeds reasonable force, but the boundaries between physical abuse and corporal punishment have been generally left to the discretion of the legal and criminal justice systems (Straus & Runyan, 1997). Moreover, many states still have exemptions from prosecution for a husband raping his wife (Rennison, 2002), such as when he does not have to use force to make her have sex (e.g., if she is physically or mentally impaired and unable to give consent).

Medical Perspectives

Maltreatment in families has been recognized not just as a human rights and a legal issue but also as a medical issue. On an international level, the World Health Organization (WHO, 1997) identifies violence in the home as a public health problem. Within the United States, professional organizations such as the American Academy of Family Physicians (2004) have also noted that family violence is a public health issue of epidemic proportions. The medical perspective on maltreatment tends to focus on recognizing symptoms, identifying causes, and providing treatment. Medical practitioners frequently emphasize the causes of maltreatment having a biological component (e.g., substance abuse, psychiatric disorders). Perpetrators are often viewed as victims themselves and more in need of treatment than of criminal prosecution. For this and many other reasons (including assumptions that the social welfare system does not always respond appropriately), medical personnel often do not report the cases of maltreatment they are mandated to report (Zellman & Fair, 2002).

Social Service Perspectives

The social service system has generally had a much broader perspective on family violence than the medical or legal systems, traditionally viewing maltreatment within family settings as a symptom of family crisis and a need for services. The social service system has been more concerned with ameliorating conditions that give rise to maltreatment than with promoting the prosecution of offenders or providing medical treatment of victims. Much of the emphasis on acts of omission (neglect) in definitions of child and elder maltreatment is derived from social service perspectives. Workers within the field have often emphasized the role of external forces—for example, poverty and discrimination (Beckett, 2003)—in contributing to family maltreatment. Of all the relevant systems, the social service system probably has the greatest familiarity with social science research relevant to family maltreatment, its causes and outcomes.

Need for Multidisciplinary Cooperation

In many cases of family maltreatment, representatives of the legal, medical, and social service professions all become involved. A coordinated approach of these various services is often hard to achieve because of the differing definitions and perspectives within these professions. Members of the legal profession want to pursue prosecution of the perpetrator if they believe they can "win" their case. Medical practitioners are more concerned with providing treatment for victims and perhaps perpetrators, but typically see it as beyond their purview to address any problems of poverty, community violence, and despair besetting the family. Social service personnel may believe that any focus on helping, prosecuting, or changing individuals is shortsighted, and emphasize the need to find better housing and employment for family members and address substance abuse problems. Perhaps in part because of the very breadth of their perspective, social service systems have been overwhelmed by family violence cases in recent decades and are not always able to respond appropriately. A number of legal cases have been brought against local social service agencies for maltreating their clients.

Consider the case of Joshua DeShaney in Box 2. How did the differing perspectives of the various relevant agencies play out in his case? At what points in the process did systems fail him? Do any of the systems seem particularly culpable? After the final critical beating, Joshua's father was arrested, indicted, tried, convicted, and sent to jail for

---

BOX 2 • *Brief of DeShaney v. Winnebago County Dept. of Social Services*

Born in 1979, Joshua DeShaney was placed in his father's custody when his parents divorced a year later. Joshua's father's second wife and neighbors reported that Joshua was frequently abused by his father. Following a police report and hospital treatment of Joshua's bruises and abrasions in January 1983, the local Department of Social Services (DSS) obtained a court order to keep Joshua in the hospital's custody. However, a child services protective team returned Joshua to his father three days later when his father agreed in writing to enroll Joshua in Head Start and enter counseling himself. A few weeks later DSS was informed that Joshua had again been seen at the hospital but concluded there was no evidence of abuse.

During 1983, a social worker visited the father's home five times. Although she observed that Joshua had bumps and scrapes on several occasions and that the father was not adhering to the terms of his agreement, she took no action. There was also no action taken when the hospital reported in November 1983 that Joshua had again been treated for suspicious injuries. When the social worker visited the home in January 1984, she was told she could not see Joshua because he had the flu. When she tried again to see him in March, she was told that he had recently fainted, but she did not request to see him. The next day Joshua's father beat him severely, causing brain damage and permanent retardation. A medical examination revealed evidence of multiple previous injuries to Joshua's head and body.

Source: Adapted from online news reports.

child abuse. Subsequently, Joshua's mother and Joshua (represented by a guardian ad litem) sued the county Department of Social Services (DSS) for depriving Joshua of "his liberty interest in bodily integrity, in violation of his rights under the substantive component of the Fourteenth Amendment's Due Process Clause" *(DeShaney v. Winnebago County Department of Social Services*, 1989, p. 1). Their argument was that by failing to intervene in a way that protected Joshua against his father's violence, the DSS violated the Fourteenth Amendment statement that "[n]o State shall . . . deprive any person of life, liberty, or property, without due process of law." Joshua and his mother lost their case and appealed ultimately all the way to the Supreme Court, where they again lost. In a dissenting opinion, Justices Brennan, Marshall, and Blackmun argued, "The most that can be said of the state functionaries in this case . . . is that they stood by and did nothing when suspicious circumstances dictated a more active role for them. [We] cannot agree that respondents had no constitutional duty to help Joshua DeShaney" *(DeShaney v. Winnebago County Department of Social Services*, 1989, p. 17). In recent times, more cases have been brought against social service agencies. Does that appear to be the best way to deal with the staggering problems of maltreatment in society today? What other approaches might be better?

Disrespect for each other's professions may often hamper cooperation among representatives from different agencies. For example, although several United States Supreme Court decisions in the post-World War II years (e.g., *Brown v. Board of Education*, 1954; *In re Gault*, 1967) provided some recognition that juveniles have rights protected by the Constitution, more recent decisions by a more conservative Supreme Court have eroded some of these rights, in part because of a decreased willingness to attend to social science data (Walker, Brooks, & Wrightsman, 1999). For example, "Justice Scalia consistently has considered social science studies to be irrelevant when deciding on constitutional law; for him, the only 'empirical' materials of relevance . . . are legislation and jury decisions" (Walker et al., 1999, p. 11). . . .

SUMMARY

. . . There is some empirical support for each of the major theories of family violence, but there are also limitations to the empirical support. None of the individual theories can account for all forms of family violence. Essentially, research designed to test the validity of the theories has been effective in identifying risk factors for maltreatment at each of several different levels of the ecological systems in which development takes place. Conversely, the reciprocal of many of these risk factors can serve as protective factors against maltreatment or the negative impact of maltreatment. For example, social support within the micro- and exosystem has long been recognized as an important protective factor, as have higher income and higher education.

Even what may seem like a simple and clear-cut case of maltreatment of one family member by another is likely to have multiple causes. For example, a father may commit incest on his prepubertal daughter because of his sexual inadequacies with adult women, *and* his wife's overt contempt for him, *and* his wife's unconscious denial that her husband is doing to their daughter what her father did to her, *and* the norms of his peer group that a man's home should be his castle, *and* his personal belief that his family should be obedient to him, *and* society's tolerance for pornography, *and* the lack of availability of appropriate services within the community, *and* inadequate funding for intervention programs for incest offenders.

Editors' Note: *References for this reading can be found in the original source.*

Credits

pp. 14–25: William Goode, "The Theoretical Importance of Family" is from *The Family*, second edition, © 1982. Reprinted by permission of Pearson Education, Inc., Upper Saddle River, NJ.

pp. 26–31: Anthony Giddens, "The Global Revolution in Family and Personal Life" is copyright 1999 from *Runaway World* by Anthony Giddens. Reproduced by permission of Routledge/Taylor & Francis Group, LLC.

pp. 32–40: Arlene Skolnick, "The Life Course Revolution" is from *Embattled Paradise: The American Family in an Age of Uncertainty* by Arlene Skolnick. Copyright © 1991 by Arlene Skolnick. Reprinted by permission of Basic Books, a member of Perseus Books, L.L.C.

pp. 40–58: Donald J. Hernandez, "Changes in the Demographics of Families over the Course of American History" is from *Unfinished Work: Building Equality and Democracy in an Era of Working Families* edited by Jody Heymann and Christopher Beem. Copyright © 2005. Reprinted by permission of the New Press. www.thenewpress.com.

pp. 59–75: Sharon Hays, "The Mommy Wars: Ambivalence, Ideological Work, and the Cultural Contradictions of Motherhood" is from *The Cultural Contradictions of Motherhood* by Sharon Hays. Copyright © 1996 by Yale University Press. Reprinted by permission of Yale University Press.

pp. 76–95: Janet Z. Giele, "Decline of the Family: Conservative, Liberal, and Feminist Views" is from *Promises to Keep: Decline and Renewal of Marriage in America* edited by David Popenoe, Jean Bethke Elshtain, and David Blankenhorn. Copyright © 1996 by Rowman & Littlefield. Reprinted by permission of Rowman & Littlefield.

pp. 95–103: George Chauncey, "How Marriage Changed" is from *Why Marriage? The History Shaping Today's Debate* by George Chauncey. Copyright © 2004. Reprinted by permission of Basic Books, a member of Perseus Books, L.L.C.

pp. 109–116: Robert M. Jackson, "Destined for Equality" is reprinted by permission of the publisher from *Destined for Equality: The Inevitable Rise of Women's Status* by Robert M. Jackson, pp. 1–23, 157–171, Cambridge, Mass: Harvard University Press, Copyright © 1998 by Robert Max Jackson.

pp. 117–128: Kathleen Gerson, "Children of the Gender Revolution: Some Theoretical Questions from the Field" is from *Restructuring Work and the Life Course*, edited by Victor W. Marshall. Copyright © 2001 by University of Toronto Press. Reprinted with permission of the publisher.

pp. 129–134: Amy T. Schalet, "Raging Hormones, Regulated Love: Adolescent Sexuality in the United States and the Netherlands" is reproduced by permission of Sage Publications Ltd. from "Raging Hormones, Regulated Love: Adolescent Sexuality and the Constitution of the Modern Individual in the United States and the Netherlands," *Body and Society*, 6(1), 2000, 75–105, Copyright © 2000 by Sage Publications Ltd.

pp. 304–315: Ellen Galinsky, "What Children Think about Their Working Parents" is a reuse of pp. 58–95 from *Ask the Children* by Ellen Galinsky. Copyright © 1999 by Ellen Galinsky. Reprinted by permission of HarperCollins Publishers, Inc.

pp. 315–324: Vern L. Bengston, Timothy J. Biblarz, and Robert E. L. Roberts. "How Families Still Matter: A Longitudinal Study of Youth in Two Generations" is from *How Families Still Matter: A Longitudinal Study of Youth in Two Generations* by Vern L. Bengston, Timothy J. Biblarz, and Robert E. L. Roberts. Copyright © 2003 Cambridge University Press. Reprinted with permission of Cambridge University Press.

pp. 329–343: Katharine S. Newman, "Family Values Against the Odds" is from *No Shame in My Game: The Working Poor in the Inner City* by Katherine S. Newman, copyright © 1999 by Russell Sage Foundation. Used by permission of Alfred A. Knopf, a division of Random House.

pp. 343–350: Arlie Hochschild, with Anne Machung, "The Second Shift: Working Parents and the Revolution at Home" is from *The Second Shift* by Arlie Hochschild and Anne Machung, copyright © 1989, 2003 by Arlie Hochschild. Used by permission of Viking Penguin, a division of Penguin Group (USA) Inc.

pp. 350–359: Kathleen Gerson and Jerry Jacobs, "The Work-Home Crunch" is from *Contexts*, Vol. 3, No. 4: 29–37. Copyright © 2004, American Sociological Association. All rights reserved. Used by permission.

pp. 360–377: Lillian B. Rubin, "Families on the Fault Line" is copyright © 1994 by Lillian B. Rubin. Originally published by HarperCollins. Reprinted by the permission of Dunham Literary as agent for the author.

pp. 377–383: Harriet B. Presser, "The Economy That Never Sleeps" is from *Contexts*, Vol. 3, No. 2: 42–49. Copyright © 2004, University of California Press.

pp. 384–397: Elizabeth Warren and Amelia Warren Tyagi, "Why Middle-Class Mothers and Fathers Are Going Broke" is from *The Two-Income Trap: Why Middle-Class Mothers and Fathers Are Going Broke* by Elizabeth Warren and Amelia Warren Tyagi. Copyright © 2003 by Elizabeth Warren and Amelia Warren Tyagi. Reprinted by permission of Basic Books, a member of Perseus Books, L.L.C.

pp. 398–421: Ronald L. Taylor, "Diversity within African American Families" is from *Handbook of Family Diversity* edited by David H. Demo et al. Copyright © 2000 by Oxford University Press, Inc. Used by permission of Oxford University Press, Inc.

pp. 422–447: Maxine Baca Zinn and Barbara Wells, "Diversity within Latino Families: New Lessons for Family Social Science" is from *Handbook of Family Diversity*, edited by David H. Demo et al. Copyright © 2000 by Oxford University Press, Inc. Used by permission of Oxford University Press, Inc.

pp. 448–469: Judith Stacey, "Gay and Lesbian Families: Queer Like Us" is from *All Our Families: New Policies for a New Century, 2/e*, edited by Mary Ann Mason, Arlene Skolnick, and Steven D. Sugarman. Copyright © 2003, 1998 by Oxford University Press, Inc. Used by permission of Oxford University Press, Inc.

pp. 469–490: Karen Pyke, "'The Normal American Family' as an Interpretive Structure of Family Life among Grown Children of Korean and Vietnamese Immigrants" is from *Journal of Marriage and the Family*, 62(1), 2000, pp. 240–255. Copyright © 2000 by the National Council on Family Relations, 3989 Central Ave. NE, Suite 550, Minneapolis, MN 55421. Reprinted by permission.